SALT WATER GAME FISHES

Angler's Guide to the...

THE RONALD PRESS

SALT WATER GAME FISHES

Atlantic and Pacific

Edward C. Migdalski
Bingham Oceanographic Laboratory
Yale University

COMPANY • NEW YORK

Copyright, ©, 1958, by

THE RONALD PRESS COMPANY

All Rights Reserved

The text of this publication or any part thereof may not be reproduced in any manner whatsoever without permission in writing from the publisher.

Library of Congress Catalog Card Number: 58–12958

PRINTED IN THE UNITED STATES OF AMERICA

To
My Wife
Bo

Preface

Like others who go on fishing expeditions to many parts of the world, I am often asked to lecture on my experiences to sporting clubs and other fraternal, civic, and industrial organizations. Wherever I go—whether I am talking to big-game fishermen or pier anglers—I am struck by the insatiable curiosity shown by members of these groups about the fishes they catch. They are, of course, interested in learning how to take more fish; but they also want to know much more than that. They ask innumerable questions about the habits of fish: what they eat, where they spawn, how deep they lie in the water, what they do in the winter, or how they can be told apart. It is to answer such questions as these that this book has been written. I hope that those who read it will find their days of fishing more interesting as well as more successful.

It also seems to me that all true anglers love to get into discussions about every kind of game fish, even those they may never see. They are interested in fishes inhabiting both the Atlantic and the Pacific, both northern and southern waters. Anglers who fish primarily for flounder are fascinated by accounts of black marlin off South America, and specialists in surf fishing for bluefish and striped bass show as much interest in the mako shark as in their own favorite species. Furthermore, I believe the majority of sportsmen possess an intelligent outlook toward fishes and fishing. They want to know the facts. Consequently, my approach in this book has been based on what I like to call "popular academics"—scientific facts put into easy language for enjoyable reading by the angler.

I have tried to give the essential information about every species of game fish likely to be caught on rod and line in the Atlantic and Pacific, with special emphasis on those of most importance to anglers of all kinds. My observations are based on the best available scientific evidence gathered from wide reading in technical publications as well as from my own work at the Bingham Oceanographic Laboratory of Yale University. But they also grow out of my personal experience as an enthusiastic angler. Aside from my own angling excursions along the Atlantic and Pacific coasts of North America, I have been lucky enough to participate in sixteen Yale expeditions to distant parts of the world. I have been able to make personal acquaintance with most members of every group of fishes included in the book, and always I have enjoyed fishing for them as much as I have observing them scientifically.

To help the angler identify the fish he catches, I have included accurate outline drawings of more than 150 different fishes, with attention specifically drawn to points of identification easily visible to the nonscientist. Never again need the fisherman confuse flounder and fluke, or black and striped marlin! Special maps have been prepared to show when and where to fish. And photographs have been chosen both for their general interest and for their clear depiction of the physical characteristics of each fish—though I am glad to say that many of them include pictures of my good friends.

As I look back over the years, I realize that many fine men and good friends have contributed to the realization of this book. I am grateful to Professors Dan Merriman at Yale and Ed Rainey at Cornell, who have taught and advised me. I especially appreciate the help of four men who, with unusual foresight and scientific interest in fishes, contributed valuable time, leadership, and funds to Yale expeditions, thus providing

Preface

me with opportunities to study the finny tribe in many parts of the world: Wendell Anderson, Stephen Sanford, Larry Sheerin, and Tom Shevlin. Many fish guides and boat men have taught me much about fishes and fishing; they vary from well-known personalities like Captain Bill Fagen to humble illiterates in primitive surroundings.

Others who, as friends and advisers, helped to make this book possible are: Charles Gage of Yale University; Lou Mowbray, Director of the Bermuda Aquarium; Professor Dillon Ripley of Yale, who taught me much on my first expeditions; Ralph Morrill and Percy Morris, two top-ranking museum men; and Frank Collver, Director of the New Haven Boys Club, who gave time and encouragement to a young boy with a craze for fishing.

Thanks are due to Bob Crandall, Hal Lyman, Pete Perinchief, the Bermuda News Bureau, the Nova Scotia Bureau of Information, and *Salt Water Sportsman* for photographic material; and to Bill Holdsworth for drawing the maps.

Edward C. Migdalski

New Haven, Connecticut
September, 1958

Contents

Introduction 3

Open-Ocean Fishes
    Billfishes 25
    Dolphins 82
    Finletfishes 89
    Sharks 169

Coastal and Inshore Fishes
    Barracudas 175
    Chub 188
    Bluefish 190
    Bonefish 207
    Cobia 212
    Codfishes 215
    Cottids 223
    Croakers 225
    Flatfishes 261
    Greenlings 273
    Grunts . . . , , 275

Jackfishes	281
Ladyfish	312
Lingcod	315
Marine Basses	316
Ocean Whitefish	358
Porgies	360
Rockfishes	369
Roosterfish	373
Seaperches	377
Shad	380
Snappers	388
Snook	405
Tarpon	408
Tripletail	415
Wrasses	417

Identification Charts 423

Appendix: The International Game Fish Association . . . 465

Glossary 473

Index 479

SALT WATER GAME FISHES

Introduction

GAME FISHES

The selection of species to be included in a book on game fishes presents a problem which may easily become controversial. The more academic-minded angler will demand to know what constitutes the author's lines of demarcation in choice of the fishes—and why? To clarify the situation and to justify the selection some discussion is necessary.

We must begin by answering what seems like an elementary question—what is a game fish? In the pursuance of an acceptable definition I have found many attitudes. Some authors include only fishes which are familiar to them. Some say, "fishes that will take a moving bait," and others insist that the bait must be artificial. Some well-known writers offer uncertain definitions, such as "a game fish is one which the angler must be proud of" or "a fish caught on rod and reel which the angler does not throw back in disgust." The most general definition given is "any fish caught on rod and reel which puts up a good fight." The inference, of course, is that a fighting fish is a fish which displays commendable resistance during the process of being dragged from its element.

In my opinion it is not imperative that a fish be taken on artificial lures, or a moving bait, or that the quarry be taken with a line of certain pound test before it is given the rank of game fish. Nor can the degree of "gameness" or ability to resist the rod and reel in the different species be a criterion; this aspect of the problem is even more controversial, and the subject then develops many ramifications. As far as I am concerned, any fish, regardless of species, which rod and reel fishermen pursue specifically is a game fish. A few of the fishes included in this book may not fall into this category. However, I feel justified in including types that are taken only incidentally but which may create interest or confusion among anglers.

IDENTIFICATION

Although experienced anglers generally recognize most of the species of game fishes they catch, it is a surprising fact that most of them cannot point out the differences in closely related species. For example, a fisherman will say, "This is a fluke, and this a flounder," but if he is asked how they differ, invariably the reply will be, "The fluke is bigger," or "The flounder has a darker back." Many anglers believe that the bluefish and snapper bluefish are different species "because the bluefish is bigger" or "the snapper is more silvery." Therefore, I wish to impress upon the angler that color and size should be subjugated to anatomical considerations when properly identifying fishes.

The use of coloration as a criterion of identification is unreliable because color in fishes is not a stable characteristic. Not only do the colors differ in shades among different fish in the same species, but also the colors themselves may change on one and the same fish—often in an astonishing manner in some types such as the groupers and snappers. Much depends upon the environment that a particular fish frequents—a light shade on sandy bottom. All fish lose their brilliant coloration upon death. The mood of a fish may affect some of its color—even spots and stripes may come and go. Seasons of the year have

Identification 5

an effect upon coloration of fishes. Spawning periods usually produce the most vivid hues. Young fish of many species possess stripes, bars, lines, or markings which gradually disappear as the fish grow older.

Nor is size a reliable guide. The fluke should not be separated from the flounder by the fact that it is a larger fish. Differentiation should be made by such points as length of the upper jaw in relation to the eye, the types of tail outlines, comparative curvatures of the lateral lines, number of spines in the fins, and the fact that the fluke faces left and the flounder faces right when lying on the bottom.

The angler should notice that the bluefish and snapper blue are the same species. It can be clearly seen that they are identical anatomically—same type of tail, same formation and location of fins, same number of fin spines and rays, etc.

All game fishes have one, two, or three dorsal fins and one or two anal fins; the number of spines or rays in the first dorsal, in the second dorsal, and in the anal are often used in identification. The first dorsal in the great majority of fishes contains hard, pointed spines and may also be referred to as the spinous dorsal. The second dorsal contains rays, which are softer than spines; this fin may be called second dorsal, soft dorsal, or rayed dorsal. Whenever present the third dorsal is usually soft rayed, or, as in the billfishes, it may be very small in comparison to the body. In some cases, the front of the second dorsal may include a hard spine.

The lateral line, which in most species extends from the gill cover to the base of the tail, is visible in most species; it may appear puckered or as a line containing pores. Sometimes the number of scales along the lateral line aids in identification.

The scientist, when attempting to identify or separate two very closely related species which look alike, investigates the internal anatomy. Obviously, this type of "positive" identification would be, in some cases, much too technical for use by the sportsman. However, there are "scientific methods" of identification which are actually quite simple. For example, I believe any angler can cut open a fish's abdomen to see whether or not

GILL RAKERS
ASSIST IN IDENTIFICATION
FIRST GILL ALWAYS USED

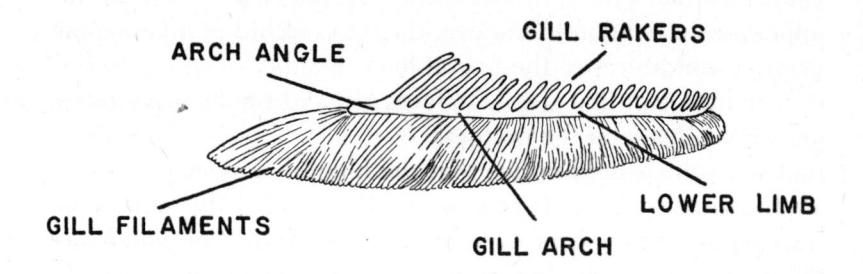

SIDE VIEW

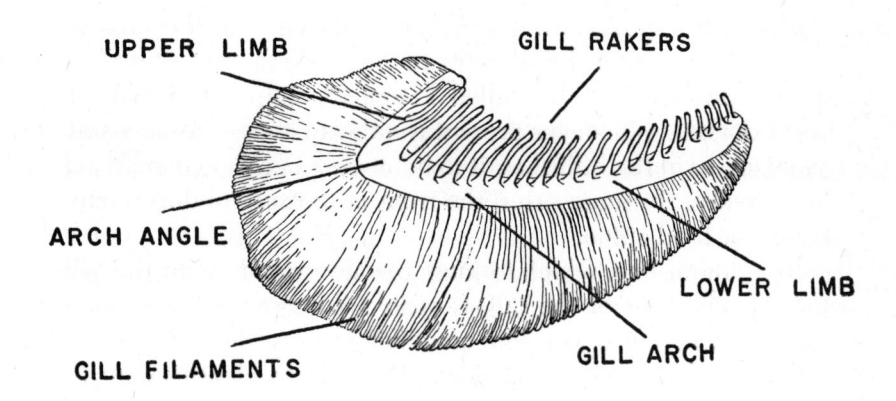

TOP VIEW

an air bladder is present or whether the air bladder is a single organ or has two lobes. In some cases the color of the lining of the stomach can be checked.

Counting the gill rakers in the upper part of the first gill arch is one of the most common methods of identification used by scientists. Any angler can impress his friends and appear very scientific by simply lifting the gill cover and counting the gill rakers. In the text, wherever necessary, the gill raker count is given with the species.

The detailed illustrations on pages 8-9 portray the points of anatomy of different types of fishes which are specially important when identifying fishes in each group.

The Identification Charts at the end of the book present scientifically accurate outline drawings of every salt water fish likely to be taken by the angler. The important identification marks are clearly indicated. A numbered reference to the appropriate drawing is given after the name of each species in the text.

CLASSIFICATION

There are many possible ways of classifying game fishes. But most of them are complex and controversial, and they are of little practical value to the angler. For the purposes of this book I have made only one division—a separation of fishes that are predominantly oceanic in habit from those that spend their lives along coastal and shore areas. Within these two major categories the groups appear in alphabetical order.

Oceanic game fishes roam the high seas and are often referred to as pelagic. The group is composed of fast-swimming, open-ocean fishes. Mostly they inhabit the ocean's surface waters and generally stay clear of coastal areas, although certain groups approach quite close to shore. Oceanic game fishes are almost entirely predacious. They seem to be constantly traveling, and they take part in long migrations. These fishes are found in warm and temperate waters and seldom, if ever, pene-

MARLIN

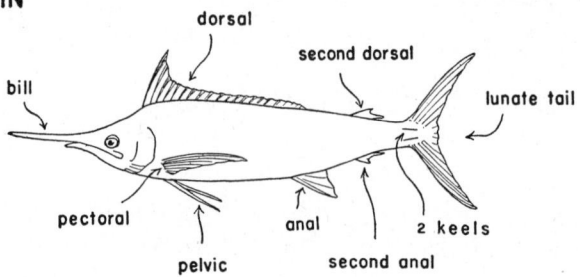

TUNA

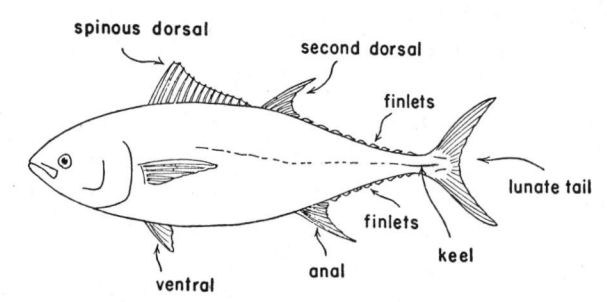

JACKFISH

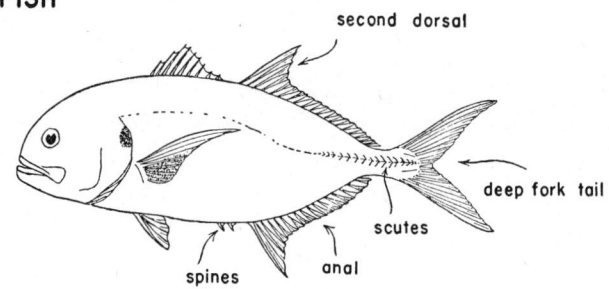

POMPANO

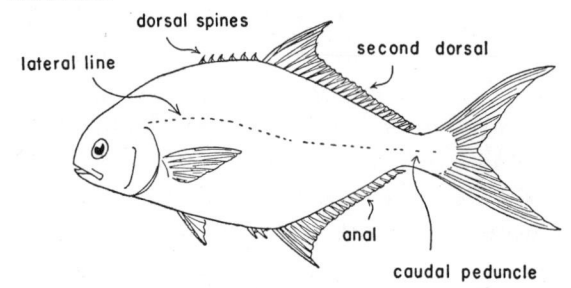

Classification 9

GROUPER

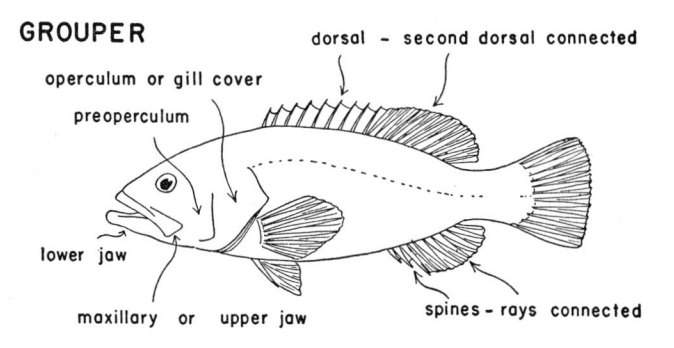

- dorsal – second dorsal connected
- operculum or gill cover
- preoperculum
- lower jaw
- maxillary or upper jaw
- spines – rays connected

ROCKFISH

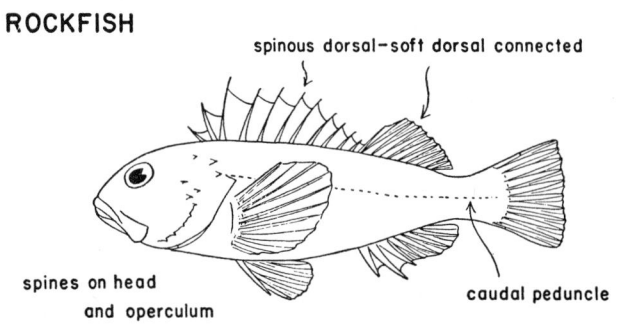

- spinous dorsal – soft dorsal connected
- spines on head and operculum
- caudal peduncle

COD

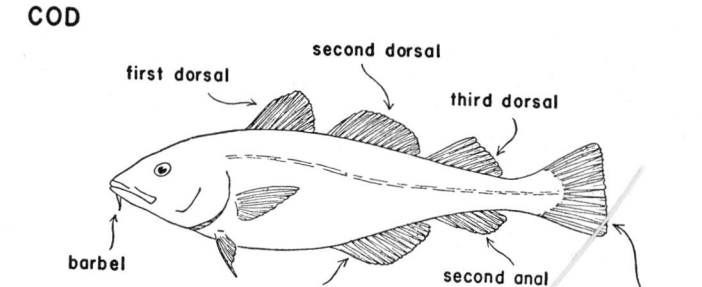

- first dorsal
- second dorsal
- third dorsal
- barbel
- first anal
- second anal
- square tail

FLATFISH

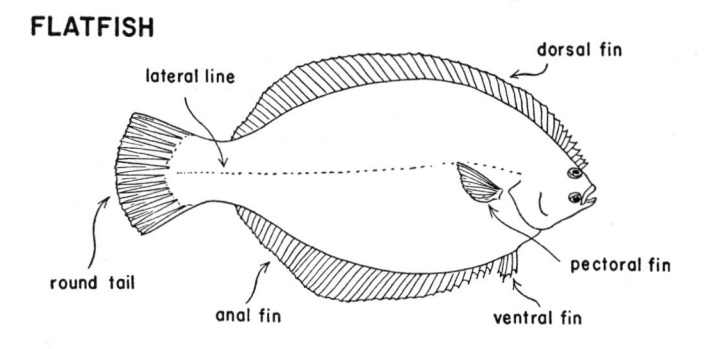

- lateral line
- dorsal fin
- round tail
- anal fin
- ventral fin
- pectoral fin

task. The common names used in this book are the ones employed by most people—at least as far as my personal experience goes. Also, I have changed a few common names in an attempt to avoid confusion.

It is even more important to be clear about scientific names. Regardless of the efforts made to present material on game fishes in a popular manner, the common names of the fishes must be accompanied by the scientific name because, as we have seen, there is so much confusion about common names—even in a fairly restricted locality. The problem becomes greater as one goes further afield, and the situation would become hopeless when considering fishes from different parts of the world if the scientific names were omitted.

The great value of employing scientific or distinctive names is simply that there is only one for each "kind" of fish; the name is in Latin and composed of two parts (a double word or binomen). The great Swedish biologist Karl von Linné (Carolus Linnaeus in Latin) introduced this system in 1758 when he produced *Systema Naturae*, in which he attempted to name in Latin all the animals of the world. The system was a success and is still used today.

The first part of the name refers to the genus; the genus is a category into which are placed fishes that closely resemble each other (we might say close relatives). The second part of the distinctive or scientific name is called the species, which in Latin means each "kind." Another way of putting it—the first part is the generic name and the second the specific name. As an example to illustrate the method, let us consider some of the marlins which are closely related one to another. We place them, the black, blue, striped, and white, in the genus *Makaira*, but each has its specific name; striped marlin is *Makaira mitsukurii;* white marlin is *Makaira albida*, etc.

Sportsmen who wish to pursue the subject of taxonomy further can find a full treatment of it in any good textbook on zoology. However, anglers are always interested in knowing to what family a certain fish belongs. The family group (Latin family name always ends in *-dae*) is composed of fishes which belong to the same genus or to closely related genera (plural for genus). For example, the marine bass family is named SERRANIDAE and is composed of sea basses, groupers, and rock basses; the family as a whole includes several different but closely related genera. The family name is given with each species in the text.

DISTRIBUTION

The geographical distribution of game fishes is influenced by a wide variety of factors. Some species have an almost cosmopolitan range while others are confined to a fairly restricted area. The wandering or dispersal of fishes is limited by water temperature, salinity, ocean currents, and also by the configuration of the coastline, underwater ridges, canyons, and deep water.

Certain game fishes can tolerate only certain temperatures of water. For example, in the eastern Pacific the cold temperature toleration of the sailfish and marlins is approximately 59° F. In other words, billfishes usually do not travel farther north than Point Conception, California, nor farther south than Valparaiso, Chile, because beyond these points the water usually drops below 59° F. The depth limits of the sailfish and marlins may also be controlled by the 59° temperature factor. An excellent example of a fairly abrupt line of demarcation formed by a temperature difference takes place off the coast of North America where the cold Labrador Current meets the warm water of the Gulf Stream. Although the water masses are close to each other, the differences in the water temperatures of the warm and cold currents act like a wall that discourages penetration by fishes inhabiting the two zones.

Seasonal variations in the temperature of the sea also influence the distribution of fishes. For example, the Atlantic mackerel, which prefers warm waters, remains in the open sea or in deep-water areas during the winter; when the inshore waters become warmer in summer, it frequents coastal areas. Another example is the occurrence of white marlin and blue marlin in waters off the Massachusetts islands in summer; when the water temperature drops, the fish leave. The seasonal occurrence of bluefish along our Atlantic coast can be followed progressively—farther north as the warm season progresses and the water temperatures go higher.

Salinity (in different areas in the seas the salt content may vary in amount per given quantity of water) is effective in preventing the dispersal of some species of fish, but it does not present an insurmountable barrier to others. The salt content of water has an important effect not only on the range of adult fishes but also on the development of drifting eggs. If winds or currents happen to force these eggs from open sea to more dilute coastal waters, the eggs sink and die.

An ocean current may carry some types of fishes almost passively, while other kinds are seen always swimming against it. Warm-water fishes may go beyond their usual northerly limits when ocean currents temporarily change their course slightly, or the fishes may appear closer to shore because of natural fluctuations of the currents. Good fishing may be had fairly close to the coast in some areas, while at a nearby shore fishes are not present within hundreds of miles because the ocean current shoots off from the coast. This situation usually exists where an abrupt and deep depression takes place in the continental outline. Underwater ridges and canyons affect, to some extent, the directional flow of currents, which in turn influence the distribution of fishes. Game fishes are never found in excessively deep places; water pressures must confine the fishes to the upper zones.

MIGRATION

The travels or wanderings of fishes, commonly referred to as migrations, are controlled, or perhaps I should say induced, by two basic factors: food and spawning. Migrations take place regularly, that is, they occur at the same season each year.

Oceanic game fishes may follow the abundance of bait schools for hundreds of miles or travel enormous distances between the spawning area in southern waters and the location of great food supply in northern waters. Bluefin tuna, for example, after reaching northern waters will seek and follow herring, sardines, or mackerel in the same localities year after year; but if the waters warm up or other water changes take place, and the bait schools depart from their usual haunts, the bluefins will leave the area and follow.

Coastal fishes like the striped bass and shad may travel short or long coastline distances before arriving in brackish stretches or fresh water rivers which fit the requirements for their spawning activities. Some species do not migrate north and south, but instead travel offshore into deep water in cold weather and inshore during warm weather. Still others may combine the inshore-offshore type of migration with a north-south movement.

Water temperature plays an important role in pinpointing the time of migrational departure or arrival of a certain species in a specific area. In other words, although some types of fishes may appear in an area at the same season annually, the exact dates are controlled by water temperature. For example, if spring weather is unusually cold in the Massachusetts area, the striped bass may arrive two or three weeks later than usual.

Some fishes make a practice of traveling with the tides, in to shore and out again, mostly searching for food. This habit should not be referred to as a migration but as a movement or tide-running. As a general rule, all fishes in a migration toward spawning do not feed. However, they may often hit a bait or lure simply as a reflex action.

SPAWNING

The matter of fish reproduction and its associated activities is generally referred to as spawning. The breeding period or spawning season is that time during which the reproductive apparatus is ripe—the eggs of the female and milt of the male. This condition may last only a few days in some species and

Spawning

extend over weeks or months in others. Most of the salt water game fishes spawn during the first part of the year.

Basically there are two types of spawning systems: external fertilization of eggs, and internal fertilization. The latter means that the young are born alive. The mako shark, Pacific coast seaperches (EMBIOTOCIDAE), and rockfishes (SCORPAENIDAE) are examples of fishes in which fertilization takes place internally and the young are born alive. Almost all the different kinds of fishes, however, fertilize externally. One type of external fertilization occurs in open waters where the fish gather in huge schools during spawning season and release their reproductive cells indiscriminately into the water. In this type of spawning (which is usually referred to as pelagic) there is no effort at matching or pairing off. Most oceanic fishes spawn in this manner. The eggs are at the mercy of currents, winds, temperatures, water salinities. In pelagic spawning the eggs of most species of fishes float freely, while in others the eggs sink to the bottom, where they are preyed upon heavily by bottom fishes. In either case, parents show no concern for the eggs, and the spawning activity seems to be nothing more than relief from the pressure of overabundant sex products.

Some species of game fishes, striped bass for example, leave the salt water and travel into fresh water rivers, often many miles upstream, to spawn. Fish undertaking this type of spawning travel are referred to as anadromous. Here again, the fertilization takes place more or less freely, but a single female may be accompanied by a few to as many as fifty males. The eggs of the striped bass are nonadhesive, slightly heavier than water, and are rolled about by the current. It is interesting to note that, generally speaking, the salt water game fishes take part in what appears to be indiscriminate spawning in groups, whereas many of the fresh water fishes prepare a nesting area and indulge in varying degrees of parental care up to actually guarding the nest and the young.

Fertilized eggs, whether in the open sea, brackish, or fresh waters, require certain conditions for successful development (correct amounts of salinity, sunlight, oxygen, agitation), but the length of the incubation period depends mostly upon water temperature. For example, striped bass eggs will hatch in about 30 hours in a temperature of 71°–72° F.; 48 hours at 64° F.; 70–74 hours at 58°–60° F.

THE OCEANS

The sciences which encompass the study of the oceans are many, varied, and too technical to delve into here in detail. However, since the fishes treated in this book are inhabitants of salt water, I will touch on the highlights of information concerning the seas which will interest anglers.

Game fishes are found in all the world's great bodies of water referred to as oceans and seas. Generally speaking, the tropical and subtropical waters contain a greater number and a more varied assortment of game fishes than do the colder waters of more northern latitudes.

The *composition* of sea water is interesting; it contains in solution gases and solids which can be recovered by evaporation. Over three quarters of the dissolved material is common salt; the remainder is made up of small quantities of almost every known chemical element (including gold and silver), the greater part consisting of sodium, magnesium, and calcium.

Salinity or the actual quantity of salt dissolved in water is one of the controlling factors in the distribution of fishes. The amount of salt per given quantity of water varies in the different seas and oceans of the world and from time to time in any specific area. Open-ocean water varies little in its salinity, being almost always between 34 and 36 parts of salt to 1,000 parts of water by weight. Close to land in some areas the amount of dissolved salt is less because of the fresh water that flows off the land. A good example is Long Island Sound, where the salt content is 25 to 28 parts per 1,000. All oceans derive their salt from the earth. Fresh water drains the land in the form of rivers and brings with it salt and other substances. The salt, now so noticeable in sea water, has been washed from the soil in minute quantities over countless centuries.

The Oceans

The salinity of sea water in warm latitudes may be considerably higher than that of the open ocean because of the constant evaporation of water at the surface and the resulting concentration of salts left behind. It is interesting to note that the highest salinities in the world for open waters are found in the Red Sea—40 parts per 1,000. The eastern Mediterranean contains more salt than the open Atlantic; in this ocean the highest salinities occur in the Sargasso Sea. The polar regions contain the lowest salinities because rain and snow dilute the surface waters.

Phosphates and nitrates, present in minute quantities, are the most important elements found in sea water. These are substances which have a great nutrient value and are responsible for development of plankton, which is the start of the food chain for fishes (*see* p. 55).

Oxygen is one of the gases dissolved in water. Without it animals cannot live. It appears that there is no area in the open sea where oxygen is not present in solution in sufficient quantity to support a large number of fishes. However, there are unique instances where this element is not present; in some areas in the Black Sea there is no oxygen below about 100 fathoms—therefore, no fish or other animals can live there. But in the open ocean life is still possible in the greatest depth where oxygen is present because of the circulation of water in the enormous ocean currents.

The *temperature* of the sea is another important factor in reproduction and distribution of fishes. Surface temperatures vary generally from about 80° F. near the equator to about 30° F. near the poles. Actually, the highest sea temperatures occur in the Persian Gulf where the water is 96°; the coldest is 28° in the polar regions. Between these two extremes all temperatures are to be found. Temperature drops with depth and varies with the change in seasons. Approximately one half mile down the temperature is about 40° F., and readings on the ocean bottom are about 35° F. The effect of the sun's rays are not felt to a depth greater than 300 fathoms; the heat rays are rapidly absorbed by the upper few inches of water; any warmth developed in the deeper waters is carried there by a mixture of warmer surface waters.

Because water requires a great amount of heat energy to rise in temperature, it retains the heat well and is slow to give it up. This is why, in some areas, the fishing may continue to be good well into the fall even though the weather may be uncomfortably cold for the angler. Water temperatures (in oceanography) are given in degrees centigrade rather than degrees Fahrenheit, which may confuse the sportsman who is accustomed to the latter. Centigrade thermometer space between freezing and boiling is divided into 100 equal parts: 0° (freezing) to 100° (boiling). The space on the Fahrenheit thermometer, between freezing and boiling, is divided into 180 equal parts: 32° (freezing) to 212° (boiling). Here is a simple formula which is easy to work and accurate enough to satisfy the angler: $(°C \times \frac{9}{5}) + 32 = °F$.

The average *depth* of the ocean is about 2½ miles; the greatest depth is approximately 6 miles. Specific areas of unusually deep waters (below 18,000 feet) are known as deeps or trenches. For example, the Philippine Trench is 35,400 feet deep, and the Puerto Rico Deep is 28,707 feet in depth. There are 57 such deeps—32 in the Pacific, 5 in the Indian Ocean, 19 in the Atlantic, and one which lies partly in the Indian Ocean and partly in the Atlantic. The fathom, used in water measurements, is equal to 6 feet.

The *density* of sea water is about 1.03 times that of fresh water; therefore, salt water exerts a greater buoyant force on bodies immersed in it (swimming is easier in salt water). Because water is almost incompressible, the increase in density with depth is extremely small. In other words, the great pressure in the depths of the ocean has but slight effect on the density of the water. The actual *weight* or *specific gravity* of sea water depends upon its temperature and salinity; warm water is lighter than cool water, fresh water lighter than salt water; higher salinities make for heavier water. The *pressure* in the sea varies with depth. Approximately every 33 feet of

The Oceans

depth the pressure is increased by 14 pounds to the square inch. Therefore, pressures in the depths of the ocean are tremendous —as much as 3 tons to the square inch.

Light plays an important part in sea life; without it no plants could survive, and all fishes are ultimately dependent upon plant life for food. Therefore, ocean areas which are rich in nutrients and have an abundance of sunlight (some areas, like Peru, have practically no rainfall) produce great quantities of plankton which attract fishes. The penetration of light in any part of the sea depends upon the strength and altitude of the sun, weather conditions, the amount of sediment and turbidity in the water.

Coastal fishes are found in waters along the *continental shelf*, which is an extension of the continental mass into the ocean. The material which forms this shelf was worked down from the land by running water and deposited in the ocean. Then the waves and currents over the centuries spread out the deposits and formed a gently sloping floor which extends outward from ten to about a hundred miles.

The oceans and seas of the world are not merely great masses of water; they are composed of huge *currents* which circulate and move the water from place to place. Ocean currents are made up mostly of the "blue water," which is a common term to big game fishermen. The forces which set these gigantic bodies of water in motion are varied; some of the important ones are the rotation of the earth, winds, heat from the sun, and polar ice. To illustrate some of the phenomena involved in the movement of ocean waters let us consider the Gulf Stream, which sees more game fishing than any other oceanic current in the world. This gigantic river of warm blue water, 50 miles wide and 350 fathoms deep, originates in the Gulf of Mexico. Actually, this current is part of a system of currents which is of continuous circulation in the Atlantic and really cannot be said to start or end anywhere. In brief, this is what happens:

1. The surface water just north of the equator is heated by the tropical sun, and salinity is raised by constant evaporation.

2. Continual winds from the northeast (Northeast Trade Winds) blow across this warm saline water and help move it (known as the North Equatorial Drift) towards the north coast of South America and then into the Caribbean Sea and Gulf of Mexico.
3. The waters become piled up at a level higher than that outside the islands of the West Indies.
4. Because these forced waters must flow somewhere in order to keep equilibrium, they push through the Straits of Florida; hence the birth of the Gulf Stream which continues at a rate of approximately four knots.*
5. As it moves northward this stream is deflected to the right, or eastward, because of the rotation of the earth; when it reaches the latitude 40° north, the current is flowing across the Atlantic due east.
6. Approaching cooler climates, it has lost a certain amount of its warmth, lost some of its speed, and has widened a good deal.
7. Ice drifting down from the polar seas on cold Labrador currents meets the Gulf Stream and cools it.
8. Cool water is heavier than warm water; therefore it sinks and is replaced by more warm water near the surface; this action causes a downward current of water.
9. The process continues while the ice melts, so that in a way the ice attracts the warm water.
10. The enormous masses of ice exert great power and cause part of the Gulf Stream, which is flowing east, to split off from the current and head north. The remainder of the east-going stream continues across the Atlantic and, because of the earth's rotation, continues right until it returns to equatorial waters where it originated.

Two types of water movement are distinguished in the great bodies of oceanic circulating water: the *currents*, which are definite bodies of flowing water, and *drifts*, which are horizontal movements of water brought about by wind action and which travel more or less in the same direction the wind is blowing.

---

* A knot is a measure of speed equal to one nautical mile per hour. The nautical mile is equal to about one and one sixth statute miles.

Louis Mowbray, director of the Bermuda Aquarium, one of the world's best scientist-anglers, discussing native fishing gear with author (left). Mrs. Migdalski looks on.

trate the colder waters of the Arctic and Antarctic. The world's largest fishes are oceanic.

Physical barriers such as mountains, dense forests, deserts, and large stretches of water are factors involved in the limitation or dispersion of land animals; the distribution of many fresh water fishes is limited by similar physical obstructions. Even though the great oceans are connected one to another, the dispersal of oceanic fishes throughout the world is also restricted by barriers. With oceanic fishes such factors as temperature, salinity, chemical properties of water, and the flow of ocean currents are the barriers of restriction.

Many of these fishes are commercially important. All are edible, and most are considered table delicacies. Without exception they will hit a trolled bait and exhibit great resistance before being boated. Examples are swordfish, marlin, sailfish, tuna, dolphin.

Coastal and shore game fishes are those which inhabit the continental shelves. Fishes of varied environments are represented in this group. Some prefer tide rips, the surf, river mouths, and fast flowing waters; others like to inhabit quiet areas, bays, or lagoons. There are warm-water fish and cold-water fish and in-between fish, reef fish, bottom fish, sandy area fish, and those that love rocky areas. Some species take part in extensive migrations; others don't travel very far from home. In other words, the coastal and shore fishes could be screened into many interesting environmental divisions, but to do so would fill another volume.

NAMES

Everyone dealing with fishes is aware of the problem of names. Some species of fish may have as many as a dozen common names. One example is the weakfish, which is also known as sea trout, spotted sea trout, squeteague, and yellow fin. An effort is being made by the American Fisheries Society and the Outdoor Writers Association to arrive at a single common name for each kind of fish, but this is a very difficult

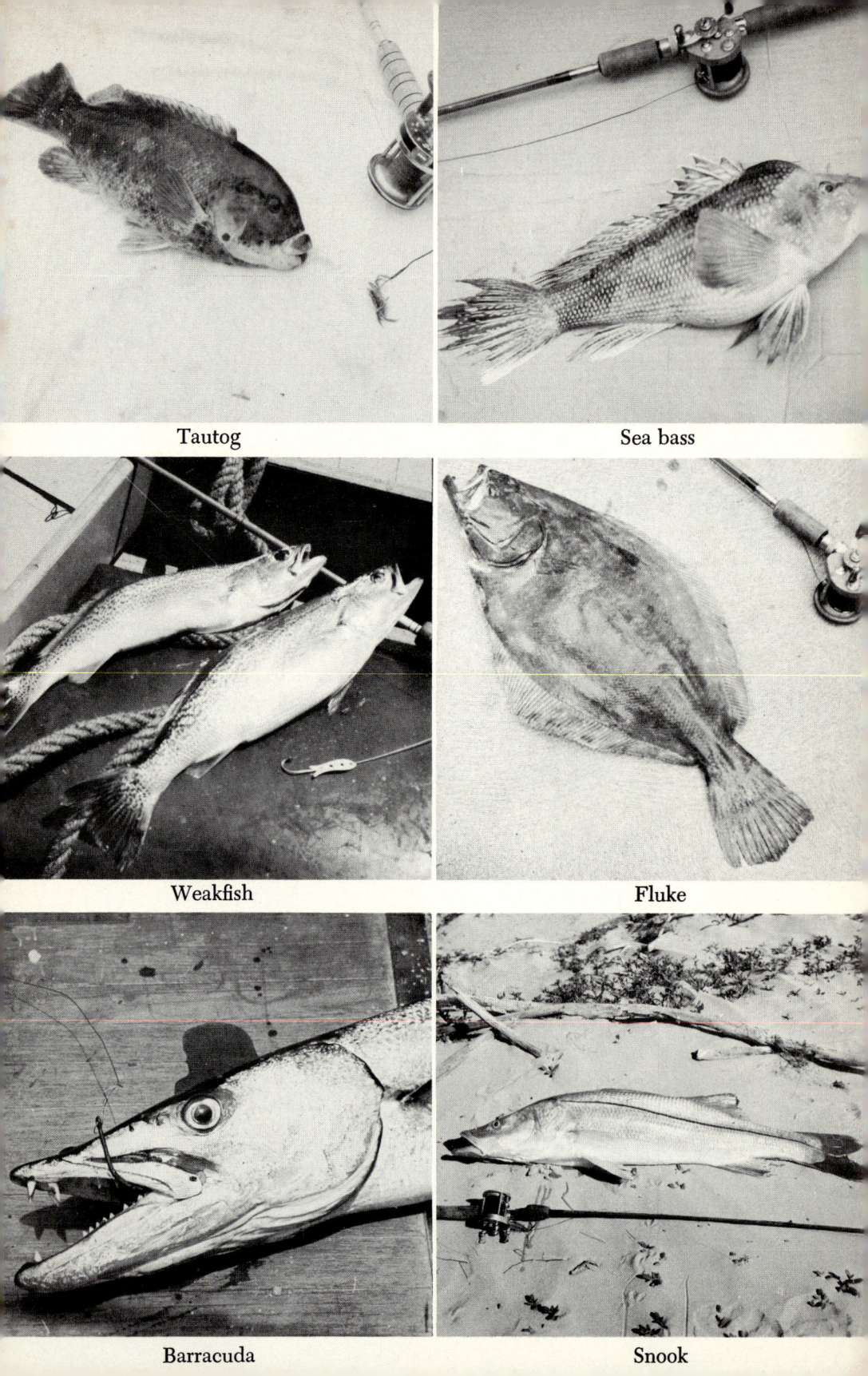

Tautog	Sea bass
Weakfish	Fluke
Barracuda	Snook

The Oceans

The movements of bodies of water in a vertical direction are of two types known as *upwelling* and *sinking*. When the density of surface water increases by cooling, it travels downward or sinks. Upwelling occurs when a deep current meets the shelving bottom or submerged bank in coastal regions. Persistent offshore winds can also bring about upwelling by blowing the surface waters outward. This movement of vertical water to the surface is of great importance because the bottom waters, which are rich in nutrient salts, phosphates and nitrates, are brought to the surface. That is why in regions of upwelling there is a great abundance of sea life.

Tides are periodic water movements familiar to all fishermen. This rise and fall of ocean water is caused by the gravitative pull of the moon and the sun. A rising tide is said to flow, and a tide that is receding is said to ebb. To put it briefly, the workings of the tide happen this way: The water is drawn or attracted by the moon from all around the earth to a point beneath the moon so that it is accumulated there. High tide takes place where this bulge of water occurs. At the same time exactly similar forces act on the hemisphere of the earth opposite the moon, causing high tide there too. Therefore, there are two high tides simultaneously on the earth—one on the side of the earth facing the moon and the other on the side of the earth away from the moon. These two high tides are responsible for the water between them being pulled away. In other words, the two regions lying on either side of the earth, midway between the two high tide areas, at the same time will be low water. Two high tides and two low tides take place every 24 hours. Because the moon moves around the earth in an elliptical orbit, the interval between one high tide and the next is not exactly 12 hours. There is a progressive change; the time of high water is not the same every day. High tide of one morning will be close to an hour later than that of the previous morning.

With the change in tides there is also a change in the range of the tides. These periods are known as spring tides (a better name would be big tides because "spring" has no association with the season of year) and neap tides. During the spring tides the high-water mark reaches its highest and the low-water mark its lowest—in other words, the range between the tide marks is greatest. On the other hand, during the neap tides the tide comes in and out at a short distance. Spring tides are in effect when the moon and sun are exerting their pulls in the same direction and the force is at its greatest (shortly after both the new and full moons). When the sun and moon are on the same side of the earth (new moon), the range of tides is at its maximum; at full moon the spring tides are less because the sun and moon are opposite one another. When the forces of the moon and sun are at right angles to one another (half moon), the range of tides is least or neap tides.

OPEN-OCEAN FISHES

Billfishes

The billfishes are large, spectacular, oceanic game fishes characterized by a prolongation of the upper jaw into a weapon commonly referred to as bill, spear, or sword. Members of the great clan are sailfishes, marlins, spearfishes, and swordfish.

Anglers are confused, and fishery technologists do not agree on many aspects regarding this assemblage of fishes—much remains to be learned. Even billfish is a controversial name. Popular books on fishing, encyclopedias for anglers, and many other publications refer to this group as speared fishes. The authors of these contributions maintain that this assemblage should not be called billfishes because a selection of small silvery fishes (houndfish, halfbeaks, and needlefish) are named billfishes. I believe their conclusions lead only to more confusion. A member within this group, *Strongylura marinus*, is named billfish, which increases the bewilderment. Besides, I have never heard an angler, guide, or boatman refer to these fishes, some of which are used for bait, as billfish; they are always called ballyhoo, skippers, halfbeaks, needlefish, scissors, and other names depending on the locale of the fishing. (A better name for this collection of small fishes would be beakfishes.)

I oppose applying the word "speared" to marlin and others, first, because types within the group are named spearfishes, which starts the mix-up. Second, to add *-ed* to *spear* in order to differentiate between the group and the particular species is not clear enough. (Also, fishery scientists have been attempting to eliminate the suffix *ed* in the common names of fishes.) Perhaps these reasons may be too academic, but have you ever heard a mate yell, "Look at that spear!"? Never. It is always "Look at that bill," Grab his bill," or "There's his bill." It is my contention that the term "billfishes" rather than "speared fishes" should be used to describe the sailfishes, marlins, spearfishes, and swordfish as a group.

The range of the billfishes seems to be restricted by definite barriers of water temperatures. Both above and below the equator these fishes are seldom found where surface temperatures fall below 59° F. For example, on the West Coast of the United States the 59° line occurs off southern California; in South America, off southern Chile. In between these two temperature lines billfishes are found. If 59° is a confining factor, then it seems likely that these fishes are restricted also to the upper layers of the water whose temperatures range above 59°.

Many stories revolve about the ferociousness of billfishes and their prowess to attack vessels. Some of the tales are without foundation, but many are backed by evidence. It is not unusual for a billfish to strike and damage a vessel, especially when the fish is hooked or harpooned. Stories of these occurrences have been documented. (*See* sections on Swordfish and Blue Marlin for specific instances.)

We know that a billfish will often plow through a school of fish, raising havoc with its bill. Often small fishes take shelter close to an ocean-going vessel and will travel alongside for hundreds of miles. Perhaps when in the excited state of feeding, a billfish may accidentally ram the vessel.

Any species of billfish can be dangerous when handled impatiently at the gaff. Also, green fish brought alongside may be especially troublesome. (A green fish is one which is forced to the gaff before being played out.) When close to the boat a fish

Billfishes 27

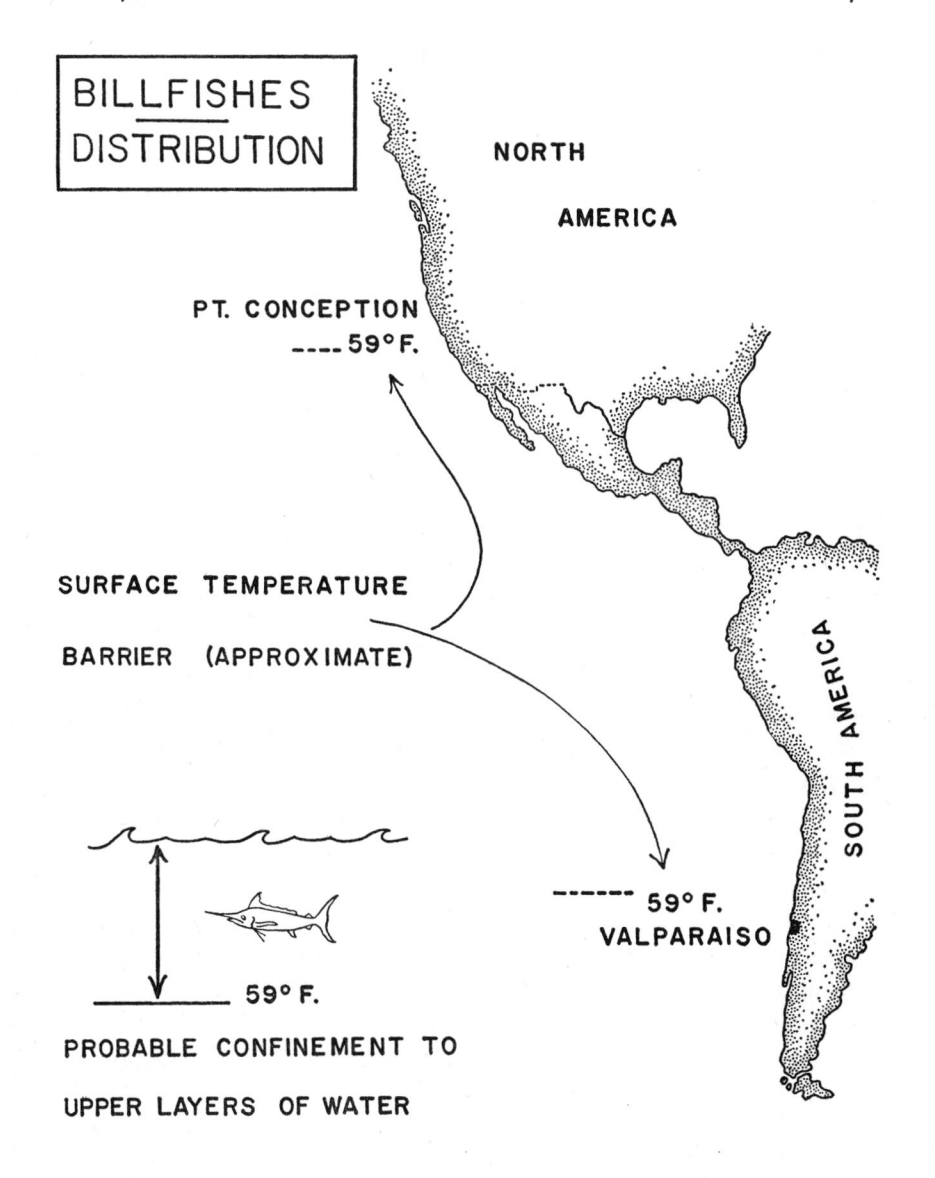

**BILLFISHES
DISTRIBUTION**

NORTH AMERICA

PT. CONCEPTION
---- 59° F.

SURFACE TEMPERATURE

BARRIER (APPROXIMATE)

------ 59° F.
VALPARAISO

SOUTH AMERICA

59° F.

PROBABLE CONFINEMENT TO

UPPER LAYERS OF WATER

in this condition may leap suddenly and do great damage to the person bent over the side attempting to use the gaff. A friend of mine, "Captain Pete," had his chest rasped by the rough edge of a leaping marlin's bill—he was lucky.

Off Cabo Blanco, Peru, we boated a large striped marlin. As it lay on deck the fish appeared to be dead, and one of the mates sat on it. Suddenly the marlin gave a flip and the mate almost went over the side. Before he could scramble away, he was hit several times quite severely. For many days he carried black and blue marks on his legs and backside. The huge fish pounded the deck until the mate grabbed the wooden persuader and in turn played a tattoo on the marlin's head.

Angling techniques employed in capturing the billfish are based upon its feeding habits. The usual method is to troll a bait from the outrigger; the bait skips and dances on the surface; the billfish is attracted and hits the bait; the line comes down from the outrigger allowing slack line. The slack line interval permits the bait to appear stunned; the fish grabs it and the angler sets the hook. But it doesn't always happen in such a cut-and-dried manner. Sometimes the fish, after hitting the bait, will wait a bit before taking it. Often the billfish will crash-strike the bait without tapping it first.

The question arises, "How much time should elapse from the moment the fish hits the bait, or from the moment of a crash-strike, until the angler sets the hook?" The angler has a choice of striking immediately or waiting about ten seconds or longer before striking. Usually the captain and the mate will influence the action the angler takes by yelling instructions like crazy men.

One school of thought maintains that the bait is always hit first with the bill; the other believes that the billfish captures the bait with its jaws while the bill action is only incidental. Some boat captains and other observers state that most baits which have been hit by a billfish and retrieved by the angler show markings or mutilations on both sides; these baits have scales missing and show marks made by the fish's jaws. They see this as evidence that the billfish grabs the bait instead of hitting it first with its bill. Often, bluefin tuna will rush a bait, grab it, and let go immediately. Anglers refer to this procedure as spit-out. Why wouldn't a billfish do the same? The fish could hit the bait with his bill, take it, let go, and thus place markings on both sides of the bait.

It is my contention that a billfish when in pursuit of live, darting fish will use his bill first to stun his quarry before picking it up in his mouth. However, when following a bait dragged by a fishing craft at a constant speed and in a fairly straight line there may be an inclination to eliminate the tap. Also, could it be that on calm days a billfish is more apt to grab a bait, and on choppy or rough days, when the bait is dancing all over the surface, the billfish would be inclined to hit it first with his bill? If a billfish is following the bait and looks it over before hitting (they often do—from side to side), he should, I believe, be given about ten seconds of free-spool. On the question of whether or not the billfish hits the bait before taking it, I believe much depends upon the fish's state of hunger. It is my opinion that the length of time between the strike and the setting of the hook should be governed by the conditions of the moment plus the experience of the angler.

The following incident may add more material for discussion on the subject. In the yellowfin tuna grounds near the equator south of Hawaii, the U.S. Fish and Wildlife Service longline vessel, the "John R. Manning," captured a huge marlin (erroneously called white marlin). The estimated weight of this fish was 1,500 pounds, and in its stomach was found a 5-foot yellowfin tuna which was speared twice through the body. The tuna was headfirst in the marlin's stomach and weighed 157 pounds. It may be that marlin hit small prey with their bills and spear the larger ones.

SAILFISHES

Found in tropical and subtropical seas of the world, sailfishes are the most popular members of the billfish clan. Everyone recognizes them immediately because these fishes carry huge sail-like dorsal fins on their backs. Popularly, as yet, the flesh is not considered desirable as food. However, when smoked it is delicious and is growing in popularity. Commercial smokehouses which specialize in preparing sailfish for sportsmen are now in vogue.

A prime favorite with a multitude of fishermen, the sailfish is the billfish easiest to catch and usually the first large fish taken by most budding big game anglers. On the other hand, this fish's leaping, skittering acrobatics after it is hooked are spectacular enough to excite the most experienced sportsman. The sailfish is fast, and attempts have been made, using a stop watch, to time the runs of a hooked sailfish. Speeds have been estimated to be as high as 100 yards per 3 seconds or about 68 miles an hour. (The accuracy of this method would be difficult to ascertain.) Nearly exclusively, the method of surface trolling for sailfish is used in all areas. However, some have been caught on hook and line several hundred feet down.

The first sailfish was described in 1876 by Brousonnet from an Indian Ocean specimen. Not many years later attention was drawn to the sailfish along the eastern coast of the United States when it was being caught on handline by anglers who went along with commercial fishermen to enjoy a day of hooking kingfish and mackerel. A Mr. Armes with Mr. Cammeron as guide, about 1898, caught the first sailfish on rod and reel in the Florida Keys. It wasn't until the 1920's however, that the Atlantic sailfish was given recognition as one of the gamest fish in existence, and it is now the leading sport fish on the coast of Florida. Today the many undertakings catering to the sportsman in quest of sailfish combine to make it a multimillion dollar industry.

Imbedded in the skin are unusual thorn-like scales similar to the marlin's; the bill is smooth on the top or dorsal surface but contains rasp-like protuberances on the sides and bottom or ventral surface; the eye is contained in a pronounced horny socket, which is capable of movement; the caudal peduncle keels are paired, and the lower jaw is not separated below the gill covers as it is in most typical fishes. The tail is large, rigid, and of a lunate type. A pair of ventral fins, long and very nar-

Sailfishes

row, are located just behind the throat region; a small second dorsal fin and a small second anal fin are present.

The beautiful shimmering colors of a sailfish are at best when the fish is jumping. The large dorsal fin is purplish blue, profusely spattered with dark spots; the dorsal surface is a typical marine-fish color of dark blue; sides are silvery with a touch of bronze, and when the fish is alive, a fairly distinct burst of golden bronze is displayed along the area where dorsal and lateral colors meet; distinct, broken narrow bars or vertical stripes are present on its sides. Often the entire fish is covered with a bronze effect, which is removed in streaks when the wire leader comes in contact with the body during the process of fighting the fish.

Scientists refer to this family as ISTIOPHORIDAE, which also includes the marlins and spearfishes. The sailfish genus *Istiophorus,* previously split into many species, has been narrowed down. Japanese fishery workers believe nine species are recorded for this genus, but American ichthyologists generally accept the possibility of five different species of sailfishes which occur in the Atlantic, Pacific, Indian Ocean and Red Sea, Japan and Hawaii, and Tahiti. However, at present, splitting the sailfishes into five groups is still more or less informed guess work, and much specific investigation has to take place before it becomes a proved fact. Here we discuss only the Atlantic and Pacific forms.

Atlantic Sailfish (2c)
(*Istiophorus americanus*)

The majority of the great horde of salt water fishermen who invade Florida's blue waters annually have an ambition to catch their first sailfish—or more sailfish. Undoubtedly this exciting fish carries the brunt of all Florida fishing in the responsibility of promoting big business fishing spending millions of dollars.

For the angler there are no complications in distinguishing the Atlantic form from other species of sailfish simply because it is restricted to the Atlantic. Identification of the sailfish is simple since it is the only fish which possesses such a huge dorsal fin, commonly referred to as the sail.

The Atlantic sailfish ranges over an extensive area. It is found in the Caribbean, the Gulf of Mexico, and has been recorded from southern Brazil to as far north as Massachusetts. However, catches north of the Virginia capes are rare, and only along the coast of Florida is the sailfish truly abundant. The inside edge of the Gulf Stream seems to be its preferred habitat.

As far as anglers are concerned the best all-year fishing area extends from Fort Pierce south to Key West. During the summer months results are better a little farther north, from Mayport, near Jacksonville, south to Cape Canaveral. The hottest spot is generally known to be an area from Fort Pierce south to Lake Worth, and in between is Stuart, which anglers consider to be the sailfish capital.

Although the Atlantic sailfish activity is mostly along the Florida coast, there are good grounds at the other side of the Gulf Stream—Walker Cay, Bimini, and Cat Cay—all in the Bahamas. Occasionally a sailfish is taken off Nassau, where few boats fish for them. Although sailfish have not been taken on rod and reel to date in Bermuda, my good friend Lou Mowbray, director of the Bermuda Aquarium, has identified them close to his boat. It is found in the eastern Atlantic along the coast of France, off Africa's Gold Coast, and also in the Mediterranean.

The average weight of the Atlantic species is approximately 50 pounds. The record on rod and reel is 123 pounds, caught off Walker Cay, Bahamas, on April 25, 1950, by H. Teetor. (The Pacific sailfish is a much larger species, with an average weight of 100 pounds and a record of 221 pounds.)

Migratory patterns of the sailfish are, as yet, not known completely. The fish are present year round in the Gulf Stream off Florida's shores, and as the weather gets warmer they migrate northward and appear off the Carolinas in August. Sailfish often swim in numbers, which indicates a schooling or migratory behavior; at most other times they travel singly or in pairs. Although the majority of the fish are encountered in the blue Gulf Stream, some are seen in the green waters, where they come in to feed on the profusion of inshore fishes. As with many other fishes, availability of food, temperature toleration, and the seeking of proper spawning conditions are primary factors in migration. We are now just beginning to get definite information on the extent of sailfish migration. One sailfish tagged December 30, 1953, was recovered early in 1956; it had gained 20 pounds, grown 12 inches in length, was 7 feet 3 inches in length, weighed 50 pounds, and was captured 55 miles from the tagging point. Another caught (by H. J. Blum of Cincinnati, Ohio) on March 9, 1957, approximately 6 miles northeast of Alligator Reef Light off the Florida Keys, was tagged off Port Aransas, Texas (Gulf of Mexico), on June 8, 1955 (tagged by Charles Urschel of the Port Aransas Rod and Reel Club). This fish, which weighed 40 pounds and measured 6 feet 10 inches when caught, had traveled at least 850 miles in 433 days.

Jack Gehringer of the U.S. Fish and Wildlife Service reports: "In the Atlantic Ocean off the coast of the United States spawning occurs from April to September in the area from south of Cuba north to the Carolinas, beyond the 100-fathom line, closely associated with the Gulf Stream, and with a northward advance as the season progresses. In the Gulf of Mexico two separate spawning areas beyond the 100-fathom line are apparent: the southeastern Gulf from April through August, and the western Gulf less clearly defined, but at least during June and probably into August."

Gilbert Voss of the Miami Marine Laboratory found that Florida sailfish spawn in fairly shallow water from April through August. As might be expected, females carrying roe during this period are rather sluggish fighters. Similar to most pelagic fishes, the eggs are fertilized at random and float freely, in this case northward along with the plankton in the Gulf Stream. Voss, and other scientists who have been investigating the sailfish, found that a single female may carry as many as 4,675,000 eggs. The gonad, a reproductive organ holding the eggs, may weigh from 3 to 5 pounds. However, as with other ocean fishes, a mere fraction of that total survives because numerous predators feed on the eggs and young as they float helplessly in the sea. The hatchlings themselves soon turn predators and feed on tiny shrimp-like copepods, which collectively are known as the milk of the sea. The baby sailfish soon find that tiny mollusks, called heteropods, make good food. Gehringer reports that sailfish larvae less than 6.0 mm. long exist on a diet of copepods (minute crustaceans). Fish larvae were the major food item of sailfish larvae larger than 6.0 mm.

Voss is of the opinion that growth of the sailfish is extremely rapid, but their length of life is short—three to four years. After spawning in southern waters, the larvae and young are carried northward to the waters off the Carolinas. (Larval sailfish are also found in other areas: for example, the Gulf of Mexico, mostly in June.) Then they work inshore—5- to 8-inch specimens are found in this area during the summer—and back southward to Florida, where they arrive as 4- and 5-foot adults in October and November. Within a year the fish may be 5 or 6 feet in length. The average sailfish, 7 feet and 25 to 60 pounds, is about two years old.

Donald De Sylva, who worked at the Miami Marine Laboratory, in further studies on the growth of the sailfish reports that a fish hatched in June will reach 56 inches and a weight of 7 pounds by November; one year—72 inches, 21 pounds; two years—85 inches, 43 pounds; three years—92 inches, 63 pounds. The average of three-year-old fish is 63 pounds, but individuals may weigh from 42 to 109 pounds. Apparently three years is old age for the sailfish and few may reach four years. Growth of the sailfish is extremely rapid, especially in the first two years of its short life span.

During one year, in the vicinity of Palm Beach, more than 2,500 sailfish were landed, many over 7 feet long. Consequently, along the Florida fishing coast great concern was shown by conservation-minded anglers because of the large number of sailfish slaughtered every year. Some of these men organized activities in clubs (Sailfish Yacht and Beach Club, West Palm Beach Fishing Club, Sailfish Conservation Club, etc.) for the purpose of encouraging the conservation of sailfish. During a sailfish derby, which is held in the first two months of the year,

1,579 fish were caught in one season by 40 boats; but because of the conservation crusade carried out by the fishing clubs, most of the fish were released. The clubs award prizes as an incentive to release fish. For example, in 1955 one person released 35 fish. During the 1956 derby, 626 fish were caught in 28 days and 507 were released—a score of 82 per cent. In the twentieth annual derby 296 fish were taken and only 60 were killed for mounting; the rest were returned to the water. Gold buttons are awarded for fish over 8 feet. One year saw over 100 of these buttons handed out. The top prize, a diamond button, is awarded to the person who catches three fish of this size. As a further incentive a red pennant is raised for each fish released (traditionally a white one is raised for a boated fish) and more publicity is given for fish liberated than for fish brought to the docks.

The findings of scientists Voss and De Sylva will undoubtedly foster the thought of revising the Florida laws pertaining to the sailfish. At present, the law prohibits possession of more than two sailfish by one person in one day. The sale of this species is also prohibited. From the studies made by the scientists it becomes apparent that fish over 7 feet have a very short life span, and natural mortality takes the great toll of larger fish. Releasing these fish is a commendable sporting practice because other anglers may get a chance to catch the same fish, but scientists question the justification of it as a wise conservation move. (Conservation does not imply the complete safeguard of a renewable natural resource, but instead it is the efficient management of that resource in a way to obtain its present fullest benefit without harming future potential.)

In association with the biological studies on the sailfish carried out since 1948 by the Miami Marine Laboratory, a tagging program was initiated. (Sailfish and marlin tagging had been tried many times before without success; for instance, in the Gulf of California several thousand sailfish had been tagged without a single return.) The program carried out by the Miami Laboratory included an area from Fort Pierce to the Florida Keys. A cattle tag was used first—a metal clamp which clipped over the fin or gill covers; this kind of tag does not harm the fish. The first tag returned was of this type. Another method, neoprene rubber rings around the bills, damaged them and was discontinued. Dart tagging is the latest method to be introduced. A plastic tube which holds a label is attached to the metal dart. The dart is jabbed into the fish from the end of a wooden pole and stays after the pole is pulled back. Whether or not this method will be successful remains to be seen; the dart may cause injury or may work itself out of the muscles of the fish. Thus far, out of 2,032 Miami tags only 5 have been recovered. The tagging of large sailfish seems fruitless because of their short life span. De Sylva suggests tagging young fish.

Adult sailfish feed almost exclusively on smaller fishes, depending on what is available, usually mullet, pilchards, and balao (pronounced ballyhoo), a small, silvery fish which is also excellent bait for other game fishes such as kingfish or king mackerel, wahoo, etc. At times needlefish, anchovies, or pelagic octopods, such as the paper-shelled nautilus, are found in sailfish stomachs. Strangely, the flyingfish, which is considered to be one of the best baits, was practically nonexistent among several hundred stomachs examined by the Miami scientists.

Billfish feeding methods are interesting (*see* first section on Billfishes). Usually a sailfish, with a rap of its bill, stuns its prey, then grabs and gobbles it. At times sailfish will gather in schools and with half-raised sails circle a dense group of bait fish. In this manner one and then another will swim through the mass of bait while whipping its bill viciously from side to side. After a large number have been killed or stunned, the sailfish slowly cruises below the bait swarm and picks off the victims.

I have had many exciting experiences with sailfishes in different oceans, but the one that I will remember until I've caught my last fish is the following. Bo, my wife and excellent fishing partner, and I were pleasantly occupied hunting sailfish in the lovely blue Gulf Stream waters off Miami Beach. While I was in the chair one of the silvery acrobats hit the bait and was soon pounding a tattoo on the teakwood deck. I intended to bring

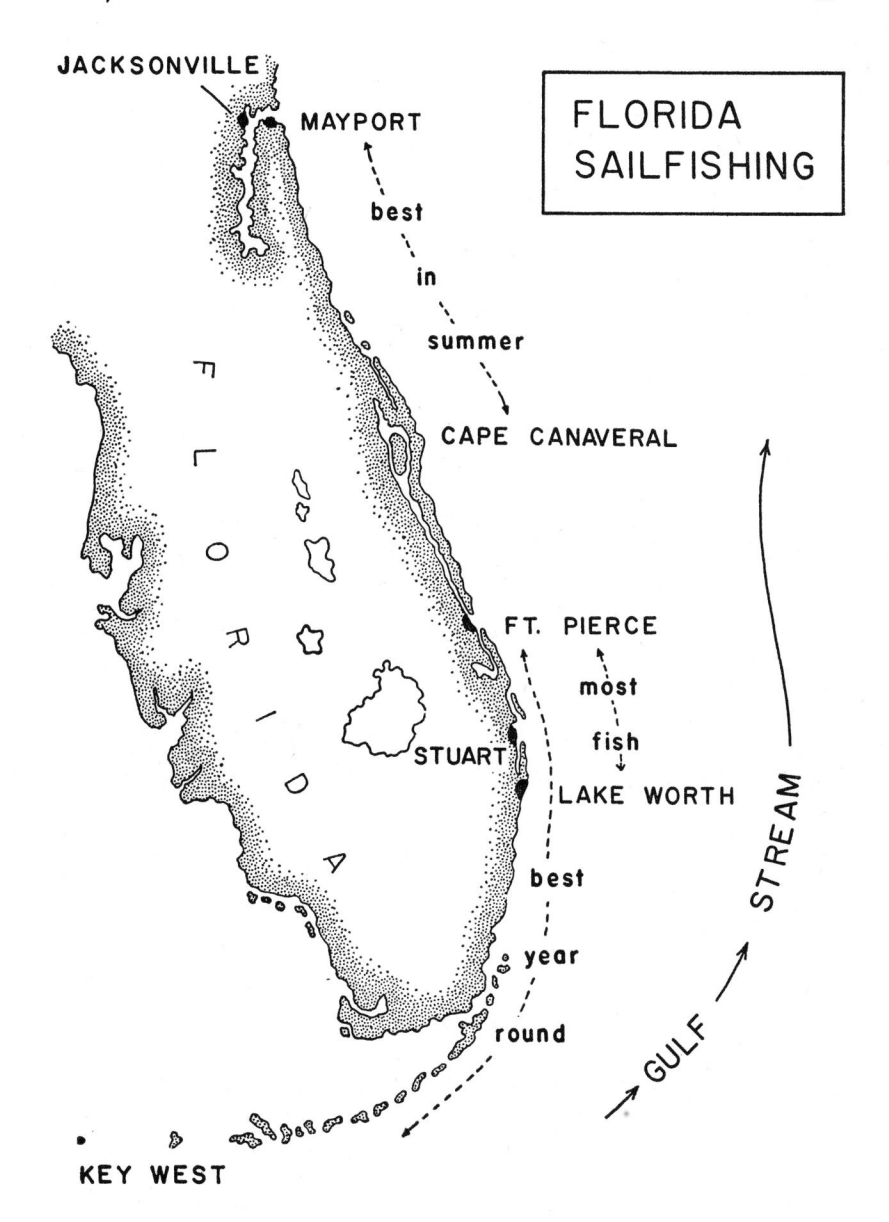

Sailfishes

FLORIDA SAILFISHING

this one ashore to get it smoked. One of the engines of the
beautiful new craft we chartered was acting up, and since our
schedule was to fish Bimini waters starting the next morning,
we decided to return to shore immediately to get the engines
checked. The mate tied her up, filled the gas tanks, washed
her down, and departed. Our film director, Kevin Donovan,
and our photographer, John Bennewitz, took off in search of a
telephone and more film. While we waited for their return,
Bo became engrossed in a book while I snoozed on the other
side of the cabin. Almost an hour passed. It was four P.M.
when I awoke and said, "It's warm—let's go up on the dock
where there's a breeze." I helped Bo up the ladder, and as we
stepped onto the pier, the boat blew up!

Pacific Sailfish
(*Istiophorus greyi*)

Similar to its smaller Atlantic cousin, the Pacific sailfish is also
a great favorite of the big game angling fraternity. Its range
is extensive—from Monterey, California, where they are rare
summer visitors, south along the coast of southern California,
Mexico, and Central America down to Cabo Blanco, Peru. Sailfish are scarce north of southern California and only rarely
caught off Peru. Water temperature seems to be the controlling
factor in the distribution of these fishes. Sailfish prefer waters
warmer than do the other billfishes.

Although some authorities claim the existence of five different types of sailfish, there is no confusion regarding the
Pacific species. Obviously, the angler does not concern himself
with the differentiation between the Atlantic and Pacific fish
for the simple reason that they occur in different oceans. However, the Pacific sailfish, which averages 100 pounds, with a rod
and reel record of 221 pounds (taken off the Galapagos Islands
by C. W. Stewart, February 12, 1947), grows bigger than the
Atlantic species, which averages 30 to 40 pounds with an angler's
record of 123 pounds. Aside from the obvious difference in

weight, there are other slighter differences which are not important to the angler.

The Pacific record fish was caught off Santa Cruz Island in the Galapagos—an area of great concentration for sailfish. Other exceptional spots for Pacific sailfishing are Panama Bay and—all in Mexico—Acapulco, Mazatlán, La Paz, Guaymas, White Frier Islands, and Les Tres Islas Marias. The fish have also been caught off the Seychelles and Madagascar in the Indian Ocean, Tahiti, Solomon Islands, and in the Philippines—Luzon, Palawan, and Samar. They are also fairly abundant around Guam, Japan, Hawaii, and Cocos Island (Costa Rica). In Panama Bay large groups of sailfish are seen during the fall cruising along with the upper portion of their tails above water. They seem to be migrating and seldom will be enticed to take a bait. These actions may indicate a spawning activity. Sailfish migrate into the Mazatlán area from May to October.

Feeding habits of the Pacific sailfish are similar to those of his Atlantic cousin: sardines, mackerel, mullet, and squid are the preferred bait.

Very little scientific work has been done on the Pacific sailfish —practically nothing is known regarding its spawning grounds, rate of growth, lifespan, etc. During a recent Yale Oceanographic Expedition to South America we caught a few sailfish off Cabo Blanco, but to find them this far south is unusual. Because of a phenomenon which occurred while we were there and which happens only rarely, a changing of currents and warming of the waters, sailfish were in evidence. (Currents off Cabo Blanco are treated in the section on Black Marlin.)

The Indian Ocean has a reputation for harboring truly gigantic sailfish (either closely related or identical to the Pacific sailfish). We hoped to prove this point during a Yale expedition to Africa in 1950. A few fairly large sailfish were taken but nothing of world-record proportions. However, two of the biggest sailfish I have ever seen followed our baits but would not hit. Although Captain Bill Fagan changed speeds on the "Manana" and tried other tricks, the fish would not take. I spoke with people in Mombasa familiar with market fishing, who said that it was not unusual for native handline fishermen to bring in very large sailfish. We explored the fishing possibilities during the months of January, February, and March. Mr. Jim Bailey, who ran a native commercial fishery at Shimoni, approximately 60 miles south of Mombasa, rendered much assistance to our expedition. I marvel at the fortitude and integrity of Jim, who organized a going fishery under primitive and difficult circumstances. (I might add that his wife, Jane, is an enthusiastic amateur ichthyologist.) Jim kept accurate records of the catches over a period of five years which show that the best fishing off Shimoni is during October, November, and December. Jim informed me that during these months natives often caught sailfish on handlines.

MARLINS

As a group marlins are considered to be the elite of big game fishes. These blue-back billfishes are the real racers of the sea with an estimated speed of 50 to 60 miles an hour. Compare this with the bluefin tuna and salmon, which are not sloths when movement is required, whose fastest has been an estimated 30 miles an hour. Marlin are blue-water fishes which prefer the warmer currents of the open seas. They are famous for their acrobatics—20, 30, or even 40 jumps displayed by a hooked fish are not rare. They are the most action-photographed group of all fishes. Often a hooked fish will jump clear of the water within close range of the boat, providing the camera man with opportunities for spectacular results. I have taken photographs of a striped marlin which jumped within 5 feet of the boat. Marlins are members of the family ISTIOPHORIDAE.

Marlins have thorn-like scales imbedded in the skin; the bill is smooth on top but contains rasp-like protuberances on the sides and ventral surface; minute teeth are present; the first dorsal, first anal, and ventral fins fit into grooves when folded; the eye is contained in a pronounced horny socket, which is capable of movement; the caudal peduncle keels are paired, and

Marlins

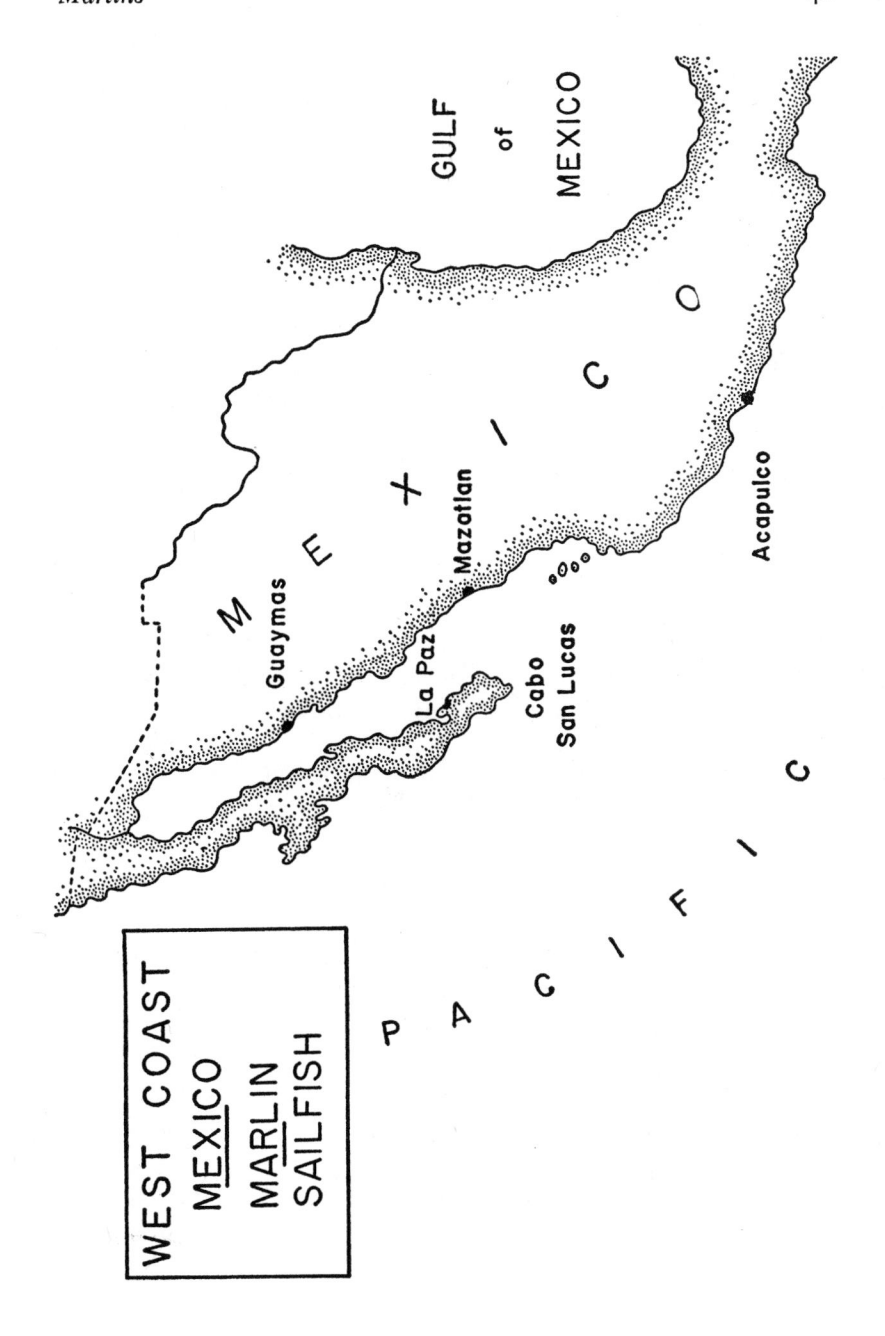

WEST COAST
MEXICO
MARLIN
SAILFISH

the lower jaw is not separated below the gill covers as in most typical fishes.

Confusion prevails among ichthyologists and fishery technologists regarding the technicalities of nomenclature, recognition of species, subspecies, etc. Over 150 years have passed since the first marlin was described, and still there is no agreement as to the number of species we should recognize. Of course, one must realize the difficulties of collecting a series of marlin for study, and because these fishes are so big, preserving them in the usual Formalin or alcohol is almost impossible.

Dick Robbins at the University of Miami and Jim Morrow of Yale are among several fishery scientists working on the marlins, hoping to unscramble the confusion. Until they do, the list below is up to date. I consider the Bermudian marlin questionable as a species. Dick Robbins treats the silver marlin, *Makaira tahitiensis*, as a synonym of black marlin, *Makaira marlina*. He states, "The name silver should now be buried and forgotten as worthless, as the first step in unscrambling the tangle," and I agree. Two types of striped marlin are now distinguished by Panama fishermen, but this remains an unsettled question.

>Atlantic blue marlin—*Makaira ampla*
>Pacific blue marlin—*Makaira mazara*
>Black marlin—*Makaira marlina*
>Striped marlin—*Makaira mitsukurii*
>White marlin—*Makaira albida*
>Bermudian marlin—*Makaira bermudae*

Each member of the marlin clan is discussed fully in the following sections.

Atlantic Blue Marlin (1b)
(*Makaira ampla*)

The blue marlin is a respected member of the giant-size game fish clan. It prefers warm areas and is found mostly in oceanic currents in Bahamian waters and Caribbean seas. This marlin is considered a prize by anglers because it is a big fish that fights

Marlins

well when hooked and may jump many times before coming to gaff.

Although scientists do not agree unanimously, the blue marlin of the Atlantic is closely related to, but slightly different from, the blue marlin of the Pacific.* Often authors may refer to this billfish as *istiophorid,* which is taken from its family name ISTIOPHORIDAE.

In the western Atlantic it is known to range from the Guiana current off the coast of Brazil into the Caribbean, Gulf of Mexico, and to as far north as Georges Bank (about the latitude of Cape Cod). It is found in Bermudian waters and on the other side of the Atlantic off France, and also off French West Africa. Much remains to be known regarding its distribution, especially off the east coast of South America.

When alive in the water, the blue marlin has a fascinating, almost cobalt blue, back or dorsal surface, which grows darker as soon as the fish dies. The fairly distinct vertical stripes also disappear quite rapidly. Its bill, like that of all marlin, is smooth on top with rough, rasp-like sides and ventral surface. Also, the bill is shorter and heavier, in comparison with the body, than that of the sailfish or white marlin. The sides are silvery, with a golden-copper effect in the live fish, and the belly is white.

A large white marlin may be mistaken for a small blue marlin and vice versa. I have seen many photographs in publications where these two species were labeled wrongly. This should not be because they are distinguished easily by the dorsal and anal fins: the blue has the anterior tips pointed, whereas the white marlin has them rounded. If you care to look closer, the lateral line is pronounced in the white marlin but cannot be seen externally in the blue. The lateral line in the blue appears as a joint network of lines mostly hidden in and under the skin; it may be called a reticulated lateral line system.

The average weight of the blue marlin is about 300 pounds. One year 112 fish taken at Bimini and Florida were weighed; they ranged from 75 to 596 pounds for an average of 283 pounds.

* Some scientists consider the blues from the two oceans as subspecies— Atlantic, *Makaira ampla ampla,* and the Pacific, *Makaira ampla mazara.*

Although the Atlantic record for rod and reel is 756 pounds (taken off San Juan, Puerto Rico, April 19, 1956, by Allen Sherman, Jr.), fish weighing over 1,000 pounds have been harpooned off Havana, Martha's Vineyard, Block Island, and Montauk.

Mrs. Wendell Anderson of Detroit, Michigan, a friend of mine and a well-known angler, tangled with a large blue marlin off Bimini; she had it whipped and alongside when sharks attacked and mutilated most of the fish. Only the head and shoulders were retrieved intact. When measurements were taken and compared proportionately with the measurements of the world's record, her fish would have been larger with quite a bit to spare. This fact, plus evidence of the 1,000 pounders harpooned, indicates a favorable possibility that a 1,000-pound prize will be taken on rod and reel in the Atlantic.

Very little has been written on the life history of the blue marlin. Spawning females have been taken off Cuba, and Ernest Hemingway has called attention to its north coast as a spawning area for this species during June and July. Ripe females also have been taken off the Bahamas in early summer, indicating a possible spawning area in the lower section of the Gulf Stream and the Caribbean. Blue marlin under 100 pounds are seldom taken.

The blue marlin is never abundant along the coast of the United States; most often it appears solitary, sometimes in pairs. Along the western Atlantic, from north to south, the areas where any noticeable angling for the blue marlin takes place are the following.

In the Massachusetts area each year more and more blue marlin are taken by anglers who fish the waters off Block Island and Martha's Vineyard. The angling effort for big fish in this locality is not great. Therefore, more billfish may be present here in the latter part of summer than one might suspect.

Occasionally a blue marlin is reported southward along the coast off Maryland or North Carolina. Only occasionally, during July and August, is the blue marlin found on the western edge of the Gulf Stream. July and August are also the best months for the blue off Bermuda. Although sport fishing is developing fast, not enough boats fish off this British Island to indicate the true abundance of billfishes.

The most productive area off the United States coast seems to be the eastern edge of the Gulf Stream—about 50 miles from Miami. Favorite spots are Cat Cay, Bimini, and Walker Cay in the Bahamas, where the best months for angling are May, June, and July—including perhaps a month earlier around Walker Cay. Actually, the blue is in greatest abundance off Bimini from early spring to mid-August. However, it is impossible to rely always on specific dates; for example, during one of my trips enroute home from South America I detoured a bit for a few days of fishing at Walker Cay in May and caught two blue and one white marlin. The next year I was there at the same time, fishing hard for five weeks, and did not see a billfish; they arrived when we departed! It may be interesting to mention that during the first trip my fishing companion lost several fish by using the quick method of striking (the accepted system in this area) as soon as possible after the fish hit the bait. Against the captain's instructions I free-spooled each fish until it was running well before I struck (as I was taught in New Zealand); we boated the three fish that came to my bait.

The waters off Texas in the Gulf of Mexico are just beginning to draw the attention of anglers, and blue marlin are occasionally taken. This is another area which is potentially rich in big game fishing. As yet the angling effort has not been expanded enough to give a true picture of whether or not the blue marlin is plentiful, but I suspect that the area may harbor an abundance of billfishes.

The fishing area off Havana, Cuba, is noted for blue marlin from July to about the middle of October. However, the fish do not seem to take a bait readily in this locality, and almost always they are headed in a westward direction against the current. It appears that spawning activities may influence their behavior. This marlin has been well known to Cubans for almost one hundred years, and Poey, a Cuban scientist, first called it Cuban black marlin. Today, as it has been for many years, a commercial fishery is built around the blue marlin in

Cuban waters. Most of the commercial boats work in the early morning and come in when the winds spring up, about noon. Their methods remain primitive; they handle an amazing amount of line—each boat usually runs about 20 lines at depths varying from 10 to 100 fathoms. The Cubans consider the flesh of the blue marlin a delicacy. Usually the largest fish are caught during the latter part of summer. When the stream is not in strong evidence, the fishing drops off; marlin are not seen at the surface, and fewer than usual are caught in the depths.

The economic boom that has taken place in Venezuela is responsible for the exploration of big game fishing off northern South America, mostly off Caracas. Alfredo "Freddie" Behrens of Caracas is one of the most interested and highly enthusiastic sportsmen responsible for the discovery of new marlin waters in the area, about 15 miles WNW of La Guaira. The waters about the islands of La Blanquilla and Margarita are also productive. The blues average 250–300 pounds (400–500 pounders have been taken), and the best angling months are from December to April, although they may be present year round. Incidentally, these waters off Venezuela also produce a great number of white marlin each season.

The pugnacity of blue marlin is a point of conversational interest among anglers. The latest documented instance that I know of regarding the so-called attack upon a vessel occurred in 1956. The incident was recorded by the Marine Laboratory at the University of Miami. During the night of February 14 or early morning of the 15th, the research vessel "Gerda" was off Bimini's west side when the crew noticed that she was taking on water faster than her usual rate. They continued the voyage by pumping at more frequent intervals. When the "Gerda" was hauled out in Miami, a blue marlin's bill was found to have penetrated her hull. One can imagine the power required to thrust that bill through two and a half inches of tough beech planking and about a half inch of pine. Fortunately, the pine was not completely broken through because a main fuel tank was directly inside. The split in the planking was about eight inches long and one quarter inch wide, which explains why the "Gerda" suddenly took on water at a greater speed.

People in many parts of the world appreciate marlin as good eating. However, the blue marlin is seldom used for food on the southeastern coast of the United States, the Bahamas, or Bermuda. I have found marlin steaks delicious, and Louis Mowbray, director of the Bermuda Aquarium, is a master at preparing them.

Pacific Blue Marlin
(*Makaira mazara*)

The Pacific blue marlin is almost identical with the Atlantic blue marlin. Externally the two fish appear the same, but they differ slightly in certain parts of the internal anatomy. The exact range of the Pacific form is not known. It is a fish which has created confusion and controversy among scientists and sportsmen alike.

Only a few years back the blue marlin was accepted as a strictly Atlantic inhabitant, but when large marlin, whose pectoral fins folded back (blue marlin pectorals fold back, black marlin do not) were reported by anglers, scientists took note. Ichthyologist Luis Rivas made a study of this Pacific fish and compared it with the Atlantic blue marlin. He found that the anatomy was identical and proclaimed the blue marlin from both oceans as the same species. He stated, "In addition to Acapulco and the Gulf of Panama, *Makaira ampla* probably occurs throughout the entire tropical and subtropical Pacific." Rivas's conclusions were based upon external characteristics of specimens from the two oceans. However, James Morrow, of the Bingham Oceanographic Laboratory at Yale University, made later studies on the internal anatomy of the pelvic girdle (that section of bones which holds the pectoral fin) and found differences in the bone structure between blues from the Atlantic and blues inhabiting the Pacific significant enough to indicate that they should be separated.

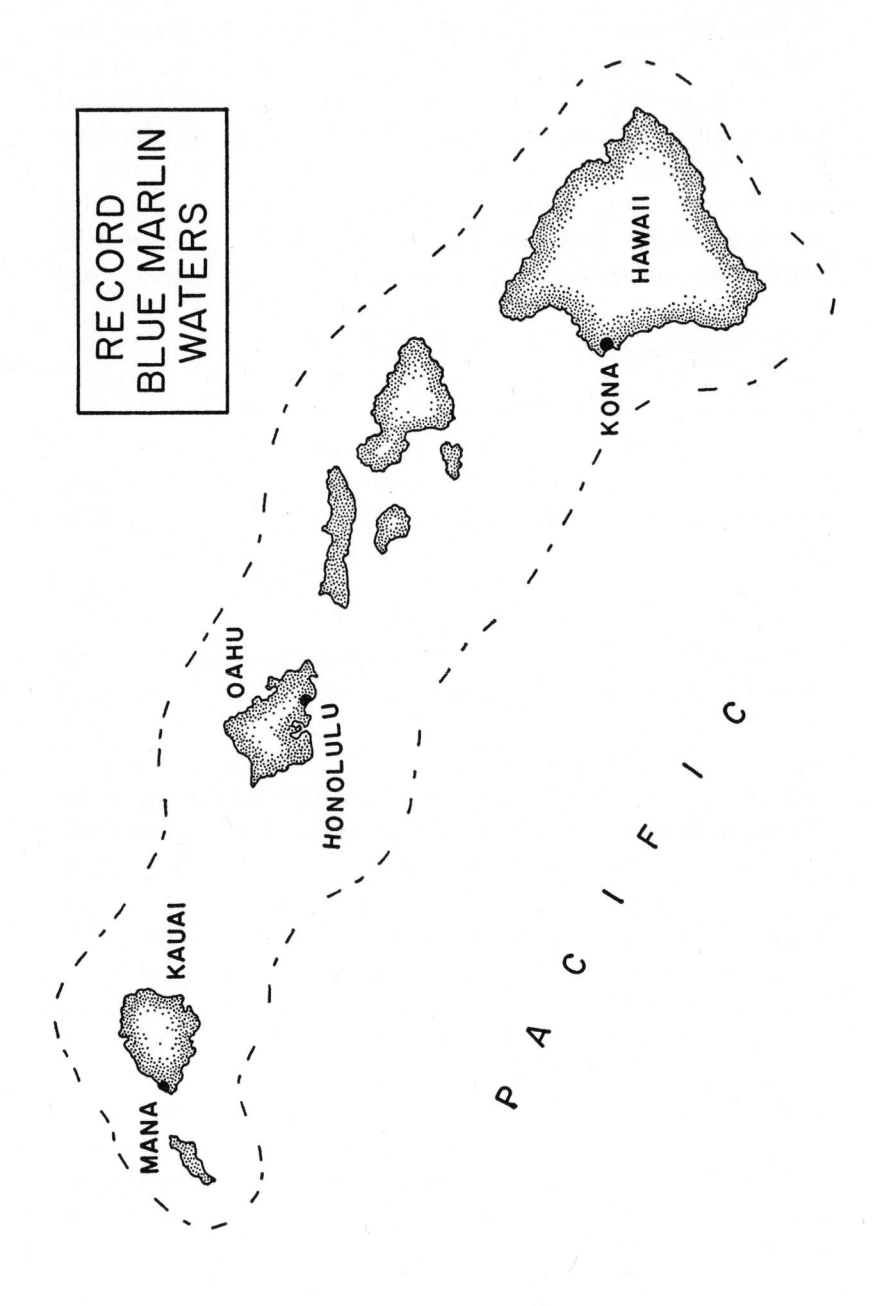

With the new turn of events the International Game Fish Association was expected either to accept the Pacific blue as another form and add it to the official list, or else to announce it as sharing the same bracket with the Atlantic blue marlin. Evidently there was no cause for immediate action, and no official word came. However, catches of unusually big blue marlin in waters off Kona, Hawaii, brought this fish to worldwide attention among anglers and scientists. The area about Kona is rich with marlin; for example, in one fishing season eight boats landed 207 marlin averaging 325 pounds each. This tremendous catch included blacks, blues, and stripers. Strangely, the largest fish caught in this locality are blues and not blacks.

On February 4, 1956, Pablo Libero, mate aboard Tacks Waldron's "Kumu," landed a 796-pound blue marlin (the Atlantic record was a fish of 756 pounds). He submitted his catch to the I.G.F.A. for official recognition as a new world record.

This started the confusion. The I.G.F.A. was not, as yet, prepared to make a decision regarding the Atlantic and Pacific forms of blue marlin. An added point of discussion is De Wayne Nelson's marlin, which was an 866 pounder. He took it off Kona in 1953. At the time the fish was thought to be a black marlin, but because of the new events this fish is now being judged as a blue marlin. Further, George Parker aboard his "Mona H" boated a 1,002-pound marlin in 1954, which he claims was a blue marlin and not a black marlin. Dr. Dale Scott of Los Angeles caught a 911-pound marlin, but no official decision has been reached on whether the fish is a blue or a black.

My opinion is that the Pacific blue marlin should be accepted as distinct from the Atlantic blue marlin and should be given a place on the official I.G.F.A. list of World Record Marine Game Fishes.

In other words, Allen Sherman's 756-pound fish should remain as the Atlantic record, and either Libero's 796-pound fish or Parker's 1,002 pounder or maybe Scott's fish (depending on I.G.F.A. technicalities) should be the present Pacific record. (*See* Atlantic Blue Marlin.)

Black Marlin (1d)

(*Makaira marlina*)

The black marlin is the world's largest game fish. Big ones, over 1,000 pounds, taken off Cabo Blanco, Peru, are no longer considered rare. The giant 1,560 pounder, the largest ever captured by rod and reel, was killed off Cabo Blanco by Alfred C. Glassell of Texas, on August 4, 1953.

This marlin is distributed mainly throughout the warmer waters of the Pacific, but it is also present in the Indian Ocean. Along the eastern Pacific this fish is distributed from southern California down into Chilean waters. It is well known in Hawaii and Fiji and in the western Pacific from Japan south to Australia and New Zealand.

Scientists do not agree, as yet, on the taxonomic technicalities involved with the scientific name of the black marlin and its relation to other marlin; therefore, the angler may be confused when encountering other scientific names for this species.* It is much darker than any other marlin; hence the name black marlin.

The black marlin is a husky fish with a robust body form, tremendous depth at the shoulder, a large lunate tail, a heavy, short, club-like bill, and a low dorsal fin. In comparison with the body the fore part of its dorsal fin has less height than any other billfish. The most striking point which will differentiate the black from other marlin is the permanently rigid pectoral fins. They cannot fold back against the body without breaking bones. The black marlin which I have seen possessed no indication of stripes or other markings, and while still alive a bronze-like coloration dominated the lateral surface of the body, gill cover, and tail.

Nothing is known concerning the spawning, migration, or other parts of the life history of this fish. Young blacks have never been found. The black giants are never seen in numbers; they usually travel alone or sometimes in pairs.

* *Makaira nigricans, Makaira mazara, Makaira marlina marlina.*

If one stops to consider that most marlin over 1,000 pounds have been taken off western South America, none of that weight off New Zealand, and the smallest in average size are found in Australian waters (although a black marlin weighing 1,226 pounds was stranded on the beach at Eden, New South Wales, April 7, 1938), the possibility appears that these fish may migrate with the currents from Australia to New Zealand to South America. Bluefin tuna, which migrate in the spring and summer along the eastern coast of the United States from southern waters to Nova Scotia, arrive in the latter spot as much heavier fish. Perhaps it may be the same with the black marlin in the Pacific. To think about these possibilities is interesting, but only much research on black marlin in these areas will tell us the facts.

Mackerel and squid are favorite foods, but the blacks will take dolphin, bonito, and any other small or medium-size fish. In New Zealand waters a dominant item of diet is the kahawai, a 2- to 4-pound mackerel-like fish.

Well-known regions for black marlin fishing are the Gulf of California, Acapulco, Canal Zone, Hawaiian Islands, Peru, Australia, and New Zealand. It appears that the greatest spot is an area off Cabo Blanco, Peru, where the world's record has been broken and rebroken six times between the spring of 1952 and the summer of 1953. About 40 fish each weighing more than 1,000 pounds have been taken in these waters.

Another unusually good spot for the blacks is off the northeastern coast of New Zealand's North Island—especially the Bay of Islands, although any fish over 500 pounds is considered a big one in this area. Recently, however, a black marlin of 904 pounds was taken by W. L. Cartaing of Auckland. He battled the fish for 16 hours. This is believed to be the longest encounter with a big game fish in New Zealand waters.

Since 1924, to and including the 1954–55 season, 328 black marlin were recorded by the New Zealand Swordfish and Mako Shark Club. For many years, 1926 to 1952, the world's record was a 976-pound fish caught by Captain L. M. Mitchell in the Bay of Islands. Many black marlin in the 800–900 pound class

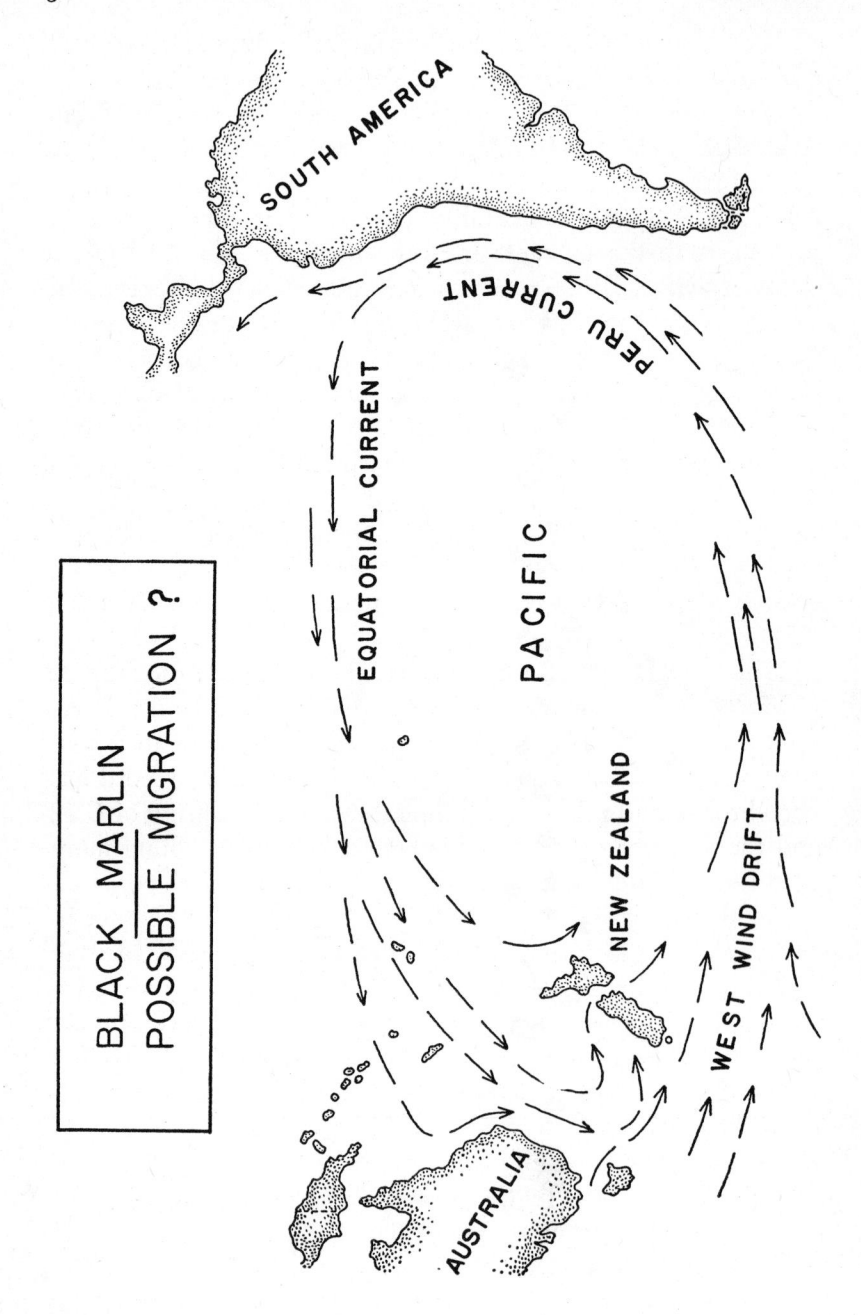

BLACK MARLIN
POSSIBLE MIGRATION ?

Left: Record black marlin—1560 pounds. Taken off Cabo Blanco, Peru, on August 4, 1953, by Alfred Glassell, Jr., of San Antonio, Texas. (Photo by Bob Turner) *Right:* A 1000-pound plus black marlin taken off Cabo Blanco by Kip Farrington, well-known author and pioneer of big game fishing.

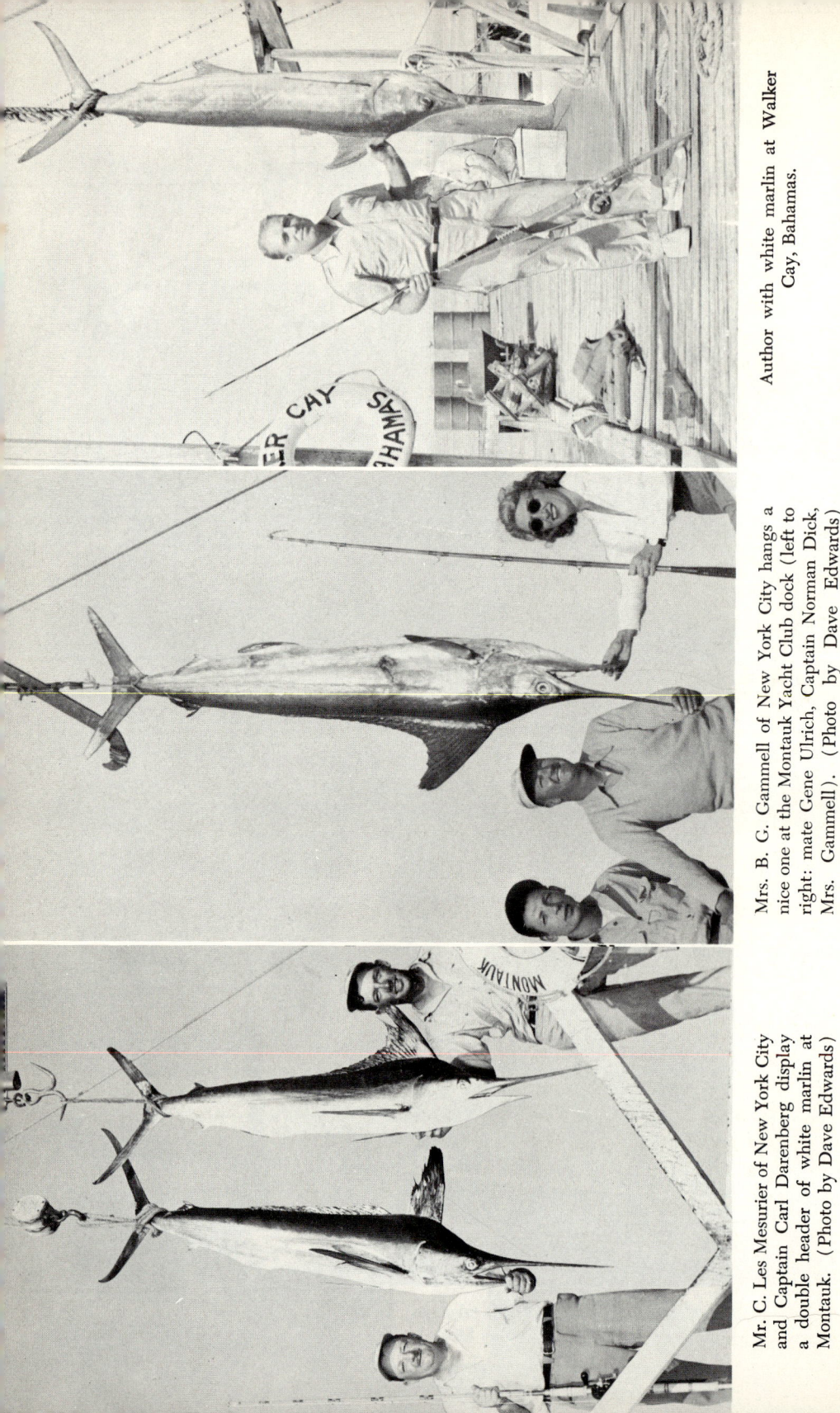

Mr. C. Les Mesurier of New York City and Captain Carl Darenberg display a double header of white marlin at Montauk. (Photo by Dave Edwards)

Mrs. B. C. Gammell of New York City hangs a nice one at the Montauk Yacht Club dock (left to right: mate Gene Ulrich, Captain Norman Dick, Mrs. Gammell). (Photo by Dave Edwards)

Author with white marlin at Walker Cay, Bahamas.

have been taken, but in the land of the Maori's they are still waiting for that 1,000 pounder.

In New Zealand waters, where the season runs about November 1 to April 20, constant surface trolling is the accepted method, but fine fish have been taken drifting with the bait many fathoms down. The Yale–New Zealand Expedition was responsible for introducing the use of outriggers to the local fishermen and guides in the Bay of Islands area; up to that time the baits were trolled a short distance directly astern, which was exciting when a marlin followed the bait about 20 or 30 feet astern.

One day while fishing from the "Rosemary" with Katie Hassel, a well-known New Zealand angler, and Captain George Warne, a huge black marlin sailed from almost directly under the boat and hit my bait on the surface. Half of his back came out of the water as he "boiled," and the spray flew high. While I gave line by free-spooling the reel, Katie started to reel in her bait in order to clear the field for me. But the fish changed its mind, dropped my bait, and came charging up and crashed Katie's bait a few feet from the boat. She battled the fish for almost four hours. Captain Warne sunk the gaff into that 500-pound black just as daylight was fading.

It may not be amiss to mention that I have been fortunate in taking part in big game fishing in many parts of the world, but as yet I have not met a fish guide with the capabilities of George Warne, captain and mate who did everything well. He ran the boat alone, rigged the baits, attended the chairs, gaffed and tailed the fish, and catered to the personal wants of the angler. To top it, he was always in good humor.

If I were asked to name another "hot spot" for black marlin I would say "Panama Bay." Most anglers who have fished this area agree that black marlin are rarely seen tailing; they usually hit the bait on a blind or crash strike. There is evidence that record marlin may be caught in this locality. In 1938 a black marlin weighing over 900 pounds was washed ashore on Taboga Island. This specimen was very thin and in poor condition. If it had been a healthy fish it would have weighed well over

1,000 pounds. The angling effort is not great, hence the lack of information on the true abundance of fish in this locality.

A story from Panama received wide publicity when Louis Schmidt, who has one arm and one leg, tangled with a huge black marlin. He fought the fish for almost two hours, but because his ill-fitting harness was cutting him badly, he had to surrender the rod to his brother, John, who completed the job. The marlin weighed 1,006 pounds and would have broken the world's record at that time. Also, it would have been the first fish ever caught on rod and reel over 1,000 pounds. The International Game Fish Association could not recognize the record since the fish was fought by two men. However, they sent Louis Schmidt a certificate of honorable mention. In this area there are other recorded instances of gigantic blacks which were fought for a long time and then lost. Here again is evidence that Panama Bay may be one of the greatest big game fishing spots in the world.

Although the coast of Chile harbors some of the largest swordfish and striped marlin, black marlin seem to be scarce; however, one specimen harpooned by a commercial boat weighed 1,440 pounds. It appears that colder water temperatures may be a barrier to the black marlin off Chile.

After reviewing the distribution and records of the largest game fish, it is obvious that Cabo Blanco, off the coast of northern Peru, is the best black marlin area in the world today. I say "today" because other grounds may be found which will prove to be just as prolific in the big fish as Cabo Blanco. Besides the black marlin, other game fishes such as the striped marlin, bigeye tuna, broadbill swordfish, and many smaller species are found in abundance.

Why is the fishing so good in this area? Let's analyze the situation. Black marlin are found in the Peru Current (also called the Humboldt after the famous German scientist), which approaches Chile somewhere near Valparaiso, flows northward along the coast of Chile and Peru, turns westward off Cabo Blanco, and loses its identity in the South Equatorial Current.

Marlins

Although the Peru Current flows close to the equator, its waters are cool. For example, surface temperature off Cabo Blanco is about 71° F., while at the same latitude out to sea the surface water temperature is approximately 5 or 6 degrees higher.

Why are these waters so cool? Is it because of the melting snows in the high peaks of the Andes? Consensus of opinion is no. The theory accepted by scientists today is that the prevailing winds blow along the coast and literally turn the water over; that is, the surface waters are driven away from the coast, and cold bottom water rises from a depth of 600 to 1,000 fathoms to replace it. This phenomenon, called upwelling, brings up water very rich in nutrients, and this is basically the cause of the abundance of big game fishes.

Let us consider for a moment the food cycle of the sea. Sea plants contain chlorophyll just as land plants do. The microscopic kind, called floating phytoplankton, are eaten by minute sea animals (zooplankton), which in turn are taken by the smallest fishes. Small fish are preyed upon by larger fish ad infinitum. Any organisms that escape being eaten eventually die and sink to the bottom, where they are consumed by scavengers such as worms and crabs. Finally, by bacterial action, the nutrients are returned to the water in a soluble inorganic form. When the upwelling brings the rich bottom waters (nutrients) to the surface, phytoplankton benefit and grow fast, and in turn the larger animals are attracted. We can put it in a nutshell by saying that the black marlin and all other game fishes abound in this area because of the vast food supply caused by the upwelling.

In rare years, traditionally every seventh, in the area about Cabo Blanco and the Peru Current, life in the sea (and on land) is disrupted by a phenomenon which at times reaches catastrophic proportions. The Peru Current seems to disappear, and the surface temperatures of the water rise rapidly. Fish move away or are killed by the warmer temperatures. The vast flocks of sea birds that depend on the huge schools of bait for food starve or fly away. This condition is known as *El Niño*, "the

CABO BLANCO BLACK MARLIN

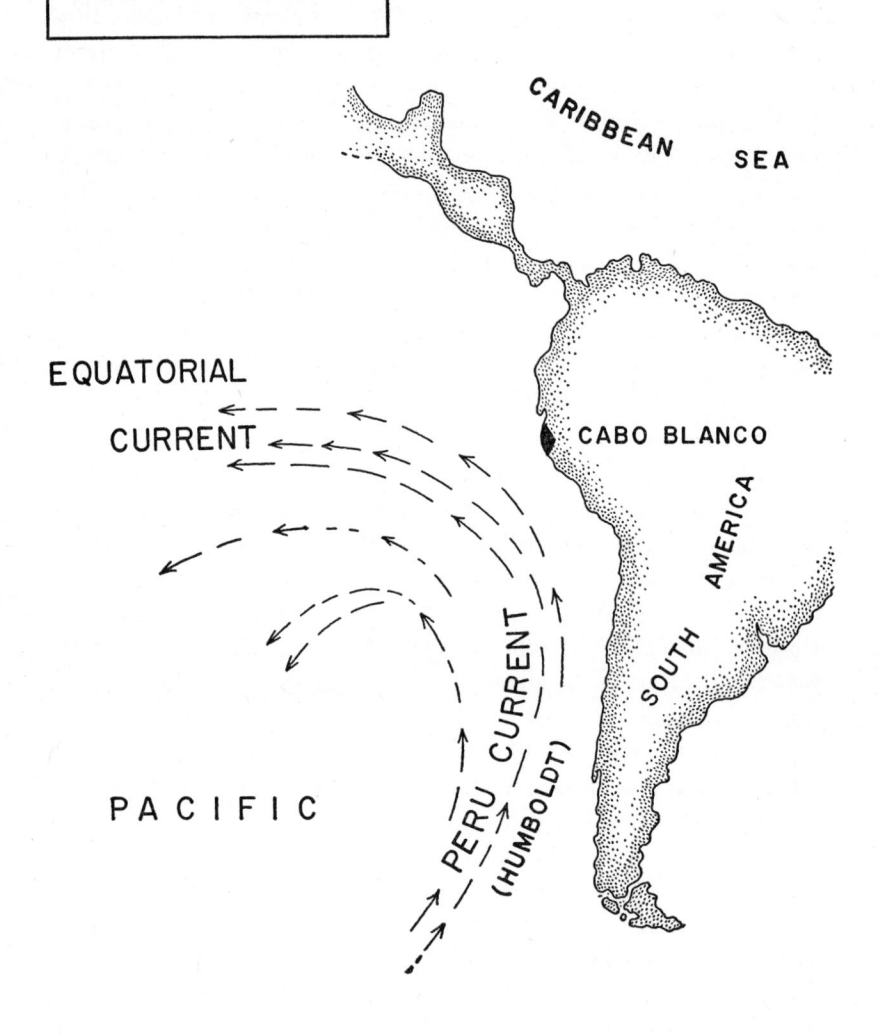

child," because it occurs shortly after Christmas. During an *El Niño* the surface water is much warmer and less salty than usual, and the Peru Current is covered with a layer of warm water about 75 feet deep. How this comes about is a matter of debate—some scientists contend that the warm waters flow down from the equatorial Pacific; others believe it comes from the Gulf of Guayaquil.

Whether fish die or leave the area because of warmer temperatures, diminished food supply, or the reduced salinity of the water can be answered only by more scientific work in the area. This phenomenon demonstrates forcefully that the presence of fishes in an area in vast numbers at one time and the almost complete absence at another may be due to causes far beyond human control.

Game fish writers state erroneously that in order to meet the billfishes off the Peru–Chile coast you must go beyond the Peru Current to get into blue waters. Oceanographers generally agree that the width of the Peru Current may be anywhere from 75 miles off southern Chile to 1,000 miles off Cabo Blanco. The current can be several colors. Usually the green water, which is the upwelling area, extends approximately 15 to 20 miles offshore; it is beyond this flow that fishermen start activity, but they fish in the Peru Current and the blue water. All native fishermen know that blue water is the most productive for big game fishes. I was first introduced to these conditions while in quest of billfish off Tocopilla, Chile. In the darkness of early morning we experienced a bumpy, uncomfortable ride of two to three hours before reaching blue water. En route, we slowed down occasionally; the mate would look closely at the water, shake his head, and we would proceed again until he was satisfied that the water was a proper blue—then we would finally fish.

Black marlin is considered a fine food fish by the natives of Peru and Chile. A gigantic specimen of 2,250 pounds was once harpooned off Cabo Blanco. Let the records fall where they may.

Striped Marlin (1c)
(*Makaira mitsukurii*)

In my estimation the striped marlin is the most active and most exciting of all the marlins. This billfish, when hooked, nearly always will not fail to jump many times in a spectacular manner. Its common name is derived from the pronounced vertical bars or stripes along its sides, and it is found throughout the warm, blue waters of the Pacific and Indian Ocean currents, where it appears in fluctuating degrees of abundance.

Although it is found in the open sea, the largest concentrations appear to be fairly close to shore—along the eastern coasts of Australia and New Zealand, the coasts of Chile, Peru, Ecuador, Panama, Mexico, southern California, the Hawaiian Islands, and the east African coast, Ceylon, Japanese coastal waters, Formosa, and the Philippines. Along the eastern Pacific it generally does not go north of Point Conception, California, although on occasion it may be found farther up the coast. From California it ranges southward to southern Chile. As with other billfishes, water temperatures colder than 59° F. (water about 70° F. preferred) seem to be a confining factor.

The most productive area for big striped marlin fishing appears to be off Chile and Peru. Going north, one finds that Ecuador has some excellent striper fishing around Salinas. The Perlos Islands off Panama produce good fish, as does Acapulco on occasion. Cabo San Lucas at the southern tip of Baja California is a spot where fish in abundance are found in season. (No accommodations or fishing facilities are available, and anglers who wish to work these waters must import a boat and supplies.) Mazatlán is another interesting area where striped marlin are plentiful from late fall to early spring. (Sailfish are present from spring to fall—one is arriving while the other is leaving.) Thousands of billfish are taken in this area. Three hundred billfish per boat per season is common—usually 60 per cent marlin and 40 per cent sailfish.

Marlins

When alive the striped marlin is a beautiful fish. It has a vivid cobalt-blue forehead and a dorsal surface only slightly darker. Its sides are pearlescent and silvery with a slight tone of shimmering bronze over the entire lateral surface. The stripes, some of which are broken, are light blue-lavender and may run from 19 to 23 in number. The dorsal fin, which is pointed, is colored lavender blue and spattered with dark spots.

The largest average-size fish come from Peru and Chile, New Zealand, and Mexico. It is interesting to note that a difference exists in the average sizes caught in areas which are far apart, for instance, Guaymas, Mexico—175 pounds; Catalina—220 pounds; New Zealand—225 pounds; Peru and Chile—about 325 pounds.

The world's record striped marlin is 692 pounds, 13 feet, 5 inches, caught off Balboa, California, by A. Hamann. The second largest ever boated was taken off Tocopilla, Chile, by George Carey; it weighed 483 pounds. Because the presence of blue marlin in the Pacific has only recently been ascertained and because of the fact that a striped marlin between these weights has never been taken, I doubt the authenticity of the species of that 692-pound fish. It appears likely that the catch was a blue and not a striped marlin. Previously, quite possibly, all large marlin which were not identified definitely as blacks were taken to be stripers. I'm also inclined to believe that Zane Grey's striped marlin, which weighed 1,040 pounds after being mutilated by sharks, was a blue marlin.

Striped marlin can easily be distinguished from the other Pacific marlins. Its pectoral fin folds back as does the pectoral of the Pacific blue; the black marlins' pectoral is permanently rigid. The striper is a slimmer fish than the blue, its bill is more slender, and the dorsal fin is higher in comparison with the body than the blue's. Its most conspicuous markings are the vivid vertical bars or stripes which, though faded, retain their presence on the dead fish.

One of the greatest known migrations of big game fishes takes place when the striped marlin enter the Gulf of California by Cabo San Lucas in the spring of the year—about March. The first part of the migration arrives off Guaymas early in April. Here, within three months anglers have taken several hundred marlin. (Flying fish is considered the best bait in this area.) In the Gulf of California, at several spots, the fish are plentiful in March, April, and May, although some marlin have also been taken off Cabo San Lucas in November and December. Striped marlin do not appear off the coast of California until some time between late June and August. They are most abundant in September, then disappear in November or December. Striped marlin usually travel alone or in pairs, and only occasionally are they found in number.

Because striped marlin are found concentrated in the areas I have enumerated (Peru, Chile, New Zealand, Mexico) this question arises: Is it an isolated population in each spot which is more or less separated geographically and genetically, or is the seasonal abundance due to a migratory pattern of a more or less homogeneous population over the Indo-Pacific area?

The discontinuity between the so-called "hot spots" may be caused by two factors—first, certain waters may be attractive to fishes because of an abundant supply of good or favorable sea conditions; thus they congregate there. Second, fishermen who catch these big fish are not in a continuous or regular line of occurrence, and we know nothing about the localities between the areas that produce fish. Undoubtedly, other grounds will be discovered as investigations broaden. As we look at the entire picture of the distribution of striped marlin in the Indo-Pacific, we come back to the question of whether or not the concentrations are separate groups. Two of Yale's fishing expeditions have thrown some light on the subject. During our trips to New Zealand and South America off the coast of Peru, Jim Morrow made a study of a number of striped marlin from both areas. He compared measurements and fin ray counts of 39 fish from Peru and 79 from New Zealand and Australia. Morrow found differences in 11 characters and a better than 70 per cent separation. Therefore, he concluded that the samples represent separate and distinct populations of the species. In other words, the groups of striped marlin present off Peru and New Zealand are not the same population.

Similar to other billfishes, striped marlin feed on smaller fishes which they slaughter with their bills. Squid is a favorite food, and stomach contents indicate feeding on bottom fishes also. The species of fish the marlin feed on depends on the location they are inhabiting at the time.

Because of the difficulties involved, scientific investigation of the striped marlin, as with other big game fishes, has been practically nil. For example, as recently as the middle forties some scientists were merely guessing at the possible existence of two kinds of marlin off the coast of Peru. Nothing is known concerning the breeding habits of striped marlin. The eggs, larvae, and young have never been found; and a specimen of less than 50 pounds has never been caught.

The first striped marlin on rod and reel was taken by Harry Willey on August 25, 1903, while fishing on his cruiser in Catalina waters. He used 300 yards of 24-strand Ashaway Line, and the fish weighed 182 pounds. The second striper was caught three days later in the same waters by Edward Llewellin, whose fish weighed 125 pounds. Some authors erroneously credit Llewellin's fish as the first—perhaps because the only available photograph is of the second fish. Actually, Llewellin was a guest aboard Willey's boat when he caught the second fish. Harry Willey's father, Captain Jacob Willey from Georgetown, Maine, commander of his ship sailing the Atlantic and later moving to California, first named the striper belaying-pin fish and later, marlin swordfish. Harry Willey still pursues striped marlin in the Pacific!

The first marlin ever caught on rod and reel in New Zealand waters was taken by a Mr. Campbell in February, 1913, estimated weight—220 pounds. Strangely, the second fish was caught the next day by Mr. F. P. Andreas. Marlin are often called swordfish in New Zealand. The reference to these first fishes was swordfish. Therefore, I was not able to identify the species. However, since the weight of the first fish was about 220 pounds, I assume it was a striped marlin.

The most picturesque, the most comfortable, and one of the most productive striped marlin areas in the world is found in the Otehei Bay area of the Bay of Islands off the northeastern coast of New Zealand. Within a short time of leaving the dock you are in beautiful blue, big game waters. Most of the time is spent trolling close to or within sight of many small islands which rise abruptly out of the sea. Years ago my first, and some of my greatest, big game fishing thrills happened in this area. The first marlin I ever hooked was a striper which jumped completely out of the water 39 times. His head and shoulders are now proudly displayed on one of my living room walls.

It was also during this first trip that I enjoyed one of the rarest of angling sights, which I haven't seen since and probably never will again. While trolling the usual two lines from the outriggers and two short lines baited with strip baits for smaller game fish, three marlin came up without notice and hit the outrigger baits and one of the short lines. All three went into the air simultaneously, time and time again, a short distance from the boat. As you can imagine, bedlam was aboard. The fish persisted in exchanging directions; the anglers, complete with rods and harnesses, swapped chairs. One marlin broke off; the other two were landed. I was one of the lucky anglers.

White Marlin (1a)
(*Makaira albida*)

Smallest of the marlins, the white marlin is a western Atlantic species which prefers the warmer blue waters of open-ocean currents. In its habits it resembles the other marlins, and as a game fish it rates high with salt water anglers. Also, no disagreements exist amongst fishery scientists as to the technicalities of nomenclature or relationship of this fish to other marlins.

The distribution of the white marlin is known to be throughout the Caribbean, Gulf of Mexico, Cuba, Bahamas, Bermuda, eastern Florida, and northward to Maryland and New Jersey.

Although the whites have been recorded as far north as Nova Scotia, these instances must be considered freak occurrences. As yet there are no records south of the Caribbean, and north of New Jersey it has been considered a straggler; but during the summer months white marlin will go along with the Gulf Stream in fairly good numbers and appear as far north as Montauk, Block Island, and the Massachusetts islands. I believe we can no longer apply the word "straggler" to the white marlin in these waters since more and more are caught every summer. On the contrary, these small billfish are almost common in this area during the warm weather months. Also, I suspect that when angling effort is greater off the east coast of South America the presence of white marlin may be recorded farther down the Guiana Current in that area.

Although the white marlin is much smaller than the other marlins, it resembles them closely in shape of body, bill, and in type and placement of fins. The lateral surfaces lack markings of any kind and appear to be silvery or white, especially when the fish jumps—hence, the name.

In size it averages 60 pounds and 7 feet in length—seldom does it exceed 100 pounds. White marlin caught off the north coast of Cuba range from 35 to 140 pounds. The world record was taken off Miami Beach, Florida, by L. F. Hooper on March 20, 1938; the fish weighed 161 pounds and measured 8 feet, 8 inches in length.

A large white marlin could easily be misidentified as a blue marlin. However, they are easily separated. The white has a slightly slimmer bill. The blue has faint vertical markings when alive. But the best way to tell them apart is to compare the dorsal and anal fins. In the blue these fins are pointed, and in the white they are rounded.

White marlin are migratory fishes, but little is known concerning their regular routes of travel and the many other aspects of migration. We know only of their approximate dates of arrival at different fishing grounds. Florida, Cat Cay, Walker Cay, and Bimini are popular angling spots during the winter months. Off Bimini and Havana and the south Florida coast white marlin first appear in late January and stay till June, with the best fishing from mid-April to mid-June. Fishing off Cuba is best during the last two weeks of May; in some years the fish may appear in the middle of March. When the Gulf Stream is running clear and strong, they are in abundance off the north coast of Cuba in the area out of Matanzas during April, May, and into June. As the late spring and early summer months get warmer, the white marlin is seen progressively farther north until they reach their northern limits in the vicinity of Block Island and the Massachusetts islands. Their usual turning point of migration is east of Nantucket. Unlike the blue marlin, the white will run in groups, and often a half dozen can be seen frolicking about near the surface. At times, during the white marlin migration off Cuba, large blue marlin will be found among them.

There are many blank spots concerning the life history of the white marlin. Females with ripe gonads have been taken off Cuba, the Bahamas, and Florida during the summer months; but as no larval specimens have been found, we can assume only that the fish may spawn in this area. A few small specimens—4 feet plus—have been taken off Florida, but no other information concerning these young fish is available. They feed on small fishes and have a taste for squid and pelagic octopods.

In 1939 the U.S. Fish and Wildlife Service carried out a tagging program in the Ocean City, Maryland, area, but there have been no recoveries. In the summer of 1956 the Woods Hole Oceanographic Institution introduced another tagging, but to date of this writing no recaptures have been reported. Perhaps the fish has a short life span similar to that of the Atlantic sailfish, and the value of tagging programs may be doubtful. This leaves us with a ton of information to be desired—life span, age of first spawning, size at maturity, specific water type preference, etc.

The most famous angling area in the entire range of the white marlin is off Ocean City, Maryland. Ocean City is located on the strip of land known as Sinepuxent Beach. A superlative often used to describe the fishing is "fabulous." Before Paul

Marlins 65

WHITE MARLIN FISHING GROUNDS OCEAN CITY

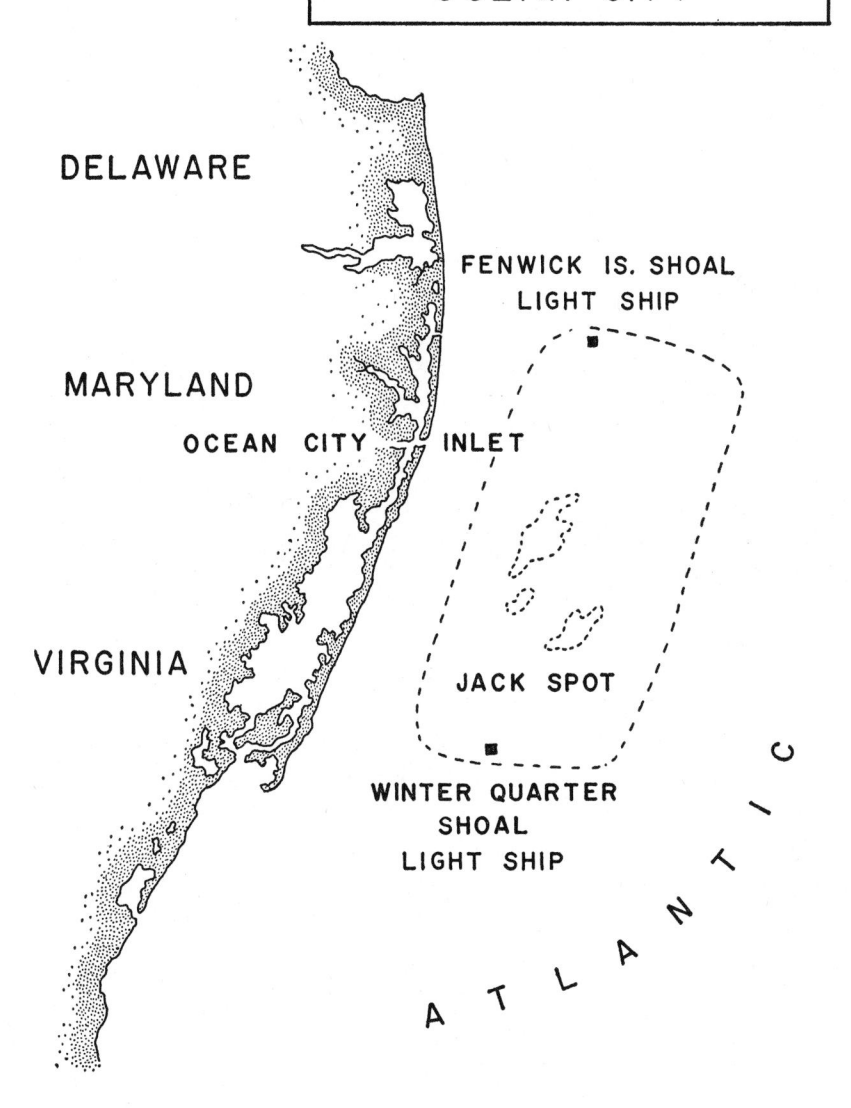

DELAWARE

FENWICK IS. SHOAL LIGHT SHIP

MARYLAND

OCEAN CITY INLET

VIRGINIA

JACK SPOT

WINTER QUARTER SHOAL LIGHT SHIP

ATLANTIC

Townsend investigated the marlin grounds off Ocean City in 1935, big game fishing in these waters was practically unknown. When he observed white marlin jumping close to shore, he procured a boat, searched, and found the fish at the Jack Spot (*see* p. 65). Named after an old market fisherman, it is a stretch of shoal water about 5 miles wide and about 2 miles long. The shoal is covered with fine brown sand and lies at a depth of from 47 to 60 feet. The Jack Spot lies 22½ miles southeast by south of Ocean City Inlet and is about 11 miles northeast of Winter Quarter Shoal Light Ship. Many finger-shaped shoals lie toward shore off the Jack Spot, with their long axes extending northeast and southwest. Marlin are also caught on these shoals, but more marlin are taken from the 10 square miles of the Jack Spot than from any other area off Ocean City. Other marlin grounds in the area which often produce good fishing are Fenwick Island Light ship and Winter Quarter Shoal Light ship and areas both east and west of the main fishing spot. To appreciate the marvelous fishing in this area one has but to read the statistics—1938 produced 910 fish, and 1,343 marlin were caught in 1939, with a single day's catch of 171 fish! In the 1956 season, up to July, about 800 fish were hooked. Five to 10 fish boated in one day is not unusual.

In the Ocean City area, as with the sailfish off Palm Beach, a great effort is being made to encourage anglers to release their fish. (Whether or not this is good conservation has not been scientifically established. *See* Atlantic Sailfish.) A fine example of the results of popularizing conservation is shown in the records. In 1939 only 84 out of 1,343 fish caught were released, but up to July in the 1956 season over 500 out of approximately 800 caught were released. A souvenir cigarette lighter is awarded to anglers for their first released fish. Conservation may be the key to a sustained sport fishery if the fishing pressure is great. The fairly new, concentrated marlin fishing off Ocean City also depicts, quite strongly, the economic importance and the value of fishing in specific areas. Hotels, motels, restaurants, charter boats, tackle shops, and many associated businesses

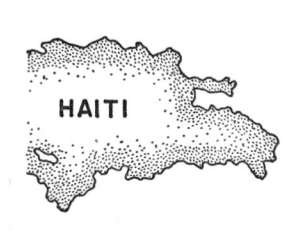

NEW MARLIN WATERS OFF VENEZUELA

have mushroomed since 1935. The white marlin is responsible for attracting hundreds of thousands of dollars to the Ocean City area.

In recent years an area north of Venezuela in the Caribbean has come into prominence as an outstanding white marlin locality (*see* Atlantic Blue Marlin). Although few boats are available to fish these waters, it appears that white marlin may be just as abundant here as they often are off Ocean City. The season is from June to December with the summer months the best; the whites average about 60 pounds.

There is a tendency for anglers and boatmen to underrate (in comparison with the larger marlin) the white marlin. Often the fisherman reels the fish close while it is still green, and the mate hurries to gaff it. Off Miami I have seen a mate lose the tip of his finger by the wire leader in a premature attempt to boat a white marlin. I have also been aboard when a hooked white marlin jumped close to the boat, landed on the stern, and then bounced back into the sea. The bill of this fish is slim and sharply pointed, and with force behind it a man could be injured seriously.

One of my most exciting experiences took place one balmy day off Walker Cay in the Bahamas when I was fishing with Laddie Sanford. He had hooked a good-sized white marlin which, after a dozen graceful, spray-flying leaps, began to show signs of weakening. Laddie started to work hard on the fish while I covered the action with his movie camera. As the tired fish approached the boat, it suddenly dashed towards the port side and I lost it in the view finder. I took the camera away from my eye in order to locate the marlin when an electrifying action suddenly took place. The marlin went into the air, not more than twenty feet from the stern, with a large mako shark close behind. Actually both fish were in the air simultaneously. The mate quickly swung the chair around so Laddie could follow the marlin. Both fish broke the surface in a mass of white water twice more before the shark clipped the marlin in two. As Laddie was reeling in the remainder of his fish, the shark returned, grabbed it within a foot of the boat, and tore off while the reel whizzed. Angler and shark then played tug of war for about ten minutes. The mako must have had the marlin by the head because the hook finally pulled out of the marlin's jaws. Laddie then turned to me and said, "Boy, I was glad to lose that fish because the movies should be terrific." I felt sheepish and didn't know what to say. The action had been so fascinating that I had completely forgotten about the movie camera!

Bermudian Marlin

(*Makaira bermudae*)

The Bermudian marlin was described * by the late Louis L. Mowbray, former curator of the Bermuda Aquarium. (His son, Louis, now heads the organization.) In this publication Mr. Mowbray states: "This exceedingly rare specimen was harpooned by Mr. T. Fox of St. David's Island, near the Northern shore of Castle Harbour, November 9th, 1927, the most unlikely place to expect such a fish, which in all probability entered the harbour from the ocean and became bewildered when among the shallow shoals. The specimen reached me late in the afternoon as Mr. Fox was taking it to the City to be placed on public exhibition. I made notes, secured a photograph, and made arrangements to purchase the specimen after it had been exhibited, but the Health Authorities ordered its instant disposal. It is the first record of any of the family in these waters, and, after comparing it with the forms likely to occur in these waters, I do not hesitate to describe it as new."

This specimen, as seen in the photograph, looks like a blue marlin, but the anterior spine of the dorsal fin is very high—one third higher than the depth of the body. Was this fish a blue marlin freak? Are there more marlin of this type in the sea? Who knows?

* 1931, *Fauna Bermudensis*.

SPEARFISHES

Very little is known about the spearfishes of the Atlantic and the Pacific. Chances of taking one on rod and reel are rare, but the angler should know that such fishes exist. Also, the subject does present itself as a conversation piece among sportsmen. Three kinds are recognized: the shortbill and the longbill spearfishes in the Atlantic and the shortbill spearfish in the Pacific. Superficially the spearfishes resemble a cross between a marlin and a sailfish. They belong to the family ISTIOPHORIDAE and possess the same type of bill, body, tail, and fin arrangement as do the other members of this group. The dorsal fin is higher than a marlin's but not as high as the dorsal of a sailfish; also it is almost of the same height throughout its length. The body shape of the spearfish resembles that of sailfish—long and slender in comparison with a marlin. Some scientists suggest that spearfishes may be a growth stage of a marlin.

Atlantic Shortbill Spearfish (2b)

(*Tetrapturus belone*)

Very few of these billfishes have been taken in the western Atlantic, and they appear to be more rare than the longbill spearfish. They have been recorded from Puerto Rico and from the Florida coast. The species is supposed to occur in European waters, but evidence is still lacking. Whether or not this spearfish is the same as the one which appears in the Mediterranean region remains to be seen. I saw only the skin of one specimen years ago, which was pointed out to me by Al Pflueger, well-known fish expert and taxidermist, in his Miami Studios.

Atlantic Longbill Spearfish (2a)

(*Tetrapturus* sp.)

This billfish is the most recently recognized addition to the billfish clan. In the summer of 1957 three specimens were taken

Spearfishes

in Florida waters—two off Islamorada in the Keys, 65 inches and 75 inches in length, and the other, off Fort Lauderdale, 65 inches long. Another spearfish was taken off Port Aransas, Texas, which weighed 33 pounds and was 78 inches long. These four fishes closely resembled the shortbill spearfish in all superficial respects except that the bill was much longer. Therefore Dick Robbins, of the Marine Laboratory at the University of Miami, named it the longbill spearfish. The Florida fish were taken on rod and reel while the anglers were trolling for sailfish. The Texas specimen was hauled, by rod and reel, from 11 fathoms of water.

Pacific Shortbill Spearfish
(*Tetrapturus angustirostris*)

Unless he is fishing in the Japan Current, the Pacific angler has but slim possibility of hooking this spearfish. I include it here to complete the group on billfishes.

A paper on the billfishes of Formosan waters by Hiroshi Nakamura has been translated from the Japanese and published by the U.S. Fish and Wildlife Service. This document includes a study of the *shortnose spearfish*. Part of the author's description follows: Upper jaw slender and short. The first dorsal is well developed, with its anterior lobe low, its central portion rather higher, the three most anterior are spines, the following eight to nine are clearly soft rays with branched tips, and the remaining more posterior ones are again spines. The pectoral fins are comparatively short. The ventral fins are represented by three rays and are moderately well developed. Along the bases of the first dorsal and first anal fins are developed grooves in the skin in which these fins can be accommodated. There are no markings on the sides of the body. The lateral line is clearly apparent. The jaws possess rasp-like teeth. A broad area of long, sharp teeth is present on the palatines (roof of mouth).

Although this fish has been studied morphologically, it is so rare around Formosa that it had no particular name. However, through the experiments of the research vessels of the Formosan

Government the species was discovered to occur in rather dense concentrations far to the east of the island, approximately 30 to 300 miles offshore in the area of the Japan Current. Spawning takes place in this area between October and December. Nothing else is known concerning the life history of this billfish.

SWORDFISH

Swordfish (2d)
(*Xiphias gladius*)

All big game anglers doff their hats in salutation to the broadbill swordfish as king of the finny tribe. Epicures toast him with raised glasses as a table delight. Commercial fishermen even find the broadbill's liver a beautiful thing; it brings good prices as a source of vitamins A and B—when tested the oil is found to be 100 times more potent than codliver oil! Ichthyologists sigh in contentment because the swordfish belongs to a worldwide single species, and there is no confusion such as exists among the marlins; no one has detected any constant differences among specimens taken from different oceans—at least, not yet. The swordfish is in a family by itself, XIPHIIDAE. Other common names are broadbill and broadbill swordfish.

The swordfish has a wide distribution and occurs in warm and temperate seas throughout the world. In the eastern Atlantic it ranges from North Cape, Norway, to, probably, Cape of Good Hope, Africa; western Atlantic—from Newfoundland to the mouth of the Rio de la Plata, Argentina; eastern Pacific—from Santa Cruz Island off California to Valparaiso, Chile; western Pacific—from Northern Japan to Australia and New Zealand. It also occurs in the Mediterranean, the Bosphorus, and the Sea of Marmora.

The broadbill has a very high first dorsal fin, which is soft-rayed, permanently erect, and deeply concave on the rear margin. It has no ventral fins such as the marlin and sailfish possess, and its long, flat, sharp-edged, and pointed sword distinguishes it easily from the marlin. The adult swordfish has no scales and no teeth; the marlin possess teeth which are minute. The very large blue eyes are set close to the sword.

When a swordfish is near the surface, its dorsal fin and upper tail stand conspicuously above the water, but the marlin, in most cases, has only the upper tail showing. However, I have seen a marlin practically motionless, floating along with its dorsal extended. Incidentally, a swordfish, when at a distance, can be distinguished from a shark because the shark has a more broadly triangular fin. Also, the broadbill's tail cuts along a direct line, whereas a shark's tail wobbles from side to side as the fish moves.

The fry differ in appearance from the adults, having only one dorsal fin and one anal fin, a rounded tail, both jaws toothed and of the same length, and no sword. Also, the fry possess skin covered with scales and spiny plates. Young fish about half a pound in weight resemble parents but retain their scales until about 30 inches in length. Small specimens such as these are caught in abundance in the Mediterranean.

The swordfish is pelagic or oceanic in habit. Generally speaking, it prefers warm waters and is usually most plentiful in areas where the temperature is higher than 60° F. However, facts show that the swordfish tolerates colder waters than the marlin. For example, swordfish have been caught on halibut lines set at depths of 200 fathoms. As many as thirteen broadbill have been caught in one day on set lines. It is not unusual for swordfish, taken on the offshore banks of the Gulf of Maine, to contain different types of deep-sea fishes in their stomachs. Since these blackfishes live outside the continental shelves, mostly below 150 fathoms, it is evident that the swordfish do some foraging at great depths far out to sea. These instances may substantiate the belief that the very large eyes of the swordfish indicate deep water habits. Also, the broadbill is found on the Newfoundland banks, which proves that they can tolerate waters as low as 50° to 55° F. Evidence indicates that swordfish frequent the depths during nightfall and surface in daylight.

The largest swordfish are taken off the coast of Chile. W. E. S. Tuker's world's record established April 28, 1940, held until Lou Marron caught the big one off Iquique, Chile, on May 7, 1953. Tuker's fish, taken in the waters off Tocopilla, weighed 860 pounds and measured 13 feet, 9 inches, while Marron's fish weighed 1,182 pounds and measured 14 feet, 11¼ inches. (The first broadbill taken on rod and reel weighed 355 pounds and was caught by W. C. Boschen off Catalina in the Pacific in 1913.)

In the north Atlantic the swordfish generally run smaller than off western South America. Occasionally, fish 500 to 900 pounds are harpooned, but the majority run between 200 and 400 pounds. In 1921 a dressed broadbill, at the Boston fish pier, weighed 915 pounds. This huge specimen was harpooned on the Georges Bank; its estimated live weight was 1,100 pounds. Another big one which tipped the scales at 1,565 pounds was harpooned off Chile. With these known weights there is plenty of encouragement for anglers to attempt to break records in both the Atlantic and the Pacific.

Swordfish have a seasonal migration, but almost nothing is known of their routes or the levels they prefer when not basking near the surface. Small swordfish (about 200 or 300 pounds) are occasionally taken off Florida, and it seems that a migration takes place past this area. They seem to be plentiful off Cuba, but not many are taken on rod and reel. The broadbill is seldom encountered in Bermuda, where only one has been landed. However, Lou Mowbray suggests that deep trolling or drifting will produce more of these fish in the future.

Swordfish are summer visitors off the northeastern coast of North America, often reported between the outer edge of the continental shelf and the inner edge of the Gulf Stream, off southern New England and the Gulf of Maine. Off Block Island, on the Nantucket shoals, and on Georges Bank they arrive approximately between the 25th of May and the 20th of June, later off the Scotian Banks (July and August), and disappear at the approach of cold weather. Louisburg, Cape Breton Island, Nova Scotia, is the center of an important commercial broadbill fishery. Very little sport fishing takes place, but the harpooning boats, on a good day, will land over 300 fish. The best time is from the latter part of July to September; but the season runs till October, and the fish are usually taken from a mile or so offshore to 25 or 30 miles to sea (average weight of the fish in this area is 265 pounds dressed).

On the Pacific side of the United States swordfish are usually not found north of Santa Cruz Islands off California, and they seem to be in greater abundance about the Channel Islands than in Mexican waters—at least commercial fishermen seem to be more successful in the former area. In late May the broadbill appear off California, and as the year progresses and water temperatures rise, more and more arrive until the peak of the season is reached sometime in September or October. During this peak period a thousand or more fish may be seen in a single month. They vanish abruptly between October and December. Where to? Nobody knows.

Along the Peruvian and Chilean coasts swordfish can be found as far out to sea as 300 miles. Seldom are they seen beyond this distance. January brings the most fish. Swordfish may fluctuate in abundance from year to year in any given locale. Their ups and downs may be attributable to the pursuit of a superior food supply in other areas, or because spawning attractions are better elsewhere, or because in previous years there was a low survival of spawned eggs due to unfavorable conditions at the time, or because ...

Although the swordfish is widely dispersed over the world's seas, the "hot spots," besides Cape Breton, seem to be off Cuba, the northwest coast of Africa, Sicily, the Bosphorus, Hawaii, Japan, and the west coast of South America down to about 200 miles south of Antofogasta, Chile.

The most popular swordfish grounds off the east coast of the United States include an area 5 to 25 miles south of Montauk Point, Long Island, from Block Island to off Southampton. Here the fish are not as big as in other localities, but the shore and angling accommodations are good, which is a rarity in other swordfishing areas. Some waters which contain broadbill cannot be fished by sport boats; the runs are too long and usually the weather is rough. Such a spot is found off Georges Bank and Brown Bank, 80 to 125 miles out of Cape Cod, where a large commercial catch is made.

Many years have passed since ichthyologist Goode produced the first summary on the swordfish, but it is just now that parts of this prized fish's spawning behavior is coming to light. Off the north coast of Cuba broadbill have been taken which contained eggs ready to be extruded. A few ripe fish have also been taken off the northeastern coast of the United States, but the occurrence is so rare that this area is discounted as a possible spawning ground. The broadbill are first seen usually on the offshore banks in the spring. It appears that they do not travel along the coast to reach this locality but arrive suddenly and directly from the open sea. Their departure in the late fall is just as abrupt. They disappear into the open Atlantic without a trace and are not seen on their offshore or presumably southward journey. In both the Atlantic and the Pacific the spawning occurs when the fish are away from the coasts between December and May. The following summer the swordfish return in a thin and generally poor condition (which indicates a post-spawning situation) and spend the summer getting fat while feeding in the rich coastal waters.

Present-day investigations are placing together pieces of the puzzle slowly but surely. Larval and juvenile swordfish have been found in the Gulf of Mexico and the Gulf Stream from Florida to Cape Hatteras. George Arata, Jr., a fishery scientist who worked on this problem, surmised that the spawning area probably extended from the lower Caribbean to the South Carolina coast and that within this area they probably spawn year round, with the height of the season in Florida and Georgia waters from April through September.

Another scientist, Edgar Arnold, Jr., collected numerous larval swordfish in the Gulf of Mexico, and he indicated that parts of this body of water serve as nursery grounds for swordfish.

Danish oceanographic expeditions have also been contributing knowledge on the broadbill. A. Vedel Tanning, one of the investigators, believes that an important breeding area lies north and northeast of the Lesser Antilles in the southern part of the Sargasso Sea because a distribution of the larval stages, smaller than 20 mm. in length, has been found in this area. Breeding areas are also indicated by records of tiny swordfish (small postlarvae) west of Sumatra, in the South China Sea, in the Celebes and Banda Seas, and off the Marquesas. The fry are usually found in water of about 75° F.

From these investigations it now appears that some spawning takes place at all seasons, but most occurs during February, March, and April in the north Atlantic. In the eastern Pacific spawning is probably at its height during these months also, but in the Mediterranean it occurs later in the year because of different temperature conditions there.

The broadbill, like other billfishes, may often be seen jumping freely, that is, when not hooked by an angler. They may jump in an effort to get rid of remora or one of the other sucking fishes—there are several types of which the remora is the most common. Market fishermen often attest to the fact that many broadbill are seen jumping just before they disappear from a locality and migrate to the unknown. Could it be that the fish may jump simply because they are frisking about? Perhaps it is a playful characteristic of the young fish.

Although swordfish may gather in certain areas, they do not school. They are always seen scattered; sometimes two fish swim together, but most often they are alone. When waters are calm, the broadbill may be seen loafing or lying quietly near the surface, with dorsal fin and upper tail visible above the water. In this state of relaxation the fish are easily harpooned. Often the boat can approach quite close to the swordfish so that the pulpit (extended harpooning platform) comes directly over the fish. When lazying on the surface swordfish are sometimes easily frightened at the approach of a small boat. Yet, they often allow themselves to be almost run down before suddenly turning from a large vessel. I have never heard of a broadbill being hit by any kind of a boat. However, there are many instances where a vessel has been hit by a swordfish—when hooked or harpooned they are dangerous.

There are many documented stories about the attacks of swordfish upon boats. Even the earliest voyagers to America noted the pugnacity of the broadbill. In 1674, Josselyn, in his *Account of Two Voyages to New England,* wrote: "and in the afternoon we saw a great fish called the Vehuella or Sword-fish, having a long, strong and sharp finn, like a sword-blade on the top of his head, with which he pierced our ship, and broke it off with striving to get loose. One of our sailors dived and brought it aboard."

The following account documented by Dr. W. E. Gudger, who has compiled many interesting ichthyological phenomena, is one of the most interesting: "Absolutely authentic is the next account which concludes with the certificate of the attending physician. The sword was preserved and sent to the U.S. National Museum. On Monday, August 9, 1886, Captain F. D. Langsford sailed out of Lanesville, Mass., in the schooner Venus (12 tons) with a crew of three men, in pursuit of a swordfish— About 11 A.M., in Ipswich Bay a fish was seen. The captain, with one man, taking a dory, gave chase, and soon harpooned the fish, throwing over a buoy with line attached to the harpoon, after which the fish was left and they returned to the vessel for dinner. About an hour later the captain, with one man, again took his dory and went out to secure the fish. Picking up the buoy, Captain Langsford took hold of the line, pulling his boat toward the swordfish, which was quite large, and not badly wounded.

"The line was taut as the boat slowly neared the fish which the captain intended to lance and thus kill. When near the fish, but too far away to reach it with the lance, it quickly turned and rushed at and under the boat, thrusting its sword up through the bottom of the boat 23 inches. As the fish turned and rushed toward the boat the line was suddenly slacked, causing the captain to fall over on his back, and while he was in the act of rising the sword came piercing through the boat

Swordfish

and into his body. At this time another swordfish was in sight near by, and the captain, excited, and anxious to secure both, raised himself up, not knowing that he was wounded. Seeing the sword, he seized it, exclaiming, 'We've got him, anyway!' He lay in the bottom of the dory, holding fast to the sword, until his vessel came alongside, while the fish, being under the boat, could not be reached. Soon the captain said, 'I think I am hurt, and quite badly.' When the vessel arrived he went on board, took a few steps, fell, never rising again."

These great fish are so big and powerful, and their swords such excellent offensive and defensive weapons, that they are known to have practically no enemies besides man. However, mako sharks seem to be able to hold their own against the mighty gladiators. One fisherman described the uneven battle between two sharks and a broadbill. He watched the sharks bite off the tail of the swordfish, making it practically helpless. Before the sharks could do further damage the fisherman harpooned the swordfish, which weighed 350 pounds. There are many recorded instances of swordfish found in the stomachs of sharks; the most amazing was the case of the nearly intact 120-pound swordfish with its sword still attached, found in the stomach of a 730-pound mako taken off Bimini, Bahamas.

The broadbill is a voracious fish, which feeds on menhaden, mackerel, herring, haddock, bluefish, hake, butterfish, and just about any small fish. Squid and mackerel are favorite foods along the coast of Peru and Chile. They have been hooked on set lines, close to bottom, baited with mackerel, which indicates that they do not live on live food exclusively. The method of securing their food is similar to that of the other billfishes. They bull through a school of fish, slashing right and left with their swords, and then turn to gobble the mangled or dead fish.

To catch a broadbill with rod and reel takes patience, skill, luck, and long days of angling effort—some anglers have tried year after year without ever being rewarded with a strike. When a fish does hit, he has to be handled skilfully because the hook tears easily out of the soft mouth. A few fish have been caught on a trolled bait, but normally the swordfish is spotted first and then the bait is presented to it. As I have stated previously, these fish appear to surface only during the daylight hours, mostly to sun themselves or to seek the warmer surface temperatures. Therefore, they don't seem to have much interest in food, and most of the time it is difficult and exasperating to try to induce them to strike. I believe that in all big game angling history less than 400 of these big fellows have been taken on rod and reel.

In pursuit of the elusive broadbill I had a heartbreaking experience in the waters of the famed Humboldt Current off Tocopilla, Chile. Upon our arrival in Tocopilla, Mr. Tuker—world champion swordfisherman at the time—instructed me on the procedures of circumventing the broadbill. Kip Farrington, well-known big game fisherman, also gave me pointers. The angler does not troll a bait hoping to raise a swordfish. When a fish is sighted, a previously rigged squid is presented to the fish "about 2 feet down and 20 feet in front of his nose." Then the fish grabs the bait and goes off about 100 yards, stops, and when he runs again, the angler sets the hook with all he has, again and again.

Fishing from the "Fortuna," a rather primitive craft with a native crew aboard, we were sliding along the smooth ocean swells when suddenly the mate let out a loud "albacora, albacora!" I looked to starboard and saw the dark form of a huge swordfish propelling itself directly to the trolled bait.

When the mate spotted the "albacora" I was trolling a feather directly off a light rod and a mackerel bait from the outrigger. One mate grabbed the small rod and reeled in the feather jig while the other was anxiously unwinding the wire leader of the squid rig. Meanwhile, I had jerked the line from the outrigger and began to reel in the bait as fast as I could—so that the squid could be put on and presented to the swordfish. Before I had reeled the mackerel ten feet the broadbill hit it in a most unorthodox manner and went off like a bat out of hell. He didn't stop; he didn't even pause! I leaned back and yanked the rod four or five times as hard as I could. That solid feeling of a well-hooked fish was there. The Chilean mate clamped my harness to the reel and adjusted the chair. After about ten minutes, as I was getting some of the line back, it went limp, parting a few feet from the rod tip. The Sanfords, who watched this activity from another boat, pulled alongside. I was so disappointed I couldn't speak. We tested the line and found that any part of it could be broken easily by hand. Later we were informed that this line, which was outfitted with the boat, had been in use for four years! I would advise any angler who survives the 100-mile, wild and dusty motor trip from Antofogasta to Tocopilla to bring his own tackle.

Dolphins

The dolphins are offshore, blue-water inhabitants of the open seas. They are distributed widely throughout the oceans of the world in warm waters. Although gregarious and fairly common, nowhere do they appear in quantities large enough to induce a commercial fishery. At one time about 20 different species were assigned to this fish, but now only 2 are recognized. The dolphin and the small dolphin comprise the family CORYPHAENIDAE.

Dolphin (11a)
(*Coryphaena hippurus*)

The dolphin is exceedingly fast and spends much time near the water's surface. As a great sport fish it is famous for its brilliant and changeable colors. Anglers agree that it is one of the most beautiful of all fishes.

Coryphaena hippurus is accepted without dispute among fishery workers as the scientific name. However, both scientific and popular writers make the common name "dolphin" appear more confusing than it is. In heraldry both the fish and the porpoise were used and both were called dolphin; this was the beginning of the confusion. Ever since, writers continue to say, "It is unfortunate that both the mammal and fish are known by the same name." As one pursues the literature on fishes it is easily seen that almost without exception every author on fishes who includes dolphin in his work repeats, in some manner, the words of the early writer pertaining to the fact that the porpoise and dolphin are confused. Some recent writers embellish their accounts with phrases such as "it is a shame" and go into a detailed differentiation of a fish and a mammal: "a mammal is suckled by its mother," etc. Some scientists now advocate dropping the name "dolphin" and introducing "dorado" instead. Nonsense! I know that the supposed great confusion regarding the name does not exist. If a dolphin is listed in a fish book no one expects it to be a mammal. When an angler states, "we are going after dolphin," or "we caught a dozen dolphin," who would think that a dozen porpoises were caught?

I have fished for dolphin in many spots in different oceans, and I have yet to find any confusion about this name. Further, the name "dorado," which has been recently inserted as a substitute, would do more harm than good because a well-known inland game fish (a characin and one of South America's best) is the dorado. In American waters the Pacific yellowtail is occasionally called dorado. If we are concerned that quiz programs —"What is a dolphin?"—are inconvenienced, and if the name must be clarified officially, I would like to suggest that "dolphin-fish" replace "dorado."

In its extensive range the dolphin prefers waters not below 70° F. and has been recorded in the Atlantic from Brazil to the outer coast of Nova Scotia. It is found in the Caribbean, the Gulf of Mexico, and in or near the Gulf Stream from Florida northward to a turning point about the Massachusetts islands. Many are now taken during midsummer in Block Island Sound off Point Judith, Rhode Island, and in the vicinity of No Man's Land off the coast of Massachusetts.

Off the west African coast (Gold Coast) it is rather rare, appearing during warm seasons and not in large schools. It is known to occur off southern Italy and Sicily. In the eastern

Pacific it ranges from the Columbia River, Oregon, down to Peru and Chile and is common in Hawaiian waters. In the western Pacific it ranges from Japan south to Australia. However, off the California coast the dolphin is seldom seen north of Catalina but is abundant in areas off Lower California, Mexico, and Panama Bay.

The dolphin possesses a laterally compressed (side flattened) elongated body, most massive and deep close behind the head, tapering to a deeply forked tail. The dorsal fin originates well forward, almost directly above the eye, and its flexible spines are 55 to 65 in number. The anal fin, which is also unusually long, numbers 26 to 30 flexible spines. Minute scales, fine teeth, and 8 to 10 gill rakers are present. The front profile of the head is blunt. An excellent example of the difference of form between male and female in some species of fishes (sexual dimorphism) is shown in the roundish head of the female dolphin and the almost vertical profile of the bull or male. (The various differences in the growth phases of the male and female were primarily responsible for the previously accepted 20 species.)

Most authors wax poetic when describing the colors of the dolphin, and I feel they are completely justified in doing so. When one looks down on a darting school in calm waters the fish appear to be almost completely vivid blue. A fish on deck, while still alive, is a wondrous thing; its beautiful transient coloration must be seen to be appreciated. The dorsal fin is purplish blue and the tail is golden yellow, but basically, in the body, I can distinguish two color phases—one, a brilliant gold-yellow and green as a background upon which prominent blue and green spots are spattered. The other phase has an intense blue background with silvery markings. As the fish flips around on a deck, a flowing but fast transition of coloration takes place, especially at the moment before the fish flips its last. Undoubtedly the fish produces these changes in coloration while alive during varying phases of excitement.

Average size is 5 or 6 pounds, although many 35 and 40 pounders are taken, but most are under 25. The world record

Right: Atlantic blue marlin taken by Laddie Sanford off Walker Cay, Bahamas. *Below:* Pacific blue marlin taken off Kona, Hawaii, from Tacks Waldron's boat "Kumu" by Pablo Libero (Waldron on right).

Left: Mrs. Wendell Anderson with a blue marlin in Bimini, Bahamas. She probably would have had a world's record if sharks had not mutilated the fish.

Right: Mr. Wendell W. Anderson, well-known big game angler, with a fine specimen of blue marlin taken off Bimini.

rod and reel fish weighed 76 pounds and was taken by R. G. Stotesbery off Acapulco, Mexico, on September 24, 1957. Big fish have also been taken in the Atlantic and Indian oceans.

Obviously the dolphin can be identified instantly, and although another species exists, *Coryphaena equisetis* (at least, at present, accepted as such), anglers do not distinguish between them. (For differentiating points between the species, *see* Small Dolphin.)

Of their migratory habits we know only the approximate dates of arrival and departure in popular fishing areas in different parts of the world. Off the Florida coast they seem to be in greatest profusion from late winter to April (and later in some years); then most move on northward during the warm summer months—North Carolina, May to October (Diamond Shoals, one of the greatest concentration areas 21 miles east by north of Hatteras); Virginia, August; Maryland, July and August (largest groups about 35 to 50 miles offshore from Ocean City); Delaware and New Jersey, August; off southern New England and the Massachusetts islands in August and early September (no longer should we term it a straggler in this area).

January to May are probably the best months in Bermuda although the fish is present the year round; in the northern Bahamas June is best, and in the central and western portions of the Bahamas February and April bring the largest groups of dolphin. In Cuban waters migratory schools, extending for half a mile or more, sometimes appear in the Gulf Stream. Off Chile large schools appear from December to June. Although dolphin appear mostly in groups, the big fish, 20 pounds or more, are found alone or in pairs.

Little is known of its breeding habits. Spawning in this species seems to spread over a lengthy period. In Bermuda waters small specimens two inches long may be found in September and October, and some adults will have partially developed roe. Great schools of young dolphin one half pound to one and one half pounds are present off Maryland southward (probably the previous year's hatch) and are a nuisance to white marlin anglers. Six immature fish, averaging almost 16 inches fork length (tip of snout to fork in tail), were taken in mid-August from a trap a quarter of a mile offshore in lower Buzzards Bay, Massachusetts. Off Callao, Peru, females with large, swollen, almost ripe ovaries were taken in February. In the West Indies spawning takes place in the spring. Young fish have color bands on the fins and body which the adults do not possess. A full-grown female will average about 2,655,500 eggs.

Without question the great food favorite is the flyingfish, which is often pursued from underneath while it is in the air; as it hits the water the dolphin grabs it. Mullet, anchovies, and sardines are also tops on the diet list and crabs have been found in dolphin stomachs.

One of the greatest known concentration areas (such areas are known as "hot spots" among anglers) for dolphin is a spot 21 miles east by north of Hatteras in the vicinity of the Diamond Shoal Light Ship. Here single boats have been known to catch over a hundred in a morning's fishing. The western edge of the Gulf Stream is usually found just inside the light ship, and anglers generally work the waters within sight of this well-known marker. Flyingfish, the favorite food of the dolphin, are present in this area in great abundance—that is why the dolphin congregate there. But what attracts the flyingfish? I believe the answer is this: When the blue ocean current (in this case the Gulf Stream) flows by or against the green littoral or shore waters, which contain far less movement, an agitated situation is created (you may call it a type of rip) whereby great numbers of crustaceans and other tiny animals are dragged from the bottom by current movement and are held temporarily swirling by water action. (No matter where you may be fishing, never pass up an area where two types of water meet—a line of demarcation is usually seen.) So again we have the food chain—flyingfish in great numbers are attracted because of the profusion of tiny invertebrates on which they feed. We go one step further and say that the little animals are there because the water is rich in nutrients.

When in quest of dolphins, captains of fishing vessels go out of their way to troll by any log, box, wreckage, or any other floating debris. Dolphin love to congregate around such objects—perhaps because of their curious nature and perhaps because smaller fish may take refuge in such floating materials. Floating weeds also attract dolphin. For example, off Bermuda, after prevailing winds from northeast to southwest have brought in huge quantities of sargassum weed, dolphin will usually be found following it.

Among anglers the dolphin rates highly. When hooked it produces spectacular resistance against rod and reel, doing a series of acrobatics on the surface of the water and in the air, mixed with flashy, skittery, bouncy runs. One of the most exciting sights in angling, I believe, is to see several of these beauties come charging from the side, with a series of quick jumps, before pouncing on the trolled bait. Usually the hooked fish will go into the air immediately and then tear off line at a fast rate. The angler who catches his first dolphin will be surprised indeed, for the fish he brings to boat will be less than half the size he expected. The dolphin has a broad flat body and will present it against the pull of the rod, creating resistance against the water. It is like trying to pull a dish broadside through the water.

It is a curious fish, and its curiosity often proves its downfall. Usually it is possible to keep a school close by if one of them is kept in the water (string it through the lower jaw on a length of line 20 to 30 feet in length). I had one unusually productive experience in this manner. We were fishing for yellowtail snappers in clear blue water and chumming with anchovies or hogmouth fry (the fry are torn in bits and mixed with beach sand). Several yellowtail had been taken when my wife, Bo, yelled, "I've got the biggest yellowtail in the ocean!" It turned out to be a large dolphin which we quickly tied in the water. There was no time for chumming, but the school kept by for close to a half hour. Our baited hooks (of whole fry) were grabbed almost as soon as they hit the water. The dolphin looked like darting blue gems as they fought for the bait. That morning remains as one of my most memorable fishing experiences.

The literature on the dolphin reveals mixed feelings concerning its table qualities. Not too many years ago some fishermen considered it a poison fish and would heave it back into the sea. Today many authors (who have never eaten one) proclaim it edible or mediocre. Some even state that if placed on ice for a few days the flesh can be made palatable. I'm amazed, for I rate it as one of the best of all sea foods. When skinned and filleted it is a dish worthy of a king's table. I might add here that as the main constituent in a fish chowder it is also tops. During our fishing expedition of several months off the east African coast our captain, Bill Fagan, who is a great "fancy chef," prepared many of these chowders aboard the "Mañana," and although I have since eaten many types of chowders in many different parts of the world, I will say that Captain Bill's dolphin chowder is "the best."

Small Dolphin
(*Coryphaena equisetis*)

The small dolphin, with a maximum length of about 30 inches, is known in the Atlantic and Pacific, and although it seems to be more abundant in warmer waters, its range is generally assumed to be the same as the larger *C. hippurus*. In the Atlantic it seems to be more common from Florida to Cape Hatteras than in the Pacific, where it is found off southern California only during the warm weather months. However, I believe that *C. equisetis* is more abundant than it seems, for anglers never attempt to differentiate between the two forms.

There is question as to whether the small form should be considered different from the larger dolphin. At present the two species are accepted as being distinguished by the following differences of anatomy:

C. hippurus—pectorals more than half the length of the head; tongue is narrow, rounded in front, and does not fill floor of mouth; dorsal fin rays 55 to 65, anal fin rays 26 to 30.

C. equisetis—pectorals about half length of head; tongue is broad, square cut in front, and fills floor of mouth; dorsal fin rays 51 to 55, anal fin rays 24 to 26.

Finletfishes

Tunas, bonitos, mackerels, and wahoo form one of the most important groups of fishes in the seas, for they supply a great amount of the world's protein food. The annual commercial and sporting catch runs to many millions of pounds. They are often referred to as the tuna-like fishes or the mackerel-like fishes, which I feel is unsatisfactory. For example, the Spanish mackerel or the cero mackerel cannot be called tuna-like. For these fishes, as a group, I would like to propose the name "finletfishes." To my knowledge, this name has never been used, and yet it is correct and descriptive. All members of this clan possess finlets; these are small, soft fins situated on the dorsal surface between the second dorsal fin and tail and on the ventral side between the anal fin and tail.

The finletfishes provide both great sport and commercial fishing in all oceans. They constitute an international resource; home to them is no particular country. Nearly all spend their lives and reproduce their young outside the territorial limits of any nation. All are swift, predacious, oceanic, schooling fishes distributed in greater or lesser abundance throughout the world's great bodies of water. These powerfully muscled, streamlined fishes generally do not jump or perform acrobatics when hooked.

Instead, they zoom off like torpedoes, and every member of the clan is capable of sustaining an amazing amount of resistance when worked with rod and reel of proper size in relation to the fish. Typically, the fight of a finletfish is a long, fast run followed by a series of smaller runs, then a tendency to circle when approaching the gaff.

This group has been split, off and on, into various families * or considered as a single natural family, SCOMBRIDAE. I prefer to accept the latter view and place the finletfishes in this family. (Often these fishes may be referred to as scombrid or scombroid, which are taken from the family name.)

TUNAS

In the oceans and seas of the world the tunas are the giants of the finletfishes. All are great game fishes, and some are ranked among the world's best. The tunas all have robust, streamlined, bullet-shaped bodies, which immediately separate them from the slender mackerels. Any tuna can be distinguished from the bonitos, skipjacks, or wahoo at a glance. Tunas have dark backs and silvery sides minus stripes, bars, dark spots, or any other pronounced markings which the other finletfishes possess.

Bluefin Tuna (3a)

(*Thunnus thynnus*)

The bluefin, one of the fastest swimming fishes in the sea and largest of the finlet tribe, commands one of the top spots in the enthusiasm of big game anglers. It is important in the world's fisheries and has been known by many names—great tuna, tunny, horse mackerel, albacore. Since 1758 it has been given a half dozen different scientific names. At present the common name "bluefin tuna" and the scientific name *Thunnus thynnus* are accepted by all fishery scientists.

* ACANTHOCYBIIDAE, CYBIIDAE, KATSUWONIDAE, SCOMBRIDAE, THUNNIDAE.

The bluefin tuna is a world-wide species, found on both sides of the Atlantic, eastern Pacific, Baltic Sea, North Sea, Black Sea, Sea of Azov, Mediterranean, Persian Gulf, and Indian Ocean. On the western side of the Atlantic it is known to range from the north coast of South America (Caribbean) to as far north as Labrador. Along the eastern side of the Atlantic the giant ranges from Norway southward to northwest Africa. It is also known to extend out from the coast as far as the Azores. In the eastern Pacific the bluefin ranges from the Columbia River southward to somewhere along the coast of Lower California and probably to the Galapagos Islands.

The bluefin is a powerful-looking fish with a full, streamlined body which tapers sharply at both ends. It has a slim caudal peduncle and yellow finlets. A keel is prominent on the lateral sides of the caudal peduncle, and the tail is "lunate." Although most bluefins have a dark blue or blue-gray dorsal surface, I have seen live fish caught off Wedgeport, Nova Scotia, whose backs were flat gray in color. The change takes place so quickly after death in fishes that most anglers never notice the true coloration. All the bluefins which I have seen alive in both northern (Nova Scotia) and southern (Bahamas) waters had a vivid yellow-gold band along the lateral surface from the tip of the snout to approximately half way along the body, where it gradually faded out. This band disappears almost immediately upon gaffing the fish. The belly and the forward half of the lateral surface below the golden band is bright silver. Most bluefins when mounted, or illustrated in books and magazines, are incorrectly colored.

The world's record for rod and reel stands at 977 pounds, but unquestionably the bluefins grow bigger. It was reported in the *Boston Transcript* for July 20, 1923, that a tuna caught off Manasquan, New Jersey, was about 14 feet long and weighed approximately 1,600 pounds. Fish of 1,000 pounds plus are not rare. Several tuna caught off Nova Scotia and brought into Boston weighed 1,200 and 1,300 pounds. Another example of a "fairly well authenticated instance," was mentioned by Sella, an Italian ichthyologist—a bluefin caught 60 to 70 years ago off

Narragansett, Rhode Island, weighed about 1,500 pounds. The fish was divided among the various hotels and fed, supposedly, 1,000 people. You can take this instance and the 1,600-pound New Jersey fish for what they are worth. I cannot find any record stating that these fish were weighed. And the round figures given lead me to believe that the weights were merely guesses. However, facts indicate that a bluefin well over 1,000 pounds will be taken eventually on rod and reel. I venture to say that the prize fish will be taken in the western North Atlantic.

The adult bluefin averages about 400 pounds. When taken in southern waters, during their northward migration, the fish are generally thinner and weigh less than the ones caught at the end of the migration in northern waters. For example, two 88-inch tuna caught off Bimini, Bahamas, in May and June averaged 415 pounds, while a fish of the same length captured in northern waters a couple of months later weighed 516 pounds. Also, three 93-inch fish taken off Bimini averaged 450 pounds, while a specimen of the same length captured in northern waters weighed 587 pounds. Data from records kept by the Tuna Guides Association of Wedgeport, Nova Scotia, and the Cat Key Club of Cat Cay, Bahamas, and used by Luis Rivas in a scientific paper, give us a definite idea of the differences in weight of tunas from southern and northern waters. The average weight of 381 bluefins from Cat Cay (May and early June 1947–1952) was 467 pounds. The average weight of 331 specimens from Wedgeport (July 1947–1952) was 506 pounds. Also from Wedgeport—729 bluefins taken during the month of September averaged 579 pounds. In other words, there is a progressive increase in weight as the fish travel from south to north, and they also gain about 7 per cent in Nova Scotian waters from July to September.

There is a great difference in maximum weight between the bluefins which ply the waters off our western coast and those which travel off the eastern coast of the United States and Canada. Although the Atlantic bluefins are known to reach 1,000 pounds plus, their Pacific cousins appear to reach a maximum of about 250 pounds.

The Atlantic and eastern Pacific bluefins are remarkably similar (except in maximum weight), but they can be distinguished by at least four internal characteristics (too technical to deal with here) and possibly by the gill raker count which is 39–41 in the Atlantic and 32–39 in the California tuna. Both have 8 to 9 dorsal finlets and 7 to 8 anal finlets. Although results of studies by scientists indicate that the California and the Atlantic bluefin should be considered distinct species, this has not as yet been formally adopted. Two other species of tuna found in the western side of the Pacific are sometimes called bluefins; these are in fact distinct species and are dealt with later in this section.

For anglers the following anatomical points can be used as means of distinguishing the bluefin from other tuna. The bluefin possesses no stripes or conspicuous markings (this separates it from the bonitos). The pectoral fin is small, about three quarters of the length of the distance between the tip of the snout and the hind edge of the operculum or gill cover (the yellowfin and blackfin tunas have comparatively larger pectoral fins). The bluefin has small jaw teeth, and the roof of the mouth along the midline possesses small teeth. The entire trunk or body of the bluefin is scaly, including the belly.

The migration of bluefin tuna along the coast of eastern North America is of great interest to anglers, commercial fishermen, and scientists. The pieces of information regarding migration are being put together slowly, and much research is necessary to complete the picture.

Large tuna are caught in the deep water off Havana, Cuba, during May. This fact indicates that the migration, which appears in the Straits of Florida along the shallow western edge of the Bahamas about the middle of May, enters from the Caribbean—through the Yucatan Channel and around the western coast of Cuba. There may be another run into the Straits of Florida from the Caribbean through the old Bahama Channel off the east central coast of Cuba. Louise Victoria Smith of the Institute of Jamaica reported a regular run of bluefins off the northeastern coast of Jamaica during February through April, from the California Banks up to Port Antonio or farther.

Apparently the northerly migration of bluefin tuna may start in the Caribbean and continue around both ends of Cuba. As they swim northward, some groups move directly into the Gulf Stream; others may go along the eastern edge of Bahama Banks, but there is no proof of this. However, I have witnessed huge schools off Walker Cay (north end of the Bahamas) headed in a northwesterly direction and moving along at a tremendous rate of speed. I assume that these bluefins did not come through the Florida Straits. I believe it would be highly improbable for migrating schools in deep water to leave their northerly movement, head east and south for many miles, and then make an about-face to return northward again to the Gulf Stream.

Is there a concentrated migration route along the eastern side of the Bahamas? After studying charts, considering all available information, and taking into account my own observations, I can offer an opinion that a portion of the schools of tuna, after leaving the Caribbean area (perhaps through the Windward Passage between Cuba and Haiti) and rounding the eastern end of Cuba, continue northward somewhere along the eastern side of the Bahamas. In many areas throughout the Bahamas the fishing is virtually unexplored. I am sure that as more of the islands are developed for tourists, sport fishing will increase, and consequently more light will be thrown on this most interesting question.

After leaving southern waters, about mid-May to the latter part of June, the bluefins probably travel deep because it is rare to have a giant bluefin reported between the Straits of Florida and northern waters. Frank Mather of the Woods Hole Oceanographic Institution reported a 600-pound tuna taken in a trap 200 miles south of Chincoteague, Virginia, and small ones are also taken off Chincoteague. Tuna are often reported off North Carolina but as yet have not been identified. In late June and early July the bluefins may be found, swimming far offshore, passing Montauk. Some groups head into Block Island Sound, where the big fellows are found in favorite spots off Watch Hill, Rhode Island, between Block Island and Rhode Island in the

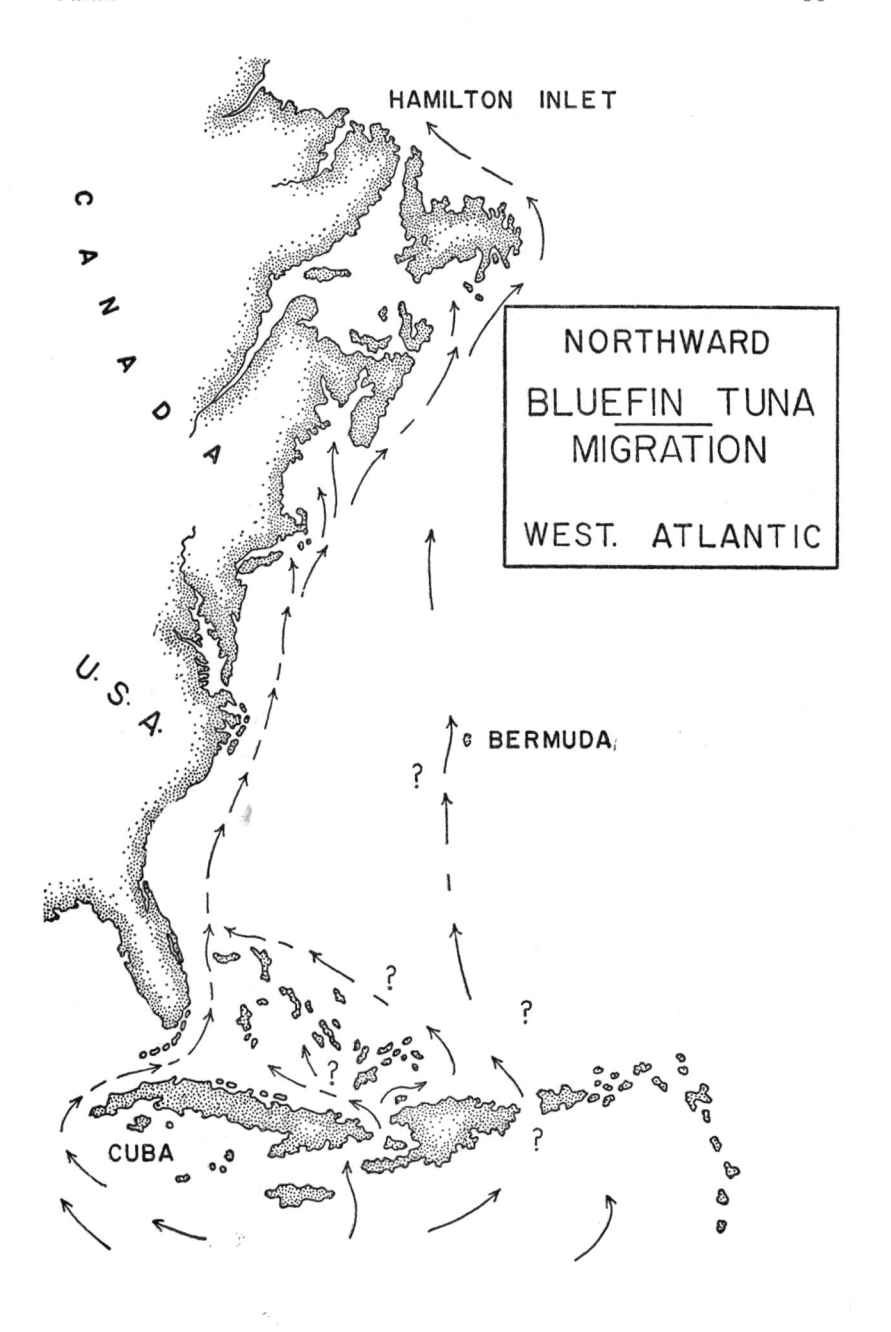

Tunas

NORTHWARD BLUEFIN TUNA MIGRATION
WEST. ATLANTIC

area off Greenhill Point and Matunuck Point. Other great angling spots in this zone are east and southeast of Block Island.

All along the eastern coast of the United States, from Ocean City, Maryland, to Cape Cod—June to October—small bluefins, from 10 to about 100 pounds, are abundant and known by all fishermen as school tuna. Many salt water anglers believe that school tuna are different from the bluefins, but the giants and the school tuna are of the same species. The "schoolies" are simply younger bluefins.

It is a curious fact that the giants come into Block Island Sound but the smaller school tuna are taken far offshore well into ocean waters. My friend George Albrecht, for over twenty years a well-known angler and guide in these waters, informs me that the angling boats look for the young tuna at the 180-foot contour line and out. This line occurs south of Block Island and Montauk Point. However, in exceptionally good years George has taken many school tuna within two to three miles of Block Island and Montauk. Some areas such as off Provincetown, Massachusetts, sometimes witness vast numbers of school tuna cavorting along inshore waters.

Groups of bluefins by-pass Block Island Sound and appear off Massachusetts and its islands; others round Cape Cod and go into the Gulf of Maine. (During an exploratory cruise into the offshore western Atlantic during June and the first week of July by the U.S. Fish and Wildlife Service research vessel "Delaware," an excellent catch of bluefin tuna was made. Tuna longline gear was used, and over 16,000 pounds of bluefins were taken 140 miles south of Georges Bank.) Many groups travel on to Nova Scotia (one of the greatest concentration areas) and farther north to Newfoundland and Labrador. Hamilton Inlet, Labrador, seems to be their most northerly outpost. When temperatures drop in October, the bluefins disappear suddenly. There is no sign of them until they appear again in the Caribbean and the Straits of Florida.

Where do the giant bluefins go when they leave the waters off Canada and northeastern United States? A plausible theory, prevalent at one time, was that bluefins crossed the ocean into

European waters. However, through studies, with comparison of anatomical measurements of bluefins from both sides of the Atlantic, it was found that the western Atlantic and eastern Atlantic tuna are of the same species but represent separate and distinct groups. Also, spawning areas (treated fully further on) present on both sides of the Atlantic indicate independent breeding populations. Therefore, from such evidence it may be inferred that no transoceanic migration takes place. We do know that the bluefins of both sides of the ocean, after their northward migration, return to warm waters. It appears that they travel far out from shore or go deep (or both) on their return to balmier waters.

Much remains to be solved concerning bluefin migrations. For example, Louis Mowbray, director of the Bermuda Aquarium, suggests the possibility of another lane of migration because bluefins are caught occasionally off Bermuda. Over the years there have been numerous reports of large schools of tuna, seen at the surface from 15 to 100 miles east of Bermuda during April and May. One specimen weighing 400 pounds was caught in a net in April. Also, a few have been taken by trolling in November and December. These occurrences of bluefins off Bermuda coincide in time with the north and south migrations along the eastern coast of the United States.

What proof do we have that the giant tuna seen along the Straits of Florida are the same groups or populations which appear in northern waters, such as off Wedgeport, Nova Scotia? We have no proof. Because the bluefins are absent in one locale when present in another (Bahamas and Nova Scotia) and seen always traveling in a northerly direction during migration, we assume that the Bahama and Wedgeport bluefins are of the same group or population. Also, the known facts concerning the progressive increase in weight further substantiates the accepted theory that the bluefin tuna definitely migrate, annually from south to north, along the coast of eastern United States.

However, logical as this theory appears to be, it remains an assumption. Tagging or marking information will provide definite facts. The inference of a south to north migration must

FINLETFISHES

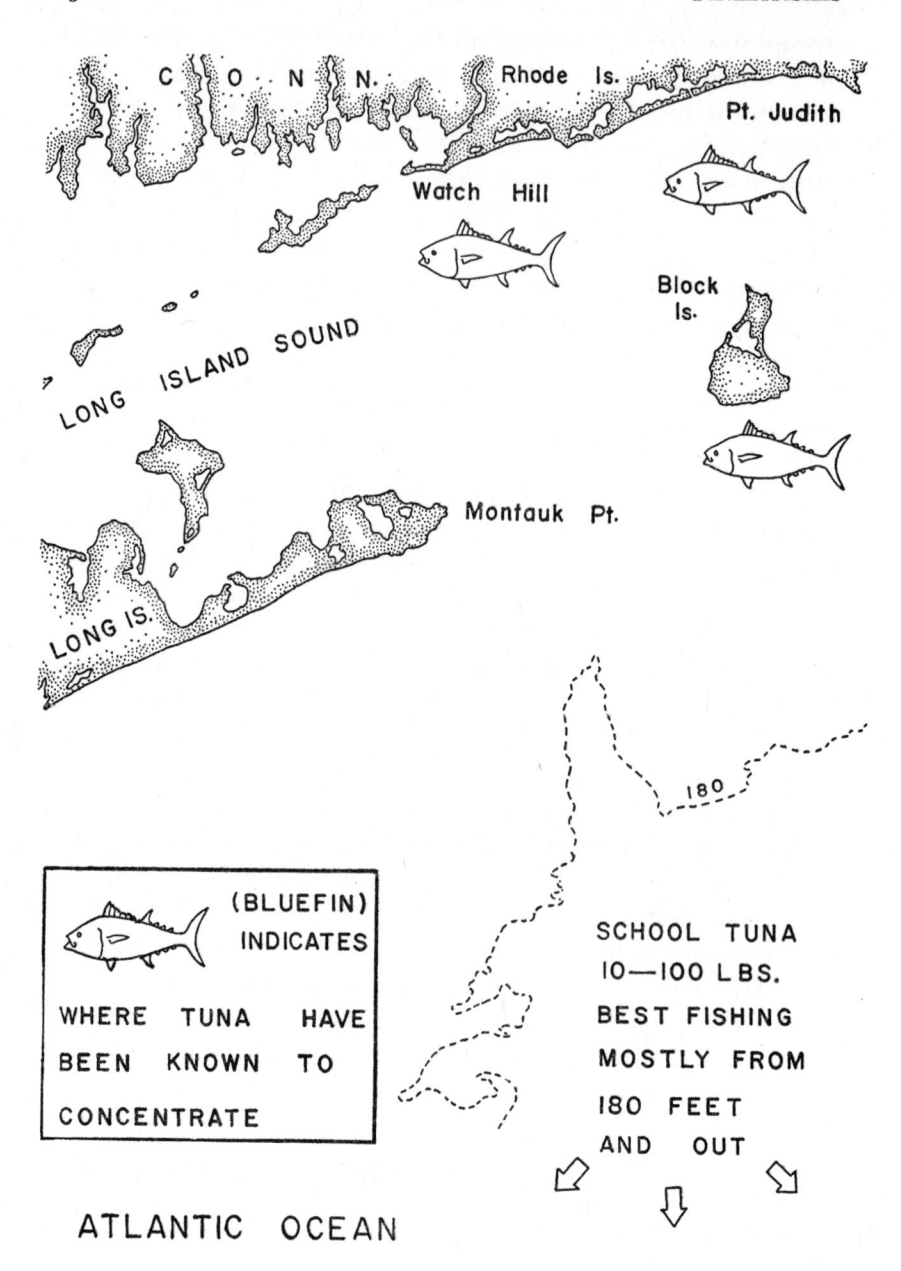

Map showing Connecticut, Rhode Island (Pt. Judith), Watch Hill, Block Is., Long Island Sound, Montauk Pt., Long Is., and the Atlantic Ocean with a 180 ft depth contour.

(BLUEFIN) INDICATES WHERE TUNA HAVE BEEN KNOWN TO CONCENTRATE

SCHOOL TUNA 10—100 LBS. BEST FISHING MOSTLY FROM 180 FEET AND OUT remain tentative until a tuna marked in the Straits of Florida is recovered in northern waters. Some writers repeat that tuna containing Bimini hooks have been caught at Wedgeport. However, this supposed evidence is not accepted by scientists because the brands and sizes of hooks used by anglers at both Bimini and Wedgeport are the same. It would be difficult to identify such a hook unless marked. Frank Mather and Luis Rivas, scientists who have worked with this problem, used marked hooks in Bimini and Cat Cay in the Bahamas in 1952 and 1953. Also, Mather used a dart-tag in 1954. But none of the marked fishes has been caught. Efforts are continuing in this direction and perhaps some day a marked fish will be recovered.

Bluefins in the European side of the Atlantic seem to have a similar migration—from south to north—after spawning. The Italian ichthyologist Sella, who studied the European bluefin, sent letters to many widely scattered institutions asking that hooks found in bluefin tuna be sent to him. He studied the different types of hooks, the country which used them, etc. By this method he collected evidence from which he deduced that European bluefins migrate from Italy to the Azores and from Spain to Norway.

Mr. Heldt, another scientist who worked on European tuna also concluded, from the recovery of hooks, that bluefins traveled northward after spawning. A Spanish hook taken from a bluefin off Oslo, Norway, indicates that the fish had traveled more than a thousand miles in less than a month!

The bluefins possess an interesting piece of anatomy, found atop the head between the eyes, which may possibly be associated with their ability to perceive direction during migration. The area of this "window" in the head may be seen and felt by hand as a slight depression. A tube leads from this window to the brain; it is called the pineal apparatus. In certain reptiles the pineal body, which reaches the surface, is called the third eye. Evidence presented by Luis Riva's study of this apparatus suggests that tuna and other related fishes may react to light by means of the pineal apparatus. It is possible that one of the factors controlling the movements of tuna in the open sea is light. There may be a correlation between sun altitudes, intensity of light, direction of rays, water transparencies, depth, and the behavior of tunas.

The spawning mystery of the western Atlantic bluefin is being unraveled, mostly through the efforts of scientists at the Marine Laboratory, University of Miami. They have discovered that at least part of the spawning grounds is located in the Straits of Florida, off the northwestern end of Cuba, and off the western edge of the Bahama Banks along the eastern side of the Florida Current (Gulf Stream). Most of the spawning activity seems to take place in the locality of Riding Rocks and Bimini. Evidence for this assumption includes the occurrence of ripe and recently spawned adult fish in these areas, plus what the Miami scientists say may be fertilized eggs and larvae. Presence of juveniles and young in the vicinity adds further credence to this belief. It is interesting to note that juveniles have been taken from the stomachs of predacious fishes, especially dolphin. The scientists also found very young specimens of bluefin, weighing as little as half a pound and about 10 inches in length, present in the vicinity from about the middle of July.

European scientists have discovered the spawning grounds of eastern Atlantic bluefins to be located mainly in the central Mediterranean. The breeding season here extends from late April through the middle of July. In the latter part of April and early May, in various parts of the Mediterranean, ripening of bluefins' gonads takes place. During this period great schools of tuna form groups, often composed of thousands of individuals, and then travel to the spawning grounds. The fish arrive about the last part of May. Actual spawning occurs during June and early July. These scientists have also discovered that breeding tuna prefer warm and highly saline waters and present evidence that spawning may take place in either shallow or deep water but close to the surface—at depths of 8 to 10 meters. Sella suggests that tuna of only 35 pounds may be sexually mature.

The spawning grounds of the eastern Pacific bluefin are not known. We may assume that they follow a pattern similar to

Above: Pacific shortbill spearfish (mounted specimen) taken off Honolulu, Hawaii. *Left:* Atlantic longbill spearfish (fresh fish, fins damaged). Top fish—taken off Bermuda; second—Fort Lauderdale, Florida; third and fourth—Islamorada, Florida Keys. Courtesy Al Pflueger, Miami, Florida. (Photos by Doris Barnes)

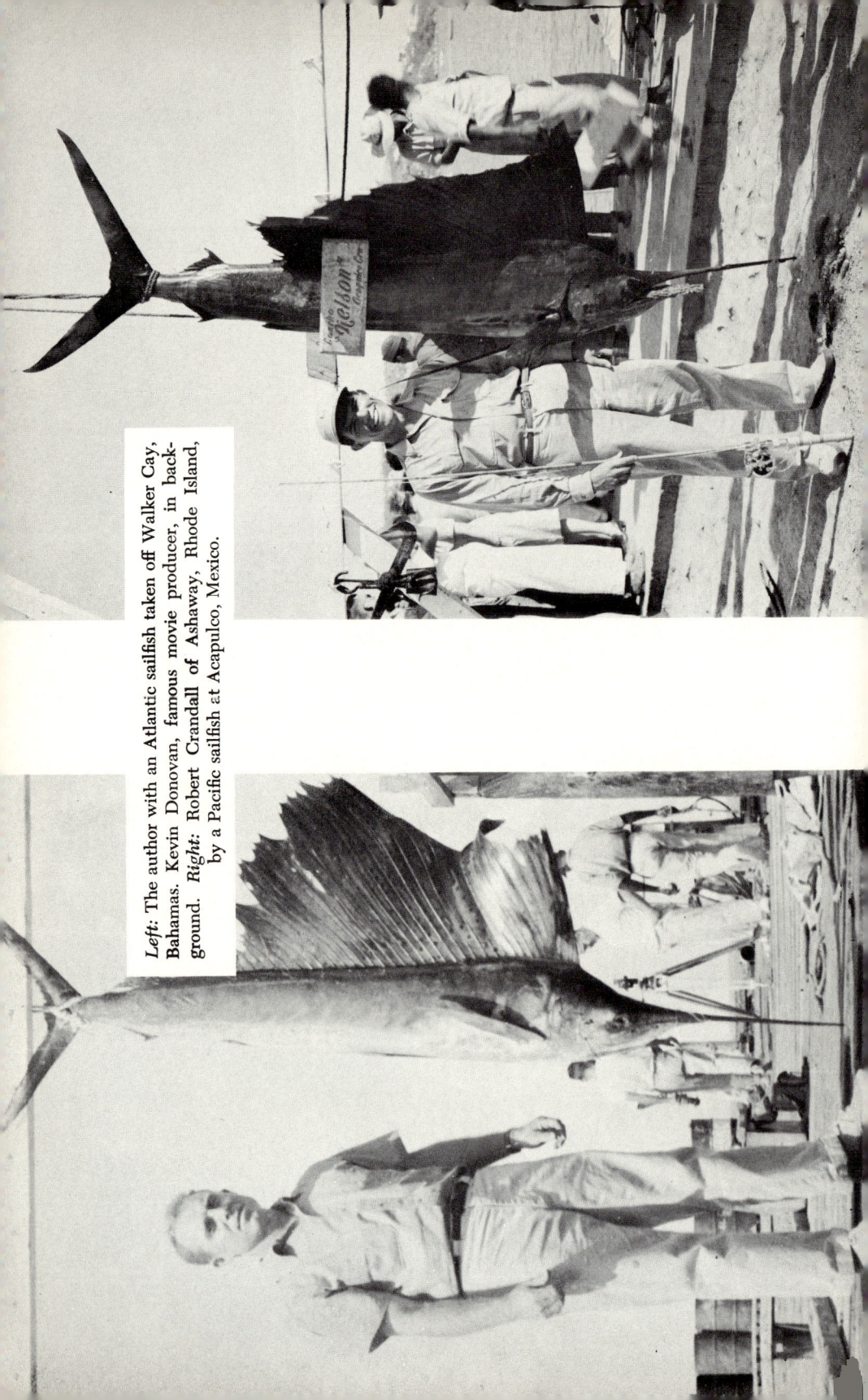

Left: The author with an Atlantic sailfish taken off Walker Cay, Bahamas. Kevin Donovan, famous movie producer, in background. *Right:* Robert Crandall of Ashaway, Rhode Island, by a Pacific sailfish at Acapulco, Mexico.

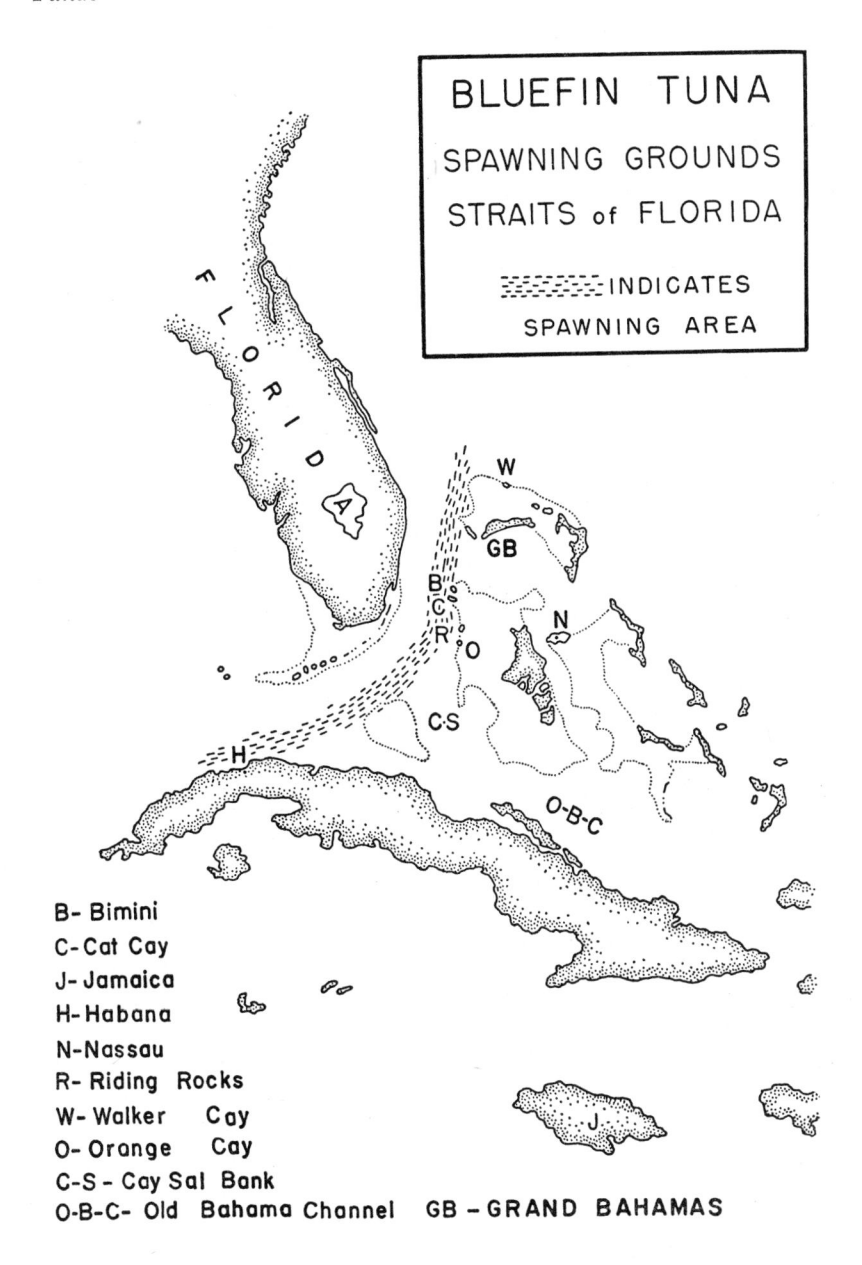

BLUEFIN TUNA SPAWNING GROUNDS STRAITS of FLORIDA

INDICATES SPAWNING AREA

B- Bimini
C- Cat Cay
J- Jamaica
H- Habana
N- Nassau
R- Riding Rocks
W- Walker Cay
O- Orange Cay
C-S - Cay Sal Bank
O-B-C- Old Bahama Channel   GB - GRAND BAHAMAS

that of their western Atlantic cousins. Since the Atlantic bluefins seek warm waters for spawning, it is probable that the spawning requirements are the same for the Pacific bluefin. After migrating as far north as the Columbia River, these scombrids return (we assume) south, swimming in deep waters to their spawning grounds—perhaps in the warm waters off Mexico and Central America. I venture to guess they do not travel farther south than the Galapagos Islands area.

As with all large game fishes, the maximum size and rate of growth of the bluefin is of much interest to anglers and fishery workers. Information from Mediterranean scientists indicates that young fry grow at an astounding rate; fish hatched in June in the Mediterranean reach a weight up to a little more than a pound by September.

One of the most popular questions asked by anglers when they see a large bluefin is "How old is it?" Therefore, I am listing statistics produced by the Italian ichthyologist Sella, who has done much work on tuna. He has made studies of the concentric rings in the vertebrae of 1,500 Mediterranean bluefins. (The vertebrae possess annual rings similar to those found in the trunk of a tree.)

SELLA'S AGE-WEIGHT RELATIONSHIPS OF MEDITERRANEAN BLUEFINS

Age in years	Weight in pounds
1	10
2	21
3	35
4	56
5	88
6	128
7	170
8	214
9	265
10	320
11	375
12	440
13	517
14	616–660

When a fish as large as a giant tuna comes aboard, everybody attempts to guess its weight, and usually wagers are made. Of course, facilities to weigh a fish of this size are not present on sporting boats, but a tape measure is easy to carry. Therefore, I have attempted to formulate a length-weight table which may help anglers estimate the weight of a bluefin when boated. Israel Pothier, amateur scientist and manager of the Tuna Guides Association at Wedgeport, Nova Scotia, presented me with data covering the landings of tuna of three seasons. This data I modified slightly with bits of information available in a few scientific papers.

Length in Inches	Weight in Pounds
55– 60	110–140
61– 65	150–185
66– 70	190–205
71– 75	208–250
76– 80	260–290
81– 85	320–400
86– 90	440–500
91– 95	510–560
96–100	570–650
101–105	670–700

The above table can be considered fairly accurate. However, as stated previously, large adults of the same length may weigh up to about 100 pounds less in southern waters than they do in colder waters two or three months later. Also, it is possible that fish of the same length caught the same day in the same waters may differ as much as 100 pounds. In other words, the angler should take into consideration whether the tuna is slim or fully developed.

As with the other species of finletfishes, bluefins travel in schools in which the individuals are of approximately the same size. The schools vary in number of fish—anywhere from about six to what appears to be more than a hundred. Bluefins spend much time near the surface, and in calm days their sickle-shaped second dorsal fins are a stirring sight as they cut through the water—I have never seen a tuna cruising along with its first dorsal extended (marlin often do). However, when chasing bait or when hooked, the dorsal may be up. When attacking bait they often jump clear of the surface and fall back explosively. They may cavort all over top water when pursuing smaller fish but seldom show above the surface when hooked. Their first run is an exhibition of power; then they go deep.

Tuna prey mostly on schooling fishes such as herring, menhaden, and sardines but will, of course, take any small fish available in their vicinity. They will also take squid and shrimp, and one is known to have gulped an 8-pound dogfish!

The behavior of migrating bluefins in the south is quite different from that of feeding tuna in northern waters. I was fortunate to observe the giant bluefins in both areas during one summer. My first sight of the southern, fast-swimming, tightly schooled, wolf-like packs was during a fish-collecting expedition off Walker Cay in the Bahamas. It was a hot, calm day in June, and under the scorching sun the water appeared as smooth as deep blue glass. We were trolling for marlin when suddenly, about a half mile to starboard, there appeared the tell-tale sign of feeding fish—wheeling and dipping sea birds. Before the baits were aboard we were headed at full speed toward the spot. In a few minutes we could see the water boiling white below the birds—giant tuna were attacking a school of small fish; the waters were churned to a froth by the big torpedo-like bodies as they jumped and dove among the bait fish. Occasionally half a dozen tuna were in the air simultaneously. The captain gunned the engines and put us ahead of the school while the mate heaved our baited hooks over the side. But we had misjudged the great speed of migrating tuna, whose feeding activity seemed to slow them only momentarily. Suddenly, before we realized it, we were directly in their path and the entire assemblage swept toward us like a huge thrashing wave. Both baits were taken, and almost immediately, both lines were cut by tuna bodies. We found ourselves in the middle of a churning deluge of fish, water, and birds. Giant tuna jumped around us. Birds were fighting and screaming. Aboard, excitement beyond description. The action was almost nightmarish—an experience of a lifetime.

As the action subsided we settled down; the mate rigged up another bait as I prepared again for battle. The captain maneuvered the boat so as to place us in position on the edge of the school. "There they are!" The mullet bait was tossed and it seemed hardly to touch the water ——wham! A tuna hit it with the force of a truck. I saw a big, blue back in a swirl of white water. I couldn't resist setting the hook three or four times with all the strength in me. Before we could do anything about it, the fish dove back into the school, and the line was again cut immediately by a fin or tail of another tuna. Mr. Sanford, with whom I was fishing, had the same experience on the next fish, and again I had another with the same result. Before the school disappeared I connected with a bruiser we managed to steer away from the school. He was on for about 15 minutes and then I could feel him going down, down. There was plenty of room for him to go, for close to the edge of Walker Cay, which is situated on the northern end of the Grand Bahama Bank, the depth of water runs from 110 to 175 fathoms. The waters were calm again as I anticipated a long tug of war with the big bluefin I had hooked. Then out of nowhere appeared a sinister-looking dorsal fin and a wobbly tail slowly propelling the water—a huge shark glided towards us. Probably attracted by our idling engine he swam up close and directly astern. The shark seemed to take interest in the light colored 39-thread line and proceeded to swim around it. His circles became smaller; he went deeper and deeper as he slowly disappeared from view. Then, zing! Like a violin string snapping, my taut line went limp. It must have been the sandpaper-like skin of the shark, for the end of the line I retrieved was frayed. Incidentally, while it is difficult to resist striking hard on a tuna, it is the consensus of opinion among big game anglers to let the tuna hook itself; the theory is that the tuna's immediate reaction will not be as great and the initial run will be somewhat diminished in violence.

The tuna fishing at Soldiers Rip, ten miles south of Wedgeport, Nova Scotia, is entirely different from pursuing bluefins off Walker Cay. The weather is usually cold, often damp and foggy. The Rip is a tidal stream with a six-knot current, about a mile wide, near Bald Tusket Island (*see* p. 107). This underwater canyon is 17 fathoms deep and harbors enormous schools of herring and mackerel—that is why the bluefins are there. No longer are the tuna in closely knit packs in swift migration; they are more or less dispersed and seeking their food somewhat individually. The usual angling procedure is to attract the tuna by chumming—that is, to form a slick by throwing pieces and whole herring over the side in hopes that a bluefin will follow the chum to the boat and the baited hook. Bamboo outriggers, one on each side of the stern, hold the lines, which are baited with herring. The usual method at Wedgeport is to troll one line with a single baited hook and the other with a rig consisting of five to eight herring tied by their noses to the wire leader with the last one containing the hook. This type of rig, which seems to be used only in Nova Scotia, is trolled on the surface about 50 or 60 feet astern. The dancing teaser-baits may be advantageous in attracting fish, but often a tuna will slam into the middle of the line of herring and escape the hook.

Sometimes two sets of teaser baits are used. Lou Mowbray, a member of the British team during the International Tuna Cup Match, had an unusual experience at the Rip when a tuna stole nearly all the baits by taking the lead herring in first one set and then the other—back and forth—and escaped the hook. To say there was excitement aboard Lou's boat would be putting it mildly! Another method popular in Nova Scotia is to keep chumming with herring until a bluefin is sighted taking the chum (the tuna will often come close to the boat), then the mate, standing on the stern, tosses a herring with a hook through its back with the hope that the tuna will take it.

In the Atlantic, sport fishing for tuna began off Liverpool, Nova Scotia, about 1871 when a schoolmaster named Thomas Patillo set out to kill a "horse mackerel." He describes his first experience in the book *Moose-Hunting, Salmon Fishing, etc.* "Prompted by the desire for a little excitement, a friend and I decided to attempt the capture of one. As we knew the gear required must be first-class, we procured two of what in fishing parlance are called 18^{ths} hemp cod-lines, each 32 fathoms long. Then we had a hook made for each out of steel three-eighths thick, 8 inches long, with a 3-inch shank, and long heavy beard.

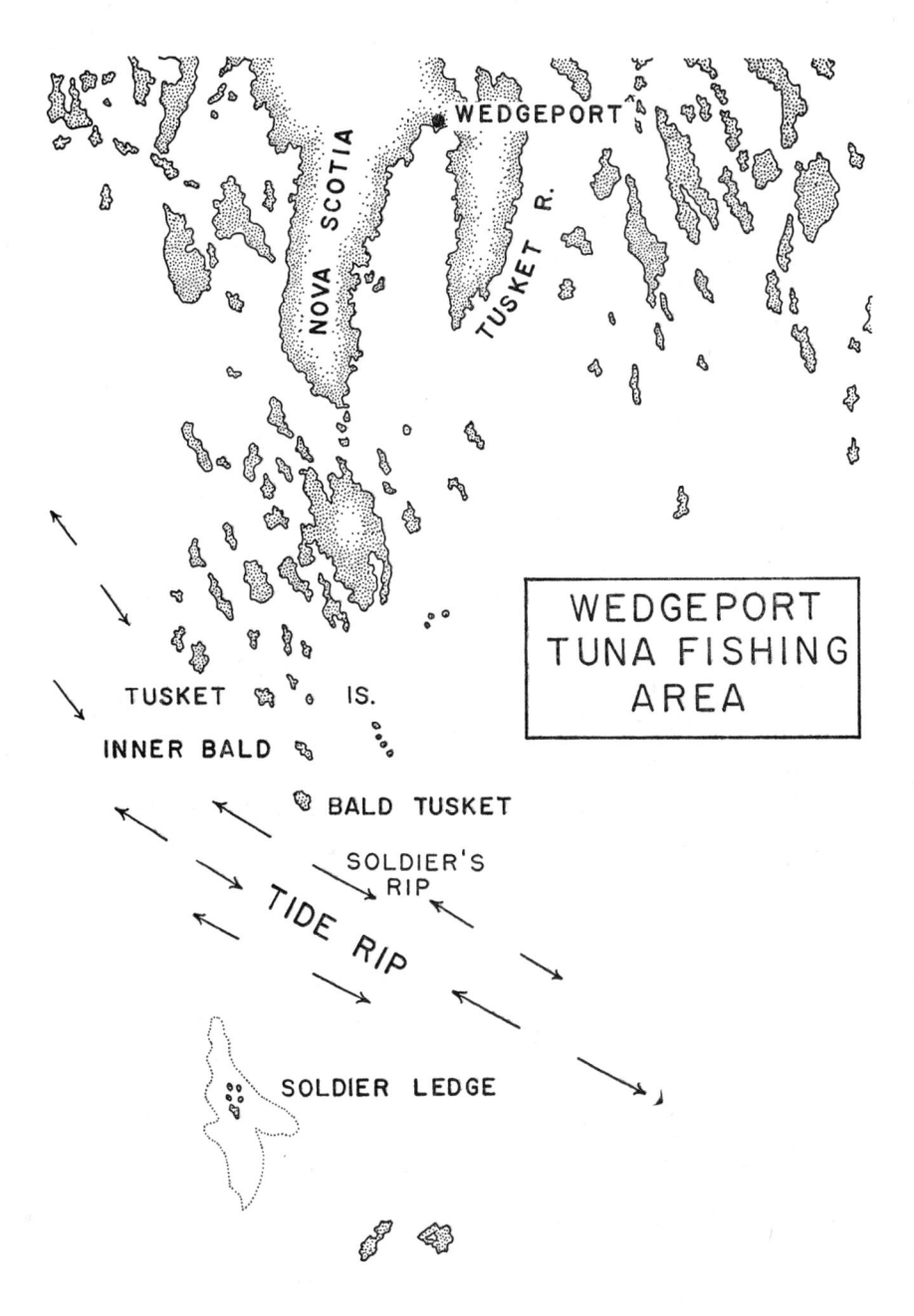

Tunas

WEDGEPORT TUNA FISHING AREA

With our lines attached to swivel-reels to run them on and off, we felt we were equipped for the expected spree, so, having secured a stiff medium low boat, we proceeded one morning quite early to the netting-ground. There we found the nets well fished, and knew by that our game would be on hand."

Tom Patillo and his friend then experienced one of the most exciting captures of a bluefin. The first fish they hooked headed directly into the commercial herring nets with a catastrophic result, "the boats came together with a heavy crash, filling the other's and washing a lot of their herrings overboard." After much verbal abuse, by "swearing" from the netters, and the loss of most of his tackle, "our freed albacore paraded himself all over the harbour, jumping dozens of times, with the line still attached to him, all through that day." Patillo courageously tried again. The second attempt also was a barrel of excitement. After several near-collisions with the herring boats, Patillo triumphed, "What a beauty! Ten feet long, weighing 600 pounds. We soon had a rope through his gills, and towed him to the shore in through the boats. The men and boys came to see him after their nets were picked, and helped us haul him up on the beach, and finished by giving three cheers, which made us feel like heroes."

Next in line for Nova Scotia tuna honors was Commander J. K. L. Ross, who, in the summer of 1908, hooked and lost 22 bluefins. He returned the next year and lost 19 more but landed the 20th which weighed 680 pounds. The longest time for fighting a tuna was recorded in 1934, when six anglers took turns with the rod and line which held a 782 pound foul-hooked bluefin. The battle continued for 62 hours before the fish was subdued. Angling history was further recorded when Ross's son-in-law, Commander Duncan Hodgson, a Canadian naval officer from Montreal, captured the world's record fish of 977 pounds on September 4, 1950.

The present-day interest in Nova Scotia's tuna fishing is attributed to Michael Lerner who interested the local fishermen in converting their lobster boats into sports fishing craft. These boats are sturdy, with a broad beam, high bow, and a cockpit of low freeboard. About 40 feet long, they are roomy and are considered now to be one of the finest types of fishing craft. Michael Lerner and Kip Farrington spread word about the great fishing off Nova Scotia. Many well-known anglers arrived and caught fish. The fame of Wedgeport grew, and the development of sport fishing gave Nova Scotia an economic boost.

Recently the giant tuna have attracted collegiate interest to Nova Scotia. The Intercollegiate Game Fish Match and Seminar sponsored by Bingham Oceanographic Laboratory of Yale University was held at Wedgeport. Teams of boys representing colleges in the United States and Canada took part in the activities. During the evenings students attended lectures and discussions given by well-known big game anglers and fishery scientists.

Our first attempt at a friendly competition among colleges in a combined sporting-academic event was held in trepidation. We knew that the academic aspects of teaching students the life history of bluefins and the correct way to handle big game tackle would be a success, but we realized that the capture of a tuna was necessary to give the initial event the proper boost.

In the three days of collegiate fishing at Wedgeport many tuna were seen as they "boiled" here and there on the surface. Excitement ran high. First, one boat and then another would report tuna in their chum slick. All boats had fish take their baits momentarily—a procedure which is commonly referred to as a spit-out.

It was twenty minutes to four when Bob Crandall, a member of the seminar faculty, and I, in the judges' boat, were preparing the four o'clock closing gun when we saw about two hundred yards away, directly off our port bow, a huge boil as if a depth charge had gone off the stern of one of the contestant's boats. A tuna had struck! Immediately there was a frenzy of excitement as the lucky boat gunned its motors and peeled off and away from the rest of the boats. The throttle was wide open as it dashed after the speeding tuna with the "Novie" gracefully splitting the rough waters. The judges' boat followed cautiously, and ten minutes later Bob and I could see the white jacket of a member of the Yale team in the fighting chair. We spotted the field glasses on it and saw that the angler was Captain Al Wood-Prince. We nosed around at a safe distance and watched Al do a tremendous job of working that tuna. Bob and I shook hands—we were sure that one of our pupils had not slept through our lectures.

The rules required that all boats were to stop fishing and to leave the Rip at four o'clock—excepting, of course, any boat which had a "fish on." The judges' boat had to return to fire off the gun. It was with reluctance that we tore ourselves away from the scene of action—we had been praying that somebody, anybody, would land one of the giant tuna. Two hours and fourteen minutes of suspense later Al boated his tuna, which won the Hulman trophy for the Yale team. Our introduction of the Intercollegiate Game Fish Match and Seminar was a great success.

Australian Bluefin Tuna
(*Thunnus maccoyii*)

One of the most abundant game fish along the southern coast of Australia, this bluefin is considered par excellence a sporting and commercial fish. Authors persist in calling it the southern bluefin tuna, a name which may be confused with tuna of other regions. Australian bluefin tuna is more appropriate because this fish is principally an inhabitant of Australian waters, and the name is not confused with tuna of other southern regions.

The Australian bluefin ranges from approximately the latitude of Sydney south to Tasmania and west to Cape Leeuwin in western Australia. It is also present in New Zealand waters.

Externally the Australian bluefin resembles the bluefin of American waters, and until recently they were considered identical. H. C. Godsil and E. K. Homberg, working for the California Bureau of Marine Fisheries, obtained three specimens of Australian bluefin tuna, which averaged 75 pounds in weight, and compared them with bluefins found along the California coast. The purpose of their study was to determine the differ-

Tunas 111

ences between the specimens from opposite sides of the Pacific. Godsil and Homberg found that the Australian bluefin is distinct from the California bluefin. The differences are found in the internal anatomy and are too technical to enumerate here. However, the California scientists point out that the vent of the Australian bluefin is small, measuring about three millimeters in diameter, whereas the vent in the eastern Pacific bluefin is twice as large. It has 34–36 gill rakers, 8–9 dorsal finlets, 7–8 anal finlets. As far as identification for anglers is concerned we need not dwell further on the anatomical differences of the Pacific bluefins because the Australian form, so far as known, is confined to Australian waters, and there is no overlap in range between the two types.

It appears that the maximum size of the Australian bluefin, with a rod and reel record of 238 pounds, is much smaller than that of the Atlantic bluefin. However, Mr. T. C. Roughley of Australia states that many claims regarding large tuna have been made by commercial fishermen and sportsmen off the coast of New South Wales. While fishing for yellowtail kingfish (*Rigificola grandis*) during November they have hooked unusually big tuna many times, but because of inadequate tackle not one has been boated. The presence of fish in the giant tuna class in this area was further substantiated by an American tuna clipper fishing the waters 20 miles east of Jervis Bay during October. The clipper encountered a school of tuna of such size that teams of fishermen using three poles attached to one terminal hook could not land them.

A migration seems to take place from New South Wales, where the fish are abundant from September to November or December, southward along the east coast of Victoria, across Bass Strait to the coast of eastern and southern Tasmania, where the bluefins are found in abundance from December to March or April. In South Australia, where the bluefin is the only species of tuna recorded thus far, they are found in greatest numbers during summer and autumn. In this area, as in the waters off New South Wales, the fish are not large, varying in size groups from 6 to 35 pounds with only an occasional fish up to 80 pounds or better. As the season progresses the bluefins travel westward into the Great Australian Bight and are found in large numbers off the southern tip of Western Australia at Albany Harbor. They are taken during late summer and early autumn weighing from 100 to 300 pounds.

Sexually mature fish are found off the south coast of Western Australia; other than that little is known concerning the spawning habits of the Australian bluefin tuna. The smallest specimens taken weighed about 4 pounds, between one and two years old, but where they come from is not known.

Reports from Australian anglers and commercial fishermen indicate that this tuna takes a lure readily. Enormous quantities of tuna are taken—about 1,000 tons a season (spring and summer) off the far south coast of New South Wales.

Much remains to be learned concerning the Australian bluefin tuna. As with other big game fish, angling effort must be increased before maximum size of this tuna can be established. Also, from the literature it appears that the really big bluefins are always encountered by accident when the angler is employing inadequate tackle. The information concerning the big ones suggests an interesting, unexplored area in which to carry out a properly equipped fishing expedition.

Pacific Bigeye Tuna (3b)
(*Thunnus sibi*)

The second largest of all tuna (Atlantic bluefin is first), the Pacific bigeye inhabits the deep tropical waters of the Pacific Ocean. For many years this tuna was confused with the yellowfin tuna, but scientists now agree that they are separate species. The Atlantic and Pacific bigeye tuna have different scientific names, but they appear to be identical (*see* Atlantic Bigeye). I prefer to use the scientific name *Thunnus sibi* rather than *Parathunnus sibi*.* Although a fine game fish, the sporting

* As suggested by Donald P. de Sylva, who made a study of the osteology of six species of tuna, which included the Pacific bigeye, and found that the group was compact and closely related, therefore warranting the incorporation of *Parathunnus* with the genus *Thunnus*.

exploitation of this species could be much greater than it is at present.

The Japanese have undertaken much research and have contributed valuable data on the bigeye in the western Pacific. According to the Japanese fisheries worker, Hiroshi Nakamura, the Pacific bigeye is spread widely from 0° to 40° N. latitude. In the tropical Pacific the greatest commercial catches have been made north of latitude 5° N. The records of the operations of Japanese longline vessels indicate that the outstanding fishing grounds are in the low latitudes—the main current area of the North Equatorial Current and the Equatorial Counter Current. Also, this tuna is presumed to be broadly distributed in the southern hemisphere waters of the Pacific Ocean and the northeastern parts of the Indian Ocean. Other known bigeye locations are found in the Banda and Flores seas (Indonesia) and off the coast of northwestern South America. Commercial fisheries operations are generally limited to waters north of 20° S. latitude.

There seems to be general agreement among scientists and commercial fishermen that the up and down distribution of the bigeye goes to greater depths than most tuna. The longlines are fished at depths of 150 to 500 feet. In Hawaiian waters, where the bigeye occurs in greatest numbers from October to May, the longline or flagline fishermen set their lines deeper for this fish than they do for yellowfin tuna (the yellowfin is most abundant from May to September). The bigeye, unlike the yellowfin, is rarely taken by surface fishing methods. The bigeye taken off Hawaii is usually a large tuna with an average weight of 157 pounds; fish under 80 pounds are rare.

Like other tuna, it has a streamlined body with a dark blue dorsal surface typical of most pelagic fishes. When first taken out of the water the greatest part of the body is iridescent, shimmering silver. The finlets are not as bright yellow as those of the yellowfin tuna. The eye in comparison to the rest of the body is large. At Cabo Blanco, Peru, when Mrs. Maurice Meyer, Jr., caught a bigeye which weighed 288 pounds, I measured the socket of the eye of the fish. From top to bottom at its widest point it was 2⅜ inches. I compared this with a measurement I had taken of a tuna caught by Alfredo Behrens of Venezuela during the International Tuna Match in Wedgeport, Nova Scotia. This fish weighed 320 pounds and the eye socket measured exactly 2 inches. In other words, the tunas were approximately the same size, but the bigeye's eye was considerably larger.

Anglers may find it difficult to differentiate the bigeye from the yellowfin tuna and the bluefin tuna. Although the bigeye has a larger eye than the other two species it takes a trained person to recognize it. The yellowfin usually has elongated second dorsal and anal fins. The bluefin tuna has a short pectoral fin, which is about three fourths of the length of the head (from the top of the snout to the edge of the gill cover). These characteristics are enough for the angler to tell the species apart. However, if in doubt count the gill rakers: Pacific bigeye, 24–28; yellowfin, 26–32; Pacific bluefin, 32–39.

Hiroshi Nakamura, the Japanese ichthyologist, states that bigeye spawn over broad areas of the low latitude waters and over long periods of time. One of Nakamura's colleagues observed, in the area of 2° N. to 9° N. latitude, 161° E. to 174° E. longitude, large numbers of bigeye which contained completely ripe, transparent eggs. Evidently the fish were close to spawning. This locality, therefore, is assumed to be a spawning spot of the Pacific bigeye tuna. The Japanese workers postulate that the main spawning areas are in the North Equatorial Current and the waters immediately south of the current.

The bigeye inhabiting the sea areas of the North Pacific from September to April have been found to possess immature gonads. From this evidence it may be assumed that the bigeyes do not spawn in the northern waters, which indicates that a migration takes place. The Japanese further announce that the minimum size at maturity is about 100 cm. and that the age groups contributing to the spawning must be at least two years old.

J. E. King and I. I. Ikehara, U.S. Fish and Wildlife Service biologists, have made a study of the food of the bigeye in the central Pacific. They have arrived at the following: the food of the bigeye consisted of 62 per cent fish, 33 per cent squid, 3 per cent other mollusks, and 2 per cent crustaceans. Major food items were pomfret, *Collybus drachme,* snake mackerel, *Gempylus serpens,* and two types of squid. This should give the angler a good idea of the type of possible baits for the bigeye.

Sports fishing for the Pacific bigeye (and the Atlantic bigeye) is still in its infancy. This tuna swims in the deep layers of water, and comparatively few are taken because most big game anglers prefer to fish the surface for billfishes. When there is no sign of marlin, the angler may give a try for tuna. It is much more enjoyable to cruise around trolling a bait or looking for marlin tails than drifting and rolling with the swells; for you must go deep for the bigeye, even deeper than for other species of tuna. It is rarely taken by surface fishing techniques such as trolling or live-bait fishing. At Cabo Blanco, Peru, where the bigeye world records come from, the baits are drifted at about 40 fathoms. Usually the boat's engine is kept running because of the strong current. Occasionally, sharks take the bait, and often, especially when drifting closer to shore, giant squid will ruin the bait. (Incidentally, I have caught giant squid with rod and line off the coast of Chile which were five and six feet in length!)

Well-known anglers, such as John Olin, who have taken many bluefins and bigeyes, claim that the bigeye is a better fighter. However, I was aboard when John worked on a bigeye off Cabo Blanco, and it appeared to me that a bluefin of the same size would certainly put up just as good a scrap.

Other outstanding "hot spots" for bigeye tuna may be discovered, but now the best area is about nine miles off Cabo Blanco, Peru. Sportsmen have named this spot Tuna Terrace. I noticed the great potential of this area during my first visit to Cabo Blanco with the Yale Expedition in 1953. At this time the angling effort for bigeye tuna was small (one or two boats for a few hours), and yet record fish were common. Mrs. Maurice Meyer, Jr. caught a 288-pound bigeye. A short time later that same day Mrs. Wendell Anderson, Jr. snared the record away from Mrs. Meyer with a bigeye of 335 pounds. The next day Mr. H. L. Woodward boated a beauty of 368 pounds, which was the largest ever taken on rod and reel at that time. In this productive area bigeye tuna in the 300-pound class are common. The world's record fish of 435 pounds was caught here by Dr. Russel V. A. Lee in April, 1957. However, tuna weighing over 600 pounds have been taken by commercial fishermen, so more rod and reel records will undoubtedly be broken at Cabo Blanco.

Atlantic Bigeye Tuna (3b)
(*Thunnus obesus*)

For many years confusion has reigned concerning the presence of bigeye tuna in the Atlantic. Scientists at times have reported the occurrence of this tuna in this ocean but later have announced it as misidentification.

During a cruise of the U.S. Fish and Wildlife Service exploratory fishing vessel "Oregon" six species of tuna were caught on longlines in the northern Caribbean. Harvey Bullis and Frank Mather, scientists aboard the vessel, have identified two of the specimens taken as Atlantic bigeye tuna. Previously, there was no record of this tuna from west of the Azores. Bullis and Mather have given the following as characteristics of the bigeye, which distinguish it from the other species of tuna: gill raker count, lower limb—19; upper limb—8 to 9, for a total of 27 to 28; predominantly yellow finlets distinguish it from the blackfin tuna whose dorsal finlets are not yellow but usually dusky brown accompanied by a dusky steel anal fin. The posterior ventral margin of the liver is striated.

The yellowfin tuna is often confused with the bigeye, but when compared side by side, the two are readily distinguishable. The bigeye has shorter second dorsal and anal fins, a much wider and deeper body, and larger eyes (*see* note on eye measurements in section on Pacific Bigeye). Bullis and Mather state that the bigeye's second dorsal and anal show dull yellow in the distal portions only, and just a trace of yellow is present on the first dorsal and ventrals. Bigeye's finlets (dorsal 8 to 9, anal

Left: Swordfish taken off Iquique, Chile, by Alfred Glassell, Jr.
Right: Swordfish taken off Cabo Blanco, Peru, by Kip Farrington.

Right: Alain Wood-Prince, Yale Fishing Team Captain, with the fish that won the first annual Intercollegiate Game Fish Match and Seminar at Wedgeport, Nova Scotia. The event is sponsored by the Bingham Oceanographic Laboratory of Yale University. (Photo by Bob Brooks) *Below:* School tuna (bluefin) taken off Block Island. (Photo courtesy of Salt Water Sportsman)

7 to 9) have a heavy band of glossy black edging, centrally a dull yellow turning to a sienna brown proximally, and black along the base. The finlets of the yellowfin are uniformly bright lemon yellow, with thin black edging. The two bigeye tuna reported by Bullis and Mather, taken off the coast of Hispaniola, are the first positive record of the species in the western Atlantic. These specimens weighed "about 175 pounds each." The world's record rod and reel fish weighed 209 pounds, 6 ounces, but individuals weighing about 275 pounds have been reported.

Mixed schooling of species was indicated when three yellowfin and one bigeye were caught on adjacent hooks on one of the "Oregon's" longlines. The Atlantic bigeye, the yellowfin, and the albacore were encountered in sizes which may be fished efficiently by the longline method and utilized in canneries. A new tuna fishery has been started in Puerto Rico, and because three species are available, the chances of commercial success are good.

The Atlantic bigeye tuna, yellowfin, and albacore are known to be abundant in the eastern Atlantic as far west as the Azores. Bullis and Mather suggest that these fishes may be distributed all the way across the tropical and subtropical parts of that ocean. The possibility appears that an extensive tuna fishery can be developed in the tropical Atlantic.

The Atlantic bigeye, like other tuna, travels mostly at depths beneath the surface where trolling lures do not reach. Therefore, big game anglers have boated comparatively few of these fish. After many years the Atlantic bigeye has been added to the International Game Fish Association's list of world record game fishes. The present record fish was taken off Madeira (a Portuguese Island off the western coast of Morocco) by A. A. dos Santos Ribeiro. However, any angler who may wish to concentrate on catching the bigeye has an excellent chance of breaking not only the "all tackle" world's record but the other line test records as well, some of which appear as blanks on the I.G.F.A. chart.

Regarding the similarities of the Atlantic and Pacific bigeye tuna, Frank Mather, who has done much work with tuna, gives me the following information: "Comparing the measurements and counts of the two Atlantic bigeye tuna we caught with those published by Royce and others for Pacific bigeyes, I found no distinct differences in external characters. Several men familiar with the Pacific form looked at our photographs and could see no difference."

Yellowfin Tuna (3c)
(Atlantic—*Thunnus albacares*)
(Pacific—*Thunnus macropterus*)

One of the most beautiful of big-game fishes, the yellowfin in the Pacific is often seen in vast schools which cover acres of water. However, it is comparatively scarce in the Atlantic and remains a most controversial species with scientists and anglers. In contrast to some other tuna, it seems to prefer surface waters. It is a commercially important species, and although widely distributed in the deep seas, it is often taken quite close to land.

Over the years this tuna has been known by at least a dozen different scientific names. At present ichthyologists refer to the Atlantic yellowfin as *Thunnus albacares* or *Thunnus argentivitatus*. The Pacific form is named *Thunnus macropterus*. It appears that eventually the yellowfin will be known only by one of these names, for, as yet, it has not been decided whether or not the Atlantic and Pacific yellowfins are identical. Only an anatomical study of many specimens from both the Atlantic and Pacific oceans will tell the story. If I were to hazard a guess, considering available literature, I would say they are the same.

The Allison tuna, with a scientific name of *Neothunnus allisoni*, was accepted formerly as a well-known and distinct species. It was differentiated from the yellowfin only by its elongated second dorsal and anal fins, which sometimes reach as far back as the tail. The original Allison tuna, taken off the coast of Florida, was named by Louis Mowbray's father in 1920 for James A. Allison of Indianapolis, Indiana. The Allison tuna's elongated fins are now considered to be a characteristic of the larger and older yellowfin tunas; therefore, the Allison is no longer a valid species. In other words, as the yellowfin becomes older its second dorsal and anal fins grow longer.

The yellowfin is a fish of temperate seas, and in contrast to the bluefin tuna it is primarily a resident of warm waters with temperatures of about 60° to 80° F. Its Atlantic distribution along the southeast coast of North America is considered to be usually from about Maryland to Florida, Gulf of Mexico, the Caribbean, and down to the northeast coast of South America to Brazil. Two specimens were taken by trolling from the research vessel "Atlantis" (Woods Hole, Massachusetts). One was caught in waters about 100 miles southeast of New York. The other was taken about 183 miles south of Martha's Vineyard.

During an exploratory cruise in the western Atlantic the U.S. Fish and Wildlife Service vessel "Delaware" caught over one ton of yellowfin tuna 135 miles south of Nantucket. While fishing 85 miles east-southeast of Cape Hatteras a catch of over a ton of yellowfins was again made. The cruise took place during June and into the first week of July. Louis Mowbray, director of the Bermuda Aquarium, has been catching some big yellowfins while experimenting with longline fishing off Bermuda.

In the Pacific the yellowfin is found off the California coast from about Point Conception southward through the Gulf of California, along the Mexican coast to the Galapagos Islands, and southward to Chile. It is also present off Hawaii, Japan, the Philippines, and Australia. The Red Sea and Indian Ocean also claim it as a resident. From the early part of the year to summer seems to be the best season along the southeast coast of North America. Louis Mowbray has discovered that the yellowfins are present all year round off Bermuda, being particularly active in May and again in September and October. Off Brazil the yellowfins are scarce, but they have been caught from January to September; the best month seems to be January.

The California season is late summer and fall—August through October. For lower California and the Gulf the best catches are made June to August. In Mexican and Central American waters yellowfins are taken all year round—more or less—with

June, July, and August generally considered the poorer months. Off Peru the early part of the year is best, while Japan's season is in the summer.

Not much is known of the yellowfin in Australian waters, and information on seasons is not definite. Zane Grey reported yellowfin tuna "all over the ocean" in January, 1936. He caught the first yellowfin off the Australian coast; it was a fish weighing 91 pounds. Yellowfins have been reported off New South Wales in October. T. C. Roughley states: "During the summer of 1950–51, 2,783 pounds of yellowfin tuna were landed at Narooma and 326 pounds at Eden, on the far south coast of New South Wales. These fish were caught by trolling and were canned at the factory in Eden."

When first taken out of the water the yellowfin is a shimmering beauty, with its fins predominantly a brilliant cadmium yellow in contrast to its deep blue back, silvery sides, and belly. It also possesses a bright golden yellow band from the tip of its snout to the tail along the lateral surface which fades quickly. Irregular spotted white markings on the lower half of the body are also present in a live fish. The body is a typical tuna-like form but with unusually long second dorsal and anal fins. The pectoral fin is longer, in comparison with its body, than the pectoral fins of other tuna, with the exception of the albacore.

The yellowfin is known to reach a weight of 450 pounds in the Pacific. However, fish that weigh over 100 pounds are not common. The heaviest fish caught on rod and reel weighed 265 pounds, while the California market size runs about 15 to 20 pounds. The largest taken from Bermuda waters was 236 pounds. Harvey Moore of the U.S. Fish and Wildlife Service found that in Hawaiian waters the yellowfin is a fish of rapid growth, demonstrating, at least during part of its life, a growth of approximately 50 to 60 pounds in one calendar year.

The older yellowfins are identified without trouble because no other tuna possesses the unusually long second dorsal and anal fins. However, the younger specimens, which do not possess elongated fins, may be confused with other tuna. The following characteristics will identify the yellowfin: body, slender and completely scaled; fins have large yellow areas; finlets unusually bright cadmium yellow (lemon yellow) with dusky edging; pectoral fin as long or slightly longer than the head. For the angler, bright finlets separate the yellowfin from the blackfin, and the rather long pectoral distinguishes it from the bluefin whose pectoral is about three fourths of the head length. The yellowfin has a gill raker count of 26–32. It has 8 to 11 dorsal finlets and 8 to 10 anal finlets.

June and July seems to be the spawning period in Bermuda waters. Otherwise almost nothing is known concerning the migration or spawning activities of the yellowfin tuna in the Atlantic. However, because of the rapid expansion of tuna fisheries in the Pacific in recent years, attention has been focused on the various species of tuna, including the yellowfin, in that ocean. Studies have been made, and more are in process, by the Pacific Oceanic Fishery Investigations of the U.S. Fish and Wildlife Service. Fred June, a scientist working on one of the projects, has found that several developmental groups of ova are present in the ovaries of individual fish during the breeding season. Based on diameter measurements of the most mature ova present, June suggests 11 arbitrary stages of maturity, which trace the maturation of the ova from the immature stage through the spawning stage. This evidence suggests that individual yellowfins mature more than one group of ova and have several spawnings during the same season in Hawaiian waters. The number of ova produced by a 100-pound fish ranges from about 2,000,000 in small females to about 8,000,000 in large females. The spawning period in Hawaiian waters during 1950, when the study took place, extended from about the middle of May to the end of October. It is interesting to note that the best catches of yellowfin tuna taken by the longline fishery were made during this period. Spawning also takes place off Central America, at least during late winter and spring.

In a more recent investigation Mr. Heeny S. H. Yuen and Mr. June found that the spawning area of yellowfin seemed to include the entire equatorial Pacific. The season extends throughout most of the year, with November, December, and

January the months of lowest spawning intensity. The size of the yellowfins at sexual maturity may be as small as approximately 2 feet but is usually greater than about 4 feet. From the age and growth rate data it may be logical to suggest that the Pacific yellowfin does not take part in extensive migrations. In general, short-lived, fast-growing fish travel shorter distances than fish that are long lived and slow growing. A yellowfin of 50 pounds has lived about 2½ years; a 100 pound fish is approximately 3½ years of age; 5 years for about 150 pounds; and in 6 years the tuna reaches approximately 200 pounds. Commercial catches in the Pacific range in size from 6 to 200 pounds; most of the fish are under 40 pounds.

The food of the yellowfin is similar to that of other tuna; it contains a diverse diet of many types of fish, squid, octopods, and crustaceans. Japanese scientists were the first to make observations on the diet of fishes in the Pacific about 1915; they found that the different species of tuna swam at certain depths and preferred certain types of food. The yellowfin also has a reputation for gluttony; often it is taken on hook and line with a stomach bulging with food.

Among anglers the yellowfin is considered a prime game fish; some prefer it over any other species of fish in the Pacific. It takes trolled surface lures readily and will hit just about anything when feeding. Off California the majority of anglers seldom boat one over 50 pounds because the fish are usually hooked with a live bait outfit which lacks the necessary line capacity to handle the fish. This tuna prefers a fast moving lure —speeds up to 9 miles an hour.

When I accompanied Louis Mowbray on one of his longline expeditions for yellowfins off Bermuda, he informed me that this fish has great potential as a sport fish in Bermuda waters. Besides being captured by the longline, the yellowfin can be lured close to the boat by chumming. Also, they can be taken by deep trolling and drift fishing. Lou states that the fish come up on the shelf, but they are much more prevalent around the off-lying banks and in really deep water.

The world's record rod and reel fish of 265 pounds was taken by J. W. Harvey off Makua, Hawaii.

Last but not least, this marvelous fish is not only beautiful in the water; it looks great on the dinner table. Its meat is white when cooked and thoroughly delicious.

Albacore (4c)
(*Thunnus alalunga*)

The albacore, an oceanic tuna responsible for a greatly fluctuating fishery, roams over vast distances. It occurs in great abundance in the Pacific but is less known in the Atlantic. For many years (from about 1870) albacore were considered an inferior fish and when caught were hit on the head and thrown back. The Japanese are credited with drawing attention to the albacore as a fine table fish, and now it rates commercially as one of the most valued of all the tunas. This "white meat tuna" or "chicken of the sea" is also a fine game fish and supports a great sport fishery in waters off California. The world record fish of 69 pounds was taken off St. Helena on April 7, 1956, by P. Allen.

If the name albacore were not so well established, I would call this fish the longfin tuna—because it possesses an unusually long pectoral fin. It has been known by several scientific names, but now *Thunnus alalunga* is accepted by up-to-date fishery scientists.

The distribution of the albacore in the Atlantic was previously considered to be confined to warm waters, rarely north of Florida and Bermuda. Scientists believed that this species might stray as far north as Massachusetts, but no positive record was known. However, a report from a cruise in the northwestern Atlantic by the U.S. Fish and Wildlife Service's research vessel "Delaware" stated, "the general distribution of tunas in the offshore area during June was found to consist primarily of small bluefin and scattered albacore *Thunnus alalunga* at the more northern stations." One albacore of 25 pounds was taken at the vessel's most northern station—about 140 miles south of Georges Bank along the 1,000-fathom line. The most southern record of albacore taken was two fish caught at a station approximately 38° N. latitude and almost directly in line south of Block Island. The albacore is found in Bahamian waters, and off Bermuda it is not uncommon. This valuable species appears to be fairly abundant and widely distributed in the northern Caribbean from midwinter through April. It also roams the eastern Atlantic and the Mediterranean.

In the eastern Pacific the albacore ranges from Alaska all the way down to Chile. It is common around the Hawaiian Islands and is distributed in the northwest Pacific over broad areas from the equator to the polar front. In Japan, during recent years, there has been a gradual increase in the landings of albacore from the southern hemisphere; however most of the albacore still come from the northern areas. Australia and New Zealand also list it as an inhabitant of their waters. Along the California coast the principal albacore fishing ports are San Diego, Oceanside, San Clemente, Newport-Balboa, Long Beach, San Pedro, and Malibu.

The albacore has a deep and wide body, large eyes, and interesting long pectoral fins, which extend past the origin of the anal fin. Freshly caught specimens, which I have seen taken off Bermuda, impressed me because the coloration differed from the typical bright silvery appearance of other tuna. Nearly the entire body of the Bermuda specimens had a dark bronze metallic tint, which appeared almost brownish.

Although albacore have been known to reach about 80 pounds in the Pacific, the rod and line record is 69 pounds, and generally the fish run from 8 to 30 pounds, with an average of about 14 pounds. In the Atlantic the largest taken off Bermuda was 62 pounds; here the probable maximum is in the vicinity of 70 pounds. Fish taken in the northwest Atlantic by the U.S. Fish and Wildlife Service's research crew ran from 25 to 48 pounds.

Identification of the species is a simple matter. Anglers know without question that they have an albacore when they spot the unusually long pectoral fins. Those who may like to know the

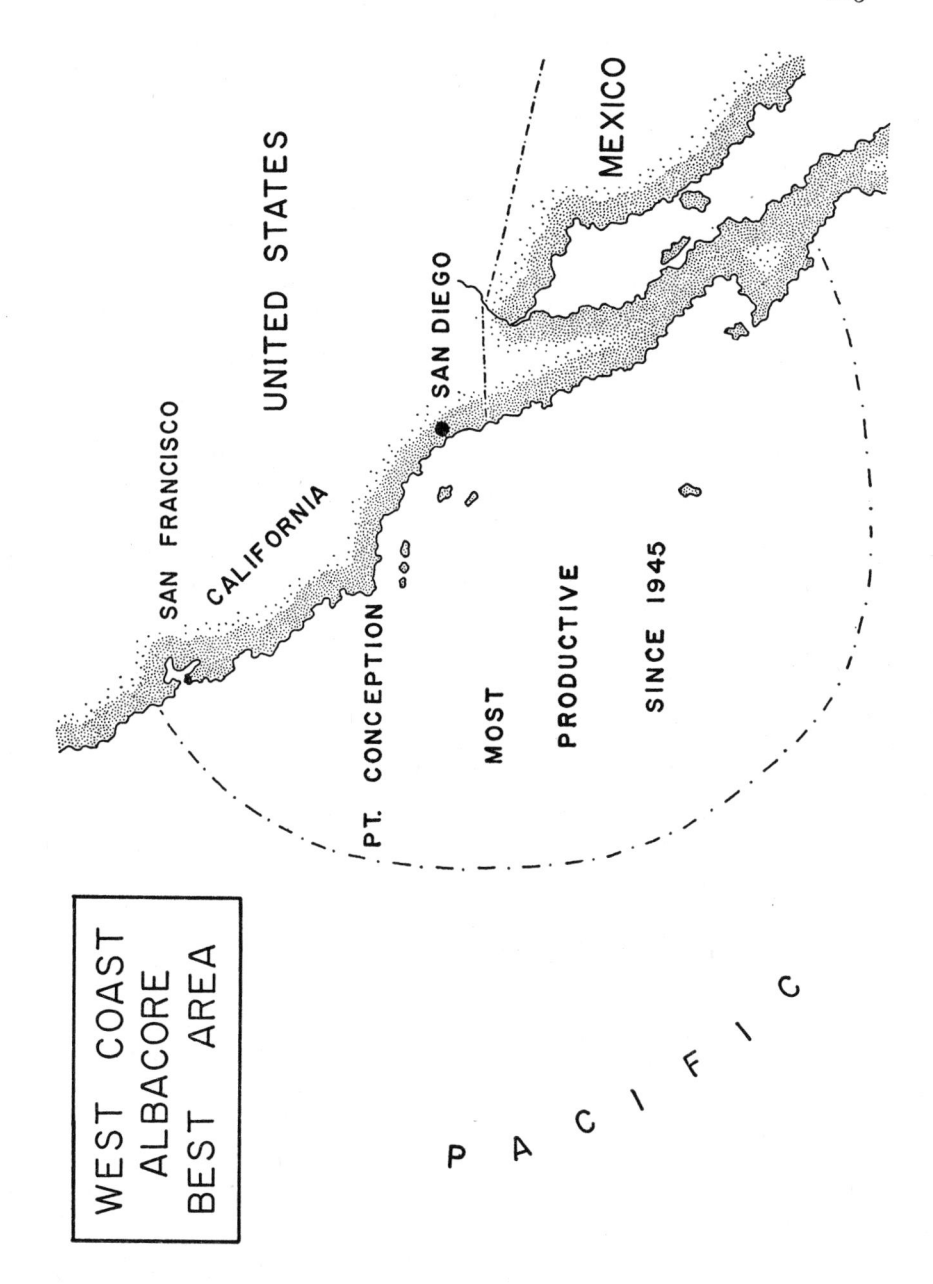

Tunas

more technical characters of identification may note the following: gill rakers, 27–31; dorsal finlets, 7 or 8; anal finlets, 7 or 8; entire ventral surface of liver striated with blood vessels; round vent (yellowfin has an oval vent); body completely scaled; air bladder present; flesh white.

Albacore make extensive migrations. Great schools travel northward along the Pacific coast of North America during late spring and summer. They first appear off the lower California coast, generally in the vicinity of Guadalupe Island. In Japanese waters two fishing seasons of different types have been developed according to the migration of the albacore: one is the pole-and-line fishing season for fish moving north from April to July; the other is the longline season from November to April for the schools moving south. These methods indicate that during the north to south migration the albacore swim deeper.

The following tag recoveries are excellent examples of the vast distances covered by migrating albacore. The first authentic record of trans-Pacific migration by this species was obtained from Japan by the California Fish and Game Department. The fish was taken on hook and line 550 miles southeast of Tokyo on June 23, 1953. This fish was one of 215 albacore tagged by the California Department of Fish and Game on August 4, 1952, 18 miles south of Los Angeles Harbor. Since the date of tagging the fish had been out 324 days and had traveled 4,900 miles west! There were two earlier recoveries, both off Morro Bay, California, from the same group of 215 tagged. Both fish had traveled about 200 miles northwest from the same point of release. One was out 30 days and the other 43 days.

The U.S. Fish and Wildlife Service reported a recapture of another tagged albacore in the Pacific. This fish was tagged on October 5, 1954, about 1,300 miles south of Hawaii and was caught 471 days later 2,370 miles away, near Japan. When tagged it weighed 15 pounds, and when again taken, it was 40 pounds. These examples not only depict the extensive migrations of the albacore but they also suggest a single population which may be migrating between America and Japan.

Albacore do not spawn along the Pacific coast of North America. Vernon Brock, who worked with albacore off Oregon, states that milt from the more mature testes of the males could be squeezed out, but no females with eggs that could be seen with the naked eye have ever been found in that area. Fish from Hawaii, taken in July, have been found to contain ripe ovaries. Albacore with mature ova have been reported also from the Mediterranean.

Anchovies, pilchards, herring, small mackerel, and other small schooling fishes are food for the albacore. Small rockfish are an important part of the diet of albacore in the eastern north Pacific; saury and squid also rate highly. As with other tuna, albacore will take all types of food, such as black cod, red feed (small shrimp-like euphausids), flatfish, jellyfish, and others, depending on what is available.

The sporting qualities of the albacore are well known; it rates high in general popularity with southern California's salt water sportsmen. When the run is on, it is difficult to reserve space on a fishing craft. This longfin tuna will take a lure trolled up to about 8 or 10 miles an hour. It is a wary fish and will often make a close pass at a lure and then turn aside. Anglers refer to this performance as "coldfish." On the other hand a "hot" school will hit practically any lure thrown at them. Sometimes, even though seen clearly under the boat, they cannot be coaxed up with chum or live bait. In such instances live bait hooked through the back and lowered to deep water will often be successful. The Japanese fishermen, when confronted with a cold school, will sometimes entice the fish to strike by using a flicker made of feathers. It is tied to a bamboo pole and skittered along the surface to simulate a surfacing school of anchovies or sardines. During this maneuver the fishermen continue to heave over live bait. A school of albacore can be excited into striking the baited hooks. Anchovies are the favorite bait because they are hardy and survive well in the holding tanks. Pilchards are also good but second to the anchovies. Herring are more difficult to keep alive and therefore not as desirable as the others. If obtainable, young rockfish would make excellent bait because they are found in good numbers in the stomachs of albacore in the northern Pacific.

Water color and temperature are definitely correlated with the presence of albacore. Most fish are encountered in Pacific blue currents with temperatures between 58° and 61° F. On occasion, they may be found in blue-green water with temperatures from about 56° to 58° F., but it seems they are never taken in green water.

Canning of albacore started in 1906 with two plants operating, one in San Diego and the other in San Pedro. From 1900 through 1935 trolling for albacore on a commercial scale was operated only in southern California, although occasionally a few fish were reported taken off southern Alaska. Off the coast of Oregon commercial trolling began in 1936 and then spread to Washington, British Columbia, and Alaska. Good numbers of fish are still taken in northern waters, but the majority of fish are caught between lower California and San Francisco within 400 miles of the coast. The fishing usually starts in June, grows in July, and is at its peak in August and September. Then it tapers off during October and November. In good years the fishing may start as early as January. When the salmon catch is slack, many of the boats from northern waters make the trip to San Diego or San Pedro. They work back north with the fish as the season advances to September, October, and November. These fishermen find it worth while to fish for the albacore; once considered a trash fish, it now brings fancy prices as one of our most highly prized fishes—sometimes over $400 per ton.

During our last visit to Bermuda, Lou Mowbray demonstrated his successful longline experiments with the albacore and introduced the sporting qualities of the fish to me. However, his wife, Nellie, has made an even more valuable contribution to my appreciation of the albacore by introducing us (my wife and me) to the tasteful delights of fresh albacore on the table— as a main dish or as an hors d'ouevre with onions and celery chopped fine, curry, fresh pepper, and mayonnaise. To all anglers who are fortunate enough to take one of these longfin tuna, I recommend without reservation fresh albacore as an unsurpassed delicacy.

Blackfin Tuna (3d)
(*Thunnus atlanticus*)

The Atlantic blackfin tuna is a small but sporting fish which has long been neglected by fishery workers. Both scientists and anglers have confused it with the albacore. It is well known to commercial fishermen and sportsmen in south Florida, Bermuda, and the Bahamas. In the West Indies it is a rather common tuna found with schools of oceanic bonito and spotted bonito. The scientific name of this tuna has been changed at least six times, but now it is accepted as *Thunnus atlanticus.*

The range of the blackfin appears to be limited to the western Atlantic. The northern limit of its usual distribution along the coast of the United States is about Cape Hatteras, where Frank Mather reported 16 specimens in October, 1952. However, the northernmost record is from off Martha's Vineyard, Massachusetts. One was taken by the "Atlantis" (research vessel, Woods Hole, Massachusetts) about 300 miles east of Cape Hatteras, but the blackfin does not appear to range very far outside the 100-fathom curve. It has been reported throughout the West Indies, Gulf of Mexico, western Caribbean (northwest corner abundant in January and February), off the north coast of Venezuela, and as far south as Rio de Janeiro, Brazil. This tuna invades Bahamian waters in great schools from May to September and is also plentiful off Bermuda, where it is an all-year-round fish. Louis Mowbray tells me that they appear in small and large groups. Sometimes the schools extend for a mile or more in length and breadth. The best months are April, May, June, August, and September.

Unlike most of the other tuna, the blackfin's finlets, which number 7 to 9 on the dorsal surface and 7 to 8 on the ventral surface, are not yellow. The dorsal ones are usually dusky brown in coloration and the anal ones are the color of dark steel. Individuals of over 25 pounds are rare. The Bermuda average is 12–16 pounds; Lou Mowbray believes the maximum weight here to be around 35 pounds. The world's record rod and reel fish of 44 pounds 8 ounces was taken by G. B. Mercorio off Capetown, South Africa, January 27, 1957.

Anglers may identify a blackfin by its dusky colored finlets or its pectoral fin, which is 0.8 to 1.2 times head length; but it may intergrade with the albacore in this respect. For a decisive characteristic in separating the blackfin from the albacore and other tuna, a gill raker count should be made. Total number on the first limb is 20–24; Atlantic bigeye has 27–28; and the albacore, 27–31. The air bladder, which in the blackfin is not divided and is wider than long, is also an aid to identification.

Not much is known concerning blackfin migrations, but their appearance and numbers fluctuate and large schools move fast. In the month of June, off Bermuda, Lou Mowbray observed a vast school of blackfin feeding on small fry and plankton—as far as the eye could see! Fish from this school contained roe about half developed. July is the poorest month for blackfins off Bermuda; it appears that they may spawn at this time. Incidentally, it wasn't until November, 1934, that blackfin tuna were known to inhabit Bermuda waters. At that time Louis Mowbray caught two specimens weighing 25 and 20 pounds.

In their food habits they are similar to other tuna, feeding on plankton, crustaceans, squid, anchovies, and other small herring-like fishes. They rush into tightly packed masses of baitfish and snap them up by the dozens, leaving bits and pieces of their victims for the birds to fight over. Anglers love the blackfin for its gamy fight on light tackle. Surface trolling seems to be the most effective method of taking this tuna. Although the meat is grayish in color, it is a fine food fish.

Tonggol Tuna (4b)
(*Kishinoella tonggol*)

The tonggol tuna is found in the western Pacific from Japan south to Australia. Superficially it resembles the Australian bluefin, but it is a much smaller fish. Beyond the Pacific it is reported from the Gulf of Aden, Kenya, Tanganyika, Ceylon, and the East Indies. In Australia it is probably the most important species of tuna around the northern half of Australia and seems to take over northward where the Australian bluefin stops.

The Australians have no problem concerning the common name of this species. They call *Kishinoella tonggol* northern bluefin, and *Thunnus maccoyii* southern bluefin simply because in Australia there is a northern and southern division in the range of the two species. This is fine for Australia, but the common name presents problems when used in other parts of the world. Because it is abundant in Japanese waters it is called Oriental bonito, which I believe is the least appropriate name used. It is also called Indian longtail tunny and long-tailed tunny, but it does not have a long tail; a portion of the body, that section between the second dorsal fin and tail, is rather slender—hence the erroneous name. Therefore, I suggest using the specific name and calling the fish tonggol tuna; it is pleasing and sounds oriental. It offers no conflict and should satisfy everyone.

Although the tonggol tuna has a more slender body, it can be easily mistaken for the Australian bluefin. They were considered identical until D. L. Serventy pointed out distinguishing characters in the tonggol tuna which separates it from any other form. It has no air bladder, and this is noteworthy for identification. The first dorsal fin usually consists of 13 spines. The gill raker count is 20–24. Dorsal finlets usually number 9; anal finlets are 8.

Fish weighing 60 pounds have been reported by fishermen. Specimens examined by Serventy weighed between 11 and 42 pounds. The average weight changes in different localities. For example, south of Sydney 20 to 25 pounds is common, while on the northern Australian coast the largest fish are about 12 pounds with the average about 5. I wonder whether there may be a correlation between size and migration.

The tonggol tuna, unlike other tuna, enters inlets freely and is taken easily with seines. Catches of up to 400 fish have been made in such a manner. Large numbers of fish have been reported at different seasons in Australia: Eden and Merimbula in February and March; Moreton Bay and Hervey Bay in late summer and throughout the winter; Shark Bay, end of June and middle of October. Little is known of its migrations or spawning activities. Tonggol is considered a good fish for canning, but Australian sportsmen claim it does not take a lure as readily as do other tuna.

Dogtooth Tuna (4a)
(*Gymnosarda nuda*)

For anglers this is a rare species, which is seldom taken on rod and reel. I list it here in order to round out the tuna group. The dogtooth tuna is also known as lizard-mouth because it possesses large teeth.

This tuna is found chiefly on the western side of the Pacific, Indian Ocean, and Red Sea. A patch of very small scales is present below the pectoral fin (this area is sometimes referred to as "pectoral corselet"). A few rows of scales are present on both sides of the lateral line. The dogtooth tuna is known to prefer coastal waters with rocky bottoms where it is a voracious feeder—mostly on smaller fish. It is a large tuna; a specimen of slightly over 151 pounds was taken off Tahiti. Mr. Trevor Beaumont had taken a 75-pound specimen on rod and reel in the Seychelles Islands area in the Indian Ocean.

BONITOS

Close cousins to the tunas, the bonitos are migratory, fast swimmers that travel in large schools in the open oceans. Like their larger relatives they possess strong, streamlined, bullet-shaped bodies which contain strength and endurance. To sportsmen this group is one of the most bewildering of all game fishes. Authors also differ on the common names for these members of the family SCOMBRIDAE. One example will suffice to illustrate this point. In the leading textbooks and handbooks on fishes a bonito known scientifically as *Katsuwonus pelamis* is given the following names (each name in a different publication): skipjack, oceanic bonito, arctic bonito, leaping bonito, striped bonito, and oceanic skipjack. The angler should not confuse a bonito with any species of tuna because tunas all have dark blue backs and silvery sides minus black spots, bars, lines, stripes, or any other conspicuous markings of this type.

Oceanic Bonito (5a)

(*Katsuwonus pelamis*)

The oceanic bonito is a tropical and subtropical fish found in the warmer parts of the oceans of the world. It is a fish of the high seas that leads a completely oceanic existence. Although considered a delicacy by the Japanese, it is not generally accepted as a food fish in the United States. Anglers rate it highly as a game fish because it demonstrates great fishing qualities when hooked.

This bonito is known by many common names; one of the most popular with guides and boatmen is skipjack because it appears to skip in and out of the water when huge schools voraciously feed on small fry. The name arctic bonito is used a great deal also, but it is a misnomer since the oceanic bonito dwells primarily in warm waters. The Australians call it striped tuna. The generic name (first part of the scientific name) has been changed several times.*

The oceanic bonito seems to be most common in the trade wind belts. In the Atlantic it has been recorded as far north as Cape Cod, Massachusetts. It is well known in the Caribbean area and in the eastern Atlantic off northwest Africa. On our Pacific Coast it is numerous south of San Diego, but it is also found north to Point Conception and the Channel Islands. Copiapo, Chile, seems to be its southern limit along the western coast of South America. Widely spread around the Hawaiian Islands and throughout the central Pacific, the oceanic bonito

* *Scomber, Thynnus, Gymnosarda, Euthynnus,* but now it is accepted as *Katsuwonus* by the majority of fishery scientists.

is also abundant off Japan, Australia, and New Zealand. It is also found in many areas of the Indian Ocean.

This member of the family SCOMBRIDAE has a typical tuna-like body tapering to a pointed nose and an extremely slender caudal peduncle. On each side of the peduncle a prominent keel is followed by a smaller one above and another below it. At a glance, the vivid black stripes, which run lengthwise along the lower half of the body, make this fish easy to identify. (The spotted bonito has stripes on the upper half.) It has a deeply concave contour of the first dorsal fin, which contains about 15 spines. The second dorsal is triangular with a concave rear edge, and the anal fin is about the same shape. Seven or 8 dorsal finlets are present, while the anal finlets may number from 6 to 8, but usually 7. There are no scales on the body except along the lateral line and in the region of the pectoral fin (corselet). The lateral line takes a sudden downward curve below the second dorsal fin (this is not so with the spotted bonito). The gill raker count is a high 51–65. The oceanic bonito has the typical basic coloration of the oceanic fishes, a dark blue back and silvery iridescent sides. Four to 6 flashy black stripes extend from the breast to the tail.

Although there is a Pacific record of a fish which weighed 43 pounds, the average is 3 to 6 pounds. The world's record rod and reel fish weighed 39 pounds, 15 ounces and was caught off Walker Cay, Bahamas, on January 21, 1952, by F. Drowley.

Because of its wide-ranging oceanic habits the life history study of the oceanic bonito is expensive and technically difficult. Until recent years very little was known concerning this fish. However, during the past decade fishery scientists of Japan, the United States, and other countries have begun extensive studies on the oceanic bonito (in association with others such as the yellowfin tuna).

Exploratory fishing conducted in the Pacific by the U.S. Fish and Wildlife Service has shown that the oceanic bonito (and the yellowfin tuna) occurs at various longitudes between the American mainland and the central Pacific. In the high seas off the shores of North and South America the oceanic bonito occurs in abundance from about latitude 32° north to 20° south. In the middle part of this range it is present at all times. However, at the northern and southern extremes of the range the fish appears only during the warmer months of the year.

Scientists who have been tagging oceanic bonitos recaptured some that showed a migration of 600 and 700 miles. These fish were at liberty for about a year. On the other hand, some fish tagged and at liberty for approximately the same length of time have shown rather short travels. The geographical distribution of oceanic bonito catches by clippers in 1953 (according to statistical areas of the Inter-American Tropical Tuna Commission) showed a concentration of oceanic bonito (and yellowfin tuna) off Lower California, in the vicinity of the Gulf of Tehuantepec (only during the early part of the year), off the coast of Central America, and in the vicinity of the Galapagos Islands. It is interesting to note that these areas correspond to regions which are known for their high production of food organisms—zooplankton and on up the food chain. The surface waters in these areas are enriched by nutrients brought up from deeper layers by upwelling.*

Although it appears in great numbers in the Pacific, often seen in vast schools for long distances, nowhere along the Atlantic Coast can it be said to be really abundant. Along the eastern coast of lower Florida this bonito makes its greatest appearance during spring and summer. In the Bahamas it is about in great schools from May to September. During the summer months anglers occasionally catch it in Long Island waters, and sometimes a stray is taken farther north.

Like other tropical scombrids the oceanic bonito spawns over a wide geographical range, and the season is quite long, with some spawning taking place throughout the year. Oceanic bonito, during their early years of life at least, combine with yellowfin tuna into mixed schools at the surface. This behavior is the basis of the successful commercial fishery in the Pacific. The occurrence of large combined schools of these fishes into

* Upwelling is treated in the section on black marlin off Cabo Blanco, Peru.

compact groups makes for their efficient capture. The two species may occur in the same area at the same time as mixed groups or in separate schools. San Diego and Los Angeles are the two leading ports for commercial activity. Investigators in the Pacific have found that the oceanic bonito feeds omnivorously on all forms of pelagic life—ranging from small crustaceans to fairly large fishes and squid.

Salt water anglers agree that the oceanic bonito is fun to catch and well worth pursuing. It will hit feather jigs trolled at a fairly good rate of speed—up to about 8 miles an hour, but live-bait fishing seems to take most fish. There is no question that the oceanic bonito, when taken on light tackle, will equal any fish of its size in fighting qualities, but my greatest thrill from these fishes comes in watching several hundred of them in a churning mass pile into a school of anchovies, sardines, or other small fishes. When feeding, the bonitos seem to go into a complete frenzy. Their usual method of attack is to surround a school of bait fishes, mass them together, and proceed to chop through them. It is an electrifying sight to see many bonitos in the air simultaneously as they dive and jump for their quarry. Many times I have been amazed to see an oceanic bonito hit a large bait, such as a big mullet, while we were trolling for giant tuna.

Atlantic Bonito (5c)
(*Sarda sarda*)

An inhabitant of the open seas, the Atlantic bonito, like the rest of its tribe, travels in schools. This "true bonito" is common along the Atlantic coast of the United States. A fine sport fish but poor on the table, it is seldom eaten because it is extremely oily. Unlike most of its cousins, the Atlantic bonito causes no confusion regarding either its scientific or common name.

This bonito ranges the open, warm parts of the Atlantic—north to Nova Scotia on the American coast and north to Scandinavia on the European coast, including the Mediterranean.

Frank Mather and Godfrey Day record one specimen taken off the northwest coast of Africa. Its southern distribution is not clear. Most textbooks state that the Atlantic bonito is found off Florida and the Gulf Coast throughout the year. Some authors list it as being present off Texas, Brazil, and the Cape of Good Hope; others believe that it is not known from the Gulf and Caribbean areas and southward.

The bonito has a dark blue back, silvery sides, and in general shape resembles the tunas, but it is not quite as heavy through the body (about one fourth as deep as it is long). Its body is completely scaled. The two dorsal fins are close together, appearing as practically confluent. Comparatively speaking, other Atlantic scombrids have a smaller mouth. The Atlantic bonito's mouth gapes back to the hind margin of the eye; its jaw teeth are large, with the 2 to 4 in the front of the lower jaw noticeably larger than the others. Its first dorsal fin has a nearly straight upper margin. It grows to approximately 3 feet and reaches a weight of 12 pounds, but the usual size is about 2 to 4 pounds.

Anglers should have no trouble identifying this fish. The large mouth distinguishes it from other species with which it may be confused. The uniform scaliness of its body and the upper sides barred with 7 to 20 narrow dark bluish bands which run obliquely downward and forward across the lateral line are also characteristics which can be used for identification. Young fish possess transversely barred dark bluish stripes, but these crossbars usually disappear before maturity. The Atlantic bonito has 20 to 22 dorsal spines, 12 to 14 gill rakers on the lower limb of the first arch, no teeth on the roof of the mouth, and no air bladder. The dorsal finlets number 7 to 8, and the anal finlets 6 to 7.

The lines of migration of this fish are not known, and it is assumed that it spawns in warm waters during the late spring and early summer. Young fish 5 to 6 inches long have been reported as common off Orient, New York, in September. As a predacious inhabitant of the open sea it feeds upon mackerel, alewives, menhaden, and other herring-like fishes, plus squid.

It swims deep in compact schools and comes to the surface only when feeding.

The Atlantic bonito is most often caught on trolled feather jigs while the angler is hoping for more desirable game. However, the bonito and its silvery skin is always welcome because it makes excellent strip bait. I have seen many species of game fish, ranging from small dolphin to 400-pound marlin, caught on strip bait cut from the sides of a bonito. When a whole bait and a strip bait are trolled a few feet apart, the strip bait will often be hit first. Great sport can be had when a school of bonito has been located, usually by trolling; the boat can then be stopped and light tackle and lures should be put into play. The most effective lures are the deep-running type. The bonito strikes savagely and puts up a great fuss when hooked.

Atlantic Spotted Bonito (5b)
(*Euthynnus alletteratus*)

Another member of the clan of finletfishes, the spotted bonito closely resembles the oceanic bonito. It is chiefly a warm-water oceanic fish widespread on the high seas. Although anglers agree that it is a first-class game fish, there is diverse opinion regarding its table qualities. Market fishermen trolling for them have been known to catch more than 5,000 pounds to a boat in a single day.

This is another bonito with a confusion of names—false albacore, little tuna, little tunny, and bonito being most permanent. "Little tuna" is not a satisfactory name since it implies that this fish is a small tuna, which it is not; the name originated from southern Europe where the fish is known as thunnine, which means little tuna. I suspect that in this area other species of bonitos are given this name also. Furthermore, anglers and boatmen rarely refer to this species as little tuna. The term "mackerel tuna" is applied by some authors because this fish possesses mackerel-like markings on its dorsal surface; since it is not a mackerel, I believe the name is a poor one. I have given the common name "spotted bonito" to this species because it will clear away the confusion. A conspicuous characteristic of this fish is the prominent spots below and posterior to the pectoral fin. No other bonito in the Atlantic possesses prominent dark spots below the midline. (The Pacific form resembles it closely.) It has been known by six or seven different scientific names, but *Euthynnus alletteratus* is now accepted by the majority of fishery technologists.

It ranges throughout the North Atlantic, along the Atlantic coast from Cape Cod Bay southward—the Gulf of Mexico, the Caribbean, down to Brazil. Also, it is abundant around Bermuda, the Bahamas, and eastern Atlantic near the Mediterranean.

In form it resembles other bonitos in having a tuna-like body and a deeply concave margin on the first dorsal fin. The spotted bonito possesses a gleaming silvery body and a dark blue dorsal surface, which has a conspicuous color pattern of wavy black markings from about the middle of the first dorsal fin to the tail. The several dark spots below the pectoral fin vary in number, size, shape, and intensity of color. The weight may be up to 10 pounds, but the average fish is about 3 pounds. Louis Mowbray of Bermuda states that this fish reaches a weight of at least 22 pounds.

An angler may easily identify this species by the dark spots below the pectoral fin, the deeply concave first dorsal fin, and the markings on the top posterior half of the body, but the more scientific minded may count the gill rakers, which are 25 to 29 on the lower limb of the first arch (the oceanic bonito has 36 to 40 on the lower limb). The spotted bonito has palatine teeth (roof of mouth); the oceanic bonito does not. The spotted has 8 to 9 dorsal finlets and 6 to 7 anal finlets.

The spotted bonito is found in large schools, often mixed with oceanic bonitos, and takes part in migrations, but as yet definite patterns of travel are not known. It is present sporadically in different areas along the Atlantic coast and may be present during the entire year. In the more northerly areas such as Massachusetts this scombrid may be in evidence as a stray from warmer waters during July and August. Off the New York,

New Jersey, and Maryland coasts great numbers are often seen during the summer. It is well known off both coasts of Florida, where it appears about April and remains for most of the summer. An idea of their numbers may be had from the reports of a certain Florida firm whose fishing operations are carried out during June, July, and August. This company states that at times two men trolling from a mackerel boat and using spoons and artificial squid as lures are able to catch from 1,000 to 5,000 pounds per day. Another example: speaking of exploratory trolling operations off the coasts of Florida and Georgia, C. B. Carlson of the U.S. Fish and Wildlife Service reported "areas from 2 to 5 miles wide and from 5 to 10 miles long, over depths of water from 10 to 14 fathoms to be literally alive with schools of little tuna (spotted bonito) varying in size from a few fish to extensive tonnage." In Bermuda waters this fish is found the year round, but it is most abundant from May to November.

From the various reports of the wide dispersion of this bonito at different times of the year, pinning down approximate migrational routes would be a difficult task. Fish taken from about October to February show small gonads. Many caught in July have freely running milt. I dissected several fish caught off Walker Cay in the Bahamas in the latter part of June, which contained ripening gonads. Indications are that this species may spawn over a wide area of warm waters during the latter part of the summer. Their stomachs contained small herring-like fishes—too far gone to be identified. Squid is known to be a favorite food.

Great sport could be had by light-tackle fishing for the spotted bonito. However, strange to say, many charter skippers purposely bypass schools of these fish because their "sports" cannot take their catch home, or because they do not know the proper method of preparing this fish (and other dark meat fish) for the table.

The next time you catch a bonito, try it this way. Remove the head and insides and then skin it. An easy method is to slit the skin along the midline of the back, around both sides of the dorsal fin to the tail and the same on the bottom side.

Loosen a bit of the skin around the head-end with a knife and simply pull the skin off; then fillet the fish. Place the meat in a bucket of brine (plenty of salt and water) and let it stay for an hour or two. This will remove the blood; drain the slabs of meat, sprinkle thoroughly with salt, and let stay over night. Broil the fish rather well, while basting with melted butter and lemon or hot bacon fat. You may prefer to place strips of bacon on top and to baste with butter. If done this way, I believe you will find the spotted bonito a delicious fish.

Peruvian Bonito
(*Sarda chiliensis*)

Oriental Bonito
(*Sarda orientalis*)

Mr. H. C. Godsil, of the California Fish and Game Department, who has investigated the Pacific bonitos, has produced some very interesting data, which will undoubtedly lead to a revision of these scombrids. It appears that three of the accepted kinds * will be eliminated as distinct species. Through exhaustive studies on the anatomy of bonitos (too technical to relate here) Godsil has concluded that the differences formerly accepted as criteria to separate the species are not valid. He has produced data which demonstrate that the California bonito and the Chilean bonito are the same fish with a priority on the scientific name of the latter, *Sarda chiliensis*, thereby eliminating *lineolata*. Since he refers to this fish as Peruvian bonito, I accept it as the common name. He states, "it is my measured opinion that such differences as exist between *Sarda lineolata* and *Sarda chiliensis* should be considered as varietal or population differences and that both varieties should be assigned to the same species." Without knowing the origin of a

* Over the years the Pacific bonitos have been known as the following: California bonito—*Sarda lineolata*, Chilean bonito—*Sarda chiliensis*, Mexican bonito —*Sarda velox*, Japanese bonito—*Sarda orientalis*, Australian bonito—*Sarda chiliensis australis*.

given specimen, one could not positively distinguish *lineolata* from *chiliensis*. Godsil further fully believes that *velox* and *orientalis* (Mexican and Japanese) will prove synonymous. He also states, "superficially it appears that *chiliensis* (Pacific) is nothing more than a geographic variation of *Sarda* (Atlantic)."

From Godsil's work it appears as a good possibility that the bonitos of the Atlantic and Pacific may be narrowed down eventually to three or perhaps two species. We can safely say at this time that there are two species of bonito in the Pacific, the Peruvian, *Sarda chiliensis* (formerly divided into Chilean and Californian) and the Oriental bonito, *Sarda orientalis* (formerly considered three different fishes—Japanese, Mexican, and Australian). Some scientists previously advocated identifying the species by the position of the dark bands on the fish's dorsal surface. However, it has been shown that the bands vary; therefore, I would advise any angler who is interested in knowing which bonito he has captured to count the gill rakers; if they number below 20 (11–14), it is *orientalis* or Oriental bonito; if the number is 20 or over (24–27), the species is *chiliensis* or Peruvian bonito.

The Pacific bonitos are found from British Columbia south to Peru and Chile, Hawaii, and Japan, down to Australia. They closely resemble the Atlantic form and have the first dorsal fin contiguous with the second. All possess the characteristic horizontal or oblique striping on the back, and the young have vague dark crossbars. As with the other scombrids, these fishes have a dark blue back and silvery sides. Seven to 9 finlets are present on the dorsal side, while the anal finlets are 6 to 7 in number. Supposedly, they run in weight up to 25 pounds.

For years there has been much confusion regarding these bonitos, and not much is known concerning their life histories. They are gluttonous predators and travel the open seas in huge schools in pursuit of small herring-like fishes such an anchovies, sardines, and smelt. Also, like the other scombrids, they love squids and crustaceans.

As in the Atlantic, these fishes make excellent strip bait (*see* Atlantic Bonito), and they also afford great sport to anglers working light tackle. They strike a lure or bait in full stride with such force that it surprises the angler. Often the bonitos will be attracted by a disturbance in the water. When a fish or two are hooked, you can bet that there is a school in the vicinity, and chumming in the area will usually provide more fish. Continuous chumming may hold the school for quite a while. Then the school may leave and flash back at varying intervals.

Black Skipjack
(*Euthynnus lineatus*)

The black skipjack of the Pacific is, practically speaking, almost identical with its close relative, the Atlantic spotted bonito (which see). There is no confusion of nomenclature with this species; neither the common nor the scientific name is disputed. It is known to roam along the coast of lower California, Gulf of California, and off the coasts of Mexico and Central America.

The general description of this fish is similar to that of the spotted bonito although more scales are present in the pectoral region (corselet). A weight of 4 to 5 pounds seems to be about average for this fish, and 10 to 12 pounds is about maximum. Dark spots below the pectoral fin, and a series of 3, 4, or 5 broad, continuous, irregular black stripes running horizontally on the back from the corselet to the tail make this fish easy to identify. The total gill raker count on the limb of the first arch is 32–41. No air bladder is present.

Not much is known concerning the life history of this species. Spawning probably takes place in late spring and early summer. Juveniles have been found off Central America by scientists Milner Schaefer and John Mahr. Like the other members of the family SCOMBRIDAE, the black skipjack is a voracious feeder; small herring-like fishes and squid are favorite food. This skipjack is a gamy fish and will produce excellent sport on light tackle, but sportsmen do not go out of their way to fish for it (*see* Atlantic Spotted Bonito).

Hawaiian Skipjack
(*Euthynnus yaito*)

As its name implies, this species is found principally in the waters around Hawaii. It closely resembles the spotted bonito of the Atlantic and the black skipjack of the eastern Pacific. Its mode of life and habits can be assumed to be more or less the same as those of its close relatives (*see* sections on Atlantic Spotted Bonito and Black Skipjack). This fish is abundant in the Philippines, where it is one of the chief commercial fishes. Most of the catch is packed in the tuna canneries. Anglers need not worry about mistaking this fish for other species of skipjack; thus far it has been found only in Hawaiian waters and in the western Pacific.

The Hawaiian skipjack, also called yaito tuna, is a small fish, usually 18 inches to 2 feet in length, which seldom weighs more than 8 to 10 pounds. It possesses the same streamlined body, dark blue dorsal surface, and silvery sides of the other bonitos and skipjacks. Black roundish spots are present below the pectoral fin. The pattern of dorsal marking is distinctive in the majority of specimens. The black bars are more oblique in the Hawaiian skipjack than they are in the other species. However, a specimen which is not marked typically would be difficult to distinguish from the other two species. The total gill raker count on the limb of the first arch is 29–34. It has no air bladder. There are other differences in the anatomy which separate this skipjack from the others, but they are too technical to enumerate here.

THE MACKERELS

Close relatives of the tunas and bonitos, the mackerel tribe is one of the most important and most popular groups of finletfishes plying the Atlantic and Pacific. Commercially, mackerel are valued for their table qualities, and sportsmen rate these fish highly for their fighting ability. They range the open sea

The Mackerels

and coastal waters in large, fast-swimming schools while searching for masses of bait fish to feed on. Their bodies are more slender than the other finletfishes.

Atlantic Mackerel (6a)
(*Scomber scombrus*)

One of the smallest of the finlet tribe, this is principally a cold-water fish. Although oily, it is delicious and is considered one of the most valuable fish of the New England coast. Anglers seek it avidly. This mackerel is often referred to as common mackerel because it is well known, but I prefer to retain the name Atlantic mackerel. No confusion exists regarding its scientific name.

A fish of northern waters, it is not known in the Gulf of Mexico or Caribbean areas but is present on both sides of the Atlantic—Norway to Spain off the European coast and from the northern side of the Gulf of St. Lawrence and Strait of Belle Isle to Cape Lookout, North Carolina, off the American coast.

The Atlantic mackerel is a fish of the open seas, but it often comes into coastal waters quite close to shore. The young will enter harbors and estuaries, but they have never been known to swim into brackish water. Although found far out on the outer portion of the continental shelf, they stay within the inner half during the fishing season. In contrast to their relatives the tunas and bonitos, they seem not to range beyond the upper part of the continental slope. The vertical range of this mackerel is down to about 100 fathoms at different times of the year. They are in the upper layers of water from spring through summer and into autumn—approximately 25 to 30 fathoms to shallower depths. At this time schools of all sizes frequently come to the surface. It seems highly probable that during warm months of the year the mackerel will be found at that level at which their food is most abundant. In commercial quantities they are never found in waters lower than 45° F.

The Atlantic mackerel is a rather handsome fish; it has a pointed nose and a body that tapers back to a very slim caudal peduncle. As with all of its tribe, the body is firm muscled, and its head is long with a large mouth. The jaws contain small, sharp teeth. The large eye has a so-called adipose eyelid, a transparent gelatinous mass in the form of two parts, a forward and a hinder, which cover the eye except for a perpendicular slit over the pupil. Five finlets are present between the second dorsal fin and tail, and 5 finlets between the anal fin and tail. This fish is silvery with its upper surface metallic greenish-blue in color. The head is usually much darker, a blue black. The dorsal surface is barred with 23–33 dark transverse bands that run down in a wavy irregular course nearly to the mid-level of the body. In fresh fish a narrow, dark streak runs from the pectoral fin to the tail.

Although the Atlantic mackerel reaches 22 inches in length, the majority of adult fish are between 14 and 18 inches long. A 14-inch fish will weigh about one pound in the spring and about one quarter of a pound more in the fall when fatter; an 18 incher will scale about 2 to 2½ pounds; and a 22-inch bruiser will push the scale hand up to about 4 pounds. One fish of 7½ pounds has been recorded.

Anglers should encounter no difficulties in identifying this fish. The Atlantic mackerel could be confused with the chub mackerel, but one distinguishing character, easily seen, separates the two—the Atlantic mackerel is silvery-sided below the midline whereas in the chub mackerel the lower part of the sides is mottled with dusky blotches. The chub has a larger eye. The Atlantic mackerel lacks a swim bladder, but the chub has a well-developed one. The Atlantic mackerel is a larger fish than the chub mackerel. The wide space between the first and second dorsal separates the Atlantic mackerel from the bonitos. Other distinguishing characteristics are 11 or 12 dorsal spines and about 30 gill rakers on the lower limb of the first arch.

The Atlantic mackerel is a migratory fish of the western North Atlantic and makes an appearance near the coast along its range in the spring. It usually shows at the surface. By the end of December the majority of mackerel have withdrawn from the coast along their entire range. It is not yet known definitely where the bulk of them go—a subject which has been widely discussed. The point of issue is whether the mackerel take part in north and south migrations in association with offshore and onshore journeys or whether they move directly into the nearest deep water and spend the winter there after they leave the coast in late autumn.

Mackerel have been found in the stomachs of cod and pollack taken in January, February, and early March in various areas in northern waters. However, winter records are considered as stray fish—not enough to suggest any great concentration of mackerel. These examples are considered freak occurrences because mackerel are never encountered in commercial quantities in temperatures lower than about 45° F. The winter grounds for cod and pollack usually are too cold, with temperatures of 35°–39° F. Also, in most years the inner part of the continental shelf as a whole—southward as far as northern Virginia—cools to 37°–40° F. at winter minimum. However, the bottom water at the outer edge of shelf is warmer than 44°–46° F. the year round—all the way to the central part of Georges Bank. Therefore, these temperatures suggest that the mackerel migration, which leaves coastal waters, winters in the deeper waters of the outer edge of the continental shelf from northern North Carolina to the mid-length of Georges Bank— 30 to 100 miles offshore according to location in waters of 50 to 100 fathoms.

The appearance of mackerel in the spring, simultaneously along hundreds of miles of coastline, and the fact that no mackerel have ever been taken outside the continental shelf or on the high seas are additional factors which support the theory that the mackerel do not travel any long distance in winter.

The mackerel of British seas winter in the deeper portions of the English Channel and southwest of Ireland on the outer edge of the continental shelf in waters nearly all deeper than 60 fathoms. European mackerel are known to hug the bottom on their spring migration and rise to the surface only when near land. However, this does not apply to mackerel of our waters because they are first sighted off Hatteras about the middle of March to the latter part of April, and as the water warms, they spread northward and shoreward and reach the waters of New England in May. Cape Cod's first arrivals are usually about the middle of May.

The Atlantic mackerel spawns off the American coast from Cape Hatteras to the southern side of the Gulf of St. Lawrence in spring or early summer. From Cape Cod northward the spawning area is confined more or less to the vicinity of the coast, but from Cape Cod southward the spawning area covers almost the entire breadth of the continental shelf. The area between Chesapeake Bay and southern New England is the most productive location, the Gulf of Maine is considered second best as a spawning area, and the outer coast of Nova Scotia the third.

The spawning activity is oceanic or pelagic and takes place wherever the fish happen to be when the gonads (sex organs) ripen. When the water temperatures warm to about 46° F. in the early spring and summer, spawning begins; most of the egg laying takes place in water temperatures of about 48° to 57° F. Spawning takes place progressively northward as the water warms: mid-April, Chesapeake Bay; May, New Jersey; June, southern Massachusetts; June, outer Nova Scotia; late June and early July, Gulf of St. Lawrence. Medium-size females will produce as many as 400,000 to 500,000 eggs, but about 50,000 are released at one time, for the members of a given school will spawn over a period of time.

Young mackerel about 10 to 11 inches long, which anglers call tinker mackerel, are in the early part of their second year of growth. In the third summer they reach about 14 inches, about 15 inches in the fourth, about 15½ in the fifth, 16 in the sixth, and only about one third of an inch more in their seventh. A 17-inch specimen is about eight years old.

Mackerel are most likely to be found where there is an abundant supply of red feed (small crustaceans called copepods); other favorite foods are shrimp, herring, and pilchards. Mackerel fluctuate wildly in abundance from year to year—perhaps

Harry Wesley Smith of Buenos Aires, Argentina, battles a 583-pound bluefin tuna during the famous International Tuna Cup Match at Wedgeport, Nova Scotia.

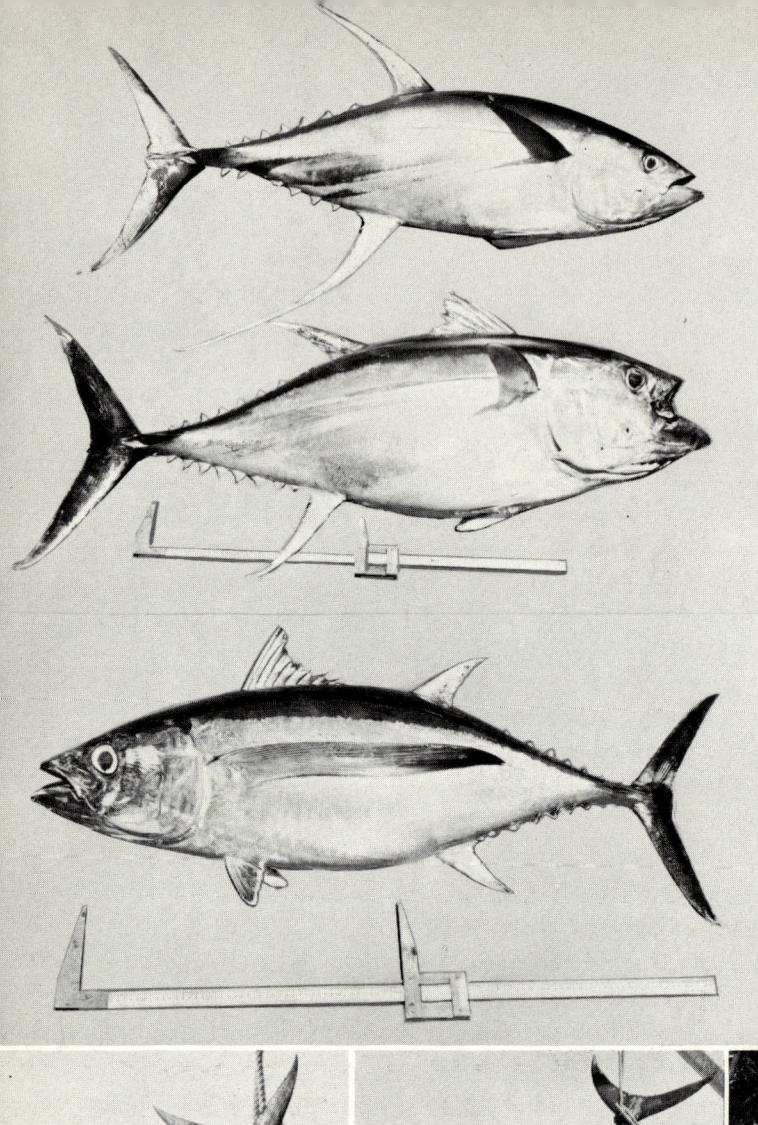

Left (from top down): Yellowfin tuna, bigeye tuna, and albacore. Photo taken by Harvey Bullis, Jr., and Frank Mather while carrying on studies of the species in the northern Caribbean. *Bottom left:* Kip Farrington, one of the pioneers of angling in South America, stands by a 302-pound bigeye tuna at Cabo Blanco. *Bottom center:* Mrs. Wendell Anderson, Jr., of Detroit, with a women's record 335-pound bigeye tuna taken at Cabo Blanco, Peru. *Bottom right:* Yellowfin tuna captured off Bermuda by Louis Mowbray, director of the aquarium.

more so than any other important food and game fish. They go through periods of great abundance which alternate with times of scarcity and almost total absence. For example, in a good year schools of unbelievable numbers, miles in length, will thrash the surface in quest of food. The next year they may be scarcer than the proverbial hen's teeth. The history of mackerel landings is a series of ups and downs. All sorts of explanations have been offered for this phenomenon—the fish have gone across to Europe, over-fishing with purse seines, etc. However, it seems most likely that the numbers of mackerel in a given year depend upon factors in the sea having a favorable or unfavorable bearing on spawning conditions and the successful growth of the eggs and larvae produced several years previously.

Mackerel are also unpredictable because the schools are constantly on the move, and there is no guessing where they may appear. This mackerel is of prime importance commercially; it is delicious to eat, but because of its oily flesh, it does not keep well. At one time commercial fishermen caught it with hook and line, attracting the fish to the boat with chum (chopped fish), but now the use of the purse seine is general. To a lesser extent floating traps, pound nets, weirs, and gill nets are also used.

Sports fishermen take a large number of the fish by trolling feathers and spoons. In most cases the boat retains its forward motion, and the fish are handlined aboard (called heave and haul). However, when a school is located and the boat is allowed to drift while the anglers spin with light tackle, excellent sport can be had. During a "hot year" it is not uncommon for charter boats consisting of three or four anglers to come in with a couple hundred mackerel. Occasionally sportsmen along the New England shore are fortunate in experiencing a run of tinkers. At this time the fish come close into shore, and men, women, and children by the hundreds will occupy all available space on bridges, piers, rocks; boat liveries put out the "no boats" sign early in the day. A favorite piece of tackle is a long, slender pole with a short line and a cork float.

However, if you want a day of tremendous sport in a rowboat, try a fly rod and a small colorado spinner with a sliver of pork rind attached to the hook. And if you really want a bucket full of the tasty tinkers, do a bit of chumming. Fish a line or two on the bottom and catch cunners; hit them over the head and place them in an ordinary household meat grinder attached to the gunwale (you can sneak this piece of equipment out when your wife or mother isn't looking) and grind the cunners into chum. If you are squeamish, purchase a can of sardines, puncture with holes, tie a line to it and dunk it over the side occasionally. If the tinkers are "in," I guarantee you a pot full!

Chub Mackerel (6b)
(*Scomber colias*)

The chub resembles the Atlantic mackerel so closely in appearance and habits that usually no attempt is made to separate them for the market. Generally it is not considered a game fish because it is not common. However, I have included it here because the chub often is found schooling with its larger cousin, the Atlantic mackerel, and many anglers are interested in identifying the species they are catching.

Since 1777 it has been known by about a dozen different scientific names. Today scientists may refer to this species as *Pneumatophorus grex, Pneumatophorus colias,* or *Scomber colias.* I prefer to use the latter. As with many other species, it has been described under the various scientific names because previous descriptions have been misinterpreted or the early descriptions were poor. The eastern Atlantic specimens, usually referred to as *colias,* and the western Atlantic inhabitants, known as *grex,* are not separable. Depending on the location, the chub mackerel may be called hardhead, tinker, bulleye, thimble-eye, or eastern mackerel. The Atlantic inhabitants are found on both sides of the North Atlantic Ocean—on the north American coast from Virginia (usually from New Jersey) to outer Nova Scotia, Gulf of St. Lawrence, and to England in the east. There is a record of one taken off Gordon Key, Florida.

The Mackerels

The chub mackerel is a smaller fish (8 to 14 inches only) than its better-known relative, the Atlantic mackerel, but unless studied closely, they appear identical. There is a characteristic color difference in the two: the Atlantic mackerel is silvery below the mid-line, whereas the sides of the chub below the mid-line, are mottled with dark blotches, and the chub has a larger eye. Other external differences are: the dorsal fins are closer together in the chub, there are 9 or 10 spines in the chub's first dorsal fin (Atlantic mackerel has 11 or 12). The chub possesses 5 dorsal finlets and 5 anal finlets. The Atlantic mackerel usually has the same but sometimes may have 4 to 6. One of the most important anatomical differences in the two species is the fact that the chub has a well-developed swim bladder, which the Atlantic mackerel lacks.

In good years (not very often) the chub mackerel appears wherever Atlantic mackerel are found. Nothing is known of its spawning or migratory habits. While traveling in dense schools the chub feeds on pelagic plankton, young herring, and other small herring-like fishes. The chub will take an angler's bait readily, but because of its scarcity, anglers are not familiar with this fish. It is possible that failure to recognize this species as different from the Atlantic mackerel has erroneously termed it scarce. As a table fish it is considered choice.

Frigate Mackerel (6d)

(Auxis thazard)

The frigate mackerel is not as widely known as most of the other mackerels. It looks as much like a bonito as it does a mackerel, and some scientists prefer to classify it with the tuna. Its habits are the same as those of the other members of its group. Anglers may occasionally hook one while fishing for other species. Although its family classification is disputed, its scientific and common names offer no conflict. It is seldom called anything but frigate mackerel.

This scombrid prefers warm seas and has a world-wide distribution. It is known from Cape Cod to Brazil, Gulf of Mexico, eastern Atlantic, and Mediterranean. In the Pacific it has been found from southern California to Central America. A fish which may be the same or a closely related species is found in the western Pacific from Japan to Australia. There is doubt as to whether there is a single cosmopolitan species of *Auxis thazard* or whether different species occur in different parts of the world.

As with the other mackerels, this species is erratic in its occurrence in various areas. Off the western Atlantic coasts it may not be seen for years; then suddenly it will appear in vast numbers. No one seems to know the maximum size of this fish; some claim that it will not go over 5 pounds, others say up to 10, and everyone is guessing.

Although its widely separated first and second dorsal fins are typical of the mackerels, other portions of its anatomy resemble the bonito and tuna. For example, it does not have the deeply forked tail of the mackerels but the lunate type which tuna and bonito possess. Also, it has a pronounced pectoral corselet. The irregular markings, which are variable, are on the dorsal surface but present only in the posterior half of the body. The eyes are large. The frigate could be confused with the black skipjack, *Euthynnus lineatus*, because the wavy, oblique lines or markings on the dorsal surface appear about the same. However, the frigate does not have the dots below the pectoral fin which the black skipjack does. The general appearance includes a dark bluish-green back and iridescent silver on the sides and belly. The gill raker count is 42–45.

Nothing specific is known concerning the migratory habits of this wandering fish, which appears in different locations on irregular occasions. Milner Schaefer and John Marr, Pacific coast scientists, have taken juveniles of the frigate mackerel off the coast of Central America, which indicates a spawning area during the early spring.

The food habits are assumed to be similar to those of other fish of this type. Small fish and crustaceans are favorites. It is valued as a food fish when available in quantity. Anglers do not go after frigate mackerel, but when accidentally taken on light tackle, it puts up the typically strong fight of the mackerel tribe. I feel that this species is taken more often than it appears to be. It is probably often mistaken for one of the other mackerel or bonito.

Pacific Mackerel (6c)
(*Pneumatophorus diego*)

Constituting one of California's top fisheries in volume, the Pacific mackerel is used almost entirely for canning, with the commercial activity centered mostly in southern California. Although large numbers are caught by sports fishermen, this species is generally not accepted as a good game fish. Like all mackerel, it is an oceanic schooling fish with erratic migratory habits. Whether or not this species is identical with other closely related mackerel is not as yet clearly known.* The common name is well established, but fishermen may call it striped mackerel, greenback mackerel, or zebra mackerel. It ranges along the western coast of North America from southern Alaska to Cape San Lucas, Mexico, into the Gulf of California, and along the mainland coast of Mexico to Banderas Bay.

The Pacific mackerel, like its Atlantic close relative (chub mackerel), possesses 5 (sometimes 4 or 6) dorsal finlets and 5 anal finlets. Its color, which is a distinctive feature, varies considerably. The innumerable, short wavy bars covering most of its back form no constant pattern, and the mottling may or may not run below the mid-line. The lower sides and belly are silvery. The rather high first dorsal fin is separated widely from the second dorsal fin. Its tail is deeply forked, and no keel is present on the caudal peduncle. The body is covered completely with small scales. The gill raker count is 26 to 29.

Compared with other fishes the mackerel grows rapidly, reaching a foot in length within three years, and a weight of three quarters of a pound. The usual size is 16 to 17 inches and

* There is a *P. peruanus* (Panama to Chile, Galapagos Islands) and *P. japonicus* (western Pacific), but they are not readily distinguishable from *P. diego.* Another form, *P. australasicus,* is a smaller fish, found in Australian waters, about 14 inches maximum.

1½ to 2½ pounds. Seven-year-old fish are common, and some reach the age of 10. Specimens 22 inches long and 3½ pounds in weight have been taken. The largest ever recorded was a fish 25 inches long which weighed 6⅓ pounds, but it is considered a freak.

The Pacific angler may possibly confuse this species with only one other fish, the frigate mackerel. However, they are easily distinguished. The frigate appears more tuna-like, its tail is not deeply forked, and its body is heavier towards the rear; the first dorsal is more or less pointed; the bars on its back are present only on the posterior half of the body. Also, the frigate has a prominent corselet and a keel on the caudal peduncle.

Mackerel are not continually abundant at any one location, and their migratory habits are erratic. Every season, at approximately the same time, there are definite periods of abundance and scarcity. Off the California coast they are not found in great numbers north of Monterey Bay. Generally the mackerel are most abundant from July through November, although they may be present the year round. The big schools seem to disappear in March, April, and early May. Their habit of fluctuating in abundance, from week to week during a season, suggests that they indulge in frequent short migrations away from shore or perhaps down to depths where they cannot be caught. They also fluctuate greatly in abundance from year to year. Some years they may be comparatively scarce, while in others they are so numerous as to glut the market. Causes for these wild fluctuations are not known. We may guess that they follow their food to different places, or that certain year classes run into unfavorable spawning conditions, or the young may drift into unfavorable waters and die in mass. Spawning takes place from late April through July, but the time of season and duration of spawning vary from year to year. Each female seems to spawn more than once a season; about 500,000 eggs per year may be produced by a single female.

The most important item of diet seems to be larval and juvenile fish, but they also feed on shrimps, copepods, and other plankton. Contrary to some of the other scombrids, mackerel do not favor squid as a major delicacy in their feeding habits.

The commercial fishery for mackerel in the Pacific is a prime example of the need for a controlled fishery—at least as far as size limits are concerned. The great majority of mackerel used for canning are taken at an early age, before they have a chance to reach two years. This illustrates the potential economic loss to all concerned in the fishery when the fish do not reach the spawning age of two or three years. If the mackerel are not taken before the age of three, they can spawn once or twice, thus increasing the possibility of maintaining a large population level. The age of this fish can be detected from the study of the unattached bony structures found in the ear, called otoliths; about 98 per cent are readable.

It is not considered a first-class game fish because, I'm sure, it is usually taken on tackle far out of proportion to its size. On light tackle it is a real struggler. The Pacific mackerel is not fussy about the proper bait at the proper time; it will snap at almost anything—worms, clams, live bait, cut bait, and artificial lures. If the angler cleans these little scrappers as soon as possible, he will be rewarded with a delicacy on the table.

King Mackerel (7c)

(*Scomberomorus cavalla*)

King mackerel is well named, for it is one of the Atlantic's prize game fish and is also rated highly by commercial fishermen. It is a bold fish that seems clever in stealing bait while escaping the hook. The king is a fairly large mackerel that prefers the deeper waters of the outer reefs and open ocean in warm waters. As *Scomberomorus cavalla* it is accepted by fishery scientists, but its common name is not stabilized. In different localities it may be known as kingfish, cavalla, or cero. Sometimes it is referred to as one of the Spanish mackerels. This member of the family SCOMBRIDAE ranges mostly throughout the tropical and subtropical western north Atlantic. Occasionally, it straggles north to Cape Cod and has been recorded from the West Indies and off Brazil.

It has an elongated, speedy looking body and more or less the same formation of fins as the other finletfishes. In color its dorsal surface is steely or iron gray, while the sides are dusky silver and the belly white. About 40 teeth are present in each jaw.

As the largest of the genus *Scomberomorus* it attains a weight of about 100 pounds and a length of over 5 feet (taken by commercial fishermen). Fish of 40 to 50 pounds caught by anglers are not rare, but the average size is about 6 pounds. Young king mackerel may possess yellow spots, which add confusion in its identification when compared with the Spanish and cero mackerels. But anglers may separate the adult king readily from the cero and Spanish mackerels because it lacks markings of any kind. If you want to be sure of your identification, look at the lateral line; the king mackerel has one which is extremely angulate and descends abruptly in the region below the second dorsal fin. The 7 or 8 gill rakers on the lower limb can also be used as a means of identification; the Spanish and cero mackerels have more. Eight or 9 dorsal finlets are present, accompanied by 8 or 9 anal finlets and 15 or 16 spines in the first dorsal fin. I might add that Donald de Sylva, working at the University of Miami Marine Laboratory, has identified one specimen as a hybrid between king mackerel and Spanish mackerel, *Scomberomorus maculatus*.

The king mackerel is a migratory fish, but the exact scope of its travels is not known. Along the Florida coast it is most abundant during winter from the St. Lucie river southward. The greatest concentration of fish is in the Florida Straits. It is also caught in fair numbers in the Bahamas during this time. As the warm season progresses the king migrates northward until the region of Cape Hatteras is reached. Although individuals and groups are found farther north, Hatteras seems to be the most northern point for the main groups of king mackerel. From early October through March there seems to be a common meeting ground of schools from the Gulf and Atlantic coastal waters in the vicinity of Rebecca Shoals east of the Dry Tortugas. At present it is not known whether fish from the Caribbean are found in this area at the same time. Like most oceanic and coastal fishes, king mackerel travel in schools according to size or age classes. Smaller fish seem to prefer to travel in blue water and tighter schools, while the large fish may be found in green waters, not in compact schools but more or less in small groups or as individuals.

Although king mackerel feed on shrimp and several species of small fishes, their favorite fish food seems to be the small silvery halfbeaks called ballyhoo, which also serve as a prime bait when properly rigged. Although it is possible to attract the king by chumming, the larger fish are usually taken while trolling with strip bait or mullet for other species. When hooked, the king puts up a great fight with long, fast runs. It is an interesting fact that a hooked king mackerel will seldom jump, and yet when pursuing a trolled bait it will often jump to an amazing height. Many times I have discussed these jumps with Captain Bill Fagan while fishing from the "Mañana." We were standing on the bridge one day when a king mackerel hit one of our strip baits and went high into the air. We agreed that the fish came up almost to our eye level. Later we placed a tape measure from the surface of the water to about the highest point of the fish jump and found that it was 16 feet! Many times king mackerel will ruin a strip bait by clipping it clean just in back of the hook, which is exasperating when trolling for sailfish or marlin. It is amazing that this fish, which must be traveling at a great rate of speed in order to sail high into the air, can nip the bait so accurately just behind the hook. When fishing in an area where king mackerel are known to abound, it is wise to use a double-hook rig with the second hook in the tail end of the bait.

King mackerel is the only member of the so-called Spanish mackerels which rates a membership in the International Game Fish Association chart of salt water game fishes. The world record rod and reel fish of 77 pounds was taken by Clinton Olney Potts, off Bimini, Bahamas, May 12, 1957.

Spanish Mackerel (7b)
(*Scomberomorus maculatus*)

One of the most important food and game fish of southern waters, the Spanish mackerel is a close relative of the cero and king mackerels. Although an oceanic species, it often frequents inshore waters. This mackerel is well known on both coasts of North America, but it is called sierra mackerel in the Pacific (*see* Sierra Mackerel). It is found in the Caribbean, Gulf of Mexico, off the north coast of Cuba, and along our southeastern coast up to Chesapeake Bay, New York, and Massachusetts. An occasional fish will straggle as far north as Maine, and it has been recorded from Panama, Venezuela, and Brazil. Spanish mackerel have been taken also in the eastern Atlantic off northwest Africa and the Canary Islands. Investigations by scientists Mather and Day indicate that the Spanish mackerel from opposite sides of the Atlantic are of the same species. The slight differences between the eastern Atlantic and western Atlantic specimens appear to be racial rather than specific. It may be that at least two different races exist with little if any interchange between populations.

The Spanish mackerel is a slender, compressed fish (body about four and one half to five times as long as it is deep) with a greenish-blue back and silvery sides and belly. It has bright golden-yellow spots on its sides. The dorsal fin is high, with the top edge receding downward almost in a straight line. This mackerel's mouth is large and possesses large conical, sharp jaw teeth. The caudal peduncle has a keel, the lateral line is wavy, and the first dorsal fin has 17 to 18 spines. Dorsal finlets number 8 or 9, and the anal finlets also number 8 or 9. The tail is deeply forked. Average weight for this mackerel is about 2 pounds with a length of 18 inches. Ten pounds seems to be the approximate maximum weight. Different authors state that fish of 20, 25, and 35 pounds have been taken, but they do not give specific names, dates, and places.

Anglers may find it confusing to distinguish the Spanish mackerel from its close cousins, the king and the cero. This is

The Mackerels

how to tell them apart: the pectoral fins of the Spanish are naked while the pectorals of the other two possess some scales. The ventral fins originate behind the first dorsal spine, whereas in the other two species the ventrals are ahead or just under the first dorsal spine. It has 32 or fewer teeth in each jaw. The golden-yellow spots are more or less round, whereas the cero mackerel's are elongated. Ten or 11 gill rakers are present on the lower limb of the first arch.

Often congregating in huge schools, Spanish mackerel are migratory in habit. Not much is known concerning the migrational routes except that there appears to be a spring and fall run along the mid-Atlantic and southern Atlantic coasts. Along the Florida coast the Spanish mackerel seems to appear in greatest abundance, with November to April the best months. Off the Texas coast it is common from March to September, with August as the month in which greatest numbers are caught. Fish usually come into the Chesapeake Bay area in May or June and are present until about September. In the latter part of summer they migrate to their northern ranges off the New York area, less regularly along the southern coasts of New England, although a few are taken nearly every summer off Woods Hole, Massachusetts. Where these migrations originate no one knows. There may be two major migrational routes, one encompassing the Caribbean and the Gulf, and the other along the Atlantic coast from Florida to Hatteras.

The spawning period seems to be a prolonged one—off Beaufort, North Carolina, for instance, from June to the end of August. In the Chesapeake Bay they spawn during late spring and early summer. The eggs are buoyant and float near the surface.

Shrimp is a favorite food, but small fishes and squid are also major items of diet. The Spanish mackerel, unlike most other scombrids, will follow bait schools into large bays, tide estuaries, and lagoons, where it can be taken by fishermen fishing from skiffs, piers, and bridges. Millions of pounds are taken annually by commercial fishermen. Some of it is salted or smoked but most is sold fresh. Unfortunately, the Spanish mackerel is nearly always hooked with tackle meant for much larger game. Or else it is taken by handline while trolling with feather jigs with the express purpose of catching it to be used for marlin bait.

Cero Mackerel (7a)

(*Scomberomorus regalis*)

The cero is a close relative of the king and the Spanish mackerel. In general appearance it resembles the latter so closely that most anglers consider them to be the same. It is a fish that swims near the surface much of the time and loves the outer reefs in warm waters. The king mackerel prefers deeper waters of the outer reefs, while the Spanish mackerel often comes into inshore waters. The cero occurs throughout the greater portion of the western north Atlantic, but catches north of Cape Florida are considered strays. It has been recorded from Cape Cod to Brazil. Off Cuba and in the Florida Straits it is abundant. In the Straits it is most numerous from spring through fall, but it is taken throughout the year from Marathon to the Dry Tortugas. It is probably present in greatest number in the Caribbean area. Aside from being confused with the king and Spanish mackerels, it is also known by other names including painted mackerel, but cero is now being more generally accepted.

Like the king and Spanish mackerel, it has a long, racy appearance, a greenish-blue dorsal surface, silvery sides, and white belly. Conspicuous golden-yellow markings are present along the sides. These markings differ from those of the Spanish mackerel in that they are not oval spots but rather elongated dashes. Usually there is a horizontal stripe, also colored golden yellow, which runs from the gill cover to the tail. Although the markings are more or less of the same type, the intensity of brightness, number, and size probably vary with age and sex of the individual. Sometimes the markings may not be visible at all. The dorsal fin spines number 17 or 18, dorsal finlets are 8 or 9, while the anal finlets are 8. In size it seems to be between the king and the Spanish mackerel. Its average weight is about

The Mackerels

2 to 5 pounds. Various authors give the maximum weight of this fish as from 20 to 35 pounds.

It is not difficult for anglers to separate the cero from the Spanish and king mackerel. At a glance it is easy to see the elongated yellow markings of the cero (Spanish has spots and the adult king has none). However, occasionally a cero may possess indistinct markings, or they may be entirely absent. Therefore, for a sure identification, count the gill rakers on the lower limb of the first arch: cero, 12 or 13; Spanish, 10 or 11; king, 7 to 9. Also, it has scales on its pectoral fins, as does the king, but the Spanish mackerel has none. The ventral fins of the cero are directly below the beginning of the first dorsal, whereas in the Spanish they are definitely behind the first dorsal spine.

Little is known concerning its migrations, which appear to be mostly confined to the Caribbean and Florida areas—southward in the winter and northward in the fall. The cero feeds predominantly on small fishes, squids, and shrimp. As with its related species, the cero is taken usually by heavy tackle when anglers are out for bigger game. It is also specifically sought after as bait for marlin and taken with handline and feather jigs while trolling. On the rare occasion when caught on suitable light tackle, it proves its worth as a game fish. Its flesh is fairly light in color, and unlike most mackerels, it is not excessively oily and does not need special methods of preparation for the table.

Sierra Mackerel

(*Scomberomorus sierra*)

The sierra mackerel of the Pacific and the Spanish mackerel of the Atlantic are very closely related, if not actually identical. Only minor differences have been found between the fishes of the two oceans (*see* Spanish Mackerel). The Pacific form ranges from Santa Monica, California, south through the Gulf of California, along the coasts of Mexico and Central America, down into Peruvian waters (I have seen vast schools which covered acres of water off Cabo Blanco and Talara, Peru). The sierra does not differ from the Atlantic form in general appearance. The coloration, including the golden markings, is similar. The Pacific species appears to attain 10 or 12 pounds in maximum weight.

Anglers should have no trouble in identifying this species. It can be confused only with the Monterey Spanish mackerel. However, in the latter species the males have no yellow markings, and although females have spots, they are not yellow but brownish. The females are also generally darker. The sierra has 10 to 12 gill rakers, whereas the Monterey has about 15 or more.

Not much is known concerning the sierra's migrations or other habits. It seems to be most abundant along the coasts of Mexico and Central America. Fish with ripening ovaries have been taken in Mexican waters at the end of March, which indicates that spawning probably takes place in late spring or summer. Here we may take a clue from the sierra's close relative, the Spanish mackerel of the Atlantic, which prefers warm inshore waters for breeding and whose spawning season lasts from six to ten weeks in certain localities. The eggs are buoyant. Like its Atlantic cousin, it is found close to shore, where a school may be spotted easily as it churns the waters white while slaughtering bait fishes. Besides small fish, squid is a preferred food.

In its southern range the sierra is taken easily almost at any time with about any type of trolled lure or bait. Big game anglers consider it a nuisance because it ruins strip baits intended for billfish. On the other hand, the sierra itself makes one of the finest baits for marlin. The long, slender body is ideal for the double hook rig. In black marlin waters off South America this mackerel can be depended upon to supply the bait. The sierra mackerel is usually taken by handlines trolled a short distance astern.

I often wondered how the sierra would react to light tackle since it always put up a great fuss when taken by handline. An excellent opportunity presented itself for a try when we found these mackerel unusually abundant during a fishing expedition off Cabo Blanco, Peru. The large schools appeared frequently here and there, and it was a simple matter to fill our bait boxes.

One day after I had finished my work on the beach I was tossing a spinning lure into the surf when a large school of mackerel appeared about a half mile from shore. I persuaded two of the friendly natives to paddle me out in their small homemade craft. When we arrived at the spot the fish were gone, but it wasn't long before we were in the midst of another thrashing school of mackerel that were cutting up bait fishes. I tossed the silver spoon into them, and just as it hit the water, I had on a mackerel. As I expected, the fish put up a dandy show, jumping clear of the water several times. Suddenly the large school disappeared while I continued to play the gamy fish. I had it quite close to the boat, and as I grabbed the line hoping to swing the fish aboard, a large mako shark zoomed up from nowhere and grabbed the mackerel right from under my nose. Half of the shark's body came out of the water and caused the little boat (and my heart) to bobble about. Rod and reel went over the side. I also lost my dignity. The natives were doubled over with belly laughs and yelling in Spanish. I was petrified.

Monterey Spanish Mackerel
(*Scomberomorus concolor*)

Structurally the Monterey Spanish mackerel is very similar to the sierra mackerel. At one time (1870–1880) it was common in Monterey Bay, California, and taken by commercial fishermen in large numbers. It was considered a delicacy, commanding high prices in San Francisco markets. It disappeared suddenly and has never returned in its former abundance. Only occasionally is one taken. (For a description of this species *see* section on Sierra Mackerel.)

School Mackerel
(*Scomberomorus queenslandicus*)

Except for larger spots this western Pacific mackerel closely resembles the Spanish mackerel and the spotted mackerel. The school mackerel is a small member of the family SCOMBRIDAE, not growing much beyond 2 feet, 6 inches. The average size is a length of about 20 inches and a weight of 3 or 4 pounds. It is primarily an inhabitant of bays and estuaries, where it is caught by trolling. (This mackerel was once considered the same as *Scomberomorus guttatus,* which is distributed from India to Japan).

Spotted Mackerel
(*Scomberomorus niphonius*)

In general appearance this fish seems to be identical with the sierra mackerel of the eastern Pacific and the Spanish mackerel of the Atlantic. It grows larger than the school mackerel and attains a length of about 3 feet, 6 inches and a weight of 7 to 10 pounds. It seems to appear in largest numbers in eastern Australian waters from December to May.

WAHOOS

The wahoos are oceanic fishes found in the warmer portions of the great oceans. They are streamlined, cigar-shaped, and renowned for their speed when hooked. Not much scientific work has been done on the life history of these fishes. It is not known whether or not they belong to a single species with world-wide distribution. There is a question regarding some mackerel-like fishes found along the western Pacific as to whether they are a species of mackerel or young wahoo.

Wahoo (7d)
(*Acanthocybium solandri*)

Without question the wahoo commands respect among salt water anglers as a top-bracket sport fish. It is a species which prefers the waters of deep reefs and the open seas; it hits hard and has a reputation as one of the swiftest of the game fishes.

Wahoos

Although known mostly as wahoo, it may have other names in different localities: ono (Hawaii), peto (Bahamas), queenfish (Caribbean), springer (Brazil). In American waters it is sometimes referred to as ocean barracuda, and because of its abundance in Bermudian waters, it is also known as "pride of Bermuda." Among taxonomists this highly specialized scombrid has provided uncertainty. By possessing finlets it demonstrates its relationship to the SCOMBRIDAE or family of finlet fishes; on the other hand, the peculiar structure of its gills resembles those of a billfish. Therefore, some scientists have advanced the theory that the wahoo may be a link between groups and have classified it in a family of its own—ACANTHOCYBIIDAE. However, I believe it has a closer affinity to the SCOMBRIDAE, and I go along with those who place it in this family.

The wahoo ranges in all warm seas and is common in the western Atlantic and Caribbean. It has been taken along the coast of northwest Africa and is known to frequent the eastern part of the equatorial Atlantic. Also, it is fairly common off northern Brazil in the Guiana current; a single capture in the Mediterranean has been recorded. Bermuda and Bahamas are favorite spots for wahoo. In American waters of the Atlantic it is caught in the Gulf of Mexico off the coast of Texas and in the Gulf Stream from southern Florida to Cape Hatteras. Known Pacific areas harboring the wahoo are found southward from the southern tip of lower California (common off Panama) to Cocos Island (Costa Rica) and Galapagos Islands (Ecuador). It is present about the Hawaiian Islands and found from Japan southward to the Philippine Archipelago down to Australia.

The wahoo is a speedy looking fish with a pointed head, slender, cigar-shaped body, and a small tail less deeply forked than in any finlet fish. The first dorsal, which has 24 to 26 spines, is elongated and nearly of an even height throughout its length. The numerous teeth are triangular in shape and closely set. It has 9 dorsal finlets and 9 anal finlets. Scales cover the entire body.

In color the back or dorsal surface of the wahoo may vary— deep blue-black, steel blue-gray, or a light golden green with a touch of blue. The sides are silvery, sometimes appearing silvery gray with a light spray of bronze, and the belly is white or silvery. Young wahoo have pronounced, dark vertical markings along the sides. Adults display vivid, irregular, dark blue-gray bars (about 25 or 30) when in a state of excitement. When boating a wahoo the vividness of these bars disappears almost instantly. Also, the wahoo is covered with what seems to be a superficial spray of bronze silver; it is scraped off easily when in contact with the wire leader. The substance is also removed when the fish is handled roughly. The upper jaw or snout is unusual in that it is movable. When the mouth is open the upper front jaw structure and tip of the snout have a pronounced tip up. Another condition which is unusual in typical fishes is found in the maxilla (upper lip) of the wahoo; it slides or folds into a type of groove in the side of the upper snout. Most of the posterior portion of the maxilla is not visible when the mouth is closed.

The wahoo is a fairly large game fish with an average size of 20 pounds. The record rod and reel fish weighed 136 pounds and was taken off East Boynton Inlet, Florida, on April 8, 1955, by R. J. Geyer. The size of schooling fish off Bermuda averages about 35 pounds, but when encountered in smaller groups the size is usually larger. One of the smallest specimens known (8 inches) was taken from the stomach of a dolphin. In the Hawaiian Islands specimens over 70 pounds are taken consistently.

Identification is easy. The movable upper snout and the numerous closely set, triangular teeth set it apart from other fishes. A look under the operculum or gill cover will show no developed gill rakers. This will add credence to your identification. All other finlet fishes possess gill rakers.

Generally the wahoo is considered to be a nonschooling fish, but Louis Mowbray of Bermuda states, "It is not an uncommon occurrence in summer, on a flat calm day, to steam through a mile or more of wahoo on the surface with the tips of their caudal fins showing. At these times the fish are seldom induced to strike." (In the Pacific it has been reported as plentiful and schooling off the Midway Islands in September and October.)

Seasonal migrations are indicated by the appearance and disappearance of this fish from certain areas, but true lines of migrations are not, as yet, known. Although it is a year-round fish in Bermuda waters, migrations are suspected by a minor run from mid-April through May, and by major abundance during September and October. Generally speaking, the wahoo is most plentiful from April through October. In the Bahamas late March and early April are considered the best time for wahoos. Along the south Florida and Miami coast they are caught with some degree of frequency from mid-winter through early summer—December through May.

Practically nothing is known concerning their spawning activities. In Bermuda waters they spawn between May and July, and off Cuba in June or July. Like all free swimming oceanic fishes the adult wahoo feeds on smaller fishes and squid. As an item of sea food the wahoo has a reputation as one of the best. The flesh is delicious; it is firm and pure white when cooked. Not often found in the markets, but when it is sold the wahoo commands premium prices.

Because it produces good eating and good sport the wahoo is a prize fish among anglers. Its fighting qualities are well known. It will hit any bait of any size, although a trolled white feather is a favorite method of angling for them. Also, strip bait or small whole bait such as a half beak skipping from the outrigger is particularly successful—6 or 7 knots of speed seems best. Like the king mackerel, the wahoo usually strikes at the second half end of the bait. Therefore, it is advisable to keep the hook well back when rigging for wahoo. Another precaution which is well worth taking when fishing in wahoo waters is to remove (or perhaps tape) bright or shiny swivels which reflect light. Wahoo often hit swivels and cause the loss of terminal tackle. They may also be responsible for the loss of a hooked sailfish or marlin in this same manner. Wahoo are often taken unexpectedly when fishing for the larger game fishes.

My introduction to wahoo was a painful one. It happened years ago, on my first fishing trip in Bermuda, aboard the Aquarium boat. We had been out all day collecting specimens with wire traps, and on our way in we trolled feather jigs with handlines. While I was letting out line, a good swirl appeared suddenly by my lure. I started to jerk the line back and forth to make the feather jig look more enticing. My technique must have been good because a big wahoo hit the feather hard on the run and kept going. I was quite excited and held onto the line until I felt something like a hot scalding iron run through my fingers. Lou Mowbray's mate landed the fish. I wore greased bandages the rest of the trip, but I posed proudly with that fish, for I thought I earned it. Now I wear gloves when trolling with a handline.

Tanguigue

(*Cybium commersonii*)

Closely resembling the wahoo in appearance and habits, the exact relationship of the tanguigue and the wahoo is not clearly known. It is probably identical with the banded mackerel of Australia. In distribution it is found chiefly in the western Pacific. In maximum size it is about the same as the wahoo. Excellent as a table fish.

Broad Banded Mackerel

(*Scomberomorus semifasciatus*)

Narrow Banded Mackerel

(*Scomberomorus commerson*)

The banded mackerels are found in the western Pacific, mostly in Australian waters. The two species, which seem to be separated only by the difference in width of dark bands on the body, closely resemble the wahoo and the tanguigue.

Sharks

Many anglers will be surprised to know that a shark does not have a true bone in its body; instead, the skeleton is composed of a cartilaginous material which is soft when compared with hard bone. Because of this fact scientists classify the shark in a group with the skate and ray—because these winged fishes also possess the same type of skeletons. One of the most accurate methods of identifying sharks is by the shape of their teeth.

Out on the water, when basking near the surface, a shark can be easily differentiated from swordfish and marlin. Compared with these fishes, the shark has a small dorsal fin and a weak, wobbly tail. The swordfish has a sickle-shaped dorsal fin that never folds and a rigid tail; both are often seen above the surface of the water. The dorsal fin of the marlin is usually folded, although I have seen a striped marlin taking life easy near the surface with its dorsal erect. In any case the marlin dorsal fin is pointed and more or less triangular; therefore it should not be confused with that of a shark or swordfish.

Many different types of sharks abound in all seas, but they are most abundant in tropical and subtropical waters. The largest fish in the world is the whale shark, *Rhincodon typus*, while the most ferocious marine fish, as far as man is concerned, is the white shark or man-eater, *Carcharodon carcharias*. The

I.G.F.A. lists the following sharks as game fishes—mako, maneater, porbeagle, thresher, and tiger. In New Zealand the hammerhead is added to the list. However, in my estimation they should all be scratched from the game fish roster except the mako. Usually big game anglers shun sharks, and boat captains will invariably speed up their crafts in order to discourage a shark following a bait. Many boatmen despise sharks to a point which is almost frightening. I have caught or seen caught every one of these species of sharks, and I would honor only the mako as a game fish. Further, it is the only shark that big game anglers will ordinarily pursue.

Mako Shark (38b)

(Atlantic—*Isurus oxyrinchus*)
(Pacific—*Isurus glaucus*)

Anyone who has witnessed the graceful leaps of a mako, as its blue and silvery body reflected the sunlight, will agree that when alive it is a handsome fish. This shark not only jumps clear of the surface in a spectacular manner but it also makes strong runs. Much of the action is near the surface, and often the mako does not give up even when hanging by the tail at the dock! Its dogged resistance to the rod plus the fact that it is a delicious table fish make the mako a first-class big game fish. Other common names for the mako are mackerel shark, sharpnose shark, and bonito shark. It is a member of the family ISURIDAE.

Although the mako prefers warm waters, it is distributed widely in the oceanic blue waters of the great oceans. Along the western Atlantic it is found from Cape Cod to Brazil, including the Bahamas and Bermuda; in the eastern Atlantic, from Norway down to West Africa. The Pacific form ranges from off California south to Chile. The mako is present around the Hawaiian Islands and along the western Pacific from Japan down to Australia and New Zealand. Except in tropical and subtropical waters (for instance, off Massachusetts), the mako is present only during the warm months of the year.

Mako Shark

Most sharks are dull brownish or grayish in color, but the mako is a beauty. When alive, its dorsal surface is a deep cobalt blue which meets the silvery sides in a sharp line of demarcation. The entire ventral surface is flat white. The mako has wicked-looking teeth which are sharply pointed; most of them curve inward. They are smooth edged without lateral denticles, and the first two in each jaw are much the largest. The teeth that follow toward the rear are broader and more blade-like.

The largest mako ever taken on rod and reel was 12 feet long and weighed 1,000 pounds; it was captured off Mayor Island, New Zealand, on March 14, 1943, by B. D. Ross. In the western Atlantic the largest specimen recorded was about 10 feet 6 inches long and was taken off St. Petersburg, Florida. Another mako of 10 feet 2 inches was captured off New York Harbor. Ernest Hemingway took one on rod and reel off Bimini, Bahamas, that weighed 786 pounds.

The mako is mostly a fish eater and is often seen pursuing mackerel and other fishes. It does not hesitate to attack and feed on larger fishes. A 730-pound mako taken off Bimini was found to have a 120-pound swordfish in its stomach (including bill!). Another specimen of about 800 pounds harpooned off Montauk had been seen attacking a swordfish. When opened the mako contained about 150 pounds of its victim.

Commercially it is sold in limited quantities, but most anglers discard it after capture. I *was* one of those anglers until Dick Stoner and his father, Art, introduced me to the mako shark delicacy. Now I will go out of my way to obtain a hunk of it. The flesh is tender, juicy, and delicious. It comes closest in taste to young swordfish. For best results I would suggest skinning the shark as soon as possible and placing the meat on ice for a day or two before eating or freezing for future use.

I like to prepare it in this manner. Slice the fish into the thickness desired. Place the steaks in a pan which contains a piece of butter; season liberally with salt and pepper. Broil eight to ten minutes and baste occasionally with butter. If you have a copper pan, the fish need not be turned over, for the copper conducts enough heat to cook the upperside. I prefer mine broiled four or five minutes on each side so that both sides get brown. Serve with a slice of lemon.

My first and most exciting encounter with a mako took place over ten years ago in the Bay of Islands, New Zealand. One of the great advantages of fishing this area, out of Otehei Bay, is that long treks to find blue water are not necessary; it is practically at the doorstep. I was fishing on the "Rosemary" with Captain Warne. We were under way for not more than fifteen or twenty minutes when he rigged up a kahawai of about 3 pounds as bait and heaved it over the side. In New Zealand, at the time, outriggers were not used; the bait danced on the surface not more than 25 to 30 feet astern. I was relaxing with my feet off the fighting chair while the butt of the rod was in the gimbal with its tip resting on the stern. I did not expect any action until we were well away from the island, so I was enjoying the sunshine. We were traveling along at good speed when suddenly I saw a big dark shadow under the skipping bait. Before I could unscramble myself a huge shark went into the air; I could see about three feet of daylight under him before he came down, with open mouth, upon the kahawai. Even today I am surprised that I had presence of mind to reach over and flick the reel drag control onto free-spool.

It was about the most exciting hour and 40 minutes of my life as that mako came out of the water four or five times. He fought close to the surface for awhile and then went deep; then again and again he thrashed around along the surface. As the mako began to tire, I would drag him alongside, and everytime I did so Captain Warne would jab a lance viciously into its back—and off the mako would go again. It seemed like hours before the gaff was deep in his side. We hauled the shark across the stern, and I was amazed to find that many hours later as we were heading in the shark was still alive. The mako weighed 321 pounds. The catching of this mako was doubly interesting to me because professional news cameramen, who were interested in our expedition, were aboard and captured the fight on film.

COASTAL and INSHORE FISHES

Barracudas

Several species of barracudas in the family SPHYRAENIDAE are found in the Atlantic and Pacific, but only one, the great barracuda, is large enough to receive the attention of anglers; the other, smaller species are obscure in comparison. All are warm-water fishes which prefer shallow, inshore reef areas and are quite similar in appearance. The characteristic long, pike-like body and outstanding dentition separate them easily from all other salt water fishes.

ATLANTIC BARRACUDAS

Great Barracuda (8a)

(Sphyraena barracuda)

The largest of the SPHYRAENIDAE, the great barracuda is a coastal fish, which prefers fairly shallow reef areas in warm seas, where it preys upon the abundant fish life. It is a long cigar-shaped fish with a wicked looking dentition. Over the years authors have built up the barracuda's reputation to surpass that of the devil himself. No other game fish has more adulterated hokum written about it than the great barracuda. It is sometimes called 'cuda and generally referred to as barracuda, but because there are other, smaller species, it is differentiated by naming it great barracuda.

In the Atlantic its centers of greatest abundance seem to be off the southeastern United States and the West Indies. Although it strays as far north as Massachusetts, it is seldom found north of South Carolina. Southward, it ranges to Brazil. Especially abundant around the Bahama Islands, this barracuda is also found off Bermuda, where it has been taken in every month of the year. In the Gulf of Mexico it is occasional. It is distributed mostly in shallow areas inshore, but large specimens are taken far out to sea; one fish was captured 270 miles from the nearest shoal water.

In general conformation the barracuda's body resembles closely that of the fresh water family ESOCIDAE—pike, pickerel, muskelunge. It is elongate, cylindrical, streamlined, and as swift as it appears to be. The tail is forked, and the other fins are small in comparison with the body. The first dorsal is insignificant and looks out of place with only 5 short spines; the second dorsal has 8 or 9 rays, while the anal, which is below it and slightly further back, contains 2 spines and 8 or 9 rays. The ventral fins originate at a point between the origin of the pectoral and first dorsal fin. The gill rakers are obsolete, and the large scales along the lateral line number 75 to 85. Undoubtedly, the wicked-looking face, long snout, and large mouth containing prominent, pointed, sharp teeth are responsible for the evil assumptions built up about this fish. The lower jaw, which extends beyond the upper, also adds to the pugnacious appearance of the barracuda.

The coloration is generally silvery along the sides, with the ventral surface white. The dorsal area may vary from light brownish green to blue or a deep blue which appears almost black. Barracudas found in open waters usually have dark backs in contrast to the reef-dwelling barracudas, which have lighter colored backs. When the fish are alive the dorsal coloration in most great barracudas extends downward in an irregular edging which produces a scallop effect, and several black spots or blotches of different sizes are usually found along the lower sides of the hind part of the body. The fins and tail are predominantly dusky or blackish gray but may be in degrees of greenish yellow or gray.

Fifty pounders are not infrequent; average size is from 3 to 15 pounds. The rod and reel record is 103¼ pounds taken off West End, Bahamas, by C. E. Benet in 1932. This fish was 5 feet 6 inches in length. Many authors have copied one another over the years, writing, "maximum size—a length of 8 feet and about 100 pounds." Obviously this statement about maximum length is erroneous since the authenticated rod and reel record fish was much shorter. Anglers do not bother to differentiate between the young great barracuda and its smaller relatives. These miniature 'cudas usually are from 1 to 2 feet in length and can be separated by the differentiating characteristics given in the next sections treating these small barracudas.

The great barracuda is not a schooling fish; it is usually seen solitary or in groups of several fish. There seems to be a northward migration along the Atlantic coast as far as North Carolina in the late spring, with the greatest concentration around the Florida Keys. Occasionally these large groups or concentrations simulate the appearance of a school. In the spring around the Keys area barracuda come into the shallow water to spawn. The females, which seem to be the larger fish, cast their eggs about, and at this time several males may be in attendance upon a single female. Barracuda are known to spawn from May to October.

The barracudas which inhabit reef areas have a diet which consists mainly of puffer, spiny boxfish, parrotfish, filefish, and triggerfish, none of which are fast swimmers. On the other hand, out at sea I have caught medium-size (14 pounds) and large barracudas (35 pounds) which grabbed a bait intended for marlin. The fact that these baits were trolled at 5 or 6 knots, bouncing on the surface, leads me to believe that the great barracuda is capable of dieting on the different types of smaller, swift-swimming oceanic fishes.

Among the fishes thought to be toxic or poisonous the barracuda seems to have the most widespread reputation. This or any other fish can produce poisoning by bacterial spoilage. However, it has been consistently associated with true fish poisoning called ichthyosarcotoxism (fish-flesh poison). This is not an allergic condition where a single person out of several consuming the flesh is affected. In true fish poisoning everyone who partakes of the fish becomes ill. Reports of barracuda poisoning in south Florida, in at least two of the many suspected cases, were followed up by laboratory analysis, and bacterial tests were undertaken on the poisonous meat by the U.S. Public Health Service. In both cases the flesh was found not to be spoiled. In other words, the cases were true fish poisoning.

The Marine Laboratory at the University of Miami has been conducting a study of the biology of the barracuda with emphasis on food habits, and it has been found that barracudas feed a great deal on such reef inhabitants as puffer, spiny boxfish, parrotfish, filefish, and triggerfish in which the liver, intestine, gall bladder, spleen, and reproductive organs are known to be highly toxic most of the time. Theories exist, though as yet not scientifically proved, that these small fishes may feed on algae that grows on the copper of old shipwrecks; or they may feed on other poisonous substances.

Actually, the flesh of the barracuda is only rarely poisonous; only a few of the many thousands eaten prove to be toxic. Donald de Sylva, who has been working with this problem at the Marine Laboratory, states: "At a certain stage during its life history, that is, at about 3 to 5 pounds, the barracuda begins to feed more and more upon poisonous fishes and also upon larger sizes of these poisonous species, which presumably contain more toxin than do the smaller sizes. At this size, then, the barracuda might become more dangerous to eat, if the theory holds." The poison may be cumulative in the body of the barracuda, for most of the poisonings occur from fish over 15 pounds. Perhaps the reason that more cases of barracuda poisoning do not occur is that most people refrain from eating the larger fish, whose flesh is coarse and not as tasty as that of a smaller specimen—

that is, if we accept the theory of toxin building up in the growing barracuda until it reaches a dangerous point for human consumption. However, many large ones are eaten without ill effect.

It all boils down to this: Many barracuda are used as food; comparatively few have been proved poisonous to eat. It appears that the larger ones may be more apt to be toxic, which indicates a possibility of cumulative toxication by their diet of poisonous fishes over a period of time. The U.S. Public Health Service and the Office of Naval Research are interested in fish poisoning. Perhaps in the not too distant future scientific investigation will produce a method of poison determination in barracuda.

Almost without exception all persons who know even a bit about fishes or fishing will swear to the fact that the barracuda is one of the most dangerous, if not *the* most dangerous, creature in the sea. Every angler is acquainted with many bizarre stories about the ferocity and viciousness of the "evil-eyed, bloodthirsty monster." One can understand that outdoor magazines must produce exciting yarns to attract readers. However, they consistently print stories similar to one which appeared in a recent issue of one of the most popular magazines in the country. This incredible tale embodied a father and son whose escape from a stalking barracuda left the former exhausted on the beach. (The son clung desperately to his father's bathing trunks during the retreat to shore.) The story was repulsive in its use of adjectives describing the evil beast and in the author's fancied assumptions about the potential killer, the barracuda. Fanciful stories are more than common. But we cannot shake a criticizing finger too vigorously at these publications when some of our most respected and most widely read books on fishes are equally guilty with contributions from reputable writers including scientists. This great aura of bloodthirsty viciousness built around the barracuda is without foundation.

Let's be specific. Let's take a few of the statements in some of the most up-to-date publications and analyze them. The caption to one photograph reads: "This five-foot barracuda on the prowl was photographed over the cruiser side in crystal clear Bahama waters about 8 feet below the surface. A savage, fearless hunter and rightly called 'tiger of the sea,' it will attack and kill fish many times its size." Any fish "many times its size" would have to be, conservatively speaking, at least 15 feet long and several hundred pounds in weight. A barracuda swallows its prey whole; it does not tear pieces like a shark. Why would a barracuda endanger its life by singly attacking a huge fish? Just for the pleasure of mutilation? It is against the laws of nature. The caption is a stupid one which promotes a character not true of the barracuda.

Another photograph has a caption, "Behind this girl is the barracuda, whose teeth support its reputation for ferocity." This statement is an assumption. The barracuda's teeth are positioned for retention of prey, not for tearing and pulling, which might be termed a ferocious action. The king mackerel, *Scomberomorus cavalla*, has a much more effective shearing dentition with its cutting type of teeth positioned side by side; yet no one ever hears of a ferocious king mackerel.

Another: "They are savage when attacking their prey and can sever in two a fish much larger than themselves." This statement is so obviously ridiculous that it requires no comment. And another: "The muttonfish was bitten in two by a larger fish, probably a barracuda, after it was hooked by an ardent angler near Miami Beach." The photograph which this caption refers to shows a fisherman holding the fore part of an unusually large muttonfish. The hind part is gone. The section of fish portrayed has almost a perfect half circle edge where it was bitten. The bite is clean and the contour continuous, which indicates, most likely, one bite. The beast responsible for this action could not have been a barracuda but a shark and a big one at that!

These captions are just a few random examples of the kind of statement that fills the literature. The following will further demonstrate the embellishments of present-day authors whose books are widely read: "Any human within reach will be menaced by a large barracuda." "Bloodthirsty, swift-striking barracuda are responsible for many attacks on bathers attributed to

A Bermuda bonefish taken on artificial lure by Pete Perinchief of Warwick, Bermuda.

Top left: Pete Perinchief, well-known angler-photographer of Warwick, Bermuda, (right) and friend display a fly rod catch of pompano. *Top right:* Leo Martin of New York smiles by his 78½-pound wahoo. *Bottom left:* Joe Brooks, author and angler, takes a barracuda on light tackle. *Bottom right:* Eugene Mayer of Bermuda with his record 20¾-pound blackfin tuna taken on 15-pound test line.

sharks." "Wherever blood has been spilled, the thickly grouped, prowling barracuda gather at once." Man-eating tigers are gentle, inoffensive creatures compared with the monsters in these statements, which lack any basis of fact.

I have fished for barracuda in various places of the Atlantic, Pacific, and Indian Oceans, and in areas where they are noted for their abundance: the Bahama Islands, the coast of Florida, and the Florida Keys. I have caught many of all sizes, from docks, wading in shallows (where at times I could see barracuda in different spots around me), from small and large boats; I have taken them on trolled baits, spoons, and other artificials and a few on streamer flies. I have fished with many anglers, natives, and guides of many years experience. Many times I have watched barracuda cruising leisurely along the beautiful shallow beaches of Bermuda where people swim almost daily. To date I have not experienced, nor have I witnessed, any unusual incident associated with the barracuda. In all my travels where these fish abound I have not been able to track down a single instance of a barracuda attack on a human being.

Once my native Bahama assistant and guide (nicknamed Conchy because of his love for raw conch meat—as he cut it for bait, he would say, "piece for de hook and piece for me, hey boss?") lost his knife over the side while in the process of removing the meat out of a conch shell. He dove into 8 or 10 feet of water and retrieved the knife. As he came over the side he pointed to his ankle which showed several shallow but nasty lacerations with the blood slowly oozing down. He immediately said "cuda"—and so it was to everyone ashore, but I know he scraped his foot against a sharp coral, for I could see his activities through the clear water.

How then has all the false reputation of the barracuda been built up? In digging through the literature I have found bits of interesting writings which will throw some light on the subject. In the *Field Book of Giant Fishes* written by Norman and Fraser in 1937 the following is quoted:

"The Sieur de Rochefort, writing in his 'Natural History of the Antilles,' published in 1665, says: 'Among the monsters greedy and desirous of human flesh, which are found on the coast of the islands, the Becune is one of the most formidable. It is a fish which has the figure of the pike, and which grows to six or eight feet in length and has a girth in proportion. When it has perceived its prey, it launches itself in fury, like a bloodthirsty dog, at the men whom it has perceived in the water. Furthermore, it is able to carry away a part of that which it has been able to catch, and its teeth have so much venom that its smallest bite becomes mortal if one does not have resource at that very instant to some powerful remedy in order to abate and turn aside the force of the poison.' Writing in 1707, Sir Hans Sloane observes that 'it is very voracious, and feeds on Blacks, Dogs, and Horses, rather than on White Men, when it can come at them in the water.' Père Labat, in 1742, confirms this curious prejudice of the Barracuda against the flesh of the white man, and adds another surprising fact: 'But a thing rather surprising,' he writes, 'yet one which is however of public notoriety, is that these same fish more often attack an Englishman than a Frenchman, when they find them both together in the water.'"

The authors, Norman and Fraser, do not venture an opinion as to whether or not they consider the above simply hogwash. It is further amazing that Norman should repeat, in all seriousness, the same paragraphs in his *A History of Fishes* published in 1948. Norman and Fraser state, "In some parts of the world, and more especially in Florida, large barracudas are more feared by the natives than sharks ... they are ferocious to a degree ... they will not hesitate to attack bathers, and cannot be scared off by splashing the water as is generally the case with sharks." Where did the English authors obtain this information? Have they been in Florida? Did they possess irrefutable information? If they did, they would have said so, being scientists. I believe I know their source of information; let's go back a little further in the literature and check the following. In 1902 Jordan and Evermann (famous American ichthyologists) in *American Food and Game Fishes,* stated, "It is as fierce as a shark and is sometimes very dangerous to bathers." They do not illustrate this

Atlantic Barracudas

point as they do with many other instances in this same publication. Could they have been influenced by the earlier writers but with reservation reproduced a modified statement? In 1907 Jordan, in his *Fishes*, turned the sentence slightly to read, "and these are almost as dangerous to bathers as sharks would be"—but again no basis of truth for this statement, which was now used as a generalization by all writers, for Jordan was a great ichthyologist.

Any investigator who has the time and inclination, I am certain, can track down the successive authors who used Jordan's weak generalization and who have changed the sentence, adding a word here and there to fit their own needs, until the progressive reputation of the barracuda grew to its present state.

There are general statements also written here and there to the effect that a wound was inspected by a physician and identified as produced by a barracuda. I have friends who are excellent dentists, physicians, and surgeons but who haven't the foggiest idea of what a fish's dentition looks like. Therefore, I cannot accept a torn flesh wound, without other evidence that the culprit was a barracuda.

I am not making a dogmatic statement that it is impossible for a barracuda to injure a person. It is possible that by chance a 'cuda might make a swipe at a shiny object, a belt buckle or wrist band, but if such instances have occurred, they must be rare because the occasions unquestionably would have drawn much publicity. I would greatly appreciate receiving any information regarding an instance where a barracuda, definitely identified, has slashed or taken a hunk out of a person. Until then, I will consider the barracuda a sinister-looking fish, interesting because of its impressive dentition, which is there for the purpose of aiding in the capture of food—interesting, too, because of the folklore which surrounds it.

As a game fish the great barracuda is fun, especially when taken on light tackle and artificial lures. However, it belies its aggressive appearance by not putting up much of a show after being hooked; smaller fish may jump, but usually the larger ones make a run or two and then come dragging in. In the Bahamas the native guides I fished with never hesitated to take a barracuda home. A great many are eaten, so they must be good. I would suggest skinning them before cooking. I cannot venture a personal opinion on the barracuda's table qualities, for I have never eaten one.

Northern Barracuda (8b)
(*Sphyraena borealis*)

Guaguanche (8c)
(*Sphyraena guachancho*)

European Barracuda
(*Sphyraena sphyraena*)

These small Atlantic cousins of the great barracuda are not considered game fishes, but because most anglers believe they are the young of the big 'cuda, I include them with a few remarks. They all are of the same family SPHYRAENIDAE and of the same genus *Sphyraena*. In some areas close to shore they are abundant. For example, in the Florida Keys I have had excellent sport, cruising slowly in among the mangrove areas catching guaguanche on fly rod and spinning outfit using tiny lures. In the grassy areas they act similar to fresh water pickerel or pike.

These miniature barracudas are not defined clearly as to species. It appears that the European Barracuda, *Sphyraena sphyraena*, is present in some areas on our side of the Atlantic and may be in abundance in the Bahamas. Another species, *Sphyraena picudilla*, may be identical with the northern barracuda. In other words, there is a need for scientific investigation regarding this group. The northern barracuda is a small fish, about a foot in length, which may be found close to shore, where it is possible to take them with seines. Its regular distribution extends much farther north than that of the other species, which only occasionally stray into cooler waters. It ranges from about Cape Cod, Massachusetts, southward to North Carolina. Another species, generally considered to be *Sphyraena picudilla*, supposedly ranges from where the northern species stops and continues in distribution southward to Brazil. Here again more investigation is necessary, for it is suspected that both species may be identical.

In general coloration it is a silvery fish with a light greenish or olive back; no dark blotches are found on the body. The underside is white. It can be separated from the other barracudas by the following characteristics: no fleshy tip on its under jaw; pectoral does not extend to the origin of the dorsal fin; small maxilla (upper jawbone or lip) does not reach the front of the eye; scales are small and number 115 to 130 along the lateral line.

The guaguanche, also called sennet, is another small type of barracuda but it grows larger than the northern form, reaching a length of about 24 inches. Its range is strictly in warm waters—from Florida, Gulf of Mexico, to the West Indies. In form, coloration, and habits it is much the same as the others, and it feeds on smaller fishes. It is easily distinguished from the great barracuda by its smaller scales and the lateral line scale count which numbers about 120. Also, the pectorals extend back to a point in front of the dorsal fin and behind the origin of the pelvic fin (the pelvics are further back in the northern barracuda). The origin of the dorsal is behind the origin of the pelvic fins, and the end of the upper jawbone just reaches below the front of the eye.

PACIFIC BARRACUDAS

Pacific Barracuda (8d)

(*Sphyraena argentea*)

The Pacific barracuda is also called California barracuda, scoots, scooter, or snake and is the only member of the family SPHYRAENIDAE to be found in California waters. It is distributed from Alaska south to Cape San Lucas and into the Gulf of California. However, it is not common north of Point Conception, California. Similar in all general respects—body shape, type of fins, and mode of life—to the Atlantic barracudas, it can be differentiated from the Mexican barracuda by the following characteristics: no bars or stripes present; dorsal and ventral fins placed further back on body—the pectoral fin does not extend close to the dorsal and ventrals. It is a medium-size barracuda with a maximum length of about 44 inches and a weight of about 10 pounds.

Off the Mexican coast this fish is taken all year round, but along the California coast only in the warmer months. It arrives in schools about March, first appearing off San Diego, north to Orange, Los Angeles, and Santa Barbara. During the latter part of summer the Pacific barracuda may be found north of Point Conception. When cooler weather takes effect—about October —the barracuda seems to vanish; perhaps it retreats into deeper water.

Spawning reaches its height in May or June. Fish with ripe sex organs are caught close to shore; therefore, it may be assumed that the spawning activity takes place inshore near the kelp beds. The eggs are cast freely by the females and fertilized by the males. All Pacific barracudas reach sexual maturity in their third year, with some of the females and most males starting a year earlier.

It is not a great game fish; nonetheless it is considered desirable and is taken by sportsmen who fish from docks and boats and use live bait mostly. In southern California it is one of the leading sport fishes, and sometimes the sporting catch exceeds the commercial catch in total poundage. It is recognized as an important food fish.

Mexican Barracuda
(*Sphyraena ensis*)

The Mexican barracuda resembles closely the other members of its group in appearance and habits. It can be separated from the Pacific barracuda by the presence of dark bars along the sides of the body. Also, the tip of the pectoral fin extends to the ventral fins and reaches a point close to the dorsal fin. In size it averages about 3 pounds, and it is reported to reach much greater weights; however, there is some doubt concerning this report. The distribution of this species is always stated as being from Lower California and the Gulf of California to Panama. Also, it is reported as being a fairly good sporting fish. However, I have caught them on bait-casting tackle off the coast of Cabo Blanco, Peru. First, this adds an extension to its accepted range, and second, I found them not exciting to catch. Truthfully, I would not give this barracuda game fish rating.

AUSTRALIAN BARRACUDAS

In Australian waters the barracudas are known as sea pikes, and eight species are reported from the area, but only two seem to be worthy of attention by anglers. The Australian publications also possess the same erroneous contentions regarding the character of the barracuda which abounds in English and American publications (*see* Great Barracuda).

Shortfin Barracuda
(*Sphyraena novae-hollandiae*)

This barracuda, also called snook in South Australia and Western Australia, ranges along the southern half of the Australian coast. It is found in ocean waters and also about inshore estuaries. Its maximum length is about 3 feet. Sportsmen take it by trolling, and occasionally it is seen in the markets. There is a minimum length requirement in taking this fish; depending upon the area, it may be 9, 11, 12, or 14 inches.

Striped Barracuda
(*Sphyraena obtusata*)

The striped barracuda seems to be closely related to the Atlantic great barracuda. It is distributed widely in the Pacific, round the Australian coast, along the East Indies, and Japan. It is a large barracuda with a rod and reel record of 51 pounds which was taken off the Great Barrier Reef.

Chub

Bermuda Chub (16c)
(*Kyphosus sectatrix*)

The Bermuda chub, also known as white chub or rudderfish, is a member of the sea chub family KYPHOSIDAE. Nowhere along its range can it be termed very abundant. Most of its reputation as a game fish has come from Bermuda, where perhaps it dwells in its greatest numbers. To some extent it is plentiful in the Bahamas. Its known range, aside from Bermuda and the Bahamas, includes the western Atlantic from Cape Cod to Brazil. It is primarily a warm-water fish.

It is a rather deep, compressed fish with a mouth that looks much too small for its body; incisor teeth are more or less flattened. The tail is forked, and the small scales cover most of the head and are present on the second dorsal and anal fins in the adult. The dorsal fin is long and contiguous; dorsal spines, 11; dorsal rays, 12; anal, 3 spines, 11 rays. Pectoral fin is short, and the gill rakers on the lower limb of the first arch number 14 to 16. The body color is brownish, bluish, or steel gray. Horizontal yellow stripes are present along the body, and yellow lines and spots are present along the snout and gill cover. Edge

Chub

of the gill cover may be blackish. Fins are dusky or dark gray; pelvic and anal may be blackish. The chub is variable in color; a spotted phase, with white spots covering the entire body, may appear suddenly on the fish. It is a medium-size fish with a maximum length about 18 inches, but most chubs taken are much smaller—about 6 to 10 inches in length.

The Bermuda chub is mostly a scavenger, nipping its food off the corals and rocks—a type of area it generally inhabits. It also feeds on marine worms, shrimp, and small fishes. Because of its small mouth and short, strong teeth, the Bermuda chub easily strips a baited hook without getting caught. The use of small hooks and only bits of bait are necessary. Perhaps the reason that this chub appears to be rare in most areas is that anglers seldom use hooks small enough to take it with any regularity. On occasion it may take an artificial fly.

Bluefish

Bluefish (10d)
(*Pomatomus saltatrix*)

The bluefish is a superb game fish; it is swift, exceptionally strong, and renowned for its sporting qualities when taken on rod and reel. It is difficult to find a better fish for the table. Yet, in spite of these outstanding characteristics, there is one facet of its nature that draws even more attention. Anglers, writers, and commercial fishermen who are acquainted with the bluefish unanimously agree that it is a voracious, cannibalistic producer of blood-stained trails.

This fish is the only member of its family POMATOMIDAE. It appears that most American ichthyologists seem to favor classifying the bluefish family close to the jackfish family (CARANGIDAE). However, others prefer to group the bluefish with the sea bass tribe because of certain similarities in the skeleton structure.

The bluefish does not have as many common names as other game fishes possess. Yet, some confusion exists regarding these names. In most areas a bluefish of several inches in length is called snapper; it is the same species as the big blue. In certain spots along the shores of Rhode Island the small bluefish is known as skipjack. Anglers often use the term "tailor" for bluefish; this fish is supposed to fit (because of size) between the snapper and the big blue. Many times I have listened to sportsmen who informed me dogmatically that the tailor is a different species or that the tailor grows only to a certain size. On the other hand, in the Chesapeake Bay region the name "tailor" may be applied to a bluefish of any size. Depending upon locality, the tailor becomes a bluefish when it reaches a weight of between 1 and 2 pounds. In other words, snapper up to 1 pound; tailor up to 2 pounds; bluefish from there on. However, I believe it would be less confusing if the small bluefish, usually caught in localities close to shore, were called snapper bluefish and bluefish of larger size, from a pound on up, were referred to as bluefish. Forget the name "tailor." A Hatteras blue is a name used in the Cape Hatteras area to indicate fish of 5 pounds or more. Also, in this locality and along the shores of Virginia and Maryland small bluefish are sometimes referred to as summer blues. Incidentally, a Boston blue is not a bluefish at all; it is a term applied by commercial interests to pollock and sometimes other kinds in order to encourage the sale of species which appear less desirable as food fishes to the public. Snapping mackerel is an old name rarely, if ever, used along our shores. Bluefish, of all sizes, are tailor in Australian waters; it is believed that the name was given to this fish because when trapped in a net it can bite its way through the mesh as easily as if tailor's shears had done the job.

The bluefish is widely, but irregularly, distributed in the warmer seas. In the western Atlantic it ranges regularly from Cape Cod (occasionally to outer Nova Scotia as a stray) down to the Gulf of Mexico and southward to Brazil and Argentina. Off Bermuda it is a rare fish; on the eastern side of the Atlantic it inhabits the Mediterranean and the waters off northwestern and southern Africa. In the Pacific it is distributed along southern Australia and New Zealand. The known areas it inhabits in the western Indian Ocean are along Madagascar and southern Africa and also along the eastern Indian Ocean and off the Malay Peninsula.

The bluefish has a fairly long, stout body and a belly with flat sides, but with a blunt edge below. The nose is moderately pointed; the caudal peduncle is medium stout and contains no keels; the tail is deeply forked; the mouth is large with a projecting lower jaw and strong, more or less conical, canine teeth which are about a quarter inch long in a 10-pound fish. These efficient "choppers" are lined in a single series in both jaws. In general structure and arrangement of fins the bluefish closely resembles the jackfishes, with two dorsal fins; the first is spiny (7 or 8 spines) and depressible in a groove; the second is soft (about 23 to 26 rays). The anal fin (25 to 27 rays) is about the same size as the second dorsal and preceded by 2 very small detached spines that are often hidden in the skin. Pectoral and ventral fins are not large. Scales cover the body and most of the head; second dorsal and anal fins also have scales. The bluefish is not outstanding in coloration; the dorsal surface is iridescent greenish blue going lighter on the sides and silvery on the belly. The fins are mostly dusky or olive, with the ventrals often whitish.

The record rod and reel fish of 24 pounds 3 ounces was taken off San Miguel, Azores, on August 27, 1953, by M. A. da Silva Veloso. However, larger fish have been recorded; the heaviest American fish known by definite record was a specimen of 27 pounds, measuring 3 feet 9 inches, taken by handline in 1903 off Nantucket. One of the largest taken in recent years was caught off Montauk, New York, in August 1951; it weighed 20 pounds. Old timers talk about blues that were in the 30 to 50 pound class, but unfortunately none of these giant fish was ever recorded. A bluefish of 10 to 15 pounds is now considered large along the American coast, but 20 pounders are not rare off the African coast, where a huge specimen of 45 pounds was reported by Phil Mayer of New York City. Hal Lyman records one he saw, which was taken off the North African coast; it weighed "just under 22 pounds." Hal estimates the weight of another bluefish he saw there "pressed 30 pounds."

Bluefish fry from ¾ inch to 3 inches in length, which are often taken close to shore along the northern range, appear to

Bluefish

be of that season's spawning. These same fry probably are the ones that grow rapidly to reach from 4 to about 9 inches (snapper blues) by fall. Although not as yet proved, it appears plausible that by the following spring the fish in this group reach a length of 8 to 12 inches. The rate of growth of older bluefish is not known, and the age at which they mature sexually has not been discovered.

The approximate length-weight ratio is as follows:

Inches	Pounds
14	1
17	2
20–21	3
24	4
28–29	8
30	10–12

Bluefish inhabit inshore and close offshore waters mostly; they travel in schools, often in vast numbers, and in some areas appear to take part in extensive migrations. Their appearance and sudden disappearance depends a great deal upon the weather; they are warm season migrants only. Water with temperatures lower than 58° to 60° seldom contains bluefish. Bluefish first appear in North American offshore waters about like this: Florida (southern), mid-winter; Carolinas, March and April; Delaware, April; New Jersey, April and May; New York, April and May; Massachusetts (southern), late May.

These migrants, which appear to be en route to northern waters, perhaps break off from the main groups and form individual sections; then they head for waters closer to shore. The bluefish require approximately 30 days to work inshore where anglers can reach them. In other words, sportsmen should add about a month to the above schedule. Usually the snapper blues come inshore earlier than the bigger bluefish and appear in great numbers in and around harbors and mouths of rivers all along the coast from Delaware to Cape Cod.

Large schools of bluefish will often remain in a locality throughout the entire summer and early fall if the food is plentiful. Along the coast from the Carolinas northward the blues usually disappear by the first part of November. Off New England the greatest portion of fish start moving southward in the latter part of October. Nearly everywhere, north and south, the best bluefishing months are in September and October. Even in Florida waters most of the bluefish leave (we assume they travel into tropic waters); some fish are an exception and remain, mostly about the mouths of inlets. Every winter a few bluefish are caught on both coasts of Florida, southward from Cape Canaveral on the east, and southward from Tampa Bay on the west. Enough bluefish are taken near Key West between mid-December and mid-February to carry commercial activities in most years. Also, commercial fishermen around Cuba take fish in January and February. Most of the Florida blues, however, possibly the Cuban also, disappear at the end of winter.

It is certain that some bluefish along their northern range off our Atlantic coast travel south for the winter (a bluefish tagged off New York in August, 1936, was recaptured off Matanzas, Cuba, in January, 1939). Whether this tagged fish was a stray, and whether fish of this type ever again come north, is not known. However, it may be possible that the main groups of bluefish along the northern range do not go south, but instead may spend the winter months in the warm zone along the outer edge of the continent. Material for this trend of thought was supplied by a bluefish that was captured off Martha's Vineyard in mid-January in 1950 by the trawler "Eugene H." Also, hauls containing from 175 to 1,400 pounds of bluefish per trip were made in the area of Hudson Gorge by other trawlers early in February of the same year. In other words, bluefish may migrate inshore at the advent of warm weather and travel offshore when water temperatures drop to their dislike.

The possibility of an interchange of bluefish from the Atlantic coast with those of the African and Mediterranean groups seems highly improbable. Bluefish in these areas are plentiful at the same time (summer and fall), which is one fact against the possibility of transoceanic travel. South American bluefish, which are seldom more than 5 pounds in weight, are probably confined to the waters off the eastern shores of the continent.

Bluefish

Nothing is known concerning the migration of snapper blues. The available information only adds confusion to the picture. As far as can be noted, the snappers appear along shore after the first offshore arrival of adult bluefish and before the adults appear inshore. The snappers disperse widely in the shallow areas of bays and inlets, and it seems that they remain in the same area throughout the summer. Toward fall the snappers head for parts unknown. Sometimes they leave before the big blues depart; sometimes they go later. Often they seem to leave an area for the winter, then suddenly reappear several days later before disappearing for the year. The abundance or decline of the larger bluefish in any given season cannot be predicted by the scarcity or the profusion of snapper blues. Sometimes snappers will be about in tremendous runs, causing optimism among anglers, but the big fellows never appear. It works the other way too; there have been seasons when the snappers were almost entirely absent, and yet the big blues were roaming about in enormous schools.

As with other game fishes (striped bass, weakfish), the larger adult bluefish of 5 or 6 pounds or more will appear in coastal waters several weeks later than the smaller adult fishes of 2 to 4 pounds. Also, the biggest ones usually leave for the south a bit earlier than their smaller relatives. Just previous to their departure the big bluefish (also the big striped bass and weakfish) gather together into schools and feed voraciously in preparation for heading out into the unknown. Obviously, the best chances of angler success for the big ones is at this time.

No other game fish can match the bluefish in the amazing cycles of abundance and scarcity along its northern range off the eastern coast of the United States (only along the northern part of its range does the American bluefish periodically fall to a very low level). Theories for this phenomenon are a dime a dozen, but as yet none has been proved. These theories cannot be correlated with regular spacing of years or anything else known. Unquestionably there is a cause (or causes) responsible for fluctuations in the supply of bluefish from year to year. Perhaps when we get to know more of the life history of the bluefish, some clues to the situation may appear. On the other hand, the cycles may be produced by complex changes in water conditions which, perhaps, man can never influence.

The spawning activity of the bluefish is still practically unknown. Written material on this important part of the life history of this fish is meager. The published facts are these. Off North Carolina in the spring, and off other spots farther up the coast in summer, large females containing eggs approaching ripeness have been taken. In June and July ripe males have been caught inside Chesapeake Bay. From this information it can be deduced that bluefish spawn from late spring through July and August, depending on specific areas. Bluefish (previously) have never been reported spawning. A clue that the spawning grounds are not too far distant has been the fact that snapper blues are regularly present in numbers inshore; also, smaller fry have been captured in Chesapeake Bay and in the Gulf of Maine.

But, some new and exciting information concerning the matter has been brought to my attention by my friend Hal Lyman, publisher of the *Salt Water Sportsman* and author of *Bluefishing*. One evening during the International Tuna Match at Wedgeport, Nova Scotia, we were firmly settled in comfortable leather chairs by a roaring fire. It had been a cold and foggy day aboard the judges' boat so Hal and I were enjoying the warmth of the burning logs and a before-dinner drink. The discussion concerning tuna spawning led to bluefish. Hal's remarks on the possible spawning activities of bluefish were so interesting to me that the next day while bouncing about on the famed Soldier's Rip I stood by while he wrote the following:

"Three years ago I received a communication from Winslow Warren of Walpole, Massachusetts, concerning a remark I made in my book, *Bluefishing*, dealing with the fact that no one knew where the fish spawned nor anything else about the spawning habits. Warren claimed that he had seen spawning blues and, as a result, I have been following up on this since. Warren and a man named Whitehead fish from early July through the season in waters to the south of No Man's Land in Massachusetts, and

Bluefish

it is here that they found the spawning fish. In my own mind, there is no doubt that they are right. To prove that they are right is something else again.

"The southern edge of No Man's is typical of our coastal islands. High cliffs drop down to the water's edge. Over the centuries these have been eroded away so that now there is a shelf, varying in depth from about 4 feet to about 15, extending from the shore out to the drop-off. This drop-off is very abrupt and goes down to 40 feet at least in most places. The deep water and even the water over the shelf is characterized by swift currents and tide rips. It is also faced on the open sea with consequent heavy swells most of the years.

"Warren and Whitehead in the summer of 1955 saw many very large—up to 11 pounds—bluefish in the clear water over the shelf. These fish were extremely difficult to catch with rod and reel. Only a cast lure, using monofilament, would do the trick. The fish caught were, in mid-July, running with roe or milt. Both fishermen observed a number of times that one fish would swim slowly along, followed closely by one or two others. Every now and then the lead fish would roll on its side and the following fish would swim about rapidly. Since both men are highly intelligent there is no reason to doubt their observations. Both agreed that the fish appeared to be spawning. As the season progressed, their catches were made much more easily, but the blues were spent in most cases.

"In 1956, I went out with Win Warren and took some of the fish myself. I did not observe the fish in pairs or groups, but several of those we caught were almost ripe, both male and female. In addition, we made several plankton hauls in the area. Bill Schroeder of Woods Hole has the results of these plus an analysis of them. However, although we gathered many fish eggs, no one is able to identify them. We also gathered many fry with the yolk sac almost entirely absorbed. The fry that, to me, might well be bluefish were distinctive. Even in such a small creature the eyes were a very bright light blue. Agassiz mentions this in the fry that he presumed were those of bluefish. In addition, the dorsal fin was extraordinarily well formed. Since no one knows what either the egg or the fry of bluefish looks like, obviously positive identification could not be made.

"I made an additional trip with Charlie Wheeler to the same grounds and we tried to collect more specimens with the intent of getting ripe fish and hatching them under artificial conditions. We took some fish but all were either not ripe or else spent. Then a storm put an end to our operations. Incidentally, roe and milt specimens were preserved along with the plankton hauls and all are in the hands of Bill Schroeder at the Harvard Museum of Comparative Zoology. I feel that everything in this matter should be under one roof, and Bill is official custodian.

"This season the blues again showed up. Just at the time they appeared to be getting ripe *every* female roe sac was observed to contain a parasite worm of some sort. And we have not been able to find a single ripe female. The roe had apparently been rendered sterile and was being absorbed. Whether the worm has this effect, of course, is a question, but if it has, it might well be an explanation, at least in part, of the bluefish cycles of abundance and scarcity.

"In all this I am theorizing a great deal. There is no *proof* that bluefish spawn off No Man's; there are just a good many indications. So here is some more theorizing to support the idea. Exceptionally large bluefish appear in various areas early in the season. They are always hard to catch at this time and always contain well-developed roe or milt. To name a few of these points: Staten Island, New York; Diamond Shoals off North Carolina; Nantucket and Tuckernuck off Massachusetts. There are probably dozens more along the Atlantic seaboard. Note that each of these areas is characterized by a comparatively shallow area, dropping off sharply with strong currents and, in the localities where the big blues appear, open to the ocean. This may be pure coincidence, but I for one do not think so.

"One more item. This year for the first time in history big blues were taken well offshore in Virginia. Here again the area was at the edge of the drop-off. Here again the fish were almost ripe. Here again they were exceedingly difficult to catch.

"Obviously all of this is slender evidence all along the line. The only way we can be sure is to collect ripe males and females, hatch the eggs, and watch development. If the fry is the little blue-eyed darlin' I collected, the point is proved."

Snapper blues feed on small crustaceans and mollusks but mostly on any fishes smaller than themselves. An effective bait is a large piece of shrimp; however, I have found that when the shrimp is fished side by side with a minnow, the snappers most often choose the minnow first. Also, these little battlers seem to prefer a silverside to the darker killifish. Other methods which I especially enjoy using for snappers are casting a tiny, silvery spinning lure from a rock jetty where the water is swirling during the changing of the tides, or else I enjoy slowly trolling a white streamer fly with a fly rod during a warm sunny day.

The favorable spots for snapper blues (where anglers should look for them) are localities where rips are created by water action, at mouths of rivers, under bridges, around jetties, piers, breakwaters, and rocks. The snappers are attracted to these spots because the turmoil of water churns up food from the bottom (tiny invertebrate life) which attracts small fishes; in turn the snapper blues concentrate on these areas to gorge themselves on the abundant food supply. Often mouths of rivers are good spots because food is conveyed by the current and pushed into the bays. Sometimes quiet areas around docks and piers are productive for snapper angling because the minnow-like fishes, which snappers love to feed on, take shelter under these constructions.

The larger bluefish will feed on schools of mackerel, menhaden, herring, alewives, and other open-water fishes. They will also take weakfish, porgies, hake, butterfish, cunners, eels, and many other kinds of fishes—and at times small crabs, shrimp, and squid. The bluefish is well known for its ferociousness, and the term "bloodthirsty" seems to be correctly applied when referring to this "chopper." A school of bluefish at the height of hitting a mass of mackerel or menhaden is an astonishing sight. The blues are not satisfied with taking their fill and quitting; instead, they continue literally to chop up the victims to pieces and leave a wake of dead and torn fishes.

In a given area the feeding habits of bluefish vary a great deal. All anglers who have been ardently pursuing these fine game fish over a period of years admit, and so do I, that angling for bluefish is one of the most unpredictable kinds of fishing. A known fact, that the early arrivals in most areas feed close to the bottom, helps little because the fish are difficult to locate. As the season progresses the blues, for the most part, feed closer to or at the surface where they can be spotted—often by the bird life that feeds on the bits of fishes left by the blues. The birds that give the clue are gulls and terns which wheel, dip, and pick up bits of bait—but do not dive. (Birds will not dive into a chopping mass of bluefish.) If birds are diving for food, the fish under them, most likely, are not blues. The schools may be in one spot and then within minutes appear slashing a bait school a half mile away. Although present in a general area of several square miles, they may travel from one spot to another at incredible speed. The frustrated angler is usually more successful if he does not dash off in hot pursuit but simply keeps fishing with a hope that the fish will appear and remain a while in the area he is working.

More or less specific areas, which bluefish inhabit in the north, differ in type from those mostly frequented by bluefish in southern waters. Whereas rips and tidal currents attract bluefish in the north (because of an abundance of food in these spots), in Florida, for example, bluefish also frequent shallow, fairly still water. The reason for this is the lack of hiding places for bait schools along miles of sandy shores. Therefore, the voracious bluefish will often search for and follow bait fish right up to shore. However, if feeding conditions are as good outside, bluefish prefer deeper waters.

Although the habits of bluefish are unpredictable from year to year in any area, a general summary concerning the fish along the shores of the United States can be made.

Bluefish

Bluefishing in the Gulf of Mexico never reaches great heights; fish taken are caught incidentally by anglers fishing for other species. The blues rarely work close into shore along Texas, Louisiana, Mississippi, and Alabama. Commercial fishermen report blues in large schools in offshore waters, but anglers as yet have made no concentrated effort to reach them.

Some bluefish are found throughout the winter along Florida's Gulf Coast—from Tampa Bay south to the Everglades. They are also present in this region during the spring and fall runs. However, in this locality bluefishing is of minor importance. Along the Keys bluefish are scarce, while along the Florida east coast, from Lower Biscayne Bay to Cape Canaveral, wintering blues are present; also, they are in evidence during the spring and fall runs. The better-known spots north of Miami are Lake Worth (the lake itself), Lake Worth Inlet, Palm Beach, Jupiter Inlet, Saint Lucie Inlet, Fort Pierce Inlet, Sebastian Inlet. Some spots such as New Smyrna Beach and Coronado Beach north of Cape Canaveral hold bluefish but to a lesser extent than the areas previously named. When the spring and fall runs are in progress bluefish are taken in an area from Cape Canaveral to the mouth of the Saint Mary's River (Florida's northern border).

Bluefishing off Georgia's coast is not well known. First, not much angling effort takes place along this area, and second, the bountiful Gulf Stream wanders away a long distance from Georgia's shores. The few spots that do receive some play by sports fishermen are Cumberland Island beaches, Jekyll Island, Sea Island, Saint Simons Island, and the Sapelo Island area.

As with Georgia, no word of exceptional bluefishing ever comes from South Carolina, mostly because angling effort is lacking, and offshore waters are practically unexplored for game fishing. The known bluefish grounds are the islands and inlets of Beaufort County. Along the North Island and South Island areas in Georgetown some beach fishing for blues takes place.

Off Cape Fear, North Carolina, which projects into the ocean, an area known as Frying Pan Shoals is good for bluefishing. Commercial fishermen have known this fact for a long time, but only in recent years have anglers shown any real interest in the locality. The Gulf Stream is only about 25 miles distant from the Shoals and the water is clear—factors which are conducive to attracting game fishes. Directly north of Cape Fear the beaches of New Hanover County are productive surf casting areas for bluefish; also, anglers who fish from the unusually long piers in this area catch their share of blues. Further north the shore area from the New River Inlet to North Carolina's border at False Cape constitutes one of the most interesting and most productive fishing localities along the Atlantic seaboard. Included in this picturesque shore line are famous Cape Hatteras and Cape Lookout. Bluefish (channel bass and other game fishes also) are attracted to the area because it is composed of a profusion of islands, reefs, bays, inlets, and lagoons, which contain miles upon miles of protected salt and brackish waters. These sheltered areas are ideal locations for the production of all types of food which game fishes love. Other factors which contribute in drawing game fishes to the vicinity are underwater reefs (such as Diamond Shoals), which abound in the area, and the drop-off which occurs only a few miles out from the reefs—a sudden difference of depth from 40 to more than 300 fathoms. Unquestionably the coastal waters of North Carolina, especially the central sections, hold some of the most attractive grounds for bluefish to be found anywhere in the world.

Angling for bluefish in the Chesapeake Bay is considered to be best during August. Top spots in the area usually are the Southwest Middle Grounds, off the mouth of the Potomac River, and off Messick, York County—both in Virginia. Some good bluefish areas are also found outside the Bay, from Cape Charles northward. The better-known spots are Wachapreague Inlet, Assateague Island, and Chincoteague Island.

The Jack Spot, off the coast of Maryland, has developed into one of the most famous fishing areas along the Atlantic coast for white marlin, but angling for bluefish can be terrific, even if considered secondary to the white marlin in this area. (*See* section on White Marlin for more on the Jack Spot.)

Delaware Bay has never been good for bluefish; however, snapper blues are usually found in abundance on both the Delaware and Jersey shores of the Bay. The Atlantic expanse of the coast—from Delaware's southern border to Cape Henlopen—does have some good bluefishing in late spring and fall. A shoal area about 15 miles offshore called the Hump is one of the best spots; Bethany Beach, Indian River Inlet, and Rehoboth Beach are also well known.

The beaches along the many miles of New Jersey's Atlantic coast have long been known for good bluefishing. This coast is so well fished that good spots are everywhere; perhaps the outstanding ones over the years have proved to be off Beach Haven Inlet, off Barnegat Inlet, Ridges off Manasquan, Shrewsbury Rocks off Sea Bright, and the Mud Hole (which is a good distance offshore).

Pollution has ruined the bluefishing (as it has for other game fishes) outside of the Hudson River and New York Harbor. On the ocean side of Long Island some good bluefishing areas remain near beaches and inlets—Rockaway, Jones, Fire Island, Moriches, Shinnecock, and Montauk Point. The latter spot, which is one of the best, in recent years has been producing the largest bluefish of any coastal area. On the inside New York waters (Long Island Sound) fishing for snapper blues is still good, but not for the big blues. When bluefish are in the Sound they seem to prefer waters closer to Connecticut's shores. A good spot, in the Cerberus Shoal area, is located about half way between Montauk Harbor and Fisher's Island.

Surf casting for bluefish in Connecticut is practically non-existent; however, snapper bluefishing is the shore angler's greatest delight in the late summer and early fall; excellent fishing is found all along the shore. The bluefish area ranges from Sachem's Head to Rhode Island, and the proved spots are Faulkner's Island; Six Mile Reef, off Clinton; Bloody Grounds, south of the mouth of the Connecticut River; Plum Gut, be-

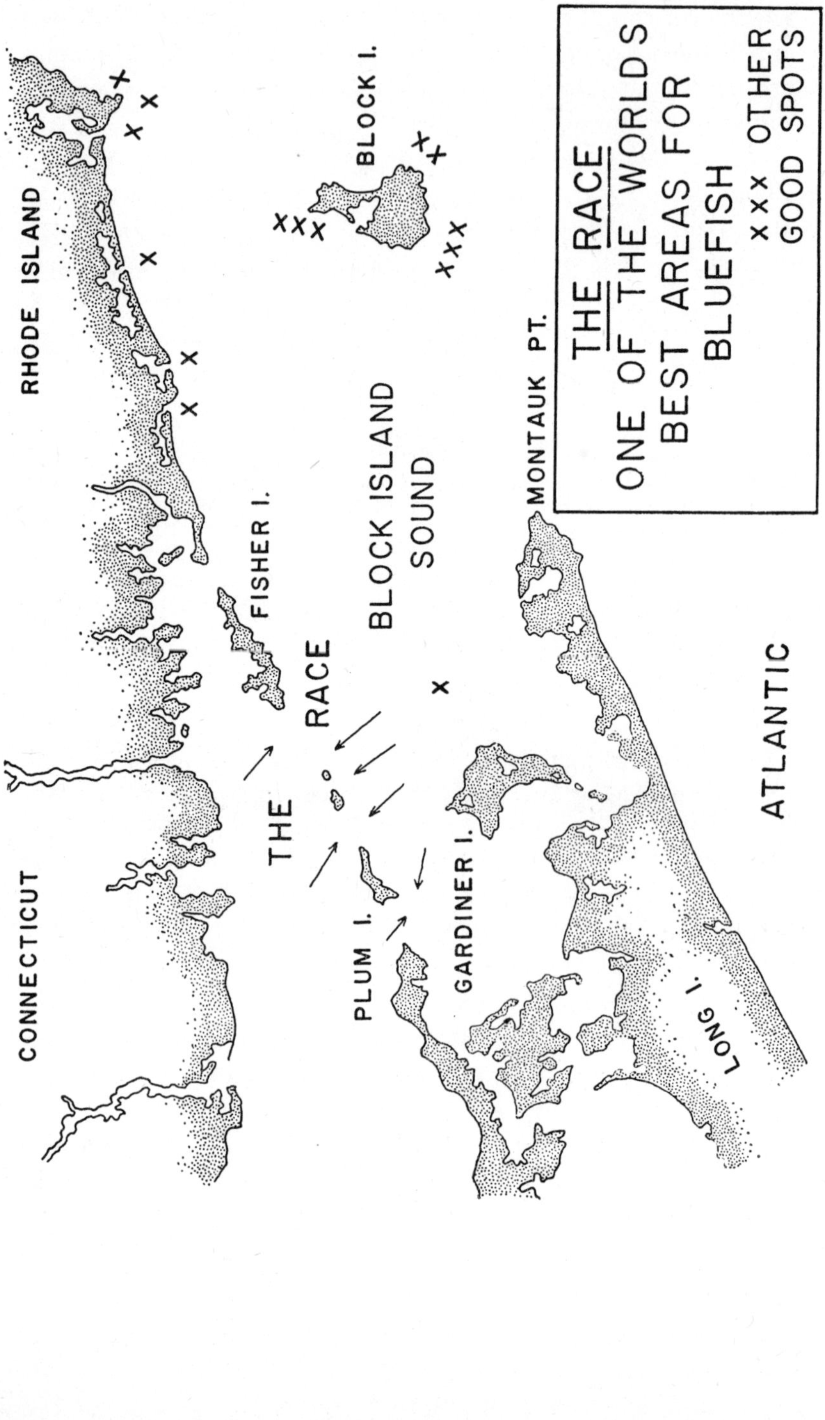
CONNECTICUT
RHODE ISLAND
THE RACE
FISHER I.
BLOCK I.
BLOCK ISLAND SOUND
PLUM I.
GARDINER I.
MONTAUK PT.
LONG I.
ATLANTIC
THE RACE
ONE OF THE WORLDS
BEST AREAS FOR
BLUEFISH
xxx OTHER
GOOD SPOTS

tween Plum Island and Orient Point, Long Island; and the Race, which is a rough body of water located between Gull Island and Fisher's Island, is the most famous spot of all. The bluefishing off the shores of Connecticut is often good enough to support a commercial fishery.

Perhaps with the abatement of pollution along the shores of Rhode Island the bluefish may return to the shore waters in abundance as they did in days gone by—especially in Narragansett Bay, where most of the small-boat fishing takes place. Favorite spots are off the inlets of Weekapaug, Quonochontaug, Charlestown, around Point Judith, the Narragansett area, Beavertail Point, Brenton Reef Rocks, and Sakonnet Point. Block Island can produce excellent bluefishing from early summer to late fall. However, it is a curious fact that in an area of such great fishing interest the angling for bluefish (and striped bass) is not fully exploited. My friend George Albrecht is one of the few experts who really work the area. He informs me that three great spots are located off the northern, southwestern, and southeastern ends of the Island; in other words, off the points of the more or less triangular-shaped island.

As far as the angler is concerned the Cape Cod Bay area is the northern end of the bluefish range along the Atlantic coast. However, in the waters of this state some of the best bluefishing takes places. The Massachusetts islands are famous fishing spots: No Man's Land, Martha's Vineyard, Chappaquiddick, Muskeget, Tuckernuck, and Nantucket (which is one of the best). Between Buzzard's Bay and Vineyard Sound lie the Elizabeth Islands, with famous Cuttyhunk at the southwestern end. Some of the largest fish recorded have come from this area. Blues come into Cape Cod Bay enroute through Buzzard's Bay, and from the outside around the northern tip of the Cape. The many islands, reefs, rips, and shoal waters in the areas mentioned make this part of Massachusetts as inviting to blues and other game fishes as are the wonderful localities along the shores of North Carolina. One of the most famous of all bluefishing areas is the Nantucket Sound rip, which is located in an expanse of water about ten miles across, between Great Point on Nantucket and Monomy Point on Monomy Island.

I advise any sportsman not fully acquainted with the various methods of angling for bluefish to read *Bluefishing* by Hal Lyman. However, through experience I would like to leave one piece of personal advice: always have your wits about you when disengaging hooks from a bluefish's mouth. The following incident happened when my brother Fritz, my father, and I were fishing for snapper blues. It was outside Faulkner's Island on a rather windy day in the latter part of summer when our favorite spot, where the waters created a rip, was rougher than usual. The little bluefish were in evidence all about us, and we had no trouble catching a pail full. Suddenly, a great commotion broke the surface at the edge of the rip, and within minutes the disturbance moved close enough for us to see bigger fish slashing into the snappers. Immediately we reeled in the shiners we were using for bait and replaced them with snapper blues from our pail. The excitement was great as we all hooked the bigger bluefish; they ran between one and a half and two pounds, with an occasional individual that went close to three pounds. Eight or nine fish were in the boat before the school disappeared. A few minutes later Pop took another of the bigger ones and was in the process of removing the hook when again the school appeared about a hundred yards away; the blues created a spectacular sight as they cut up snappers on the surface. We were watching the great sight when suddenly Pop let out a yell. The feeding blues had diverted his attention from the one he had in hand. The bluefish tore his index finger close to the first joint. The incident happened eighteen years ago, but Pop still claims that Fritz and I were more concerned about leaving while the fish were hitting than about bringing him in for surgical attention. Pop lost the forepart of his index finger of his right hand, but now he displays his shortened finger almost proudly wherever fishermen gather.

Bonefish

Bonefish (9c)
(*Albula vulpes*)

Unquestionably the silvery, wary, bottom-living bonefish ranks with the best of the world's game fishes. It is found in the clear, warm waters of tropical and subtropical seas and often feeds in shallow areas where sometimes schools are located in water but a few inches deep. Authors usually wax eloquent when writing about the sporting qualities of the bonefish. *Albula vulpes* (white fox) is well named because it is usually one of the most wary of fishes. It is in the family ALBULIDAE.

The bonefish has a world-wide distribution. In the Atlantic it has been recorded from Cape Cod, Massachusetts, down to Venezuela. However, any angler who seeks the bonefish will find it abundant enough only in the Florida Keys, the Bahamas, Bermuda, Cuba, and Puerto Rico. In the eastern Pacific it occurs from about San Pedro, California, to Panama. The Hawaiian Islands are noted for producing big ones, and bonefish are found on the other side of the Pacific—Japan and Australia.

The live bonefish presents a beautiful, shimmering, pearlescent coloration. Sometimes it may be completely silvery white;

at other times it may have a light greenish back and tints of light green or light blue along the sides, and a few widely scattered spots may be present on the body. Also, about 9 indistinct bars may be seen on the dorsal surface. The fins are usually translucent flesh color, light dusky or light gray. Without doubt the white fox rates as one of the fastest of game fishes, but yet the shape of its body belies its ability for fast propulsion through the water. It is a rather thickset fish, and the body is roundish in cross section. The head with its blunt nose, projecting upper jaw, and small mouth, which is directed for efficient feeding on the bottom, are typical characteristics of a more sluggish type of fish. The body is completely scaled. Bands of small teeth are present on the jaws, and patches of coarse teeth on the back of the tongue and roof of the mouth aid in crunching small shellfish. Dorsal fin contains 16 to 18 rays; anal has 8, and a large adipose eyelid is present in the adults.

Unusually large bonefish have been taken in Bermuda, Bahamas, and Hawaiian waters. The world record fish of 18 pounds 2 ounces was taken off Mana, Kauai, T. H., on October 14, 1954, by William Badua. However, the average size is 2 to 4 pounds.

Bonefish usually travel in schools or in small groups, but I have seen them dispersed in one's, two's, and three's in separate bays and coves. Not much is known concerning its life history. In the areas they inhabit they seem to be present the year round. Young bonefish resemble larval eels in having a small head and transparent body (leptocephali). Also, as with the eels, during development the body shrinks in length and gradually changes into a form which can be recognized as a tiny bonefish. After hatching, the fish move offshore with the currents and then spend their early life as open ocean planktonic forms, returning to the shallow water as juveniles.

As the anatomy of its jaws and mouth suggest, it is a bottom feeder. The prolonged, blunt snout aids in snubbing out food secured in the sand or mud: sand fleas, crabs, worms, mollusks. Most of its feeding is done in shallow water during the incoming tide and to a lesser extent during part of the ebb tide. Often it will appear in large groups in water so shallow that its dorsal fin and upper tail extend out of the water. Sometimes a portion of its tail can be seen as it grubs in the mud, nose down. Anglers call this activity mudding or tailing. Often darkened areas (muds), where bonefish have stirred up the bottom, can be spotted a good distance off—always a welcome sight to fishermen. It is at these times of feeding in shallow water that most bonefish are taken. However, an occasional fish may be picked up by blind casting into deeper water.

The bonefish has a reputation for being wary and extremely fast when hooked—and it well has to be, for its habits of feeding require it to be ever on the alert and prepared to beat a fast retreat at the slightest, unusual disturbance in the water. Undoubtedly these habits of extremely shallow water feeding and the necessity for hasty retreats are the factors in the evolution or development of the bonefish into one of our speediest game fishes despite its bottom-feeding habits.

The use of light tackle (in order to cast a small bait or tiny lure), plus the fact that most of the time a hooked bonefish can be watched as it zips along, adds a great deal to the charm of this type of angling. I have fished for bonefish in the Florida Keys, Bermuda, and the Bahamas; to me it is a most intriguing fish because the fisherman may choose a method of angling which ranges from the easy to the ridiculously difficult. The method of approach may be designated by the circumstances of the angler: his allotted time for fishing, his finances, his degree of proficiency with the type of tackle required.

Let's take the easiest way first. A competent guide is secured who knows the water where the fish are feeding, the tides, wind direction, and how to pole a boat in shallow water. Usually at low tide a skiff is taken to the fishing area, then the angler waits for the incoming tide. Bonefish will start cruising in; the fish can be detected by ripples in the water or by their protruding fins as they nose along. They may be attracted to an area within casting distance by chumming with pieces of conch meat or other fresh bait. The fisherman casts a baited hook into the group of feeding fish and waits for the gentle tug which indicates bonefish activity at the end of the line. If the angler can keep ahead of a mud, as the bonefish travel along feeding slowly, and if he operates quietly so as not to frighten the fish, it is possible to take several before the school is "spooked."

A less expensive method is for the angler to inquire from local inhabitants the whereabouts of sand bars and flats where bonefish are known to feed. Then he can wade slowly, and if fish are spotted working along, he can toss the bait ahead of their direction of travel and wait until the fish find it. A gentle twitch of the rod tip will move the bait slightly and assist in attracting the fish. The bait cannot be heaved close to the bonefish because most of the time in clear water the fish will zoom off at the slight disturbance even if the angler is out of sight and a long cast away.

A spinning outfit and light artificial lure, I believe, is the most satisfying method of taking the bonefish although it is not as productive as using bait. Tiny lures can be cast a long distance. The angler may cast into an area where fish are known to be, or he may cast a lure a respectable distance from a sighted fish. The lure is allowed to rest on the bottom and then is retrieved in a manner to simulate live food.

The fly rod method is the most exasperating. Regardless of how good an angler is with a rod, if he is honest I'm sure he will agree with me. Many thrilling stories concerning the capture of bonefish on fly rod and the accompanying photographs which usually appear in popular magazines are exaggerated or faked. In clear water, where it is possible to spot a bonefish, the fish is extremely cautious. If the angler is in the water up to his hips it is difficult to get out shooting line even if wind conditions are perfect (and it is also difficult to spot fish from that angle). If he is standing in a boat, unusually long casts have to be made, which again are difficult without false casting and frightening the fish. Also the heavy GAF or GBF torpedo head, fly-casting line stands out in clear water. Then the fly has to sink, usually to the bottom, before it can be twitched to imitate a small live bait. In most cases the capture of bonefish on true fly rod tackle is a matter of pure luck rather than a superior angling skill.

One of the most delightful days of fishing I have ever experienced occurred in Bermuda in quest of this elusive fish. Pete Perinchief, fishing expert and one of Bermuda's top anglers, introduced my wife, Bo, and me to an unusually pleasant method of hunting bonefish. We toured the island in Pete's station wagon from one lovely cove to another and walked along cliffs and beaches—all the while searching for the shadowy form of bonefish. And we found them—sometimes one, occasionally three or four in an area. First, we studied the cruising pattern of the bonefish; then, while we stood on a cliff well above, one of us would cast a spinning lure 60 or 80 feet ahead of the fish. As the shadowy figure approached the lure the rod tip was given action and the bonefish invariably showed enough interest to follow the lure as it was being retrieved. I was amazed when bonefish were often spooked by a tiny lure which was plunked many yards away. We had two strikes but caught no fish. However, during the course of the day, as we hunted from cove to cove, we stopped at attractive waterside inns for lunch and for tea, with a couple of swims at lovely beaches. The next time I have an allotted time for bonefish in Bermuda I'm going to call on my friend Pete, but in my kit I will carry some bait!

Cobia

Cobia (11c)

(Rachycentron canadus)

Contrary to its sluggish appearance the well-marked and, at times, voracious cobia is well worthy of its acceptance by anglers as a game fish. Cobia holds a spot on the official list of the International Game Fish Association. It is a member of the family RACHICENTRIDAE and probably has more common names than any other popular game fish. The scientific name is not questioned. The western Pacific form is labeled *Rachycentron pondicerianum*. However, cobia is recognized by many different common names depending on the locality: cabio, coalfish, crabeater, black bonito, lemonfish, ling, black salmon, sergeantfish, cubby yew, bacalao, and black kingfish.

It has a wide distribution although it is found mostly in tropical seas. In the western Atlantic it is known to range from New Jersey down to Brazil. (A stray fish may appear as far north as Massachusetts.) It is abundant in the Gulf of Mexico and the West Indies and is found as a rare visitor in Bermudian and Bahamian waters. Along the eastern Atlantic it is present off Cape Verde Islands, Senegal, and Guinea (northwest

Winslow Tuttle walks off with a 46-pound Connecticut striped bass.

Mrs. Laddie Sanford holds another big striped bass she took off Montauk Point, Long Island, New York.

Mrs. Robert Crandall with a striped bass which had enough poundage to earn her a place in the "Nifty Fifty" club. It was taken off Cuttyhunk, Massachusetts.

Mrs. George Albrecht stands by the 39-pound Charleston, Rhode Island, striped bass which rated her the I.G.F.A. women's record in the 20-pound line test category. Well-known angler George Albrecht is on right.

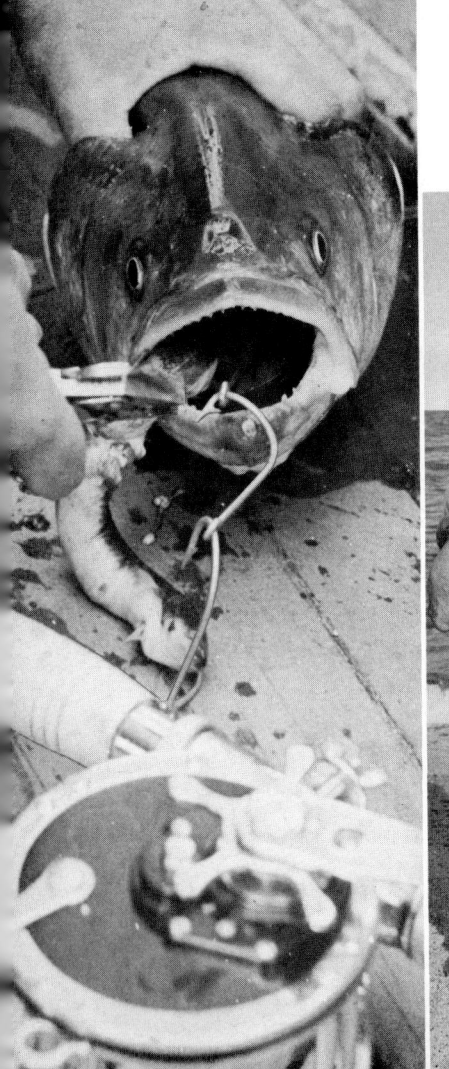

Above: A big bluefish taken on a Hopkins jig. *Left:* A bluefish taken by trolling with a rigged eel. Angler using pliers to remove hooks. *Below:* Joe Pol and Roger Fafard of Woonsocket, Rhode Island, with bluefish weighing 10½ to 17½ pounds, taken on surface plugs at Provincetown, Massachusetts.

Cobia

Africa). In the western Pacific the cobia is found in Australian waters northward to Japan.

In appearance cobia strongly resembles the remora or shark sucker; even in coloration they are more or less similar. In some respects both species have the same habits of lingering close to large floating objects and large fish such as sharks. It has a long fusiform body, long, low flat head, lunate or moderately forked tail (adults), breast fins, and long second dorsal and anal fins. The first dorsal consists of 8 low, stout spines which are unconnected by membrane and depressible in a groove. The scales are very small and the lateral line is wavy in the region of the pectoral fins. The second dorsal fin contains 26 soft rays and the anal, 23 to 26. Gill rakers below the angle of the first gill arch number 7 to 9. Young fish—up to about 4 inches—have a convex tail and use their pectoral fins for propulsion, but as the cobia grows older the pectorals become relatively fixed in position. In coloration the dorsal surface varies from light to dark brown, sides are silvery, and the belly is white. A dark lateral band or stripe extends from the snout to tail; below this a usually less distinct narrower band is present. Fins are mostly dark.

Cobia is a fairly large game fish averaging in size from 10 to 15 pounds. In some areas of the Gulf of Mexico specimens of 50 to 70 pounds are not rare. The Chesapeake Bay area also produces large fish. The rod and reel world record of 102 pounds was taken off Cape Charles, Virginia, on July 3, 1938, by J. E. Stansbury.

Anglers should have no trouble identifying cobia, for it is a rather unusual fish being mostly dark brown with dark stripes. Remora or shark sucker (the only fish cobia resembles closely) has a type of suction disc atop its head, and the cobia does not. (The suction disc is used as a device by which the remora may attach itself to other large fish.)

Practically nothing is known of its life history. Of its migrations we know little—only where it may appear in certain areas at certain times. In the lower Chesapeake it comes in about late June, and boat skippers specialize in cobia fishing (here it is called black bonito) during July and August. Along the Florida east coast it is taken mostly from early spring through summer and infrequently through the winter. In the waters of the Gulf of Mexico it seems to be in its greatest abundance (where most catches are usually made) during May, June, and July. Along Florida's west coast from about Romano Bay northward to about Tampa Bay cobia are in evidence the year round. Biloxi, Mississippi, Mobile, Alabama, and other Gulf ports send forth many party boats which favor cobia fishing from early spring through summer.

The cobia takes two types of food. It seeks crabs, crawfish, flounders, and eels close to or on bottom; shrimp and squid are favorite foods; and it will pursue fishes such as menhaden and occasionally a swift-swimming fish such as the Spanish mackerel.

Favorite spots for cobia are the vicinity of buoys, under barges, around breakwaters, pilings, and often around wreckage. They seem to be attracted to large floating objects in a manner similar to dolphin. Often they can be seen swimming leisurely around an area in more or less of a pattern. Although cobia prefer offshore waters I have taken them rather close to shore off Port Aransas, Texas. Here also I have seen them swimming in a regular pattern around a buoy when they ignored completely all our offerings—from live shrimp (with a bobber) to silvery spinning lures. On the other hand, they will often strike savagely at a trolled lure. George Rieger, cobia fisherman of long standing, finds good fishing off Louisiana. He has fished some schools where occasionally a fish would clear the water after being hooked. It is good eating prepared fresh, but some prefer it smoked.

Codfishes

Pollock, cod, tomcod, and haddock are cold-water fishes found mostly in northern parts of the Atlantic and Pacific. They are members of the family GADIDAE and as a group are referred to as codfishes. Commercially they are of great value but only of minor importance as sporting fishes. Truthfully, the only member of this group that should rate as a game fish is the pollock, which will take a lure trolled along the surface, at mid-depths, or close to the bottom. It fights well and is certainly a sporting fish. The cod is listed in the official I.G.F.A. records of game fishes; some anglers, however, question its rating as a game fish. Cod, tomcod, and haddock are often taken by sports fishermen, mostly by handline. They are fun to catch but do not present any resistance to being dragged out of their element. After a tug or two these bottom dwellers are hauled up like wet sacks.

Pollock (35d)

(Pollachius virens)

The pollock is an active, cold-water fish inhabiting both sides of the north Atlantic. It may be found at any level between bottom and surface, depending on season and food supply. It is gradually becoming a prized sport fish in many localities off our northeastern coast. It is a member of the family GADIDAE. Another common name often used is Boston bluefish. In Great Britain it is called coalfish or green cod. Along the North American continent it is distributed from the southeastern part of the Gulf of St. Lawrence and northeastern Nova Scotia southward to New Jersey. It seems to appear in greatest abundance in the Gulf of Maine and in some areas off Nova Scotia. Rarely is it taken south of Long Island and never below Chesapeake Bay.

It closely resembles its relatives in having 3 separate dorsal fins, 2 anal fins, and a pair of small ventrals located ahead of the origin of the pectoral fins. However, it can be differentiated easily from the cod, tomcod, and haddock. It has a forked tail with sharp corners, a pointed snout, and a pale lateral line. A small chin barbel may be absent in large specimens. Other characteristics are a plump body, slender caudal peduncle, a mouth of moderate size, and a projecting lower jaw. The first dorsal fin contains 13 or 14 rays; second dorsal, 21 or 22 rays; third dorsal, 19 or 20 rays. First anal fin has 24 to 28 rays, and the second has 20 or 21 rays. In coloration pollock are olive, dark brown, or greenish brown, going paler on the sides to gray or yellowish, with a silvery gray belly. Young fish are darker than the older ones.

The record rod and reel fish weighed 36 pounds and was taken off Montauk, New York, by William E. Davis on May 28, 1957. Not many exceed 30 pounds; 15 to 20 pounders are common, but the average fish is from about 4 to 8 pounds. A pollock 24 inches in length will weigh about 4 to 5 pounds; 30 inches, 8 to 9 pounds; 35 inches, 14 to 21 pounds; 40 inches, 25 to 35 pounds. Weights of large fish of a given length vary greatly depending upon the condition of the fish.

Pollock spawn in late fall and early winter, usually between November and January. The eggs are buoyant and are laid in water from 150 to 300 feet deep. About 225,000 eggs are produced by an average female. However, more than 4,000,000 eggs were reported in one fish of 23½ pounds. Incubation takes about 9 days at temperatures of approximately 43°; 6 days at 49°.

Fish hatched in midwinter are about 1 to 2 inches long the following spring and reach 3 to 5 inches in the summer. The approximate age-length ratios are these:

Age	Length in Inches
1	5– 7
2	12–13
3	17–18
4	21–22
5½	25
6½	27
7½	28
8½	29
9½	30

It is known that pollock reach an age of at least 19 years. Pollock seem to feed mostly on small fishes and free-swimming, shrimp-like crustaceans; they destroy great quantities of small herring, young cod, young haddock, young hake, and other small fishes. Undoubtedly the pollock can be termed a voracious fish, for a 9-inch specimen is capable of gulping 77 herring up to 2½ inches in length for one meal!

Seldom, if ever, are large pollock caught on the surface when the temperature is higher than 52° F. Yet, they may be plentiful a few fathoms deeper, where the water is cooler. This should be a clue for anglers who prefer trolling for their sport. Small fish of 8 or 9 inches—called harbor pollock—don't appear in numbers where the water is warmer than about 60° F. On the other hand, pollock of all sizes will take temperatures as low as 32° F. Spawning takes place when water temperatures drop to about 47° to 49°. These facts show that water temperatures play a major role in influencing many factors in the life history of fishes, including distributional barriers.

It is amazing that the pollock resembles the cod and haddock so closely and yet differs so widely when taken on rod and reel.

Just one trip to a pollock fishing area will convince any angler that pollock are capable of a high rating as a sporting fish. My most memorable day of pollock fishing occurred off Wedgeport, Nova Scotia, during the second day of our annual Intercollegiate Game Fish Match and Seminar sponsored by Yale University. We were coaxed away from the bluefin tuna fishing for a while by the exciting sight of hundreds of screaming and wheeling gulls and terns as they dipped to pick up small pieces of silvery fish. Enormous groups of frenzied pollock were crashing huge schools of bait fishes on the surface. Bob Crandall of Ashaway, Rhode Island, and I, as judges of the match, decided to include the pollock for scoring in the competition for the huge Hulman trophy. We limited the four competitive boats to an hour and a half of fishing. Just two rods per boat were permitted to fish at one time. The students used feather jigs trolled on the surface or spoons a few feet down. It was a grand sight to see one boat and then another in the midst of acres of pollock which thrashed the surface almost to a froth. The boys yelled and whooped while their light tackle was strained almost to breaking point. The Nova Scotian captains were forced to slow down their boats to practically a standstill so that the anglers could be in a position to fight the fish.

After Bob and I weighed the pollock at the dock and my wife tabulated the scores, we were more than surprised that 860 pounds of big pollock were taken in such a short time. I feel that in Nova Scotia, especially off Wedgeport, an untapped resource remains which has the potential of being a great attraction for tourist anglers who prefer the less expensive type of ocean fishing. Fishing for pollock can be very interesting sport.

Because of that great pollock day off Wedgeport, I developed an interest in this fish. While Charlie Gage, Jim Babb, and I were en route to Canada for some salmon fishing, I made a point of asking questions concerning the pollock everywhere we stopped along the coast, especially in Maine, where all salt water anglers are acquainted with this fish. The consensus of opinion was, "We like to catch pollock, but nobody eats them, and we never will." This attitude about the table quality of the pollock aroused my curiosity, for my opinion is that, although coarser than the highly prized cod, it certainly is just as tasty.

It was during the last International Tuna Cup Match at Wedgeport that I became convinced that many anglers are passing up some good eating. For me one of the highlights of the match is to have a fish-chowder lunch aboard the judges boat. During a lull in activity a line is dropped over the side, and the first cod or haddock is immediately cut up for the pot. On a cold, foggy day on the Rip a hot, fresh chowder is an extraordinary delight. One day I asked Bob Crandall, José Martin, and the other officials my stock question pertaining to the pollock and its eating qualities. Their opinions were the same as those of Maine anglers. Among our catch the next day we had several pollock. The captain and I managed to substitute pollock for cod or haddock in the chowder while the attention of those aboard was diverted. As usual, everyone raved over the chowder, but it was pollock they were eating. We informed them of the substitution after the chowder was finished. I saved the unused cod and haddock to prove it to the doubtful judges.

Incidentally, to make a delicious chowder with a minimum of fuss we do it this way aboard the Nova Scotian fishing boats: Slice some onions and drop them into a large pot where a chunk of butter is sizzling. Wait until onions are brown; then add water. When it boils, cut up a few potatoes and throw them in. When they are about done, add the fish which has been cleaned and skinned. Drop the whole fish into the pot if it fits; otherwise, cut it in two. You will know the chowder is done when the flesh can be removed easily from the bones. Remove the bones and break up the large chunks of fish into bite size portions, add salt and pepper, and stir for a minute or two.

Cod (35a)
(*Gadus callarias*)

The cod is not a game fish, but so many boats go in search of this fish during the off season that a few words concerning it will not be amiss here. It is one of the most important commercial fishes distributed on both sides of the North Atlantic. Along the eastern coast of North America it is found from Greenland and the Hudson Straits south to North Carolina. However, it is not common in the southern part of its range. From New England northward it is abundant. Adults may be present occasionally near the surface when chasing small fishes, but usually they are taken in deep water—normally about sixty feet in the summer. During their first year young cod may live in shallow water, and adults may come into shallow areas during winter.

In other words, they are cold-water fishes which may range from the surface down to at least 250 fathoms. The cod has 3 dorsal fins, 2 anal fins, small pectorals, a square tail, and a barbel on its chin. Other characteristics of the cod are a light colored lateral line and spots over the top and the sides of the body.

Cods may grow to tremendous size. A 211¼-pound fish that was over 6 feet long was taken on longline off Massachusetts in May 1895. Another huge one which weighed 138 pounds dressed (about 180 pounds otherwise) was caught on Georges Bank in 1838. Other specimens of 100 to 160 pounds have been recorded as taken off Massachusetts. However, cod approaching 100 pounds are unusual. One of the largest New England cod in recent years weighed 90 pounds and was taken off the coast of Maine in July 1922. Any weight over 50 to 60 pounds is now rare. Big fish are now considered as about 25 to 35 pounds. Shore fish average between 6 and 12 pounds. Any fish of 5½ to 6 feet will weigh 100 pounds or more. The largest one caught on rod and reel weighed 57 pounds 8 ounces

Cod

and was taken off Ambrose Light, New York, on December 24, 1949, by J. Rzeszewicz.

Roughly the approximate length-weight relationship is as follows:

Inches	Pounds
20	3
25	6
30	9
35	17
40	23
45	32
50	45
55	55

Although some populations of cod appear to be more or less sedentary, most take part in extensive migrations. It is only during the autumn, winter, and early spring that cod are caught off the coasts of southern New England, New York, New Jersey, or farther south. The fish that winter along this southwesterly extension of the cod's geographic range appear off southern Massachusetts in mid-October, off western Long Island and off the coast of New Jersey in November. With the coming of warm weather they head back eastward again in the first part of May.

It is well known that the cod is a prolific fish; a female about 40 inches long may produce 3,000,000 to 4,000,000 eggs annually. Larger fish lay more eggs: a 50-pound fish over 8,000,000 eggs, while a specimen of 75 pounds will produce well over 9,000,000. The eggs are buoyant and float freely. Along the western Atlantic a one-year-old fish is about 6 to 8 inches in length; three years about 20 inches; five years about 30 inches; and seven years about 36 inches.

The cod lives and eats predominantly along the bottom. Mollusks, crabs, lobsters, sea cucumbers, blood worms, squid, and small fishes are its main items of diet. The great value of the cod commercially is so well known that I need not dwell upon it here.

Tomcod (35b)
(Microgadus tomcod)

Haddock (35c)
(Melanogrammus aeglefinus)

The tomcod and haddock are closely related to the codfish. They are not considered game fishes, although taken by hand-line fishermen. Both are delicious on the table and commercially important. These fishes are of interest to the angler only because they so closely resemble the pollock and cod. Many sportsmen cannot distinguish the codfishes. Separation of the tomcod and haddock from the codfish and pollock is quite simple. The haddock is the only member of the group which possesses a conspicuous black lateral line plus a dark spot in the region of the pectoral fin. The tomcod is the only member of the group that has dark markings or mottlings along the dorsal surface and on the fins.

Cottids

Cabezone

(Scorpaenichthys marmoratus)

The cabezone is a Pacific member of the large family COTTIDAE, which are found in profusion in the Atlantic and Pacific. Although many kinds are taken incidentally by anglers, this group cannot be termed game fishes. The cabezone is the only member of the tribe which is important commercially (California). The cabezone is included here because it reaches a length of about 30 inches and a weight of 20 to 25 pounds, which makes it a fish welcomed by sportsmen. Most of the other cottids (also called sculpins) are small fishes.

Because of its large head the cabezone is also called *bullhead*. The body is robust and without scales, and the skin has a wrinkled appearance. The dorsal fin has 11 spines and 18 rays; anal fin has thick soft rays but no spines; a stout spine is present in front of the eye; pectoral fin is large; tail slightly convex; a fleshy flap is present on the middle of the snout, and a pair of longer ones back of the eyes. The mouth is broad and contains many small sharp teeth. Color is extremely variable—dark brown, reddish or greenish above, lighter below, and turquoise, green, or white on the belly; body mottled or blotched with darker and paler shades. The flesh and lining of mouth are a translucent turquoise green.

Croakers

The croakers comprise a group of diversified fishes—weakfishes, croakers, drums, whitings—found primarily along sandy shores in warm seas. Some are inhabitants of reefs while others are almost entirely oceanic; a few species are found in fresh water. About 150 species make up the family SCIAENIDAE, but comparatively few are of interest to anglers. They range from small reef fishes to types that migrate fairly long distances and grow to large size. All are fine table fishes, and many are of considerable economic importance. Several representatives of this group rank with the elite of our smaller game fishes, especially in the opinion of surf and shore fishermen.

Several outstanding characteristics separate the sciaenids into a distinct group. They are easily identified by the lateral line which follows along the body onto the tail and extends to its edge, and by having not more than 2 spines in the anal fin. The spinous and soft rayed dorsal fins are not widely separated; in some species they are attached and appear as one. Another outstanding characteristic is internal—a peculiar specialization of the air bladder which is capable of being operated as a resonating chamber for sound production. (The rather loud drumming sounds are produced by rapid contractions of certain abdominal muscles against the gas-filled air bladder.) From the croaking sounds which most of these fishes emit when caught comes the name "croaker." A few species lack the swim bladder and are voiceless.

WEAKFISHES

Along the Atlantic shores of the United States the weakfish and the spotted weakfish are two of the most popular of all small game fishes that come into shore areas. In the waters of the eastern Pacific, from southern California to Peru, at least 15 different species of the genus *Cynoscion* are found. They closely resemble and possess characteristics of their Atlantic relatives.

Along the coast of southern California the white sea bass is the only member of the clan worthy of mention as a game fish. Most of the others are found in greatest abundance in Mexican waters and southward. The totuava is a giant weakfish that interests sportsmen because of its size. Undoubtedly, if the angling effort were greater in the undeveloped areas of Mexico and Central America, some of the other species would be as popular with anglers as the Atlantic weakfish. However, at present they are not important from a sporting viewpoint, but some are worth listing.

All weakfishes have more or less the same basic coloration: dorsal surface may be grayish, bluish purple, bronzy, or olive; sides are silvery burnished with metallic iridescence; fins usually liberally colored with yellow or orange; underside is white.

Weakfish (17a)

(*Cynoscion regalis*)

The weakfish is the most economically important member of the entire croaker family SCIAENIDAE of the United States. It is a great favorite with sports fishermen all along the Atlantic seaboard, and it is an important commercial species along the middle Atlantic States. It is known by several common names:

Weakfishes

gray trout, squeteague, sea trout, yellow fin. By far the most popular name is weakfish. When taken by rod and reel the hook pulls through the fish's "weak" jaws if the angler does not use a landing net; hence the name. The principal range of the weakfish is confined to the western north Atlantic from Massachusetts to the east coast of Florida, with the peak of abundance along the Chesapeake to New York area.

The weakfish is attractively colored with a dorsal surface of dark olive-green or dark greenish blue. The back and sides are burnished with purple, blue, green, gold, or copper. The many small spots flow together, more or less, and form irregular lines which run downward and forward. These vaguely outlined spots may be black, dark green, or bronze. The underside is white and often has a spray of yellow orange. The dorsal fins are dusky, usually tinged with yellow. The tail is dusky or greenish with the lower edge of its base yellowish. Ventrals and anal are yellow; pectorals may be light greenish yellow or light yellow.

The slim, shapely body, stout caudal peduncle, and fairly broad, slightly concave tail give it the superficial appearance of a trout. The scales are thin and extend onto the head and cheeks. Reduced scales are present on portions of the fins. The face is long and smooth; there is no sharp spine on the preoperculum. The mouth is large. The upper jaw holds 2 enlarged recurved teeth and the lower jaw protrudes. In adults the first dorsal fin with 10 spines is close (but not attached) to the long second dorsal, which contains 26 to 29 rays. The anal fin is short with 2 slender spines and 11 or 12 rays. The long gill rakers number 11 to 13 on the lower limb of the first arch. The number of vertebrae is 25. The ventrals are located below the pectorals. The female makes no sound, but the male is capable of producing a drumming voice by well-developed abdominal muscles which work against the air bladder. These muscles are lacking in the female. In adults the male's thickened abdominal walls can be felt.

The world record rod and reel fish weighed 17 pounds 8 ounces and was caught at Mullica River, New Jersey, on September 30, 1944, by A. Weisbecker, Jr. However, fish over 12 pounds are rare, and the average range from about ½ to 4 pounds. I have found, by weighing weakfish at a dock on the Connecticut shore, that anglers tend to overestimate the weight of these fishes. Often a flatly stated "4 pounds" proved to be exactly half that weight. Females usually are larger than the males in a given school.

Scientists Henry Bigelow and William Schroeder produced the following table which can be a guide to anglers possessing a measure but no scale.

Inches	Pounds
12 –14	⅔– 1
14 –16	1 – 1½
16 –18	1¼– 1¾
18 –20	1⅝– 2½
22 –23½	3½– 4⅓
25½–27½	5 – 6
30 –32	9½–11

Along the southern part of its range, the Carolinas, the weakfish is a resident species, but in its northern distribution its appearance is strictly seasonal. In the mouth of the Chesapeake Bay area the season usually starts from the middle of April and continues to the middle of November. Sometimes good catches are made in December. It appears in the New York–Connecticut area in spring, spends the summer inshore, and then withdraws into deeper waters at the beginning of cold weather; the average time, depending on weather conditions, is from May to middle of October. Occasionally good catches are made later. Fishing activity takes a sharp drop with the advent of cool weather. In years when it comes as far north as Cape Cod it appears about June and remains till about September. The weakfish is known to be a fish sensitive to cold, and chilling waters undoubtedly send them away from the middle Atlantic and New England coasts in autumn.

It now appears that the New York–southern New England areas are populated by two groups of weakfishes. The native fish, which spawn during spring in the area, migrate offshore into deeper water when cold weather arrives. The evidence of this offshore rather than southward migration has been suggested by the capture of weakfish in the deep waters between Chesapeake Bay and Cape Hatteras during the winter months in the past 20 or more years. Draggers have picked up small fish in 50 to 55 fathoms of water off Rhode Island during January and February. Although evidence seems to indicate that the weakfish which summer in northern shore waters move into deep water to escape the winter, there is another group of weakfish which come up from southern waters. The following abstract appeared in a scientific paper by A. Perlmutter, W. Miller, and J. Poole which summarizes the subject:

"A reported scarcity of weakfish in New York waters led to the initiation of a study of this species by the New York State Conservation Department in 1952. Based on data collected both by Nesbit in the early 1930's and by the present investigators, it was found that the resource of weakfish available to New York fishermen consists of both locally-spawned and southern-spawned fish. Weakfish are abundant in New York waters only when the southern-spawned stock is large. In recent years this stock has been smaller than ever before in the history of fishery, and the New York fishery has depended mostly on locally spawned fish. For New York to enjoy once more the abundant weakfish supply of the 1920's would necessitate an increase in the stock of southern-spawned fish. The feasibility of increasing this stock can only be determined through cooperative study by the conservation agencies of those states whose waters contribute, in important measures, to the weakfish resource."

Weakfish are schooling in habit and love shallow, sandy shore waters including bays and salt marsh creeks during the summer stay along their northern range. They run into river mouths but not into fresh water. Schooling movement is demonstrated when a group of anglers in one area will suddenly get strikes and fast action; then a lapse of time will take place until another school swims by. Weakfish may be found on the bottom, close to the surface, or in between, depending on where the food is found.

Spawning takes place from May to October along the middle Atlantic coast, with the greatest production of eggs between mid-May and mid-June. Males and females mature at 2 to 3 years of age when about 10 to 13 inches long. Eggs have been taken in tow nets in different localities where water temperatures ranged from 60° to 70° F. The spawning activity takes place usually at night in large estuaries or close to mouths of rivers. The eggs are buoyant and incubation takes 36 to 40 hours at a temperature of 68° to 70° F.

During their first summer weakfish fry grow at such a variable rate that they may be anywhere from 4 to 6 inches in length in the fall at about 6 months of age.

It appears that weakfish grow at about the following rate:

Inches	Years
8–10	1
10–12	2
13	3
15	4–5
18	5–6
22	6–7
24	9
30	12

Weakfish feed chiefly on silversides, anchovies, killifishes, herring, butterfish, menhaden, scup, and other small fishes. Shrimp and worms are favorites, and crabs, squid, and mollusks are also taken. The items of diet, of course, depend on what is available in the vicinity. Small menhaden seem to be the most general important single item of diet.

Along the southern New England coast a vast number of salt water anglers eagerly await the first word of the arrival of the weaks. It is as popular a game fish with bridge fishermen and row boat enthusiasts as it is with owners of larger craft and charter boat fishermen. On any spring weekend along the Connecticut coastline, where I do most of my fishing for weaks, a raft of boats of all types can be seen in favorite spots along shore—mostly near mouths of rivers where, on the changing tides, rips are created by fast-moving waters. Sometimes we get best results fishing a worm close to, on, or about two feet off the bottom, or they may be hitting best just under the surface where a float keeps the bait at the desired depth. The advent of spinning gear has greatly enhanced the pleasure of fishing for weakfish, and if an angler does not mind taking less fish than the bait fisherman, he can have some pleasurable fishing by using small artificials. Usually in the early season most of the fish close to shore (and often in surprisingly shallow water) run about 8 to 10 inches in length and are year-old fish. Most of the older fish, which are usually caught farther offshore (good spots are found where the tide rips around rocks and islands), are ripe at this time.

My wife and I enjoy fishing for weakfish because we like to make up picnic-like fishing parties, usually consisting of from two to four couples. It is great fun to be well supplied with food and beer and to take time out for a picnic on the lee side of a huge rock or small island. A friendly pool on the largest or most fish adds to the enjoyment.

Many of my fishing friends who previously held no interest in the weakfish as a table fish have changed their minds. Bo and I take a pail of ice along, and when a fish is boated, we throw it into the pail. As soon as there is a lull in strikes I clean the fish. When we arrive home the fish are still firm. I know of no other species that gets softer and loses flavor faster than the weakfish. However, the quick ice method sustains firm flesh and produces a delicacy. Another tip, if you catch a good string and wish to replenish the fish compartment of your freezer with future good eating, is to do it this way: skin the fish (weakfish are a bit more difficult to skin than other fish so a sharp knife helps), then dip it for 15 to 20 seconds in a solution containing 4 fluid ounces of concentrated lemon juice per gallon of water. Allow the excess to drain off before wrapping. It is not necessary to skin the fish; scale it instead—although I prefer to skin all types of fishes before cooking. If you do not intend to freeze the fish, it may be dipped in a slightly weaker solution of 3 fluid ounces of concentrated lemon juice in a gallon of water. Plan it with your favorite vegetables plus a split baked yam into which a hot sauce of butter, wine, and brown sugar has been mixed. Sip a glass of white wine and you have a meal fit for a king!

Spotted Weakfish (17b)
(*Cynoscion nebulosus*)

Along the coastal waters of the Chesapeake Bay area, the southeastern states, and the Gulf of Mexico, the spotted weakfish is an important food and game fish. Like the weakfish, *Cynoscion regalis,* its cousin of more northern waters, it is a great favorite with shore fishermen and especially popular with anglers who love to wade and fish along sandy shores. It has several conflicting common names; the most often used are sea trout, spotted sea trout, spotted squeteague, spotted trout, speckled trout, and speckles or specs. Of course the weakfishes are not trout at all, but members of the croaker family SCIAENIDAE; therefore, any common name which includes "trout" is inappropriate. True trout, the brook and brown trouts, move to and from salt water and are called sea trout along the southern New England shores. Most popular books on fishes give the range of this fish as from New York south to Texas or to the Mexican border. However, the spotted weakfish is a warm-water species and is not often found north of the lower Chesapeake Bay; I can vouch for its being farther south than the Mexican border, for I have taken a great many on rod and reel down along the Mexican coast.

In its general shape and fin arrangement it is similar to the weakfish (which see). In superficial appearance it differs by having distinct roundish black spots on the upper body which are not aligned as in the weakfish. Also, the spots are present on the soft dorsal and tail. Another point of differentiation is the absence of scales along the base of the soft dorsal and anal fins. Gill rakers are comparatively short—8 on lower limb of first arch. In coloration the dorsal surface is basically grayish with the same sort of dorsal coloration of burnished blues and purples as the weakfish, sides are silvery, and underside is white. Fins are principally light greenish yellow.

The spotted weakfish I have caught along the Mexican coast were on the average much larger than the weakfish I have taken off Connecticut shores, but the rod and reel record of the former is less than that of the latter by 2 pounds 5 ounces. The record fish weighed 15 pounds 3 ounces and was taken off Ft. Pierce, Florida, on January 13, 1949, by C. W. Hubbard. Fish up to 8 or 10 pounds are not unusual, and I have seen some specimens taken in nets by Mexican commercial fishermen that certainly would come close to, or surpass, 15 or 16 pounds. A fish about a foot long (anglers call them one pounders) will weigh in the vicinity of 9 or 10 ounces. A fish in good plump condition measuring 25 inches will scale in at about 8 pounds.

It is evident that the spotted weakfish does not travel great distances. The migration seems to consist of a retreat into deeper water when cold weather arrives. In some areas the spotted weakfish appears to be present the year round. Tagged fish have been recovered about 50 miles from the tagging point.

The growth rate of the spotted weakfish has been tabulated as being almost the same, but not quite as fast, as the weakfish, *Cynoscion regalis*. The approximate ratios are these:

Inches	Age
8	1
10	2
12	3
14	4
16	5
18	6
19	7
20	8

Some reach sexual maturity by the second year and most by the third. A mature fish is about 10 to 12 inches in length and less than a pound in weight.

Spawning takes place from early April until the middle of November, with the height of the season from May to July inclusive. Most of the spawning activity takes place in fairly shallow waters of inland bays, lagoons, and passes. It is at this time that a great slaughter takes place in the Mexican lagoons, where commercial fishermen spread nets for long distances and draw them in while wading the shallow waters. I have seen several boatloads come in with one haul. With the native market fishermen there is no such thing as size selectivity. The eggs are demersal and adhere to the bottom vegetation in quiet waters. The young seem to prefer grassy bottoms, undoubtedly because of the profusion of food. A female about 2 feet long is capable of producing more than 1,000,000 eggs. Grass shrimp, by far, is the favorite food of the spotted weakfish. Other items of diet are silversides, menhaden, mullet, and other small fishes.

Several areas are well known for harboring an abundance of spotted weakfish, and although these spots are well advertised, there is plenty of elbow room. Cocoa, Florida, likes to be called "Salt Water Trout Capital of the World"—and perhaps rightly because every year more than 1,000 spotted weakfish weighing between 6 and 12 pounds are caught by anglers. Furthermore, records show that large specs are caught during almost every week of the year. Most of the fish are taken by wading fishermen using spinning tackle and artificial lures. The majority of fish are taken along the river banks. Some of the best fishing may be had along the Merrit Island Causeway, which spans the Indian and Banana Rivers. The mud flats and rivers inside Canaveral Harbor also receive much play from wading fishermen. The Cocoa area is unusual in that an excellent fishing area is available to anglers which does not demand boats and motors, and wading along, casting a lure, is in my estimation one of the most satisfying methods of angling.

Another well known "hot spot" for the spotted weakfish is a long arm of protected water—a shallow saline bay, a little over 100 miles long and 2 to 5 miles wide—between the Texas mainland and long, thin Padre Island. It is named Laguna Madre and extends from Corpus Christi Bay to within a short distance of the Mexican border. Wading and boat fishing for spotted weakfish are popular and productive in this area. There are other spots, not as easily accessible as Cocoa and Laguna Madre, that produce an unusual abundance of large-size spotted weakfish. One such area is Eight Pass in Mexico, where the

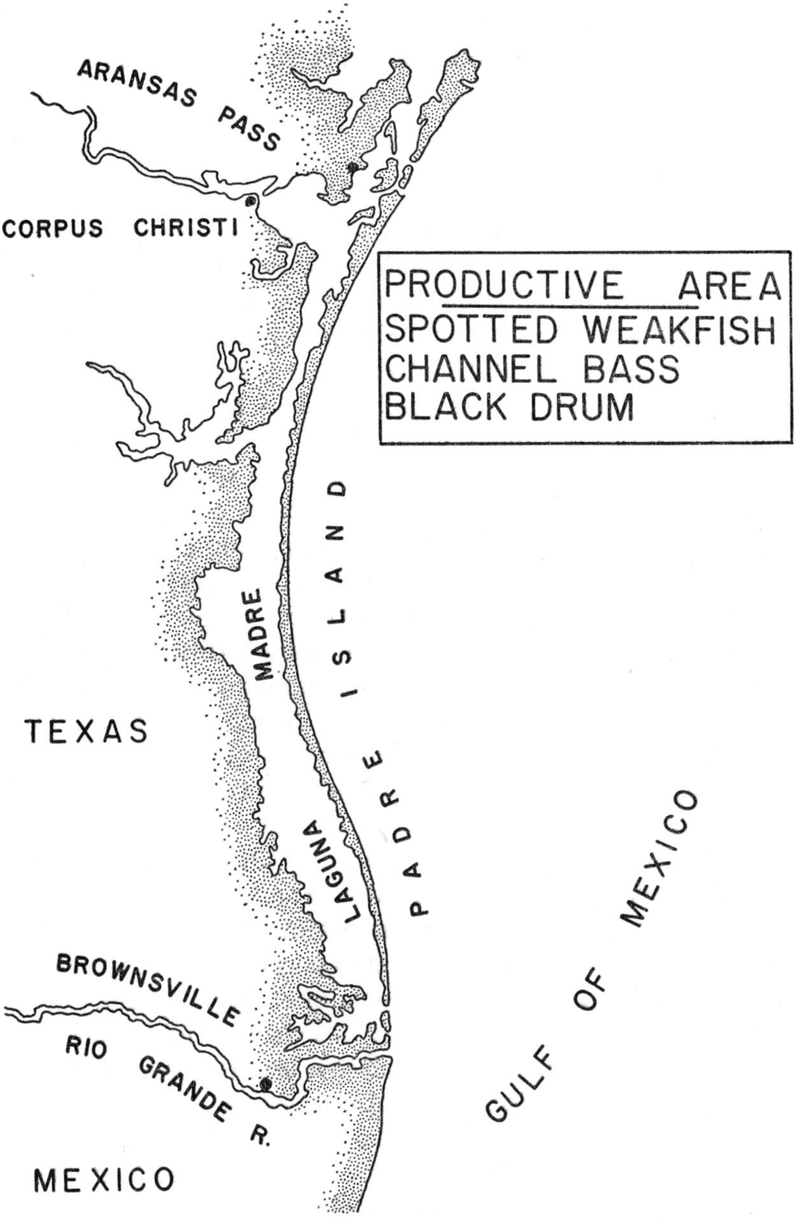
ARANSAS PASS
CORPUS CHRISTI
PRODUCTIVE AREA
SPOTTED WEAKFISH
CHANNEL BASS
BLACK DRUM
MADRE
PADRE ISLAND
TEXAS
LAGUNA
GULF OF MEXICO
BROWNSVILLE
RIO GRANDE R.
MEXICO

water comes through a fairly narrow pass into a shallow, sandy lagoon approximately 4 miles across. It is loaded with spotted weakfish—and at times with channel bass, snook, and tarpon.

Sand Weakfish

(*Cynoscion arenarius*)

Of lesser importance than its two larger cousins (weakfish and spotted weakfish), the sand weakfish is a Gulf of Mexico representative of the family SCIAENIDAE. It is known also as sand squeteague, sand trout, and white trout. The sand weakfish is not as widely distributed as the other members of its group, being more or less confined close to shore along the Gulf Coast of the United States.

Its body shape and fin arrangement are similar to those of the other weakfishes, and because it lacks conspicuous dark spots, the sand weakfish is not incorrectly identified as a spotted weakfish or the more northern weakfish. It closely resembles the silver weakfish, which is also found in its range, but they can be separated easily by anatomical characteristics. The sand weakfish has 11 soft anal rays, sometimes 10 or 12. Dorsal soft rays number 26, commonly 25 or 27, rarely 24 or 28. Gill rakers in total count usually number 14 or 13, frequently 15, and very infrequently 12. The middle rays of the tail are extended slightly. The coloration is pale, straw or yellowish on the dorsal surface, and the sides are silvery—no dark spots present. Sometimes the dorsal surface scales are covered with tiny spots which produce a dusky effect. In size it is slightly larger than the silver weakfish with a maximum length of about 15 to 16 inches and a weight seldom more than a pound.

It does not seem to take part in extensive migrations but moves from bays into the Gulf's deeper waters upon the arrival of cooler weather. Spawning takes place from April to September. Like the other weakfishes it has a definite preference for shrimp, but other invertebrates are also found in its diet, and occasionally small fishes are included. The sand weakfish is good eating, but its small size discourages its use. It is not considered a game fish and most are taken accidentally by anglers.

Silver Weakfish
(*Cynoscion nothus*)

The smallest of the weakfish group, this member of the croaker family SCIAENIDAE, is not as well known as the spotted weakfish or the weakfish. However, it is taken both by market fishermen and anglers. It is also called silver squeteague, bastard trout, and sand trout. From Chesapeake Bay it is distributed southward, along Florida and the Gulf Coast to Texas. The silver weakfish is not considered common north of North Carolina.

In general shape and fin arrangement it resembles the other weakfishes. However, its pale coloration, usually straw on the dorsal surface and silvery sides (sometimes a faint indication of irregular rows of spots), minus conspicuous dark spots, separates it from the spotted weakfish and the weakfish. It may be confused with the sand weakfish, *Cynoscion arenarius*, which frequents the same general range, although the latter seems to prefer inshore waters while the silver weakfish is taken offshore mostly. The silver weakfish has predominantly 9 anal soft rays, sometimes 8, and infrequently 10 in specimens from the Atlantic coast only. The soft rays in the second dorsal fin number 28 or 29, frequently 27, less frequently 30, and rarely 31. The eye is noticeably larger than in the other species. The gill rakers in total count on the first arch number mostly 13, frequently 12 or 14, rarely 15. Another distinguishing character is the number of vertebrae, which is nearly always 27, rarely 26.

The silver weakfish spawns from June to August at sea, and its food consists of shrimp and small crustaceans. Although taken on hook and line, it does not have the reputation of being a game fish.

California White Sea Bass (17c)

(*Cynoscion nobilis*)

In southern California the white sea bass rates as one of the top sport fishes in general popularity. It is also a valuable market species. Undoubtedly this croaker is the most important member of the family SCIAENIDAE in California waters. It is closely related to the weakfish of the Atlantic and Gulf of Mexico. White sea bass is a misnomer, for it is not a member of the bass family. A more appropriate name would be white sea croaker. However, it is known almost exclusively as California white sea bass; therefore I believe more harm than good would be done, in this case, to change the name. It is also known as sea trout. It is distributed from Alaska as far south as Chile (I have taken it surf casting off Cabo Blanco, Peru). In California waters the white sea bass seems to be most abundant from Santa Barbara to Lower California.

In body shape and fin arrangement it resembles closely the weakfishes of the Atlantic (which see). Like the spotted weakfish it has no scales along the base of the dorsal and anal fins. Also, it does not have enlarged canine teeth in the upper jaw (the short fin sea bass, which it resembles closely, possesses a pair of enlarged canine teeth in the upper jaw). The tail is slightly concave, and the pectoral fin is more than one half the length of the head. The lower jaw protrudes, and two spines are present in the anal fin. In coloration the white sea bass is coppery blue-green above, pearlescent on the sides, going to white below. The first dorsal is translucent whitish gray; second dorsal is translucent light brownish yellow; tail is transparent yellow containing no spots. The anal and ventral fins are whitish yellow; pectorals are whitish. A dusky spot is present on the anterior base of the second dorsal and inner base of the pectoral. No spots on the body. The record rod and reel fish weighed 83 pounds 12 ounces and was taken off San Felipe, Mexico, on March 31, 1953, by L. C. Baumgardner.

Weakfishes

However, California white sea bass in the 40 to 60 pound class are rare.

The white sea bass may be found the year round in different places, but they usually prefer to frequent kelp beds quite close to shore and around islands. From May to about September they are in greatest abundance, with better fishing taking place southward as cooler weather progresses. Usually heaviest landings take place during summer and early fall months. Spawning takes place in the vicinity of kelp beds from early spring until the middle of summer. Males usually spawn for the first time when about 2 feet long, and the female when a few inches longer. Items of diet are small fishes, crabs, shrimp, and squid. I have taken the white sea bass while boat fishing with bait off San Diego, California, and by surf casting lures off Cabo Blanco, Peru; and I found it to be a fighting fish as good as the weakfish of the Atlantic coast. There is also a similarity in table quality; it should be iced as quickly as possible.

Totuava (17d)

(*Cynoscion macdonaldi*)

The totuava is an interesting member of the family SCIAENIDAE, apparently confined to the Gulf of California from its northern end south to about Guaymas. It is the largest of the croakers along North American shores and is in demand by the Chinese for its swim bladder, which they consider a delicacy.

It looks like a huge weakfish and can be separated from the rest of the Pacific clan by the lack of spots or bars; the tail has the middle rays extended; no scales are present on the soft dorsal fin, which has 24 or 25 rays, or the anal, which has 7 rays; the first dorsal contains 9 spines. The first and second dorsals do not appear to be contiguous, but if one examines closely it will be noticed that the fins do meet. Teeth are small but profuse. Its coloration in general respects also resembles other weakfishes. The dorsal surface is olive or purplish bronze;

sides are silvery. The entire fish seems to be burnished with metallic iridescence. The mouth is yellowish. Smaller specimens are generally lighter in coloration.

Because the area where most totuava are taken is primitive, the weights of this species have not been properly recorded. However, maximum size seems to be in the vicinity of 200 pounds plus, and large fish, in the 50- to 100-pound class, are common.

The totuava resembles other weakfishes in being primarily a coastal fish with a love for shore waters, although larger ones rove farther out. It is often found in shallows and along mouths of rivers. Although the early arrivals appear in the Gulf of California in October or November, maximum numbers are usually reached in March. Totuavas vanish in April or May; perhaps a migration takes place to the south and deeper water. As with other members of its group, favorite foods are small fishes, shrimp, and crabs.

The totuava will come more into prominence as a game fish because the formerly inaccessible good fishing areas are now being frequented more often by anglers. At one time the overworked commercial fishery for this species was thought to be the culprit in diminishing drastically the supply of fishes. The swim bladders of totuava are in demand for oriental dishes; consequently, large amounts of these bladders were shipped to San Francisco for use by its fairly large Chinese population, and were also exported to China. In times of fish abundance the swim bladders are taken out and the rest of the fish is wasted.

Shortfin Sea Bass

(*Cynoscion parvipinnis*)

Santa Barbara Islands to Guaymas—common only in Gulf of California. Separated from California white sea bass in having enlarged canine teeth in upper jaw. No scales on soft dorsal or anal fin. Tail S-shaped or slightly concave. Mouth whitish.

White Corbina
(Cynoscion albus)

El Salvador to Ecuador. Reaches at least 40 pounds. Mouth cavity whitish. Pectoral fin reaches almost to the tip of the ventral. Tail has middle rays extended. No scales on dorsal and anal fins. Popular small game fish of Panama.

Corbina Blanca
(Cynoscion stolzmanni)

Panama to Peru. Four to 5 feet maximum length. Less than 24 rays in dorsal fin. Short pectoral—barely reaching past middle of ventrals. Middle rays of tail sometimes extended. Enlarged canine teeth present. No scales on dorsal and anal fins. Lining of gill cover is black. Commercially important.

Yellow Corbina
(Cynoscion phoxocephalus)

Panama to Peru. Two to 3 feet maximum length. Lining of mouth yellow. Lining of gill cover black. Enlarged teeth in center of upper jaw, near front. Tail slightly concave in adults.

Gulf Corbina
(Cynoscion othonopterus)

Gulf of California. About 2 feet maximum length. Soft dorsal and anal fins with scales along base. Tail slightly concave or square cut. Commercially important, shipped to United States. Game fish on light tackle. San Felipe anglers take many.

Striped Corbina
(Cynoscion reticulatus)

Lower California to Panama. About 15 inches. Said to reach twice that length. Differs from others in having dorsal surface and upper sides covered with dark brown or black stripes. Second dorsal and anal minus scales. Tail with extended middle rays. Lining of mouth orange.

Orangemouth Corbina
(Cynoscion xanthulus)

Gulf of California to Mazatlán. Maximum length about 3 feet. Mouth colored bright orange-yellow. Lining of gill cover black. Pectoral fins reach nearly to the tips of the ventral fins. Middle rays of tail extended.

DRUMS AND CROAKERS

Many fishes in the croaker group possess common names which include in part the words "drum" or "croaker." There is no method of differentiating one from the other; they are all members of the family SCIAENIDAE. The common names are a matter of choice in different areas.

Channel Bass (18b)
(Sciaenops ocellatus)

Both the sporting fraternity and commercial fishermen speak in glowing terms when discussing the channel bass, and it well deserves good words; for it is one of the most important coastal food and game fishes confined to the southeastern portion of the North American continent.

Most of my fishing for this member of the croaker family SCIAENIDAE has been along the Gulf coast—off Texas and Mexico —where I have never heard it called anything but redfish; and it is a more appropriate name for this species because it is not a bass. However, farther north along its range it is known as channel bass; every book and the International Game Fish Association charts list it under the latter name. Although I feel that a better name is redfish, I use channel bass in order to avoid confusion. Red drum is also popular, and in some areas the smaller ones are called puppy drum. It is widely distributed along the Atlantic and Gulf coasts—from the Delaware capes down into Mexican waters, but occasionally strays may be found as far north as New Jersey.

The channel bass is a snub-nosed fish possessing large scales and contiguous dorsal fins; the first dorsal usually numbers 10 spines, about 25 rays are in the second dorsal, and 7 or 8 rays in the anal. The short gill rakers number 8 or 9 on the lower limb of the first arch. This fish is identified at a glance. Almost without exception a prominent round or oval black spot is present on the top posterior portion of the caudal peduncle. Occasionally a specimen may possess more than one black spot. When alive it is rather pleasing in coloration. The dorsal surface is olive green or bluish green tinged with bronze. The coppery reddish pink or pearlescent reddish pink sides gradually go lighter to a white belly. Dorsal and caudal fins are dusky; anal and ventrals white; pectorals usually bright rusty on outer side. Young fish and those inhabiting sandy bottom areas are usually lighter in color. After death most channel bass fade to a flat red.

The record rod and reel fish weighed 83 pounds and was taken off Cape Charles, Virginia, on August 5, 1949, by Zack Waters, Jr. In the surf, fish of 10 to 30 pounds are not uncommon, but fish taken along quiet waters of bays, ponds, inlets, and lagoons usually weigh much less. Fish taken in Gulf waters are usually less than 5 pounds and rarely reach 30 or 40 pounds. On the other hand, along the North Carolina coast, school bass seldom weigh less than 15 pounds, and 50 pounders are not rare.

From the comparatively little scientific work that has been done on the channel bass it appears that they do not make extensive north and south migrations, but instead they travel inshore during the warm season and go into deeper offshore waters when cold weather arrives. A tagged fish was recovered 10 miles from its tagging point; another made a 65-mile movement in 13 days. In late March schools of channel bass appear off the Carolina beaches and usually feed (mostly on pilchard and menhaden) at the surface, from the breakers to a few miles out. As the weather gets warmer the fish are in evidence further north, until in June they are spread throughout the lower Chesapeake, and from Cape Charles, Virginia, to Cape May, New Jersey, in the surf. Big channel bass in profusion summer in the deeper waters along the eastern shore of Virginia —from Cape Charles City to Cape Charles. Along the beaches and inlets of North Carolina, from the latter part of summer through the fall, runs of small channel bass, called puppy drum, make an appearance. Big fish feed in the surf until December.

In the Gulf area channel bass are known to spawn in the vicinity of mouths of passes, and perhaps they choose this type of locality in other areas. The activity takes place in early fall and winter—September or October through December. The channel bass reaches maturity at a length of 28 or 29 inches although bull redfish have been known to spawn when 25 inches in length. The approximate growth rate is this:

Inches	Age
12	1
20	2
24	3
28	4
32	5

By far the most popular item of diet on the list of the channel bass is shrimp; crabs and small fishes are next.

The channel bass is usually considered a surf fish because it provides great sport for the surf casting fraternity. However, it is also taken from many types of fishing craft ranging from small rowboats to luxury cruisers. Along the North Carolina coast in the spring large numbers of channel bass are caught from boats following the edge of schools. As the season advances more fish are taken along the beaches and in tideways close to shore. In Florida, where the channel bass may be most abundant, they school from Mayport to Cape Canaveral in the early summer. In some Florida localities it appears to be a year-round resident. Also along the Texas coast heavy concentrations of the fish are noticeable in the early spring.

Left: 65-pound tarpon taken on fly rod by Julian Crandall of Ashaway, Rhode Island, at Islamorada, Florida Keys. Captain Ev Carey, guide, at right. *Right:* Winslow Tuttle, Captain, Yale Fishing Team, with another Florida Keys tarpon.

A limit catch of Connecticut River shad taken by Jim Galligan of the Connecticut Fish and Game Department, Winslow Tuttle, and the author. (Galligan on left, Winslow on right in bottom left photo.)

The channel bass indulges in a rather slow fight, with sustained resistance to rod and reel rather than being a flashy actor with long runs; it never clears the surface—at least I have never seen one jump. Instead, as it takes a bait or lure, it heads for the bottom, and when taken along shore its dogged type of pull plus the action of the surging surf produces a challenge to light tackle anglers.

Black Drum (20a)

(*Pogonias cromis*)

One of the world's largest croakers, the black drum is a member of the family SCIAENIDAE. Like the other members of this group, it is primarily an inshore fish that loves to spend most of the time close to the bottom. As a game fish it rates a listing in the International Game Fish Association records. In some areas it is also a valuable market fish. Its distribution has been recorded from Cape Cod southward to Argentina. However, it is a fish which prefers warm waters, and its usual range is not farther north than New Jersey. Along Hatteras to New Jersey and over the northern localities of Florida's east and west coasts it is fairly common, and it may be termed abundant along the coasts of Texas and Louisiana.

The black drum presents a hump-back appearance, with a high back and an outline that rises sharply from the head. The snout is blunt, and the ventral outline is almost straight. The tail is squarish, and the scales are large. Underneath the lower jaw (chin) numerous short barbels are present. Throat possesses large, flat, pavement-like teeth (crushes shellfish). Dorsal fins are contiguous, the first with 10 long, slender spines and the second with 20 to 22 rays. Anal fin has 2 spines—the second greatly enlarged—and 6 or 7 rays; tail is square-tipped. Gill rakers are short, 14 to 16 on lower limb of first arch. The pectorals are long and pointed, and the ventrals are also unusually long. Color of a live adult fish is silvery, with a generally iridescent appearance. The dorsal surface is dusky or brassy. The ventral side is grayish white. All fins are dusky or black, and the entire fish turns dark after death. Young fish possess 4 or 5 wide dusky bars which disappear in the adult.

The record rod and reel fish weighed 94 pounds 4 ounces and was taken off Cape Charles, Virginia, on April 28, 1957, by James L. Johnson. However, much larger specimens have been recorded. A 146 pounder was taken by handline at St. Augustine, Florida. Average size is 1 to 3 pounds.

Its migration seems to be to offshore in cold weather; inshore when warm weather arrives. It is schooling in habit, and like most of the croaker family, it inhabits sandy beaches, inlets, tideways, bays, and lower stretches of large rivers. It is found around bridges and piers. Also, offshore trawls catch them regularly.

In the Gulf of Mexico spawning takes place from February to May. Most activity takes place close to or in the entrances of bays and lagoons. Large females will lay about 6,000,000 eggs. The black drum is noted for its ability to produce loud purring or drumming sounds, especially during the breeding season. A one-year-old fish is about 10 inches in length, or slightly less. At two years of age it has gained about 5 inches and is sexually mature.

As the position of the mouth indicates, most of its feeding takes place on or close to the bottom. However, on occasion it feeds near the surface where it may take pilchard and small menhaden. The usual items of diet are shrimp, crabs, and clams. It can crush shells without difficulty. Black drum are considered pests by oyster growers and are believed to do great damage to oyster plantings in short order.

Anglers take the black drum on artificial lures. However, clams, mussels, and squid fished on the bottom are by far the best baits. Resistance to rod and reel is not spectacular. Most of its efforts are expended close to the bottom in a dogged fight. If taken in the surf, the water action helps in producing runs. It is not a great game fish; its size is the chief interest to anglers —big ones are often taken. There is a difference of opinion regarding its table qualities. It is taken commercially, mostly by handline or trotline which contains many stout hooks. These

NO. CAROLINA
FAMOUS
GAME FISH GROUNDS

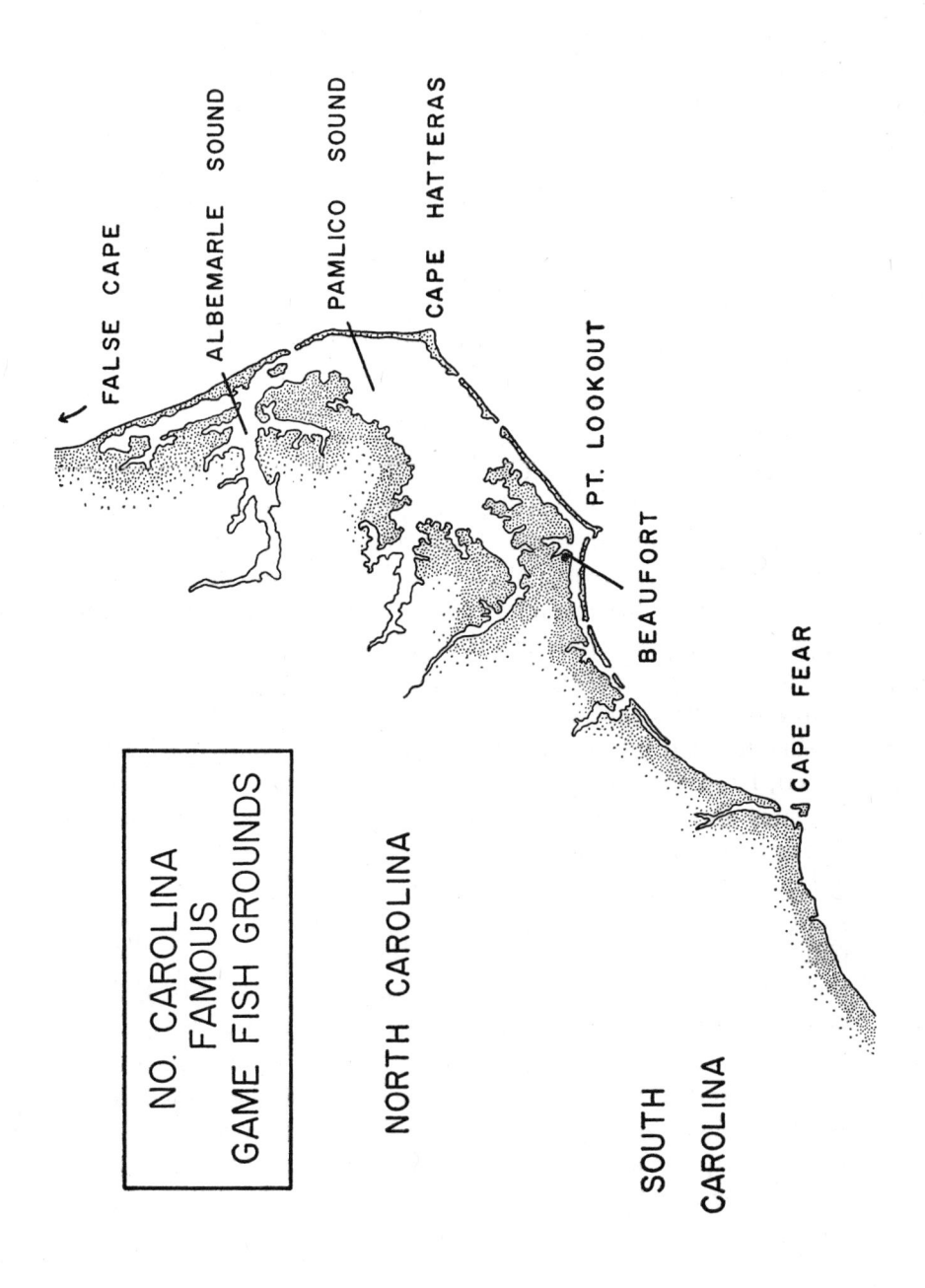

FALSE CAPE
ALBEMARLE SOUND
PAMLICO SOUND
CAPE HATTERAS
PT. LOOKOUT
BEAUFORT
CAPE FEAR

NORTH CAROLINA

SOUTH CAROLINA

lines are set, usually across inlets, and allowed to stay overnight. I find it fair or mediocre eating; the larger ones are a bit coarse.

Atlantic Croaker (19a)
(*Micropogon undulatus*)

In appearance and habit the Atlantic croaker is similar in many respects to the black drum and spot. It is appreciated more as a food fish than a game fish and appears in markets throughout most of its usual range. Unexperienced anglers find no difficulty in catching the Atlantic croaker in quantity. This plus tasty eating combine to make it a popular fish. It is one of the smaller members of the family SCIAENIDAE, and in several localities it is known as hardhead, especially around the Chesapeake. It is found in greatest abundance from the Delaware capes to Hatteras. North of New Jersey it is not common, but its range extends to Massachusetts in the north. Southward it is distributed around Florida to the Gulf of Mexico and to Texas.

The Atlantic croaker, like its close cousins, is a husky fish with a high back and a mouth more or less adapted for bottom feeding (called inferior). The dorsal fins are contiguous; first dorsal, 10 spines and second dorsal, 28 or 29 rays. Anal fin has 2 spines and 8 rays. Tail with middle rays extended, which makes it appear double concave. Pectorals long in adults. The preoperculum is serrate (toothed on edge); chin has a row of short slender barbels, and small teeth are present in the jaws. Gill rakers are short, 14 to 16 on lower limb of first arch. In color the Atlantic croaker is a silvery fish tinged with gray or green on the dorsal surface and white along the underside. A live fish has a metallic or iridescent sheen. Brown or brassy spots are abundant on the dorsal fins, on the back, and on the sides of the body mostly above the lateral line. The spots are arranged in wavy, oblique bars on the sides. In larger and older fish the spots are less distinct. It reaches a weight of about 8 pounds. However, a fish of 6 pounds is unusual, 3 or 4 pounders are numerous, but the average is more in the 1-pound class.

Like the other croakers, its migrations are mostly offshore in cold weather and inshore when the warm months arrive, although some north-and-south movement may take place. In late March it appears from Hatteras to the lower Chesapeake when it comes close inshore; many make their way slowly northward to New Jersey as the weather gets warmer.

Spawning takes place over a fairly lengthy season, from August to December in the Chesapeake Bay area. It is later in the Gulf of Mexico, from about October to February along the coast of Texas. Eggs carried by individual females are numerous—close to 200,000 eggs in a large female. One-year-old fish are about 6 inches long and about 8 inches when two years old, at which time they become sexually mature.

It prefers to feed over hard or shell bottom, and its main items of diet are worms, crustaceans, shellfish, and other invertebrates. It feeds on the bottom as the inferior mouth and barbels or feelers on the chin indicate. Like the other croakers, it has the ability to emit croaking sounds. These are produced by muscle pressure on the air bladder.

Although the Atlantic croaker is more of a food fish than a game fish (Maryland and North Carolina have an annual yield over 50,000 pounds for market), it is appreciated by anglers; it is easy to catch and worth while to bring home. It puts up a good scrap on light tackle, but the bait has to be on or close to the bottom. Often the Atlantic croaker will feed under a school of fish such as the striped bass. At times, in the Chesapeake area, they are taken in such great quantity by commercial fishermen that the market is glutted, and prices drop so low that fishing is not profitable. Flesh of this croaker is firm, white, and tasty.

Spot (18d)

(*Leiostomus xanthurus*)

The spot is a small but desirable pan fish which is caught by anglers fishing close to shore; it is also one of the more important food fishes taken commercially along the mid-Atlantic coast. Its common name, spot, is derived from a prominent black or dusky marking above the pectoral fin close to the edge of the gill cover. It is a member of the family SCIAENIDAE and is also known as croaker. Although its range is from Cape Cod to Texas in the Gulf of Mexico, it usually does not range farther north than southern New Jersey. It appears to be in greatest profusion along the coasts of lower Chesapeake Bay, Virginia, and North Carolina. In this area it is important commercially (8 to 10 million pounds are taken annually). In its range southward it is never really abundant. At times it may ascend fresh water streams, but usually it is found in salt and brackish water.

The spot has a short but steep body, a rounded snout, and a high back with an outline that rises sharply from the head. The tail is slightly forked. The dorsal fins are contiguous, and the first dorsal contains 10 spines; second dorsal 30 to 34 rays; anal fin has 2 spines and 12 or 13 rays. Adults have tiny teeth present in upper jaw. Gill rakers are short, with 22 or 23 on the lower limb of the first arch. The gill cover lacks spines, and the absence of barbels helps distinguish this fish from other croakers. The dorsal surface is iridescent bluish gray and sides are silvery going paler below. Twelve to 15 oblique yellowish bars are prominent along the back going downward and forward. In many of the older fishes these bars are fairly indistinct. The fins are mostly pale yellow and dusky. The large black, sometimes yellowish black, shoulder spot is present in almost all fish. The spot is a small fish—7 to 9 inches in average length and a maximum size of about 15 inches and a weight of about 2 pounds.

Its migrations are similar to those of other sciaenids: mostly offshore in cold weather and inshore during the warm months. In the lower Chesapeake it arrives in early spring, and in some more southern areas it appears to be a year-round resident. It is a schooling fish, and groups swim together rather compactly. Females make no sound, but males are capable of emitting a faint drumming noise which is much less noticeable than in other species of croaker. Most of the spot's feeding is done near the bottom; it has a preference for grass shrimp, worms, some small mollusks, small minnows, and vegetable matter.

Spawning takes place during winter, from December to the latter part of March in the Gulf of Mexico and late fall and early winter north of North Carolina. The larger fish migrate offshore to spawn. A one-year-old fish is 5 or 6 inches long and 7 to 8 inches at two years of age when it spawns.

When the fish are hitting, anglers using small hooks and bait may catch a great many fish in a short time. Fish taken along the Atlantic coast are slightly larger on the average than the Gulf fish. There always seems to be an abundance of this species for the market; they are sold fresh or salted, and many tons are turned into fish meal. Best catches in haul seines are made from April to November.

Silver Perch (20c)
(*Bairdiella chrysura*)

The silver perch is a small, tasty member of the croaker family SCIAENIDAE. It is a food fish often taken by anglers but not considered a game fish. I include it here because it is often mistaken for the popular white perch, *Morone americana*—a sea bass. Obviously the common name is a misnomer, for this fish is not a perch. It is also called sand perch, white perch, yellowtail, and yellowfin croaker. Its general range is from New York (sometimes Massachusetts) south along the coast to Texas. Migrations are like those of other sciaenids in being confined mostly to offshore-inshore travels, depending on season (shallow water in warm weather, deeper water in winter). Often it frequents brackish and fresh waters, and most of its meanderings are close along shore.

Anglers often mistake this fish for the white perch because, between the two, there is a close resemblance in general shape and coloration. However, one easy-to-see characteristic separates them: the silver perch has the lateral line extending onto the caudal fin. Other characteristics are 2 spines and 9 or 10 rays in the anal fin; dorsal fins contiguous, first with 11 or 12 spines, second with 19 to 21 rays; gill rakers long, 14 to 16 on lower limb of first arch; preoperculum serrated; prominent teeth in both jaws; no barbels on chin. Color generally silvery with the dorsal surface varying in shades of olive or blue-gray; sides and belly bright silvery; fins mostly yellowish; small black dots on body. The silver perch is small with a maximum size of a bit over 9 inches; average size is 7 or 8 inches in length and about a quarter pound in weight.

Spawning in the Gulf of Mexico takes place from April to June, and in the Chesapeake area in late spring and early summer. Eggs are small and produced in large numbers, one female possessed approximately 52,800 eggs. Three-year-old fish are sexually mature. It feeds close to the bottom most of the time on small crustaceans and, to a lesser extent, on worms and small fishes. Anglers take many with shrimp or cut bait. Commercially it is taken in fairly large quantities.

Spotfin Croaker (19d)
(*Roncador stearnsi*)

The spotfin croaker, found along the coast of California, closely resembles its relative the yellowfin croaker in form and habit. It is a popular game fish which rates a place on the protected list and cannot be taken commercially. It is known by other names—surf fish, spot, golden croaker. SCIAENIDAE is its family name. The spotfin is distributed from Point Conception in Southern California southward into Lower California waters. Typical with croakers, the spotfin loves sandy shore areas, bays, sloughs, and surf. The main items of diet are small crustaceans, worms, and fishes.

It grows much larger than the yellowfin croaker with a maximum length of about 3 feet and a weight up to 12 pounds. The snout is rounded, blunt, and projects over the lower jaw; tail is squarish; dorsal fins are contiguous; first has 10 spines, second has 24 rays; anal has 2 spines (second spine stout) and 8 rays; pectoral fin about as long as head; no barbel on chin; large black spot at base of pectorals. Color is metallic blue-gray or brassy

Drums and Croakers

on the dorsal surface, going light silvery below. Indistinct dark wavy lines extend downward and forward from the back.

This is another favorite sport fish with anglers along shore— from boats, piers, bridges, and especially in the surf. Fishing takes place throughout the year, but the peak season is in late summer. The spotfin is primarily a bottom feeder, and best catches are made on clams, crabs, and mussels.

Yellowfin Croaker (19b)
(*Umbrina roncador*)

The yellowfin croaker is considered a tasty sport fish by California anglers. The fishing season extends throughout the year but reaches a peak in late summer. It is on the protected list, being illegal to take by nets or to sell on the market. It is a member of the croaker family SCIAENIDAE, and is also commonly known as surf fish. Usually its range is from Point Conception southward into the Gulf of California. As with most croakers it inhabits shallow, sandy bottom areas in bays and sloughs and sometimes in the surf. Most of its food consists of crustaceans, small worms, and fishes.

Maximum size—16 inches in length and 5 pounds in weight. The snout is rounded and conical, extending beyond the lower jaw. Dorsal fins are contiguous: first with 10 spines; second with 27 rays; anal fin 2 spines (second large and thick), 7 rays; short barbel on chin. Color is silvery gray with brassy and iridescent hues; silvery below; back and sides with dark wavy lines extending downward and forward; dorsal fins dusky, other fins yellowish.

Black Croaker (20b)
(*Cheilotrema saturnum*)

The black croaker, a member of the family SCIAENIDAE, is a fine table fish but not often taken by anglers. Distributed from Point Conception south along the Mexican coast into the Gulf of California. Other common names: Chinese croaker, surf fish,

SO. CALIFORNIA
FAMOUS
GAME FISH GROUNDS

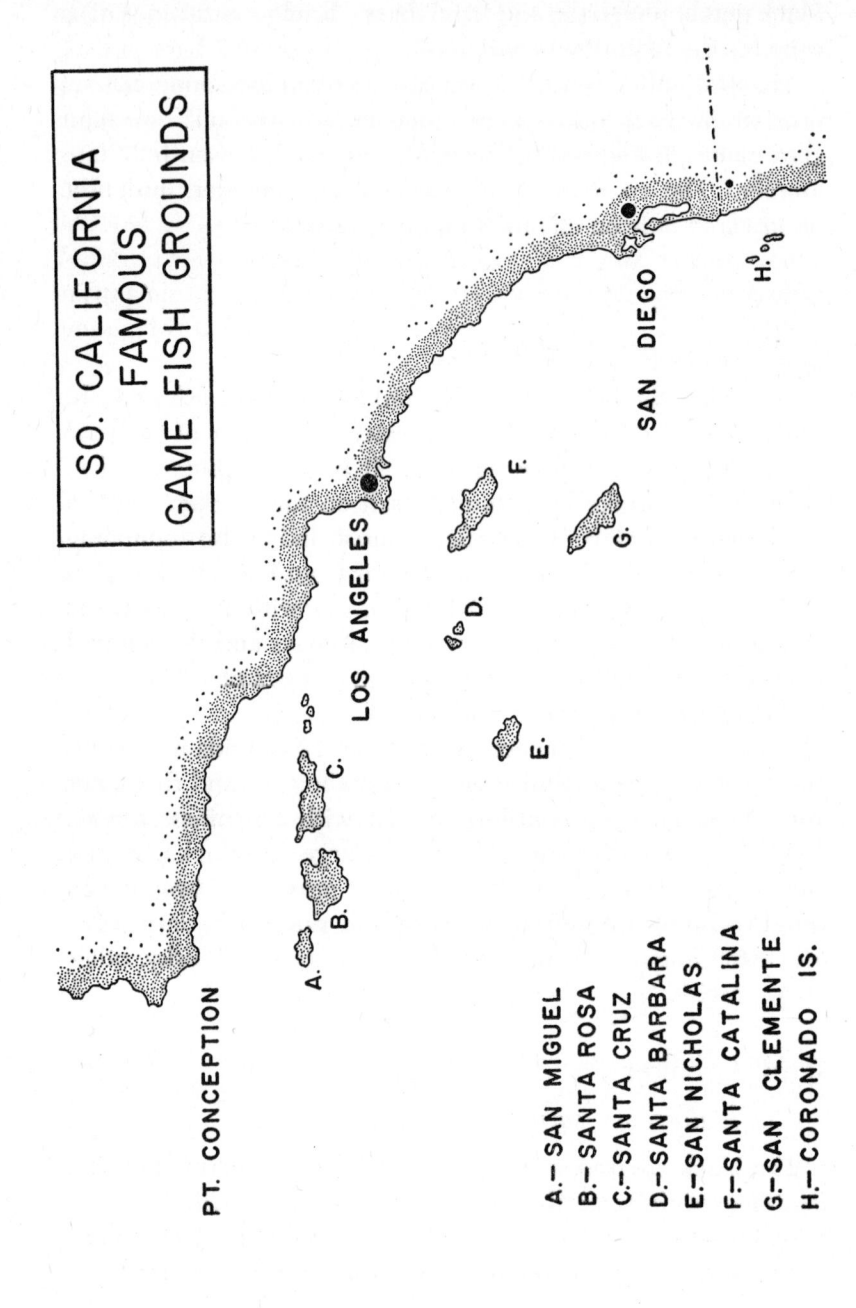

PT. CONCEPTION
A.
B.
C. LOS ANGELES
D.
E.
F.
G.
SAN DIEGO
H.

A.—SAN MIGUEL
B.—SANTA ROSA
C.—SANTA CRUZ
D.—SANTA BARBARA
E.—SAN NICHOLAS
F.—SANTA CATALINA
G.—SAN CLEMENTE
H.—CORONADO IS.

black perch, blue bass, and black bass. *Sciaena saturna* is often used for the scientific name.

Snout rounded but not as blunt as in other croakers; face and head profile slightly concave; high back; squarish tail; dorsal fins contiguous, first dorsal with 9 or 10 spines, second with 27 rays; anal has 2 spines, 7 rays; pectoral shorter than head; no barbel on chin; back edge of operculum jet black. Color is blackish with coppery tinge; silvery below with dark specks; broad, indistinct band across body from front of second dorsal to ventral fins; fins dusky, tips of ventrals and anal black. Maximum length about 15 inches.

California Kingfish (19c)

(*Genyonemus lineatus*)

Generally not considered a game fish but taken in large numbers by anglers and commercial fishermen. Also known as kingfish, tomcod, shiner, and white croaker. It is a member of the family SCIAENIDAE. Distributed from Vancouver south to central Lower California.

Snout rounded, blunt, and extends beyond lower jaw; tail squarish; dorsal fins contiguous—first has 12 to 15 spines, second has 21 or 22 rays; anal fin 2 spines and 11 rays. Pectoral longer than ventral. Color silvery gray with iridescent tinge; fins yellowish; black spot under upper base of pectoral. Faint wavy lines extend from back downward and forward. Maximum size: length a bit over a foot; weight about 1¼ pounds.

WHITINGS

King whitings are members of the croaker family SCIAENIDAE, found along the Atlantic and Gulf coasts of the United States. They are fairly small but excellent food and game fishes. Three are recognized: northern, southern, and Gulf—all of the genus *Menticirrhus*.

They resemble each other closely and differ only in minor detail; anglers and commercial fishermen do not bother to differentiate them. Whitings have the same general arrangement of fins as do the weakfishes. The tail has a characteristic outline with the lower half rounded and the upper half concave. The first dorsal is high and pointed. The snout is blunt and the upper jaw extends beyond the lower. A barbel is present on the chin, lips are fleshy, and no canine teeth are present. The body is deepest below the first dorsal fin. The whitings possess no air bladder and therefore make no sounds. This is a marked difference from the rest of the croaker family. They are good eating, and many are taken by shore anglers. The California corbina is a closely related member of the clan.

Northern King Whiting (18c)
(*Menticirrhus sexatilis*)

Also known as kingfish and king whiting. It ranges from Cape Cod southward to Florida and occasionally strays to Maine. However, it is most abundant from New York south to Chesapeake Bay.

First dorsal fin 10 spines; second has 24 to 27 rays; anal fin with 1 long spine and 8 rays. In adults the third spine of the dorsal fin is usually prolonged and filamentous at the tip (longer in larger fish than small ones). The pectoral fin reaches or goes beyond the tip of the pelvic fin. Color is dark gray, dusky, or lead color; often dorsal surface is almost black. Sides and portions of back are iridescent; yellowish white or creamy below. About 6 or 7 irregular dark bars are marked across the sides, running downward and forward from the back. Usually the first one or two bars, on the nape, run downward and backward to meet the next bar (running in the opposite direction) to form a **V** above the base of the pectoral fin. Also, usually a dusky longitudinal streak is present above the light belly. Fins are dusky or blackish with the first dorsal, anal, pectorals, and ventrals tipped white or grayish white. Maximum size: length about 18 inches and weight about 3 pounds. Average fish run from 10 to 14 inches and ½ to 1½ pounds.

Northern king whiting appears along shore and migrates

northward in the spring. When cold weather arrives in the fall it disappears. During its stay it is confined to inshore waters and often enters mouths of rivers. This whiting runs in schools close to the ground and prefers hard or sandy bottom areas where it feeds on shrimp, crabs, small mollusks, worms, and small fishes. Spawning takes place from June to August.

Southern King Whiting
(*Menticirrhus americanus*)

This whiting is also known as southern kingfish. It is a member of the croaker family, SCIAENIDAE, and closely related to the northern king whiting. It is distributed from New Jersey southward to Florida and less frequently over the Gulf Coast to Texas. Usually it is not common north of Maryland. In late summer it may be found in areas inhabited by the northern king whiting.

The southern king whiting is distinguished from the northern whiting, which it resembles closely, by the smaller number of rays in its anal fin, 7; northern whiting has 8. None of the dorsal spines is elongated. The pectoral fin reaches or goes beyond the tip of the pelvic fin. In coloration it is silvery gray above and white or creamy below. Six or 7 indistinct bars run downward and forward from the back, but the first ones do not form a V above the pectoral fin as in the northern whiting. Maximum size is about 17 inches and a weight of about 2½ pounds. However, average fish weigh about a half pound.

As with the northern whiting, it arrives in the spring, spreads northward, and departs in the fall when cool weather sets in. Spawning takes place off North Carolina from April to June, usually on the outside bank shores but occasionally inside. It prefers a sandy or hard bottom, where it roams in schools and feeds on shrimp, crabs, small mollusks, worms, and small fishes.

Gulf King Whiting
(*Menticirrhus littoralis*)

The Gulf king whiting, also known as surf whiting, is similar in most respects to the northern and southern king whitings and is most abundant, as the name indicates, in the Gulf of Mexico. It belongs to the croaker family SCIAENIDAE. Commercially it is not as well known as the southern whiting. It ranges from the Chesapeake Bay southward into the Gulf. In contrast to its close relative, the southern king whiting, it prefers shallow water.

In shape and arrangement of fins it resembles closely the other whitings. However, it possesses no colored bars or mottlings along the body. Instead, it is silvery gray on the back with bright silver sides and almost white beneath. The breast scales are smaller than those on the sides, and the pectoral fins do not come close to reaching the tips of the pelvics. In the northern and southern whitings the pectorals reach as far as or beyond the pelvic fins; also the scales in the chest region are not reduced in size. Maximum size seems to be about 18 inches in length and about 2 pounds in weight, but the average fish is much smaller—about a half pound to a pound. Like the other whitings this species spawns in the latter part of spring and early summer. It prefers hard or sandy bottoms and feeds almost solely upon small crustaceans. Anglers are most successful when using shrimp or cut bait.

California Corbina (18a)
(*Menticirrhus undulatus*)

The California corbina is an excellent food and game fish closely related to the whitings of the Atlantic coast. It is highly esteemed by anglers in southern California, where it rates as the most popular surf fish. For many years it has been placed on the protected list and cannot be taken commercially. Other popular names are California whiting, corbina, surf fish, sea trout. It is of the same genus as its Atlantic cousins and of the same croaker family, SCIAENIDAE. It is distributed mainly from Point Conception south into the Gulf of California.

In body shape and fin arrangement it resembles the Atlantic whiting (which see). Anglers may confuse this fish with the yellowfin croaker, but there are characteristics which separate

Whitings

them clearly. Corbina: 1 weak spine (rarely 2) front of the anal fin; tail profile—concave top half and convex bottom half; long flattened body with large pectoral fins. Yellowfin croaker: 2 strong spines at front of anal fin; tail with a slightly concave profile; body high and pectoral fin small. The dorsal surface is iridescent or metallic blue-gray, going to dusky or gray on the sides and white below. Wavy dusky lines, running downward and forward, are formed by tiny dark points on the center of the scales. Often these lines are partially or entirely indistinct. Fins are dusky. Maximum size appears to be about 18 or 20 inches, with a reported weight of 8 pounds.

Like most members of the family SCIAENIDAE, and especially the whitings, the corbina is a bottom-loving fish with a preference for sandy beaches and shallow bays. It feeds mostly on crustaceans and mollusks. Turbulent surf water, where food is constantly disturbed, is the area most frequented by feeding corbinas. Therefore, surf anglers do well.

Mulloway

(*Sciaena antarctica*)

One of the world's largest croakers, family SCIAENIDAE, the mulloway is an important food and game fish of Australia. Kingfish, butterfish, and river kingfish are other common names, depending upon the area. It has a wide distribution and is present in all states of the Commonwealth. Sometimes found in the deeper reef areas, most often it frequents mouths of estuaries. It likes deep holes in rivers and often ranges far up, and sometimes beyond, tidal influence. Its maximum size is about 6 feet in length with a weight of about 100 pounds. Specimens in the 50- to 60-pound class are fairly common and 80 pounders are not rare.

The mulloway feeds on squid, octopus, and crustaceans but seems to prefer small fishes. It has a ravenous appetite and is known to destroy large numbers of various members of the herring family. Its large size and strong runs when hooked give this fish a high rating with Australian anglers. A legal minimum size is placed on the mulloway ranging from 13 to 18 inches in different parts of Australia.

Teraglin

(*Atractoscion atelodus*)

Another popular Australian member of the family SCIAENIDAE, the teraglin is a valuable food and game fish. It is found along the coasts of New South Wales and southern Queensland and differs from most of its relatives by preferring offshore areas, often as much as 15 or 20 miles. Rarely does it inhabit inshore localities, as the mulloway does, but it may range along rocky reefs. Average weight is about 4 to 5 pounds, and the maximum size appears to be about 3 feet, with a weight of 20 pounds.

The teraglin is known for its fine flavor, but as a game fish it has not reached its potential. Nearly all fishermen catch it with handline although it demonstrates all the qualities of a good rod and reel fish. It has a minimum legal size of 14 inches in Queensland and 15 inches in New South Wales.

Flatfishes

FLOUNDERS, FLUKES, HALIBUTS

The flatfishes comprise a large group of commercially important fishes. This tribe includes the halibuts, flukes, flounders, turbots, and soles. It is hardly necessary to state that the outstanding characteristic of this group is the flat body, that is, compressed from side to side, but perhaps many anglers have not realized that the different species swim either on one side or the other—being right-sided or left-sided flatfishes. When young they look much like other fish larvae, but during the course of development the skull twists and one eye migrates to the other side of the head so that finally both eyes are on one side. The entire underside of the body is usually white or light gray while the top side is colored, usually in dull brown like the bottom on which they are found. The very long dorsal and anal fins, which run along the edges of the body, are also characteristic of this group.

The flatfishes are an unusually large tribe with more than 300 species known worldwide; at present at least five different families are recognized. They range in size from a few inches in length to enormous fish (halibut) of hundreds of pounds. Nearly all spend most of their lives on or close to the bottom, feeding predominantly on invertebrate life, although some species are very active and voracious attackers of small fishes. Most are inhabitants of salt water; a few types may be found occasionally in brackish and fresh water.

Although they contribute greatly to man's food supply, not many are known as sporting fishes. The few that are of interest to anglers or taken by rod and reel are the following.

Atlantic Halibut (40a)
(*Hippoglosus hippoglosus*)

This member of the family HIPPOGLOSSIDAE inhabits the cold, deeper waters of the north Atlantic. It is a valuable commercial species and well known for its vitamin-bearing oil besides being a fine table fish. Only accidentally is it caught by sportsmen. When taken, however, its size creates so much interest that a few words concerning the giant of flatfishes are not entirely out of place in a book on game fishes.

Chiefly an arctic and subarctic fish, the halibut ranges from New York northward to northern Norway, northern Iceland, and to southwest of Iceland. West of Greenland it is important to the Eskimos. Many are taken off the south coast of Newfoundland, on the Grand Banks—and perhaps Labrador. Large ones are not uncommonly reported off Nova Scotia. The most southerly record along the western side of the Atlantic was a stray fish 6 feet long that was taken in a net near Reedville, Virginia.

Besides being, by far, the largest of the flatfish clan the halibut has other outstanding characteristics; it is narrower than most of the other flatfishes, and it lies on its left side—it faces right; its large mouth gapes back to the eyes and contains sharp curved teeth. Its tail is concave, and the lateral line is arched abreast of the pectoral fin. The dorsal fin contains 98 to 105 rays; it starts abreast of the eye and continues almost the entire length of the fish. The anal fin is shorter, with 73 to 79 rays. The top side is sometimes uniformly dark, almost black, but more often it is chocolate to olive, or slate brown. Young fish are lighter and more or less mottled. Usually the underside is pure white in small fish, but larger specimens are more or less blotched with gray.

There are definite records pertaining to the huge size the halibut reaches. In June, 1917, Captain A. S. Ree took one off Cape Ann, Gulf of Maine, which must have weighed about 700 pounds because it tipped the scales at 615 eviscerated (head still attached) when brought into the Boston fish pier. A more recent report (1957) comes from Grimsby, England, where a halibut weighing 504 pounds was taken; it is one of the largest reported from English waters. However, fish of over 300 pounds are rarities anywhere in the north Atlantic. Full-grown females average about 100 to 150 pounds. Males usually run smaller; those brought into New England ports weigh from 50 to 200 pounds.

A fish 3 feet in length will weigh about 12 pounds; 4½ feet about 60 pounds; 5 feet about 100 pounds; 6 feet about 160 pounds; 6½ feet over 200 pounds.

Like all flatfishes it spends most of the time close to or on the bottom but occasionally will come to the surface. Usually it prefers sand, gravel, or clay bottom, and it is known to inhabit depths down to at least 400 to 500 fathoms. The halibut is a voracious feeder, preying mostly on other fishes—cod, haddock, cusk, rosefish, sculpin, grenadier, silverhake, flounder, mackerel, and other cold-water fishes. Also, it will take crabs, lobsters, clams, and mussels. The halibut in turn is preyed upon by seals and the Greenland shark. A female weighing about 200 pounds produces about 2,180,000 eggs. In the eastern Atlantic, halibut spawn in March, April, and May. Most activity takes place in April, but some females may ripen as early as the end of January and some as late as June. Unquestionably, if the halibut frequented waters that were available to anglers it would be rated as a top game fish.

Pacific Halibut
(*Hippoglosus stenolepis*)

A close relative of its Atlantic cousin, the Pacific halibut is also a huge flatfish which reaches a weight of about 500 pounds. It ranges from central California north to the Bering Sea. On the other side of the Pacific it is distributed to northern Japan. In general anatomy, size, and color it resembles the Atlantic halibut closely (which see). It is a desirable commercial fish, but it holds no spot on any list of game fishes only because it does not inhabit waters which are readily available to anglers.

Northern Fluke (39a)
(*Paralichthys dentatus*)

This flatfish is a favorite sport fish with anglers along the northeastern coast of the United States. It grows to good size, raps a bait or lure smartly, and is a fine table fish. Many publications list this fish as summer flounder, but I believe it should be northern fluke because anglers do not refer to it by any other name—at least in all the areas I have fished for it, from Long Island to Maine. It is a member of the family PARALICHTHYIDAE and has a close Atlantic cousin in the southern fluke and a Pacific relative in the California halibut. Its distribution is chiefly from Maine to South Carolina with its northern range mostly south of Cape Cod (it is a rare straggler north of the Cape).

The northern fluke is left handed, that is, it lies on its right side and the eyes are on the left side. It has a large mouth containing sharp teeth. The shape of the body is narrower than in most flounders. The dorsal fin, which originates ahead or opposite the eyes, has 85 to 94 dorsal fin rays, and the anal fin has from 60 to 73 rays. The margin of the tail is rounded, or double concave when not extended. The underside is white, and like most flatfishes it is brown, gray, or dusky above with

Flounders, Flukes, Halibuts

mottlings of pale and dark. It may or may not be marked with spots darker than the background color. Usually about 10 or 12 oscillated dark spots are present. The northern fluke has the ability to adapt its coloration, more or less, to the actual colors of the bottom it inhabits. A wide range of tints can be assumed —from nearly white on white sand through various hues of gray, blue, green, orange, pink, and brown to almost black. Also, the variegations on its upper surface can be a fine or coarse pattern depending on the bottom.

The world record rod and reel fish weighed 20 pounds 7 ounces and was taken in Block Island Sound on July 8, 1957, by Maggie Fredriksen. The largest definitely recorded weighed 26 pounds, but the average size is about 2 to 4 pounds. The approximate length-to-weight ratios are about as follows:

Inches	Pounds
15–16	1–1¼
17–18	2–2¾
20	3–3½
22	4
27	8
30	10
37	20

Spawning takes place offshore in the late fall, winter, and early spring. It is a fierce, rapid, predacious fish feeding mostly on smaller fishes of various kinds as well as on squid, crabs, shrimp, other crustaceans, and worms. The fluke spends most of its life on or close to the bottom, and during its stay along inshore waters it prefers sandy or muddy bottoms. It has the ability to bury itself quickly in the sand up to its eyes.

Anglers take most fluke during the warm months when the fish come to inshore waters. Many are taken along open coasts, in bays and harbors, and smaller ones are often caught from docks, piers, and bridges. Occasionally some may run into fresh water rivers. However, the greater proportion of the larger fish are found farther offshore in depths of 8 or 10 fathoms or deeper. It is one of the best of the flatfishes on the table, and commercially it usually brings the highest prices—next to the halibut. Without doubt it is the gamest of our flatfishes and will readily take live bait or artificial lures. Often I have seen one follow my bait and grab it close to the surface, and I have also witnessed fluke jump clear of the water in wild dashes into schools of small bait fishes.

Southern Fluke
(*Paralichthys lethostigmus*)

The southern fluke, called flounder or mud flounder by some fishermen, is the southern representative of the northern fluke. It is the only flounder of commercial value along the southern states. The general distribution of this flatfish is from North Carolina southward to Corpus Christi, Texas. It is common throughout its range. Along the coast of our southern states it is the largest flounder. Market fish are usually between 12 and 20 inches. The maximum size appears to be about 30 inches. However, records are scarce; the southern fluke may grow to a larger size. In most respects the southern fluke closely resembles its northern cousin. However, it can be differentiated by its spots which are diffuse, none especially prominent, and not definitely occilated. Further, a count of the gill rakers on the lower limb of the first arch will positively distinguish *lethostigma* and *dentatus* in every case; southern fluke have 8 to 11 rakers; northern fluke, 13 to 18. Not much is known concerning the life history of this species. Spawning probably takes place in the late fall or early winter.

From North Carolina to Texas this fluke makes up a fairly important commercial fishery. Along sandy shore areas spearing is the most common method of capturing this fish; the operation is known as gigging, floundering, or flounderlighting and is usually done by poling a boat along the shallows or wading at night with a light. Dark, calm nights, when the incoming tide brings the fish into the shallows, are best. Southern fluke are also taken in quantities in haul seines, gill nets, and shrimp trawls.

California Halibut (40b)
(*Paralichthys californicus*)

Although belonging to the same genus and resembling closely the fluke of the Atlantic, this species is commonly called halibut in California, a name which properly belongs to a distinct and quite different species of flatfish. Bastard halibut, Monterey halibut, chicken halibut, southern halibut, and alabato are other common names. It is distributed from Tomales Bay, California, to Magdalena Bay, Lower California. San Diego seems to be the area of greatest abundance; it is also abundant at Monterey and taken in moderate commercial quantities at San Francisco.

The California halibut is the largest of the genus *Paralichthys* in American waters. The largest specimen recorded weighed 58 pounds and was 4 feet 10 inches in length. Like the Atlantic flukes, this fish faces left and has a high arch in the lateral line above the pectoral fin. The jaws are large and hold strong sharp teeth. The maxilla reaches to or beyond the hind border of the lower eye. About 100 scales are present in the lateral line. Little is known concerning its life history. Spawning occurs from February to July, with greatest activity taking place in May. The California halibut is one of the most important food fishes on the coast of California and Lower California. The commercial catch is obtained mostly in water 3 to 20 fathoms in depth. It is one of the most desirable sport species in southern California and ranks among the top game fishes in total poundage taken annually.

Fourspot Fluke (39b)
(*Paralichthys oblongus*)

This flatfish closely resembles the fluke in form and habit. It ranges from the eastern part of Georges Bank southward to the coast of South Carolina. Between southern New England and Delaware Bay it is found in its greatest abundance.

The fourspot can be distinguished easily from the northern fluke by its four oblong and very conspicuous black spots on the top side. They are edged with pale pink; two are located at each side of the body close to the margin. Also it has fewer fin rays—dorsal 72 to 86; anal 58 to 72 (northern fluke—dorsal 85 to 94; anal 60 to 73). The dorsal surface, other than the conspicuous spots, is colored in shades of browns and dark grays similar to other flatfishes. Occasionally specimens have been taken whose undersides were dark rather than white and marked with four spots similar to the ones on the upper side. It is a much smaller fish than the northern fluke. The bulk of the specimens captured are about 12 inches or less. Maximum about 16 inches. Because of its small size it is not important commercially. Taken by anglers incidentally.

Lenguado

(*Paralichthys brasiliensis*)

Along the Atlantic coast of South America the lenguado is probably the most abundant species of *Paralichthys*. The common commercial flounder along the coasts of Brazil, Uruguay, and Argentina appears to be this flatfish. The lenguado is mottled with brown and may be spotted. Distinguishing characters are gill rakers on lower limb of first arch 14 to 17; dorsal rays 68 to 78; anal rays 54 to 60. Maxilla reaches up to or past the eye, and the large mouth contains strong canine teeth. Maximum size is not recorded. Argentine sportsmen who catch the fish surf casting claim it to run to about 50 pounds, but a 10 pounder is considered large.

Winter Flounder (39c)

(*Pseudopleuronectes americanus*)

The winter flounder is the most common shoalwater flatfish along the coast of North America from the coast line out to the offshore fishing banks. It is the thickest, meatiest, and tastiest of all the flatfishes. Not only is it one of the most valuable commercial fishes in the western north Atlantic but it is also of great importance as a gamefish, and thousands of anglers

Flounders, Flukes, Halibuts

catch tons of them each year. Other common names are flatfish, flounder, blackback flounder, lemon sole, mud dab, and black flounder. It is a member of the family *Pleuronectidae* and ranges along the north Atlantic coast from Labrador to Georgia.

The winter flounder is a right-sided species. It is easily separated from the yellowtail flounder by its lateral line which is nearly straight (yellowtail lateral line takes a high curve above the pectoral fin). Also the dorsal profile of its head is less concave, its nose is more blunt, eyes are farther apart, and it has fewer fin rays—dorsal 60 to 75, anal 45 to 58. (Yellowtail— dorsal 76 to 85, anal 56 to 63 rays). The mouth is small, the gape does not reach the eye, the lips are thick and fleshy, and the tail is round. Usually this flounder has a dark back, but as with other flounders the color varies in shade according to the type of bottom the fish inhabits. It may be dusky, dark brown, reddish brown, greenish brown or olive, dark slate, or almost black. This flounder can be plain in color, vary with mottlings, or marked with spots of darker shades of the ground color. Underside is usually flat white with a slight bluish cast, and the caudal peduncle may have a yellowish tinge. Occasionally a fish may be taken which has dark blotches on the underside.

The largest recorded winter flounder caught inshore was 22¾ inches. Another authentic report is 20 inches and 5 pounds. However, fishes longer than 18 inches inshore are unusual. A fish from 12 to 15 inches is considered good size. However, out on Georges Bank winter flounder of larger size are taken; many 4 to 6 pounders are caught, and one of 8 pounds and 25 inches was recorded.

The winter flounder is one of the most stationary fishes along the north Atlantic coast. Its migrations seem to be only seasonal movements from deeper water in the summer back to shoal water in the winter. Extensive marking experiments have been carried out in Long Island Sound, along southern New England, and along the coast of Maine. Ninety-four per cent of the fish recaptured were taken in the general area where the fish had been tagged. A few fish have been recaptured after traveling some distance (Block Island to Georges Bank); this seems to be an exception, but it demonstrates that some interchange takes place between inshore and offshore populations. Generally, along the southern New England coast the fish come into shoal water in the early spring and depart when the water begins to warm up. They return again in the fall and depart when the water becomes uncomfortably cold in winter. They may descend to depths of 30 to 50 fathoms during the cold season. Farther south (south of New York), where the coastal waters are warmer, these flatfishes migrate into deep water during the summer and back into shoal areas for the winter.

Spawning takes place mostly on sandy bottom during winter and early spring—in New England from January to May inclusive. Farther north (Maine) spawning occurs from about the first of March to around the first week in May. Average females produce approximately 500,000 eggs annually. However, fish slightly over 3 pounds can carry nearly 1,500,000 eggs. The eggs are not buoyant but sink to the bottom and stick together in clusters.

Winter flounder feed mostly on shrimp, amphipods, sea worms, small crabs, and other crustaceans. Occasionally they also take squid and small fish. Along the New England shores in spring, the winter flounder is one of the first species of fish to be taken by scores of anglers. Of recent years the handline has given way to spinning outfits. On light fishing gear this flatfish produces an excellent fight. Aside from boat fishing, the angler can take them off rocks, jetties, bridges, and piers. However, the most productive method, and one that I use, is to drift along slowly in a rowboat and either troll or cast but drag the bait and sinker along the bottom. The slight disturbance of a sinker dragged along the sand or mud will often attract flatfish in the vicinity. They will take a variety of baits—clams, mussels, snails, squid, shrimp, and both marine and angle worms.

Many anglers turn up their noses at flounder fishing, especially when the stocked trout season opens. However, I must confess that although I love trout fishing, I am one of the crazy clan that awaits with keen anticipation the joys of rainy day fishing for the "flats" in the cold weather of early spring.

Yellowtail Flounder (39d)
(*Limanda ferruginea*)

The yellowtail flounder, also called rusty dab, is a commercial flatfish of North American continental waters from the lower part of Chesapeake Bay northward to the north shore of the Gulf of St. Lawrence. Although it is one of the most valuable of flatfishes, it inhabits waters much too deep to be of interest to anglers. Only occasionally is one taken on rod and reel.

It is right sided, has a small mouth, pointed snout, thin body, and eyes set close together. The dorsal fin has 76 to 85 rays; the anal has 56 to 63 rays and is preceded by a short, sharp spine pointing forward. The top side is reddish, brownish, brownish red, olive, or dusky and profusely spotted with irregular rusty spots. The tail and the margins of the long fins are yellow. The underside is white with the caudal peduncle yellowish. Maximum size is about 18 inches; average is about 15 inches. It is more sluggish than other flatfishes. Excellent on the table.

Starry Flounder (40d)
(*Platichthys stellatus*)

Along the Pacific coast of the United States this flatfish, a member of the family PLEURONECTIDAE, is a valued commercial fish. It provides much sport for anglers and rates highly as a small game fish. It has a wide distribution from southern California to Alaska, and on the other side of the Pacific to Japan and Korea. The starry flounder is a broad flatfish that may face right or left, and its lateral line is almost straight. The most obvious distinguishing characteristics are dark bars on the long fins and dark broad stripes on the tail. Also, rough plates are scattered on the top side which gives this fish a name of grindstone or emery wheel in some areas. Color is dark brown to nearly black on the top side and white to creamy underneath. Orange-yellow or reddish orange areas are present between the dark bands on fins and tail. Maximum size is about 20 pounds. Food consists of crabs, shrimp, worms, clams, and small fishes. Spawning takes place in late winter and early spring.

This flounder seems to prefer shallow water areas and often moves into brackish or fresh water rivers. Most of the fish taken by anglers are caught still fishing using the usual bait, clams or worms. However, during one expedition to Unimak Island in the Aleutians, Larry Sheerin and I experienced some wonderful sport with the starry flounder. We were fishing primarily for dolly varden trout as we cast small spoons into a fairly large and rapid river which emptied into the sea a couple of miles farther down. We caught many good-sized dolly varden, which put up a splendid battle in such cold swift water, but the occasional, large starry flounders that grabbed our lures out-scrapped the trout!

Diamond Flounder (40c)
(*Hypsopsetta guttulata*)

This Pacific flatfish of the family PLEURONECTIDAE is caught mostly by sportsmen fishing in the bays of southern California. It is not important commercially. It ranges from northern California south into the Gulf of California. The diamond flounder is a wide flatfish with a body shaped more or less like a diamond. Instead of being oval the outline of the body is angular with the widest points on either side about mid-body. It faces right. The lateral line is almost straight; the mouth is small, and the color of the top side is brown, greenish brown, olive-brown, and mottled with paler shades. Maximum size is about 4 pounds and a length of 18 inches.

Greenlings

There are several species of greenlings which resemble each other closely. All are fine eating and interesting because of their vivid coloration. As a group greenlings cannot be termed game fishes; most are taken incidentally, bottom fishing in deep, rocky waters. Two species are caught by hook and line in fairly good numbers and are worth listing here.

Greenling

(*Hexagrammos decagrammus*)

The greenling, also called rock trout and seatrout, is a fish of our Pacific coast from Kodiak Island south to Point Conception, California. It is no relation to trout but is a member of the family HEXAGRAMMIDAE. The greenling is a spectacularly colored fish; male and female coloration is quite different. Both have a background of browns and grays, but the head and fore parts of the male are covered with large light blue spots, each surrounded by a ring of small reddish spots, while the back, sides, and head of the female are covered closely and uniformly with round, reddish spots. The dorsal fin appears to be divided but is not; dorsal spines number 21 or 22, rays, 24. Anal fin has

1 spine and 23 or 24 rays. The tail is squarish, and the pectoral fin is unusually large. Other distinguishing characteristics are two pairs of fleshy flaps on top of the head and 5 lateral lines. It is not a large fish; maximum length about 20 inches.

Atka Mackerel (31d)
(*Pleurogrammus monopterygius*)

The atka mackerel or atkafish is a fine food and game fish found mostly in the vicinity of kelp beds in the cold waters around the Aleutian, Pribilof, and Shumagin Islands off Alaska. Not a mackerel, it is a member of the Greenling family HEXAGRAMMIDAE. It is a striking fish with conspicuous black vertical bars over a yellow or gray body. The dorsal fin is unusually long, being almost the entire length of the body. The anal (minus spines) and pectoral fins are also large, and the tail is forked with rounded tips. Maximum size is around 4 pounds. Often 2- to 3-pound atka mackerel can be seen finning over acres of water when feeding on tiny crustaceans. At this time they may afford great sport because they will take a small brown fly and put up a fine scrap before being boated. They are well known for their fine table quality, and the natives along the Aleutians capture tons of them with handline. The fish are preserved for future use by drying and salting.

Grunts

The grunts, members of the family HAEMULIDAE, are small- to medium-size fishes which closely resemble the snappers but do not have teeth in the roof of the mouth. The genus *haemulon* contains many species. The name "grunt" is derived from the grunting sound these fishes are capable of producing. It is made when the upper pharyngeal teeth (throat) grate against the lower teeth. The swim bladder also acts as a sound-making device. Yellow color is found in various degrees in most of the species, and many have splashes of red on the inside of the mouth. When young, some of the species have two or more horizontal dark lines along the sides.

Although grunts form rather large schools during the breeding season, they usually travel singly or in small groups. Most of their feeding is done at night on small fishes, crustaceans, and other small invertebrates. The members of the family have a world-wide distribution in warm seas. In the western Atlantic they range from about North Carolina down to Argentina but are most abundant from Florida southward. Grunts are present along the Gulf Coast, and in the Pacific they occur from California south to Ecuador. Grunts are marketed and valued as fine food but cannot be termed game fishes. However, anglers close to shore catch many; therefore I list the most popular ones as an aid to identification by fishermen.

Margate (26d)
(*Haemulon album*)

Bermuda, West Indies, Florida to Brazil. Body color is pearl, pearl gray, or gray; three horizontal dark bands may or may not be present—most prominent one runs from the snout, through the eye, and along the body to the tail. Mouth has an orange-red lining. The back has a steep profile; tail is forked. Dorsal fin has 12 spines, 16 rays; anal 3 spines, 8 rays. Gill rakers 12 to 13 on lower limb of first arch. Average fish weigh less than a pound, but maximum size is in the vicinity of 18 inches and 8 pounds. The margate likes coral reefs and fairly deep water. It is an important food fish in the Florida Keys and Cuban markets.

Bluestripe Grunt (26b)
(*Haemulon sciurus*)

Also called yellow grunt. Bermuda, West Indies, Florida to Brazil. Color yellowish, occasionally with irregular dark vertical bars; sides of head and body with horizontal blue stripes. Fins may be translucent yellow, greenish, or black. Tail may be black with a yellowish or greenish posterior margin. Inside of mouth orange-red. Young may have dark blotch on caudal peduncle. The color is changeable and the background may be grayish. The first dorsal has 12 spines and 16 to 17 rays; anal 3 spines and 8 or 9 rays. Gill rakers 16 to 18 on lower limb of first gill arch.

White Grunt (26c)
(*Haemulon plumieri*)

Also gray grunt. Bermuda, West Indies, Cape Hatteras to

ook taken by Larry Sheerin of San Antonio, Texas, at Eighth Pass, Mexico.

Above: A couple of dolphins taken off Bermuda showing the differences in the head profile—female, right; male or bull, left.

Right: Hal Lyman, publisher of the Salt Water Sportsman, with a dolphin taken off Exuma, Bahamas. (Photo by Jarvis Darville)

Brazil (introduced to Bermuda in 1924). Deep through the body, large mouth, large scales above lateral line. Color varies from blue-grayish to bronzy, often pale; head yellowish with numerous thin blue lines. Spray of yellow sometimes present along lateral line; dark spots on scales form lines running upward and rearward. Inside of mouth red. Dorsal fin bluish gray edged with yellow; second dorsal and tail yellowish gray. Dorsal fin 12 spines, 15 or 16 rays; anal 3 spines, 8 or 9 rays. Gill rakers 14 or 15 on lower limb of first arch. Maximum size about 4 pounds, over 2 pounds rare; average about 5 ounces. Spawns on the bottom in August and September in large schools. Eggs without parental care. Feeds mostly at night on crustaceans and worms. Taken commercially.

Gray Grunt

(*Haemulon macrostomum*)

Also striped grunt, streaked trout, black grunt. Bermuda, West Indies, Florida to Panama and Colombia. Large mouth, deep body, long snout. Dorsal fin 12 spines, 15 to 17 rays; anal 3 spines (second large) 8 or 9 rays. Gill rakers short, 16 or 17 on lower limb of first arch. Color background may be dusky gray or silvery greenish gray above going to light silver below. Four or 5 conspicuous horizontal dark streaks along sides. Dorsal and anal fin greenish yellow, tail dusky or greenish yellow. Pectoral fin bright yellow. Inside of mouth flesh color. Maximum size about 15 inches and a weight of 2 pounds. Feeds mostly at night on small crabs, worms, and fishes.

French Grunt (26a)

(*Haemulon flavolineatum*)

Also yellow grunt. Bermuda, West Indies, Florida Keys to Brazil. Large scales below lateral line. Dorsal fin 12 spines, 14 or 15 rays; anal 3 spines, 7 or 8 rays. Gill rakers 13 or 14 on lower limb of first arch. Base color grayish blue; bright yellow stripes over most of body; those above lateral line are parallel to it; those below lateral line run upward and rearward. Fins are bright yellow; inside of mouth is red. Average weight is about one half pound; seldom exceeds 12 inches in length.

Ronco (27b)

(*Haemulon parra*)

Also, sailor's choice. Southern Florida to Brazil. Color variable; usually base is gray, silvery gray, or light olive green with small brown spots on scales forming lines covering most of body. Lower sides usually covered with fine dark specks; head and fins dark. Inside of mouth orange. Second dorsal and anal fins possess scales. Spawns during summer over rocky bottom. Feeds usually at night on worms, crustaceans, and other invertebrates. Average size about one half pound. Valuable food fish.

Black Margate

(*Anisotremus surinamensis*)

Also pompon. West Indies, Florida to Brazil. Not common anywhere. It is the largest of the grunts; fish of several pounds have been taken, but the average is in the vicinity of 1 to 2 pounds. There is confusion regarding its maximum size—publications list it up to 20 pounds, but this weight is doubtful. The black margate has a very deep body, small mouth, thick lips, large scales, and the inside of the mouth is white; these are definite distinguishing characteristics. General coloration is dusky or grayish; each scale is brownish on its anterior portion and grayish white on the outer border. The color contrast is quite conspicuous. Fins are dusky or blackish. When the fish is alive, a dark, wide vertical band is present on the fore part of the body. Anglers catch the black margate only occasionally; it seems to swim in mixed schools with other fishes which frequent waters close to shore.

Porkfish (27c)

(Anisotremus virginicus)

Bermuda, West Indies, Florida to Brazil (introduced in Bermuda). Deep body, small mouth, thick lips, steep face and head profile. Dorsal fin 12 spines, 16 or 17 rays; anal 3 spines, 9 or 10 rays. Gill rakers 13 to 15 on lower limb of first arch. Easy to identify. Basic coloration and fins bright yellow. Conspicuous blue horizontal lines along body. Two black bars add sharply contrasting colors. One bar extends from the end of the jaw, through the eye, and over the head; the other goes from the front part of the dorsal fin to the pectoral fin. Not a large fish; most specimens under a pound; maximum length about 12 inches and a weight of about 2 pounds. Like other grunts it feeds mostly during the night on crustaceans, worms, and small fishes. Spawns during summer in schools.

Sargo (27d)

(Anisotremus davidsonii)

Also named perch, black croaker, china croaker, blue bass, bass. A Pacific grunt closely related to the Atlantic members of the same genus. It ranges from Point Conception, California, south into central Lower California. Deep body, small mouth, thick lips, no teeth on roof of mouth; dorsal fin 11 or 12 spines; anal 3 spines, 10 or 11 rays. Color entirely iridescent silvery with grayish tinge above; dorsal surface, head, and sides sometimes with indistinct blotches; dark vertical band across body. Generally taken during warm weather in shallow water.

Pigfish (27a)

(Orthopristes chrysopterus)

Also called sailor's choice. Bermuda, Gulf of Mexico, Florida to North Carolina; strays to New York and Massachusetts. Most numerous in North Carolina and Virginia. Deep body, pointed snout, thin lips. Dorsal spines 12 or 13, rays 15 or 16; anal 3 spines, 12 or 13 rays. Gill rakers 12 on lower limb of first arch. Blue above going to silvery to white below; each body scale has a blue center and a bronze spot on the edge of each scale thus forming stripes on the back and sides of the fish. The stripes above the lateral line extend upward and backward while those below are more or less horizontal. The snout and head contain lines and bronze spots. Second dorsal, anal fin, and tail are edged dusky or blackish; pectorals and ventrals yellowish. The pigfish is small, usually from 4 to 6 inches in length but may reach about 15 inches. Often used as bait; excellent for tarpon.

Jackfishes

The jackfishes or carangid fishes (from the family name CARAN-GIDAE) comprise a large family of warm-water, open-sea fishes, many of whose members love to inhabit inshore areas. The group embraces some well-known game fishes of jacks, amberjacks, and pompanos. Other peculiar-looking members of this clan such as lookdown, moonfish, and threadfin are caught incidentally by anglers. The rest of the jacks, which are not game fishes, but round out the family are pilotfish, banded rudderfish, jumper, leatherjack, and scad.

This group is closely related to the mackerels and possesses anatomical similarities such as two dorsal fins, first hard-spined and the second soft-rayed; ventral fins at the breast; a slender caudal peduncle; and a deeply forked tail. The jackfishes differ in not having a series of well defined finlets, and the spiny dorsal fin is not large but is rather small and inconspicuous. Most of the carangids have a series of sharp scutes along each side of the caudal peduncle which may inflict a nasty wound to a careless angler. They rove usually in closely packed schools and are located easily when chasing small fish, for they create a commotion on the surface which can be spotted from a long distance. Only a few are of commercial value, but most (jacks, amberjacks, pompanos) are prized by anglers because of their sporting qualities. They seldom jump, but produce a strong, dogged fight characterized by short but powerful runs.

Of all the game fishes the jackfishes are, without question, the least understood. There must be a couple hundred different species in the world, but even those that are common along our coasts remain question marks. Scientific literature, in attempting to differentiate species, subspecies, and other relationships, creates a jargon of confusion. Many genuses of convenience have been established. Any taxonomist who attempts to straighten out this group has a long, difficult task ahead of him. Many of the species, even in the most common genus (*caranx*) change with age, and thus misidentification comes about. To make matters worse, these changes vary in the different species. It is even possible for some aged individuals to lose their dorsal fin spines completely. Also, the anal fin is preceded by 2 or 3 spines which may be lost in old age. I have selected only those carangids which are usually taken by anglers in the Atlantic and Pacific.

JACKS

Jack Crevally (14b)

(Caranx hippos)

The jack crevally is one of the most common of the carangid fishes. It is a fine game fish but worthless for the table. Common jack or crevalle are other common names, and in Bermuda it is known as horseeye jack. The Pacific form is known as *Caranx caninus;* however, the differences between these jacks of different oceans are so slight that I prefer not to differentiate them. It ranges along both coasts of America. On the western side of the Atlantic it is found from Brazil, the Caribbean, Gulf of Mexico, along Florida's coasts, where it is abundant all year, to as far north as Nova Soctia as a stray. It also inhabits Bermudian and Bahamian waters. In the eastern Atlantic it is known to be abundant along the African Gold Coast. Along

Jacks

the eastern Pacific it ranges generally from the Gulf of California southward to Peru. It is also found in Hawaiian waters and along the western Pacific.

It is bluish green or greenish bronze on the dorsal surface, with light golden or silvery sides growing lighter below. Sometimes the lower side has a yellowish tinge or yellow splotches. Young fish have 5 or 6 dark crossbars. The adults have a pugnacious-appearing, sharply rounded head. A conspicuous black spot is present on the upper hind edge of the operculum. The long, curved pectoral fin has a less distinct dark blotch on its lower anterior portion. The dorsal fin contains 8 spines, and the second dorsal has about 20 rays. The anal fin, with about 17 rays, is preceded by 2 short, detached spines. Prominent scutes are present along the posterior portion of the lateral line and the caudal peduncle. The breast is scaled only in a small triangular patch in front of the ventral fins.

Most of the individuals I have seen, in schools along shore, averaged 2 to 3 pounds. Out in the open deeper waters I have taken them about 6 to 8 pounds. However, the species reaches 20 and 25 pounds, and Lou Mowbray states that they reach a size of 35 pounds in Bermudian waters. Nothing is known about the life history of the jack crevalle. It is a voracious eater, hacking into schools of small fishes with abandon. On light tackle it is a great fish, and in Bermuda they are caught mostly at night in tideways, particularly in summer.

Blue Runner (14a)

(*Caranx crysos*)

The Atlantic blue runner is a small jack which prefers warm waters. It is common and seems to be recognized by most southern salt water anglers. This jack is also known as hardtail jack, but this is no improvement on the name blue runner since all jacks possess a hard tail. Admittedly the blue runner is more green than it is blue, but because this jack is nearly always called blue runner, I retain that name here. Another small jack, *Caranx ruber*, resembles and is closely related to the blue runner, but anglers do not bother to differentiate between the two species. However, they can be separated easily (*see* Runner). The Pacific form, green jack, *Caranx caballus,* is perhaps identical with the blue runner (*see* Green Jack). *Caranx crysos* ranges from Brazil to Nova Scotia, occasionally being found in Bermuda waters and abundant in the Bahamas. It appears to be the most common jack to appear in northerly waters off Massachusetts.

In coloration it is similar to the Pacific green jack—over all bronze green and silvery along the sides. A dark spot is present on the upper edge of the operculum. The pectoral fins are long, the breast is scaled, and 42 to 50 scutes are present along the posterior portion of the lateral line and caudal peduncle. The second dorsal fin contains 23 to 25 rays and the anal 19 to 20. Gill rakers number about 24. Other jacks—crevally, yellow, horseeye—have fewer gill rakers, 13 to 18. Average weight for this species is about 1 pound, and 2 or 3 pounds may be considered large, but it is known to reach a weight of 6 pounds and a length of 2 feet.

Like all the other jacks the blue runner is migratory, but definite routes and seasons are not as yet known. It is a gregarious fish and often found in its northern range in mixed schools with the jack crevally. Off Florida it may be mixed with groups of runners. Mostly, it prefers inshore waters although encountered occasionally offshore. Its favorite food is shrimp, tiny fishes, and small crabs. Although not a large fish, it is a commendable fighter and will not give up even after being boated. Similar to the dolphin, it continues to beat a fast tattoo on the deck. It is often used as bait by big game anglers.

Runner

(*Caranx ruber*)

The runner is another small member of the jack family, about a foot in length and often confused with the blue runner. Usually *Caranx ruber* has a more southern distribution than its close cousin *Caranx crysos,* with a range from West Indies to

Florida and occasionally to North Carolina. In color the runner is blue-gray, but often its body has a greenish tinge. It has a vivid, dark blue band along the base of the dorsal fin. The lower lobe of the caudal fin has a dark bar. (In Bermuda where *Caranx ruber* is called green jack, Louis Mowbray states, "the green jack has a neon green stripe along the base of the dorsal fin.")

It is no wonder that anglers do not differentiate between the runner and blue runner because these two species appear identical and both have 23 or more gill rakers on the lower limb of the first arch. However, they can be separated easily. The runner possesses scutes which are not as pronounced and are fewer in number (30–35) than those of the blue runner (42–50). Like all jacks, the runner is a fine scrapper on light tackle. In Bermuda it is quite common and commercially important.

Green Jack

(Caranx caballus)

The green jack is a Pacific form which is found from San Pedro, California, to Peru. It is a small, slim fish about 15 inches in length with a greenish tinge to most of the body going silvery ventrally. A black spot is present on the operculum edge. The gill raker count on the first gill below the angle is 25 to 30. Another distinguishing characteristic is the scaled membrane between the first 5 or 6 rays of the second dorsal fin. This fish resembles the blue runner of the Atlantic and the two may be closely related. On light tackle it is very sporty. Another carangid, *Caranx ruber,* is called green jack in Bermuda waters.

Yellow Jack (14c)

(Caranx bartholomaei)

The yellow jack is an Atlantic and Caribbean species which ranges from the West Indies to as far north as Cape Cod, where it is considered a straggler. This jack is found in Bermuda and

Bahama waters and is well known off Cuba, Florida, and North Carolina. Another common name for *Caranx bartholomaei* is bar jack.

This fish is sometimes listed as reaching a maximum size of 15 inches; others list it as from 3 to 15 pounds. Its coloration is typically that of a jack with a light bluish green dorsal surface and silvery sides containing a golden yellow tint. The yellow coloration is more pronounced after death. The gill raker count is 17 to 19; the rather weak scutes along the caudal peduncle number from 22 to 35; the ray count is 26 to 28 in the second dorsal fin and 22 to 24 in the anal.

Gwelly

(*Caranx guara*)

In the Atlantic this fish is known to inhabit Bermuda's waters, and it has been recorded from the Mediterranean. It may possibly be present in the Pacific. Practically nothing is known concerning this species. Therefore I am quoting Louis Mowbray: "worthy of mention because of its change in habits with age is another jack, known locally as gwelly. It is *Caranx guara*. Very game and fair eating. Generally a yellow-gray in color, with a large sickle-shaped pectoral fin. In its younger stages, e.g. 10 inches, it resembles most of the conventional jacks. However, from this size it changes its feeding habits and grubs along the bottom like a bonefish or channel bass feeding on worms and tiny mollusks. This causes the mouth to become very large and flabby, and due to its stamina, a difficult fish to land on any tackle because the mouth tears easily. Maximum size is about 15 pounds. They spawn in June."

Horseeye Jack

(*Caranx latus* or *Caranx sexfaciatus*)

There is great confusion regarding this species. Some authors list it as an Atlantic species only. Others consider it to be an inhabitant of the Atlantic and the Pacific. *Caranx latus* is

Jacks

listed in a recent publication on the fishes of the Texas coast, but the author gives its range as "the tropical Atlantic and the Indo-Pacific areas." One author states the head is strongly convex; another illustrates this fish with a slanted head profile. From all descriptions it appears that the horseeye jack and the jack crevally are similar in every respect except for the amount of scales on the breast. In Bermuda the *Caranx hippos* is known as horseeye jack. Perhaps the reader is confused about this species. I am, and so is everyone else!

Spotted Jack (15d)

(Caranx stellatus)

The spotted jack, known as blue crevally or lua in the Pacific (koli-koli and karambesi, East Afria), is one of the most colorful of the carangid fishes. Its dorsal surface is bluish green, and its sides are silvery. Dark spots are scattered over most of the body. To my knowledge it is the only *caranx* or typical jack which is liberally spotted; therefore I believe that a less confusing name is spotted jack. In the eastern Pacific it has been taken from Mexico to Panama. It is also present in Hawaiian waters and the Indian Ocean. *Caranx stellatus* is the largest member of the jack family and reportedly grows to about 150 pounds. During the Yale–East African Expedition, while fishing off Pemba Island (north of Zanzibar), Tom Shevlin caught one that weighed 78 pounds, and I took another which tipped the scales at 72 pounds. We caught many of them in the Indian Ocean and found that even on marlin tackle the larger ones demonstrated unusual fighting qualities.

Pauu'u

(Caranx ignobilis)

Also known as ulua and karambesi, this fairly large jack is an Indo-Pacific inhabitant common around the Hawaiian Islands. It has the typical jack coloration but no spot on the gill cover. The scutes are many and prominent. It has scales on the cheek and upper part of the gill cover. A small patch of scales is present on the breast. Not as large as *Caranx stellatus*, it reaches a length of about 2 feet and is great on light tackle.

Bigeye Jack
(*Caranx marginatus*)

Not a well-known Pacific jack. It has been recorded from Mazatlán, Mexico, to Panama, and Hawaii. This jack probably ranges elsewhere in the Pacific, but no investigations have been conducted into this species. Its chief distinguishing marks are blackish dorsal and anal fins which have white tips on the longest rays. The second dorsal contains 19 or 20 rays, and the anal fin has 14 to 16 rays. The bigeye jack attains a length of approximately 3 feet, takes any type of artificial lure, and rates as a game fish.

Cavalla
(*Caranx ajax*)

The cavalla is a solitary, shallow water fish found around the Hawaiian Islands. Also called white ulua because of its silvery color; it has a white patch on the lower part of the pectoral fin. It is a large carangid reaching a weight of about 15 pounds. This Hawaiian jack is fairly common and holds both commercial and sporting interest.

Silver Trevally
(*Caranx georgianus* or *Usacaranx georgianus*)

This jack occurs in all Australian states and reaches a weight of about 10 pounds, but the average is approximately 2 pounds. The silver trevally usually congregate in channels in the surf where anglers cast for them. It is of unusual, fine quality on the table and as a smoked fish is considered excellent. It holds distinction as one of the world's few salt water fishes that commands a legal size limit—11 inches in New South Wales, 12

Jacks

inches in Queensland, 8 inches in Victoria, South Australia, and Western Australia.

Turrum
(Caranx emburyi)

One of the best sporting fish in Australian waters (Queensland). It is a large jack known to reach a weight of about 70 pounds with an average size of 20 to 30 pounds. The Down Under anglers considered the turrum a splendid game fish; it puts up great resistance to the rod and reel for lengthy periods of time. *Caranx emburyi* is also one of the most beautiful fish off Queensland, of a flashing, iridescent, and pearlescent coloration.

Bludger
(Caranx gymnostethoides)

Considered a good fighter by Australian anglers, but not edible and a pest in some areas.

Great Trevally
(Caranx fosteri)

One of the largest of jacks growing to about 80 pounds and a length of 4 feet. Also one of the commonest along the coast of Queensland, present during all seasons.

King Trevally
(Caranx speciosus)

Another common Australian jack that grows to a length of about 3 feet.

Cuban Jack (14d)
(Hynnis cubensis)

The Cuban jack, also called African pompano, is a beautiful but rare fish. It is found off Florida, Bermuda, Bahamas, Cuba, and the West Indies. Most Cuban jacks caught by anglers are taken in the upper keys during winter, although this fish is present the year round. Off Bermuda and the Bahamas it is taken only occasionally, usually by trolling offshore. It has a typical carangid body with breast fins, large pectorals, deeply forked tail, and bony scutes along the lateral line before the tail. It differs from other jacks in that it has no first dorsal fin. Another outstanding feature is the nearly vertical front profile of the head. The dorsal surface has a light blue-green cast, while the over-all pearlescent and iridescent hues on most of the body of this fish produce a most striking coloration. This large jack averages approximately 10 pounds in weight, but 30 pounds is not unusual, and the maximum appears to be in the vicinity of 40 pounds.

A large Cuban jack is identified easily because of its coloration and lack of a first dorsal fin. In smaller specimens the first few rays of the soft dorsal and anal fins are extremely long and threadlike. It seems likely that the threadfin, *Alectis crinitus*, may be the young stage of the Cuban jack. Not enough specimens have been studied for scientists to arrive at definite conclusions. A close relative in the Pacific, the goggleeye, *Hynnis hopkinsi*, resembles closely the Atlantic species. Nothing is known concerning the life history of this fish.

As a game fish it is indeed a prize, not only because it fights well and is of good size, but because it is rather rare and of unusual coloration.

Goggleeye Jack

(*Hynnis hopkinsi*)

The goggleeye is a close relative of the Atlantic's Cuban jack and is known from Mexico and Panama. Its soft dorsal fin contains 18 rays, the anal fin has 14 rays, the first gill on the lower angle has about 12 gill rakers. (For a description *see* Cuban Jack.)

Mackerel Jack (15a)
(*Trachurus symmetricus*)

Because of the appearance of enormous numbers of mackerel jack off the coast of southern California in recent years, this fish has suddenly developed into an angler's delight. It also is important commercially.

In nearly all publications that include this jack its common name is given as California horse mackerel or jack mackerel. The authors state, "this is not a mackerel"; then they go on to explain why it is a member of the jack group. To remedy this confusion and unnecessary wordage is a simple matter. Horse mackerel, as a name, suggests a large fish of the finlet tribe and is obviously inappropriate; therefore it should not be used. The name "jack mackerel" has been used extensively, and I can appreciate the reluctance of authors to change it. However, why not reverse jack mackerel into mackerel jack? To me it seems ideal: it calls the fish a jack, which it is, instead of a mackerel; and no other fish holds that name.

The distribution of this member of the family CARANGIDAE appears to be from British Columbia down to Cape San Lucas, Mexico, but it undoubtedly ranges farther south. However, there is question concerning its identity in its extreme southern distribution. A fish which may be the mackerel jack or another species similar to it is found as far south as Chile.*

The mackerel jack's fin arrangement, deeply forked tail, and series of scutes along the lateral line are characteristics of the jack family, but the body of the fish is slender—more like that of a mackerel. The dorsal fins are close together, and the anterior portions are almost of the same height. The lateral line bends down abruptly just above the vent. Its first dorsal fin contains 8 spines; second dorsal has 1 spine followed by 31 soft rays,

---

* The mackerel jack has a close cousin on the other side of the Pacific; found mostly off Japan; it is given the scientific name of *Trachurus japonicus*. Some scientists believe that an Atlantic species, *Trachurus lathami*, is identical with *Trachurus symmetricus*, while others believe they are separate species.

and the anal has 1 spine plus 27 soft rays and is preceded by 2 minute spines. In coloration it is greenish blue iridescent on the dorsal surface, sometimes mottled with darker shades. The sides and belly are silvery. The large eye, mackerel shaped body, narrow caudal peduncle and carangid fin arrangement are all identification points, but the best is the lateral line which contains scutes along its entire length.

In the commercial catch since 1947 most of the fish have measured about 8 to 15 inches in total length. However, on occasion quantities of large mackerel jacks appear in the inshore waters of southern California. These fish, which come in only for a month or two each summer, range from 18 to 30 or more inches and up to about 5 pounds in weight. Although the mackerel jack makes seasonal appearances in fluctuating abundance, its migratory routes, inshore-offshore or along the coast, are not known.

Spawning takes place from March through October, but the peak of this activity does not usually occur until May and June. Off California and Baja California it can be found mostly from March through July. About 50 per cent of the two-year-old females spawn, but not until age three (about 14 inches in length) are 100 per cent of the females mature. Individual females spawn more than once during a season. Spawning takes place in the open ocean far from shore. Similar to most oceanic fishes the mackerel jack spawns in the upper layers of water (from the surface down to about 300 feet). These top layers of water are warmer than the deeper zones and better supplied with food. The eggs and larvae are found in greatest abundance off southern California and Baja California. However, they are also found north and south of these areas.

In recent studies John Fitch of the California Department of Fish and Game found that in both juvenile and adult mackerel jacks 90 per cent of the food consisted of small crustaceans [*] found in the upper layers of water. At times mackerel jacks feed heavily and almost exclusively upon juvenile squid and anchovies. It is interesting to note that in Fitch's investigations

[*] Euphausids, large copepods, and pteropods.

Jacks

mackerel jacks, which have been taken a considerable distance offshore, were found to be stuffed with lantern fishes which live at some depth in the ocean. However, these mackerel jacks were attracted to a bright light suspended from the boat's stern at night. The lantern fish were probably also attracted to the light and were captured by the jacks near the surface rather than in the depths.

During the routine sampling of the commercial catch off California the otoliths (ear bones) were found to be satisfactory for age determination. Some of the larger mackerel jacks were estimated reliably to be over 30 years of age!

Mackerel jack has always been taken to some extent off southern California by anglers; previously it was considered a minor game fish. However, in 1953 vast schools appeared in the inshore waters off southern California. In that year, during the month of August, 196,300 were taken, and since then this jack has become one of the major and prized sport fishes of California. Anglers prefer large anchovies as bait, and on light tackle this fish displays all the fine fighting qualities of the jack family.

The California Department of Fish and Game has been recording the approximate number of mackerel jacks caught by sports fishermen.

Year	Number	Best Month
1947	4,500	September
1948	2,400	August
1949	2,900	August
1950	600	July
1951	200	July
1952	4,400	May
1953	196,300	August
1954	19,400	June
1955	39,600	May

Bigeye Scad

(*Trachurops crumenophthalmus*)

This species is not considered a game fish. I include it here because it resembles closely the mackerel jack and may be confused with it. The bigeye scad occurs in the warm waters of the Atlantic and Pacific. In the Atlantic it ranges as far north as Nova Scotia. In the eastern Pacific it is found from Cape San Lucas to at least as far south as Panama. It is also present throughout the Gulf of California. This scad is a member of the jack family CARANGIDAE and grows to about 2 feet in length in the tropics, and from 10 to 15 inches in more northern waters.

It has a large eye with a well-developed adipose eyelid. A small black spot is present on the upper, posterior edge of the gill cover. The bigeye scad can be distinguished easily from the mackerel jack by the presence of a little fleshy knob on the shoulder girdle just under the gill cover. Its first dorsal fin contains 8 spines; second dorsal has 1 spine followed by 23 to 26 soft rays. The anal has 1 spine plus 20 to 23 rays and is preceded by 2 stout detached spines. Other scads, named mackerel scads of the genus *Decapterus*, are present in the Atlantic and Pacific. These resemble *Trachurops* but are separated easily because they possess a single finlet between the second dorsal fin and tail, and anal fin and tail.

Samsonfish (12d)

(*Seriola hippos*)

The samsonfish inhabits Australian waters off the coasts of New South Wales, southern Queensland, and along the south and west coasts of Western Australia, where it is known as sea kingfish. At one time it was fairly common off New South Wales and sold in markets, but it has been reduced drastically in numbers. This jack is one of the world's few salt water fishes which commands a legal minimum size—14 inches in Queensland and 15 inches in Western Australia. In general body shape it resembles more closely a typical jack, *Caranx*, than it does other fishes of the genus *Seriola*. Another closely related jack, also called samsonfish, is a different species, *Seriola simplex*. Maximum length for the samsonfish is about 2 feet. Australian anglers prize it as a fine sporting fish.

Leerfish (15b)

(*Hypacanthus amia*)

In the eastern Atlantic the leerfish is known from northwest Africa, Portugal, and occasionally as a stray off northwest Europe. Although it is a member of the jack family and its fin arrangement is carangid, its body is not that of a typical jack. The leerfish has an almost pointed face, which is unusual in the jack family, and the body is more elongated in shape. The first dorsal fin spines are low, of even height, and almost separated from each other. The skin is leathery, and the dark, prominent lateral line is unusual in its wavy formation along the body. In coloration the leerfish has a bluish gray back going light towards the belly. This is a large carangid attaining a weight of about 70 pounds, but most fish taken are between 2 and 20 pounds. Occasionally found in offshore schools near the surface and inshore in the vicinity of rocks and surf, it is a fine game fish which takes either bait or artificials readily. It is a good food fish found in European markets.

Talang (15c)

(*Chorinemus lysan*)
(*Chorinemus tol*)
(*Chorinemus sancti-petri*)

This is a slim mackerel-like member of the CARANGIDAE. There is confusion regarding its distribution and specific relationships. At present some scientists divide it into three species. Along the western Pacific it is found from Japan to Australia, and it is also present in the Indian Ocean. It has the same general arrangement of fins as do the other jacks; the dorsal fin contains 6 or 7 dorsal spines which are almost separated. Two spines precede the anal fin, and no scutes are present along the lateral line. The dorsal surface is bluish green, the sides are silvery, and the belly is white. Usually 5 or more dark spots, resembling finger prints, are present above the lateral line just posterior to the head. It is marketed commercially and is taken on rod and reel. Off Mombasa, Kenya, where it is called queenfish, we caught many of them on trolled feathers. They produced excellent sport on light tackle.

Rainbow Runner (16a)
(*Elagatis bipinnulatus*)

The rainbow runner is an oceanic fish which belongs to the family CARANGIDAE but looks more unlike a jack than any other member of the clan. However, it fights as well, or better than its cousins, and rates top ranking as a game fish. It has a world-wide range in warm ocean waters, but nowhere can it be called common. In the Atlantic it is distributed from the West Indies to occasionally off Long Island, New York, but mostly it is found along the Gulf Stream off Miami, among the reefs of southern Florida, and in the Gulf of Mexico. It is also recorded off Africa. In the Pacific it roams from Cape San Lucas, Baja California, to the Galapagos Islands, Ecuador, the Hawaiian Islands, and Australia.

Rainbow runner is an excellent name for this fish because its coloration is startling. In the course of collecting fishes in the Indian Ocean I caught several of these speedy swimmers and made color notes while they were still alive. The dorsal surface is a vivid, greenish cobalt blue, developing lighter as it approaches the lateral line. A bright sky blue streak, approximately one-half inch wide in an average fish of about 20 inches, starts at the snout, follows along below the eye and along the entire body to the anterior part of the tail. Between this sky blue stripe and the dorsal fin is a line of Prussian blue sharply defined but slightly undulating. It is approximately one quarter of an inch wide and runs the length of the body from above and back of the eye to the tail. Below and adjacent to the half-inch sky blue streak is a one-quarter inch line of bright cadmium yellow which also runs the length of the fish. The entire lower lateral and abdominal surfaces are pure flat white, includ-

Jacks

ing the lower jaw. The fins and tail are predominantly translucent greenish yellow. The average size of the rainbow runner seems to be about 2 feet in length and a weight of about 3 pounds. However, it is known to reach a weight of approximately 12 pounds.

Identification of this carangid is not difficult. Like the pompanos and amberjacks, which are also members of the CARANGIDAE, it possesses no bony scutes along the lateral line near the tail. It can be distinguished from the pompanos and amberjacks by the presence of a single finlet which follows the second dorsal and anal fins. Also, its bright yellow and blue horizontal streaks cannot be missed.

The food of the rainbow runner consists mostly of small fishes and crustaceans. Because it is not a common fish practically nothing is known concerning its life history. It may spawn during spring off Pensacola, Florida.

I have taken the rainbow in the Atlantic, Pacific, and Indian oceans, and I can attest to its good sporting qualities. This jack hits a trolled bait or lure in a convincing manner and makes several runs before giving in. I can also recommend it as a fine table fish.

Lookdown (16b)

(*Selene vomer*)

If I had not experienced pleasant hours of fun catching the lookdown on light tackle off a bridge in the Florida Keys I would not list it here as a game fish. The lookdown is distributed in the warm waters of the east and west coasts of North America and is common along the Atlantic from Chesapeake Bay southward. Although it is a warm water fish, it occurs as a stray to the Gulf of Maine and Nova Scotia.

The lookdown is one of the most peculiar looking of the jack family, CARANGIDAE. It possesses a very thin, flat body (compressed from side to side), a long face, high forehead, and an almost vertical, frontal face profile. The mouth is set low, and the eye is high, giving the fish a grotesque appearance. The rest of the body is carangid in type with a short, insignificant first dorsal fin and long second dorsal and anal fins. The first few spines of the second dorsal and anal fins are elongated into long filament-like structures. The ventral fins are tiny, the caudal peduncle is narrow, and the tail is deeply forked. When first pulled out of the water the lookdown appears to be completely covered with pearly iridescence. The coloration is facinating, for it changes with every slight turn of the fish's body; it catches the light from different angles and produces amazing effects. Because of these great reflections it is difficult to take a color photograph of the lookdown in bright sunlight.

It is not a large fish. The average length is from 8 to 10 inches, but it is known to reach a weight of about 4 pounds and a length of 18 inches.

The lookdown is usually found over hard or sandy bottom, and especially around pilings and under the many bridges along the Florida Keys. It feeds mostly on small crabs, fishes, shrimp, and marine worms. Often it can be seen milling around in small schools close to the bottom.

I had my first contact with the strange lookdown during a fishing trip along the Florida Keys with a group of student members of the Yale Fishing Club. One afternoon with nothing else planned we secured some shrimp and drove to the nearest bridge at Grassy Key with no thought in mind but to catch anything that would take our bait. Before the afternoon was out we had a pail full of lookdowns. These fragile looking fish put up a good fight and were fun to catch. We were further delightfully surprised when, upon the advice of a local fisherman, we fried them at our camp. They were delicious.

AMBERJACKS

The amberjacks, like the other members of the family CARANGIDAE, are top sport fishes on rod and reel. They are warm-water, oceanic fishes which prefer the outer reefs in deeper water and rarely come inshore. There are a dozen or more kinds of amberjacks found in the world's tropical or semitropical waters. As yet, these members of the genus *Seriola,* are not defined clearly. In the Atlantic one, two, or three species are recognized, depending on the views of individual scientists: amberjack or great amberjack, *Seriola lalandi;* horse-eye amberjack or amberjack, *Seriola dumerili;* and falcate or Bermuda amberjack, *Seriola falcata.* In the Pacific three or four species are generally recognized: amberjack, *Seriola lalandi;* Pacific amberjack, *Seriola colburni;* yellowtail, *Seriola dorsalis;* and Mazatlán yellowtail, *Seriola mazatlana.*

Amberjack (12a)
(*Seriola lalandi*)

This carangid which is listed for both the Atlantic and Pacific is the largest of the amberjacks. Several species of amberjacks have been recognized, but present indications are that *Seriola lalandi* is the only species that attains any size in the western Atlantic. In Bermuda it is called great amberjack, and some scientists consider *Seriola lalandi* and *Seriola dumerili* synonymous. It ranges from Brazil northward to the Carolinas during the summer and sometimes to Massachusetts, where it is considered a stray. Off Florida it is fairly common; at times off Puerto Rico, the Bahamas, and Bermuda it is abundant.

The amberjack is a fairly elongated fish—not as deep through the body as a typical jack (*Caranx*). However, its fin arrangement is similar to that of a typical jack, with an insignificant first dorsal fin, lengthy second dorsal and anal fins, and a forked tail. It has 30 to 34 rays in the second dorsal fin. The dorsal surface is a light purplish blue, with a grayish or a bronze hue. The sides are silvery with a touch of yellow. When the fish is alive a prominent bronze band extends from nose to tail; it soon fades when the amberjack is boated. A narrow dark band runs diagonally from the mouth to the eye and continues to join a similar band from the other side, atop the posterior part of the head. These stripes, which form an inverted V on the face and head, are called fighting stripes or feeding stripes by anglers. When it chases bait or a lure these facial markings are outstanding. However, they usually disappear when the fish is taken aboard. In the Atlantic, anglers should have no trouble separating this fish from the other jacks. Its elongated body, pronounced stripes (when alive), and small number of gill rakers, 10 to 14, on the lower limb of the first arch set it apart from its relatives.

This amberjack is the largest of the group with an average weight of 5 to 15 pounds. It commonly reaches 50 or 60 pounds. The rod and reel record is 120 pounds 8 ounces taken off Kona, Hawaii, on October 25, 1955, by C. W. McAlpin. The largest amberjack captured off Bermuda weighed 171 pounds dressed.

Practically nothing is known of its life history. In the more northerly areas it seems to appear in greatest abundance during the warmest months. However, it is common in the Bahamas from December to April and off Bermuda from September to April, when fish up to 12 pounds arrive in large schools. The larger fish, between 12 and 20 pounds, appear in groups while the largest are always found in pairs. Because schools of half-pound fish appear in August, Lou Mowbray suggests that this amberjack spawns in Bermuda waters. It feeds mostly on small fishes such as anchovies and small squid but will also take crustaceans. In some areas the amberjack is not considered good eating but in Bermuda it is known as a choice table fish and commands premium prices when sold.

A trolled bait or lure will take the amberjack close to the surface, but for chances of greatest success with rod and reel the use of live bait and fresh squid is recommended. Other top baits are large shrimp and live small fishes such as mullet, bluestripe grunts, pinfish, and pilchards.

An outstanding experience which I had with amberjack occurred off Walker Cay in the Bahamas in the month of June. About two or three miles off the island an old wreck lies on the bottom. I say "about two miles" because I do not know its exact location. Only a couple of the native guides can find the spot; they will take you there but will not disclose the wreck's position. During one calm day we arrived at the choice spot when the sea was flat and clear as crystal. We anchored, chummed a bit with ground fish, and then fished over the wreck. Countless fishes of many species were seen below. Among them a group of large amberjack was swimming leisurely. Our strip bait attracted many different fishes, but the swift amberjack always hit first. They hit hard and fought strenuously. It was thrilling to see large fish dash up, take the bait, and speed off with it. After catching about 15 amberjacks between 3 and 4 feet in length they suddenly, as if by a signal, quit striking. For a while they continued to investigate the baits but would not touch them. From then on we caught other fishes—yellowtail snappers, groupers, hogfish, snappers, etc. The amberjacks still swam below, but they completely ignored our offerings.

Horseeye Amberjack
(*Seriola dumerili*)

There is confusion regarding this species. Some ichthyologists maintain that *Seriola dumerili* and *Seriola lalandi* are the same fish, and the choice of name seems to be a matter of preference. However, Lou Mowbray of Bermuda is of the opinion that *Seriola dumerili* is a separate species. He contends that the horseeye amberjack reaches a weight of about 60 pounds (Bermuda rod and reel record—54 pounds) and is not as elongated in shape as *Seriola lalandi*. He states: "The color is dark gray-brown with a longitudinal amber-to-chocolate stripe through the eye to the tail. This stripe is not always visible on this or the former species (*Seriola lalandi*). The horseeye never appears other than in small groups or singly and prefers the area beyond the shallow reefs. It is more game than either of the other species, though it is not so highly prized as food."

Falcate Amberjack
(*Seriola falcata*)

Especially abundant around Bermuda, the falcate amberjack is distributed in warm oceanic waters. Its most northerly record of occurrence is off Atlantic City, New Jersey. Another common name for this fish is Bermuda amberjack, and in Bermuda it is also known as common bonito. (This species may be identical with *Seriola rivoliana,* one of the Mediterranean forms.) In habits, form, and coloration it differs only slightly from the other amberjacks. Its second dorsal fin contains 29 rays, and the gill raker count is 16 or 17 on the first gill arch below the angle. It is the smallest of the amberjacks with a maximum weight of about 12 pounds. In Bermuda the falcate amberjack rates highly as a sporting fish and is also considered excellent for the table. It can be taken by trolling or still fishing.

Pacific Amberjack (12b)
(*Seriola colburni*)

The Pacific amberjack is a close relative of the other amberjacks and resembles them in form and habits. As with the other species, this jack is strictly a warm-water fish. In the Pacific it ranges from Cape San Lucas, Mexico, through the Gulf of California southward around the Mexican Islands, down to about Panama. In form it resembles *Seriola lalandi* except for its longer first rays of the second dorsal and anal fins (about two thirds the length of the head). It is darker in coloration than the yellowtail (*Seriola dorsalis*) and lacks the yellow-bronze stripe of the latter. The second dorsal fin contains 28 to 31 rays, and the gill raker count is 13 to 16 on the first gill below the angle. It seems to be in the same size class as the *Seriola lalandi,* with fish in the 30-pound class not rare; specimens over 100 pounds have been taken. Its food habits are the same as those of other amberjacks—chiefly small fishes, squids, and crustaceans. Practically nothing is known concerning its life history.

Yellowtail (12c)
(*Seriola dorsalis*)

Anglers who patronize the party boats in southern California waters will almost unanimously agree, I'm sure, that the yellowtail is their greatest sport fish. The yellowtail is not only one of the finest of game fishes; it is also important commercially. It is grouped with the amberjacks and is a member of the family CARANGIDAE. Like the rest of its tribe, it is a warm-water, open-ocean fish. It is also known as Pacific yellowtail, California yellowtail, and amberjack. In Australia and New Zealand it is called yellowtail kingfish or kingfish (*Seriola grandis*). The popular Atlantic yellowtail, *Ocyurus chrysurus*, of the snapper family, LUTJANIDAE, is no relation to the yellowtail, *Seriola dorsalis*.

This amberjack ranges from central California (rare north of Point Conception), south along the Mexican coast, into the Gulf of California, along Panama, the Galapagos Islands, Ecuador, down to Chile. On the other side of the Pacific the same yellowtail or a close relative * is found in Australian and New Zealand waters.

The yellowtail is similar to the other amberjacks in that it has the same type of fin formation, forked tail, and lack of prominent scutes along the caudal peduncle. However, it is more streamlined. The body is not as deep as the amberjacks, and its head is longer. A low, blunt keel is present on each side of the caudal peduncle. It has a grayish green dorsal surface and silvery sides. A bright, yellowish bronze band runs from the snout to the tail. The fins are yellowish with a touch of light green, and the tail is yellow. It is differentiated from the Mazatlán yellowtail by the fewer gill rakers. On the first gill arch below the angle *Seriola dorsalis* has 15 to 17, while *Seriola mazatlana* possesses 21 or 22.

Off southern California the average-size yellowtail runs approximately 15 to 20 pounds, with fish of about 35 pounds not uncommon. Yellowtails which usually take top prizes in the various fishing derbies weigh in the 50- to 60-pound size. How-

---

* Investigators in Australian waters found that the liver oil from *Seriola grandis* is about 36 times more potent in vitamin A, and 110 times more potent in vitamin D than standard cod-liver oil. Another interesting item is that a minimum legal size of 14 inches is placed on this fish in New South Wales and Queensland and 15 inches in South Australia. In the other Australian states there is no size limit.

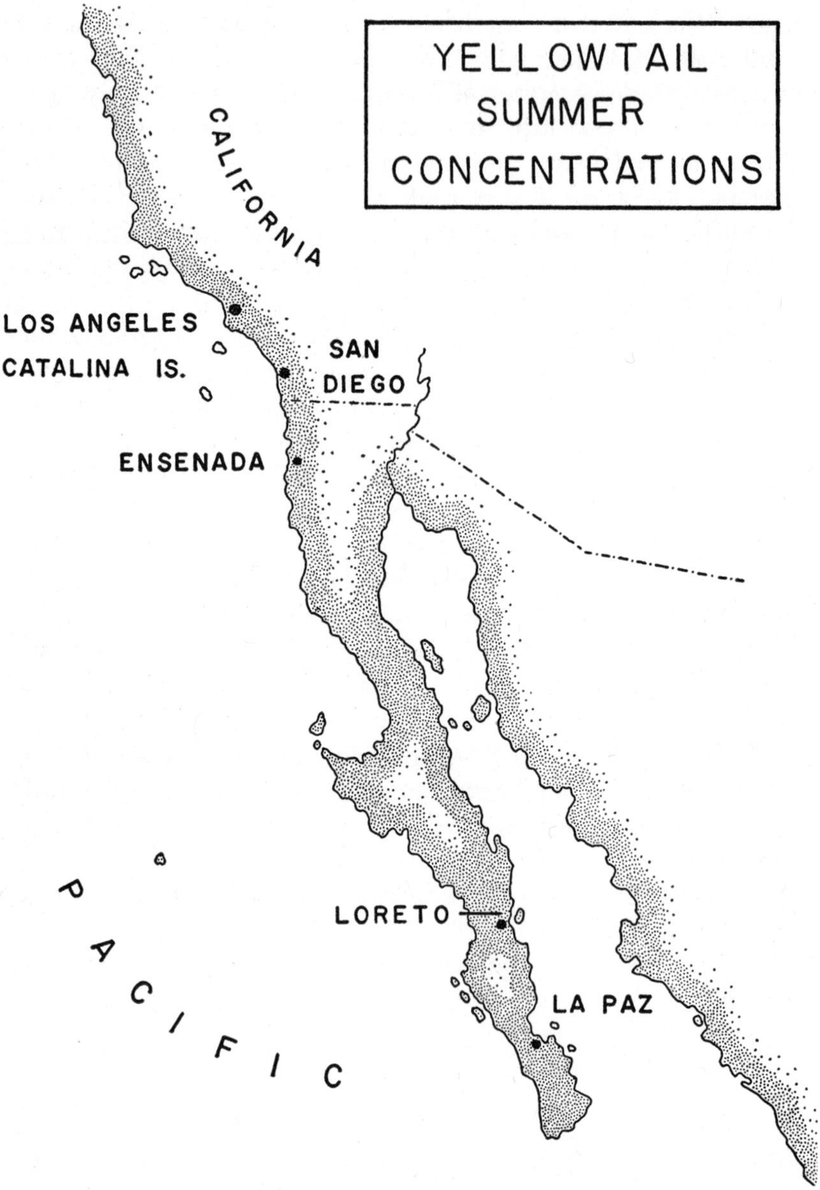
YELLOWTAIL
SUMMER
CONCENTRATIONS
CALIFORNIA
LOS ANGELES
CATALINA IS.
SAN
DIEGO
ENSENADA
LORETO
LA PAZ
PACIFIC

Amberjacks

ever, the world record for rod and reel, 105 pounds 12½ ounces, was taken at Bahia de Topolobampo, Mexico, by M. A. Yant on April 30, 1955.

Migrations of yellowtails appear off southern California from mid-March (sometimes in late February) and remain through October, and at this time this amberjack is considered by many anglers to be the top game fish of the area. In the fall they vanish. During the autumn and winter the yellowtail may be found farther south, in the Gulf of California and along Baja California. Whether this fish migrates up and down the coast is not known. In Australian and New Zealand waters the months of October, November, and December see most fish.

In the eastern Pacific spawning takes place mostly during the early spring, but practically nothing else is known concerning the life history of the yellowtail. It feeds on small schooling fishes—anchovies, smelts, sardines, mackerel. Shrimp and squid are taken also.

The yellowtail will hit a trolled lure or bait. I have taken it in New Zealand waters while fishing for marlin with large baits trolled from outriggers. Although it usually will not jump, this fish puts up a commendable show with fast runs and deep dives. Many yellowtails are taken by party boat fishermen. Aboard one of these large craft the sport is exciting, especially when an angler has to follow his fish over the heads of the other fishermen who line the rails. When a school is located, chumming continues while the anglers fish with live bait. During the peak of the season party boats out of San Diego are jammed with enthusiastic fishermen. Most of the boats fish off kelp beds off La Jolla or off Catalina and San Clemente islands. Other notable fishing spots are the Coronado Islands in Mexican waters (about 20 miles out of San Diego), off Ensenada, Mexico, and in the Gulf of California from Loreto down to La Paz.

June is usually the most productive month for yellowtail fishing. Live anchovies are used more than any other bait, and the number of yellowtail taken at the Coronado Islands in the last few years average about 40,000 fish per season. A new record was set in this area on March 10, 1957, when 2,214 fish were taken by 15 boats. The previous high was 1,916 set on June 7, 1956.

Mazatlán Yellowtail
(*Seriola mazatlana*)

The Mazatlán yellowtail is known to range from Mazatlán to the Galapagos Islands, Ecuador. It closely resembles the yellowtail, and it has also been confused with the Pacific amberjack. The angler need not concern himself with this carangid, but any one fishing in the area below Mazatlán should report any *Seriola mazatlana* taken, because practically nothing is known of this fish. It has a steep profile and a ridge that runs along atop the head, and it possesses 21 or 22 gill rakers below the angle of the first gill arch. (Yellowtail has 15 to 17 gill rakers, and Pacific amberjack has 13 to 16.) Another species, the Peruvian amberjack, *Seriola peruana*, was described from an immature specimen, and not much is known concerning it.

POMPANOS

The pompanos are a group of popular shore fishes which mostly inhabit sandy beaches in warm-water areas. They are unusually fine game fishes when taken on light tackle, but even better when served on the table, for these members of the family CARANGIDAE are considered a gourmet's delight. Anglers may refer to any of the species as pompano, for not enough scientific investigation has taken place to eradicate some of the confusion regarding the individual kinds. The pompanos can be distinguished easily from the other jacks because their bodies are roundish, usually deep from top to bottom, and thin from side to side.

Atlantic Permit (13d)
(*Trachinotus goodei*)

The Atlantic permit is the largest of the pompanos and one of the finest of light-tackle game fishes. It roams primarily in shallow, sandy areas in the inshore waters of warm seas. A purely Atlantic species, this carangid is found in its greatest abundance along the Florida Keys on the east coast from Cape Florida down to the Dry Tortugas, and the Florida Gulf Coast south of Tampa Bay. However, it is also known from North Carolina, usually in the fall, and stragglers are occasional off Massachusetts. In Bermuda waters it is rare, but well known in the Bahamas, where large specimens are taken. It ranges along different types of areas—through inlet passages, Gulf passes, along the offshore edges of sandy flats—and appears to prefer rocky areas or hard sandy bottoms covered with pebbles. Great pompano is another name for this member of the jack family, but in nearly all southern areas it goes by the name of permit. There are four other members of the genus *Trachinotus* which resemble each other closely. It may be that the permit is a full grown or an extremely large specimen of the pompano, *Trachinotus carolinus,* or round pompano, *Trachinotus falcatus,* but only scientific work on many specimens would ascertain this possibility.

In some respects the permit (and other pompanos) resembles the jacks in that it possesses a side-compressed, rather oval body with a narrow caudal peduncle and a deeply forked tail. In placement and structure of fins it looks very jack-like. The first dorsal spines are very low and almost separate, and the second dorsal and anal fins are long, almost reaching the tail. Also, 2 or 3 short spines are present ahead of the anal fin. Its coloration is variable, especially between fishes taken in shallow sandy areas and those caught in deeper waters. The former have a silvery blue back or dorsal surface with silvery sides going ventrally into a yellow. The deep-water fish lose most of the blue and yellow but retain much of the silvery iridescence and some of the blue on the back. The fins are dusky blue, but often the dorsal fin and tail are almost black.

It is a large pompano, growing close to 50 pounds with an average of approximately 12 pounds. The world record catch on rod and reel is 42 pounds 4 ounces, taken off Boca Grande, Florida, by R. H. Martin on September 11, 1953. Aside from its much larger size, the permit can be distinguished from the pompano by its fewer dorsal rays, 19 to 20, and fewer anal rays, 17 to 19.

Nothing is known of the life history of this carangid. It feeds on small fish, crabs, crawfish, shrimp, and mollusks. It is usually seen alone or in pairs, either in the shallow inshore waters or offshore in deeper waters. The permit may grub in the mud for its food and often roams the shallow flats in a manner similar to that of bonefish. In the shallow areas it seems to feed best during the last part of the flood and the first part of the ebb tide.

Although it is mostly a question mark with fishery scientists, this slab-sized speedster is noted among southern fishermen for its game qualities. It will hit either artificial lures or bait. Often permit are hooked by anglers seeking bonefish. On light tackle it is supreme, but although it has been known for years as a tremendous game fish, not many anglers possess the know-how to take this jack consistently. To any angler whose ambition is to hang one of these fish on light tackle I would recommend, as of prime importance, a good native guide who knows well the waters which hold permit. It is the bonefish guides and fishermen who are primarily responsible for elevating the permit from the occasional or casual list to a rank of importance as a select game fish. It was previously taken only by chance by surf fishermen or others in quest of snook, channel bass, or tarpon. Bridge fishermen in the Florida Keys also hook one occasionally.

Pacific Permit

(*Trachinotus kennedyi*)

The Pacific permit is another large member of the carangid fishes considered a true pompano. It is called palometa on the Pacific coast—Magdalena Bay, Gulf of California, and Panama. However, since it grows to be 2 feet in length and because its appearance cannot be distinguished readily from that of the Atlantic permit, I believe it would be less confusing in the lit-

Above: The late Fred Holliday (left) and the author holding a yellowtail in the Bay of Islands, New Zealand. (Photo by T. W. Collins) *Right:* Spotted jack taken in the Indian Ocean by Tom Shevlin, leader of Yale East African Expedition. Spotted jack also inhabits the Pacific.

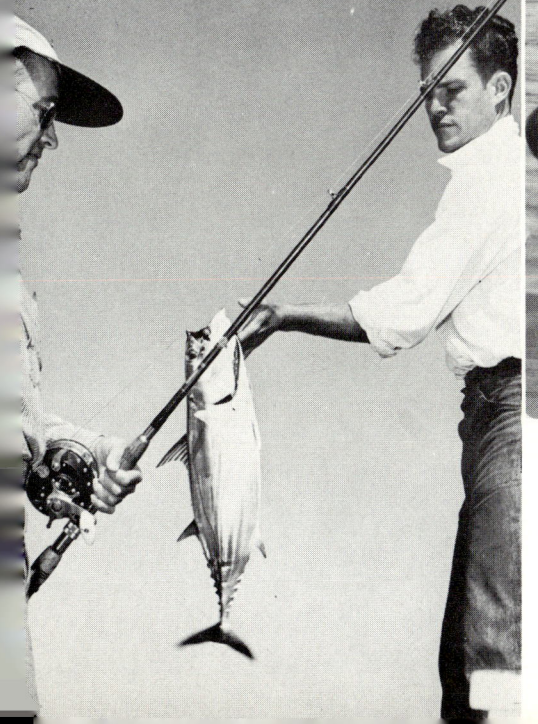

Left: Hal Lyman, publisher of Salt Water Sportsman, left, and guide Basil Albury of Exuma, Bahamas, with an oceanic bonito. (Photo by Jarvis Darville) *Above:* José Martin of New York and Cuba with a yellowfin grouper taken at Walker Cay, Bahamas. Native guide "Bookey" on right. (Photo José Martin)

Top left: Rockfish taken off California. (Photo by Leon D. Adams) *Top right:* Laurrie Perrin enjoys fishing off California for greenling. Dad Merle Perrin in background. (Photo by Leon D. Adams) *Directly above:* Roosterfish taken off Cabo Blanco, Peru, by Mrs. William Sidley of Encampment, Wyoming.

erature to apply the common name Pacific permit rather than palometa. It is considered a great game fish although not easily or commonly taken by anglers. As with the Atlantic form, *Trachinotus kennedyi* is a table delicacy (*see* Atlantic Permit).

Pompano (13a)
(*Trachinotus carolinus*)

One of the choicest of all marine, shallow water fishes, the pompano is an epicure's delight which always commands high prices in the markets. Only in recent years, and mostly because of spinning tackle, has this carangid been generally accepted as a fine game fish to be taken by bridge, pier, and surf anglers. *Trachinotus carolinus* is a western Atlantic species with a range from Brazil to Massachusetts. In its northern limits it appears as a stray. Its distribution is mainly from Texas in the Gulf of Mexico, along Florida's west coast, where it reaches its peak of abundance, around to North Carolina.

The pompano has a typical jack-like body and closely resembles the permit. It has a grayish silvery blue dorsal surface, silvery sides, and lower parts sprayed with yellow, including the ventral and anal fins. The forehead is bluish, the dorsal fin is dusky, and the tail is dusky yellow. The maximum weight is about 8 pounds and the length about 18 inches. An average fish will weigh in the vicinity of 1 pound, although 3 pounders are common. The pompano can be distinguished from its close relatives by its more numerous dorsal and anal rays—about 25 dorsal and 22 anal. No dark crossbars are present as in the longfin pompano. The adult has no teeth. Its gill rakers are very short with a count of 7 or 8 on the lower limb of the first arch, and the lateral line is nearly straight.

In the spring, pompano appear in the Gulf of Mexico from Texas to Louisiana, where they are found in greatest abundance during the summer. In Florida waters, migrations of any extent seem to be nonexistent although it comes inshore to spawn. The spawning season seems to be in the late spring and early summer. Nothing more is known concerning the pompano's life history. It feeds on small fishes and crustaceans, especially shrimp and sand fleas. The pompano loves shallow, warm waters, which sometimes proves its downfall during sudden, lengthy cold spells. It cruises along beaches, often very close to shore, and into inlets and shallow lagoons. In North Carolina the pompano is commercially important, and sometimes taken in inshore pound nets along Maryland waters.

The pompano, like the permit, has only in recent years become generally known to the ordinary run of bridge and pier fishermen because the know-how of hooking these splendid fish on light tackle has been spread. Either bait or artificials are effective. The best baits are shrimp and sand fleas. For an artificial, a small yellow feather jig is hard to beat. With a light spinning outfit it is possible to cast this lure effectively from piers and bridges that abound along Florida's coast. The excellent scrap a pompano produces when hooked on light tackle plus the fact that it is rated as one of the best table delights, places it high on the list of game fishes among discerning anglers.

Round Pompano (13b)

(*Trachinotus falcatus*)

Except for its slightly different shape in being deeper through the body, and slight differences in coloration, the round pompano, *Trachinotus falcatus,* is quite similar to the pompano *Trachinotus carolinus.* The round pompano ranges mostly in warm waters of the western Atlantic shores in the area from North Carolina down the Florida coast and along Florida's west coast. As a stray it may appear around Cape Cod, and as far south as Brazil. It is also found in the West Indies.

This pompano is a smaller fish than its close relative *Trachinotus carolinus,* seldom going over 3 pounds. In coloration it has an over-all silvery color with a bluish tinge. In young fish the fins are edged with black but dusky or blue-gray with lighter margins in adults. Distinguishing characteristics are 19 to 20 dorsal fin rays, 17 to 19 anal fin rays. The last rays of these fins are elongated and falcate in shape. The lateral line is less straight than in the pompano. In its habits and mode of life the round pompano appears to be identical with *Trachinotus carolinus*. When taken on light tackle it also gives a fine account of itself, and on the table it is just as delicious.

Palometa (13c)

(*Trachinotus palometa*)

The palometa is another small pompano with more or less the same habits as the other pompanos. Also, it prefers the same type of warm waters as its close relatives. It is accepted by the name gaff-topsail pompano, which I believe is much too cumbersome as a common name. Another name is longfin pompano, which may be confused with the round pompano because it also possesses elongated fins. Therefore, I prefer palometa; this name is used widely by fishermen.

Its distribution is practically the same as that of the other pompanos along the western Atlantic—Florida, the West Indies, and as far south as Argentina. It is common off Bermuda's south shore, mostly from July to September where it is prized as a light-tackle fish. Another carangid called pompanito, *Trachinotus rhodopus*, is recorded in the Pacific from Mexico, Panama, and the shores of Colombia; it appears to be identical with the Atlantic form.

The palometa is one of the few carangid fishes that can be recognized immediately by the four, narrow, dark vertical stripes or bars. The lateral line is almost straight from the upper edge of the gill cover to the tail. It is undoubtedly one of the most beautiful of the game fishes. The dorsal surface is a dark silvery blue with silvery sides. It has a yellowish belly and a bright orange breast. The elongated portions of the dusky gray second dorsal and anal fins are almost black. The outer portions of the forked tail are also dark. This combination of vivid and opposing colors plus the graceful lines of the palometa make it a striking fish as it comes flopping out of the surf and onto the beach when hooked.

Ladyfish

Ladyfish (9b)

(Elops saurus)

The ladyfish, an energetic, bright, silvery, coastwise fish, which often travels in schools, is found in warm seas. It resembles a small tarpon. Although anglers do not specifically seek it as game, they enjoy its acrobatics when one is hooked; nearly all are taken while sportsmen are attempting to capture other types. Perhaps the ladyfish can be termed "incidental game fish." Among the other popular names for this member of the family ELOPIDAE are ten pounder and bigeye herring. The former is obviously a misnomer because this fish seldom exceeds a few pounds, and the latter is also inappropriate because "the lady" is not a herring. In my meanderings in different areas where this fish is taken I found ladyfish to be the name most often used. The scientific designations as to species are, as yet, not clear. *Elops affinis*, the Pacific form, is probably the same as the western Atlantic *Elops saurus*. Also, other species appear to be present in the eastern Atlantic (west African coast), western Pacific, and waters about the Hawaiian Islands.

Ladyfish

In the Atlantic it is distributed mostly from North Carolina southward along the coast of Florida, Gulf of Mexico, the Bahamas, and the Caribbean. As a stray it appears as far north as Massachusetts. In the eastern Pacific *Elops affinis* ranges from California down to Ecuador. Sometimes it is found in bays and lagoons, and occasionally it may move into fresh water streams.

The ladyfish is slender but not as compressed in body shape as the tarpon. It has a large mouth, large eye with a prominent adipose eyelid in adults, and a deeply forked tail. The dorsal fin has soft rays; the other fins also resemble those of the tarpon and bonefish in type and placement. It has a lateral line; the lower jaw projects slightly beyond the upper, and small teeth are present on the jaws, roof of the mouth, and tongue. A sheath of scales is found along the base of the pectoral and anal fins. The dorsal fin contains 22 to 24 rays, while the anal has 15 or 16. Gill rakers below the angle of the first gill arch number about 14.

Anglers may confuse this fish with a bonefish or a small tarpon. However, an easy point of differentiation is the bony plate present on the throat of the bonefish between the lower jaws, located easily. Also, the ladyfish has much smaller scales and lacks the extended last dorsal fin ray characteristic of the tarpon. It has a large mouth which does not face downward as in the bonefish, and the maxilla or upper jaw extends beyond the eye.

In coloration it appears silvery all over, but the dorsal surface may be light olive or light greenish blue, while the underside is white and may have a yellowish tinge. Fins and tail are dusky, sometimes with yellow, and often all the distal portions are black with the posterior edge of the tail a dark bluish gray.

Maximum length of the ladyfish is about 3 feet; most of the ones I caught averaged about 16 to 20 inches in length and from 1 to 3 pounds in weight. It prefers to feed upon shrimp, squid, and small fishes. The ladyfish, after hatching, quickly develops into small leptocephali (young form, body transparent and head small); then it changes (metamorphosis) by shrinking into juveniles which resemble the adult form. Leptocephali of the ladyfish were obtained from Haiti by the Miami University Marine scientists and raised to juveniles which were fed brine shrimp.

The ladyfish is versatile; it may be encountered in waters close to shore where anglers "hit into them" while wading. Sometimes a school is located in the vicinity of bridges or piers. It may feed near the surface or close to the bottom depending on where its food is found. This fish is taken by anglers using various lures such as spoons and feather jigs, but live bait and cut bait fished on the bottom often take ladyfish. Although it is primarily a shore living species, I have taken it several miles out to sea on large feather jigs meant for larger game. Even when caught accidentally on heavy tackle, it displays great jumping ability plus some exciting dancing and skittering along the surface before being brought alongside. Light spinning tackle is the most enjoyable and most efficient sporting method of taking this fish. It is captured by commercial fishermen along Florida's west coast, but there is disagreement as to its table qualities; some claim the flesh to be musty and tasteless. I find the fish to be fair eating, but it possesses many small bones which dims its popularity for table use. As with many other fishes, the taste and attractiveness for the table depend upon the cooking method employed.

Lingcod

Lingcod
(*Ophiodon elongatus*)

A Pacific coast fish of wide distribution, the lingcod is an important commercial and sport fish from Alaska south to Lower California. It is most abundant north of Point Conception, California. Not a cod, it is a member of the family OPHIODONTIDAE. Among the other more popular common names are Pacific cultus, cultus cod, greenling, leopard cod, and buffalo cod.

The long body and head are finely scaled, and the large mouth contains canine-like teeth. A large fleshy flap is above each eye. The dorsal fin is long with a deep notch. Tail is squarish, and the pectoral fin is large. In coloration it is extremely variable, depending upon its habitat. Background usually with shades of green, tan, blues, and grays. Darker blotches are outlined in orange or light blue. Spots are also present over the body—brown, green, orange, or yellow. Body whitish below. Flesh of the lingcod may be turquoise green to whitish. The green is not harmful. Maximum size is over 4 feet in length and about 70 pounds in weight. Fishing takes place throughout the year, and no specific seasons seem to be known. It is one of the leading sport fish of central California.

Marine Basses

The marine basses consist of a world-wide group—nearly all are members of the large family SERRANIDAE, which is related to the popular fresh water family of basses, CENTRARCHIDAE. The marine and fresh water families closely resemble each other in body form, fin arrangement and other anatomical structures. However, technical characteristics distinguish the groups into separate families. Generally, the carnivorous assemblage of salt water bassfishes is divided into categories: sea basses, giant sea basses, groupers, and rock basses. Although the great majority are inhabitants of warm, tropical, and subtropical seas, a few species range into cold waters as far north as Nova Scotia and the St. Lawrence River.

There is no other large group of fishes where the individual species resemble each other so closely as in the bassfishes. The general appearance of the members of the SERRANIDAE is usually accepted as the most typical or the most fish-like of fishes. They all have large mouths containing teeth, and the maxillaries (upper lips) are prominent. Most species have a spinous first dorsal fin connected with the second dorsal, which contains rays. The pectoral fin is roundish (pointed or angular in snappers). The dorsal fin is usually deeply notched between the spines, and the anal fin usually has 3 spines with several soft rays. (The third spine is often deeply imbedded and difficult to see.) There is a great diversity of coloration among them, and with individuals the color changes are astounding. The basic color, spots, stripes, bands, and other markings may appear in different degrees of vividness or may disappear—all depending on the changing emotions of the individual fish.

Rock bass is a good name for any one of the serranids because they prefer rocky areas and reefs. The striped bass, sea bass, and white perch take part in rather extensive migrations, but the rest of the bassfishes are more or less sedentary in habit; they usually inhabit an area which is not affected by tidal flow or rips, but they may take part in some movement offshore-inshore. Most of the time is spent close to the bottom, and among their items of diet will be found fishes, shrimps, and crabs.

Of the many species of marine basses only a few can be truly termed game fishes. For example, in Bermuda the SERRANIDAE form the largest related group of fishes in numbers—about 28 types recorded—but Lou Mowbray, who knows more about Bermuda fishes than any other person, lists, in his paper, "The Gamefishes of Bermuda," only one species of serranid—the rockfish, *Myctoperca bonaci.* I suspect that he lists this fish only because it creates interest as one of the largest of the sea basses, although on occasion it will grab a bait and produce strong, dogged resistance to the rod. Actually, only three of the SERRANIDAE can be rated as game fishes—striped bass, *Roccus saxatilis;* white perch, *Morone americana;* and sea bass, *Centropristes striatus.* Although the others—groupers and rock basses—are not sought after as game fishes, they will take a baited hook and occasionally a lure trolled slowly, usually close to the bottom. However, they will produce only a tug or two on the line and then come up like a wet sack. Many of the groupers and rock basses are important, excellent food fishes and are taken for this reason. Also, some are caught by accident by anglers fishing for other species. Therefore, I will treat only the more common ones.

SEA BASSES

Although the term "sea bass" may be correctly applied to any member of the family SERRANIDAE, it is used here as one category in the method of separating the marine basses into groups for better understanding. The fishes that fall into this division are striped bass, sea bass, and white perch. These three sea basses are very popular with anglers, who seek these fishes avidly and specifically by several different methods of sport fishing. Commercially they are also important.

Striped Bass (10a)
(*Roccus saxatilis*)

The striped bass is one of the most valuable fish that inhabit the coastal waters of North America. It is a gregarious sea bass that loves to roam in schools close to rocky and sandy shores; seldom is it found more than several miles from the coast line. It is a fish of the surf, tidal rips, bays, estuaries, and of brackish and fresh waters; some stocks may be found upstream as far as 200 miles from salt water. An unusually successful population of landlocked stripers is established in the Santee-Cooper Reservoir of South Carolina. Between anglers and commercial fishermen it has been, and persists to be, a fish of great controversy. The striper is a game fish of first rank, and anglers pursue it with all types of angling methods—trolling, surf casting, still fishing, and to a limited extent, fly casting. The financial return to those involved in supplying the varied wants of striped bass sportsmen is in the millions of dollars. In recent years sport fishing for striped bass has developed into one of the most popular of all angling pursuits along both coasts of the United States.

Magazine literature concerning the methods of taking this fish on rod and reel has become voluminous. To any angler interested in good, up-to-date accounts of striper fishing I recommend checking *The Salt Water Sportsman* published in Boston. For the angler who would like a general introduction to the life history of the striped bass I have summarized facts presented by my former Ichthyology instructors, Professors Dan Merriman of Yale and Ed Rainey of Cornell, and other scientists.*

Within the last hundred years the striped bass has shown a gradual decline in numbers, a fact substantiated by available data. However, unusually successful hatchings, which lead to good fishing a few years later, are produced occasionally. The biological, chemical, and physical conditions which make for a highly successful hatching are not understood, although there has been a correlation with subnormal temperatures in some years.

The majority of sportsmen have no idea—or care not—about the major cause of the ruination of the striped bass (and of other game fishes as well). The usual cry of the sporting fraternity is over-fishing by commercial fishermen. The depletion of the striped bass along the east coast may be the result of many factors (destruction of breeding and feeding areas, dams, and siltation are primary reasons), but the greatest factor responsible for the gradual annihilation of the game fishes that inhabit our coastal shores and rivers is pollution. Concentrated effort by organized sportsmen to induce an interest in the abatement of pollution is sadly lacking. The disinterest of anglers in the situation is appalling! The isolated instances along the Atlantic seaboard where some action is actually taking place gives some hope, but unless a much greater effort is expended, and soon, it will prove to be an almost impossible task to resurrect our river and coastal fisheries.

There are many places along the east coast where pollution is ruining, or has ruined, productive fish areas. In the Roanoke River an outstanding spawning area for striped bass has been

---

* I recommend that sportsmen interested in delving deeper into details read "The Striped Bass," by Edward Rainey, Ernest F. Tresselt, Edgar H. Hollis, V. D. Vladykov, and D. H. Wallace. *Bingham Bulletin*, Vol. XIV, Art. 1, published by the Bingham Oceanographic Laboratory of Yale University.

hurt severely by paper mills dumping waste into the lower stretches of river; whether more than a small percentage of fry are able to survive the trip downstream to the foraging grounds in Albemarle Sound is doubtful.

The Weldon, North Carolina, striped bass hatchery is the only successfully operating one of its kind in existence. This hatchery was established in 1906, and operations since then have been more or less continuous. North Carolina sportsmen have supported the theory of hatchery restocking in hopes of perpetuating the run of striped bass in the Roanoke River and of re-establishing the runs of other rivers. However, every ichthyologist or fishery biologist knows that the results obtained from stocking species like the striped bass, where enormous numbers of eggs are produced by the female, are negligible. In other words, it is a consensus of scientific opinion that the operation of any striped bass hatchery is fruitless. Here is another example of misdirected effort by sportsmen. If the fish hatchery were forgotten and more emphasis placed on pollution abatement, progress would be shown in the increase or resurrection of striped bass in the Roanoke and other rivers. Incidentally, the striper rates as a game fish in the area above the bridge at Weldon and as a commercial fish below—where large numbers are taken during the spawning season. It is indeed an amazing fact that any fish reach the spawning grounds in the Roanoke. At least 5,000 nets are set in Albemarle Sound alone; and further, the fish must get by haul seines, miles of pollution, skin net fishermen, and baits and lures.

The Delaware River is being killed by both industrial and domestic pollution. The lower Hudson River is also greatly polluted. Both sport and commercial fishing are greatly reduced by sewage pollution. For example, in 1948 and 1949 stripers were plentiful in the lower Hudson, but their flesh was so affected by pollution that few were utilized as human food. The Merrimac has been practically snuffed out as a spawning area for striped bass by pollution and dams. The once proud Connecticut could be returned to a great river, not only for striped bass but other game fishes as well (even salmon), if pollution could be abated and the construction of dams controlled wisely. It appears that the only unspoiled areas remaining for the reproduction of the striped bass are some of the larger tributaries of Chesapeake Bay.

Around 1934 the striped bass stock reached an all time low. However, since 1936 striper fishing has been fairly good to excellent from Massachusetts down to North Carolina. Because of the increase in the bass population along the east coast, anglers perked up and took notice. Some sportsmen with unusual foresight began to drum up scientific interest in the striped bass. They wanted studies made on this bass while the population was large enough to be investigated. Among them were Hal Lyman, publisher of *The Salt Water Sportsman* (also a fine angler and amateur scientist) and A. Heaton Underhill. They approached Professor Ed Rainey of Cornell, and with their backing he undertook a preliminary review on what was already known about striped bass. The result was the publication on "The Striped Bass" mentioned previously.

Actually, scientific interest in the striped bass developed in the 1930's. On the Pacific coast E. C. Scofield produced the first important biological treatise in 1931. Along the Atlantic, Dan Merriman, now director of the Bingham Oceanographic Laboratory, initiated a study of the striped bass in 1936. His work was published in 1941 by the U.S. Fish and Wildlife Service as "Fishery Bulletin 35," and remains one of the best scientific contributions on the striped bass. Also in 1931, the U.S. Fish and Wildlife Service undertook bass studies in the Chesapeake Bay region.

The striped bass is a member of the sea bass family SERRANIDAE. Scientists for many years have referred to it as *Roccus lineatus,* but evidence indicated that this name belonged to a related Mediterranean species; therefore, *Roccus saxatilis* is presently accepted by all fishery workers. Back in 1884 this serranid was called squid hound. "Striped bass" is used from New Jersey to Nova Scotia. From New Jersey southward it may be known as striper, rockfish, rock, or greenhead. Along the Pacific coast it is known as striped bass.

Sportsmen have no difficulty in identifying the striped bass, for at a glance, the prominent 7 or 8 narrow, lateral stripes set it apart. The white perch, *Morone americana,* could be confused with a young striper in the Atlantic. However, they are easily separated; the dorsal fins of the white perch have a deep notch between them but are connected; the dorsal fins of the striper are separated. Other characteristics of the striper are stout body, rather deep and keelless caudal peduncle, tail slightly forked, moderately pointed nose, and a projecting lower jaw. The first dorsal fin has 9 or 10 spines, second has 12 or 13 rays, and anal has about 11 rays preceded by 3 spines. The color of the striper differs with the type of area it inhabits—lighter when the fish frequents sandy areas, and darker when it is taken in rivers and deeper rocky areas. The dorsal surface may vary from a light tan to a dark olive or bluish green, going lighter and silvery along the sides down to a flat white underside. The body of the freshly caught bass possesses a bronze or pinkish iridescence. The longitudinal stripes are produced by markings on the individual scales. The lowest stripes are not as distinct as the upper ones. Ventral fins are white; others are dusky or greenish olive.

The record rod and reel fish weighed 73 pounds and was taken by C. B. Church in Vineyard Sound, Massachusetts, on August 17, 1913. The largest California striped bass on record is 78 pounds. However, bigger fish have been recorded. By definite account several of the largest known weighed about 125 pounds each and were taken at Edenton, North Carolina, in April 1891. One of 112 pounds was caught at Orleans, Massachusetts, many years ago. Fish that are usually caught by anglers weigh from three to 40 pounds; 25 to 45 pounds is not unusual, and in recent years about 65 pounds is about tops. Contrary to popular opinion the big fish are not "bulls" (as called by anglers) because females usually grow larger than males and most fish over 30 pounds are females. The approximate length-weight relationship is this:

Inches	Pounds
12–13	¾
18–20	2¾– 3
24	5
30–32	10 –15
33–36	18 –20
43	30
47–48	40
50–51	50

The sex of some species of fish can be seen by differences in the external anatomy; for example, the profile of the bull dolphin's head is square while that of the female is round. No way is known whereby the male and female striped bass can be differentiated externally. Some females reach maturity at four years, more than half are mature at five years, and practically all are mature at six. It appears that most females in the Atlantic mature when 17 or 18 inches long; a five-year-old female in California waters measures about 22 inches. Females do not always spawn every year. A small female, about three pounds, will produce approximately 4,000 eggs; a large fish, 50 pounds, will contain about 5,000,000 eggs. The majority of males spawn at about 10 or more inches. April and May are the main months of the spawning migrations; the schools that take part consist of fish that are almost ready to breed. The spawning areas vary from riffles in swift water to fairly quiet tidal areas. Ideal spawning grounds are rather extensive localities with some current and a nearby nursery where food is abundant. Along the east coast the tidal mouths of the Chesapeake Bay seem to be best suited for spawning requirements. Off the western coast the lowland section of the Sacramento and San Joaquin Rivers in the San Francisco Bay area are excellent spawning and nursery grounds.

Several weeks before spawning the stripers move upstream to fresh water; males reach the spawning grounds first and are usually smaller and always more common than females. A single female, of any size, may be accompanied at spawning by a few to as many as 50 males. The eggs are spherical, nonadhesive, slightly heavier than fresh water and greenish in color. They are deposited during the thrashing and splashing near the surface, an activity commonly referred to in some areas as "rock fights." At the time of laying, the eggs are one sixteenth of an inch in diameter. The length of the incubation period depends on water temperature: 71°–72° F., 30 hours; 64° F., 48 hours; 58°–60° F., 70–74 hours. At the end of the first year the young average from 2 to 5 inches.

In their first and second years they roam about feeding in small groups, but usually by the end of the second summer they congregate in fairly large schools. When they grow older and bigger they may be gregarious to some extent, but they tend to lie alone or separated from each other when feeding among rocks in or close to the surf or in areas where some current is running.

The striped bass has a wide temperature tolerance and can take low temperatures as shown by the population that roams the cold waters of Nova Scotia, New Brunswick, and the St. Lawrence River. Off the Niantic River, Connecticut, most of the stripers appear in the spring and depart in the fall when the water is 43° to 46° F., but some fish winter in southern New England estuaries, and netters have taken them through the ice in rivers from New Jersey southward. The schools off North Carolina start moving when temperatures are about 44° to 46° F. During an unusually warm August and early September, many dead bass were found in eastern Connecticut rivers. It appears that the maximum water temperature for the striped bass is about 77° to 86° F. This degree of temperature toleration was further substantiated by the fact that a movement of tagged fish from the Niantic and Thames Rivers out into cooler coastal waters was noted at the time the river water reached its maximum temperature.

Although the striped bass is definitely coastal in habitat, occasionally the fish is reported being present far offshore; for example, the dragger "Captain Bill," in February, 1949, captured an 18-inch specimen about 70 miles to the southward of Block Island in about 70 fathoms. Also, during migration they cross the open east end of Long Island Sound.

Sea Basses

Freaks or anatomical abnormalities in the striped bass are sometimes reported. Occasionally, a pug-headed striper is sent to the Bingham Oceanographic Laboratory for identification. Two such specimens have been brought to my attention within the last year and are now preserved. A pug-headed striper is unusual, but specimens of pug-headed fish are known in collections—both striped bass and other species. A pug-headed striper has a grotesque head, which ends in a blunt snout with the lower jaw projecting far beyond the upper. The tongue protrudes to its normal length, lying exposed on the floor of the mouth. In other words, the lower jaw looks normal while the upper appears as if it had been cut off and grown over.

Anglers will be interested to know that the "funny looking" pug-headed striper is not the result of an injury; failure of the bones to harden or properly develop results in these facial abnormalities. Since the condition arises in the embryo, scientists believe that it is a type of genetic disturbance and may be transmitted, that is, the factors for pug-headedness may be passed on from generation to generation. (It is known that pug-headed dogs reproduce their kind.) Although the theory of inherited pug-headedness in stripers is plausible, as yet it has not been proved.

Another deviation from the normal which has been known to occur in stripers is hermaphroditism, a condition whereby both male and female organs are present in one body. Of the bass sampled by scientists Morgan and Gerlach in Coos River, Oregon, 3 per cent were found to be hermaphrodites. In some fish both organs were ripe and in spawning condition at the same time. In all cases the testes was the forepart and the ovary the posterior portion of the gonad. Schultz reported a hermaphroditic striped bass taken on the Pacific coast which contained the ovary on the left side and the testes on the right. He was of the opinion that the fish would have produced both sexual products.

Another condition which is not rare amongst striped bass, and one which is brought to my attention occasionally by anglers, is the "white eye." The lens is clouded, milky, or dead white. The cataract is almost always in both eyes and may be the result of a deficiency in diet. Dan Merriam reported that large numbers of stripers which he had taken in the Thames and Niantic Rivers were affected with cataract of the eye. During June, 1951, there appeared a condition of skin eruption on stripers in the Thames and Niantic Rivers; it was diagnosed as lymphocytis by Ross Nigrelli of the New York Zoological Society.

Following this general introduction on the striped bass are two sections, "Striped Bass in the Atlantic" and "Striped Bass in the Pacific." I have made this division so that the angler will find it less confusing to read about facts pertaining to the striped bass in waters separated by a continent.

Striped Bass in the Atlantic

In the Atlantic the distribution of striped bass ranges from the St. Lawrence River, Canada, southward to the St. Johns River in northern Florida, and in the Gulf of Mexico tributaries of western Florida, Alabama, Mississippi, and Louisiana. The center of abundance is from Cape Cod to northern North Carolina, including Chesapeake Bay.

The greatest nursery and spawning grounds along the east coast are Chesapeake Bay and its tributaries, Pamlico Sound, North Carolina, upper Delaware Bay, and the lower Hudson River. In Connecticut rivers and areas farther north spawning may occur occasionally, but these cases do not contribute to the major stock to any extent. Spawning takes place in fresh, or virtually fresh, water in rivers from early April in Alabama to June and early July in New Brunswick, and mostly when water temperatures range from 58° to 70° F.

Along the Atlantic coast, from 1933 to 1940, many bass were tagged. The recoveries indicated that the stripers move out of their wintering localities in the Chesapeake, New Jersey, and New York areas in the late winter or early spring and migrate northward and eastward to New England, and possibly to southern Canada. This stock usually remains in New England waters during the summer, and then about the middle of September begins to travel southward and westward back to New York and New Jersey. By November and December they arrive in the Chesapeake Bay area and possibly North Carolina. Bass two or more years of age make these migrations. In the fall movement the greatest portion of the migratory group heads southward, but certain sections break off from the main group and spend the winter in localities like the lower Delaware River and tributaries of Delaware Bay, in New Jersey's coastal rivers, and in the lower Hudson River, New York. It is interesting to note that one of these wintering groups, composed of hundreds of bass, was found frozen in the ice on January 26, 1939, near Stony Brook on the north shore of Long Island. Certain small parts of the summer stock remain and winter for at least one season in the coastal waters of New England from Maine to Connecticut.

Striped bass are fairly inactive during the winter; large groups gather in deep pools near the mouths of rivers, in brackish bays, and in estuaries. When in this situation the fish are open to capture by scoop nets and gigs of different types. Few are taken by sporting methods because the bass are in a state of quiescence and usually do not feed.

When they leave their wintering areas—often as early as the first half of March in the waters of New Jersey and farther south —the run northward is joined by wintering populations from various northern regions such as the Hudson River, Long Island, and southern New England. Apparently individual stripers or units of the general population do not always winter in the same region in successive years. For example, some of the stock that winter in New Jersey one year may winter in a more northern area or in a locality as far south as Chesapeake Bay.

Although carnivorous and voracious, feeding mostly on other fishes, the striped bass also consumes large quantities of invertebrates, especially crustaceans. Usually, all fish in a given school will feed periodically and at about the same time. In salt water young fish feed mainly on shrimp and marine worms, and it does not take long (when they are about 3 inches in length) before they shift to a diet primarily of small fishes. The silverside is the common summer food in Connecticut; menhaden, killifish, and shrimp are also on the preferred list. In the Chesapeake Bay area the most common items of diet are anchovy, menhaden, spot, and croaker. As with most fishes, spawning bass eat little or nothing.

Tagging returns and observations by scientists and sportsmen have contributed to our knowledge of the dates of arrival, areas of occurrence, and schooling behavior of striped bass. In the northward movement the approximate dates of arrival of the first schools are as follows: New Jersey, middle of April; Long Island, New York (south side), third week of April; Rhode Island, fourth week in April; Cape Cod, Massachusetts areas, first to third week in May. The following is a condensation of available information on the striped bass in the most important and most interesting areas along its Atlantic distribution.

In *Quebec* a rather large population is present in the St. Lawrence River which is believed to be indigenous (that is, a native population), since no tagged fish as yet have been recovered outside the St. Lawrence. All the stripers tagged in the Quebec area were taken within approximately 50 miles up or down stream.

Nova Scotia bass are found mostly in the various rivers, river mouths, and bays along the western shoreline. The best known areas are the Annapolis River, which is a tributary to the Digby Basin, and the Shubenacadie Lake and River tributary to the Minas Basin. After years of scarcity the bass increased sufficiently in these rivers so that sport fishing perked up in 1949 and 1950. It appears that these populations may be resident. Bass in the Shubenacadie are interesting because the fish are taken in the fresh waters of the river and lake where they are known to spawn. Some large fish remain in the lake throughout the year and behave like a landlocked population. About a thousand fish are taken by sports fishermen in the lake and river; fish as large as 50 pounds have been recorded. Other known bass producers are the Gaspereau, Bass, and Bear rivers.

Sea Basses

The outer coast of Nova Scotia also has striped bass populations; known areas are the head of Mahoney Bay, the head of Chedabucto Bay, as well as Mira Bay and other harbors of Cape Breton.

Striped bass in the waters of the St. John River, *New Brunswick*, are known to be more plentiful than anywhere along the eastern part of the coast of Maine. Stripers are sometimes taken in St. John Harbor between April and June.

In *Maine* a few stripers are caught here and there—Casco Bay, Kennebec River, St. George River, and off Georgetown in August. In most years at the Bangor Pool (head of the estuary of the Penobscot) anglers take some stripers. These fish are caught by anglers fishing specifically for them and also accidentally by salmon fishermen. Other spots where stripers have been seen in Maine are Belfast River, Searsport Harbor (farther down Penobscot Bay), between Mount Desert Island and the mainland in August (near Hancock-Sullivan Bridge), Winter Harbor, Narraguagus, and St. Croix.

New Hampshire is an unimportant bass area, although some are taken in Hampton Harbor.

Undoubtedly, *Massachusetts* has some of the greatest of striped bass fishing. The Cape Cod, Cuttyhunk, and Martha's Vineyard areas are well known for some of the best bass angling waters in existence and for producing the biggest fish. This is the land of beach buggies, surf casting, bass tournaments, and crazed striped bass addicts. There are many excellent striped bass spots in Massachusetts Bay: First Encounter Beach, Brewster Flats, Billingsgate, Wellfleet Harbor, Sandy Neck, Cape Cod Canal, Spring Hill, Scorton Creek, Barnstable Harbor, Chequessett, Pamet River, Duck Harbor, Wood End. The ones that are considered best year in and year out are the canal area, which is usually the most heavily fished, and the Billingsgate locality where often over a hundred boats fishing for stripers can be counted at one time. The stripers usually appear in Massachusetts waters in May. However, weather affects the time of arrival. For example, the unseasonably cold weather in the spring of 1956 caused the Cape Cod Bay bass to appear

ONE OF THE BEST AREAS FOR STRIPED BASS

MASSACHUSETTS BAY

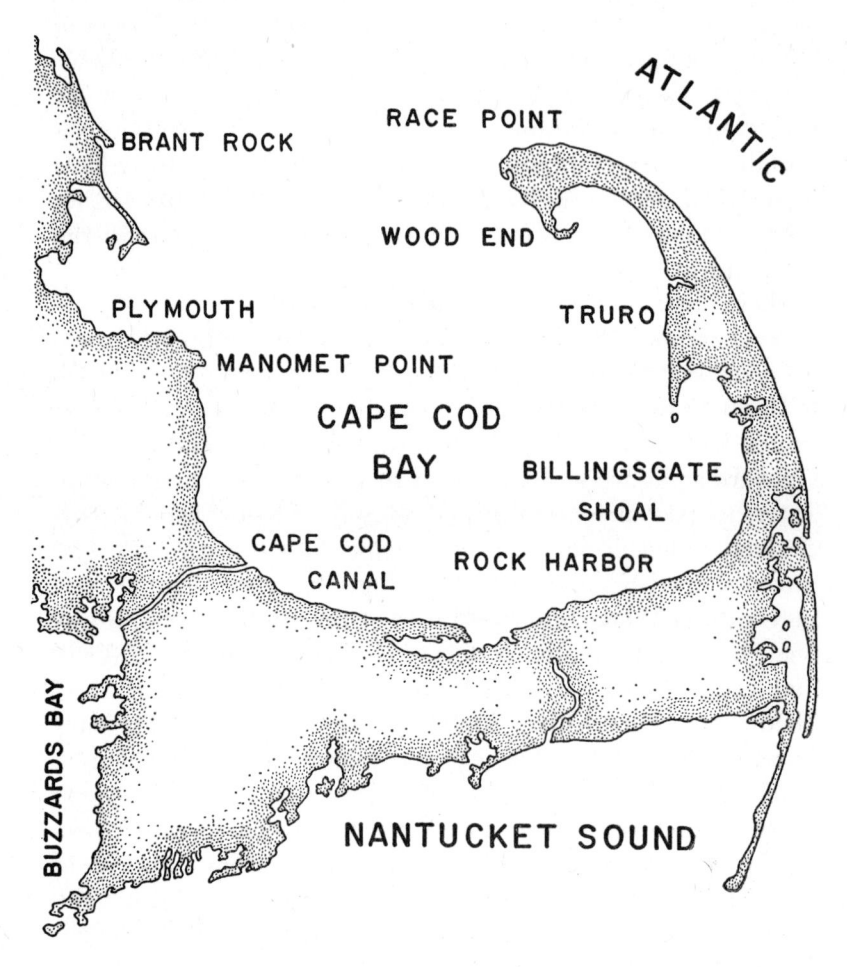

BRANT ROCK
RACE POINT
ATLANTIC
WOOD END
PLYMOUTH
TRURO
MANOMET POINT
CAPE COD BAY
BILLINGSGATE SHOAL
CAPE COD CANAL
ROCK HARBOR
BUZZARDS BAY
NANTUCKET SOUND

Sea Basses

in the first week of June. Successful fishing was established on June 26, and good catches were reported for the next six weeks. Although the north shore of Massachusetts Bay appears to be an attractive area for bass, actually it is not; catches are small and scattered during most summers. However, the enclosed waters from a few miles north of Cape Ann to and including the mouth of the Merrimac River are good enough to rank second to the Cape Cod Bay region.

Rhode Island also may boast of its exceptional striped bass localities with fish in the 50-pound class not rare. The spots that are famous along this coastline are Napatree Point, Watch Hill, Weekapaug, Quonochontaug, Charleston Inlet (one of the best locales along the Atlantic coast), Matunuck, Point Judith, and Beavertail Point. Block Island is also a noted striper fishing area. However, much of the water around the island does not receive enough angling effort to explore fully its bass fishing potential.

Striped bass along the *Connecticut* shore generally are not as large as they run in the neighboring states. An angler may say that he intends to fish specifically for stripers in any of the following areas: Norwalk Islands, Sherwood Island Park or Bedford Point in Westport, Seaside Park in Bridgeport, Woodmont, Pond Point in Milford, Connecticut River, Niantic River, Thames River, Mason Island off Mystic. An occasional bass is taken in other places, but the above named are the known productive areas.

The Montauk Point section at the eastern tip of Long Island, *New York,* is one of the more famous striped bass fishing areas; the north side of Shagwong Reef is good, and so is the area off Wilderness Point, Fishers Island. A commercial fishery existed in the Hudson River for many years. However, it is now prohibited by law. One hundred striped bass less than 16 inches were tagged and released in the Hudson River off South Nyack during the first part of April, 1940. Within four days some were caught in shad nets in the vicinity of the George Washington Bridge. However, there is a population of adult bass that travels as far upstream as Albany. The Hudson River spawning area in 1955 was found to include the region from Bear Mountain up river to Cruger Island. Most spawning apparently took place in the West Point areas in fresh water; eggs were found from mid-May through mid-June. The main nursery locale was the brackish portion of the river which includes an area from Newburgh south to the George Washington Bridge.

Winter groups start to move out of local *New Jersey* waters as early as the first part of March. The stripers migrate to New England and remain there during the summer, and in the fall they move southward to winter in several places along the coast (some may go as far as Chesapeake Bay). Scientists Wallace and Neville, who worked on the striped bass in this area, pointed out that recommendations for the prohibition of winter fishing in New Jersey would not necessarily improve the summer catches. However, it is possible that the restriction might be a contributing factor in improved summer fishing farther north. The scientists further stated that the prohibition or restriction of striper fishing, especially by certain types of commercial gear either permanently or during closed seasons within a year or over a period of years, would not necessarily assist significantly in rehabilitation of the striped bass.

In the *Chesapeake Bay* area the striped bass is the most valuable of all the fishes taken. Most of the basic migratory stock on the Atlantic coast is produced in the Bay, but the migratory part of this population appears to be comparatively small—about 10 per cent or less at the two-year-old stage. Schooling takes place from June to mid-September near the surface in open parts of the Bay. From mid-October to late November there is an inshore movement of schools. In the fall a general movement southward takes place, mostly along the western side of the Bay. In winter general concentrations occur in deeper parts of the Bay, but in mild weather some are taken in shallow areas. In the spring, movement northward in the Bay again takes place. The Chesapeake Bay fish under two years of age are not migratory. Contrary to the situation in other wintering localities, where the striped bass are mostly inactive during the cold

Sea Basses

months, many of the Chesapeake Bay bass continue to feed. In the winter of 1936–1937 certain schools moved up and down the entire length of the Bay.

Apparently, the sex ratio (that is, the number of males to females in schools) changes with the season. In the Chesapeake Bay area males comprised 55 per cent of all bass sexed, but the percentage varies from about 50–50 in August, to a predominance of males (about 83 per cent) in March. (Of the fish checked in Long Island and New England waters in summer about 90 per cent were females.) This data from both areas was taken 1936–1937.

Maryland reaps a substantial amount (about 75 per cent) of the Chesapeake Bay striped bass harvest; the catch rates third in quantity but first in dollar value. Here sport fishing is also a major industry. About 200,000 anglers fish yearly in Chesapeake waters for striped bass with a resultant income of about $500,000 to the people who cater to sportsmen. Besides Maryland the greatest commercial catches of bass are made in the waters of Virginia, Delaware, and North Carolina.

Bass spawned in *North Carolina* contribute little to the schools that run northward to New England. Also, indications are that there is little interrelationship between populations of North Carolina and Chesapeake Bay.

In *South Carolina* the Santee-Cooper Reservoir has developed a remarkable new inland fishery for landlocked striped bass. The area consists of two artificial lakes on the Santee and Cooper rivers that are connected by a diversion canal six and one half miles long. The construction of the Pinopolis Dam cut off the upstream population of stripers from access to the sea. However, research studies indicate few if any of the landlocked fish migrated to and from the sea even when no barriers were present. Apparently they moved back and forth within the original waters—the upper hundred miles or so. (Many attempts at transplanting ocean stripers into fresh water have taken place in hopes of establishing permanent populations. As yet no attempt has proved successful.) Stripers from the Santee-Cooper system, both above and below the Pinopolis

Dam, have been used for transplantings to other inland waters, but these efforts have also proved fruitless.

In appraising factors known to be critical in the life history of stripers in the Santee-Cooper Reservoir it appears that the following conditions are necessary for successful striped bass reproduction: the fertilized eggs and newly hatched larvae must remain suspended in well-oxygenated water so that they will not perish from smothering. A certain amount of water flow or turbulence is necessary to keep the eggs from sinking to the bottom, where they would be destroyed by sediment. The length of time the eggs and larvae must remain suspended is important—70 hours minimum to a maximum of about 6 weeks. A current of one mile per hour and a reservoir system 100 miles or more are probably minimum requirements for successful striped bass breeding. Perhaps areas of less than 100 miles in length may fill the bill if enough turbulence is present.

Accumulated data illustrate the presence of a great striper fishery in the Santee-Cooper reservoir. About one tenth of the anglers who fished it were checked by the 1957 creel census; they took 28,272 stripers. Therefore, the total number caught is approximately 282,000 or more bass. The fish averaged slightly over 5 pounds each; in other words, about 1,500,000 pounds or 10 pounds of striped bass per acre.

The striped bass has never been common in *Florida;* from 1946 to 1949 five bass weighing from 3 to 13 pounds were reported caught in the St. Johns River. It appears that stripers never invade the waters of southern Florida.

The striped bass that inhabit the *Gulf of Mexico* are not found in salt water but in fresh or brackish coastal rivers. In recent years a fairly good sport fishery of stripers weighing from 5 to 40 pounds has been noted at Coosa River at Wetumpka and in the Tallapoosa River at Tallassee, Alabama. These are fresh water localities several hundred miles from the Gulf of Mexico. Any exchange between the striped bass populations of the Gulf and the Atlantic does not appear feasible.

The fight that has been raging between sporting and commercial interests concerning the conservation of the striped bass along the Atlantic coast is a bitter one. Caustic accusations from both sides come forth, and court cases have erupted. Periodically, sportsmen along the Atlantic coast yell loud and clear, demanding that the striped bass be ordained a strictly game fish with no commercial catches allowed. One of the most publicized harangues pertaining to the problem took place in New Jersey, where a showdown hearing was held. Sportsmen, commercial fishermen, and scientists took part in the discussions. The case was dropped because the scientists testified that no data was available concerning commercial fishing as the cause of the depletion of the striped bass stocks. While the controversy continues hot and heavy, there are indications that the sportsmen will eventually win their fight to place the striped bass on the select list of the protected game fishes.

The economics of the striper in the Atlantic involves millions of dollars. From a sporting viewpoint the striped bass is one of the most desired of coastal sport fishes, and the recent much-publicized statistics on the tremendous economic value of sports fishing need not be repeated here. However, the striper is also of great value commercially, especially in the Chesapeake Bay region, where it is the most valuable of all fishes taken.

Sport fishing for striped bass from New Jersey to Massachusetts holds great interest among anglers, and the activity is extraordinarily heavy. In some states in the northern range of the striped bass protective laws have been in effect which place a minimum legal length of 16 inches (measured from the tip of the nose to the fork of the tail) on the taking, sale, or possession of bass. The theory behind this legislation is that the fish will be given an opportunity to spawn at least once before being taken by anglers or commercial fishermen.

Striped Bass in the Pacific

The striped bass is an important game fish on the Pacific coast of the United States, especially along California. Although an introduced species, it is now well established. Since 1935 it has been proclaimed strictly a game fish; commercial fishing is prohibited, and anglers may take the striper throughout the year along its entire range.

Back in the late nineteenth century S. R. Throckmorton, at that time chairman of the California Fish Commission, became interested in the sporting potential of the striped bass. He was responsible for the transplanting of bass into California waters from the Navesink River, New Jersey. The fish were sent— 135 fish in 1879 and 300 in 1882—across country in one of the early transcontinental trains. The planting of these striped bass in San Francisco Bay turned out to be one of the most successful introductions ever attempted. Within ten years stripers were being taken for market, mostly by gill netting. In twenty years the commercial catch alone was 1,234,000 pounds. Commercial fishermen took 1,784,447 pounds in 1915.

The enormous commercial catches attracted the attention of California sportsmen, and they began to organize opposition to the commercial catch of striped bass. In 1926 C. H. Wagner started the agitation to make the striped bass strictly a game fish. His proposal was endorsed unanimously by the Alameda Rod and Gun Club, and in turn the Associated Sportsmen of California continued the struggle to place the striper on the protected list. After many years of controversy the sportsmen's campaign met with success. In 1935 Governor Merriam signed the Cronin-Fisher-Andreas Bill, which put the law into effect. It is interesting to note here that this course of events took place despite the findings of biologists that the striped bass population could support both a commercial and a sport fishery on the coast of California.

At present the range of the striped bass along the Pacific coast is from Orange and San Diego Counties in Southern California to Grays Harbor, Washington. Reports of stripers occurring in Alaskan waters are unconfirmed. A population of bass is centered about Coos Bay, Oregon, with small runs in the Coquille and Umpqua rivers, but the greatest concentrations are found in San Francisco Bay and Delta areas of Central California. The largest California striped bass on record is 78

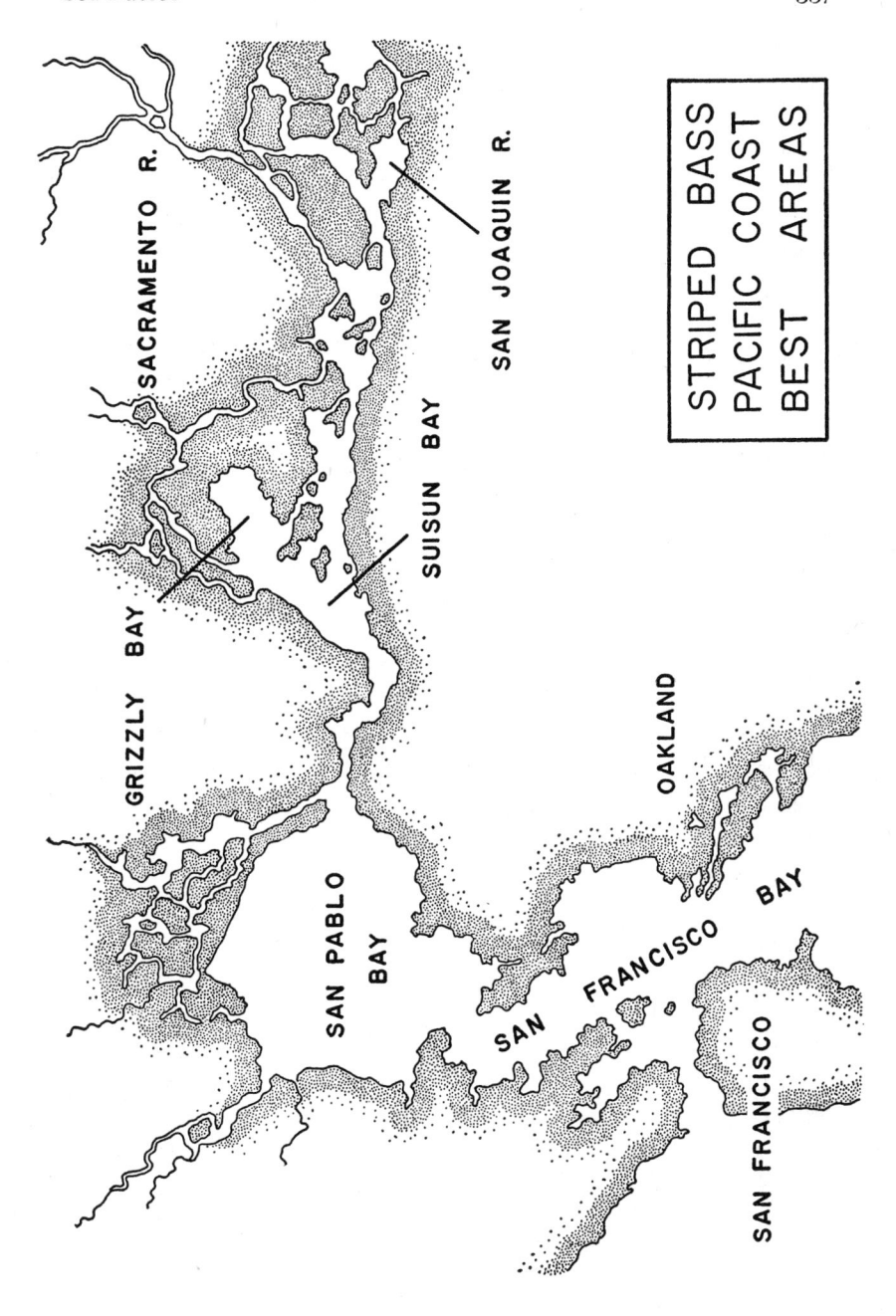

STRIPED BASS
PACIFIC COAST
BEST AREAS

pounds. Fish of about 25 pounds are not rare; average is in the vicinity of 4 pounds.

The migration pattern in the San Francisco area is as follows: Large fish are in the lower bays during the summer months and probably enter the ocean to some extent at this time. During September and October large schools of big stripers pass through San Pablo Bay and Carquinez Straits into Suisun Bay and into the Sacramento and San Joaquin deltas, where they spend the winter. In the spring they disperse out over the Delta and into tributary rivers to spawn; they are probably joined at this time by striped bass from the ocean and lower bays. After spawning the stripers return down river rapidly. Large fish may be taken in San Pablo Bay during May and June. They remain in San Francisco Bay and adjacent brackish and salt waters for the summer.

The recoveries of tagged fish in Coos Bay, Oregon, showed an upstream migration in April–June and a second movement (feeding migration) into the sloughs in fall. The natural establishment of populations in Coos Bay, Oregon, and Columbia River indicates coastwise travel.

In California waters some female striped bass first spawn in their fourth year, the majority in their fifth, 98 per cent in their sixth year, and 100 per cent thereafter. A female at five years of age is about 22 inches long. Many males reach sexual maturity at two years of age (about 11 inches long). In Coos Bay, Oregon, it was found that some females were mature at three years of age, more than half at four years, and 100 per cent at five years or older. Mature males were found in all year-classes including one-year-olds. Spawning takes place in water where a fairly good current flows. The most important spawning ground in California appears to be the San Joaquin River between the Antioch Bridge and the mouth of Middle River, together with other channels in this general area. The Sacramento and Feather rivers are also important spawning areas. In Oregon the Coos River is the major spawning site. Biologists Morgan and Gerlach discovered that in the Coos Bay area there was a predominance of females in late April and early May, while in early April, late May, and throughout June males were more common.

Generally, striped bass feed very little or not at all during spawning. Both males and females appear to feed heavily after spawning. It is well known that the striped bass is a voracious feeder. In the San Francisco Bay area it has eaten practically every marine form found in the locality. Some of the most common items of diet are small Pacific herring, smelt, anchovies, splittails, striped bass, shad, gobies, carp, and perch, together with crustaceans and mollusks such as crabs, shrimps, periwinkles, and clams—plus other forms such as worms. In Coos Bay, Oregon, blennies and flatfishes were also found in striped bass stomachs, and some small salmon and trout are taken when making their seaward journey. Striped bass feed most heavily during the spring and summer months and generally have a greater appetite when in salt water. Striped bass do not feed very actively when the water is cold; many fish may be present, but angling is poor. However, occasional good catches have been made during the winter.

From 1919 through 1935 the catch of striped bass in California waters was stabilized at between 500,000 and 1,000,000 pounds per year. Since 1935, bass have been caught by more than 100,000 anglers each year, and more than 1,000,000 stripers are taken annually. Other statistics: 2,000,000 days spent angling for stripers; value of the sports fishery in 1953 was approximately $18,000,000.

Sea Bass (10c)

(*Centropristes striatus*)

A great favorite with both the offshore party boat devotees and inshore small craft fishermen, the Atlantic sea bass is the "old reliable" along the northern seaboard. It is a good-looking fish, fine eating, and always enjoyed by the occasional fisherman as well as the enthusiast. It is a true member of the marine bass family SERRANIDAE and occasionally is mistakenly called blackfish. The common name "sea bass" is well established throughout most of its range. Some lists have this fish as black sea bass. I have fished for it during many seasons in widely separated areas of its range, and I have not as yet heard it called black sea bass. Since there seems to be no reason to add "black," I prefer "sea bass." Adult males develop a fleshy hump on their backs in front of the dorsal fin. Anglers refer to these males as "humpies" or "humpbacks."

This sea bass is a strictly salt water species distributed along the Atlantic coastal waters of the United States from northern Florida to Cape Cod with strays to Maine. It ranges inshore-offshore from close in to the coastline in only a few feet of water out to about the 70-fathom coutour line depending on the season of year. The main sea bass grounds are off the coasts of North Carolina, Delaware, New Jersey, and western Long Island.

Several features distinguish it easily from the other basses. The dorsal fins are continuous and appear as one, therefore separating this species immediately from the striped bass and white perch. Another good field mark is the unusually large pectoral fin, with a broad and round tip which may just about reach the anal fin. The ventrals are also larger than those of any other fish which might be confused with the sea bass—these fins originate ahead of the pectorals. The 10-spined, rounded first dorsal fin originates slightly in front of the rear corner of the gill cover and has 1 sharp flat spine near its posterior extremity. The second dorsal containing 11 rays is also rounded and very flexible. Three short spines are followed by 7 soft rays in the anal fin. The tail is also rounded, and in large fish one of the upper rays is extended much beyond the others. This distinguishing mark varies from fish to fish but is a characteristic of the sea bass.

Like all other bottom-dwelling marine bassfishes, the sea bass varies widely in color. The background coloration may be grayish, dusky brown, or a deep blue-black, and the belly is paler or may be whitish. The bases of the exposed parts of the scales are lighter in coloration than their margins, which produces a longitudinal series of dots and an appearance of being

A 26-pound pollock taken on a feather jig by Mrs. Ed Migdalski off Wedgeport, Nova Scotia.

Haddock

Pollock

Cod

All taken off Wedgeport, Nova Scotia, on a large nickle-plated spoon jigged off the bottom.

Sea Basses

barred. Several series of whitish spots mark the dorsal fins while the other fins are dusky and mottled. Large males at spawning time have much bright blue, especially around the eyes and hump on the back. At this time the females are a darker and duller blue. In July the females are more brownish in color. Average weight for this serranid is about a pound, and commonly, 5 pounds is not exceeded. The world record rod and reel fish weighed 8 pounds and was taken at Nantucket Sound, Massachusetts, on May 13, 1951, by H. R. Rider.

Apparently sea bass do not make extensive migrations. Most of their travels are offshore-inshore. Off New Jersey, Long Island, and southern New England they appear inshore during the first or second week in May, and then return offshore in the latter part of October or early November. They spend the winter offshore along the 30- to 70-fathom zone. It seems that a temperature preference of 46° to 47° F. guides their depth and distance travels. It also appears that some of the populations which summer off New Jersey and northward may combine the offshore migration with a southward movement. Off Virginia and northern North Carolina great quantities of sea bass are taken by the winter trawl fishery (from January to April), and only small numbers are taken at this time off southern New England.

When the sea bass are inshore they usually frequent hard bottom areas and depths of approximately 20 fathoms. They also are often found around rocks, pilings, and submerged wrecks. Spawning takes place in May along the North Carolina coast and the middle of May to the end of June off New Jersey, Long Island, and southern New England. The eggs float.

Some of the aspects of the life history of the sea bass are interesting. A hermaphroditic (containing male and female organs) condition exists which scientists have also found to be the case in other members of the family SERRANIDAE. Any fisherman who has caught more than a few sea bass has noted that the larger fish are always humpback males (the sexes can be distinguished by the differences in the shape of the head, body, and fins). Nathan Lavenda, who made a study of the sexual differences and hermaphroditism in the sea bass, found that females predominate in the younger age groups, gradually diminishing until the tenth year, after which they disappear, but males live on for at least ten more years. He found regressive ovarian tissue (disappearing female egg tissue) in the male in association with the sperm duct. These facts, Lavenda states, suggest a hermaphroditic change after the fifth year (female to male). Many instances of true hermaphroditism have been described by European scientists. It seems that most cases occur in the SERRANIDAE and to a lesser extent in the SPARIDAE (scups and porgies).

It is a valuable fish both commercially and from a sporting viewpoint. Along the New Jersey coast it is taken from May to November in large numbers by commercial fishermen and by anglers from the New York area. Other areas which get a great play for the sea bass from sportsmen are North Carolina, Delaware, Montauk, Long Island, off Block Island, and in the vicinity of Buzzards Bay. Many boats from Connecticut shores also find good fishing in Long Island Sound, returning with tubs full when the fish are running.

No elaborate tackle is necessary when the sea bass are close to shore (usually smaller fish); they can be taken on light tackle. But farther out heavier tackle is necessary, for a weight is required to bring the bait to the bottom. This does not deter the fishermen since most of them enjoy the reel and pump action. Cut squid is excellent bait, and it should bump along on the bottom. The sea bass is an excellent table fish. With me it is a favorite to skin, fillet, and pack away in the deep freeze for use at least weekly.

White Perch (10b)

(Morone americana)

The white perch is a rather small member of the marine bass family SERRANIDAE found in salt, brackish, and fresh waters. It is confined to the Atlantic seaboard and rates as a favorite pan fish with anglers in areas close to the sea, especially in the spring when great schools come into rivers to spawn. It is also a valuable market fish wherever abundant in tide waters. Maryland and Virginia count it important commercially. The Chesapeake Bay area and all its tributaries are about the greatest productive areas. It is commonest in brackish waters, and greatest numbers are taken in the lower sections of tributary streams. It is truly a coastal fish and considered a nuisance in some New England lakes.

In the Chesapeake Bay area the common name "white perch" is used, but other names are used also: bluenose perch, gray perch, black perch. In other areas it is also known as silver bass, silver perch, and sea perch. However, outside this area, nearly everywhere, it goes by the name of white perch. Since this fish is not a true perch of the family PERCIDAE, the common name is obviously a misnomer. I have given thought to the possibility of suggesting a more appropriate common name, perhaps something descriptive or adding "bass" to make it white perchbass. However, because it is well known throughout almost its entire range as white perch, I believe any change in its name would do more harm than good.

It is strictly an inhabitant of shores, rivers, salt water ponds, and lagoons along the eastern United States from the Gulf of St. Lawrence and Nova Scotia to South Carolina. Its natural range has been extended inland to include almost all eastern states. However, the white perch is not abundant on the extremities of its range and ordinarily is not considered common north of Cape Cod. Favorite spots for white perch, aside from mouths of rivers, are the salt water and brackish ponds which are usually formed by being cut off from the sea by sand bars. These ponds or sand bowls eventually "salt out." From these the range of the white perch has been expanded to many inland streams and lakes. In fresh water it prefers medium depths (10 to 20 feet) and sandy bottoms minus vegetation close to clean gravel or rocky shores.

The white perch resembles its cousin the striped bass more closely than it does the typical members of the marine bassfish family, the groupers. It is a deeper bodied fish than the striped bass (two and a half to three times as long as deep) but has the same number, outline, and arrangement of fins. Also, its body is more flattened sidewise than that of its larger relative. Its head is noticeably concave and its mouth is small. There is no space, but a deep notch, between the 9-spined first dorsal fin and the second dorsal, which contains 1 spine and 12 rays. The anal fin has 8 to 10 rays preceded by 3 stout spines. The ventral fins are placed below the pectorals, and each contains 1 stout spine at its forward margin. The ventrals and the pectorals are larger in comparison to the body than those of the striped bass.

In general coloration the white perch may be dark or light, depending upon its habitation. Usually the dorsal surface is silvery gray, grayish green, or olive, with lighter tints along the sides going to silvery or white on the belly. Fins are usually more or less dusky, and the ventrals and anal may have a rosy tinge at the base. The young have dusky vertical bars above and slightly below the lateral line. These disappear as the fish grows older. The average size is 8 to 10 inches in length and less than a pound in weight. Larger specimens reach 15 inches in length and a weight of 2 or more pounds. One of 4 pounds 12 ounces was taken in Belgrade Lakes, Maine. Anglers should not confuse the white perch with the young striped bass because the perch has a chunkier body, dorsal fins not separated, and no lateral stripes.

The white perch is not known to take long migrations up and down the coast; instead it migrates up the rivers to spawn in early spring. It is rather closely restricted in its seaward range, and although found in undiluted sea water, it is much more plentiful in ponds connected with the sea and in the brackish waters of bays and river mouths. Usually it is not a bottom fish but travels in small schools, wandering from place to place. Mostly, the white perch is a year-round resident wherever found. During the cold weather of winter this serranid gathers in groups in the deeper sections of bays and creeks where it spends the season in a sluggish condition.

Spawning takes place April, May, and June. The fish which live in salt water swim into fresh or brackish water to spawn. The eggs sink in masses and adhere to any object they come to rest upon. The short incubation period lasts six days at 52° F. When in salt or brackish water the white perch feeds on all kinds of small fish fry, young squid, shrimp, crabs, other invertebrates, and spawn of other fishes. In fresh water it feeds on nymphs, insect larvae, water fleas, other insect forms, minnows, and other small fishes.

In some respects the white perch is considered destructive because it loves to eat the spawn of other fishes. Swarms of young white perch have been seen following spawning alewives around shores of ponds and devouring their spawn as soon as it was dropped. Also, in fresh water areas large white perch invade the shallows and prey upon minnows, yellow perch, fingerling smallmouth bass, and other small game fishes.

Along many rivers it is a popular opening season fish when it leaves the salt water and deep sections of rivers and arrives in the more shallow areas of bays and rivers. Often the snow may be falling when enthusiastic anglers, with numb fingers, line the banks when the "white perch are running." Bobber fishing with live bait—grass shrimp, worms, minnows—is a popular method of taking the fish. Bits of crab and small pilchard are also effective, but spinning outfits with tiny lures are becoming more and more popular. In shallow ponds fly rod enthusiasts can take the white perch on large colored bucktails, small wet flies, and tiny spinners. The white perch is not only an excellent sporting fish, but is also excellent eating.

In the eastern Atlantic a closely related species, the gray bass, *Morone labrax*, is common off the west coast of England, where it is a popular fish. It is also known off Morocco. The gray bass grows larger than the white perch with an average weight of 5 pounds and a maximum of about 15 pounds.

GIANT SEA BASSES

The giant sea basses are king-size groupers, part of the family SERRANIDAE, generally not considered game fishes. However, the giants are of interest to anglers because of their unusual size. They are spotted Jewfish of the western Atlantic and eastern Pacific, black Jewfish of the western Atlantic, giant black sea bass of the eastern Pacific, and the barramundi of Australia. The first three are sedentary, sluggish fishes found in tropical and subtropical waters, on or close to bottom, in the vicinity of reefs, rocky areas, break waters, around submerged wrecks and pilings of deep water bridges. Occasionally, one may put up noticeable resistance to being dragged out of its element, but usually it is nothing more than the heavy weight which gives the angler trouble. Although the Australian form is usually placed with the SERRANIDAE, it is a member of another family, LATIDAE. It is esteemed as a fine game fish.

Spotted Jewfish (28a)
(Promicrops itaiara)

Along the Atlantic coast the spotted Jewfish may be known as Jewfish, Florida Jewfish, and Warsaw grouper; in the eastern Pacific it is called southern Jewfish, Junefish, and giant bass. It is the largest of the marine basses, SERRANIDAE, in the Atlantic and Pacific. Undoubtedly, its size is the dominating factor in angler interest. The world record rod and reel fish weighed 551 pounds and was taken on June 29, 1937, at Galveston Bay, Texas, by G. Pangarakis. However, much larger fish have been taken by fishermen using heavy handlines. Fish of 200 or 300 pounds are common. The maximum weight of this species is listed in different publications as being 600, 700, and 800 pounds. In the Atlantic it is found along the entire Florida coastline, the Gulf of Mexico, and the West Indies down to Brazil. It is considered rare in Bermuda. In the Pacific it ranges along Lower California, the Gulf of California, south to Panama.

The body is bass-like with a broad head and widely separated "pop-eyes." The 11 dorsal fin spines are very short (and shorter than the rays of the second dorsal), a characteristic which separates this species from the black Jewfish. The second dorsal contains 15 or 16 rays; anal fin has 3 spines and 8 rays, pectoral fin is large with a roundish edge. The lateral line scales have 4 to 6 strongly radiating ridges. The 9 or 10 developed gill rakers are short and thick. In coloration the small- and medium-size fish are usually dusky with a profuse sprinkling of dark spots over the entire head and anterior portion of the body. The larger fish may be darker than the smaller specimens, and the spots may be faded or entirely absent. This fish may take on lighter hues if frequenting the vicinity of light sandy bottom areas.

As a food fish it is good, used mostly in chowders or steaked, but in my estimation it doesn't rate as a game fish, regardless of its size. Southern fishermen in the Florida Keys fish for it with large, strong hooks attached to a chain and quarter-inch manila rope. Often they lose their rigs. It is not a good idea to fish for them with rod and reel.

Black Jewfish (28c)

(*Garrupa nigrita*)

This is another Atlantic member of the SERRANIDAE that reaches large size; 100- and 200-pounders are not uncommon. Its range and habits are similar to those of the spotted Jewfish although this species may stray slightly further north. It is distinguished from the spotted Jewfish by the much higher dorsal fin spines, which number 10 or 11. The second dorsal contains 14 or 15 rays, and the anal has 3 spines and 9 rays. Gill rakers are short and thick and number 12 to 14 on the lower limb of the first gill arch. Not a game fish, but I list it here because fishermen try to capture one "just for the fun of it" with rope, chain, large hook and large bait. Makes good chowder.

Giant Black Sea Bass (28b)

(*Stereolepis gigas*)

The giant black sea bass, also known as Jewfish, California giant sea bass, and black sea bass, is an inhabitant of the eastern Pacific, recognized as a good food fish, and noted for its size. It is distributed from about Central California at the Farallon Islands south to Magdalena Bay, Lower California; not common north of Point Conception.

As with the other giant sea basses, this species draws the interest of anglers only because of its large size—500 or 600 pounds. It cannot be confused with other marine basses in the area because the second dorsal is much shorter than the first dorsal. There are 11 spines in the first dorsal fin and 10 rays in the second dorsal—an outstanding characteristic (bassfishes usually have more dorsal rays than dorsal spines). The anal has 3 spines and 8 rays. The first dorsal is not as high as the second dorsal. In coloration the adults are uniformly dark brown or black with light patches on the throat and lower surface of the tail. The dorsal and anal fins are blackish with transparent edges. Ventrals are black, and the pectoral fin is dark with white areas between the fin rays, or pale and transparent. Its habits and mode of living are similar to those of its Atlantic cousins, and although anglers catch the giant black sea bass with rod and reel, it doesn't rate as a game fish.

Barramundi

(*Lates calcarifer*)

Although Australian scientists place the barramundi in the family LATIDAE, rather than SERRANIDAE, it is generally considered with the groups of marine basses. It is favored as one of the finest food fishes in Australian waters and taken by market fishermen using handlines, traps, and nets. As a game fish it is also regarded highly. It is also known as giant perch, palmer, and cockup. The name "barramundi" was used by the aborigines of Queensland for other fish with large scales; unfortunately white Australians have used the name widely with confusion. However, since the fish is so well known in North Queensland, where it is abundant, fishery scientists there prefer to keep the name "barramundi."

The distribution of this fish includes the East Indies to India, China, and Japan. It is plentiful along the northern Australian coast up to Western Australia. The oblong body of the barramundi resembles more closely that of a perch than a bass. Its face is long with eyes close to the snout. The mouth is fairly large and contains fine teeth. The first dorsal contains 8 spines and the second dorsal has 11 rays; anal has 3 spines and 8 or 9 rays. In Australian waters fish of 60 to 100 pounds are not rare, and specimens up to 120 pounds have been taken. However, it does grow larger; a fish taken from the Bay of Bengal weighed 580 pounds.

The barramundi inhabits salt, brackish, and fresh waters usually in and around mouths of rivers; occasionally it moves to sea. There is a minimum legal size of 20 inches on this fish in Queensland. It has all the characteristics of a good game fish, often schooling and slashing into groups of small fishes. The use of live bait is effective, and artificials are also successful. The barramundi strikes hard and when hooked makes runs and may leap high in the air in an effort to shake the hook.

GROUPERS

The grouper section of the family SERRANIDAE includes the many species of bass-like fishes which usually do not school, but rather are present in groups confined to specific localities. They live most of the time close to the bottom and seem to lead slow, serene lives, usually in one area, or even one spot, for lengthy periods of time. Wherever found they seem to be present the year round, preferring waters filled with rocks and reefs. They are not usually sought as game fishes but will take baited hooks and upon rare occasions lures trolled slowly close to the bottom. As a food item nearly all groupers are excellent. This assemblage of fishes is sometimes further split into several different categories and variously known as Jewfish, grouper, rockfish, rockbass, hind, cabrilla, kelp bass, sand bass, sandfish, gag, graysby, coney, hamlet, and others. Each has a spinous dorsal fin connected with the second or soft dorsal fin. The body shape, fin arrangement, and other characteristics are considered the type for typical marine basses. Although they are not game fishes, I list the most common species which are often taken by fishermen using hook and line.

Black Grouper
(*Mycteroperca bonaci*)

Also called rockfish. Atlantic. Brazil to Florida, stray to Massachusetts. West Indies. Bermuda. Color is dusky olive, brownish, or black, with darker quadrate-shaped blotches on the sides. Most of body covered with small bronze or yellowish spots. Pectoral fins never with yellow tips or edges. Large heavy body. Dorsal spines 11, second dorsal 16 to 18 rays. Anal spines 3, rays 11 to 12. Gill rakers on lower limb of first arch, 9 to 12. About 110 scales in lateral line. Grows to approximately 4 feet and about 100 pounds.

One of the few groupers which may be classed as a game fish. It is included in the game fishes of Bermuda. Off the Florida Gulf coast it is taken by anglers anywhere from one half mile to ten miles offshore. Cut and live bait used. Fishermen in the Keys often troll the outer reefs with strip baits. Artificials such as spoons and other deep-running lures are effective. It is a strong fish, which displays more stamina than the other groupers and puts up a commendable show unless it heads into the rocks before the angler has control of the situation.

Yellowfin Grouper (29b)
(*Mycteroperca venenosa*)

Also rockfish, yellow grouper, rock grouper. Atlantic. North Carolina south to West Indies. Bermuda. Color variable. Several color phases. Most usual: dusky olive or grayish on back and sides, white below. Spots all over body and fins; those on dorsal surface and tail darker or black, red on head and belly. The red phase is bright scarlet above, becoming gray on lower sides and head. Sides are reticulated with enclosed darker portions of red or black. Tips of pectoral fins edged with yellow or orange yellow. Tips of membranes of spinous dorsal fin also yellow. Always spotted. High forehead, slightly concave tail (rock hind has low forehead and rounded tail). Scales about 125 in row from operculum to base of tail. Dorsal spines 11, second dorsal 16 rays. Anal 3 spines and 12 rays. Gill rakers 11 on lower limb of first gill arch. Maximum size about 36 inches. The yellowfin grouper has many color phases which had scientists splitting it into different species. Although often caught by bridge fishermen in the Florida Keys, it is principally a reef fish.

Gag

(*Mycteroperca microlepis*)

Atlantic. North Carolina to Florida, Gulf Coast. Color variable. Several color phases. Usually pale or grayish white. Mottlings on back and sides faintly discernible. Tail, dorsal, and anal fins edged with white. Pectorals and ventrals dusky. Other color phases may be in shades of green-blue or violet. Small scales, about 140 in row from operculum to base of tail. Maximum size about 3 pounds. Occasionally will fight well if on light tackle but usually escapes into rocks. Good eating.

Golden Grouper and Leopard Grouper (28d)

(*Mycteroperca pardalis*)

Both are same species, different color phases. Pacific. Gulf of California from Cape San Lucas, Mexico to Banderas Bay. Ground color in leopard grouper varies—brown, gray, olive green, golden brown. Completely covered with small reddish brown spots. Golden phase is over-all yellowish orange and may have few black blotches on sides and back, or may have black on entire back. Maximum size about 3 feet. Twenty-one or more gill rakers below the angle of the first gill arch.

Broomtail Grouper (30c)
(*Mycteroperca xenarcha*)

Also spiketail grouper. Pacific. Lower California; Gulf of California southward to about Galapagos Islands. Only member of Pacific serranids with end of tail toothed. Three phases—gray broomtail grouper, pinto broomtail grouper, spotted broomtail grouper. Reaches a weight of about 60 pounds.

Colorado Grouper
(*Mycteroperca olfax*)

Pacific. Panama to Galapagos Islands. Two color phases. Brown colorado grouper: dark olive brown on back, sides and head spotted with purplish brown; belly is gray brown; also may be mottled brown. Yellow colorado grouper: entire body and fins colored in different hues of yellow orange. Second dorsal spine higher than the others. About 13 gill rakers below the angle of the first gill arch. Maximum size about 3 feet.

Rock Hind (29c)
(*Epinephelus adscensionis*)

Also garrupa. Atlantic. Florida to Brazil. West Indies. Bermuda. Color variable. Usually olive or greenish gray background, orange-red dots over body and fins but sparse on tail. Large whitish or pale spots present besides the orange-red spots. Dorsal and anal fins without dark edge. Maxilla without scales. Second dorsal spine shorter than third. Dorsal fin 11 spines, second dorsal 17 rays; anal 7 or 8 rays. Gill rakers short, 15 to 18 below angle of first gill arch. Pores in lateral line 55 to 60. Maximum size about 18 inches. Taken often on handline. Good food fish.

Red Hind (30b)

(*Epinephelus guttatus*)

Also rock hind, cabrilla. Atlantic. North Carolina to Brazil. West Indies. Bermuda. Color variable. Usualy reddish with entire body covered with red spots. Second dorsal, anal and caudal fins broadly edged with black or bluish black. Inside of mouth is red. Distinguished from the rock hind by having scales on the maxilla. Dorsal spines 11, rays 16; anal has 3 spines, 8 rays. Gill rakers 15 to 17 on lower limb of first gill arch. Small size, rarely larger than 16 to 18 inches. Maximum weight about 5 pounds.

Red Grouper

(*Epinephelus morio*)

Atlantic. Florida to Brazil. Stray to Massachusetts. West Indies. Bermuda. Color variable. Several color phases. Usually reddish brown above, lower part of head and breast pinkish. Lateral dark blotches present. Orange-red spots about the eye. Pectoral fins pale, other fins colored like body and edged with white. First dorsal fin with 11 spines is high in front, second dorsal 16 or 17 rays. Anal 3 spines, 8 rays. Gill rakers 13 to 18 on lower limb of first gill arch. Caudal fin lunate rather than rounded. Maximum weight about 40 pounds, average 1 to 5 pounds.

Nassau Grouper (29a)

(*Epinephelus striatus*)

Also hamlet. Atlantic. North Carolina to Brazil. West Indies. Bermuda. Color variable. Background of browns, grays or greens. May be plain or with regular vertical dark bands. Conspicuous dark bands from snout through eye and over head, and from snout to dorsal fin. These bands fade in different degrees and may also be totally absent. Small brown or black dots about the eye. Prominent dark blotch on upper surface of caudal peduncle. Body much lighter when over sandy bottom. Dorsal spines 11 or 12, second dorsal 16 or 17 rays. Anal 3 spines, 8 rays. First dorsal spine is low, but the second is as high as the others. Gill rakers are short and number 15 or 16 below the angle of the first gill arch. Maximum weight appears to be about 10 pounds. Average approximately 2 to 4 pounds.

Spotted Cabrilla
(*Epinephelus analogus*)

Pacific. Lower California; Gulf of California. Mexico south to Galapagos Islands. Color variable. Typical fish usually reddish all over. Profusely covered with darker spots over body and fins. Fins have greenish hue. Several dark, wide bars may be distinct, indistinct, or completely absent. Differs from other cabrillas in having 10 spines, rather than 11 in dorsal fin, rays about 16 or 17. No light spots. Inner teeth in jaws are long, slender, and conspicuous. Maximum weight about 20 pounds. Excellent food fish. Commercially important.

Flag Cabrilla
(*Epinephelus labriformis*)

Pacific. Cape San Lucas, Lower California to Galapagos Islands. Color variable. It may be grayish green dorsally and paler on sides and belly, or an over-all reddish coloration. Back and sides always covered with whitish spots and dots. Background mottled with light gray. Mouth lining is red. Dorsal spines 11 (instead of 10). Anal fin rays 8 or 9. Maximum length about 20 inches.

Coney (30a)
(*Cephalopholis fulvus*)

Atlantic. Florida to Brazil. West Indies. Bermuda. Color variable. Several color phases. Background color may be red, brown, light yellow, or cream. Most of the head and body covered with small white, blue, or black spots. Soft dorsal fin and tail in all color phases edged with white. Dorsal fin 9 spines, rays 15. Anal 3 spines, rays 8 or 9. Gill rakers 12 to 14 on lower limb of first gill arch. One of the smallest groupers. Average length about 9 inches. Maximum length about 1 foot.

Graysby (29d)
(Petrometopon cruentatus)

Atlantic. Florida to Brazil. West Indies. Bermuda. Color variable. Several color phases. Background may be reddish, whitish, brown, or dusky bars. Spots over head, fins, and body are rusty, dark brown, or black. Dorsal spines 9, soft dorsal rays 14. Anal 3 spines, 8 rays. Gill rakers on lower limb of first gill arch 9 to 11 plus rudiments. Pores in lateral line 50 to 55. Another small grouper—maximum length about 1 foot.

Sandfish
(Diplectrum formosum)

Also sandperch. A common, small serranid that makes up in fight for its tiny size. Atlantic. Tropical waters northward to the shores of Florida and Gulf coast as far as Texas. Strays to North Carolina. Coloration is light brownish yellow above going lighter below to almost silvery. Fins are barred, mottled and marked with yellows and reds. About 7 or 8 dusky brown vertical bars extend down from the back fading away towards the belly. Three prominent broken blue lines are found on the dorsal surface, and usually about 3 light tan lines are present below the mid-side of the body. Adults have blue lines on upper head and below the eye. Body is elongated, dorsal fins long, anal lobes of caudal fin moderately extended. Dorsal fins appear continuous with no notch between first and second dorsal fin. First dorsal contains 10 spines and second dorsal 12 rays. Another distinguishing characteristic is the presence of strong spines on the preoperculum.

It is common in protected shore waters, usually over sandy, pebbly, rocky ground, or shallow grassy areas. Although small, 5 to 7 inches average with a maximum of about 12 inches, it is a desirable food and game fish which will take almost any natural bait. On light tackle it is fun comparable to the small fresh water bluegill. Also, it is excellent pan fried.

ROCK BASSES

The rock basses are a group of serranids found in the eastern Pacific from California south to Peru. They all inhabit waters close to shore in the vicinity of rocks, sandy beaches, kelp beds, and bays. These fishes are recognized by several characteristics: dorsal spines are 10, of which the first two are short followed by 2 conspicuously long spines; dorsal rays number 13 to 15; anal fin has 3 spines and 7 rays. Pectorals are large, with a rounded edge. The tail has a more or less straight margin. In weight they may range from 1 to 30 pounds. Squids, crustaceans, and small fishes are their main items of diet. They are taken occasionally by sportsmen but generally are not considered game fishes. They are good eating, but only of minor importance commercially. All are of the genus *Paralabrax*. Only three are known well enough to be of interest to the angler.

Sand Bass (31b)

(*Paralabrax nebulifer*)

Also kelp bass, California sand bass, Johnny Verde. Pacific. From central California to Magdalena Bay, Lower California; not common north of Point Conception, California. Generally greenish gray or greenish brown, with irregular and sometimes indistinct, vertical dusky bands on the sides. Underparts white or grayish. Area below eye may have small brownish yellow spots. No deep notch present between connected first and second dorsal fins (as in the kelp bass). Third dorsal spine conspicuously longer than the rest (another mark distinguishing it from the kelp bass). Teeth are present in the roof of the mouth, and about 70 scales are in a row along the lateral line. Maximum length is about 20 inches.

Kelp Bass (31a)
(*Paralabrax clathratus*)

Also sand bass, rock bass, cabrilla. Pacific. From central California to Cape San Lucas, Lower California. Found mostly around kelp beds. Usually brownish gray or greenish gray. Dorsal surface and upper sides mottled with broad blotches of darker gray or brown. Lower sides and underparts silvery with a yellowish tinge. Fins tinged with yellow. Deep notch present between first and second dorsal fins (separates it from the sand bass and spotted rock bass). Third and fourth spines about same length, which is also a good identification characteristic. Has teeth in roof of mouth. It is one of the more important food fishes in southern California and is taken in large numbers by sportsmen using live bait.

Spotted Rock Bass (31c)
(*Paralabrax maculatofasciatus*)

Pacific. From southern California to Mazatlán, Mexico, and Gulf of California. Olive or greenish brown on dorsal surface going lighter below and white on belly. Vague, dusky bars extend from the back downward almost reaching the white of the ventral surface. Prominent spots cover entire fish including fins, but not on the belly. Body shape and fin structure quite similar to the sand bass. The first and second dorsal fins do not have a deep notch between them; this distinguishes the rock bass from the kelp bass. The profuse spotting and about 90 scales in a row along the lateral line separate it from the sand bass (which has about 70). Maximum length about 18 inches.

Ocean Whitefish

Ocean Whitefish (16d)
(*Caulolatilus princeps*)

The ocean whitefish, distributed from central California into Lower California and southward down to Peru, loves rocky and sandy areas. It is not a relative of the fresh water whitefish, but is the only member of the blanquillo family, BRANCHIOSTEGIDAE along the California coast. As a sport fish it is fair, but as food it is a fish of note and is taken in considerable quantity by commercial fishermen. The fishing season extends the year round, but best catches are made in the winter and early spring.

Also known as blanquillo, it is recognized easily by its blunt snout; large eyes; single, long, almost even dorsal fin which has no notch between the spinous (9) and soft rays (24) portions; anal fin long with 2 spines in front (23 rays); no teeth in roof of mouth, but large canines present toward the rear of the jaws. Tail slightly concave. Color a light brown on back and sides gradually going lighter below. Live fish usually have indistinct mottling along the back and sides. Pectoral fins are blue-gray with a yellowish streak along the center; dorsal and anal fins are yellowish and have a blue streak near the edge.

Other fins are yellowish. Sometimes a fish of general yellow-orange coloration is taken. Maximum length appears to be about 35 to 40 inches. I caught eight or ten of these fishing on bottom with bait off Cabo Blanco, Peru, but they were between 14 and 18 inches in length. It appears that this may be the average size—at least in that area.

Porgies

The porgies of the western Atlantic are deep bodied, compressed, small but energetic members of the family SPARIDAE. They are excellent food fishes; row boat anglers take especial delight in catching them. When taken on light tackle porgies demonstrate a surprisingly strong resistance to rod and reel and are easy to catch on almost any kind of cut bait or worms. It is an excellent fish to seek when introducing youngsters to the art of salt water fishing, for when the fish are hitting, there is not much waiting between bites.

Northern Porgy (24a)

(Stenotomus versicolor)

This porgy is an important food and small game fish westward and southward of Cape Cod. Commercial landings range from 3,000,000 to about 6,000,000 pounds annually in southern New England and perhaps slightly less in New York. Thousands of salt water anglers each year look forward to the arrival of the porgies. They are fun to catch and are worth taking home. Another common name (not in the New York to Massachusetts area) is scup, and some authors list its scientific name as *Stenotomus crysops*. The usual range of the northern porgy is along the east coast of the United States from South Carolina to Cape Cod; it straggles to Maine and was introduced in Bermuda.

It is a deep-body fish with a short snout, small mouth, a steep profile, and a slightly concave head. The scales are rather large, thick, and firmly attached. Eyes are situated high on the side of the head, and the margins of its gill covers are rounded. The moderately high, continuous dorsal fin contains 12 spines (first much shorter than others) and 12 rays. A groove along the back is present where the dorsal fin can be laid back. The anal fin contains 3 spines and 11 or 12 rays; it is also depressible into a groove. Tail is deeply concave or lunate. Pectorals are very long and pointed. Color is bright shimmering pearlescent over entire body; darker on the dorsal surface going lighter to a white belly. About 12 to 15 indistinct horizontal stripes flecked with light blue may be present on the back and sides. A light blue streak follows the base of the dorsal fin. Head is silvery and may have dusky blotches. Dorsal, caudal, and anal fins are dusky flecked with blue; pectorals are pale and transparent; ventrals are white or dusky. Average size is 10 to 12 inches in length and ½ to 2 pounds in weight. They do get larger—about 16 inches and 3 or 4 pounds.

Along the Chesapeake Bay area porgies arrive inshore in early April and farther north to southern Massachusetts a month later. Usually they depart in October, although some hang on till November, with rarely a few in December. Porgies winter off Virginia and northern Carolina in deep water—20 to 50 fathoms (some are taken at depths of 90 fathoms). Commercial trawlers make large catches from January to April. It seems that the porgies which appear in the more northern range migrate southward and offshore of Chesapeake Bay and northern North Carolina. Also, in recent winters large numbers have been taken off southern New England, indicating that part of the northern group moves offshore when cold weather arrives and returns close to shore in spring.

Porgies are known to be quite sensitive to low temperatures. Large numbers of both small and large fish have been known to perish when sudden cold weather has hit shallow water. They prefer water temperature of at least 45° F. during winter. Porgies hug the coast closely during the warm summer weather —never more than five or six miles from shore. They usually travel in schools. Young fry may come in close to shore in only a few feet of water, but adults will be found in water not shallower than 1 or 2 fathoms, and no deeper than 15 or 20 fathoms. They have a decided preference for smooth bottom rather than rocky areas.

Most of the food is taken off the bottom—crustaceans, worms, small squid, other bottom invertebrates, and sometimes fish fry. Anglers find that porgies will bite greedily on bits of clams, cut squid, and marine worms. During the early season, in spawning time, porgies do not feed much. Spawning along southern New England takes place from May to August but mostly in June. By November the young may be as long as 4 inches; then they do not grow much until the following spring. The approximate age-length ratios are these:

Years	Inches
1	4¼
2	6¼
3	7⅞
4	9
5	9¾

Porgies are favorite fishes along the Connecticut and Rhode Island coasts in the early summer. I like to fish for them because no elaborate rigs or preparations are required. The necessary equipment is a light spinning or bait-casting outfit and enough lead to take the bait to the bottom. Many of my friends also love to catch porgies, but seldom eat them. They admit that the fish are good eating but too much trouble to clean. My refrigerator always contains plenty of these succulent fishes in season; I also freeze some for future use and find it no arduous task to clean them. Here is how I do it. A permanent part of my tackle box is a large pair of heavy-duty scissors. When the day's fishing is over and we are still out on the water, I clean each fish with a few quick strokes of the scissors: first the head; then I insert one point into the belly and cut one side of the abdominal wall, up high; then the other side. A couple of snips for the tail and fins close to the body is next. Using a wire basket I rinse the fish in salt water. It requires but a few minutes to clean a bushel full.

When you arrive home don't scale the porgies. Simply turn up one end of the skin with your thumbnail or a knife and peel it off. You may have to slit some skin with a knife before attempting to remove the skin. In the skinning procedure a small piece of cloth under the thumb and finger facilitates a good grip. If you have a pair of pliers handy, use them instead of your fingers. Try this system once and I'll bet that you no longer try to avoid cleaning the fish by passing them on to your neighbors. On the other hand, if you want to make a hit with them, present the fish cleaned. Scissor cleaning and skinning the fish is easy, not time consuming nor messy, and the neighbors will not throw the fish into the garbage pail as soon as you leave their door!

Southern Porgy
(*Stenotomus aculeatus*)

The southern porgy, also called scup and fair maid, so closely resembles its northern counterpart that fishermen do not attempt to separate the two. Nowhere is the southern form as numerous, or as commercially important, as its northern cousin. It prefers warm waters and is distributed from Cape Hatteras south and into the Gulf of Mexico to Texas. The interested angler may differentiate easily between the two species; the southern fish has a pectoral fin about as long as its head, while the northern porgy has a shorter pectoral. In every other respect they are alike except the anterior profile is not as steep in the southern porgy as it is in the other. It is slightly smaller in maximum size, but a fine food and game fish.

Saucereye Porgy (24d)
(*Calamus calamus*)

Although small, the saucereye porgy is appreciated as a food fish in Key West, Florida, and in the West Indies. It is also distributed northward to North Carolina. In shape and arrangement of fins it resembles the other porgies. It can be distinguished from its relatives by its small scales, which number 54 to 58 along the lateral line, deep body, and elevated back. The dorsal fin contains 12 spines and 12 rays; anal has 3 spines and 10 or 11 rays. The 6 or 7 gill rakers below the angle of the first gill arch are small and blunt. General coloration is silvery with bluish reflections. The base and center of each scale are golden, forming horizontal stripes. A deep violet streak is present below the eye. Fins are pale, indistinctly blotched with orange. As with the other porgies, color may change in intensity depending upon the type of bottom and surroundings the fish is inhabiting. Maximum size is about 15 to 18 inches and about a pound in weight. However, most of the fish taken weigh less than one half pound.

Grass Porgy (24b)
(*Calamus arctifrons*)

Primarily a southern fish with a range generally from Florida, the Gulf Coast, to Texas, and southward to the West Indies, the grass porgy is not abundant anywhere. It is not a large fish, seldom exceeding 2 pounds. Scales are large and number 45 to 53 in the lateral line. Its coloration is striking. The body is usually olive or grayish with wide, dusky vertical bars on the sides and a wide dusky or olive band from the end of the gill cover to the tail. The fore part of the cheek is yellow, and the fins are mottled with black. Yellow spots may be present along the lateral line. The common name is derived from the fact that the grass porgy prefers grassy bottoms, close along shore in water 2 to 3 fathoms deep. Although most of its feeding is on

Porgies

crabs and shrimp, some vegetable matter is also consumed. As a food fish it is excellent and puts up a good scrap on light tackle.

Jolthead Porgy (24c)
(*Calamus bajonado*)

The jolthead is one of the largest porgies, reaching a maximum of about 8 pounds. Some reports state "to about 14 pounds." Its general range is from the West Indies to North Carolina. However, it strays farther north. Color is dull brassy on the back; silvery on the sides with blue markings. A faint blue stripe is present below the eye. Fins are usually plain, pelvics may be dusky, tail may be barred. Dorsal fin has 12 spines, 10 to 12 rays; 3 anal spines and 10 to 11 rays. The 6 gill rakers are short and blunt. Fairly small scales number 54 to 58 along the lateral line. In its southern range it is taken commercially in traps and by handlines.

Sheepshead Porgy (25b)
(*Calamus penna*)

Also known as littlemouth porgy, it is a small fish not exceeding a foot in length. It is found from Florida to the West Indies, and belongs in the family SPARIDAE. Named sheepshead porgy because it resembles somewhat the sheepshead *Archosargus probatocephalus* in having several dark vertical bars along the body. Rest of the body is olive or greenish and silvery. It has 45 to 53 scales along the lateral line. An excellent pan fish and taken commercially.

Pinfish (25d)
(*Lagodon rhomboides*)

The small pinfish can hardly be called a game fish. However, it is important commercially and is one of the chief bait fishes used in angling for tarpon. Along the east coast of the

United States it ranges from North Carolina southward and strays as far north as Cape Cod. It prefers grassy shallow areas. It is a member of the porgy family SPARIDAE and is also called bream. The name pinfish is derived from the sharp, slender dorsal fin spines which are pin-like. The dorsal surface is olive or greenish and the sides are silvery; a round dark spot is found on the shoulder. Numerous horizontal golden stripes extend along the body, and 4 to 6 dark vertical bars are present. Fins yellowish; first dorsal and anal may have blues and browns. Dorsal fin contains 12 spines, 11 rays; anal 3 spines, 11 rays. Gill rakers 18 to 20 below angle of first gill arch. Average size is 6 inches; maximum about a foot. Spawns during autumn and winter. Mostly considered a nuisance by anglers because it has the ability to "skin" a hook of its bait and because its sharp spines cause uncomfortable handling. Commercially it is too small to be profitable as a food fish, but many tons are taken because they yield a high-grade oil in the reduction plants.

Sheepshead (25a)
(*Archosargus probatocephalus*)

The sheepshead is one of the most popular members of the porgy family, SPARIDAE. Anglers consider it an excellent game fish. The range of this fish is rather extensive along the Atlantic and Gulf coasts of the United States from Texas to Cape Cod. It strays northward to the Bay of Fundy. However, it is rare north of New York. The sheepshead resembles the porgy closely, being deep of body and flattened sidewise. The profile is also similar. The dorsal fin is long, 11 or 12 spines and 11 to 13 rays; anal fin, 3 spines and 10 or 11 rays; dorsal and anal are depressable in a deep groove; pectorals are long and pointed; scales are large; eyes located high on the sides of the head. The sheepshead can be differentiated from the porgies by its tail, which is not deeply forked; the ends are rounded, not pointed. Dorsal spines are alternately stout and slender, and its teeth are much broader. Other distinctive characteristics are a thicker body, and 7 broad dark brown or blackish vertical bars present on a grayish, greenish yellow, or bronzy background. Fins are dusky, bluish green, or yellowish green.

Maximum size is about a length of 30 inches and a weight of 20 pounds. Average is about a pound or slightly more. The sheepshead is a resident in Florida waters with only seasonal movements to shore and offshore, but northward of Hatteras it is a migratory fish and to a lesser degree along the coasts of Texas and Louisiana, where it appears only during the warm weather of mid-summer. The migratory sheepshead is a large fish—10 to 12 pounds and occasionally as high as 18 pounds. In the areas of the Carolinas it arrives about May and stays through November. It travels in small groups and schools and prefers hard or rocky bottoms, inshore reefs, stone jetties, bridge and pier pilings. Other favorite spots are around old wrecks, sunken logs, breakwaters, and mangrove areas. Occasionally it is found in brackish waters and even fresh water rivers such as the St. Johns in Florida.

Spawning occurs along sandy shores in the early spring. Main items of diet are crabs, shrimp, young oysters, soft clams, mussels, barnacles, marine worms, and small fishes. Many are taken commercially with haul seines, pound nets, and handlines. Anglers sometimes find it difficult to land a sheepshead because its mouth is hard and the fish feeds with caution. A quick strike is necessary when a bite is felt, and chumming an area induces the fish to bite more freely.

Bermuda Bream (25c)

(*Diplodus argenteus*)

The Bermuda bream is a silvery member of the porgy family, SPARIDAE. It is distributed in Bermuda, the West Indies, Florida, to Argentina. A pretty fish, it is steel blue above, silvery on the sides and below. A conspicuous black spot is present on the anterior dorsal part of the caudal peduncle. Five or 6 narrow vertical blackish bars are present on the body, and in between these are narrower and shorter bars; the bars may be absent. Fins are light greenish gray. Dorsal spines number 12, and rays 14 or 15; anal has 3 spines, 13 or 14 rays. Gill rakers are 10 to 11 on the lower limb of the first gill arch. Maximum size is about 20 inches. This bream usually travels in schools close to shore and is commonly found around harbors. Good eating and a fine sport fish on light tackle.

Rockfishes

California rockfishes are not considered game fishes in the true sense of the word. However, within the last ten years rod and reel fishing for rockfishes has increased to such a great extent along the California coast that they have gradually become one of the more important groups of fishes sought by anglers. Therefore, any up-to-date publication on game fishes should not disregard them. Statistics indicate the surprising rise of rockfishes taken in California waters. In 1947 rockfishes comprised 9 per cent of the 2,500,000 fish taken by anglers. By 1955 over half (55 per cent) of 3,000,000 fish caught by sportsmen consisted of rockfishes. Commercially this group is also important; all are good for the table, and presently between 12,000,000 and 13,000,000 pounds are taken annually. It is the leading market fish in California.

Some rockfish frequent fairly shallow waters, at times close to shore, but many are found only in deep water; some occur in water as deep as 3,000 feet. The young of different rockfishes occur in great abundance and distribution along the California coast; some appear as far as 300 miles offshore. Young rockfishes are valuable as food for many oceanic, mid-water and bottom fishes; they provide an important part of the diet of some great game fishes such as the king salmon and albacore.

Rockfishes and scorpionfishes form the family SCORPAENIDAE, presently acknowledged as one of the most important families in California's coastal waters. The family consists of forty-nine species in the genus *Sebastodes,* two in the genus *Sebastolobus,* and one in the genus *Scorpaena.* Sportsmen find that rockfishes look very much alike in general appearance and are difficult to distinguish as to separate species. Several characteristics distinguish the rockfishes from other types: a bony support extends from the lower part of the eye across the cheek just under the skin; body is covered with scales; the dorsal fin is deeply notched and contains 13 strong, sharp spines (sculpin has 12). The 13th spine is closely attached to the soft or rayed portion of the dorsal fin. Three sharp spines are present in front of the anal fin. Five preopercular and 2 opercular spines are present, usually strong and sharp. All rockfishes bear live young. Coloration varies greatly. They range from the Gulf of California northward to Alaska. On the other side of the Pacific they are distributed down to southern Japan. The following are the most common and most distinctive rockfishes caught by anglers along the coast of California.

Blue Rockfish (32b)
(*Sebastodes mystinus*)

Also priestfish, bluefish, blue perch. Body color bluish black and mottled; fins dark. No spines top of head. Dorsal fin spines lower than rays. Maxillary extends to hind part of pupil. Inside lining of belly is black. Maximum about 21 inches. Santo Tomas, Baja California, to Bering Sea.

Vermillion Rockfish (33c)
(*Sebastodes miniatus*)

Also red rock cod, red snapper, barracho. Body color vermillion or brick red, mottled; fins red. Inside lining of belly is white. Maxilla extends to back of eye. Maximum about 30 inches. Guadalupe Island, Baja California, to Vancouver Island, British Columbia.

Boccacio (32c)
(*Sebastodes paucispinis*)

Also salmon grouper, grouper, rock cod. Body color light olive-brown on back, pink on sides. Broad, convex space between eyes. No spines on top of head. Lower jaw projects. Anal fin 9 rays. Inside lining of belly white or silvery. Maxilla reaches rear of eye. Maximum about 36 inches. Ensenada, Baja California, to Queen Charlotte Sound, British Columbia.

Canary Rockfish (32d)
(*Sebastodes pinniger*)

Also orange rockfish, red rockfish, codalarga, yellow snapper, fantail. Body color gray mottled with orange; fins orange. Inside lining of belly is pale. Slightly concave space between eyes. Lower jaw projects, knob on tip. Maximum about 30 inches. Cape Colnett, Baja California, to Dixon Entrance, British Columbia.

Quillback Rockfish (33b)
(*Sebastodes maliger*)

Also orange-spotted rockfish, brown rockfish, speckled rockfish. Body color slaty-brown mottled with yellow and orange-brown; fins dark. High spinous dorsal fin, deeply notched. Lower anterior of body spotted with orange-brown. Silvery white inside lining of belly. Maximum about 24 inches. Monterey, California, to Southeast Alaska.

Yellowtail Rockfish (33d)
(*Sebastodes flavidus*)

Also yellowtail rock cod, green snapper, gialota. Body color grayish brown, light gray on sides, white belly, sides brown speckled, blotches on back. Convex between eyes. No spines on head. Lower jaw projects. Anal fin with 8 rays (rarely 7). White inside lining of belly. Maximum about 26 inches. San Diego, California, to Vancouver Island, British Columbia.

Chilipepper (33a)
(*Sebastodes goodei*)

Also red rock cod, johnny cod. Body color pinkish red, fins pink. Convex between eyes. No spines on head. Lower jaw projects. Silvery white inside lining of belly, also small black spots in small specimens. Maximum about 22 inches. Magdalena Bay, Baja California, to Eureka, California.

Black Rockfish (32a)
(*Sebastodes melanops*)

Also black rock cod, black snapper, black bass, black rockfish, nero, cherna. Body color black on back, gray with black mottlings on sides; fins dark; ventrals lighter. Broad convex space between eyes. No spines on top of head. Maxilla extends to hind border of eye. Silvery white inside lining of belly, sometimes few black specks. Anal fin normally 8 soft rays. Maximum about 20 inches. San Miguel Island to Southeast Alaska.

Sculpin Rockfish (34a)
(*Scorpaena guttata*)

Also scorpion, scorpionfish, bullhead. Body color brick red to brown mottled with olive and brown; dark spots over head, body, and fins. Many spines top of head. Dorsal fin sharp, spines 12. Three spines front of anal. Maximum about 17 inches. Point Abreojos, Baja California, to Point Arguello, California.

Left: Larry Sheerin of San Antonio, Texas, with spotted weakfish at Eighth Pass, Mexico. *Right:* Chico, one of our Mexican assistants, holding a channel bass taken by the author.

Seabass and Bo Migdalski.

Fluke (light colored phase) and George Albrecht.

Porgy and George Albrecht.

Fluke (dark colored phase) and police commissioner Dave Leach of New Haven, Connecticut.

Tautog and Captain Pete Grazioso of the well-known "Papeeta II."

Weakfish and Bo Migdal[ski]

Roosterfish

Roosterfish (11b)
(*Nematistius pectoralis*)

Almost entirely confined to the eastern Pacific, the roosterfish is one of the best but least known of all the great game fishes. The comparatively few anglers who have tangled with this fish commend it highly for its fighting qualities. It is named roosterfish because of its high dorsal fin, which resembles a rooster's comb. If you disregard the unusual dorsal fin, this fish resembles closely, and possesses many characteristics of, the jack family, CARANGIDAE. However, because of the differences in fin structure the roosterfish is placed in a family all its own, the NEMATISTIIDAE. Ranging southward from southern California (seldom encountered north of the Coronado Islands), it is found down to Peru. The roosterfish can be met almost anywhere along the route from Mexican waters to Peru, with Ecuador as perhaps the area of its greatest concentration.

It possesses a body which closely resembles that of a jackfish except for the first dorsal fin which has 7 long, thread-like spines (11 to 15 inches long in a fish whose length is 51 inches), and the caudal peduncle lacks the keels or scutes present in most jacks. I counted the rays of one fish: the second dorsal had 29, and the anal fin 17. The pectoral is long, and its tail is deeply forked. In color, the dorsal surface is creamy green when the fish is alive, and the entire sides and belly are pearlescent, with a white underjaw and throat. A prominent black spot is present on the lower anterior portion of the pectoral fin. Four vivid, dark bluish bars or bands, approximately 1½ to 2 inches in width, are prominent while the fish is alive; these fade almost immediately after the fish is gaffed. One bar is directly on the forehead and reaches from eye to eye; another is present over the back part of the head and covers most of the hind portion of the operculum; the third starts from the front dorsal, goes down and backward, and fades away below the pectoral fin; the fourth originates below the last two spines of the dorsal fin and extends down and back to the tail. The ventral and anal fins are flat white (not colored as in most illustrations), and the pectoral is translucent whitish yellow. The base of the dorsal is creamy green and light blue, and the second dorsal is very light translucent gray with a touch of green. The tail is predominantly greenish yellow. We caught roosterfish from 12 to 22 pounds along the shore at Cabo Blanco, Peru, but the world record taken off the same area is a flat 100 pounds taken by M. Barrenechea on January 12, 1954. Anglers will immediately identify the roosterfish because no other game fish possesses such extremely long dorsal fin rays.

Practically nothing is known concerning the life history of this fish. We know that on occasion it may be found out to sea, but mostly it prefers the coastal area, often amazingly close to shore in sandy and in rocky areas. When chasing bait it moves swiftly with extended dorsal fin, which often shows above the surface of the water. Roosterfish always seem to be traveling fast in compact groups. Because it is aggressive, fast, and seen chopping up schools of bait fishes, we assume that its dominant food must be the small silvery schooling fishes such as anchovies.

From many days of angling experience for the roosterfish I can say without reservation that it possesses all the qualities necessary to term it one of the world's great game fishes. During a Yale Expedition to the area off Cabo Blanco, Peru, Dan Merriman, director of the Bingham Oceanographic Laboratory, and I, with the aid of Cap Sewall, who ran our small launch, did some exploratory fishing while securing specimens. We found that an area approximately three miles south of the Cabo Blanco Club house, close to shore was intermittently boiling with roosterfish. After trying the usual salt water lures we found that the common red-and-white fresh water spoon was by far the most successful. The fish in this general locality were mostly in a rocky area where the water grew wild and crashed high against sharp and crusted rock formations.

It was always exciting fishing. While trolling we hooked fish unexpectedly, but most of the time we came to the fish after spotting them chopping up a bait school in a great commotion. The individual dorsal fins—all fully extended—were an electrifying sight as they cut and crossed in all directions. When our spoons were sighted several would come simultaneously, and the strike would be hard and ferocious. These roosterfish would occasionally jump clear of the water, but mostly they ran deep and when approaching the boat would suddenly dash under it—all of which makes wonderful sport.

One afternoon, as Dan, Cap Sewall, and I were in the midst of a school, the launch's engine stalled. During the excitement of the fishing we had not realized our proximity to the jagged and steep rock walls which had thunderous waves smashing against them. Cap Sewall immediately jumped into the engine compartment and began to work furiously as the heaving sea carried us closer and closer to the roaring breakers. As I was giving thought to the proper time to jump from the launch before perhaps being smashed with it, the engine gurgled and started. We zoomed out of there on full throttle! Anyone fishing in the area could find the spot easily because just to the right of it a rather large, white, wooden cross is wedged rigidly in the sand and rocks and stands out most conspicuously. Here a couple of natives were battered to death when their small boat went beyond control. It is the custom of these people to erect a cross wherever a fatal accident happens. We fished there again, but we kept a safe distance from the crashing surf in water where an anchor could hold!

Seaperches

Well known along our Pacific coast from Alaska south into Lower California, the seaperches, also called surfperches, are small fishes which prefer shallow inshore waters, usually in the surf, along rocky areas or sandy shores. They are not true perch but members of the family EMBIOTOCIDAE. Commercially, seaperches are taken in fairly good numbers with the heaviest landings usually made in the ports of San Francisco and Los Angeles. Although welcomed by sportsmen because of their fine flavor, as pan fishes they generally are not rated as game fishes.

Distinguishing characteristics for this group are these: more or less oval, compressed body; no teeth in roof of mouth; anal fin with 3 spines and 15 or more soft rays; dorsal fin contiguous with not more than 11 spines. Maximum size is about 18 inches, but the average fish is less than 10 inches. Most of the species are silvery; a few are brightly colored. The EMBIOTOCIDAE is a family of fishes which are of unusual interest because the females bear live young. (Nearly all the other bony fishes spawn eggs which are fertilized externally.)

Seaperches are caught by sportsmen throughout the year. However, they are on the protected list and can be taken commercially only within certain dates, usually about May to the middle of July. The most popular species along the California coast are the following:

Rubberlip Seaperch (37a)
(*Rhacochilus toxotes*)

Very thick lips, white or pink. Spiny dorsal lower than soft dorsal. Maximum 18 inches. Central and southern California.

Barred Seaperch (36a)
(*Amphistichus argenteus*)

Vertical bars and spots. Anal fin appears divided into two sections. Dorsal spines about three quarters as high as dorsal rays. Maximum about 16 inches. Central and southern California.

Pile Seaperch (36c)
(*Damalichthys vacca*)

Tail deeply forked. Sharply elevated first dorsal rays. Maximum about 16 inches. Alaska to northern Lower California.

Striped Seaperch (37b)
(*Taeniotoca lateralis*)

Concave tail (not forked). Striped horizontally with orange and blue. Black specks above. First dorsal ray twice the height of highest dorsal spine. Maximum about 15 inches. Alaska into central Lower California.

Black Seaperch (36b)
(*Embiotoca jacksoni*)

Thick reddish-brown lips. Enlarged scales between pectoral and ventral fins. Dorsal spines shorter than dorsal rays. Maximum about 14 inches. Central California to central Lower California.

Walleye Seaperch (37d)
(*Hyperprosopon argenteum*)

Black tipped ventral fins. Large eyes. Longest dorsal spines higher than dorsal rays. Maximum about a foot. Straits of Juan de Fuca south into Lower California.

White Seaperch (37c)
(*Phanerodon furcatus*)

Tail deeply forked. Dorsal spines slender, the last the longest and almost as high, if not as high, as first ray. Body less oval than other seaperches. Anal fin usually with dusky spot. Maximum about 12 inches. Vancouver Island to southern California.

Rainbow Seaperch (36d)
(*Hypsurus caryi*)

Long abdomen. Tail moderately forked. Longest dorsal spine about three quarters length of first dorsal ray. Striped horizontally with red, orange, and blue. Blackish blotch on soft dorsal and anal fins. Maximum about 12 inches. Coast of California.

Shiner Seaperch (38a)
(*Cymatogaster aggregata*)

Middle dorsal fin spines are high, higher than rays. Large scales, less than 50 along lateral line. Tail moderately forked. Maximum about 6 inches. Alaska south into northern Lower California.

Shad

Shad (11d)
(*Alosa sapidissima*)

The shad is the largest member of the herring family, CLUPEIDAE, found along both coasts of the United States. For generations it has been famous as a table delicacy, but its full potential as an extraordinary game fish has not as yet been realized. Many authors do not recognize the shad as a game fish; obviously they have never taken one on rod and reel, because the anglers whom I know that have been introduced to shad fishing with light tackle unanimously agree that it is top sport fishing. This fish is also called American shad and white shad, but throughout most of its range it is known as shad. Along the Atlantic coast the shad is distributed from the St. Lawrence River and Lake Ontario to the St. Johns River in Florida. The most northerly record of a stray is from Bull's Bay, near St. John's, Newfoundland. It is most abundant from Connecticut to North Carolina.

This is a typical member of the herring tribe and possesses the herring-like characteristics: deep body, sharp saw-edged belly, deeply forked tail, large scales, soft-rayed dorsal and anal

Shad

fins. The shad closely resembles some of its cousins, but it can be separated easily from them by the long upper jaw (maxilla) which reaches to below the rear edge of the eye and by the front of the upper jaw, which is deeply indented. The shad has no teeth on the roof of the mouth, but the sea herring does. Adult shad have no teeth at all, although the young possess small ones in the jaws which may remain until the fish is about a foot long. The shad differs from the hickory shad in having a larger mouth. Its most obvious difference from the alewife and blueback is the upper outline of the lower jaw; slightly concave, without a sharp angle in the shad, but deeply concave with a pronounced angle in the others. The lining of the shad's belly is pale; the lining of the blueback's belly is sooty or blackish, while the alewife's is pale like the shad's. Blueback and alewife are much smaller fish than the shad. The shad is generally silvery with a bluish green back; the sides are silvery going whitish below. A dusky spot is present close behind the upper edge of the gill cover, and usually one or two longitudinal rows of indistinct dusky spots follow it.

The shad is a large herring, reaching a length of about 30 inches. Adult males weigh from 1½ to 6 pounds, females from 3½ to 8 pounds. Large fish of 12 pounds are occasionally reported, but they are rare. For the angler who has a tape measure but no scale, the following may be used as an approximate guide:

Inches	Pounds and ounces
8	3
12	10
15–16	1 5
20	2 8
23–24	4 8

The approximate length-age relationship is as follows:

Inches	Years
5– 6	1
9–10	2
13–14	3
15–16	4
18–19	5
24	6

The shad is a schooling fish that spends most of its life at sea but runs up into fresh water streams to spawn. The spent fish return to salt water as do their fry. In salt water they may be seen in great numbers, but they never re-enter fresh water until spawning time, though some may appear occasionally in brackish water. At times, large schools may appear near the surface, but upon the arrival of cold weather they vanish. Young shad (shad of the year) probably winter close to their parent rivers, and perhaps the larger ones winter in deeper water farther away from the coast. It is known that adult shad inhabit deep waters; fish of 4 to 6 pounds have been trawled off Nova Scotia in March at about 50 fathoms. Also, shad were taken at 68 fathoms on the eastern part of Nantucket Shoals. Recoveries of tagged shad indicate that the species travels for lengthy distances along the coast. A fish tagged in Chesapeake Bay was recaptured 39 days later at Race Point, at the tip of Cape Cod; another was recaptured near Gloucester. A shad tagged in the Hudson River was taken near Portland, Maine. Three out of 1,380 tagged in New York Bay were captured in the Bay of Fundy after 37 days, 75 days, and 85 days respectively. One fish recaught at St. John's, New Brunswick was tagged off Fire Island, New York, 39 days previously. Eighteen out of 236 shad tagged near Mount Desert Rock, Maine, in August, 1947, were retaken the following spring at points scattered along the different streams from Connecticut to Altamaha in Georgia. In the next two springs fish from this same batch were recaptured in the Connecticut and Hudson Rivers, on the New Jersey coast, and in the Pamlico River, North Carolina. Out of 431 shad tagged farther west along the Maine coast in summer and fall of 1948, 3 were recaptured in the Hudson River, 3 in Chesapeake Bay, and 1 in Pamlico River, North Carolina. The fishes that take part in this movement winter somewhere between their northern feeding grounds, from where they have disappeared by the middle of fall, and their southerly breeding streams, which they do not touch until spring. Where and how they pass the winter is not known.

Curiously, shad are known to make very long journeys that cannot be fitted into any regular pattern of movement or migration. For example, a fish tagged in the lower St. Lawrence River (Canada) was retaken 258 days later on Brown Bank (about 200 miles east of Cape Cod); another from the same group was retaken in Cumberland Basin, near Amherst, Nova Scotia, after 322 days; a third had traveled 1,200 miles when taken 444 days later at the tip of Cape Cod. Also, fish tagged on the coast of Maine in August and September of 1948 were recaptured in the Medway River, Nova Scotia, in the Miramachi River of New Brunswick two years later, and a third off Tor Bay, Nova Scotia, in 1951. Evidently shad may travel many miles offshore, since fish have been captured 50 to 60 miles off eastern Nova Scotia, 40 to 50 miles off the coast of Maine, 25 to 90 miles off southern New England, and about 110 miles out on Georges Bank.

In the Atlantic coastal rivers the mature fish run upstream in spring or early summer; dates depend on temperature—when the water has warmed to 50°–55° F. Therefore, the shad travel gradually into the streams from south to north along the coast as the season progresses. The usual schedule is Georgia, January; Pamlico Sound and Albemarle Sound tributaries, March; Potomac, April; Delaware to Canada, April, May, and June. Shad may begin their run in the Hudson River the latter part of March or the first of April; the run is usually finished before the end of June. In the Connecticut River the run is usually in full swing by the middle of April.

In the early season the males, called "bucks," outnumber the females, called "roe shad," but as the season progresses the females become more numerous. In large rivers shad may run far upstream—about 200 miles in the St. John River, New Brunswick; about 300 miles in the Altamaha in Georgia; about 375 miles in the St. Johns River, Florida. Unfortunately the runs that previously extended hundreds of miles in other rivers have now been reduced to only a few miles by the retarding forces of dams and pollution.

Spawning takes place a short time after the fish enter fresh water. Shad choose shallow sandy or pebbly grounds for depositing eggs. During this time it appears that the fish pair off and swim side by side; most of the spawning activity occurs between sundown and midnight. The emaciated, spent adult shad begin their return journey to the sea immediately after spawning. Male shad mature after three or four years; females may spawn anywhere from four to seven or eight years of age. After spawning they do not die, but spawn again. Whether or not shad return to the parent river as salmon do is not definitely known. An average female will produce about 30,000 eggs. From 150,000 to 250,000 eggs may be spawned by a large female. The eggs are transparent, pale pink or amber, semibuoyant, nonadhesive, and deposited free in the water. About three millimeters in diameter, the eggs absorb water, sink to the bottom, and are carried and rolled about by the current. They hatch in 12 to 15 days at 52° F., in 6 to 8 days at 63° F. Larval development appears to be more successful in brackish water than in pure fresh water. The young shad remain in the river until fall (October or November) and then migrate to the sea. They may be from 1½ to 5 inches in length at this time and resemble their parents. In the past, fish culturists have cultivated many millions of shad eggs to hatching and liberated them in streams in hopes that populations may again be built up. As yet no evidence has been shown which would indicate any permanent increase of shad in the stocked areas.

Like other herring fishes, the shad is primarily a plankton feeder. Stomachs which have been examined contained small crustaceans (copepods, amphipods), tiny shrimp, larval stages of barnacles, and fish eggs. Occasionally small fishes will be eaten. It appears that little or no food is taken just previous to spawning. However, shad will take artificial lures readily during their spawning runs up river.

The shad was introduced successfully on the Pacific coast of the United States in 1871. Now it ranges from Alaska to southern California, but it is not common south of Monterey Bay. Along the coast of California it is a commercial species of minor

Shad

importance, and Pacific anglers have not, as yet, explored rod and reel fishing for shad to its full potential. Most of the shad on both coasts are taken by gill netting. An unusually interesting method of netting remains, to a minor extent, along the famous Minudie's sand flats of Nova Scotia. Gill nets are rigged vertically and set about 6 feet off the ground; they are placed about two miles offshore during low tide. The operation is controlled by the unusual tides of the Bay of Fundy, which in Cumberland Basin rise as high as 28 feet. Twice in every twenty-four hours the fishermen make a trip across the flats at low tide by horse and wagon. They shake the fish down from the high nets and load the catch into the wagon. The practice is dying out, and only a few fishermen now take part in this picturesque and once flourishing activity.

In Colonial times the shad along the Atlantic coast were in great abundance, with fish running in vast numbers into almost every river of consequence. As with many other fishes, the disappearance or decline of shad in recent years along the Atlantic seaboard has become shockingly apparent. Since 1900 the catch has dwindled to less than one third of its former yield. In 1950 the Atlantic States Marine Fisheries Commission initiated a coastwise shad restoration project. The studies revealed that the gradual disappearance of shad along the Atlantic coast was almost entirely the result of the exclusion of shad from their spawning areas by the construction of dams. These dams and pollution have been wiping out the shad.

One would have to go back many years to the day when one of our greatest shad rivers, the Connecticut, was free of pollution, and general conditions were favorable for game fishes to reproduce fully. A spark of hope was ignited when a commercial concern recently took interest in the conservation of fishes in this body of water. The Holyoke Water Power Company of Massachusetts installed a fishway which permitted 7,700 shad to pass upriver in 1956; above this spot, for 107 years previously, shad were cut off from a stretch of river 30 miles long—their ancestral spawning grounds. The Holyoke Company was awarded the Conservation Service Award of the U.S. Department of the Interior for its cooperation in developing the new fishway. Recently the U.S. Fish and Wildlife Service announced that a phenomenal increase in the sport fishing for shad in the Connecticut River had taken place since 1950. During that year it was estimated that between 5,000 and 10,000 shad were taken from the river by sport fishermen. By 1957 the shad harvested by anglers amounted to 35,000. About one fourth of the fish caught were returned to the river alive; therefore, the total number of shad caught was in the vicinity of 50,000. One of the factors contributing to this great increase was boat fishing; also, many new locations were found to be productive.

It is indeed sad and discouraging to know that the commendable conservation efforts of the Holyoke Company may be ruined by another water company lower down the river. The new menace is a dam which a light and power company proposes to build at Windsor Locks. Competent biologists have estimated that the shad run in this once beautiful river may be reduced as much as 50 per cent by the dam. My personal opinion is that the scientists have given a conservative estimate. The dam will not only prevent shad from entering spawning areas farther up stream (fish ladders, if installed, would help the situation only partially), but it will concentrate the existing pollution of the river above the dam to an extent that would be harmful, I dare say, to fish life.

When taken on light tackle and tiny artificial lures (red flies or red, yellow, or white beads are best) the shad produces amazing resistance to the angler's tackle. The swirling waters of the river add to the excitement, and a net is required for successfully landing the fish. Our last trip out by the falls at the Enfield Dam was not unusual. My friends Jim Galligan of the Connecticut State Fish and Game Department, Winslow Tuttle of New York, and I had our limit of six fish each in short order—we caught many more. Light fly rods and spinning outfits were suitable tackle, and we enjoyed the battling tactics of each fish.

In the Connecticut River the shad is proclaimed a game fish, a category it rightfully deserves. The season usually opens about the middle of April and continues into June. The Enfield Dam area at Suffield sees many hundreds of anglers during a season. One of the best locations on the Connecticut River is open to the public through the courtesy of the Windsor Locks Canal Company. The area is patroled, and the licensed angler pays a fee of 25 cents per day. The fishermen may use only single-hook lures and must show their fish to the attendant at the checking station. If more dams are constructed, this tremendously important shad fishery may be wiped out—even before its full potential is realized.

Most anglers believe a shad is too bony and throw back the bucks, keeping only the females for the roe. I find that the flesh of the shad is not as uncomfortable to eat as general opinion indicates it to be. The extra effort of picking a few bones is well worth the delicious meat. The shad, as a gourmet's delight, was appreciated to a greater extent during colonial days. For example, Thomas Jefferson had a reputation as a great shad cook. I would have loved one of the old Virginia shad bakes. Each fish was nailed to a plank and lined against the walls of a big outdoor fireplace. The chef occasionally basted the fish with a long-handled swab, which was dipped in lemon juice and butter. As the fish cooked the guests chose a shad and ate off the plank, using it as a dish.

Snappers

The snappers comprise a large, world-wide family, LUTJANIDAE, of warm-water fishes found in tropical and subtropical regions. Valued for both their commercial and sporting qualities, they prefer to live close to the bottom most of the time, along shore and offshore rocky areas, around islands and big rocks, in sloughs, mangrove locales, and sometimes close to shore along surf and sandy beaches. It appears that most of the species do not migrate lengthy distances and seem to be present the year round in the areas they inhabit.

Snappers all have, more or less, the same feeding habits and will take small fishes, crawfish, crabs, and marine worms. They appear to be voracious but cautious. Often the angler cannot coax them to take any type of bait or lure. Usually chumming with ground bait will attract and induce them to strike.

They are not too distantly related to the grunts and sea basses. Snappers possess certain characteristics which help in separating them into a distinct group: breast fins below the pointed pectoral fins (most bassfishes, SERRANIDAE, have roundish pectorals); the dorsal fin, which contains about 10 spines, is connected with the second or soft dorsal fin; the anal fin contains 2 or 3 spines adjacent to and followed by about 8 or 9 soft rays. Tails may be forked, slightly forked, or slightly concave. The eyes are high on the head; the mouth is large with strong, sharp, canine-like teeth. Two nostrils are present on either side of the snout; the body is covered with large scales, and a lateral line is present. The coloration of snappers often changes with environment, which leads to confusion in identification. There are many species which, as yet, are not clearly defined to scientists. Sometimes identification has to be made on details such as the shape of the tooth patch in the roof the mouth. Very little investigation has been carried out with this group. Here we will discuss only those species of snappers which are of interest to anglers.

All snappers caught on rod and reel, regardless of their size, put up a fine scrap. Often they will make a strong run or two and then attempt to head for the rocks. They are not only fun to catch, but I also rate them as one of the best of food fishes.

ATLANTIC SNAPPERS

Red Snapper (22b)

(*Lutjanus aya*)

The red snapper is a valuable commercial fish, which is distributed along the tropical and subtropical waters of the western Atlantic. This member of the LUTJANIDAE inhabits depths of 150 feet or more, and because of this fact, handlines are used almost exclusively for its capture. Although most red snappers are taken by commercial vessels, sporting craft often hunt specifically for this species. Whether or not this snapper is a game fish is a debatable point. Although the common name "red snapper" is well established, commercial interests in the Gulf of Mexico area call it the Pensacola snapper. The scientific aspects concerning this species are not clear. It has been previously split into several species, but now the opinion of most scientists is that they are all of the same species. Also, whether the correct scientific name is *Lutjanus aya* or *Lutjanus black-*

fordii remains a matter of opinion. It is distributed mostly in the deep offshore banks of the Gulf of Mexico, Florida east coast, Caribbean, Bermuda, and Bahamas. Along the western Atlantic it is known to reach northward to South Carolina and southward to Brazil.

The red snapper is a distinctive fish, and as its name implies, the body coloration is mostly vivid red. The upper portions of the body are tinged bluish green when the fish comes out of the water. The lower portions of the body are lighter; fins are predominantly red but paler; dorsal fin and tail may be edged with a thin black streak; base of the pectoral fin has a dark marking, and the iris is a bright red. Because of its general over-all red coloration anglers do not have any difficulties identifying this fish. It might be confused with the mutton snapper, but the mutton snapper has a distinctive black spot on the body below the anterior portion of the soft dorsal fin. The red snapper has a black spot or splotch on the base of the pectoral fin. Ten spines are present in the first dorsal fin, 14 or 15 rays in the second, and the anal fin has 3 spines and 8 or 9 rays. The gill raker count is 16 to 17 including rudiments.

The average size is between 5 and 10 pounds, but fish in the 25-pound class are not rare. Occasionally a specimen of 35 or 40 pounds is taken. Practically nothing is known concerning its life history. Spawning probably takes place from April to July. It feeds mostly on shrimp, crabs, shellfishes, and small fishes. It is taken in greatest quantities from the Gulf of Mexico and marked chiefly through the port of Pensacola. Handline is the method used for taking red snapper commercially. It is one of the most important food fishes of the United States, with the annual catch termed in millions of pounds. Besides being available in quantities, it is famous for its delicious flavor. Some epicures rate it the best of all fishes.

I have taken the red snapper off Bermuda and the Bahamas, where we used stout line rigged with five or six whole anchovies on a single hook. The first three or four fish were fun, but after hauling yards and yards of line plus a heavy sinker, plus a 12- or 15-pound fish time and again, the fun ceased and the action took on the aspects of labor. The red snapper is more of a food fish than a game fish.

Muttonfish (22a)
(*Lutjanus analis*)

The muttonfish is a good-looking, fairly large member of the snapper family which usually inhabits deep waters—up to about 200 feet. However, it is also taken in medium and fairly shallow reef areas, especially around islands. It is classed as a game fish and is also excellent on the table. The muttonfish is a member of the snapper family, LUTJANIDAE. A more appropriate common name for it would be mutton snapper. However, it is so widely known as muttonfish that I believe it inadvisable to change the name and introduce confusion. It ranges in warm waters along Florida, Gulf of Mexico, Bahamas, West Indies, and southward to Brazil. Occasionally the Gulf Stream will carry a stray as far north as Massachusetts.

In shape it closely resembles the red snapper and may be mistaken for it. The muttonfish has different color phases which often are factors in misidentification. In a live fish, about 7 darkish vertical bars may be present. These fade almost immediately after boating the fish. Its dorsal background color may be greenish brown, olive, or bronze olive; sides are lighter and may be silvery or yellowish; the breast and belly have a tinge of red. The dorsal fin is yellowish with red or pink at the base. The moderately forked tail usually has a yellowish upper part and a reddish lower section. The other fins have a pink or reddish tinge. Iris is red. Often, blue lines or marks are present on the head. A small black spot is located on, or slightly above, the lateral line under the anterior rays of the soft dorsal fin. The anal fin, which is sharply angular, contains 8 soft rays, and the gill rakers below the angle of the first gill arch number 7 or 8 (not counting rudiments). To anyone not familiar with the red snapper and muttonfish—especially the dark reddish phase of the muttonfish—the two species can be confused. The V-shaped patch in the roof of the mouth of the muttonfish is without the backward median projection which the red snapper possesses. Also, the muttonfish has a dark spot on the body below the second dorsal, while the red snapper has the dark splotch on the base of the pectoral.

In average size it is approximately 4 to 6 pounds. Fish in the 15-pound class are not rare, and the maximum weight seems to be about 25 pounds. It feeds mostly at night and prefers small fishes and crustaceans. As a rule, muttonfish do not school. However, there is evidence that the muttonfish may do so during spawning time. Nothing much is known concerning the life history of this fish. Off party boats, fishermen take muttonfish in the catch almost throughout the year. Cut bait fished on or close to the bottom produces best results. However, I have experienced tremendous sport by trolling strip bait, down deep, along the outer reefs off Walker Cay Island in the Bahamas. The muttonfish hit hard and fought well. A good tight line was necessary to prevent the fish from diving into the rocks and cutting the line. The chef at the Walker Cay Club produced an unusual delicacy with the muttonfish.

Mangrove Snapper (21a)
(*Lutjanus griseus*)

Closely related to the cubera, dog snapper, and schoolmaster, the mangrove snapper is the most common member of the family LUTJANIDAE. It is the most numerous snapper found in shallow shore waters, but it is also present in the deeper outer reefs in some areas. Evidence indicates that it is chiefly a night feeder. Other popular common names are gray snapper, pargo, and Pensacola snapper. However, fishermen in the areas where this snapper is most numerous call it mangrove snapper. Therefore, I prefer to use that name. Its distribution coincides with that of most of the other western Atlantic snappers: Florida, the West Indies, southward to Brazil. Occasionally a straggler is taken as far north as Massachusetts. It is also abundant in

Atlantic Snappers

the Bahamas and Bermuda, and the Gulf of Mexico, especially around Texas shores.

Like its close cousins its coloration varies with the environment. Basic colors may be from a deep brownish red, lighter in different stages, to almost grayish white. The grayish background coloration phase may have reddish brown hues. Usually, faint vertical bars extend partially down from the back. Mangrove snappers which are found along muddy looking banks in mangrove and cypress waters are darker all over in appearance, while fish caught over light sandy areas are grayish white with a suggestion of reddish coloration, and the bars are either absent or just faintly discernible. The dorsal fins and tail are grayish, and the pelvic and anal fins are grayish or whitish pink. The pectoral is almost colorless, but may have a pinkish or yellowish hue.

Distinguishing characteristics are these: canines in the upper jaw are larger than in the lower; the arrangement of teeth in the roof of the mouth is anchor shaped with a backward projection present; body form is more elongated than in other snappers. The pectoral fin is fairly short—two thirds head length. Dorsal spines are 10, dorsal rays number 13 or 14; anal fin has 3 spines and 8 rays. The gill raker count is 7 or 8 below the angle of the first gill arch.

In many areas, close to shore, it may run only 8 or 10 inches in size. Two to 3 pounders are common, but average size is about a pound. The maximum weight of this fish is not known. Many unusually large fish thought to be mangrove snappers are dog snappers or cubera. Not much is known concerning its life history. Spawning takes place during July and August. During the day large numbers of mangrove snappers in closely knit groups can be seen, but when dusk arrives they begin to disperse and start to feed. Crustaceans and small fishes constitute most of the items in their diet.

The mangrove snapper is a favorite with pier, bridge, and shore fishermen, for it ranges over shallow banks, flats, around pilings, under docks, in channels under overhung banks, and in holes along mangrove shores. It is an excellent sport fish that rates highly as a food fish. It will hit trolled lures and almost any type of bait, but shrimp seem to be best. Occasionally anglers pursue this snapper with fly rod and bucktails or streamer flies. The fly is allowed to sink and then is retrieved in a jerky manner to simulate a live shrimp.

I am sure that many shore fishermen at times have experienced the same frustration that I have when fishing for larger mangrove snappers. I have seen schools of these scrappers leisurely milling around in "holes," ignoring completely all my offerings thrown into their midst. The geographical area or the location means nothing when they don't care to take a bait. I've tried for them in the Florida Keys, Bahamas, Bermuda, and the Gulf of Mexico when I felt so frustrated I would have used a hunk of dynamite. However, I have learned that if one cares to do some serious mangrove snapper fishing, the time to do it is at nightfall.

Cubera

(*Lutjanus cyanopterus*)

The cubera or Cuban snapper is a large member of the family LUTJANIDAE and resembles closely the mangrove snapper and is distributed from south Florida to Brazil and common off Cuba. Its background color is grayish, with indistinct bars on the young fish. Fins are dusky or grayish, except for the anal fin which is reddish. Large canines, about equal in length, are present in both jaws. The arrangement of teeth in the roof of the mouth is without a distinct backward projection. Five gill rakers (not counting rudiments) are present on the lower limb of the first arch. Cubera grows much larger than the mangrove snapper, with fish 30 to 60 pounds not uncommon, also specimens of over 100 pounds have been reported. Above average-size fish are taken usually off ledges in medium depths. The exceptionally large mangrove snappers reported at times previously most likely were cuberas. Live bait seems best in taking this giant lutjanid.

Dog Snapper (21c)
(*Lutjanus jocu*)

The dog snapper is closely related to the mangrove snapper and the schoolmaster. It is not as abundant as its cousins, but has the same living habits and type of environment as they do. Similar to most members of the LUTJANIDAE, it is confined to warm tropical and subtropical waters. This Atlantic species ranges from Florida southward to Brazil; an occasional stray appears in northern waters (Massachusetts).

The ability to produce different color phases is a characteristic of the snapper family, and the dog snapper is no exception. It will take on lighter or darker hues of coloration in accordance with its environment. It may have a background color of silvery gray, or coppery bronze; or it may be an over-all brown tinged with mahogany red. Seven or 8 vertical bars may or may not be present; also, if present, the degree of color intensity varies considerably. The dorsal, pectoral, and caudal fins are reddish orange, while the pelvic and anal fins are light orange-yellow. Beneath the eye an irregular marking of light blue, which may be continuous or broken, is distinctive and may be used as a mark for identification. Seven or 8 gill rakers, not counting rudiments, are present below the angle of the first gill arch. The tooth patch on the roof of the mouth has a backward projection along the median line.

Most publications list the dog snapper as having an average weight under 2 pounds, with a maximum of 20. A scientist, J. L. Baughman, who studied the snappers off the Texas coast, reports records of this fish as being no less than 48 pounds, while others weighed 72, 100, and 110 pounds respectively. Perhaps these big snappers may be the kind that are known as cubera.

Commercial fishermen at Key West and other Florida ports take great numbers of dog snappers during the fall and winter seasons. However, not many are taken by anglers, and opinions on the table qualities of this fish differ. I took one off

Walker Key, Bahamas, and because the dog snapper is considered not palatable, or even poisonous in some areas, I was interested in my native guide's reaction to this fish. He took it home and ate it; the next day he informed me that it was delicious. Many of the beliefs concerning fishes thought to be poisonous stem from the lack of refrigeration in warm areas.

Schoolmaster (21b)

(*Lutjanus apodus*)

The schoolmaster is closely related to the mangrove snapper, cubera, and dog snapper and has the same distribution and living habits as its relatives. It is one of the smaller and more common snappers. In the western tropical Atlantic it ranges along Florida, the West Indies, Bermuda, Bahamas, and the Canal Zone, down to Brazil. It is also present off West Africa. Occasionally a stray will be found as far noth as Cape Cod. It also occurs in fresh water miles from brackish areas.

The schoolmaster is not as brightly colored as some of the other snappers, but none the less it is a handsome fish. All fins are yellow, greenish yellow or orange-yellow. This snapper also has different color phases, with the degree of coloration changing with the type of environment—sandy, rocky, marshy. The most common phases are a pale yellow, a grayish blue, and a barred or banded phase. When the bands are present (about 8) they may exist on the dorsal surface, or they may extend along the sides of the body. The area in between the bands is usually a grayish silver. A characteristic color of orange-yellow and hues of red are usually present about the head. It has large canine teeth in the upper jaw.

The schoolmaster, the mangrove snapper, and the dog snapper are sometimes difficult to distinguish. In the roof of the mouth they all have the anchor shape tooth patch with the backward stem. However, the angler can differentiate them: lateral line scales, schoolmaster, 39 to 44; dog snapper, 45 to 49. Also, no markings below the eye as in the dog snapper. The pectoral fin is smaller in the mangrove snapper (less than two thirds head length) than it is in the schoolmaster or the dog snapper. The schoolmaster's canine teeth (only in the upper jaw) separate it from the cubera, which has canines in both jaws (and no backward stem in the tooth patch in the roof of the mouth). Ten spines are present in the first dorsal fin, 14 rays in the second; anal fin has 3 spines and 8 rays. The gill rakers number 7 or 8 below the angle of the first gill arch not counting rudiments.

Usually it weighs less than a pound; 6- or 7-pound fish are taken occasionally. There are reports of fish weighing much more, but whether these large specimens have been properly identified is a question. The schoolmaster gathers in schools during the day but disperses at night for feeding. Like the other snappers, it prefers shrimp, crabs, and small fishes. Wherever present, it is one of the shore fisherman's favorites; although small, this snapper is fun on light tackle and goes well on the table. I have had most luck with shrimp as bait.

Lane Snapper (23b)
(*Lutjanus synagris*)

The lane snapper is a small but nifty member of the family LUTJANIDAE, popular with anglers who fish from shore, off bridges, sea walls, and docks. Its distribution is similar to that of most lutjanids in the tropical western Atlantic—from Florida down to Brazil—and also the Gulf of Mexico, the Caribbean, and Bermuda. Although it is common along shore, it may be found also offshore over shallow reefs; its mode of life, choice of food, and habitat resemble those of the mangrove snapper. They often school together.

The lane snapper, like the yellowtail snapper, is fairly slender in comparison to the typical snappers. It is beautifully colored an over-all rosy red. Several horizontal yellow stripes are present along the sides, and short yellow stripes run diagonally down and forward from the dorsal fin. A black roundish marking is present on the dorsal surface below the second dorsal fin; hence it is also known as spot snapper. The pectoral fin is light pink; the pelvic and anal fins are yellow or orange; the dorsal fins are yellowish pink, while the tail is pinkish red with a thin black margin. The first dorsal contains 10 spines; the second dorsal numbers 12 rays, and the anal has 3 spines and 8 rays. Gill rakers below the angle of the first gill arch number 8 to 11.

The average lane snapper weighs less than a yellowtail snapper—usually under a pound. However, specimens of about 4 pounds have been taken. On light tackle it is fun to catch these active little snappers, which will take cut bait or shrimp and can be taken the year round in Florida waters. It makes an excellent pan fish, which adds to its popularity.

Yellowtail Snapper (23a)
(*Ocyurus chrysurus*)

With anglers the yellowtail snapper is one of the most popular of the smaller game fishes. Although a member of the family LUTJANIDAE, it does not conform in superficial appearance to the general body shape of the rest of the members of the family. It is primarily a reef fish, important commercially, especially in the Florida Keys. In the tropical western Atlantic it ranges from Florida to Brazil and also is present in the Gulf of Mexico, Bahamas, and Bermuda. It is especially abundant around the Florida Keys and Bermuda.

This is one snapper that cannot be confused with any other of its tribe. Its body is slimmer, the caudal peduncle is elongated and narrow, and the tail, which is always a bright yellow, is large in comparison with the body and deeply forked. A prominent yellow stripe starts at the nose and extends the entire length of the body, growing wider as it goes back until it includes the caudal peduncle and tail. The dorsal surface is light blue with elongated yellow dashes which appear as broken lines. The belly is white, and all fins are yellow. The iris is red. Unlike the other snappers there is not much variation in coloration. The gill rakers, which are long, number about 20 below the angle of the first gill arch.

Atlantic Snappers

Unlike most of the lutjanids the yellowtail snapper does not hug the bottom most of the time. It usually inhabits moderate depths and swims about 5 or 6 feet off the bottom. Also, contrary to its cousins, it often feeds on the surface and mostly on schools of small fish, shrimp, crabs, and worms. Its average size is about 1 pound or less, but it may reach about 4 or 5 pounds.

Yellowtail snappers are versatile. I have caught them with cut bait while they were swimming lazily around a wreck close to the bottom in a fairly shallow reef area in the Bahamas. Another time, off Bermuda, close to the deep drop-off, we chummed them to the surface with hog-mouth fry (small silvery fish) which were crushed and mixed with sand.

Another observation, which I made in Bermuda, concerns the feeding action of the yellowtail snapper while traveling in dense schools. Many evenings in Bermuda during the month of July, my wife, Bo, and I lounged with the Mowbrays on their lovely outdoor patio, which was high, overlooking Harrington Sound. While enjoying our before-dinner drinks we waited for the arrival of the yellowtails. To me it was one of the most wonderful sights in all Bermuda. As the sun was setting and the shadows grew longer, sky and water took on beautiful hues of blue, pink, and gold. The waters at that time of day were calm, and a soothing stillness prevailed. The quietness would be broken suddenly by the rapid and exciting slap, slap, slap of fish crashing bait on top water. Then we could see, often close to shore, an area of water churned white by the fleeing, frantic bait fish and the pursuing, ravenous, slashing yellowtails. Just as suddenly as it arrived the action would cease. After a short while the slaughter would again take place at another spot.

Vermillion Snapper (23c)
(*Rhomboplites aurorubens*)

Other names are chub-head snapper, night snapper, and bastard snapper. The vermillion snapper is a handsome little member of the family LUTJANIDAE, with a maximum length of about 15 inches. This snapper is a warm-water fish, which frequents the Atlantic from South Carolina to Brazil. It is fairly common off Bermuda and present in the Gulf of Mexico and West Indies.

As the name indicates, it is vermillion or reddish pink in color, going paler below. The dorsal surface may have darker lines running obliquely forward and downward, and narrow yellow streaks may run along the sides below the lateral line. The first dorsal fin usually contains 12 spines; the anal has 3 spines and 8 rays. The tail is edged with black. About 18 long gill rakers are present below the angle on the first gill arch. This snapper is not as common as some of the other members of its family. However, it is an active fish and good on the table.

PACIFIC SNAPPERS

Because the eastern Pacific snappers are distributed in waters which do not receive a significant amount of angling, knowledge concerning them is meagre. Like their Atlantic cousins they are restricted to warm tropical and subtropical waters— Lower California, Gulf of California, Mexico, Panama, and some species down to Ecuador. Except for a few widely separated areas, sport fishing throughout this zone, comparatively speaking, is practically nonexistent. Also, very little is known concerning the western Pacific snappers. In the Australian area they are called sea perches, and T. C. Roughley states that there are about 40 species of the family LUTJANIDAE. Along the Great Barrier Reef the snappers are particularly abundant and provide good fishing for anglers. However, there is little detailed information concerning the individual species of the area.

Striped Pargo (22c)

(Hoplopagrus guntheri)

One of the best of game fishes, the pargo is well known for its fighting qualities, especially in the area off Cape San Lucas,

Guaymas, and several other spots in the Gulf of California and Panama. It is found in only one area in the world—the eastern Pacific, from the coast of Lower California, including the Gulf of California, down to Panama. Because of its close relationship to the snappers, most scientists include it in the family LUTJANIDAE; however, some prefer to place it in another family, HOPLOPAGRIDAE. In many areas in the Gulf of Mexico and the Caribbean the mangrove snapper, dog snapper, muttonfish, and others are grouped together and referred to indiscriminately as pargo.

Its general fin arrangement is similar to that of the typical Atlantic snappers, but it has an unusually long pectoral fin which, in the adult, reaches beyond the anterior spines of the anal fin. Ten spines are present in the first dorsal, 14 or 15 rays in the second dorsal. The anal fin consists of 3 spines and 9 rays. In coloration its dorsal surface may vary from dark green to bronze green. The sides may be silvery red or light maroon growing darker along the sides and belly. The fins and tail are light green, or yellowish green, with hues of red. Seven or 8 wide vertical bands, which help in identification, are conspicuous and colored dusky or maroon. The Pacific pargo cannot be mistaken for another snapper because of the unusual position of its tubular, anterior nostrils. They are situated just above the upper lip and project beyond the end of the snout. The second or rear nostrils are located in front of the eyes. Another peculiarity of the pargo is a knobby projection present in the forward portion of the operculum (the gill cover). The preoperculum (the "cheek" or forward part of the gill cover) has an indented edge which fits around the knobby projection.

The average size is about 4 or 5 pounds, but anglers have reported specimens taken that weighed well over 100 pounds. Deep trolling with a spoon is usually the most productive method for the angler. When hooked, the striped pargo makes several deep runs, usually heading for the rocks, before being boated.

MEXICAN SNAPPERS

The striped pargo seems to be the only snapper along the eastern Pacific known well enough to be considered a good game fish. About a half dozen other species which range along Lower California, Gulf of California, and Central America will take lures. Not much is known about them, but they grow large enough to be noticed by sportsmen. To give them game fish status is debatable.

Pargo Prieto
(Lutjanus novemfasciatus)

Also called dog snapper, but may be confused with the Atlantic dog snapper. Brownish red all over including fins, which may be lighter. Body shape, head, and fin arrangement resemble Atlantic mangrove snapper. Larger teeth than any other eastern Pacific snapper. Crescent shape patch of teeth in roof of mouth sometimes with slight backward projection. One of the largest of the eastern Pacific snappers reaching a weight of about 80 pounds.

Colorado Snapper
(Lutjanus colorado)

Closely resembles dog snapper in body shape, fin arrangement, and coloration. Teeth less conspicuous. Pectoral fin in adults reaches as far back as the anus. Rear nostril long and narrow (round in dog snapper). Does not reach the large size of dog snapper.

Jordan's Snapper
(Lutjanus jordani)

Brighter in coloration than the dog and Colorado snappers— vivid pinkish red on back going silvery on the sides, belly whitish. Pale pink vertical bars may be present. First dorsal and second dorsal almost same height throughout and appear as one. Third, fourth and fifth spines higher than the others. Long pectoral fin reaches to the anus. Maximum length about 36 inches.

Mullet Snapper

(*Lutjanus aratus*)

Coloration appears similar to Jordan's snapper, but darker on back with distinctive brown striping. Body more elongated and pectoral fin much shorter than in Jordan's snapper. Only Pacific coast snapper with dorsal fin containing 11 spines.

Spotted Rose Snapper

(*Lutjanus guttatus*)

Also red snapper, flamenco. Color variable. Rose pink on back and sides going to golden yellow below. Tail maroon or reddish. Yellow stripes present along lower part of sides in some specimens. Greenish or brownish spots present on scales of back and sides, which give an appearance of oblique stripes on the back and lateral stripes on the sides. Head is also spotted. Dark spot, which may be prominent or barely discernible, present above lateral line below anterior rays of soft dorsal fin. Tooth patch in roof of mouth anchor shaped with short backward projection. Maximum length about 30 inches.

Pargo Amarillo

(*Lutjanus argentiventris*)

Also called yellowtail snapper, but may be confused with Atlantic yellowtail snapper which it does not resemble. Outline and general appearance of body and fins resemble closely those of Atlantic red snapper. The eye is large. May be distinguished easily by coloration—pinkish rose on the front half of body and mostly a pinkish yellow or yellow on the rear half.

Fore part may vary in color and extent of pattern (dorsal surface may be tinged with bronze or gray), but rear half is always more or less yellow. Bright blue dots under eye may form a line. Crescent tooth patch in roof of mouth with long backward projection. Maximum length about 24 inches.

Snook

Snook (9d)

(*Centropomus undecimalis*)

The snook is an excellent and unusual game fish; it is available to the most diversified group of anglers and appreciated by all, from the "fancy" fly rod purist to the cane pole fisherman sitting on a canal bank. Although found in the warm waters of the Atlantic and Pacific this coastal fish has made its best reputation along the shores of Florida and Gulf of Mexico. It is a member of the family CENTROPOMIDAE. Robalo is another name commonly used. Some scientists have split the Atlantic and Pacific snook into at least a dozen species—all based on differences in length of fins, number of spines or rays, slight differences in gill raker counts, etc. However, these differences may be environmental or geographical and thus a problem for the taxonomists; the angler is safe in calling it a snook.

The snook is a coastal fish. It hugs the shore and prefers brackish areas. Occasionally it strays into nearly fresh waters. Many are taken by anglers far up rivers and in drainage canals such as abound in southern Florida. It also frequents inlets, channel banks, under mangrove banks, around bridge and pier pilings. Rocky areas, sandy shores, and jetties of stone and rock are also spots where the snook can be found. In other words there are large populations spread in different types of locales throughout its range. In the western Atlantic it is distributed from the St. Johns River in Florida into the Gulf of Mexico and southward to Venezuela. On the other side of the ocean it is known to occur off West Africa. The Pacific distribution is from Lower California southward to Peru (I have watched Kip Farrington take several surfcasting off the beach at Cabo Blanco).

The snook has a long body, concave head and face profile, and a projecting lower jaw. It has a high back, almost straight ventral surface, and a deeply forked tail. The first spinous dorsal fin is well separated from the second or soft dorsal. In coloration it does not vary much. The sides are nearly always silvery, and the underside is white. The dorsal surface may be straw, tan, or greenish yellow. The dark, conspicuous lateral line extends onto the tail. All fins except the dark dorsal fins are whitish.

Although a keener interest in the snook is beginning to be shown, not much of its life history is yet unfolded. There seems to be a migration in south Florida waters, although a resident population is there. The migration takes place in the spring and stems from the direction of the West Indies. Migrating schools swim at the surface and are composed of adult fish. Scientists at the University of Miami have been studying the snook, and many fish were tagged, both by scientists and anglers. The first batch of fish recovered were all captured within a mile from the tagging point. Some of them had been at large for a couple of months prior to capture. It appears that this population of snook does not move extensively. Food items are fishes, shrimp, crab, freshwater crayfish, and minnows.

The record rod and reel fish weighed 50½ pounds and was taken at the Gatun Spillway, Panama, on January 2, 1944, by J. W. Anderson. The Atlantic record is 49½ pounds and was taken at Marco, Florida, in June, 1926, by S. Caine. The average weight is in the 2- to 4-pound class and 20 pounders are not rare. Snook about 30 inches in length may be as much as six years of age although some may reach this size at three years. The bulk of the snook caught are two- and three-year-olds.

In Florida, where it was often taken in quantities, the snook has been proclaimed an official game fish and placed on the protected list. No longer can it be taken commercially, and no longer can the greedy angler make a slaughter. The daily bag limit is 4 fish, each to measure 18 or more inches, and there is a possession limit of 8 fish.

Snook seem to favor dusk and night feeding, and often excellent catches can be made at dawn. I have taken part in nights of fishing for snook in Mexico where we caught and released fish of all sizes as fast as we desired. When hitting, the snook is not choosy about the type of lure you throw. However, I have seen times in Florida when I emptied my tackle box at fish that I could see, but they would completely ignore all offerings. When hooked you cannot "horse" the snook, for the hook tears out of the soft mouth fairly easily. Often it will jump a couple of times when first hooked, and many are lost at this point. Most of the fight is dogged and strong. The edges of the operculum (cheek plates) are sharp, and the angler should take notice when handling a flopping fish. One of our Mexican assistants, Chico (our duck guide who knew nothing of fish), in trying to be helpful grabbed a large snook that my pal Larry Sheerin had dragged onto the beach. The blood which covered the snook did not come from the fish but from Chico's hand which was rather severely gashed.

Tarpon

Tarpon (9a)
(*Tarpon atlanticus*)

"The silver-king, greatest of game fishes" is a phrase often used to describe the tarpon. Whether it rates as the greatest is debatable. However, it certainly is the most available of our great game fishes, and because of its exciting jumping after being hooked, it surely is one of the most spectacular of the larger gamesters. It also holds the distinction of being the only one of our highly respected game fishes which is almost completely ignored as a food fish. It has been previously known by several scientific names which held the genus *Megalops*, but now *Tarpon atlanticus* is well established. One of the earliest common names was tarpom; also big scale, silver king, and others such as sabalo are occasionally used. But due to the great interest sportsmen have in this fish the name tarpon is rapidly supplanting all others, and it is now most commonly used. The tarpon and its close relatives, the bonefish and ladyfish, are usually described as soft-rayed, herring-like fishes (which also includes shad, herring, anchovy, salmon, trout, and smelt). The tarpon's family name is MEGALOPIDAE.

It is primarily a coastal fish of wide distribution in tropical and subtropical waters. For example, along the Atlantic seaboard it is found regularly in large numbers in Florida waters, but it has been reported from every state along the Atlantic, all the way to Nova Scotia, where it was twice recorded. It is common throughout the Gulf of Mexico and the Caribbean, is present southward to Venezuela, British Guiana down to Brazil, and Argentina as a stray. On the other side of the Atlantic it is well known off the northwestern coast of Africa. It is present in the Bahamas and appears regularly in small numbers in Bermuda's waters. In the Canal Zone area the tarpon is abundant, and it has invaded the west coast of Central America through the Panama Canal. The boundaries of distribution and extent of establishment of the species in the Pacific are not completely clear. The tarpon ascends fresh water rivers (not to spawn), sometimes a distance over 100 miles. Although the tarpon is a salt water fish, it is known for its ability to survive in fresh water.

The tarpon does look like a giant herring. It is a big, compressed, silvery fish with a huge up-tilted mouth lined with bony plates. It has a protruding lower jaw, with a bony plate located between its branches. There is a profusion of tiny teeth, and the large eye has an adipose eyelid. The tail is well forked; the deeply falcate anal fin is long with 19 to 23 rays; a single soft-rayed dorsal fin is located in the middle of the back and contains 12 to 15 rays, the last of which is long and filamentous. This latter characteristic plus the very large and heavy scales are good points of identification. Also, there is a long filament which originates above the pectoral fin close to the gill opening; another shorter one is present above and close to the origin of the ventral fin. Gill rakers, which are long and slender, number 32 to 36 on lower limb of first gill arch. The body coloration is a concentrated bright silver with the dorsal surface a light bluish green. The pectoral and ventral fins are whitish, sometimes tinged with yellow or flesh color. The other fins are dusky or light greenish yellow.

The world record rod and reel weight stands at 283 pounds; the fish was taken at Lake Maracaibo, Venezuela, on March 19, 1956, by M. Salazar. This specimen was 7 feet 2⅗ inches in length. Many fish over 150 pounds have been caught on rod and reel, and close to a dozen fish over 200 pounds have been reported by anglers. There is an assumption that the tarpon reaches a weight over 300 pounds. The largest known tarpon measured 8 feet 2 inches in length and weighed an estimated 350 pounds. This fish was netted by fishermen at Hillsboro River Inlet, Florida, on August 6, 1912. Since the rod and reel record was a foot less in length and weighed 283 pounds, a sound indication appears that the maximum weight is over 300 pounds.

No positive data exist concerning the spawning habits of the tarpon. Eggs have been collected which appear to be tarpon eggs, but all attempts to hatch them were unsuccessful. From observations made by Charles Breeder and by scientists of the University of Miami Marine Laboratory it appears that spawning normally takes place in salt or brackish water in areas close to shore during the summer months. The tarpon gather in great schools in spots which are now notable for angling, probably because spawning conditions are more favorable than at other areas. The Florida Keys, Boca Grande Pass, Tampico, Mexico, and Aransas Pass, Texas, are among the best known.

Tarpon have been observed milling in a circle, and after this action the water appeared milky. It seems that fertilization takes place at this time. The fertilized eggs sink to the bottom. A single female may carry 10,000,000 or more eggs. Soon after hatching the larvae migrate or are carried by currents into pools and lagoons close to the sea where they spend most of their first year of life. Often during the spawning period heavy rainfall carries the young fish into inland stretches of water which later become landlocked. The fish then may return to the sea the following year, but there are instances where the tarpon are permanently cut off from exit. Such a situation occurred at Deep Lake, Florida, and in some of the lakes of Andros Island, Bahamas.

In their first year of life the young become distributed in fresh and brackish waters in a variety of types of canals, rivers, and bays. It appears that a few years later as the tarpon approach maturity they go out to sea, where they gather in schools in preparation for spawning. The schools disperse after spawning. Where do they go then? Perhaps they migrate long distances in salt water, or they may disband into deeper offshore waters, where the angling effort is not great, or they may return to fresh or brackish water. Only a tagging program will tell the story.

Some tarpon are resident the year round in the lower Florida Keys, but a migratory pattern is suggested in a northward movement along the Mexican coast in March, and from Cuba through the Florida Keys and Florida's Gulf Coast in April and May. Lake Nicaragua, a body of fresh water in Central America, holds many tarpon as does its outlet the San Juan River, which is about 110 miles long.

The reason the young tarpon (also adults) are capable of survival in landlocked bodies of water which may be muddy or lack enough oxygen to harbor other types of fishes lies in their breathing apparatus. Tarpon possess gills, but they also have a fairly large air bladder which is connected to the gullet. This apparatus contains lung-like tissue which suggests a similarity to the true lungs of higher vertebrates. The tarpon comes to the surface at intervals to gulp air.

Most of the stomachs examined by scientists have been empty. Either the food is disgorged while the angler is playing the fish or the fish are around where anglers can catch them during or at the time approaching spawning when the fish may not feed. Tarpon are known to feed on shrimp, crab, sea catfish, mullet, and other fishes.

I need not dwell on the fighting qualities of the tarpon, for sporting literature bulges with accounts of the game properties of the silver king. In recent years a complete about-face has taken place concerning the appropriate tackle to use in circumventing the tarpon in a sporting manner. For many years the tarpon was taken on heavy tackle, but at present the use of any tackle except a spinning outfit, bait-casting rod, or fly rod is frowned upon by sporty anglers. "Rave notices" are now common pertaining to the angler who takes a large tarpon of over 100 pounds on light bait-casting tackle or fly rod. Unquestionably, an angler must possess skill in order to do the trick, but if the tarpon, which is a powerful fish, zipped off on a sustained run, very few indeed would be landed on such light tackle. A hooked tarpon literally jumps itself to death while fighting in a localized area. This is the type of action which makes the tarpon a great game fish, for the leaps are spectacular, and it is thrilling to catch one on light tackle. The tremendous resistance displayed by a hooked fish is also an outdoor photographer's dream. There is no other splendid game fish which can be recorded with movie equipment under such favorable conditions—usually good sunlight, calm waters, and beautiful scenery. Above all, it is a great shimmering sporty fish that makes the spray fly with its leaping antics.

I have enjoyed many days of tarpon fishing in several different areas, yet two of these tarpon angling experiences stand out above the others. And as I reminisce I realize that these incidents portray vividly the two extremes in the joys and benefits of fishing. One was a quiet, soul-soothing, contemplative type of angling in circumstances of awesome beauty. Larry Sheerin, a pal of mine from San Antonio, Texas, and I were collecting fish for Yale University at a wonderful spot in Mexico called Eight Pass. After the day's work was done we picked up our rods and walked along the clean sands, which were absorbing lovely pink hues from the setting sun, to our favorite spot; the narrow pass of the miles-wide, lake-like lagoon. Every evening toward dusk the pass was busy with tarpon pushing through the concentrated area, and long weaving lines of pelicans were silhouetted against the mellow sun which seemed to be setting into the lagoon for a night of rest. The only sounds that broke

Tarpon

the stillness were an occasional squawk of a gull and the gentle lap, lap of the tide against the shore.

Larry and I, hip-deep in water, raised a tarpon with almost every cast. Usually the plug was thrown after several jumps—sometimes the fish missed it. Occasionally we landed a tarpon and then released it. Every fish we hooked jumped, and every jump was silhouetted clearly against the fading sun. As the tarpon hit the air its flashing body threw off sprays of water which seemed to play with the colors of the blue sky and crimson sun.

The other occasion was a hilarious one of noise and excitement. I had taken the Yale salt water fishing team from Wedgeport, Nova Scotia, where we won the Intercollegiate Tuna Match, down to the Bahamas; our match with the Nassau Anglers Club was not completed because of a hurricane. From there we traveled to a fish camp in Grassy Key, Florida.

We fished all day in boats in different areas and caught many types of fishes, but we always looked forward to the bridge fishing at night. Tarpon were splashing all over the place. Many fish hit our lures and were lost before Win Tuttle set the hooks into one that stayed on. (Incidentally he got his fish by walking along the bridge trolling a yellow feather jig.) Then the circus began—in the dark. All of the team members converged on him offering advice, mostly facetious. After scrambling back and forth along the bridge for half an hour Win finally persuaded the tarpon to the end of the bridge, and then we all stumbled down to the water's edge with everyone yelling encouragement. As the fish was reeled in close it still had enough stuff left to clear the water occasionally. Every time the tarpon came by, Al Wood-Prince, the team's captain, made a swipe at it with a short ineffective gaff, and every time the fish felt the touch it went into the air. All the while the boys whooped like a bunch of Comanches. Win maneuvered the exhausted fish up close to the rocks, but all hands that were trying to reach the fish could not do it. So Win did a surprising thing. He yelled "to hell with you guys," dropped his rod, and jumped into the water—which proved to be deeper than anticipated. With a couple of strokes he was by the fish and with an effort heaved the tarpon upon the rocks. The fish jumped like mad. It fell in between a couple of boulders and back into the water. Win again tossed it ashore. This time the boys heaved it farther up the bank and then all floundered over the flopping fish until they pegged it to the ground. I laughed so hard my sides pained for several days. Although everyone but Win claimed the fish as a team effort, he posed proudly by it the next day, and that photo appears in this book.

Tripletail

Tripletail (30d)

(*Lobotes surinamensis*)

The tripletail, well known along the shores of northeast Florida as chobie, can be called a marine bass. It is a close relative of the SERRANIDAE but is placed in a separate family, LOBOTIDAE. Similar in general mode of life and choice of warm waters to most of the marine basses, it also takes a baited hook readily.

    The common name is derived from the unusual placement of the second dorsal and anal fins which are located posteriorly on the body close to the tail. When these fins are folded back they produce a superficial appearance of three tail lobes, hence, tripletail. On the western Atlantic coast it ranges primarily from northern Florida southward along the coast and around to the Gulf of Mexico as far as Louisiana. Occasionally it is found off Texas, and to South Carolina in its northern range. Strays may be found as far north as Cape Cod, Massachusetts. In southern distribution it reaches as far as Uruguay. It is present in Bermuda, and on the other side of the Atlantic it is found off West Africa and in the Mediterranean. A similar species is found in some areas on both sides of the Pacific.

Color is variable. It may be dusky greenish, dark brown to light brown, or pale tan. The lower sides may be silvery. Young specimens show mottled coloration. All of the fins except the dorsal are darker than the body. Several dark bands or bars are present on face and head. The tripletail has a rather deep, large, compressed body. The pectoral fins are fairly small and rounded on the edges; the pelvic fins are placed posterior to the origin of the pectoral. Small eye, short snout, small rough scales, and protruding lower jaw are also characteristics of identification. The first dorsal fin contains 12 spines and is depressible into a shallow groove; second dorsal has 15 or 16 rays. The anal has 3 spines and 11 or 12 rays. Gill rakers on the first gill arch below the angle number 11 plus 4 rudiments. Fish of 30 inches and 25 pounds are not uncommon, but the average is much smaller—about 5 pounds. Maximum weights for this fish are given anywhere from 35 to 50 pounds.

The tripletail seems to be a fish which inhabits different types of waters; it may be found in the shallows and it may enter river mouths. Often it frequents waters as deep as 25 fathoms, and sometimes it schools and feeds along surf areas and beaches. It likes rocky areas and may be located around submerged wrecks and pilings. It may occur solitary, in a small group, or in schools. It is primarily a bottom fish with a choice of food in shrimp, crustaceans, and small fishes. Spawning occurs in summer. Compared with other bass-like fishes the tripletail is not often hooked by anglers, but when taken on light tackle it is a scrapper. It may take an artificial lure, but baits are by far the best producers. Most authors state that this fish is "edible," but the several that I have eaten were excellent.

Wrasses

Although the wrasses constitute one of the largest families of fishes in the world—between 400 and 500 different species—very few are pursued with rod and reel. Only three are worth mentioning as fishes preferred by anglers. However, the tautog is one of the most popular game fish to be found in the northwestern Atlantic.

Tautog (34b)

(Tautoga onitis)

The tautog, or blackfish, as it is known over a good portion of its range, is one of the most important game fish sought by shore fishermen along the rocky areas of the northeastern United States. It is a member of the wrasse family, LABRIDAE. Although distributed from South Carolina (called oysterfish in Maryland and Virginia) to Nova Scotia, it is taken in greatest abundance along the coasts of Connecticut, Rhode Island, and Massachusetts.

The tautog is a stout fish with an unusually broad caudal peduncle and a tail which is not much wider. The head profile is rather steep and the nose is blunt; lips are thick. The spinous and soft-rayed portions of the dorsal fin are connected: 16 to 17 spines, 10 rays. The anal has 3 spines and 7 or 8 rays. Each ventral fin has 1 stout spine. The tail is slightly rounded at the corners; pectoral, pelvic, and anal fins are roundish. Stout, conical jaw teeth are in two series. The 2 or 3 front teeth in each jaw are larger than the others. Two groups of flat, rounded, crushing teeth are present in the rear of the mouth. The tautog is a dark fish with a variety of background colors—grayish, grayish brown, dusky, deep gray, brownish black. It is profusely mottled with the same type of colors but darker. The mottlings or blotches are more sharply defined in younger fish. The belly is usually lighter, and the chin is whitish. Degree or intensity of coloration depends upon the type of bottom the tautog frequents. Lighter bottom, paler fish.

The record rod and reel tautog weighed 21 pounds 6 ounces; it was taken off Cape May, New Jersey, on June 12, 1954, by R. N. Sheafer. The heaviest fish on record was a 22½ pounder, which measured 36½ inches in length. Fish 12 to 14 pounds are unusual; 2- to 4-pounders are common.

The tautog is popular with the average salt water angler because it hugs the coast and can be taken close to shore. North of Cape Cod it usually does not range farther than a couple of miles offshore and seldom frequents water deeper than 5 to 10 fathoms in this area. However, southward they may be found as far as 10 to 12 miles off Long Island and in deep water.

This fish prefers rocky shores, breakwaters, boulders, submerged wrecks, piers, docks, and mussel beds. Occasionally good numbers are taken over sandy or smooth bottom at fairly good distances from any rocky locality. Some groups of tautogs follow the incoming tide above low water level around rocks and ledges to feed on the abundance of blue mussels along the intertidal zone and drop back to deeper water when the tide starts to move out. These fishes are referred to as tide runners. When tautog are through feeding they often slip into a hole in the rocks where they lie (sometimes several together) taking life easy until the incoming tide again awakens their interest. They do not take part in extensive migrations; it is mostly an

Wrasses

offshore movement into deep water when the cold weather arrives in November. In the spring the fish make an appearance about April. Some anglers believe that the tautog arrive during apple blossom time. The cold season is spent in deeper water lying amongst eelgrass, in the shelter of rocks. The young may take refuge in empty oyster and clam shells. Tautog are susceptible to drops in temperature, and good numbers have been known to perish when caught in shoal water during a sudden cold spell.

Favorite items of diet are mollusks (especially mussels), barnacles, crabs and hermit crabs. Marine worms are also taken. Green crabs, hermit crabs, fiddler crabs, and sea worms make excellent bait. Spawning takes place about June, and the eggs float. Nothing is known of their rate of growth, nor at what age they mature. Large ones, 8 to 10 pounds in weight, may be about the same number of years of age.

Every fisherman experienced with the tautog has his favorite fishing hole. The area of productive fishing may be fairly small and sharply defined. Often a matter of dropping the baited hook a few feet to the right or left makes a difference. These holes may be located in rocky areas immediately adjacent to the shore or within easy reach by rowboat. Along the Connecticut and Rhode Island shores the tautog is accepted as a fine food and game fish. During the season, catches of a bushel or two per boat are not unusual. I rate it as one of the best for the table.

Recently anglers in Yarmouth County, Nova Scotia, were pleasantly surprised to discover that the tautog abounds "inland." Waters of the Tusket River flow in and out of Eel Lake (near Wedgeport) thereby forming a type of salt water lake. Here local anglers and tourists have made large catches of tautog. The general opinion is that these fishes have suddenly invaded this body of water. However, the fish may have been there long before being discovered. It is a most interesting situation to find the tautog so far from its usual habitat.

The cunner *Tautogolabrus adspersus*, a close relative of the tautog, is considered a pest by all serious fishermen; it has a small mouth and many sharp teeth and the exasperating ability to steal bait intended for other fishes. Also, it is a nuisance because it possesses sharp needle-like spines, which make the fish difficult to remove from the hook without pricking the hands. However, many young anglers (and adults too) take great delight in using proper tackle and catching cunners, which are always about in great profusion. In the old days (about 1870) the cunner was a favorite pan fish, but it is seldom eaten these days. The flesh is tasty, but the many small bones discourage its use as a food fish.

Hogfish (34c)
(*Lachnolaimus maximus*)

The hogfish is a warm-water member of the wrasse family, LABRIDAE, and like its cousins prefers rocky areas. Nowhere along its range is it abundant, and perhaps only in the Florida Keys is it caught with any regularity. However, it is an interesting fish because of its unusual body shape and coloration. It seems to be a conversation piece whenever taken by an angler. The hogfish is present in Bermuda and is distributed from North Carolina, where it is considered a stray, southward to Florida, Panama, and the West Indies.

It is recognized easily by its hog-like head and face profile, deep body, and the unusually long 3 or 4 dorsal fin spines. The tips of the tail, second dorsal, and anal fins are extended. The dorsal fin contains 13 or 14 spines, 11 rays; anal fin, 3 spines, 10 rays. The cleft in the mouth of the male is much wider than the females. The incisor teeth are long and set at different angles, which gives the fish an appearance of requiring dental care. Heavy grinding teeth are present in the throat. The body color is highly variable. Usually the base color is some shade of red, anywhere from deep mahogany to pink, and mottled with yellow; or the base color may be predominantly yellow with red mottlings. The second dorsal, anal fins, and tail may, or may not, be barred with blue. The gill cover may have bright hues of blue. A prominent black spot is almost

Wrasses

always present on the back just below the second dorsal (at least I have never seen one without it).

The hogfish is usually found around coral reefs, rocky areas, submerged wrecks, and often in the shelter of seafans. It does not school, but is easily recognized when swimming among different types of bottom fishes. Like most of the reef fishes the hogfish does not migrate any distance; it has been known to inhabit certain restricted areas for long periods of time. Main items of diet are mollusks, barnacles, crabs, shrimp, and other invertebrates. It is an excellent food fish and a good scrapper on light tackle.

California Sheepshead (34d)

(*Pimelometopon pulcher*)

The California sheepshead is an odd-colored and odd-shaped member of the wrasse family, LABRIDAE, and like the other members of this tribe it prefers rocky bottom and rocky shore areas. It is also called redfish, fathead, and humpy. Monterey Bay to the Gulf of California is its usual distribution.

The California sheepshead is a rectangular shaped fish with an awkward-looking mouth, big chin, and large, conspicuous canine-teeth which slope obliquely forward. The facial profile is steep; the male develops a prominent fatty hump on his forehead during the breeding season. The dorsal fins are contiguous with about 11 or 12 stout spines which are shorter than the soft rays. Three spines are at the front of the anal fin. The color of the female is dull red or maroon, sometimes with blackish areas, and, rarely, all black; chin is white. In the male the head and about the posterior half of the body are black or purplish black; the soft-rayed portion of the dorsal fin, the anal fin and the tail are also black. The tail has a white edge. Ventral fin is black and white; pectoral is dusky. The anterior part of the dorsal fin is reddish, and the chin is white. Maximum size about 36 inches in length and approximately 30 pounds in weight.

Commercially it is minor; most fish are landed at Los Angeles and Santa Barbara. Fishing takes place throughout the year, but best catches are made during the winter months. Many are taken by anglers, especially at Santa Catalina Island. Not a great game fish, but fun to catch. Its main point of interest with fishermen is its bizarre appearance.

IDENTIFICATION CHARTS

Identification Charts

WHITE MARLIN — 1a
- not pointed (dorsal fin)
- 2 keels
- conspicuous
- not pointed

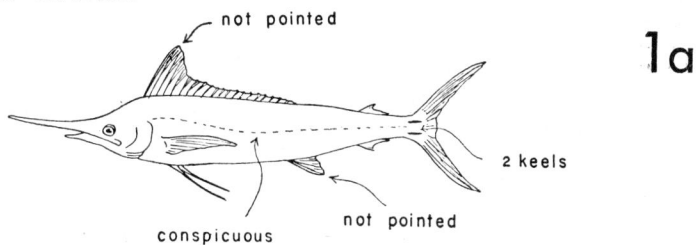

BLUE MARLIN — 1b
- pointed (dorsal fin)
- 2 keels
- pointed
- indistinct bars when alive

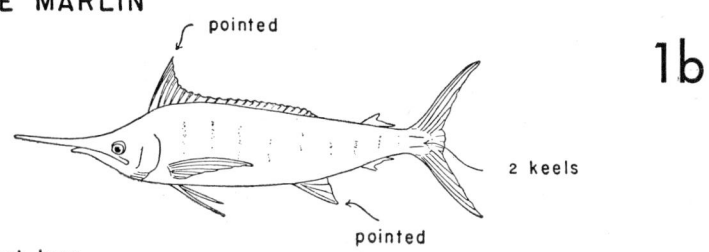

STRIPED MARLIN — 1c
- high
- spots
- 2 keels
- vivid stripes

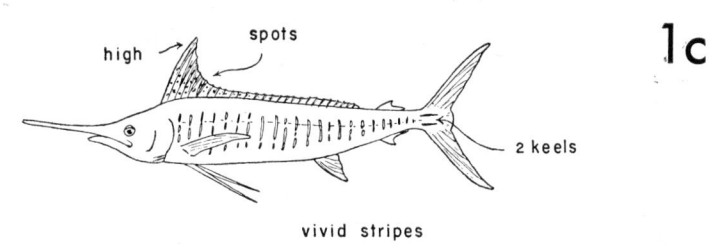

BLACK MARLIN — 1d
- deep body
- low
- 2 keels
- heavy club-like
- cannot fold against body
- no stripes

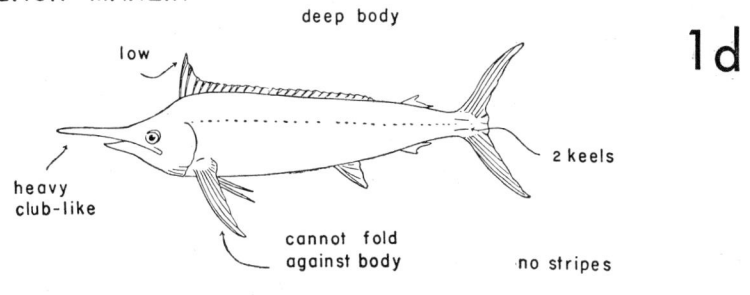

426   IDENTIFICATION CHARTS

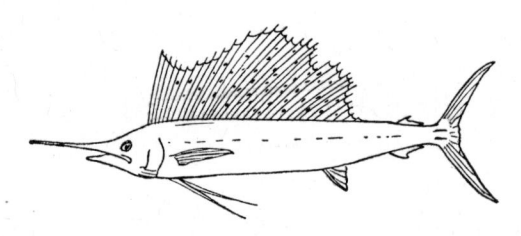

2a LONGBILL SPEARFISH
long
2 keels
slim body

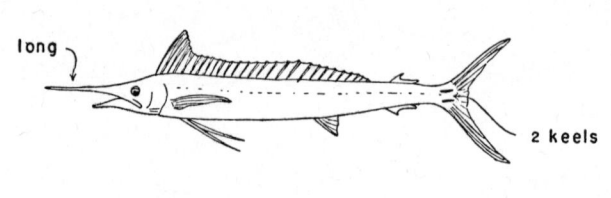

2b SHORTBILL SPEARFISH
short
2 keels
slim body

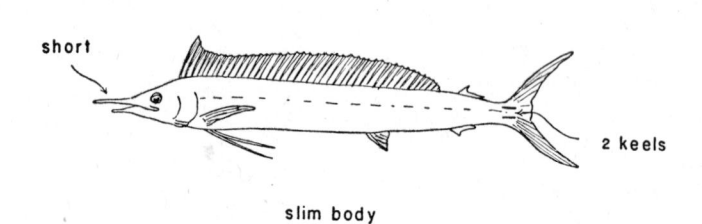

2c SAILFISH

2d SWORDFISH
no scales
does not fold
sickle shape
large blue eye
single large keel
TOP VIEW

Identification Charts

BLUEFIN TUNA

13–14
8–9
keel
7–8

gill rakers
Atlantic 39-41
Pacific 32-39

about 3/4 length of head

yellow finlets

3a

BIGEYE TUNA

large eye
8–9
7–9

GILL RAKERS
Atlantic bigeye 27-28
Pacific bigeye 24–28

yellow finlets (black edges)
bright yellow
black edge

3b

YELLOWFIN TUNA

long
8–11
8–10
long

GILL RAKERS
26–32

as long or longer than head

slender body completely scaled

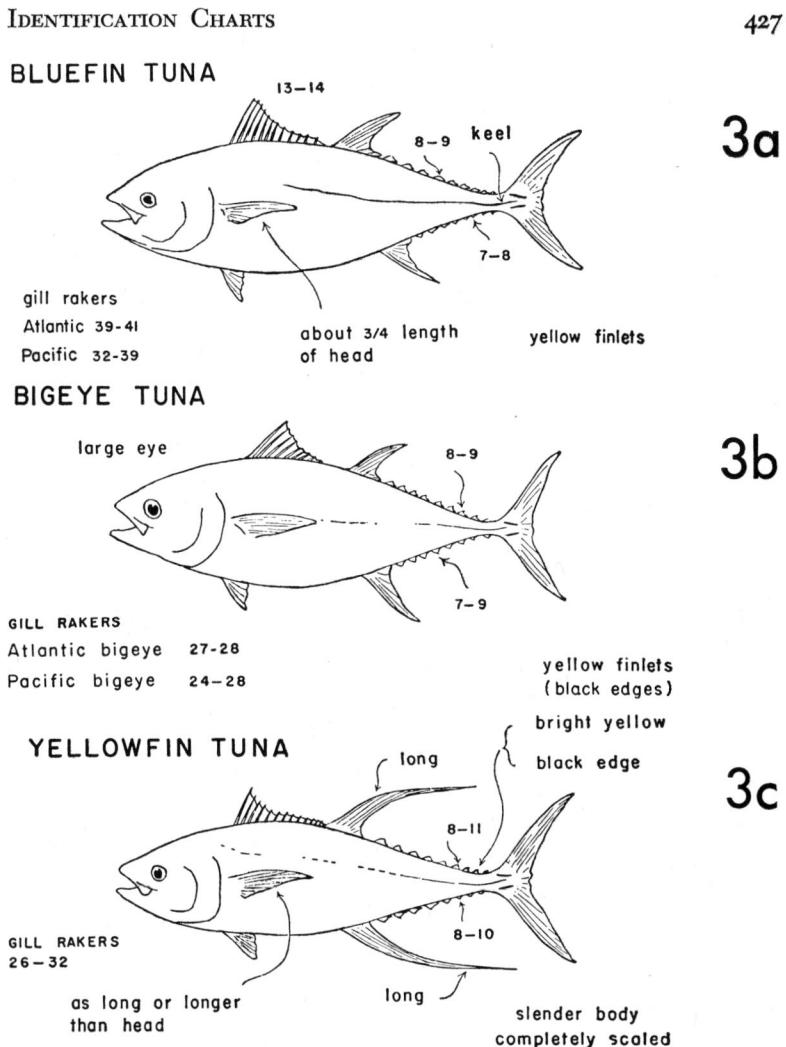

3c

BLACKFIN TUNA

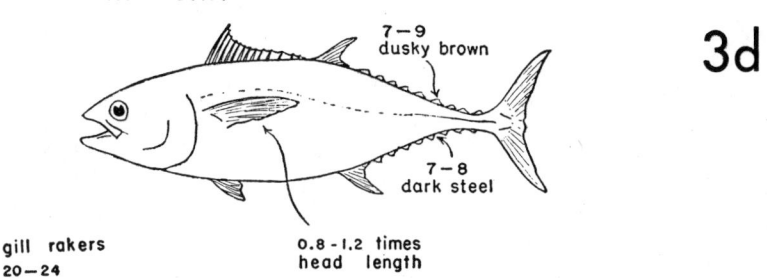

7–9 dusky brown
7–8 dark steel

gill rakers
20–24

0.8 - 1.2 times head length

3d

IDENTIFICATION CHARTS

4a DOGTOOTH TUNA

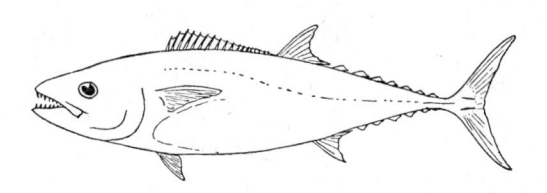

large teeth

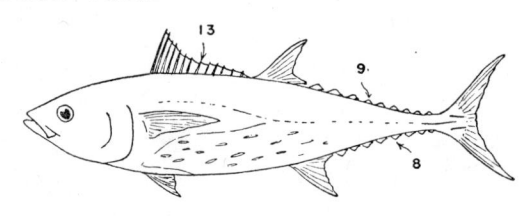

4b TONGGOL TUNA

gill rakers
20—24

no air bladder

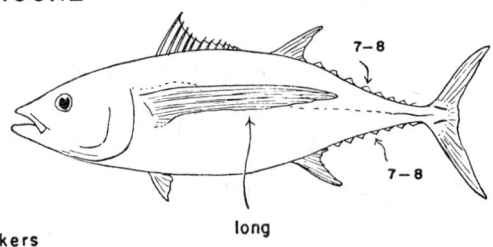

4c ALBACORE

gill rakers
27—31

long

IDENTIFICATION CHARTS

OCEANIC BONITO

5a

gill rakers
51-65

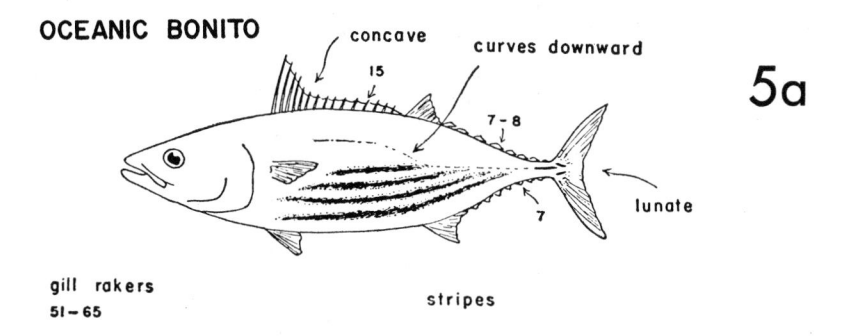

concave
15
curves downward
7-8
7
lunate
stripes

ATLANTIC SPOTTED BONITO

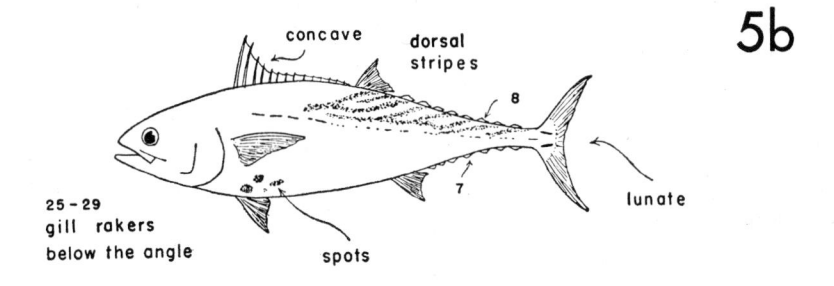

5b

concave
dorsal stripes
8
7
lunate
25-29
gill rakers
below the angle
spots

ATLANTIC BONITO

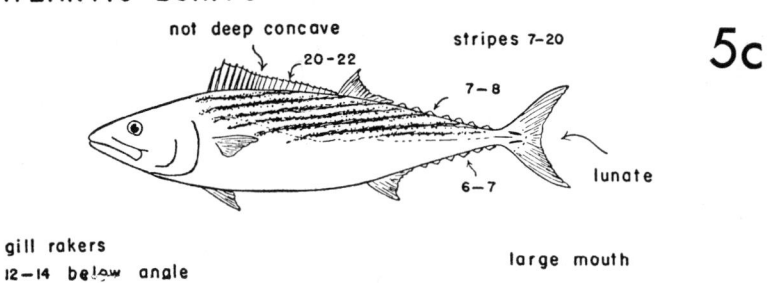

5c

not deep concave
20-22
stripes 7-20
7-8
6-7
lunate
gill rakers
12-14 below angle
large mouth

IDENTIFICATION CHARTS

6a ATLANTIC MACKEREL

- pointed
- 11–12
- wide
- 9–15
- 5
- no keel
- deep fork
- adipose eyelid
- gill rakers 30 below angle
- no swim bladder

6b CHUB MACKEREL

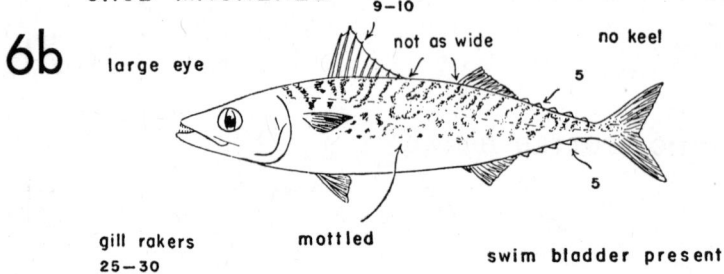

- large eye
- 9–10
- not as wide
- 5
- no keel
- 5
- gill rakers 25–30
- mottled
- swim bladder present

6c PACIFIC MACKEREL

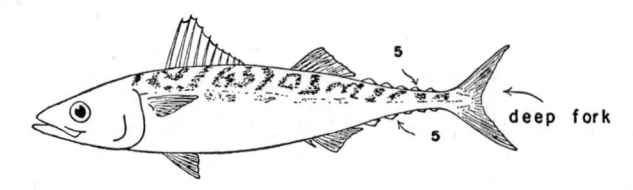

- 5
- deep fork
- 5
- GILL RAKERS 26–29
- no keel

6d FRIGATE MACKEREL

- eyes large
- dorsal posterior markings
- 7
- 7
- lunate
- GILL RAKERS 42–45
- pectoral corselet pronounced

Identification Charts

CERO MACKEREL

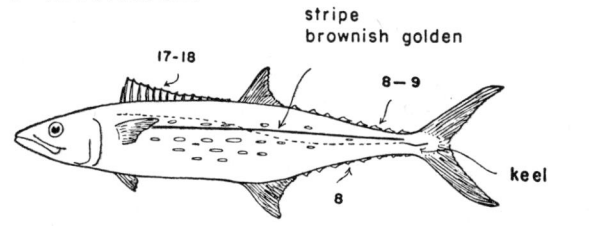

stripe brownish golden
17-18
8-9
keel
gill rakers
12—13 below angle
8
yellow markings elongated and in rows

7a

SPANISH MACKEREL

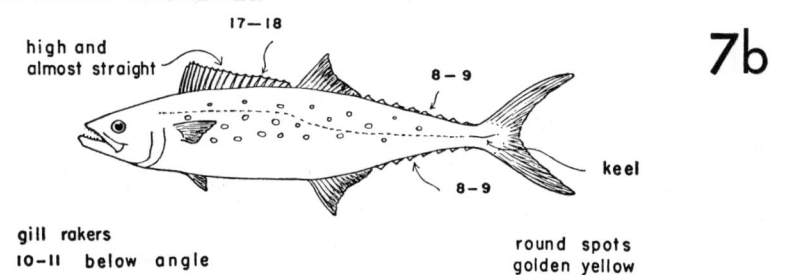

17-18
high and almost straight
8-9
8-9
keel
gill rakers
10-11 below angle
round spots golden yellow

7b

KING MACKEREL

15-16
angular
7-9
7-9
keel
GILL RAKERS
7—9 BELOW ANGLE
no spots

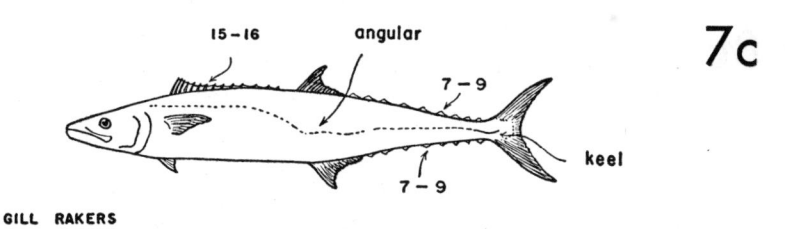

7c

WAHOO

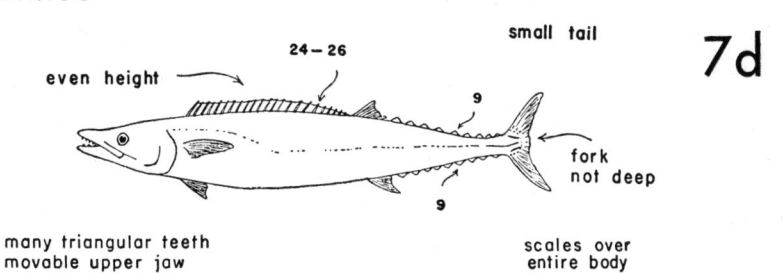

small tail
24-26
even height
9
9
fork not deep
many triangular teeth
movable upper jaw
scales over entire body

7d

GREAT BARRACUDA

8a

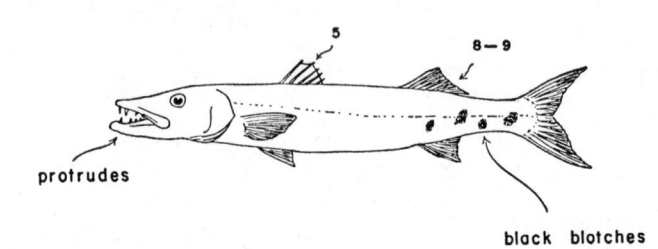

protrudes — 5 — 8–9 — black blotches

NORTHERN BARRACUDA

8b

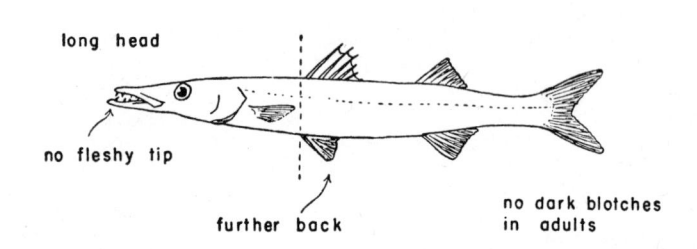

long head — no fleshy tip — further back — no dark blotches in adults

GUAGUANCHE

8c

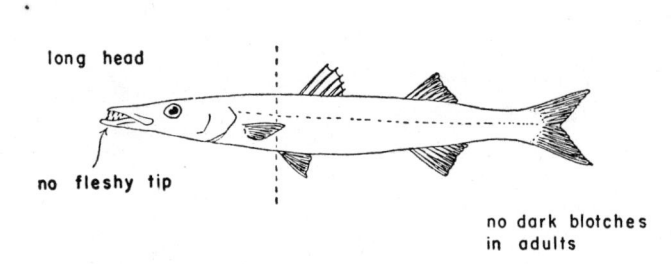

long head — no fleshy tip — no dark blotches in adults

PACIFIC BARRACUDA

8d

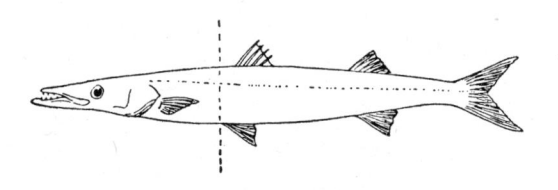

no bars or stripes

Identification Charts

TARPON

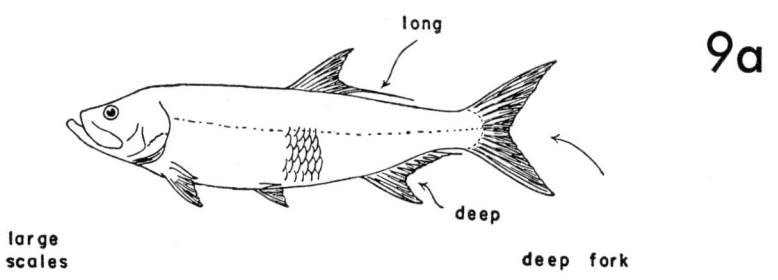

9a

long
deep
large scales
deep fork

LADYFISH

9b

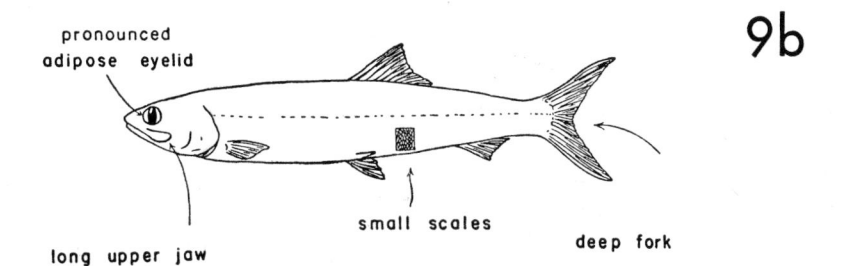

pronounced adipose eyelid
small scales
deep fork
long upper jaw

BONEFISH

9c

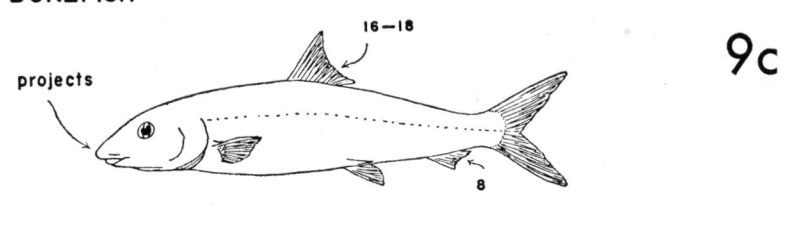

16—18
projects
8
adipose eyelid
completely scaled

SNOOK

9d

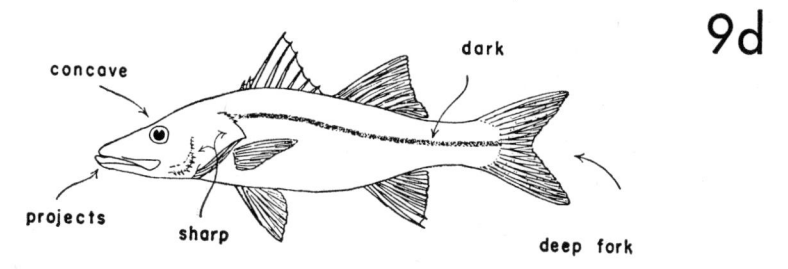

dark
concave
projects
sharp
deep fork

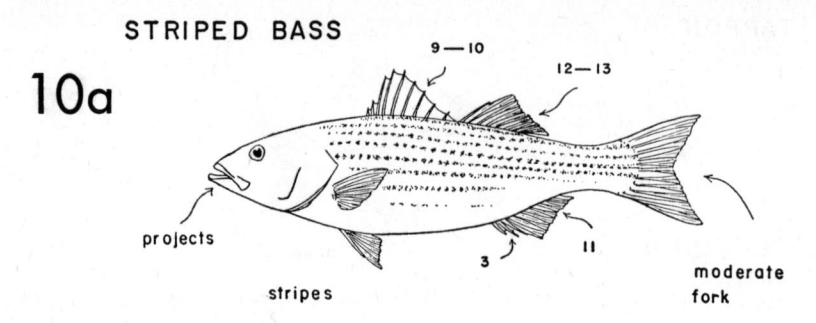

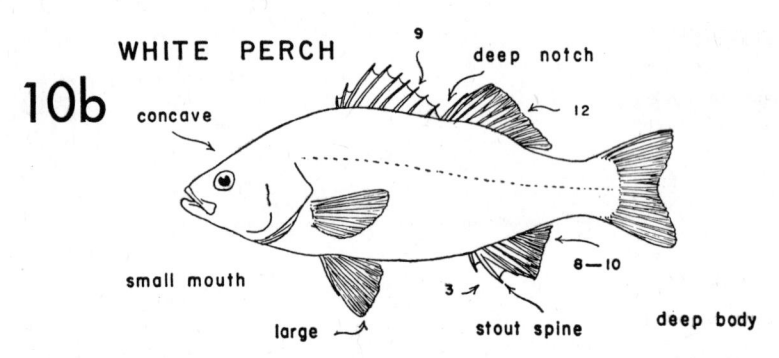

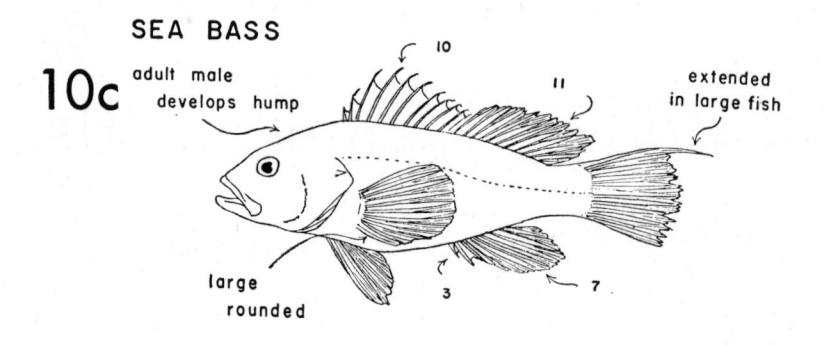

Identification Charts

10a STRIPED BASS

projects · stripes · 9–10 · 12–13 · 3 · 11 · moderate fork

10b WHITE PERCH

concave · small mouth · large · 9 · deep notch · 12 · 3 · stout spine · 8–10 · deep body

10c SEA BASS

adult male develops hump · large rounded · 10 · 11 · 3 · 7 · extended in large fish

10d BLUEFISH

sharp teeth · projects · 7–8 · 23–26 · 25–27 · no keel · no finlets · deep fork

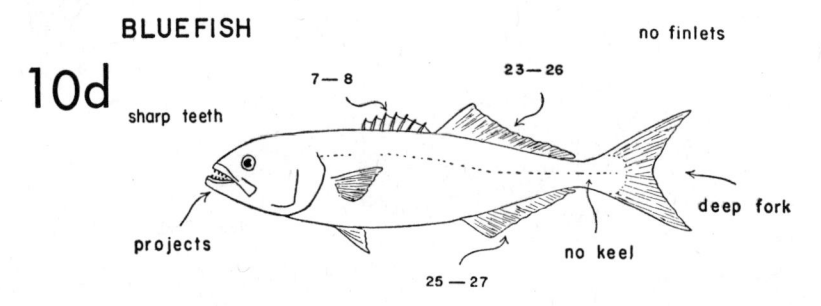

IDENTIFICATION CHARTS 435

11a

male — long dorsal — long anal — deep fork

DOLPHINFISH

female

11b

ROOSTERFISH

7
29
no keel or scutes
17
deep fork

11c

COBIA

flat head — wavy — 8 — 26 — lunate
7–9 gill rakers below angle — dark band — 23–26

11d

SHAD

adult no teeth
indented
long upper jaw — large — deep fork

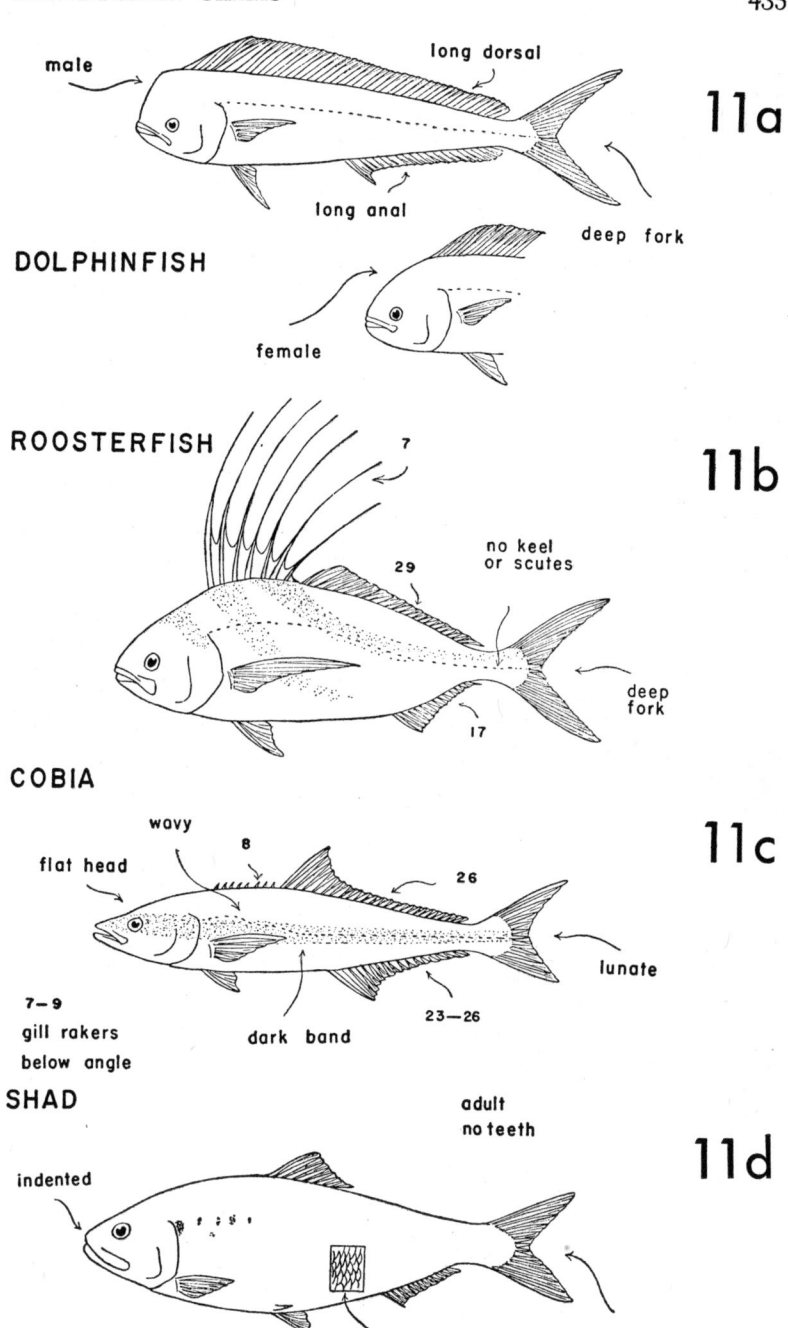

IDENTIFICATION CHARTS

12a AMBERJACK
dark band
30–34
10–14 gill rakers below angle
bronze band when alive

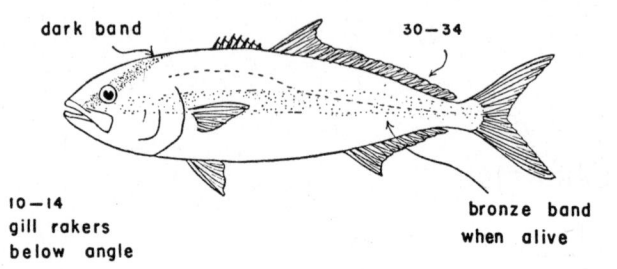

12b PACIFIC AMBERJACK
28–31
13–16 gill rakers below angle
no bronze band

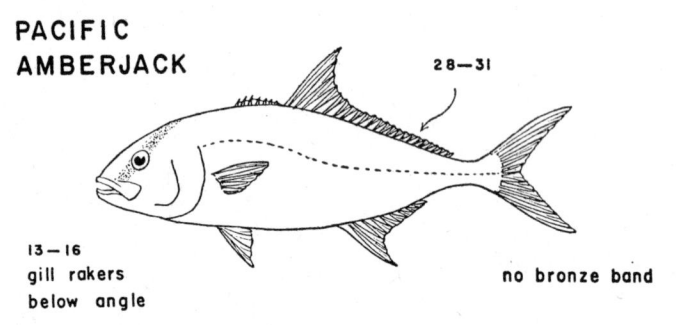

12c YELLOWTAIL
yellow
15–17 gill rakers below angle
yellow band
blunt keel no scutes

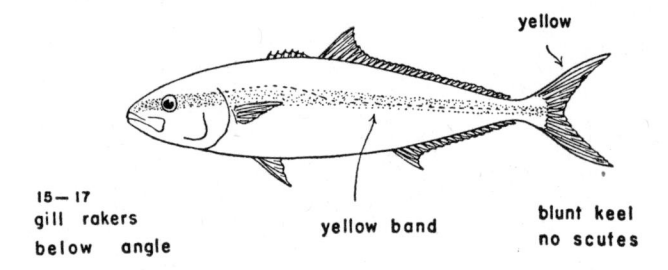

12d SAMSONFISH

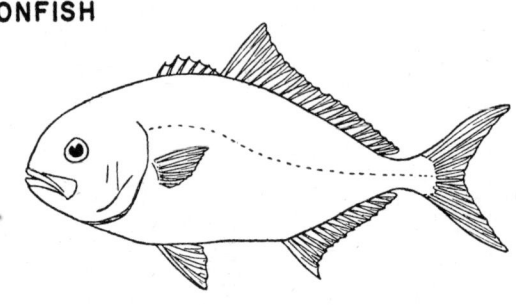

IDENTIFICATION CHARTS 437

POMPANO

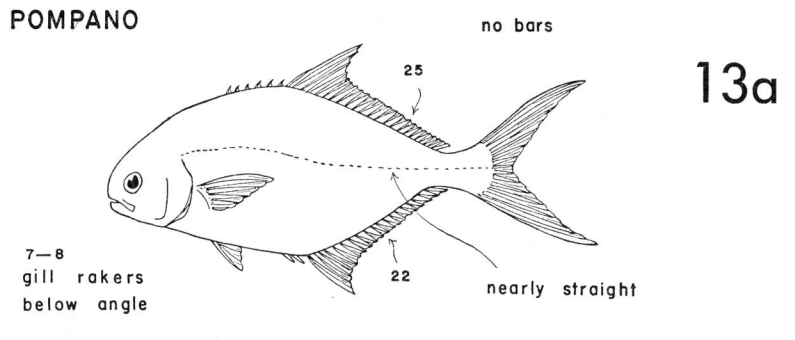

no bars
25
7—8 gill rakers below angle
22
nearly straight

13a

ROUND POMPANO

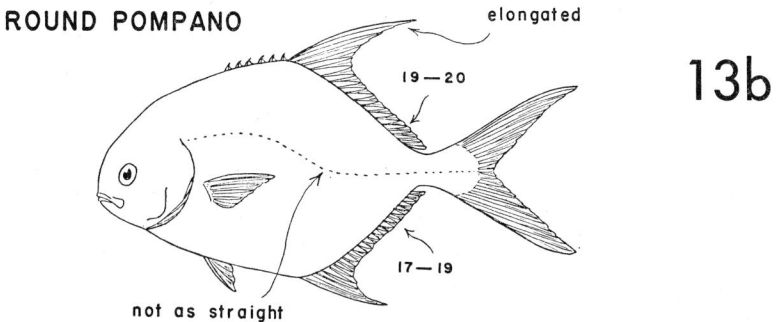

elongated
19—20
17—19
not as straight

13b

PALOMETA

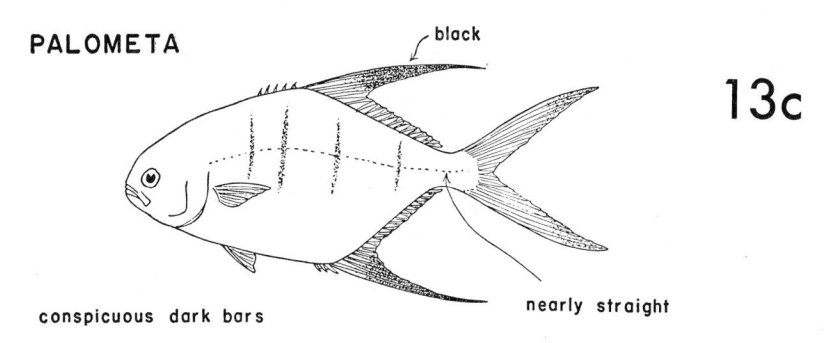

black
nearly straight
conspicuous dark bars

13c

ATLANTIC PERMIT

19—20
17—19

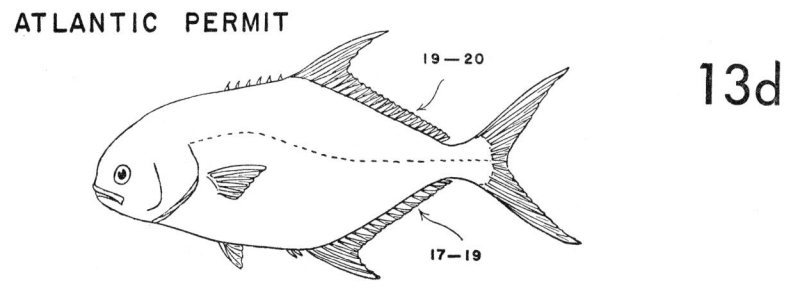

13d

IDENTIFICATION CHARTS

14a BLUE RUNNER

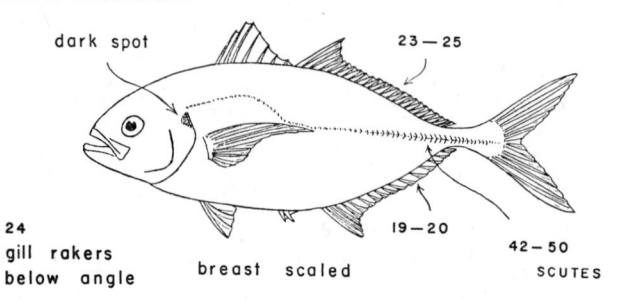

- dark spot
- 23–25
- 24 gill rakers below angle
- breast scaled
- 19–20
- 42–50 SCUTES

14b JACK CREVALLY

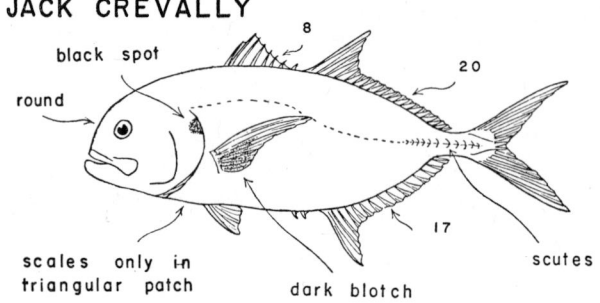

- black spot
- 8
- 20
- round
- scales only in triangular patch
- dark blotch
- 17
- scutes

14c YELLOW JACK

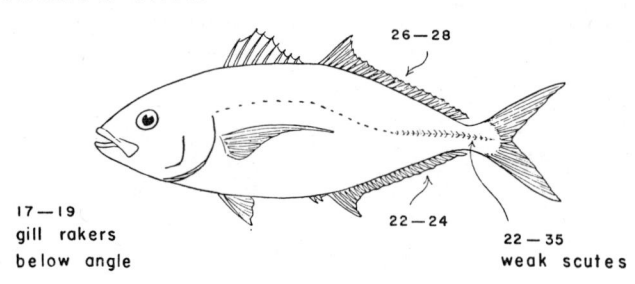

- 26–28
- 17–19 gill rakers below angle
- 22–24
- 22–35 weak scutes

14d CUBAN JACK

no spiny dorsal fin

- profile
- scutes

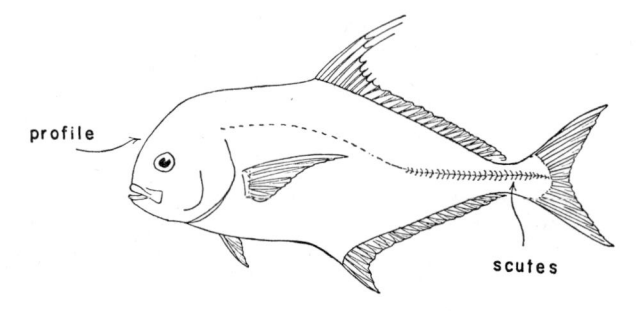

IDENTIFICATION CHARTS 439

MACKEREL JACK

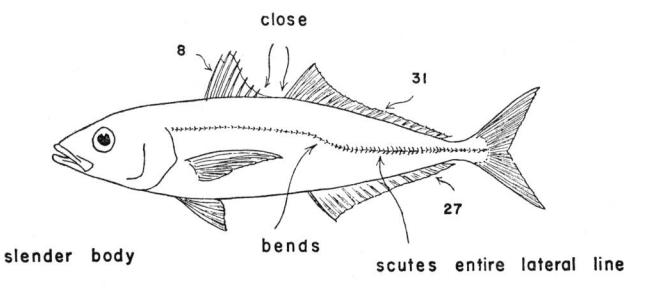

15a

- 8
- close
- 31
- slender body
- bends
- 27
- scutes entire lateral line

LEERFISH

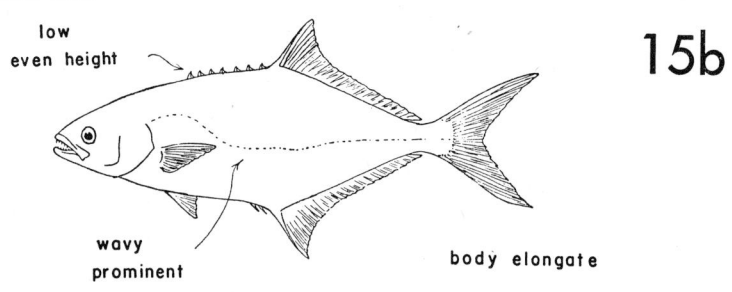

15b

- low even height
- wavy prominent
- body elongate

TALANG

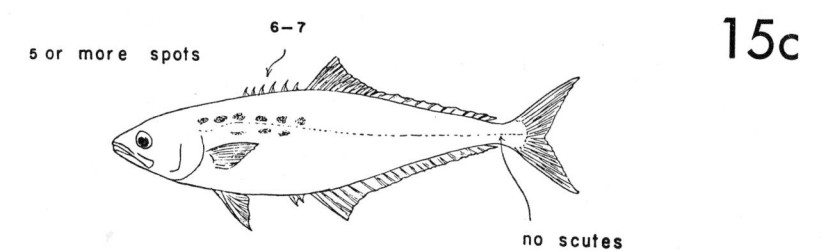

15c

- 5 or more spots
- 6–7
- no scutes

SPOTTED JACK

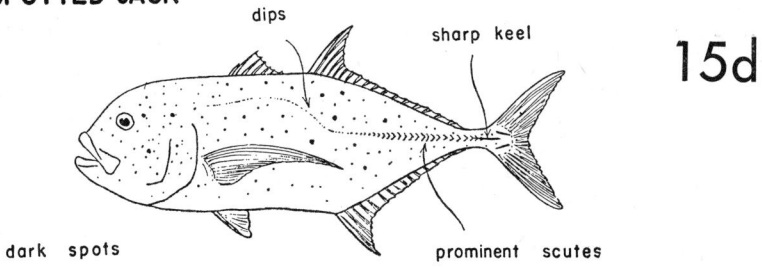

15d

- dips
- sharp keel
- dark spots
- prominent scutes

Identification Charts

16a RAINBOW RUNNER
- blue
- one
- yellow
- one
- no bony scutes

16b LOOKDOWN
- low
- elongated
- high forehead
- long face
- narrow
- tiny
- deep fork

16c BERMUDA CHUB
- 11
- 12
- deep body
- small mouth
- 14-16 gill rakers below angle
- 11

16d OCEAN WHITEFISH
- 9
- single
- 24
- blunt
- 23
- concave
- large eye

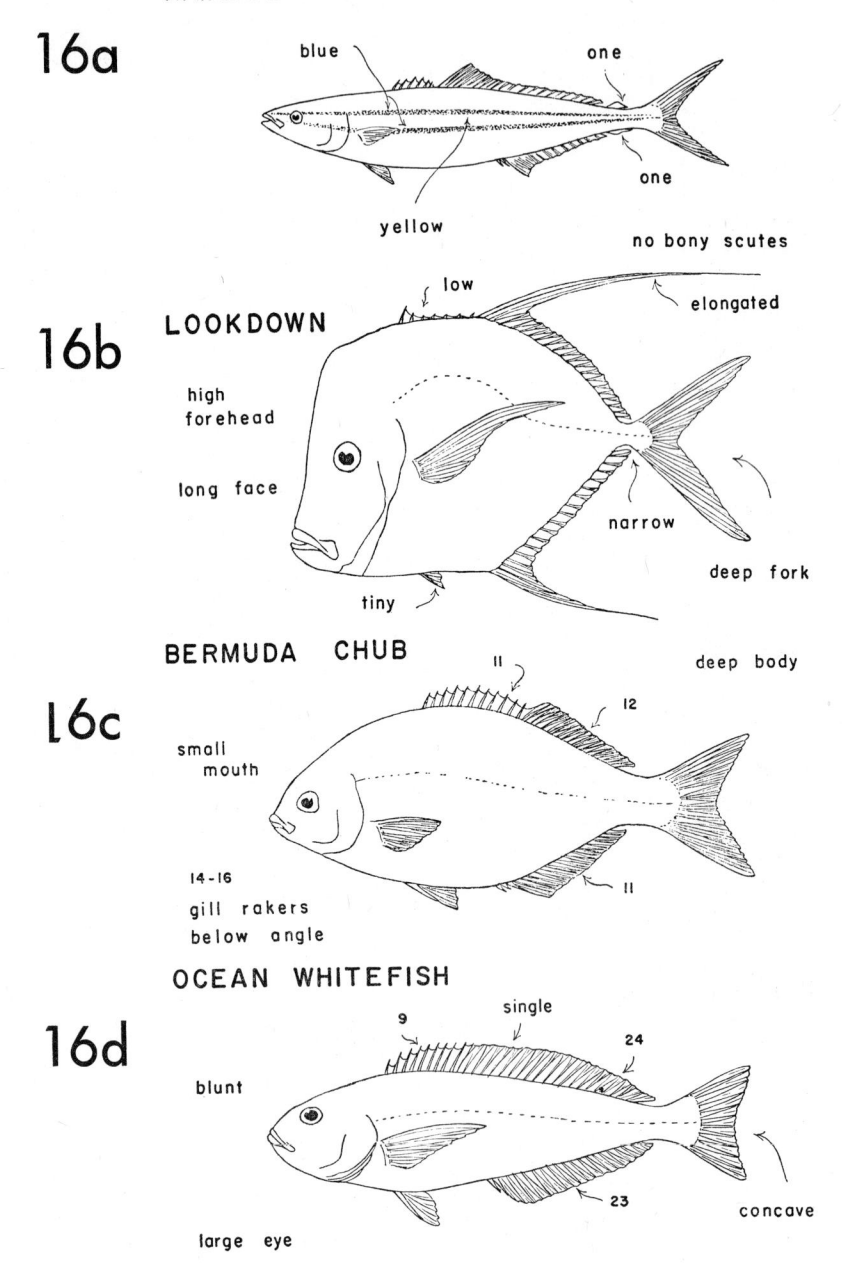

Identification Charts

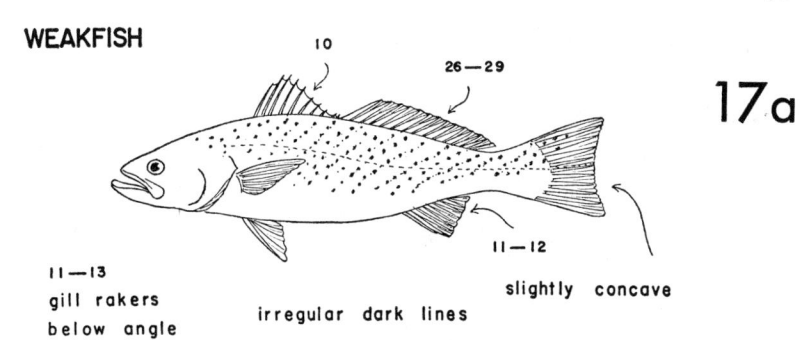

WEAKFISH

17a

10
26—29
11—13 gill rakers below angle
irregular dark lines
11—12
slightly concave

SPOTTED WEAKFISH

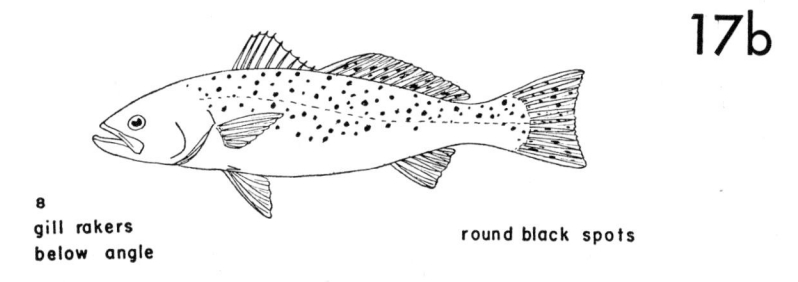

17b

8 gill rakers below angle
round black spots

CALIFORNIA WHITE SEA BASS

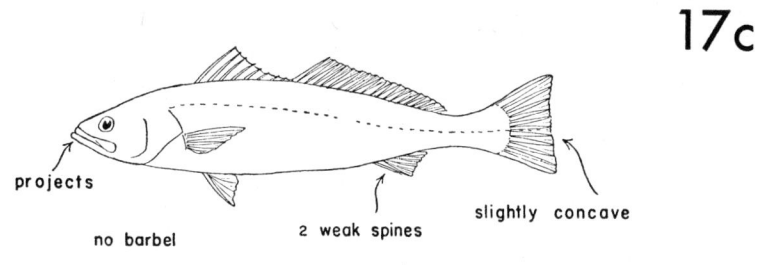

17c

projects
no barbel
2 weak spines
slightly concave

TOTUAVA

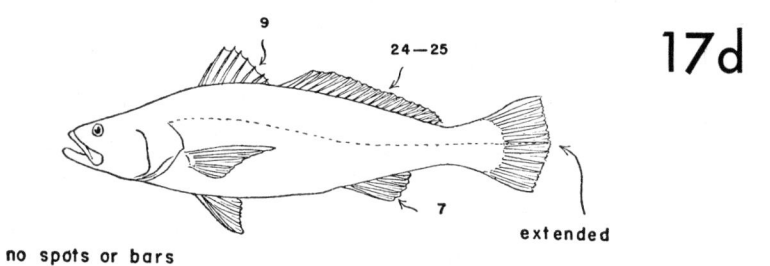

17d

9
24—25
7
extended
no spots or bars

IDENTIFICATION CHARTS

18a CALIFORNIA CORBINA

projecting — concave — barbel — large — one weak spine — convex

18b CHANNEL BASS

snub nose — 10 — connected — 25 — gill rakers 8—9 below angle — 7—8 — prominent black spot

18c NORTHERN KING WHITING

form V — long in adults — 10 — 24—27 — extent of pectoral — 8 — dark bars

18d SPOT

high back — black spot — 10 — connected — 30—34 — no barbels — 2 — 12—13 — slightly forked — gill rakers 22-23 below angle

IDENTIFICATION CHARTS 443

ATLANTIC CROAKER

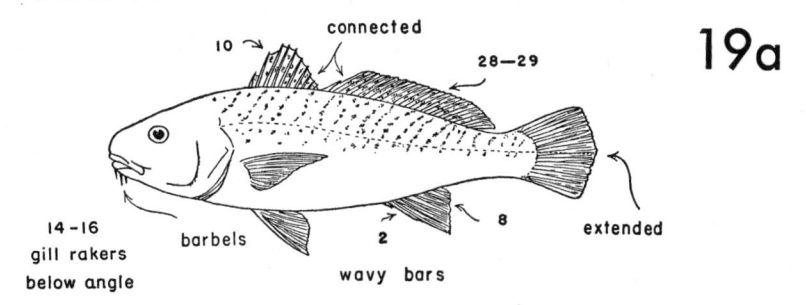

19a

- 10
- connected
- 28–29
- extended
- 14–16 gill rakers below angle
- barbels
- 2
- wavy bars
- 8

YELLOWFIN CROAKER

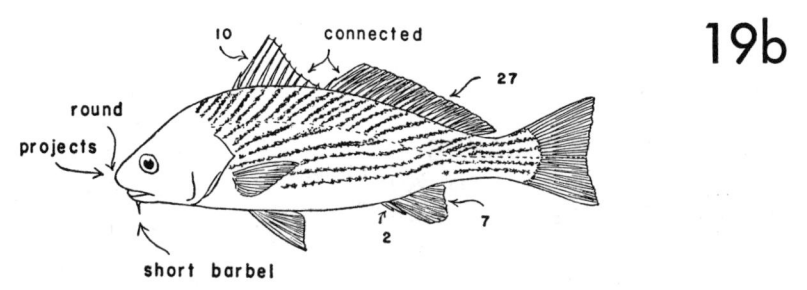

19b

- 10
- connected
- 27
- round
- projects
- short barbel
- 2
- 7

CALIFORNIA KINGFISH

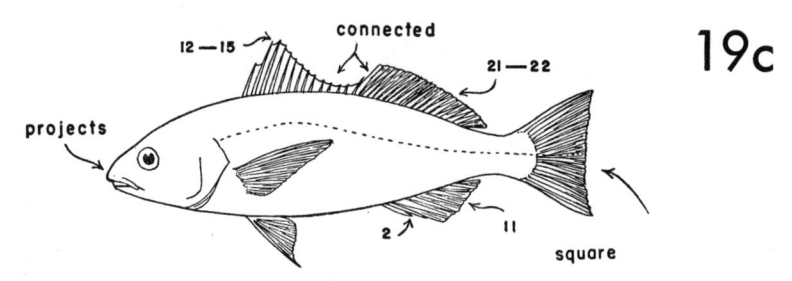

19c

- 12–15
- connected
- 21–22
- projects
- 2
- 11
- square

SPOTFIN CROAKER

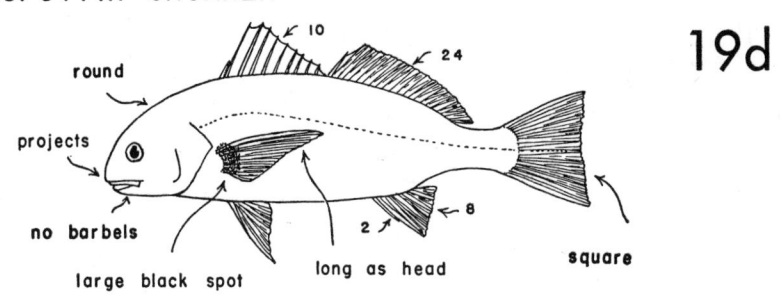

19d

- 10
- 24
- round
- projects
- no barbels
- large black spot
- long as head
- 2
- 8
- square

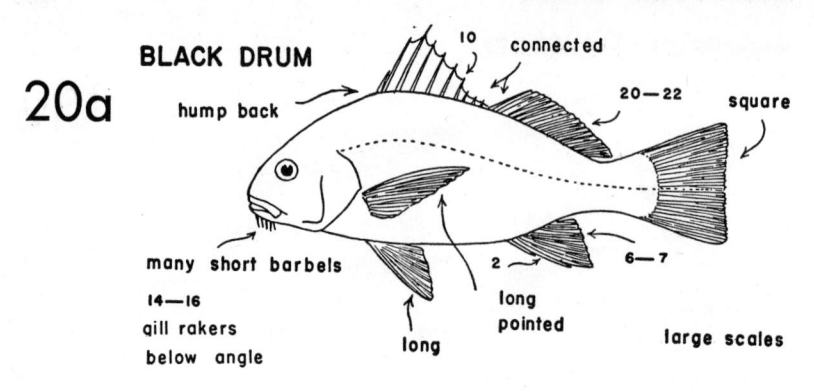

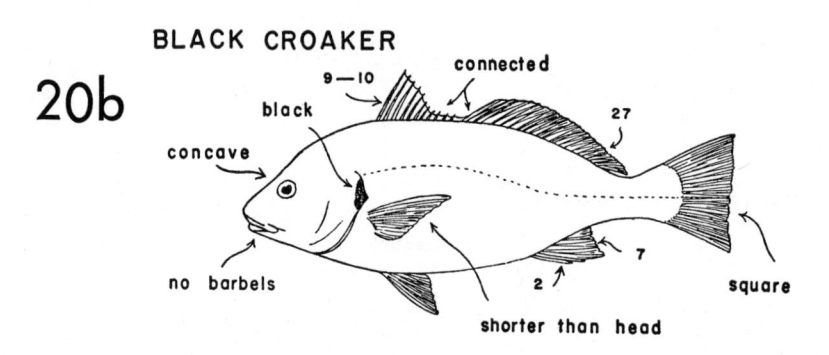

444   IDENTIFICATION CHARTS

20a   **BLACK DRUM**

hump back — 10 — connected — 20—22 — square
many short barbels
14—16 gill rakers below angle
long
2
long pointed
6—7
large scales

20b   **BLACK CROAKER**

9—10 — connected — 27
black
concave
no barbels
2
7
square
shorter than head

20c   **SILVER PERCH**

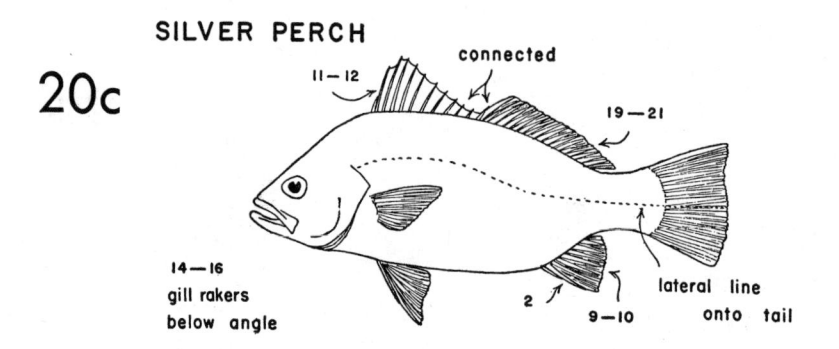

11—12 — connected — 19—21
14—16 gill rakers below angle
2
9—10
lateral line onto tail

IDENTIFICATION CHARTS 445

MANGROVE SNAPPER

21a

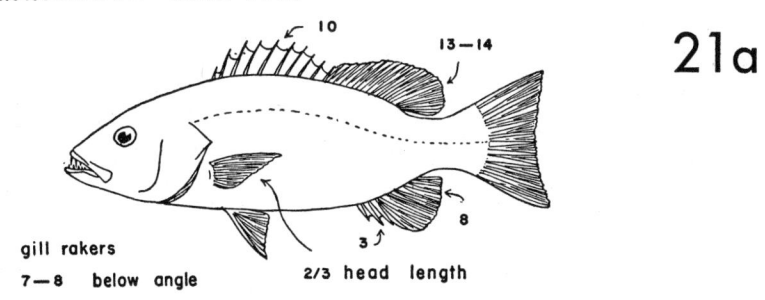

gill rakers
7—8 below angle

2/3 head length

SCHOOLMASTER

21b

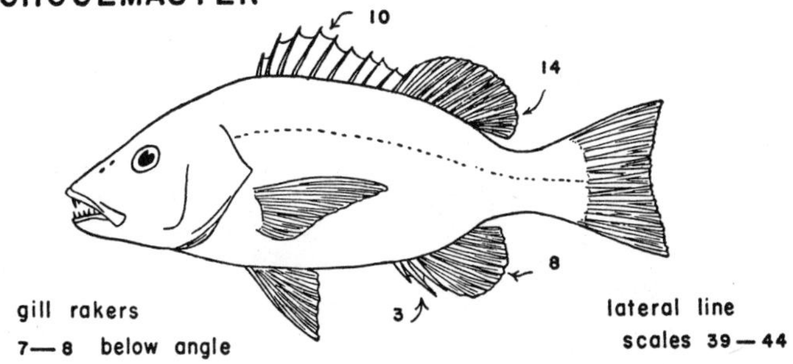

gill rakers
7—8 below angle

lateral line
scales 39—44

DOG SNAPPER

21c

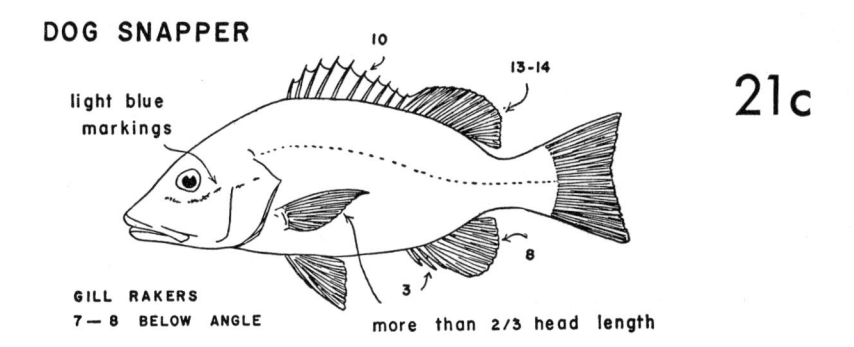

light blue
markings

GILL RAKERS
7—8 BELOW ANGLE

more than 2/3 head length

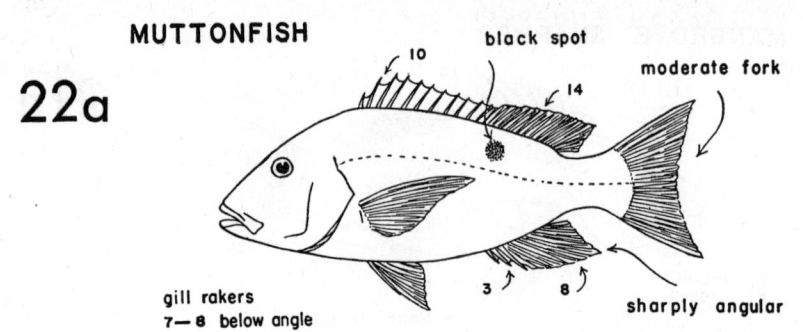

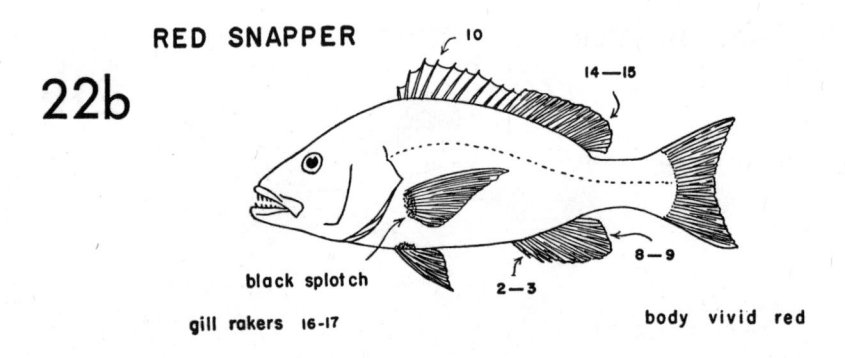

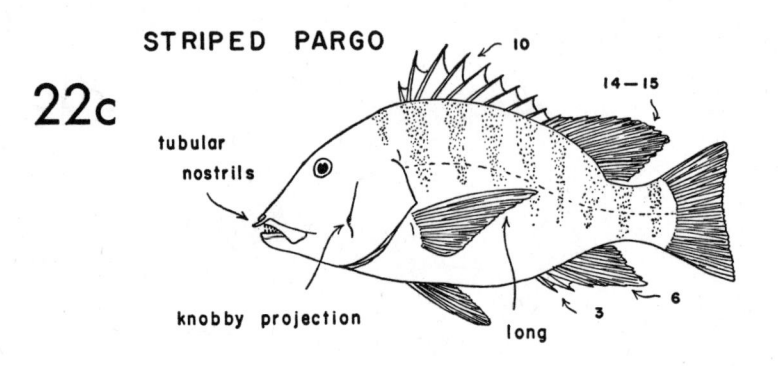

446 IDENTIFICATION CHARTS

22a **MUTTONFISH**

black spot · 10 · 14 · moderate fork · sharply angular · 3 · 8 · gill rakers 7—8 below angle

22b **RED SNAPPER**

10 · 14—15 · black splotch · 2—3 · 8—9 · body vivid red · gill rakers 16-17

22c **STRIPED PARGO**

tubular nostrils · 10 · 14—15 · knobby projection · long · 3 · 6

IDENTIFICATION CHARTS 447

YELLOWTAIL SNAPPER

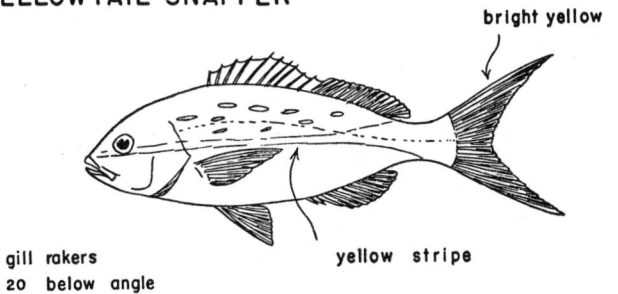

bright yellow

23a

gill rakers
20 below angle

yellow stripe

LANE SNAPPER

black spot
10
12

23b

gill rakers
8—11 below angle

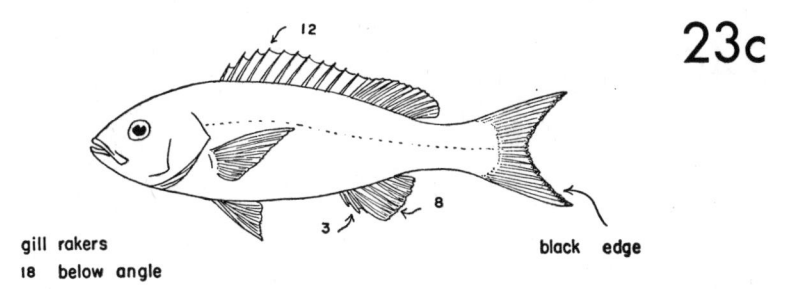

3   8

yellow stripes

VERMILLION SNAPPER

12

23c

gill rakers
18 below angle

3   8

black edge

448　　　　　　　　　　　　　　　　　　IDENTIFICATION CHARTS

24a NORTHERN PORGY

concave

small mouth

deep body

12

12

11-12

long pointed fins
barred or spotted

deeply concave

24b GRASS PORGY

dark bars

large scales

deep

lateral line scales 45-53

24c JOLTHEAD PORGY

small scales

12

10-12

10-11

3

lateral line scales 54-58

24d SAUCEREYE PORGY

back elevated

small scales

12

12

gill rakers below angle 6-7

3

10-11

lateral line scales 54-58

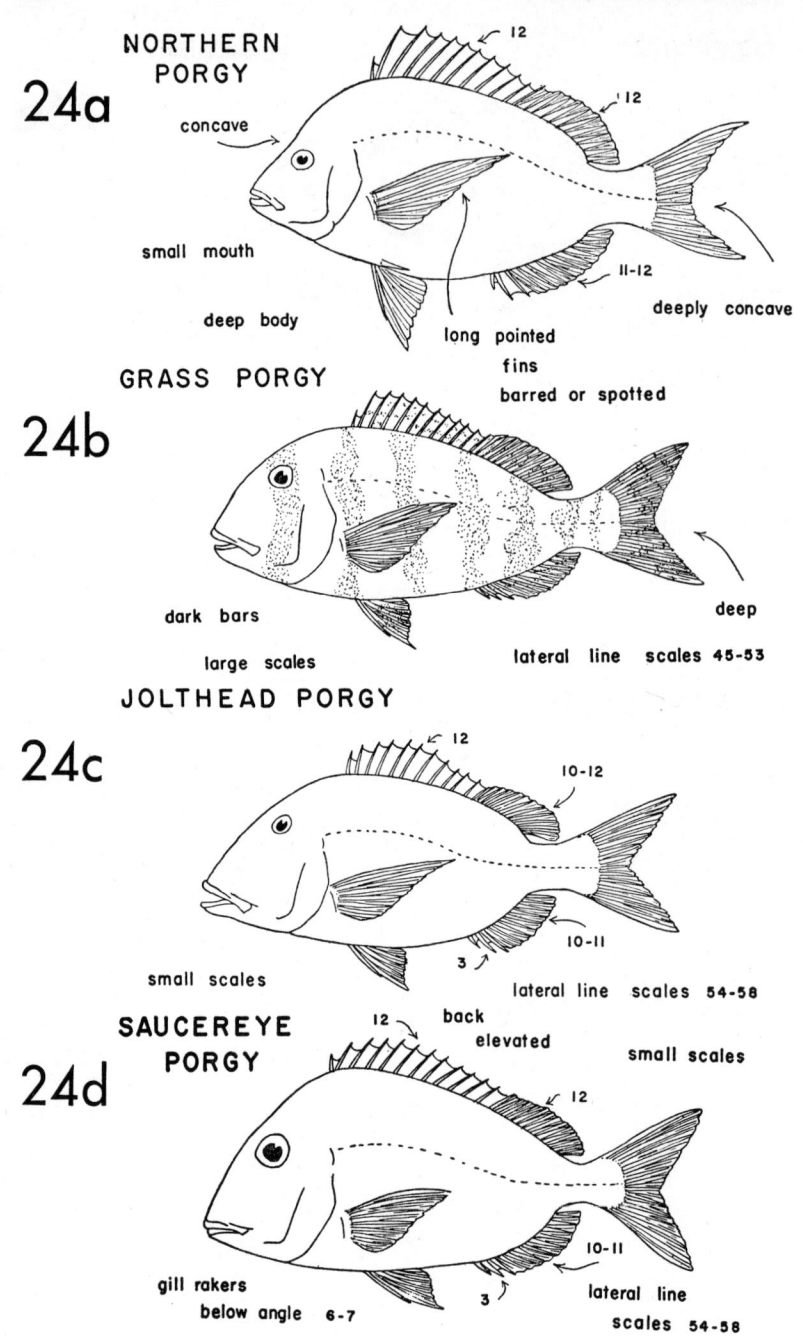

Identification Charts

SHEEPSHEAD

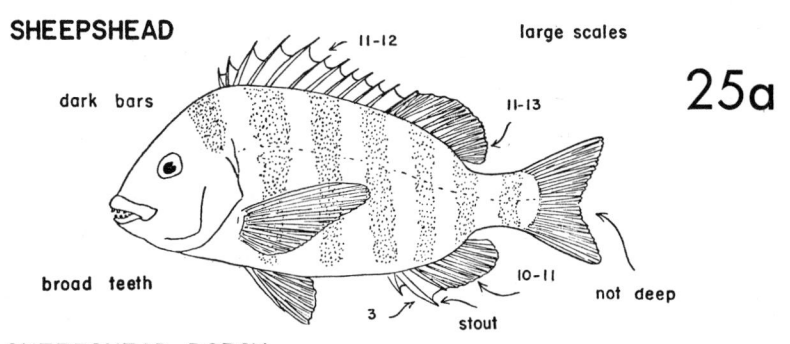

- 11-12
- large scales
- dark bars
- 11-13
- broad teeth
- 3
- stout
- 10-11
- not deep

25a

SHEEPSHEAD PORGY

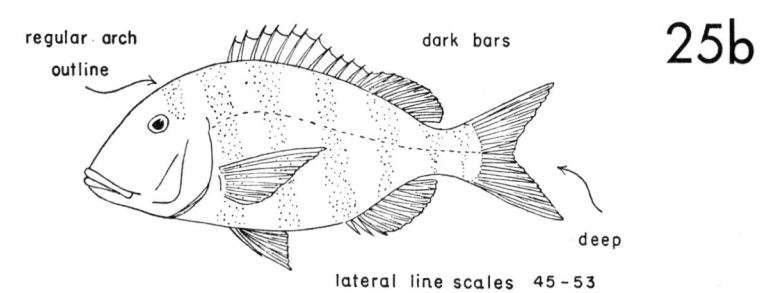

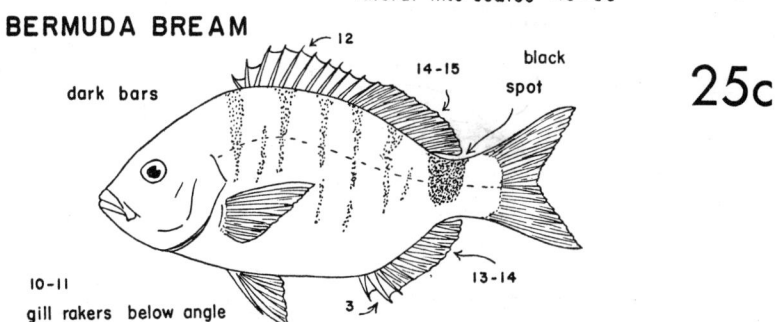

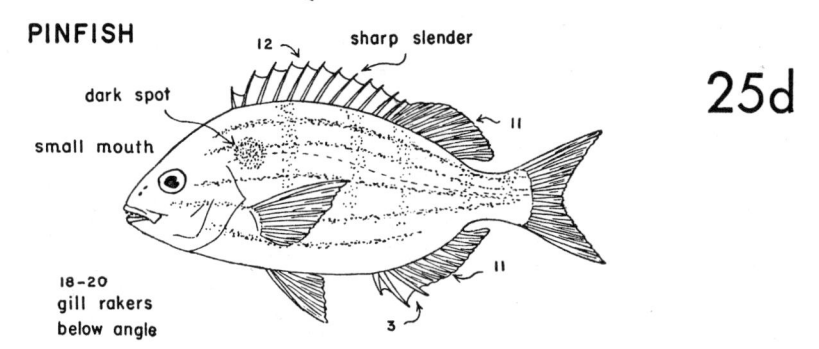

- regular arch outline
- dark bars
- deep
- lateral line scales 45-53

25b

BERMUDA BREAM

- 12
- dark bars
- 14-15
- black spot
- 10-11 gill rakers below angle
- 3
- 13-14

25c

PINFISH

- 12
- sharp slender
- dark spot
- 11
- small mouth
- 18-20 gill rakers below angle
- 3
- 11

25d

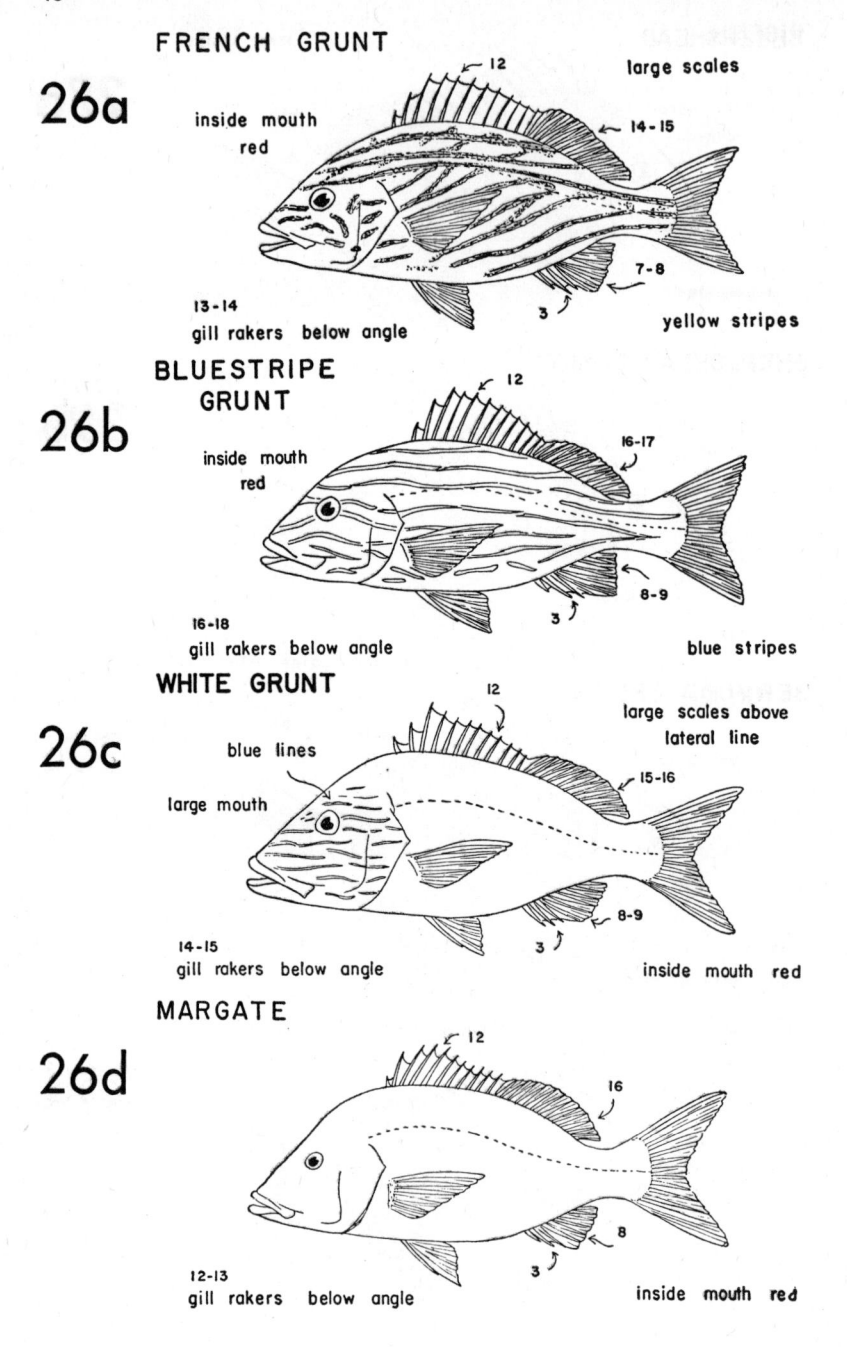

Identification Charts

26a FRENCH GRUNT
- 12
- large scales
- inside mouth red
- 14-15
- 7-8
- 3
- 13-14 gill rakers below angle
- yellow stripes

26b BLUESTRIPE GRUNT
- 12
- inside mouth red
- 16-17
- 8-9
- 3
- 16-18 gill rakers below angle
- blue stripes

26c WHITE GRUNT
- 12
- large scales above lateral line
- blue lines
- 15-16
- large mouth
- 8-9
- 3
- 14-15 gill rakers below angle
- inside mouth red

26d MARGATE
- 12
- 16
- 8
- 3
- 12-13 gill rakers below angle
- inside mouth red

IDENTIFICATION CHARTS 451

PIGFISH 27a

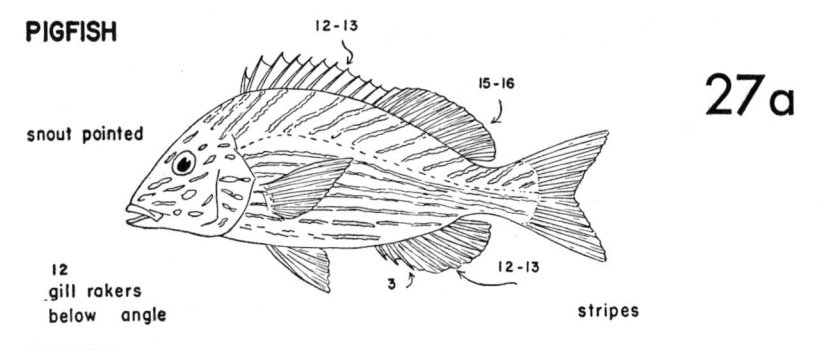

snout pointed
12-13
15-16
12 gill rakers below angle
3
12-13
stripes

RONCO 27b

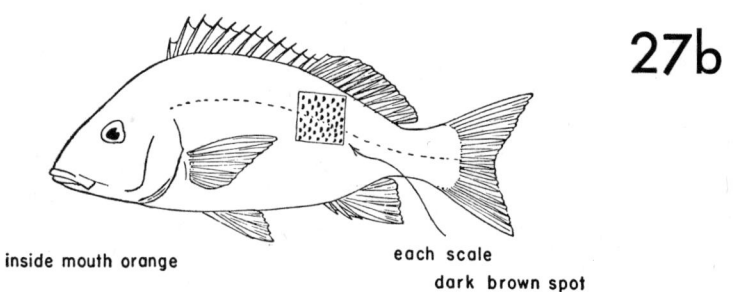

inside mouth orange
each scale dark brown spot

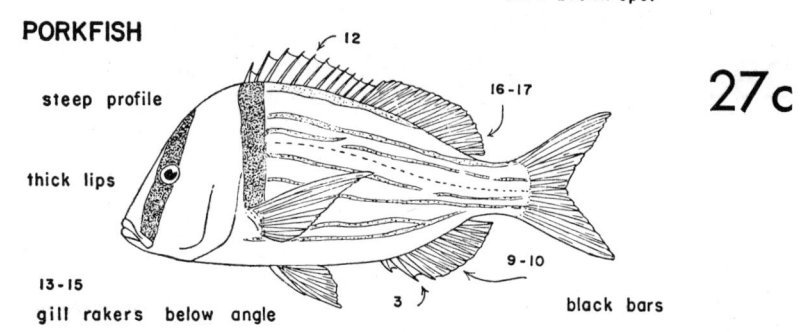

PORKFISH 27c

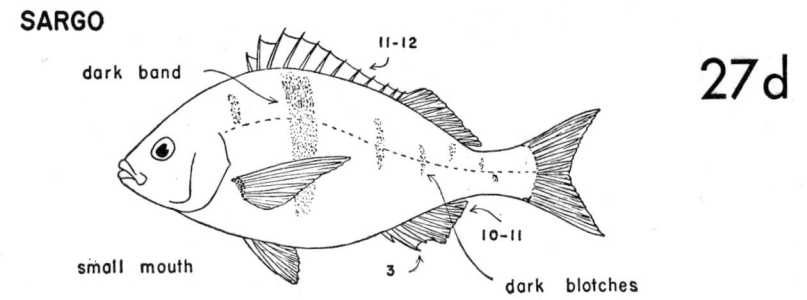

steep profile
thick lips
12
16-17
13-15 gill rakers below angle
3
9-10
black bars

SARGO 27d

dark band
11-12
small mouth
3
10-11
dark blotches

452　　　　　　　　　　　　　　　　Identification Charts

SPOTTED JEWFISH

28a

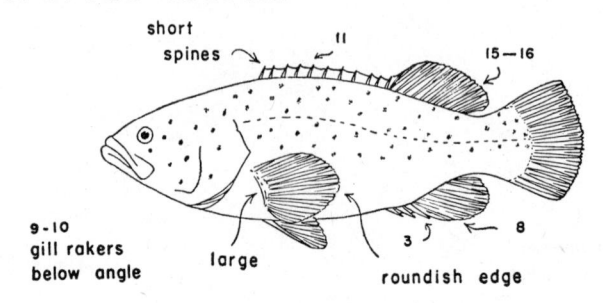

short spines — 11　　15—16

9-10 gill rakers below angle　　large　　roundish edge　　3　　8

GIANT BLACK SEA BASS

28b

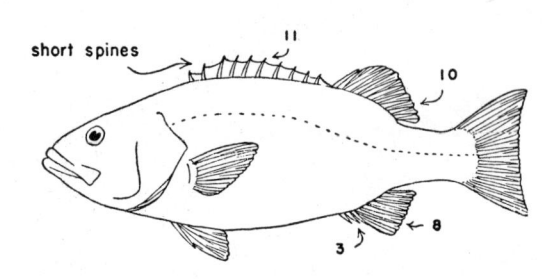

short spines — 11　　10

3　　8

BLACK JEWFISH

28c

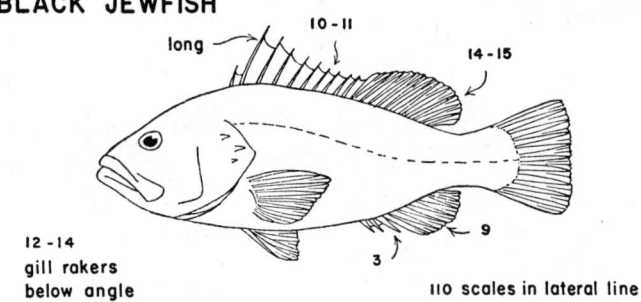

long — 10-11　　14-15

12-14 gill rakers below angle　　3　　9

110 scales in lateral line

GOLDEN GROUPER

28d

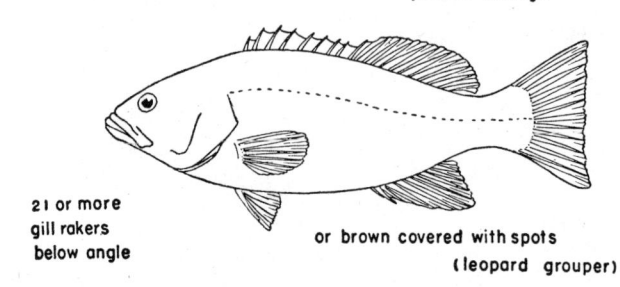

yellow-orange

21 or more gill rakers below angle

or brown covered with spots
(leopard grouper)

Identification Charts

NASSAU GROUPER

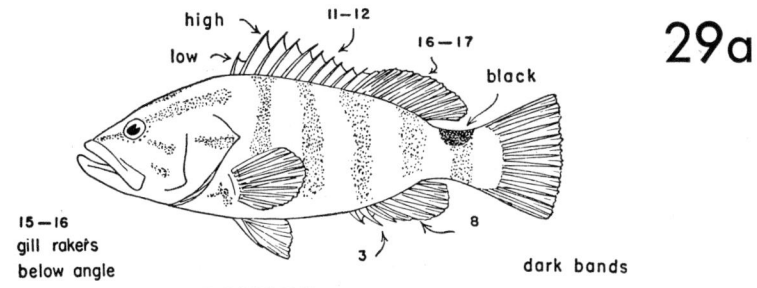

high, low, 11–12, 16–17, black
15–16 gill rakers below angle
3, 8
dark bands

29a

YELLOWFIN GROUPER

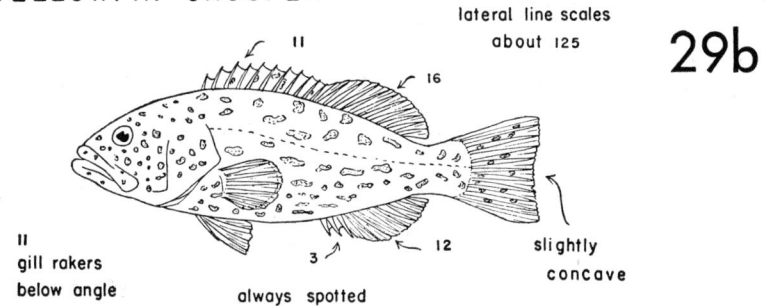

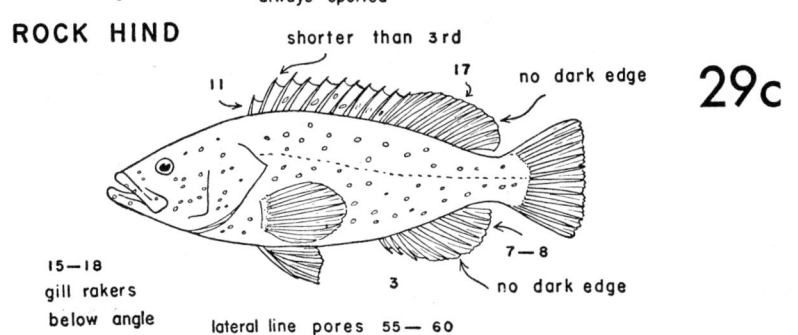

11, 16, lateral line scales about 125
11 gill rakers below angle
3, 12, slightly concave
always spotted

29b

ROCK HIND

shorter than 3rd
11, 17, no dark edge
15–18 gill rakers below angle
3, 7–8, no dark edge
lateral line pores 55–60

29c

GRAYSBY

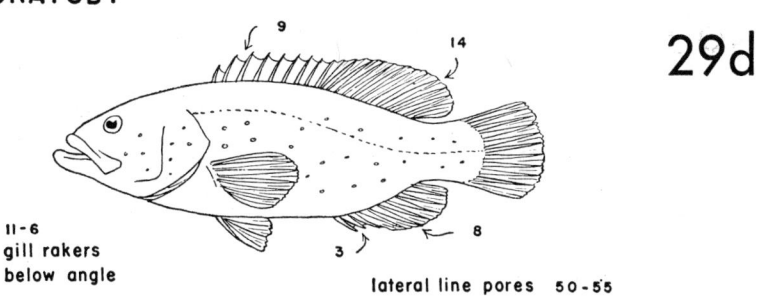

9, 14
11-6 gill rakers below angle
3, 8
lateral line pores 50–55

29d

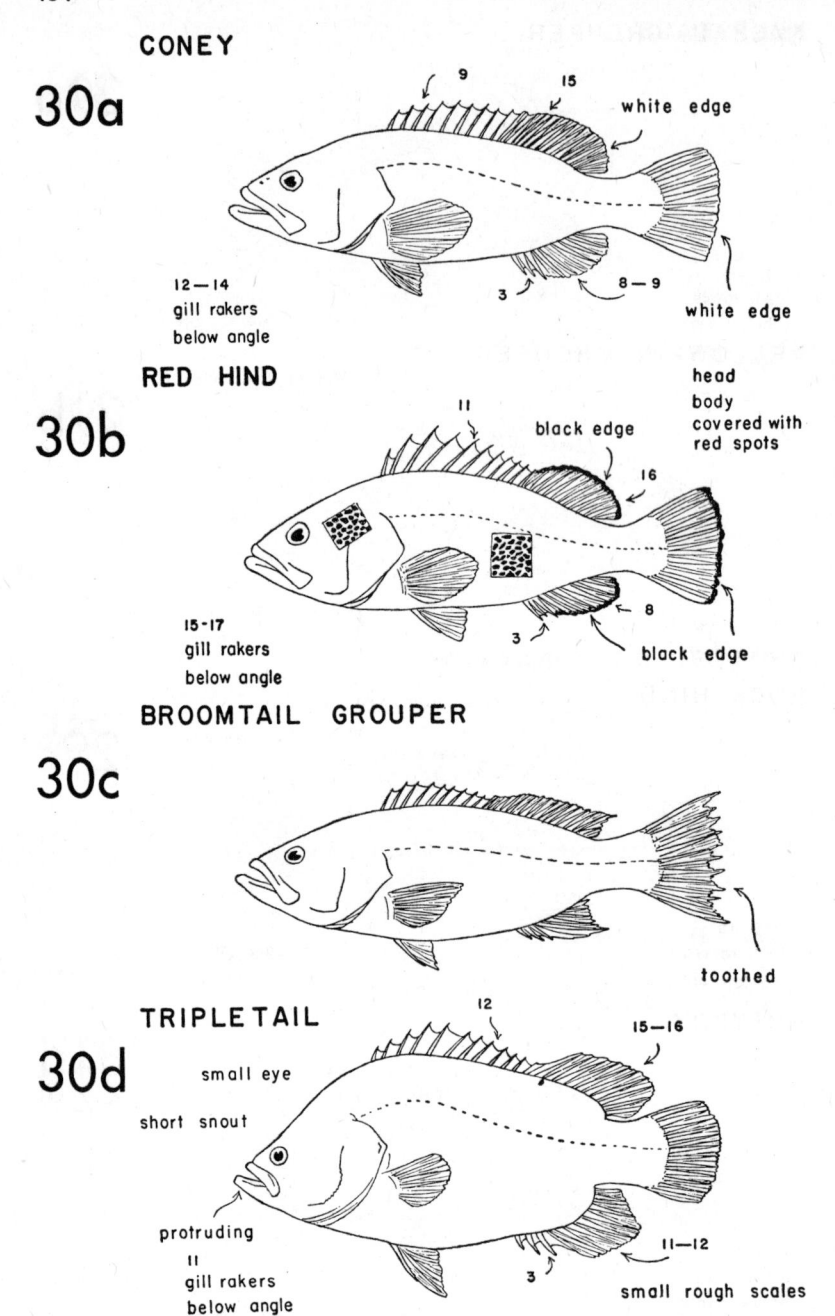

IDENTIFICATION CHARTS

30a CONEY

9, 15, white edge
12—14 gill rakers below angle
3, 8—9, white edge

30b RED HIND

11, black edge
head body covered with red spots
16
15-17 gill rakers below angle
3, 8, black edge

30c BROOMTAIL GROUPER

toothed

30d TRIPLETAIL

12, 15—16
small eye
short snout
protruding
11 gill rakers below angle
3, 11—12, small rough scales

IDENTIFICATION CHARTS

KELP BASS

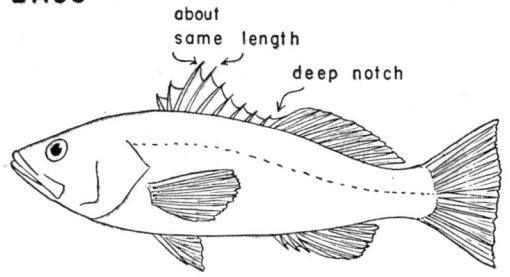

about same length
deep notch

31a

SAND BASS

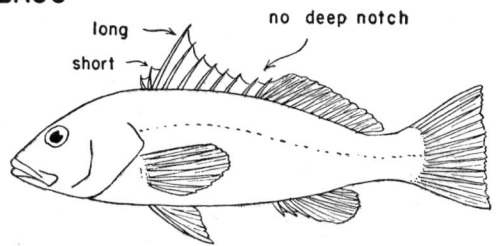

long
short
no deep notch

31b

lateral line scales about 70

SPOTTED ROCK BASS

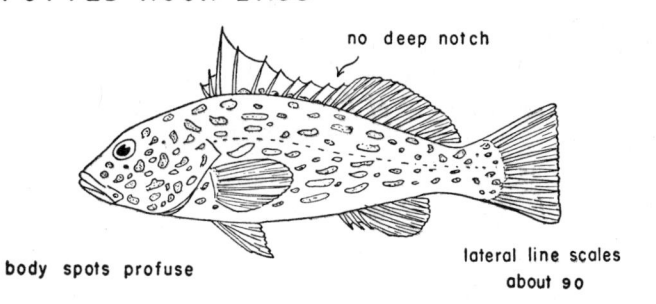

no deep notch

31c

body spots profuse
lateral line scales about 90

ATKA MACKEREL

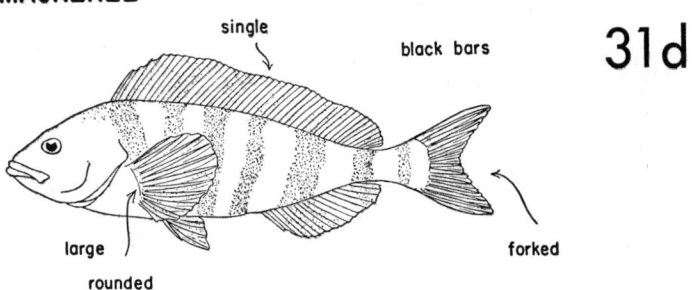

single
black bars

31d

large rounded
forked

32a BLACK ROCKFISH

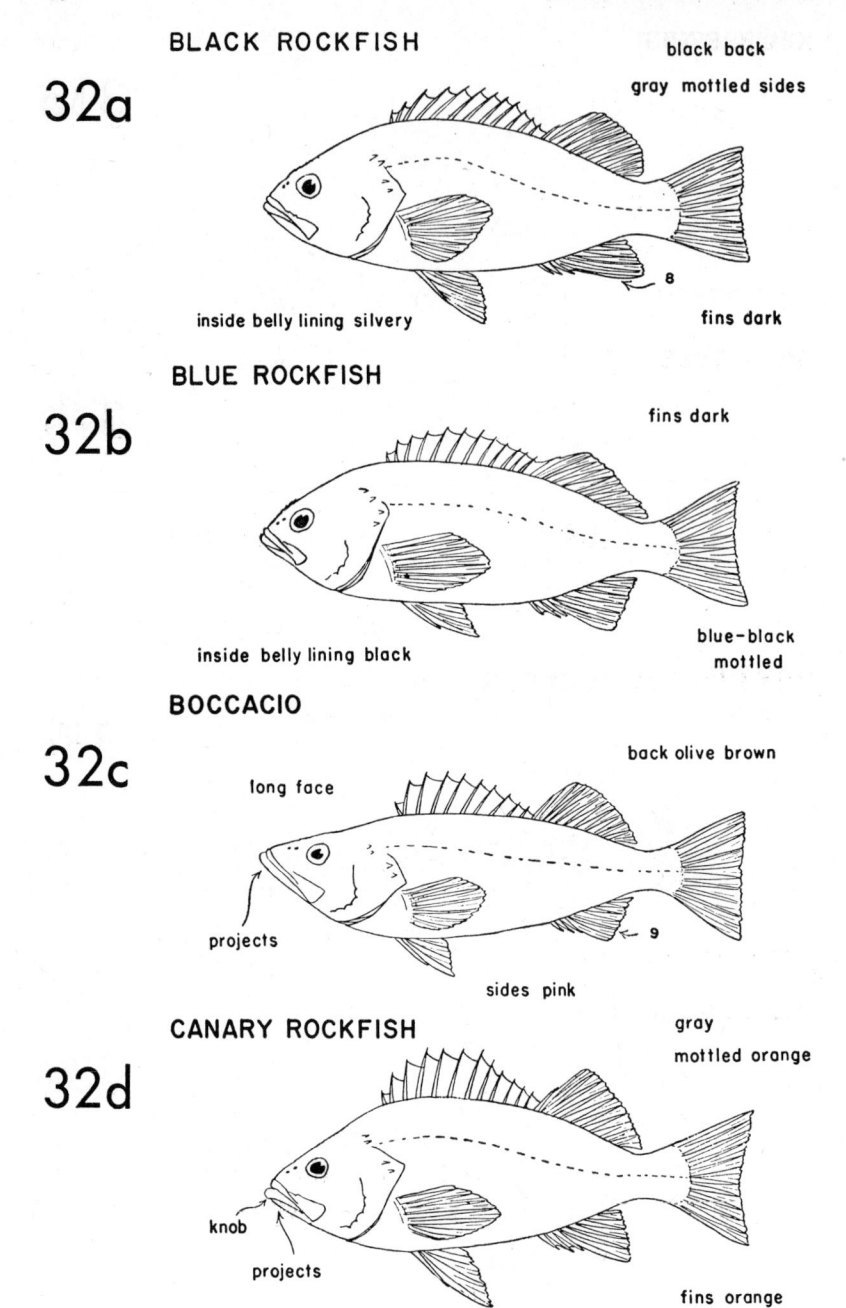

black back
gray mottled sides
inside belly lining silvery
fins dark

32b BLUE ROCKFISH

fins dark
inside belly lining black
blue-black mottled

32c BOCCACIO

long face
back olive brown
projects
sides pink

32d CANARY ROCKFISH

gray mottled orange
knob
projects
fins orange

IDENTIFICATION CHARTS   457

CHILIPEPPER

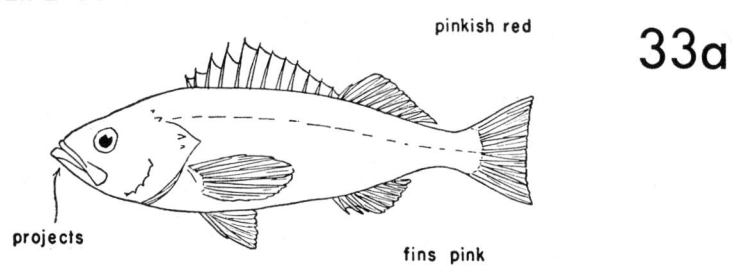

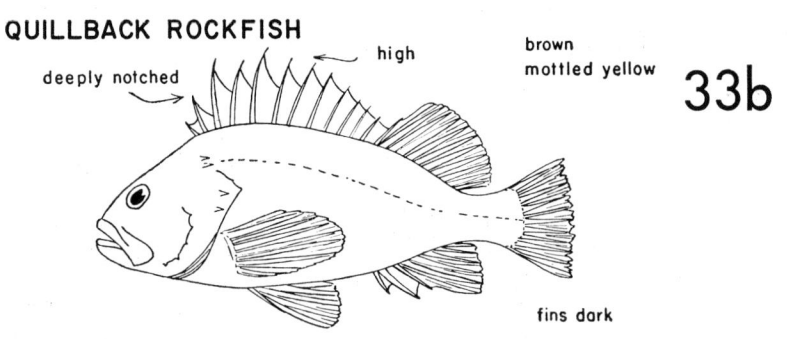

pinkish red

33a

projects

fins pink

QUILLBACK ROCKFISH

high

brown mottled yellow

33b

deeply notched

fins dark

VERMILLION ROCKFISH

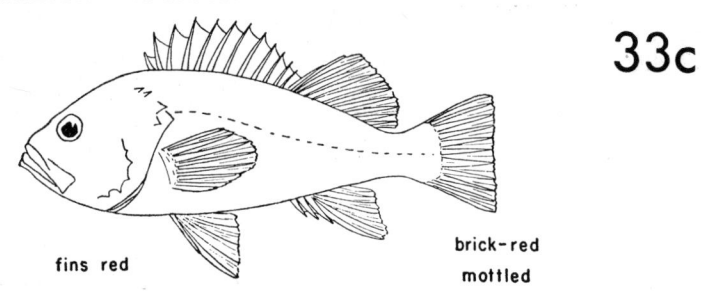

33c

fins red

brick-red mottled

YELLOWTAIL ROCKFISH

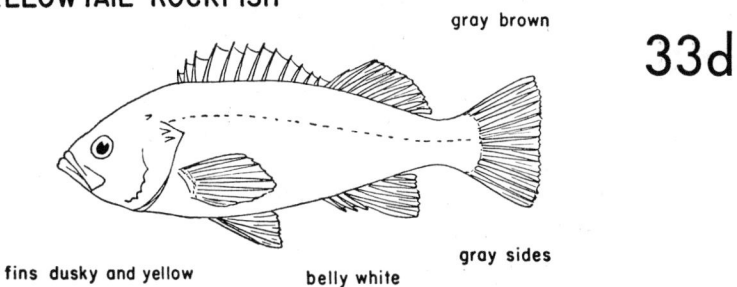

gray brown

33d

fins dusky and yellow   belly white   gray sides

Identification Charts

34a SCULPIN ROCKFISH
12 sharp spines
many spines top of head
red or brown mottled

34b TAUTOG
16-17 connected
10
body mottled
3
7-8
round fins

34c HOGFISH
long spines
13-14
11
deep body
3
10
extended fins

34d
short 11-12 black
steep
male
black red 3

CALIFORNIA SHEEPSHEAD
female

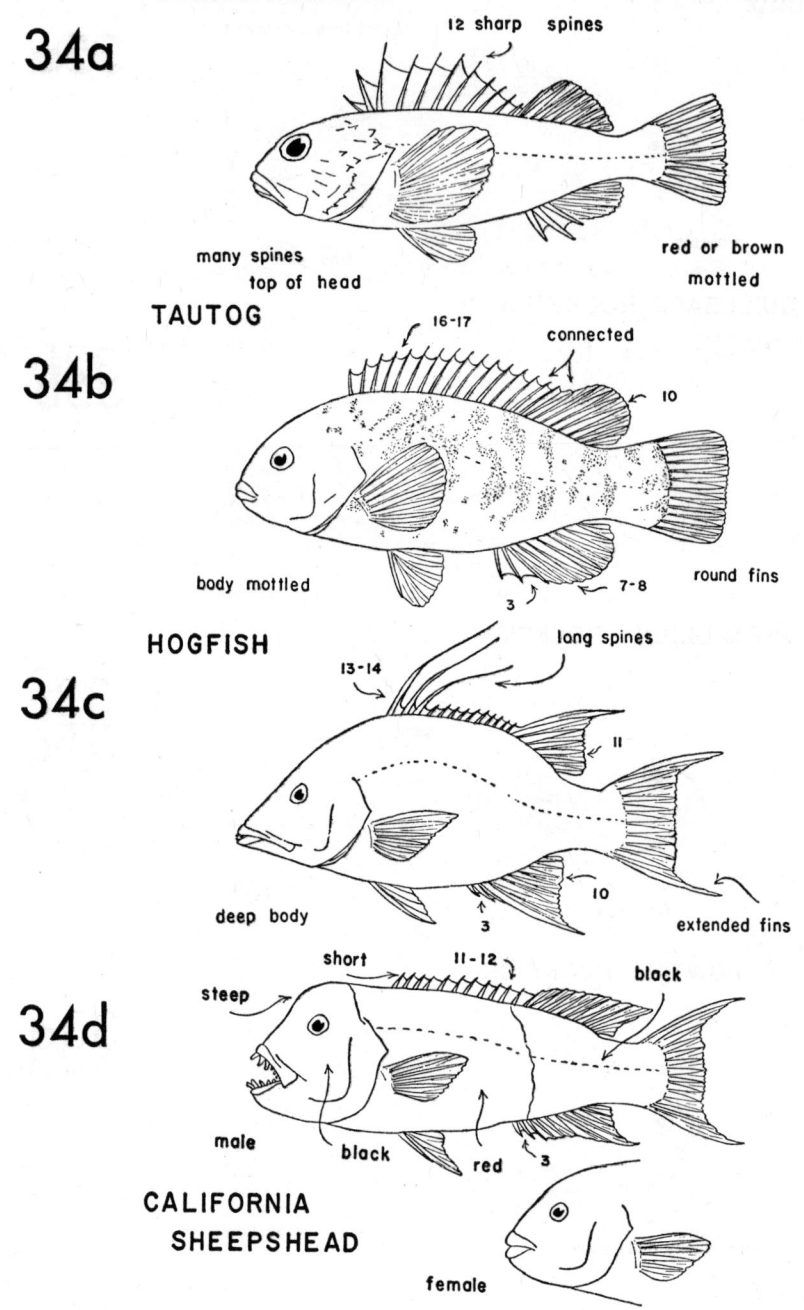

IDENTIFICATION CHARTS   459

COD

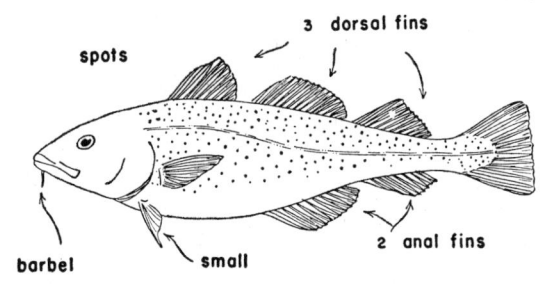

spots — 3 dorsal fins

barbel — small — 2 anal fins

35a

TOMCOD

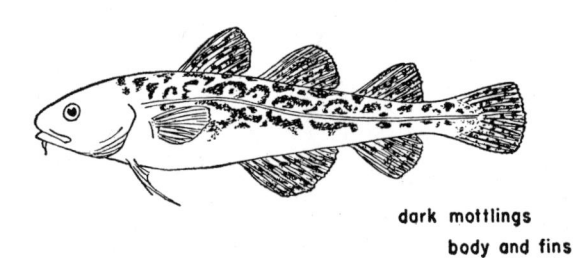

dark mottlings body and fins

35b

HADDOCK

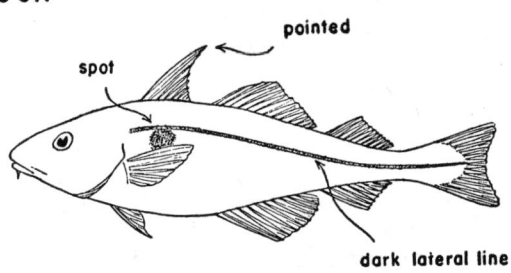

spot — pointed

dark lateral line

35c

POLLOCK

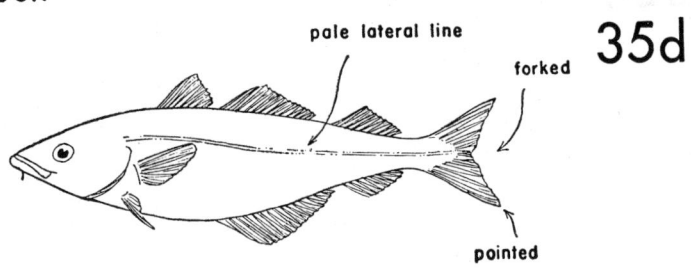

pale lateral line — forked

pointed

35d

Identification Charts

36a BARRED SEAPERCH
bars and spots — appears divided

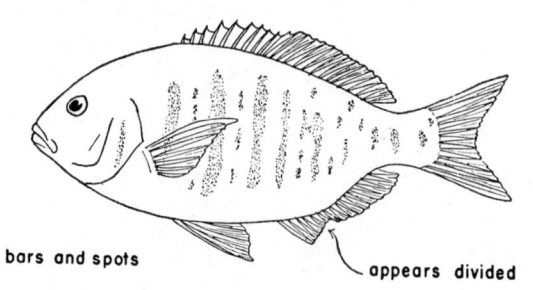

36b BLACK SEAPERCH
short — thick reddish lips — enlarged scales

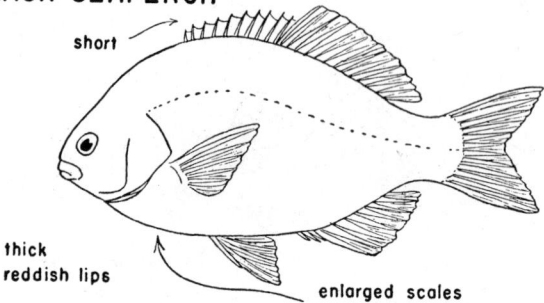

36c PILE SEAPERCH
elevated — deep fork

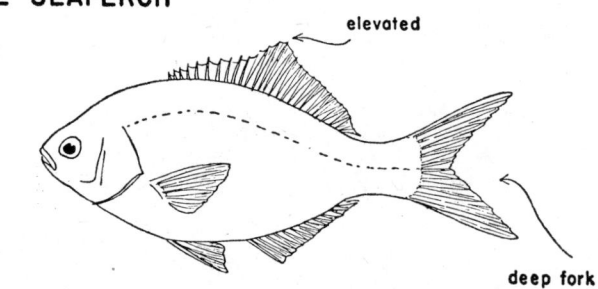

36d RAINBOW SEAPERCH
dark blotch — stripes — long abdomen — dark blotch — moderate fork

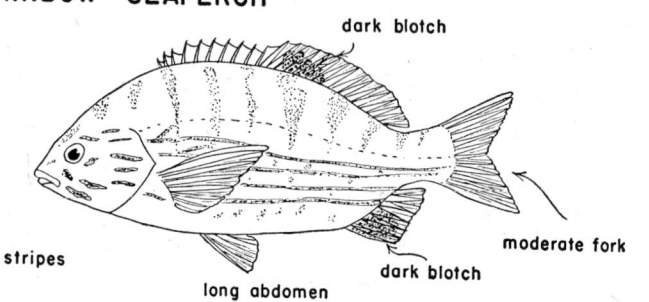

Identification Charts

RUBBERLIP SEAPERCH

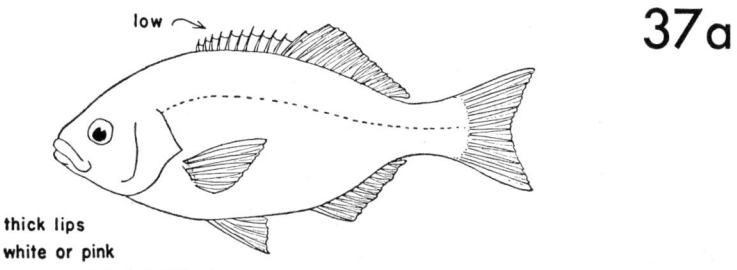

low

thick lips
white or pink

37a

STRIPED SEAPERCH

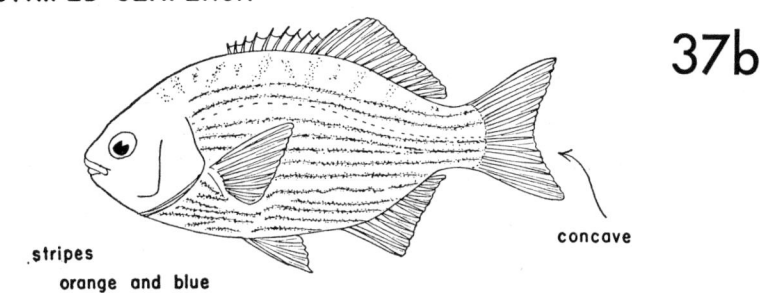

stripes
orange and blue

concave

37b

WHITE SEAPERCH

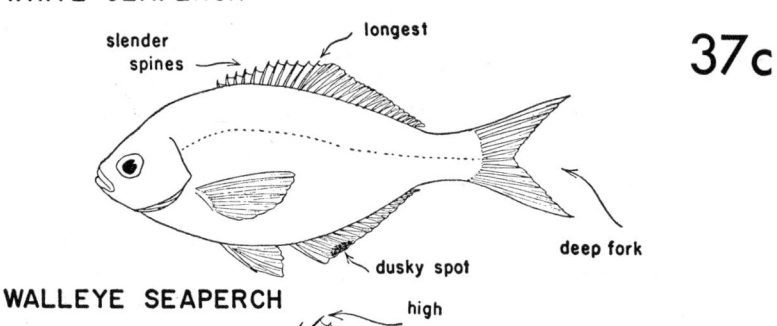

slender spines

longest

dusky spot

deep fork

37c

WALLEYE SEAPERCH

large eye

high

black

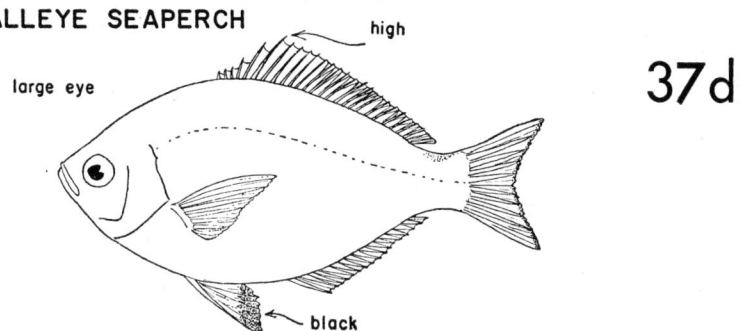

37d

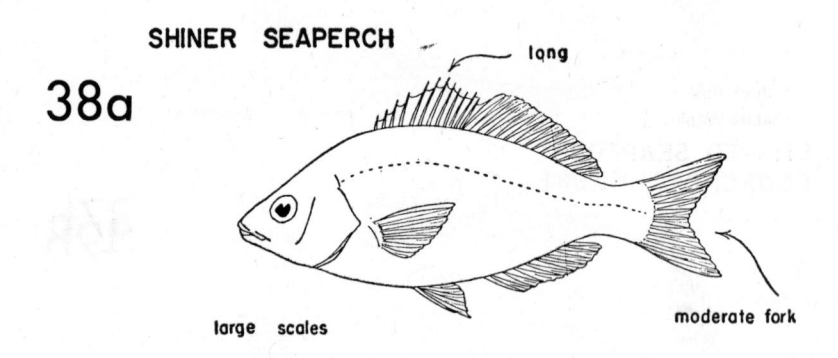

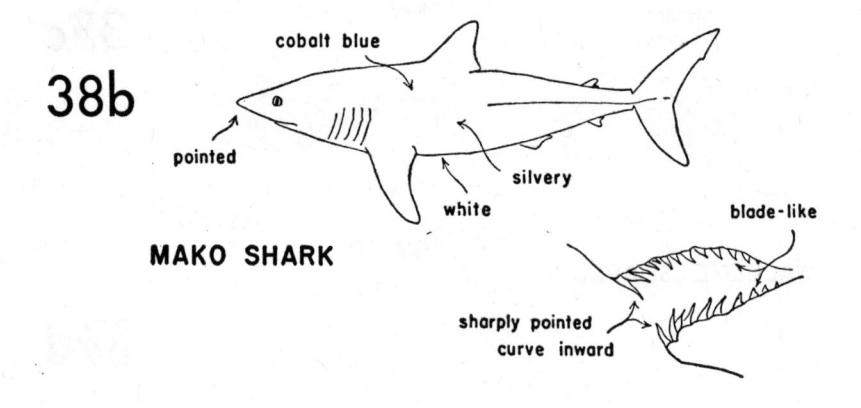

Identification Charts

38a SHINER SEAPERCH

- long
- large scales
- moderate fork

38b MAKO SHARK

- cobalt blue
- pointed
- silvery
- white
- blade-like
- sharply pointed curve inward

Identification Charts

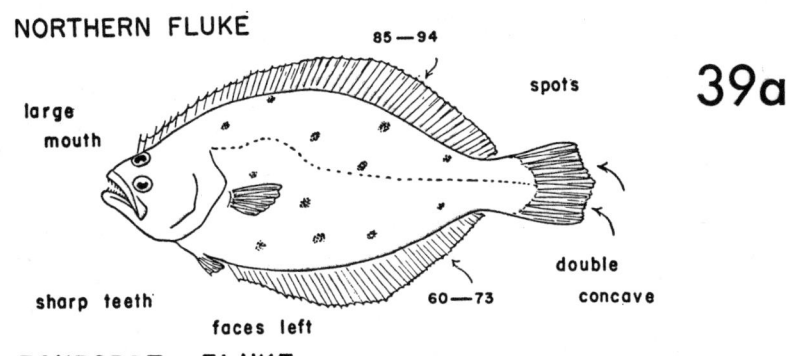

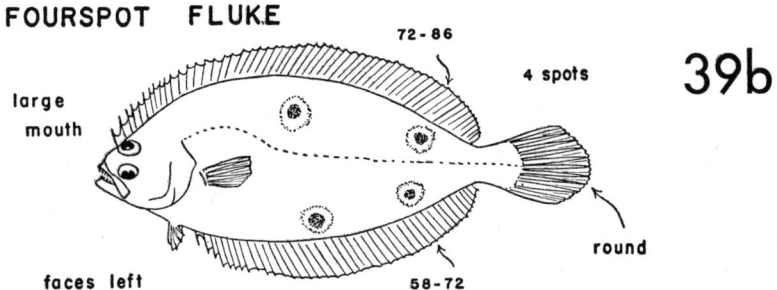

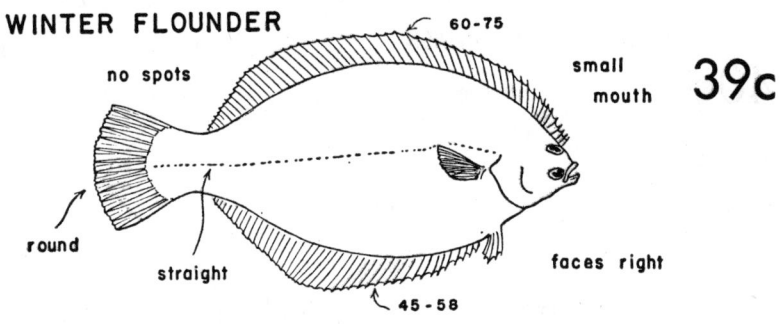

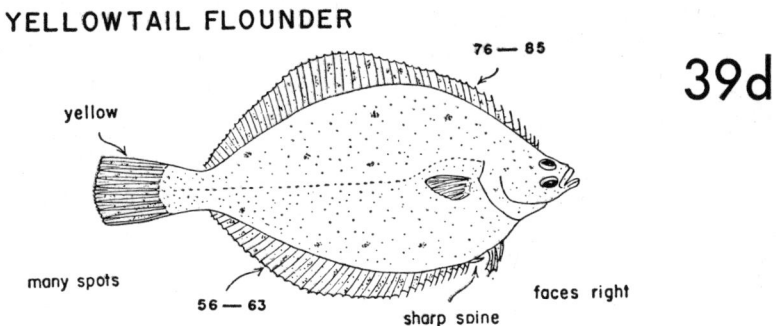

NORTHERN FLUKE

large mouth · 85—94 · spots · 39a
sharp teeth · faces left · 60—73 · double concave

FOURSPOT FLUKE

large mouth · 72-86 · 4 spots · 39b
faces left · 58-72 · round

WINTER FLOUNDER

no spots · 60-75 · small mouth · 39c
round · straight · 45-58 · faces right

YELLOWTAIL FLOUNDER

yellow · 76—85 · 39d
many spots · 56—63 · sharp spine · faces right

IDENTIFICATION CHARTS

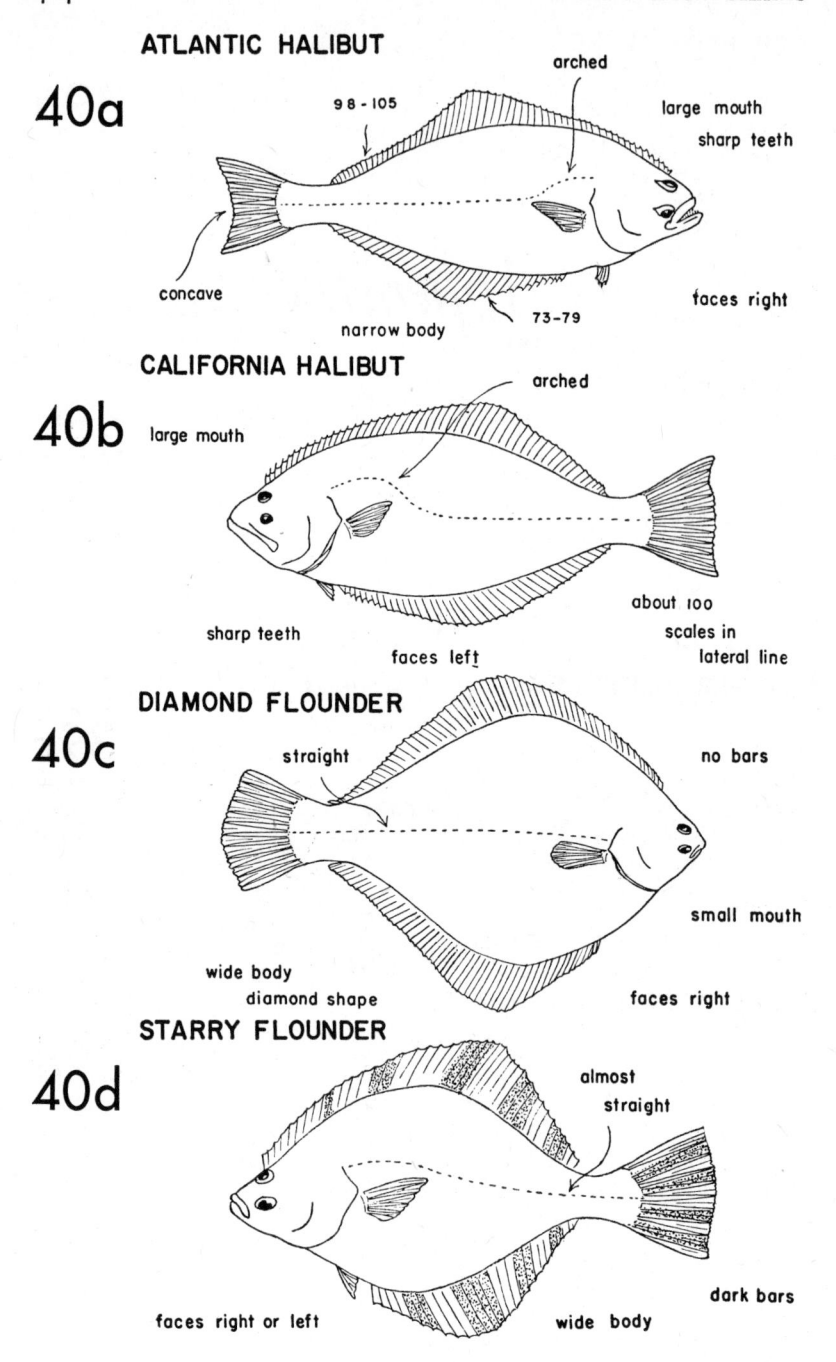

40a ATLANTIC HALIBUT
- 98-105
- arched
- large mouth
- sharp teeth
- concave
- narrow body
- 73-79
- faces right

40b CALIFORNIA HALIBUT
- large mouth
- arched
- sharp teeth
- faces left
- about 100 scales in lateral line

40c DIAMOND FLOUNDER
- straight
- no bars
- small mouth
- wide body
- diamond shape
- faces right

40d STARRY FLOUNDER
- almost straight
- dark bars
- faces right or left
- wide body

Appendix

THE INTERNATIONAL GAME FISH ASSOCIATION

Every fisherman has an interest in weight records of fishes, especially the largest of each kind caught on rod and reel. Therefore, I recommend that anglers who are not familiar with the International Game Fish Association make acquaintance with it, for this organization is the official keeper of world records.

The idea of documenting the weights and measurements of the largest fishes caught on rod and reel was fostered by Van Campen Heilner, one of the pioneers in the development of sport fishing in salt water. It was during a warm, lazy weekend of fishing with Van in Long Island waters when he told me some of the interesting history of keeping world records of fishes.

Van became interested in the maximum weights of game fishes in the early 1920's and began to gather information from fishing clubs, individuals, and records of fishing contests. After much research he compiled a list which thereafter was published annually with new records added. For ten years the list was accepted as "official." However, as salt water sport fishing developed, more and more records were received, and the task became too great for one person to handle. Then he solicited the help of John Nichols and Francesca LaMonte of the American Museum of Natural History in New York City. Because of the great interest shown by anglers, the International Game Fish Association was formed in 1939 with headquarters at the museum, and the compiling of salt water records was transferred to that organization. Since its inception, from an inauspicious beginning, the I.G.F.A. has developed world-wide recognition as the clearing house for all matters pertaining to marine angling statistics. There is a flow of information coming into the offices of the I.G.F.A. which has proved to be of great value not only to sportsmen, but also to scientists involved in the study of fishes and other marine life.

Annually the I.G.F.A. publishes "World Record Marine Game Fishes," a list which includes weight, length, and girth of each fish, the names of the lucky anglers, dates and places of capture. Records for seven different line tests make up the classes. These categories are based on the breaking strain of lines, as follows: all tackle, 130 lb., 80 lb., 50 lb., 30 lb., 20 lb., and 12 lb.

The chart may be obtained by writing to the Secretary of the I.G.F.A. at the American Museum of Natural History, New York 24, New York. The particular game fishes which make up the chart attended to by the I.G.F.A. are listed below (as they appear in the chart). I have included only the "all tackle record" weights and the dates of capture. This list will serve to give an angler some idea as to whether or not his catch might merit further inquiry.

INTERNATIONAL GAME FISH ASSOCIATION
WORLD RECORD
MARINE GAME FISHES

Fish	Scientific Name	Weight	Date
Albacore	*Thunnus germo*	69 lbs.	April 7, 1956
Amberjack	*Seriola lalandi*	120 lbs., 8 oz.	Oct. 25, 1955
Barracuda	*Sphyraena barracuda*	103¾ lbs.	1932
Calif. Black Sea Bass	*Stereolepis gigas*	514 lbs.	Aug. 29, 1955
Calif. White Sea Bass	*Cynoscion nobilis*	83 lbs., 12 oz.	March 31, 1953
Channel Bass	*Sciaenops ocellatus*	83 lbs.	Aug. 5, 1949
Giant Sea Bass	*Promicrops itaiara*	551 lbs.	June 29, 1937
Sea Bass	*Centropristes striatus*	8 lbs.	May 13, 1951
Striped Bass	*Roccus saxatilis*	73 lbs.	Aug. 17, 1913
Blackfish or Tautog	*Tautoga onitis*	21 lbs., 6 oz.	June 12, 1954
Bluefish	*Pomatomus saltatrix*	24 lbs., 3 oz.	Aug. 27, 1953
Bonefish	*Albula vulpes*	18 lbs., 2 oz.	Oct. 14, 1954
Oceanic Bonito	*Katsuwonus pelamis*	39 lbs., 15 oz.	Jan. 21, 1952
Cobia	*Rachycentron canadus*	102 lbs.	July 3, 1938

Appendix

Fish	Scientific Name	Weight	Date
Cod	Gadus callarias	57 lbs., 8 oz.	Dec. 24, 1949
Dolphin	Coryphaena hippurus	75½ lbs.	Dec. 10, 1950
Black Drum	Pogonias cromis	92 lbs.	Aug. 27, 1955
Summer Flounder	Paralichthys dentatus	20 lbs., 7 oz.	July 8, 1957
Kingfish	Scomberomorus cavalla	76½ lbs.	May 22, 1952
Blue Marlin	Makaira ampla	756 lbs.	April 19, 1956
Pacific Black Marlin	Makaira mazara	1560 lbs.	Aug. 4, 1953
Silver Marlin	Makaira mazara tahitiensis	755 lbs.	Nov. 21, 1953
Striped Marlin	Makaira mitsukurii	692 lbs.	Aug. 18, 1931
White Marlin	Makaira albida	161 lbs.	Mar. 20, 1938
Permit	Trachinotus goodei	42 lbs., 4 oz.	Sept. 11, 1953
Pollack	Pollachius virens	33 lbs., 8 oz.	June 28, 1956
Roosterfish	Nematistius pectoralis	100 lbs.	Jan. 12, 1954
Atlantic Sailfish	Istiophorus americanus	123 lbs.	April 25, 1950
Pacific Sailfish	Istiophorus greyi	221 lbs.	Feb. 12, 1947
Sawfish	Pristis pectinatus	736 lbs.	Sept. 4, 1938
Mako Shark	Isurus oxyrhynchus Isurus glaucus	1000 lbs.	Mar. 14, 1943
Man-Eater or White Shark	Carcharodon carcharias	2536 lbs.	April 11, 1955
Porbeagle Shark	Lamna nasus	68¾ lbs.	Feb. 5, 1949
Thresher Shark	Alopias vulpinus	922 lbs.	Mar. 21, 1937
Tiger Shark	Galeocerdo cuvier	1382 lbs.	Feb. 22, 1939
Snook or Robalo	Centropomus undecimalis	50½ lbs.	Jan. 2, 1944
Swordfish	Xiphias gladius	1182 lbs.	May 7, 1953
Tarpon	Tarpon atlanticus	283 lbs.	Mar. 19, 1956
Allison or Yellowfin Tuna	Thunnus albacares	265 lbs.	July 31, 1937
Atlantic Big-Eyed Tuna	Thunnus obesus	209 lbs., 6 oz.	Sept. 24, 1954
Pacific Big-Eyed Tuna	Thunnus sibi	400 lbs.	Jan. 6, 1956
Blackfin Tuna	Thunnus atlanticus	25 lbs., 12 oz.	Oct. 4, 1956
Bluefin Tuna	Thunnus thynnus	977 lbs.	Sept. 4, 1950
Wahoo	Acanthocybium solandri	136 lbs.	April 8, 1955
Weakfish	Cynoscion regalis	17 lbs., 8 oz.	Sept. 30, 1944
Spotted Weakfish	Cynoscion nebulosus	15 lbs., 3 oz.	Jan. 13, 1949
Yellowtail	Seriola dorsalis or Seriola grandis	105 lbs., 12½ oz.	April 30, 1955

Appendix

Cable Address: "Museology New York"

INTERNATIONAL GAME FISH ASSOCIATION
The American Museum of Natural History, New York 24, N. Y.

FORM FOR RECORDING RECORD GAME FISH CATCHES

Must be signed by the angler before a notary and accompanied by a clear photograph showing full length of specimen. In case of sharks, photograph must show teeth and open jaws.

SPECIES.................................... WEIGHT......................................

LENGTH..........................

GIRTH...................................(At thickest part of body, usually at shoulder.)

DATE CAUGHT.......................TIME REQUIRED...............................

WHERE CAUGHT.................................,..................................

NAME OF ANGLER (Print)..

PERMANENT ADDRESS: (Street) ....

                 (City) ....

                 (State or Country)..

If a member of an angling club, give club's name:..

....

TACKLE USED (Every item must be filled in by the angler)

Make of rod.......................................Tip weight...........................

                                            Tip length............................

Make of reel......................................Butt length..........,..............

Make of line....................... Size...........Type of gaff..........................

Length of trace or leader.................

Number of hooks......................

Lure or bait used......................   **Sample of actual line used must be attached to this claim.**

Method of catch (trolling, casting, etc.).............

When completely filled out, mail by quickest means to address at top of this blank.

Appendix

Name of Boatman or Guide...................................Boat....................

Signature of Boat Captain, Boatman or Guide...............................

Address ....

....

Name of Weighmaster...

Address ....

....

Signature of Weighmaster.. ....

Location of Scales...

If verified by club, give name and location:..................................

Witness (preferably club officer or member of International Committee, IGFA)...............

....

Address ....

....

AFFIDAVIT OF ANGLER

I, the undersigned make oath and say that the above named fish was brought to gaff by me without assistance and that the above information and statements are true.

SIGNATURE OF ANGLER..

Sworn to before me this...................day of...................., 19....

Notary signature..............................

....

SEAL

I have included the I.G.F.A. Rules and a sample of the "Form for Recording Record Fish Catches" for two reasons. First, it will acquaint anglers with the type of information that should be secured as soon as possible after capture of the fish. Secondly, all tournaments and fishing matches use the I.G.F.A. tackle rules; therefore, the reproduction of these regulations will serve a practical purpose.

RULES

(By-Laws and complete Rules are printed in the Rule Book of the IGFA)

ALL CLAIMS MUST BE ACCOMPANIED BY A TEN YARD SAMPLE OF THE ACTUAL LINE USED IN MAKING THE CATCH. If a double line was used, five yards from the double line must be included with five yards of the line next it. If less than five yards was doubled, the entire double line must be included in the ten yards. The sample must be in one piece. In light tackle claims, the entire double line taken from the end of the knot must be submitted.

Records are based on the wet testing strength of the line, whether linen or synthetic. NO CLAIMS WILL BE ACCEPTED WITHOUT LINE SAMPLE.

Claims must be filed on the IGFA form. These may be obtained from headquarters, International Committee members or Member Clubs.

Whenever possible, photographs should accompany the claims. Claims for the following fishes MUST be accompanied by a photograph: Sharks, Channel Bass, Drums, Tunas, Bonitos, Kingfish, Marlins, Permits, Jacks, Yellowtails.

TIME LIMIT: Claims for fish caught in North American waters will not be accepted by the IGFA if the date of the catch is more than 60 days before the date of receipt of claim by the IGFA; in other waters the time limit is three months.

TACKLE RULES

1. Records are based on the wet tensile strength of the line used, whether linen or synthetic. Testing is done by a professional testing company.
2. The leader and the double line on all weights of tackle up to and including the 50-pound line test class, shall be limited to 15 feet of double line and 15 feet of leader. For heavier tackle, the line shall not be doubled at the trace end for more than 30 feet and the trace shall not exceed 30 feet. (*This rule is pending vote on revision.*)
3. Rods must be in accordance with sporting ethics and customs. Rods giving the angler an unsporting advantage will be disqualified. Tubular metal and all glass rods are permitted.
4. No more than two single hooks may be attached to the leader or trace at any one time. These must be attached separately at least a shank's length apart, and must be imbedded in or attached to the bait. The dangling or swinging hook is prohibited.

    A bottom rig of two hooks on two leaders one set for the bottom, the other some two or three feet above it is permitted as long as the upper hook is far enough above the bottom to remain free and clear of fish taken on the bottom; the set must be such that a fish on one hook cannot be fouled by the other.

Appendix

5. Plugs are permitted only if they comply with the above rules.
6. The use of any float is prohibited other than a small balloon, bladder, or cork which may be attached to the line or leader for the sole purpose of regulating the depth of the bait or for drifting of the bait.
7. A detachable gaff not exceeding 8 feet in length may be used for boating a fish, but the length of rope or wire attached to the head of same must not exceed thirty feet and the prong or blade must be fixed and single.
8. The angler must hook, fight, and bring the fish to gaff unaided by any other person.

    Acts of persons other than the angler in adjusting reel drag or touching any part of the tackle during the playing of the fish, or giving aid other than taking the leader or trace for gaffing purposes, or in replacing or adjusting the harness disqualifies a catch. Only one person is permitted to hold the leader. (*This rule is pending vote on revision.*)
9. Resting the rod on the gunwale of a boat while playing a fish is prohibited. Harness may be attached to reel or rod; the use of a rod belt is permitted.
10. Changing rod or reel or splicing line or renewal or addition thereto during playing of a fish is prohibited.
11. Use of the double-handled reel is prohibited.
12. The following acts or omissions will disqualify a catch:
    A. Failure to comply with rules or tackle specifications.
    B. Broken rod.
    C. Acts of persons other than the angler, as specified in Rule 8.
    D. Handlining, or using a handline or rope attached in any manner to line or leader for the purpose of holding or lifting a fish.
    E. Shooting, harpooning or lancing any fish, including sharks, at any stage of the catch.
    F. Mutilation by sharks or other means.
    G. Gimbals must be free-swinging.

Shore Fishing: Any fish caught on regulation tackle from the shore is eligible to compete with the other catches in its line class.

Backing: In the event that two lines of different test strength spliced or tied together are used in taking a fish, that catch shall be classified under the heavier of the two lines and a sample of both lines must be submitted.

Only fish caught in accordance with these
rules will be accepted as claims.

WEIGHING

Any individual protest as to method of weighing or manner in which a fish was caught should be made to the accredited local club or unit, or to an International Committee member. It will then be transmitted to headquarters for consideration.

The fish must be officially weighed on land by a recognized official of the area or by an accredited weighmaster and on attested scales. The actual tackle used must be exhibited to the weighmaster at the time of such weighing. In addition to the boatman and weighmaster, there must be one more witness to the weight. Weighing fish on yachts is only permissible when it is impossible to get to land scales. An affidavit for such weighing, with exact measurements sworn to by the angler before a notary public and attested by at least two witnesses will be given consideration by the IGFA. (*This rule is pending vote on revision.*)

RETURN THIS CLAIM FORM TO THE IGFA
The American Museum of Natural History
New York 24, New York

Glossary

Adipose eyelid. Thin, transparent protective covering of the eye.
Air bladder. Respiratory or hydrostatic organ present along the top side of the abdominal cavity (*see also* Swim bladder).
Algae. Primitive, chlorophyll-bearing water plants. The group includes green plants from the microscopic diatoms to seaweeds and kelps.
Amphipods. Small crustaceans, such as sand fleas, usually having seven pairs of legs.
Anal fin. The single fin on the underside between anus and tail.
Angulate. Angular in shape.
Anterior. Forward or toward the front.
Arch. See Gill arch.

Barbels. Soft, thread-like appendages found on the jaws, chin, or nostrils of certain fishes; commonly referred to as "whiskers" or "feelers."
Beach buggy. Auto modified to travel on sandy beaches and rigged to hold fishing tackle.
Blue current. Open ocean current, as opposed to greenish, inshore waters.
Brackish water. A mixture of fresh and salt waters.
Branchiostegal rays. Rays or supports in the skin located below and rearward of the gill cover.
Buck. Large male fish, usually shad.
Bull. Large male fish; sometimes mistakenly applied to big female striped bass.

Canines. Conspicuous, dog-like teeth, usually sharp and longer than other teeth.

CARANGIDS. Members of the jackfish family CARANGIDAE.
CARNIVOROUS FISHES. Species that capture live fishes as a primary means of subsistence.
CARTILAGE, CARTILAGINOUS. Gristly tissues softer than bone, such as the skeleton of a shark.
CAUDAL FIN. Tail.
CAUDAL PEDUNCLE. The narrow area of a fish's body immediately preceding the tail.
CEPHALOPODS. Marine mollusks such as the snail, mussel, oyster, squid, and octopus.
CHUMMING. Throwing chopped or ground-up bait into the water to attract game fishes.
CHUM SLICK. A trail of chum created by throwing bits of fish into the current.
COASTAL FISHES. Species that inhabit areas close to shore.
CONTINENTAL SHELF OR SLOPE. The area off the edge of a continent which is covered by comparatively shallow water. This may extend for miles before ending in a drop-off.
COPEPODS. Small, oar-footed crustaceans.
CORSELET. Scaled area located in the region of the pectoral fin in certain fishes whose bodies are otherwise practically scaleless.
COTTIDS. Members of the sculpin family COTTIDAE.
CRUSTACEANS. Group of animals with an external skeleton instead of a backbone; crabs, lobsters, barnacles, sand fleas, etc.

DEMERSAL FISHES. Species that live near the bottom most of the time.
DEMERSAL EGGS. Eggs that sink to the bottom, as opposed to pelagic eggs that float in the sea.
DORSAL. Pertaining to the back or top side.
DRAG CONTROL. Mechanism which controls the amount of pressure placed on the outgoing line in a fishing reel.
DRESSED FISH. A fish that has been gutted and cleaned, in preparation for cooking.
DROP-OFF. The more or less abrupt outer edge of the continental shelf where it meets deep water, usually in the form of oceanic currents.

EMBRYO. The early stage of life inside the egg before the fish has developed any distinctive form.
ESTUARY. An area at the mouth of a river where it meets the sea, usually with an indentation in the coast line.
EUPHAUSIIDS. Small, shrimp-like crustaceans.

FALCATE. Sickle-shaped. Applied to fishes, the term usually describes a type of tail or fin.
FAMILY. A major group of similar fishes, subdivided into genera (*see* GENUS, SPECIES).
FATHOM. Six feet; a measure of length used in marine terminology.

Glossary

FINGERLING. Young fish; between the larval and adult stages of development.

FINLETS. A series of small fins present on the tail end of the dorsal and ventral surfaces of certain fishes such as tunas, bonitos, mackerels, wahoo.

FINNING FISH. A fish close to the water's surface with its dorsal fin and/or tail visible above water.

FLAGLINE. A long set-line baited with many hooks, rigged with floats, and marked by flags.

FORAGING GROUNDS. Areas which attract fish because of the food supply.

FREE-SPOOLING. Letting the reel run freely without any pressure or drag on the line.

FRY. Young fish (*see* FINGERLING).

FUSIFORM BODY. A shape or form which tapers from the middle toward each end.

GAFF. A large hook, with a long wooden handle, used to boat a fish as it is brought alongside.

GENUS. Major subdivision of a family, containing closely similar species; the first part of the scientific name.

GILL ARCH. The arch of cartilage to which the gill rakers and gill filaments are attached.

GILL COVER. The outer portions of the face behind and below the eye.

GILL FILAMENTS. The main body of the gill attached to the back edge of the gill arch.

GILL NET. Net with a mesh just large enough to hold a struggling fish behind the gills.

GILL RAKERS. The short, more-or-less rigid appendages attached to the front edge of the gill arch.

GILL RAKER COUNT. Counting the gill rakers as a means of identifying fishes.

GIMBAL. A metal socket in the forepart of the angler's chair which accommodates the butt of the rod.

GONADS. Sex glands, as a male's testes or female's ovaries.

HAUL SEINE. Seine which catches anything larger than the meshes of its net.

HERMAPHRODITISM. A condition where an individual contains both male and female sex organs.

HETEROPODS. Microscopic mollusks important in the food of some fishes.

ICHTHYOLOGIST. One who studies fishes scientifically.

ICHTHYOSARCOTOXISM. Poisoning due to eating contaminated fishes.

INVERTEBRATES. Lower animals which lack a backbone, as opposed to vertebrates which have backbones.

JIGGING. Snagging fish by means of up-and-down jerking of a handline to which a lure or a cluster of hooks is attached.

KEEL. Longitudinal ridge or process present along the hind portion of the caudal peduncle. Some fishes have a pair of keels on each side.
KELP. Type of large coarse seaweed.

LARVAE. The early form of a fish after it leaves the egg. The larva is unlike its parent in form.
LATERAL LINE. A conspicuous line present along the sides of most fishes. It is composed of continuous grooves or canals containing special sensory organs which communicate with the exterior through pores in the scales.
LEPTOCEPHALUS. Type of fish larva with a transparent, leaf-like form.

LITTORAL. Pertaining to fishes or waters that are close to shore.
LONGLINE. Type of long set-line which may be baited with hundreds of hooks. Used mostly by commercial fishermen.
LUNATE. Crescent-shaped.
LUTJANIDS. Members of the snapper family LUTJANIDAE.
LYMPHOCYSTIS. Fish disease characterized by wartlike growths on the body and fins of fishes.

MAXILLA, MAXILLARY. Upper jaw bone.
METAMORPHOSIS. Change from one shape or form to another.
MILT. Sperm or seminal fluid of a male fish.
MOLLUSK. Group of soft-bodied invertebrate animals protected by a calcareous shell; snails, clams, mussels, oysters, squid, etc.
MONOFILAMENT. Single-strand fishing line made of plastic-like materials.
MUDDING. Feeding action of bonefish in shallow water as they nose around in the mud seeking food. The action muddies the previously clear water.

NYMPHS. Pre-adult stage of certain insects.

OCEANIC FISHES. Species which inhabit the open-ocean waters or currents.
OCTOPOD. Tiny eight-armed mollusks.
OMNIVOROUS. Taking food of all kinds indiscriminately; used of fishes which are not too selective in their feeding habits.
OPERCULUM. Gill cover.
OSTEOLOGY. Science or study of the bones of the skeleton.
OTOLITHS. Ear bones.
OUTRIGGER. A pole-like projection from the side of a fishing boat to which the angler's line is attached. The outrigger keeps the bait dancing on the surface of the water at a desired distance from the boat.
OVA. Eggs.

PALATINE. Pertaining to the bones of the palate in the roof of the mouth.
PECTORAL. The fin closest to the edge of the gill cover, or to the area around this fin.

Glossary

Pectoral girdle. A set of bones in the skeleton which supports the pectoral fin.

Pelvic fins. A pair of fins located along the belly behind the pectorals.

Pharyngeal teeth. Crushing type of teeth present in the throat area behind the palate.

Phytoplankton. Tiny free-floating aquatic plants.

Pineal apparatus. Tube-like structure present between the eyes of bluefin tuna and some other finlet fishes. Light entering through the thin surface-skin may influence the migrations or other actions of these fishes.

Plankton. Tiny plant or animal life which floats freely in the sea.

Pound net. An arrangement of nets supported upon stakes to form a fish trap.

Preoperculum. The "cheek" or fore part of the gill cover; usually divided from the rest of the gill cover by a sharp line or ridge.

Pteropod. Tiny mollusks important in the food of some fishes.

Pug-head. Distorted condition in which the upper jaw and head of a fish are short, blunt, and not fully developed.

Pulpit. In marine terminology, elevated platform on a boat.

Purse seine. Net used in open waters to encircle a school of fishes. The bottom of the net is then pursed to prevent the fish from diving and escaping.

Reef. A ridge or accumulation of sand, rocks, or coral at or close to the surface of the water.

Riffle. A stretch of shallow, choppy water caused by a shoal or rocky obstruction under the water.

Rip. A violently agitated strip of water caused by tide- or wind-action or by a current meeting an underwater rock formation.

Roe. Eggs of a fish. A term used for a female fish.

Roe fish. Female fish, usually carrying roe.

Salinity. The amount of salt in a given volume of water, usually expressed in parts per thousand.

Sciaenids. Members of the croaker family Sciaenidae.

Scoop net. Open-mouth triangular or cone-shaped net with a handle.

Scutes. Series of keeled, bony shields usually found in the tail end of the fish along the lateral line. In some fishes they are sharp and dangerous to handle.

Sea fan. Type of coral which branches into a fan-like form.

Sedentary fishes. Species that live most of their lives in a given area and do not migrate.

Seine. A long net having floats at the top edge and weights at the bottom.

Serranids. Members of the sea bass family Serranidae.

Serrate. Notched, like a saw.

Sexual dimorphism. Difference in form or color between the male and female in the same species.

SHOAL. Shallow area in any body of water.

SLOUGH. Backwater, bayou, inlet, or pond in which water backs up; an area which receives tidal waters and loses it when the tide ebbs.

SPAWN. Eggs of fishes; also the act of depositing and fertilizing eggs.

SPECIES. Scientific term for a group of identical fishes to which the same name is applied—black marlin, bluefish, striped bass. The species is indicated by the second part of the scientific name.

SPIT-OUT. Fish's action in grabbing a bait and releasing it immediately.

SPOON. A flat or slightly curved spoon-like artificial lure usually made of metal.

STRIP BAIT. A flexible strip of fish skin attached to a hook in such a manner as to act alive when trolled behind a boat.

SUBSPECIES, SUBSPECIFIC. Subdivision of a species. Subspecies are distinguished only by minor differences in character and geographical range.

SWIM BLADDER. A balloon-like structure, located in the upper part of the abdominal cavity immediately below the backbone, which assists in controlling the depth at which a fish swims; in some species it produces sound, and in still others it is associated with sense of hearing. It also has a relation to air breathing in certain fishes.

TAILING FISH. Fish swimming close to the water's surface with its tail visible out of the water.

TAGGING. Method scientists use to investigate migrations of fish by attaching tags to the fish and releasing them.

TAXONOMY. The science which embodies the principles of classification of fishes (and other animals) in relation to each other.

TOXIC. Poisonous.

TRAWLER. A vessel used for capturing fish with a trawl net.

UPWELLING. The phenomenon of bottom ocean waters rising to the surface and replacing top waters pushed away by wind or currents. Upwelling carries water rich in nutrients from the bottom.

VENT. The anus. The external opening of the alimentary canal.

VENTRAL. Pertaining to the bottom side, or underside.

VERTEBRATES. Animals with a backbone and an internal skeleton.

WEIR. A series of bars close together across a stream to trap fish.

YEAR-CLASS. A group of fish all of which were hatched in a certain year.

ZOOPLANKTON. Tiny free floating and drifting animal life of the sea (also analogous life forms in fresh water lakes).

Name Index

Agassiz, Louis, 197
Albrecht, George, 96, 205
Anderson, J. W., 406
Anderson, Mrs. Wendell, 44, 115
Andreas, F. P., 61
Arata, George, Jr., 76
Armes, 30
Arnold, Edgar, Jr., 76

Babb, Jim, 218
Badua, William, 208
Bailey, Jane, 40
Bailey, Jim, 40
Barrenechea, M., 374
Baughman, J. L., 395
Baumgardner, L. C., 238
Beaumont, Trevor, 132
Behrens, Alfredo, 46, 114
Benet, C. E., 177
Bennewitz, John, 38
Bigelow, Henry, 228
Blum, H. J., 33
Boschen, W. C., 74
Breeder, Charles, 410
Brock, Vernon, 127
Brousonnet, 30
Bullis, Harvey, 116, 117

Caine, S., 406
Cammeron, 30
Carey, George, 59
Carlson, C. B., 140
Cartaing, W. L., 51
Church, C. B., 322
Crandall, Bob, 109, 110, 218, 219

Davis, William E., 216
Day, Godfrey, 137, 152
De Sylva, Donald P., 34, 35, 36, 112, 156, 178
Donovan, Kevin, 38
Drowley, F., 134

Evermann, B. W., 182, 183

Fagan, Capt. Bill, 39, 88, 157
Farrington, Kip, 80, 109, 406
Fitch, John, 292
Fox, T., 69
Fraser, F. C., 181
Fredriksen, Maggie, 265

Gage, Charlie, 218
Galligan, Jim, 386
Gehringer, Jack, 33, 34
Gerlach, A. R., 325, 338

Geyer, R. J., 166
Glassell, Alfred C., 50
Godsil, H. C., 110, 111, 141, 142
Goode, 76
Grey, Zane, 59, 120
Gudger, Dr. W. E., 79

Hamann, A., 59
Harvey, J. W., 123
Hassel, Katie, 53
Heldt, 99
Hemingway, Ernest, 44, 171
Hodgson, Commander Duncan, 108
Hollis, Edgar H., 319
Homberg, E. K., 110, 111
Hooper, L. F., 63
Hubbard, C. W., 232

Ikehara, I. I., 114

Jefferson, Thomas, 387
Johnson, James L., 246
Jordan, D. S., 182, 183
Josselyn, 78
June, Fred, 121

King, J. E., 114

Labat, Père, 182
Langsford, Capt., 78
Lavenda, Nathan, 341, 342
Lee, Russel V. A., 116
Lerner, Michael, 108, 109
Libero, Pablo, 49
Llewellin, Edward, 61
Lyman, Hal, 192, 196, 206, 321

Mahr, John, 143
Marr, John, 152
Marron, Lou, 74
Martin, José, 219
Martin, R. H., 307
Mather, Frank, 94, 99, 116, 117, 128, 137, 152
Mayer, Phil, 192
McAlpin, C. W., 300
Mercorio, G. B., 130
Merriam, Governor, 336
Merriman, Daniel, 319, 321, 326, 375
Meyer, Mrs. Maurice, Jr., 113, 115, 116
Miller, W., 229
Mitchell, Capt. L. M., 51

Moore, Harvey, 120
Morgan, A. R., 325, 338
Morrow, James, 42, 47, 60
Mowbray, Louis, 32, 47, 74, 106, 119, 122, 128, 130, 165, 168, 283, 285 286, 300, 301, 317, 399
Mowbray, Louis L., 69, 118
Mowbray, Nellie, 129

Nakamura, Hiroshi, 71, 113, 114
Nelson, De Wayne, 49
Nesbit, 229
Neville, W. C., 332
Nigrelli, Ross, 326
Norman, J. R., 181

Olin, John, 115

Pangarakis, G., 346
Parker, George, 49
Patillo, Thomas, 106, 108
Perinchief, Pete, 211
Perlmutter, A., 229
Pfleuger, Al, 70
Poey, 45
Poole, J., 229
Pothier, Israel, 103
Potts, Clinton Olney, 157

Rainey, Ed, 319, 321
Rebiero, A. A. dos Santos, 117
Ree, Captain A. S., 263
Rider, H. R., 341
Rieger, George, 214
Rivas, Louis, 47, 92, 97, 99
Robbins, Dick, 42, 71
Rochefort, Sieur de, 181
Ross, B. D., 171
Ross, Commander J. K. L., 108
Roughley, T. C., 111, 120, 400
Royce, 118
Rzeszewicz, J., 220

Salazar, M., 410
Sanford, Laddie, 68, 80, 105
Schaefer, Milner, 143, 152
Schmidt, John, 55
Schmidt, Louis, 54
Schroeder, Bill, 197, 198, 228
Schultz, 325
Scott, Dr. Dale, 49
Sella, M., 91, 99, 100, 102
Serventy, D. L., 131

Name Index

Sewall, Captain, 375
Sheafer, R. N., 418
Sheerin, Larry, 272, 407, 412, 413
Sherman, Allen, Jr., 44, 49
Shevlin, Tom, 287
Sloane, Sir Hans, 182
Smith, Louise Victoria, 93
Stansbury, J. E., 213
Stewart, C. W., 38
Stoner, Art, 171
Stoner, Dick, 171
Stotsbery, R. G., 85

Tanning, A. Vedel, 77
Throckmorton, S. R., 336
Townsend, Paul, 65
Tuker, W. E. S., 74, 80
Tuttle, Winslow, 386, 413

Underhill, A. Heaton, 320
Urschel, Charles, 33

Veloso, M. A. de Silva, 192
Vladykov, V. D., 319
Voss, Gilbert, 33, 34, 35

Wagner, C. H., 336
Waldron, Tacks, 49
Wallace, D. H., 319, 332
Warne, Capt. George, 53, 171
Warren, Winslow, 196, 197
Waters, Zack, Jr., 243
Weisbecker, A., Jr., 228
Wheeler, Charlie, 198
Whitehead, 196, 197
Willey, Capt. Jacob, 61
Willey, Harry, 61
Wood-Prince, Al, 110, 413
Woodward, H. L., 116

Yant, M. A., 305
Yuen, Heeny, S. H., 121

Subject Index

Generic and species names of fish are indicated in italic type; family names are differentiated by the use of small capitals.

ACANTHOCYBIIDAE, 165
Acanthocybium solandri, 164
Acapulco, Mexico, 39, 47, 51, 58, 85
Aden, Gulf of, 131
Africa, 32, 39, 58, 72, 75, 83, 91, 133, 137, 158, 165, 170, 191, 192, 194, 212, 282, 295, 296, 312, 409, 415; *see also* East Africa; French West Africa; Gold Coast; South Africa; West Africa
African pompano, 289
Alabama, 201, 214, 326, 334
Alabato, 267
Alameda Rod and Gun Club, 336
Alaska, 124, 128, 153, 185, 238, 271, 272, 274, 315, 336, 370, 371, 372, 377, 378, 379, 384
Albacore, 80, 90, 108, 117, 120, 123-29, 130, 369, 428
 false, 138
Albany, New York, 332
Albany Harbor, Australia, 112
Albemarle Sound, North Carolina, 320, 383
Albula vulpes, 207
ALBULIDAE, 207
Aleutian Islands, Alaska, 272, 274
Alewife, 137, 199, 345, 381
Alligator Reef Light, 33

Allison tuna, 118
Alosa sapidissima, 380
Altamaha, Georgia, 382, 383
Amberjack, 281, 282, 297, 298-306, 436
 Bermuda, 299, 302
 falcate, 299, 301-2
 great, 299
 horseeye, 299, 301
 Pacific, 299, 302, 306, 436
 Peruvian, 306
Ambrose Light, 220
American shad, 380
Amherst, Nova Scotia, 383
Amphipods, 270, 383
Amphistichus argenteus, 378
Anchovy, 36, 86, 87, 127, 130, 136, 142, 230, 292, 305, 328, 374, 408
Andros Island, Bahamas, 411
Anisotremus
 davidsonii, 279
 surinamensis, 278
 virginicus, 279
Annapolis River, 328
Antofagasta, Chile, 75, 81
Aransas Pass, Texas, 410
Archosargus probatocephalus, 365, 366
Arctic bonito, 133

483

SUBJECT INDEX

Argentina, 72, 191, 245, 268, 275, 311, 367, 409
Assateague Island, Virginia, 202
Associated Sportsmen of California, 336
Atka mackerel, 274, 455
Atlantic barracuda, 175-85
Atlantic bigeye tuna, 112, 115, 116-18, 130
Atlantic blackfin tuna, 129-30
Atlantic blue marlin, 26, 42-47, 49
Atlantic bluefin tuna, 92, 93, 100, 102, 111
Atlantic bonito, 136-38, 142, 429
Atlantic City, New Jersey, 301
Atlantic croaker, 248-49, 443
Atlantic halibut, 262-63, 264, 464
Atlantic longbill spearfish, 70-71
Atlantic mackerel, 145-50, 151, 430
Atlantic mako shark, 170-72
Atlantic permit, 306-8, 437
Atlantic shortbill spearfish, 70
Atlantic snapper, 389-400, 401, 402
Atlantic spotted bonito, 138-40, 143, 144, 429
Atlantic States Marine Fisheries Commission, 385
Atlantic tuna
 eastern, 97
 western, 97, 102
Atlantic yellowtail, 303
Atractoscion atelodus, 260
Auckland, New Zealand, 51
Australia, 50, 51, 58, 60, 72, 84, 110, 111, 112, 119, 120, 124, 130, 131, 132, 133, 134, 142, 152, 153, 164, 165, 168, 170, 187, 191, 207, 213, 259, 260, 288, 289, 294, 295, 296, 303, 305, 346, 348, 349, 400; *see also* South Australia; Western Australia
Australian barracuda, 187
Australian bluefin tuna, 110-12, 131
Australian bonito, 141 *fn.*, 142
Auxis thazard, 151-52
Azores, 91, 99, 116, 117, 192
Azov, Sea of, 91

Bacalao, 212
Bahama Banks, 94, 100
Bahama Channel, 93
Bahamas, 32, 42, 44, 45, 46, 62, 63, 64, 68, 79, 85, 91, 92, 93, 94, 97, 99, 100, 104, 124, 128, 134, 135, 139, 140, 156, 157, 165, 170, 171, 176, 177, 180, 181, 183, 184, 188, 207, 208, 209, 212, 282, 284, 286, 289, 290, 299, 300, 307, 313, 390, 391, 392, 394, 396, 398, 399, 409, 411, 413
Bahia de Topolobampo, Mexico, 305
Bairdiella chrysura, 251-252
Baja California; *see* Lower California
Balboa, California, 124
Bald Tusket Island, 105
Ballyhoo, 25, 36, 157
Baltic Sea, 91
Banana River, Florida, 234
Banda Sea, 77, 113
Banded rudderfish, 281
Banderas Bay, Mexico, 153, 351
Bangor Pool, Maine, 329
Bar jack, 286
Barnacles, 286, 384, 419, 420
Barnegat Inlet, 203
Barnstable Harbor, 329
Barracho, 370
Barracuda, 175-87
 Atlantic, 175-85
 Australian, 187
 California, 185
 European, 184-85
 great, 175-84, 187, 432
 Mexican, 186-87
 northern, 184, 432
 ocean, 165
 Pacific, 185-87, 432
 shortfin, 187
 striped, 187
Barramundi, 346, 348, 349
Barred seaperch, 378, 460
Bass, 279; *see also* Sea bass
 black, 255, 372
 blue, 255, 279
 channel, 202, 236, 242-45, 286, 308, 442
 giant, 346
 gray, 345
 kelp, 350, 356-57, 455
 marine, 316-57
 rock, 316-17, 350, 356-57
 spotted, 357, 455
 sand, 350, 356-57, 455
  California, 356
 silver, 343
 smallmouth, 345

Subject Index

striped, 195, 205, 318-39, 340, 343, 344, 434
Bass River, Nova Scotia, 328
Bass Strait, 111
Bastard halibut, 267
Bastard snapper, 399
Bastard trout, 237
Bay of Bengal, 349
Bay of Fundy, 366, 382, 385
Bay of Islands, 51, 62, 171
Beach Haven Inlet, 203
Bear Mountain, New York, 332
Bear River, Nova Scotia, 328
Beaufort, North Carolina, 159
Beaufort County, North Carolina, 201
Beavertail Point, Rhode Island, 205, 331
Becune, 182
Bedford Point, Connecticut, 331
Belaying-pin fish, 61
Belfast River, Maine, 329
Belgrade Lakes, Maine, 344
Bengal, Bay of, 349
Bering Sea, 264, 370
Bermuda, 32, 43, 44, 45, 46, 62, 69, 74, 85, 87, 97, 119, 120, 121, 122, 123, 124, 128, 129, 130, 139, 140, 151, 165, 166, 167, 168, 170, 176, 181, 188, 191, 207, 208, 209, 211, 212, 276, 277, 279, 282, 283, 284, 285, 286, 289, 290, 299, 300, 301, 307, 311, 317, 346, 350, 352, 353, 354, 355, 360, 367, 390, 392, 394, 396, 397, 398, 399, 400, 409, 415, 420
Bermuda amberjack, 299, 302
Bermuda Aquarium, 32, 47, 69, 97, 119
Bermuda bream, 367-68, 449
Bermuda chub, 188-89, 440
Bermudian marlin, 42, 69
Bethany Beach, Delaware, 203
Big scale, 408
Bigeye herring, 312
Bigeye jack, 288
Bigeye scad, 293
Bigeye tuna, 54, 427
   Atlantic, 112, 115, 116-18, 130
   Pacific, 112-16
Billfish, 25-81
Billingsgate, Massachusetts, 329
Biloxi, Mississippi, 214
Bimini, 32, 43, 44, 45, 46, 63, 79, 92, 99, 100, 157, 171

Bingham Oceanographic Laboratory, 47, 109, 319, 321, 325, 375
Black bass, 255, 372
Black bonito, 212, 214
Black croaker, 253, 255, 279, 444
Black drum, 245-48, 444
Black grouper, 350
Black grunt, 277
Black jewfish, 346, 347, 452
Black kingfish, 212
Black margate, 278
Black marlin, 42, 47, 49, 50-57, 59, 162, 425
Black perch, 255, 343
Black rock cod, 372
Black rockfish, 372, 456
Black salmon, 212
Black Sea, 91
Black sea bass, 340, 348
   giant, 346, 348, 452
Black seaperch, 378, 460
Black skipjack, 143, 152
Black snapper, 372
Blackback flounder, 269
Blackfin tuna, 116, 121, 129-30, 427
   Atlantic, 129-130
Blackfish, 73, 339, 417
Blanquillo, 358
Block Island, 44, 63, 64, 74, 75, 96, 124, 205, 269, 324, 331, 342
Block Island Sound, 83, 94, 96, 265
Bloody Grounds, 203
Bludger, 289
Blue bass, 255, 279
Blue crevally, 287
Blue marlin, 26, 42-49, 63, 64, 69, 425
   Atlantic, 26, 42-47
   Pacific, 42, 43, 47-49, 59
Blue perch, 370
Blue rockfish, 370, 456
Blue runner, 283-84, 285, 438
Blueback, 381
Bluefin tuna, 28, 40, 51, 90-112, 121, 218, 427
   Atlantic, 92, 93, 100, 102, 111
   Australian, 110-12, 131
   California, 93, 111
   Mediterranean, 102
   northern, 131
   Pacific, 92, 102, 114
      eastern, 93, 100, 111
      southern, 110, 131

Bluefish, 79, 190-206, 370, 434
  snapper, 191, 193, 195, 199, 203, 206
Bluenose perch, 343
Bluestripe grunt, 276, 300, 450
Boca Grande, Florida, 307
Boca Grande Pass, 410
Boccacio, 371, 456
Bonefish, 207-11, 286, 308, 313, 408, 433
Bonito, 51, 89, 132-44, 151-53
  Arctic, 133
  Atlantic, 136-38, 142, 429
  Australian, 141 fn., 142
  black, 212, 214
  California, 141, 142
  Chilean, 141, 142
  common, 302
  Japanese, 142
  leaping, 133
  Mexican, 142
  oceanic, 129, 133, 134-35, 136, 429
  Oriental, 131, 141-42
  Pacific, 139, 141, 142
  Peruvian, 141, 142
  spotted, Atlantic, 138-40, 143, 144, 429
  striped, 133
Bonito shark, 170
Bosphorus, 72, 75
Boston blue, 191, 216
Boston fish pier, 74, 263
Boxfish, spiny, 177
BRANCHIOSTEGIDAE, 358
Brazil, 32, 43, 83, 119, 128, 137, 139, 150, 156, 158, 160, 165, 170, 176, 185, 188, 191, 212, 268, 276, 277, 278, 279, 282, 284, 299, 309, 310, 346, 350, 352, 353, 354, 355, 390, 391, 392, 394, 395, 396, 397, 398, 400, 409
Bream, 366, 367
  Bermuda, 367-368, 449
Brenton Reef Rocks, 205
Brewster Flats, Massachusetts, 329
Bridgeport, Connecticut, 331
British Columbia, 128, 142, 291, 370, 371, 372
British Guiana, 409
Broad banded mackerel, 168
Broadbill swordfish, 54, 72-73, 74, 76-77, 79-80
Brook trout, 232

Broomtail grouper, 352, 454
  gray, 352
  pinto, 352
  spotted, 352
Brown Bank, 76, 383
Brown Colorado grouper, 352
Brown rockfish, 371
Brown trout, 232
Buffalo cod, 315
Bulleye, 150
Bullhead, 223, 372
Bull's Bay, 380
Butterfish, 79, 199, 259
Buzzards Bay, 86, 205, 342

Cabezone, 223-24
Cabio, 212
Cabo Blanco, Peru, 28, 38, 39, 50, 51, 54, 55, 57, 113, 115, 116, 162, 163, 187, 238, 358, 374, 375, 406
Cabo San Lucas, Mexico, 58, 60
Cabrilla, 350, 353, 357
  spotted, 354
Calamus
  arctifrons, 364
  bajonado, 365
  calamus, 364
  penna, 365
California, 26, 38, 49, 50, 58, 59, 60, 61, 72, 74, 75, 84, 110, 119, 120, 122, 123, 124, 126, 127, 128, 133, 136, 152, 153, 154, 161, 163, 170, 185, 186, 207, 222, 226, 238, 252, 258, 264, 267, 271, 272, 273, 275, 279, 285, 291, 292, 293, 302, 303, 305, 313, 315, 322, 323, 335, 336, 338, 348, 356, 357, 358, 369, 370, 371, 372, 373, 377, 378, 379, 384, 422
  Gulf of, 35, 51, 59, 60, 119, 143, 153, 161, 185, 187, 239, 240, 241, 242, 253, 258, 272, 283, 302, 303, 305, 308, 346, 351, 352, 354, 357, 370, 400, 401, 402, 421
  Lower; see Lower California
California Banks, 93
California barracuda, 185
California bluefin tuna, 93, 111
California bonito, 141, 142
California Bureau of Marine Fisheries, 110
California corbina, 256, 258-59, 442

SUBJECT INDEX

California Fish and Game Department, 126, 141, 292, 293
California Fish Commission, 336
California giant sea bass, 348
California halibut, 264, 267, 464
California horse mackerel, 291
California kingfish, 255, 443
California sand bass, 356
California sheepshead, 421-22, 458
California white sea bass, 238-39, 441
California whiting, 258
California yellowtail, 303
Callao, Peru, 86
Canada, 92, 96, 109, 326, 327, 383; see also names of provinces
Canal Zone, 51, 396, 409
Canary Islands, 158
Canary rockfish, 371, 456
Canaveral Harbor, 234
Cape Ann, Maine, 263, 331
Cape Breton Island, Nova Scotia, 74, 75, 329
Cape Canaveral, Florida, 32, 194, 201, 244
Cape Charles, Virginia, 202, 213, 243, 244, 246
Cape Cod, Massachusetts, 43, 76, 96, 133, 148, 151, 156, 160, 170, 184, 188, 191, 193, 228, 245, 250, 256, 264, 285, 310, 326, 328, 329, 340, 343, 360, 366, 382, 383, 396, 415, 418
Cape Cod Bay, 139, 205, 329, 331
Cape Cod Canal, 329
Cape Colnett, Lower California, 371
Cape Fear, North Carolina, 201-2
Cape Florida, 160, 307
Cape Hatteras, North Carolina, 76, 85, 86, 119, 128, 148, 156, 159, 165, 191, 202, 229, 245, 248, 249, 276, 363, 367
Cape Henlopen, 203
Cape Leeuwin, Australia, 110
Cape Lookout, North Carolina, 145, 202
Cape May, New Jersey, 244, 418
Cape of Good Hope, 72, 137
Cape San Lucas, Mexico, 153, 185, 291, 294, 296, 302, 351, 354, 357, 400
Cape Verde Islands, 212
Capetown, South Africa, 130
Caracas, Venezuela, 46

CARANGIDAE, 190, 281, 282, 287, 291, 294, 295, 296, 297, 298, 299, 303, 306-9, 311, 373
Caranx, 282-89, 294, 299
  ajax, 288
  bartholomaei, 285-86
  caballus, 284, 285
  caninus, 282
  crysos, 283-84
  emburyi, 289
  fosteri, 289
  georgianus, 288
  guara, 286
  gymnostethoides, 289
  hippos, 282, 287
  ignobilis, 287
  latus, 286
  marginatus, 288
  ruber, 283, 284-85
  sexfaciatus, 286
  speciosus, 289
  stellatus, 287, 288
Caribbean Sea, 32, 42, 43, 44, 62, 63, 66, 76, 83, 91, 93, 94, 96, 116, 119, 124, 128, 133, 139, 145, 157, 158, 159, 160, 165, 390, 397, 401, 409
Carolinas, 32, 33, 34; see also North Carolina; South Carolina
Carquinez Straits, 338
Casco Bay, Maine, 329
Castle Harbour, Bermuda, 69
Cat Cay, Bahamas, 32, 45, 63, 92, 99
Cat Key Club, 92
Catfish, sea, 411
Caulolatilus princeps, 358
Cavalla, 155, 288
Celebes Sea, 77
Central America, 38, 102, 121, 135, 143, 226, 402, 409, 411; see also names of countries
CENTRARCHIDAE, 316
CENTROPOMIDAE, 405
Centropomus undecimalis, 405
Centropristes striatus, 317, 339
Cephalopholis fulvus, 354
Cerberus Shoal, 203
Cero mackerel, 155, 156, 158, 159, 160-61, 431
Ceylon, 58, 131
Channel bass, 202, 236, 242-45, 286, 308, 442
Channel Islands, 75, 133

Chappaquiddick, Massachusetts, 205
Characin, 83
Charleston Inlet, Rhode Island, 331
Charlestown, Rhode Island, 205
Chedabucto Bay, Nova Scotia, 329
Cheilotrema saturnum, 253
Chequessett, Massachusetts, 329
Cherna, 372
Chesapeake Bay, 148, 158, 159, 191, 196, 202, 213, 216, 227, 228, 232, 237, 248, 249, 250, 251, 256, 258, 271, 279, 321, 323, 326, 327, 328, 332, 333, 335, 343, 361, 382
Chicken halibut, 267
Chile, 26, 50, 54, 57, 58, 59, 60, 72, 74, 75, 79, 80, 81, 84, 85, 115, 119, 124, 133, 142, 153, 170, 238, 291, 303
Chilean bonito, 141, 142
Chilipepper, 372, 457
China, 240, 349
Chincoteague, Virginia, 94
Chincoteague Island, 202
Chinese croaker, 253, 279
Chobie, 415
Chorinemus
  lysan, 295
  sancti-petri, 295
  tol, 295
Chub
  Bermuda, 188-89, 440
  white, 188
Chub-head snapper, 399
Chub mackerel, 146, 150-51, 153, 430
Clams, 246, 252, 263, 272
Classification, 7-10
Clinton, Connecticut, 203
CLUPEIDAE, 380
Coalfish, 212, 216
Cobia, 212-214, 435
Cockup, 348
Cocoa, Florida, 234
Cocos Island (Costa Rica), 39, 165
Cod, 9, 147, 215-22, 263, 315, 459
  black rock, 372
  buffalo, 315
  cultus, 315
  green, 216
  johnny, 372
  leopard, 315
  red rock, 370, 372
  rock, 371
    yellowtail, 371

Codalarga, 371
Codfish, 215-22
"Coldfish," 127
Collybus drachme, 115
Colombia, 277, 311
Colorado grouper, 352
Colorado snapper, 402
Columbia River, 84, 91, 102, 338
Common bonito, 302
Common jack, 282
Coney, 350, 354-55, 454
Connecticut, 203, 205, 228, 230, 232, 320, 324, 327, 328, 331, 342, 362, 380, 382, 385, 417, 419
Connecticut River, 203, 331, 386, 387
Connecticut State Fish and Game Department, 386
Cooper River, 333
Coos Bay, Oregon, 338
Coos River, 325
Coosa River, 334
Copepods, 34, 148, 154, 292, 384
Copiapo, Chile, 133
Corbina
  blanca, 241
  California, 256, 258-59, 442
  gulf, 241
  orangemouth, 242
  striped, 241
  white, 241
  yellow, 241
Cornell University, 319
Coronado Beach, Florida, 201
Coronado Islands, 305, 373
Corpus Christi Bay, 234
Coryphaena
  equisetis, 85, 88
  hippurus, 82, 88
CORYPHAENIDAE, 82
Costa Rica, 165
Cottid, 223-24
Crabeater, 212
Crabs, 86, 199, 208, 214, 221, 230, 239, 240, 244, 246, 253, 256, 263, 265, 270, 272, 277, 284, 308, 317, 345, 365, 388, 390, 397, 398, 399, 406, 411, 419, 420, 421
Crawfish, 214, 308, 388, 406
Crevalle, 282
Crevally
  blue, 287
  jack, 282-83, 284, 287, 438

Subject Index

Croaker, 225-60, 328
  Atlantic, 248-49, 443
  black, 253, 255, 279, 443
  China, 253, 279
  golden, 252
  spotfin, 252-53, 443
  white, 255
  yellowfin, 251, 253, 258, 259, 443
Cronin-Fisher-Andreas Bill, 336
Cruger Island, 332
Crustaceans, 86, 115, 122, 130, 136, 142, 148, 152, 199, 217, 237, 252, 253, 259, 265, 270, 275, 278, 279, 292, 297, 305, 308, 310, 362, 384, 393, 416
Cuba, 33, 44, 45, 62, 63, 64, 74, 75, 76, 85, 93, 94, 100, 158, 160, 161, 194, 207, 286, 289, 394, 395, 410
Cuban jack, 289-90, 438
Cuban snapper, 394
Cubby yew, 212
Cubera, 392, 393, 394, 395, 396, 397
Cucumbers, sea, 221
'Cuda, 176
Cultus, Pacific, 315
Cultus cod, 315
Cumberland basin, 383, 385
Cumberland Island, 201
Cunner, 150, 199, 419
Current(s), 20
  Equatorial Counter, 113
  Florida, 100
  Guiana, 43, 63, 165
  Humboldt, 54, 80
  Japan, 71, 72
  North Equatorial, 113, 114
  Peru, 54-57
Cusk, 263
Cuttyhunk, Massachusetts, 205, 329
Cybium commersonii, 168
Cymatogaster aggregata, 379
Cynoscion, 226
  albus, 241
  arenarius, 236-37
  macdonaldi, 239
  nebulosus, 232
  nobilis, 238
  nothus, 237
  othonopterus, 241
  parvipinnis, 240
  phoxocephalus, 241
  regalis, 226, 232, 233
  reticulatus, 241-42

  stolzmanni, 241
  xanthulus, 242

Dab
  mud, 269
  rusty, 271
Damalicthys vacca, 378
Decapterus, 294
Deep Lake, Florida, 411
Delaware, 85, 193, 203, 243, 248, 333, 340, 342, 383
Delaware Bay, 203, 267, 326, 327
Delaware River, 320, 327
Diamond flounder, 272, 464
Diamond Shoals, 85, 198, 202
Digby Basin, 328
Diplectrum formosum, 355
Distribution, 12-13
Dixon Entrance, British Columbia, 371
Dog snapper, 392, 393, 395-96, 401, 402, 445
Dogfish, 104
Dogtooth tuna, 132, 428
Dolly varden trout, 272
Dolphin, 51, 82-88, 100, 138, 214, 284, 323, 435
  small, 85, 88
Dorado, 83
Drifts, 20
Drum, 242-55
  black, 245-48, 444
  puppy, 243, 244
  red, 242
Dry Tortugas, 157, 160
Duck Harbor, Massachusetts, 329

East Africa, 88, 287
East Boynton Inlet, Florida, 166
East Indies, 131, 187, 349
Eastern Atlantic tuna, 97
Eastern mackerel, 150
Eastern Pacific bluefin tuna, 100, 111
Ecuador, 58, 165, 241, 275, 296, 303, 306, 313, 373, 400
Eden, New South Wales, 51, 120, 132
Edenton, 322
Eel, 199, 208
Eel Lake, 419
Eight Pass, Mexico, 234, 412
El Niño, 55
El Salvador, 241
Elagatis bipinnulatus, 296
Elizabeth Islands, 205

ELOPIDAE, 312
Elops
 affinis, 312
 saurus, 312
Embiotoca jacksoni, 378
EMBIOTOCIDAE, 377
Enfield Dam, 386, 387
England (Great Britain), 150, 216, 263
English Channel, 147
Ensenada, Lower California, 305, 371
Epinephelus
 adscensionis, 352
 analogus, 354
 guttatus, 353
 labriformis, 354
 morio, 353
 striatus, 353
Equatorial Counter Current, 113
Eskimos, 262
ESOCIDAE, 176
Euphausids, 127, 292
Eureka, California, 372
Europe, 138, 295
European barracuda, 184-85
European mackerel, 147
European tuna, 99
Euthynnus
 alletteratus, 138, 139
 lineatus, 143, 152
 vaito, 144
Everglades, 201

Falcate amberjack, 299, 301-2
False albacore, 138
False Cape, North Carolina, 202
Fantail, 371
Farallon Islands, 348
Fathead, 421
Faulkner's Island, 203, 206
Feather River, 338
Fenwick Island Lightship, 66
Fiji Islands, 50
Filefish, 177
Finletfish, 89-168
Fire Island, 204
First Encounter Beach, Massachusetts, 329
Fisher's Island, 203, 205, 331
Flag cabrilla, 354
Flamenco, 403
Flatfish, 9, 127, 261-72
Flores Sea, 113

Florida, 30, 31, 32, 34, 35, 36, 43, 45, 46, 62, 63, 64, 68, 70, 71, 74, 76, 83, 85, 100, 119, 123, 128, 135, 137, 140, 150, 156, 159, 160, 161, 165, 166, 167, 171, 178, 180, 181, 182, 185, 193, 194, 200, 201, 214, 227, 232, 234, 237, 244, 245, 246, 248, 256, 257, 275, 276, 277, 278, 279, 282, 284, 285, 286, 289, 296, 297, 298, 299, 307, 309, 310, 313, 314, 326, 334, 340, 346, 350, 351, 352, 354, 355, 364, 365, 367, 380, 383, 390, 391, 392, 394, 395, 396, 398, 405, 406, 409, 410, 411, 413, 415, 420
 Gulf of, 350
Florida Current, 100
Florida jewfish, 346
Florida Keys, 30, 33, 35, 71, 177, 181, 184, 201, 207, 209, 276, 277, 278, 297, 298, 307, 308, 310, 347, 350, 351, 394, 398, 410, 411, 420
Florida Straits, 93, 94, 96, 97, 99, 100, 156, 160
Flounder, 214, 261, 263, 264, 266, 268-72
 blackback, 269
 diamond, 272, 464
 mud, 266
 starry, 271-72, 464
 summer, 264
 winter, 268-70, 463
 yellowtail, 269, 271, 463
Fluke, 261, 266, 267-268
 fourspot, 267-68, 463
 northern, 264, 265-66, 267, 463
 southern, 266
Flyingfish, 36, 60, 86
Food cycle, of the sea, 55, 57
Formosa, 58, 71
Fort Lauderdale, Florida, 71
Fort Pierce, Florida, 32, 35, 232
Fort Pierce Inlet, 201
Fourspot fluke, 267-68, 463
France, 32, 43
French grunt, 277, 450
French West Africa, 43
Frigate mackerel, 151-53, 154, 430
Frying Pan Shoals, 201
Fundy, Bay of, 366, 382, 385

GADIDAE, 215, 216
Gadus callarias, 220

Subject Index

Gaff-topsail pompano, 311
Gag, 350, 351
Galapagos Islands, 38, 39, 91, 102, 119, 126, 135, 153, 165, 296, 303, 306, 352, 354
Galveston Bay, 346
Garrupa, 352
Garrupa nigrita, 347
Gaspereau River, 328
Gatun Spillway, Panama, 406
Gempylus serpens, 115
Genyonemus lineatus, 255
Georges Bank, 43, 74, 76, 96, 124, 147, 220, 267, 269, 383
Georgetown, Maine, 61, 329
Georgetown, South Carolina, 201
Georgia, 76, 140, 201, 269, 382, 383
Gialota, 371
Giant bass, 346
Giant black sea bass, 346, 348, 452
Giant perch, 348
Giant sea bass, 316, 346-49
　black, 346, 348, 452
　California, 348
Gloucester, Massachusetts, 382
Goggleeye jack, 290
Gold Coast, 32, 83, 282
Golden croaker, 252
Golden grouper, 351, 452
Gordon Key, Florida, 150
Grand Bahama Bank, 105
Grand Banks, 262
Grass porgy, 364, 448
Grassy Key, Florida, 298, 413
Gray bass, 345
Gray broomtail grouper, 352
Gray grunt, 276
Gray perch, 343
Gray snapper, 392
Gray trout, 227
Grays Harbor, Washington, 336
Graysby, 350, 355, 453
Great amberjack, 299
Great Australian Bight, 112
Great barracuda, 175-84, 187, 432
Great Barrier Reef, 187, 400
Great Britain; *see* England
Great pompano, 307
Great trevally, 289
Great tuna, 90
Green cod, 216
Green jack, 285
Green snapper, 371

Greenback mackerel, 153
Greenhead, 322
Greenhill Point, Rhode Island, 96
Greenland, 220, 262
Greenland shark, 263
Greenling, 273-74, 315
Grenadier, 263
Grimsby, England, 263
Grouper, 9, 316, 317, 344, 349-56, 371
　black, 350
　broomtail, 352, 454
　gray, 352
　pinto, 352
　spotted, 352
　brown colorado, 352
　colorado, 352
　golden, 351, 452
　leopard, 351
　Nassau, 353, 453
　red, 353
　rock, 350
　salmon, 371
　spiketail, 352
　Warsaw, 346
　yellow colorado, 352
　yellowfin, 350-51, 453
Grunt, 275-280
　black, 277
　bluestripe, 276, 300, 450
　French, 277, 450
　gray, 276
　striped, 277
　white, 276, 450
　yellow, 276, 277
Guadalupe Island, 370
Guaguanche, 184, 185, 432
Guam, 39
Guaymas, 39, 59, 60, 239, 240, 401
Guiana Current, 43, 63, 165
Guinea, 212
Gulf Coast, 137, 201
Gulf corbina, 241
Gulf king whiting, 257-58
Gulf Stream, 32, 33, 36, 44-45, 63, 74, 76, 83, 85, 86, 94, 100, 165, 201, 202, 296, 391
Gull Island, 205
Gwelly, 286
Gymnosarda nuda, 132

Haddock, 79, 215, 216, 217, 219, 222, 263, 459
HAEMULIDAE, 275

Haemulon, 275
  album, 276
  flavolineatum, 277
  macrostomum, 277
  parra, 278
  plumieri, 276
  sciurus, 276
Haiti, 94, 314
Hake, 79, 199, 217
Halfbeak, 25, 157, 167
Halibut, 261-67
  Atlantic, 262-63, 264, 464
  bastard, 267
  California, 264, 267, 464
  chicken, 267
  Monterey, 267
  Pacific, 264
  southern, 267
Hamlet, 350, 353
Hammerhead shark, 170
Hampton Harbor, 329
Hancock-Sullivan Bridge (Maine), 329
Harbor pollock, 217
Hardhead, 150, 248
Hardtail jack, 283
Harrington Sound, 399
Harvard Museum of Comparative Zoology, 198
Hatteras blue, 191
Havana, Cuba, 44, 63, 93
Hawaiian Islands, 29, 31, 39, 45, 49, 50, 51, 58, 75, 84, 113, 119, 123, 124, 127, 133, 142, 165, 166, 170, 207, 287, 288, 296, 300, 312
Hawaiian skipjack, 144
Herring, 79, 104, 106, 108, 127, 148, 151, 199, 217, 230, 312, 380, 384, 408, 409
  bigeye, 312
  sea, 381
Hervey Bay, 132
Heteropods, 34
HEXAGRAMMIDAE, 273, 274
Hexagrammos decagrammus, 273
Hickory shad, 381
Hillsboro River Inlet, 410
Hind, 350
  red, 353, 454
  rock, 352, 353, 453
HIPPOGLOSSIDAE, 262
Hippoglosus
  hippoglosus, 262
  stenolepis, 264

Hispaniola, 117
Hogfish, 301, 420, 458
Hogmouth, 87, 399
Holyoke Water Power Company, 385-86
HOPLOPAGRIDAE, 401
Hoplopagrus guntheri, 400
Horse mackerel, 90, 106
  California, 291
Horseeye amberjack, 299, 301
Horseeye jack, 282, 284, 286-87
Houndfish, 25
Hudson Gorge, 194
Hudson River, 203, 320, 326, 327, 331, 332, 382, 383
Hudson Straits, 220
Hulman trophy, 110, 218
Humboldt Current, 54, 80
Hump, the, 203
"Humpbacks," 340
"Humpies," 340
Humpy, 421
Hynnis
  cubensis, 289
  hopkinsi, 290
Hypacanthus amia, 295
Hyperprosopon argenteum, 379
Hypsopsetta guttulata, 272
Hypsurus caryi, 379

Iceland, 262
Identification, 4-7
India, 164, 349
Indian longtail tunny, 131
Indian Ocean, 30, 31, 39, 50, 58, 91, 113, 119, 132, 134, 181, 191, 287, 295, 296, 297
Indian River, 234
Indian River Inlet, 203
Indo-Pacific area, 60, 287
Indonesia, 113
Inter-American Tropical Tuna Commission, 135
Intercollegiate Game Fish Match and Seminar, 109, 110, 218
Intercollegiate Tuna Match, 413
International Game Fish Association, 49, 54, 117, 157, 170, 212, 215, 242, 245
International Tuna Cup Match, 106, 114, 196, 219
Ipswich Bay, 78
Iquique, Chile, 74

Subject Index

Ireland, 147
Islamorada, Florida, 71
Islands, Bay of, 51, 62, 171
Istiophorid, 43
ISTIOPHORIDAE, 31, 40, 43, 70
Istiophorus, 31
    americanus, 31-38
    greyi, 38
ISURIDAE, 170
Isurus
    glaucus, 170
    oxyrinchus, 170
Italy, 83, 99

Jack, 281, 282-98, 299, 300, 306, 307, 373
    bar, 286
    bigeye, 288
    common, 282
    Cuban, 289-90, 438
    goggleeye, 290
    green, 285
    hardtail, 283
    horseeye, 282, 284, 286-287
    mackerel, 291-94, 439
    spotted, 287, 439
    yellow, 285-86, 438
Jack crevally, 282-83, 284, 287, 438
Jack mackerel, 291
Jack spot, 66, 202, 203
Jackfish, 8, 190, 192, 281-311
Jacksonville, Florida, 32
Japan, 31, 39, 50, 72, 75, 84, 119, 120, 124, 126, 130, 134, 142, 152, 164, 165, 170, 187, 207, 213, 264, 271, 291, 295
Japan Current, 71, 72
Japanese bonito, 142
Jekyll Island, 201
Jellyfish, 127
Jervis Bay, 111
Jewfish, 346, 348, 350
    black, 346, 347, 452
    Florida, 346
    southern, 346
    spotted, 346-47, 452
Johnny cod, 372
Johnny Verde, 356
Jolthead porgy, 365, 448
Jones Beach, New York, 204
Jordan's snapper, 402-3
Jumper, 281

Junefish, 346
Jupiter Inlet, 201

Kahawai, 51, 172
Karambesi, 287
Katsuwonus pelamis, 133
Kelp bass, 350, 356-57
Kennebec River, 329
Kenya, 131, 296
Key West, Florida, 32, 194, 364, 395
Killifish, 199, 230, 328
King mackerel, 36, 155-57, 158, 160, 161, 180, 431
King salmon, 369
King trevally, 289
King whiting, 256
    northern, 256-57, 442
    southern, 257, 258
Kingfish, 30, 36, 155, 255, 256, 259, 303
    black, 212
    California, 255, 443
    river, 259
    southern, 257
    yellowtail, 111, 303
Kishinoella tonggol, 130-32
Kodiak Island, 273
Koli-koli, 287
Kona, Hawaii, 49, 300
Korea, 271
KYPHOSIDAE, 188
Kyphosus sectatrix, 188

La Blanquilla Island, 46
La Guaira, Venezuela, 46
La Jolla, California, 305
La Paz, Mexico, 39, 305
Labrador, 91, 96, 262, 269
LABRIDAE, 417, 420, 421
Lachnolaimus maximus, 420
Ladyfish, 312-14, 408, 433
Lagodon rhomboides, 365
Laguna Madre, 234
Lake Worth, Florida, 32, 201
Lake Worth Inlet, 201
Lane snapper, 397-98, 447
Lanesville, Massachusetts, 78
Lantern fish, 292
Lates calcarifer, 348
LATIDAE, 346, 348
Leaping bonito, 133
Leatherjacket, 281
Leerfish, 295, 439

Leiostomus xanthurus, 249
Lemon sole, 269
Lemonfish, 212
Lenguado, 268
Leopard cod, 315
Leopard grouper, 351
Leptocephali, 208, 313
Les Tres Islas Marias, Mexico, 39
Lesser Antilles, 77
Limanda ferruginea, 271
Ling, 212
Lingcod, 315
Little tuna, 138
Little tunny, 138
Littlemouth porgy, 365
Liverpool, Nova Scotia, 106
Lizard-mouth, 132
Lobotes surinamensis, 415
LOBOTIDAE, 415
Lobster, 221, 263
Long Beach, California, 124
Long Island, 44, 63, 75, 94, 135, 171, 192, 203, 205, 216, 220, 264, 296, 327, 328, 331, 333, 340, 341, 342, 418
Long Island Sound, 204, 269, 324, 342
Long-tailed tunny, 131
Longbill spearfish, 426
  Atlantic, 70-71
Longfin pompano, 311
Longfin tuna, 123, 127
Lookdown, 281, 297-98, 440
Loreto, Mexico, 304, 305
Los Angeles, California, 49, 136, 186, 377, 422
Los Angeles Harbor, 126
Louisburg, Nova Scotia, 74
Louisiana, 201, 245, 309, 326, 367, 415
Lower California, 58, 84, 91, 135, 143, 187, 238, 241, 252, 255, 267, 279, 292, 296, 305, 315, 346, 348, 352, 354, 356, 357, 358, 370, 371, 372, 377, 378, 379, 400, 401, 402, 406
Lua, 287
LUTJANIDAE, 303, 388, 389, 391, 392, 394, 395, 397, 398, 399, 400, 401
Lutjanus
  analis, 391
  apodus, 396
  aratus, 403
  argentiventris, 403
  aya, 389
  black-fordii, 389-90
  colorado, 402
  cyanopterus, 394
  griseus, 392
  guttatus, 403
  jocu, 395
  jordani, 402, 403
  novemfasciatus, 402
  synagris, 397
Luzon, Philippines, 39

Mackerel, 30, 39, 51, 79, 80, 89, 106, 137, 140, 144-64, 168, 199, 200, 263, 281, 305
  atka, 274, 455
  Atlantic, 145-50, 151, 430
  broad banded, 168
  California horse, 291
  cero, 155, 156, 158, 159, 160-61, 431
  chub, 146, 150-51, 153, 430
  eastern, 150
  European, 147
  frigate, 151-53, 154, 430
  greenback, 153
  horse, 90, 106
    California, 291
  jack, 291
  king, 36, 155-57, 158, 160, 161, 180, 431
  Monterey Spanish, 162
  narrow banded, 168
  Pacific, 153-55, 430
  painted, 160
  school, 163-64
  sierra, 161-63, 164
  small, 127
  snake, 115
  snapping, 191
  Spanish, 89, 155, 156, 157, 158-60, 161, 163, 164, 431
    Monterey, 162
  spotted, 163, 164
  striped, 153
  tinker, 148, 150
  zebra, 153
Mackerel jack, 291-94, 439
Mackerel scad, 294
Mackerel shark, 170
Mackerel, tuna, 138
Madagascar, 39, 191
Madeira, 117

SUBJECT INDEX 495

Magdalena Bay, 267, 308, 348, 356, 372
Mahoney Bay, 329
Maine, 61, 158, 218, 219, 220, 256, 263, 264, 269, 270, 327, 329, 331, 340, 344, 360, 382, 383
  Gulf of, 73, 74, 96, 148, 196, 216, 263, 297
Makaira
  albida, 62
  ampla, 42
  ampla ampla, 43
  ampla mazara, 43
  bermudae, 42, 69
  marlina, 42, 50
  marlina marlina, 50
  mazara, 42, 47, 50
  mitsukurii, 42, 58
  nigricans, 50
Mako shark, 170-72, 462
  Atlantic, 170-72
  Pacific, 170-72
Makua, Hawaii, 123
Malay Peninsula, 191
Malibu, California, 124
Man-eater shark, 169, 170
Mana, Kauai, 208
Manasquan, New Jersey, 91, 203
Mangrove snapper, 392-94, 395, 396, 401, 402, 445
Maracaibo, Lake, 410
Marco, Florida, 406
Margarita Island, 46
Margate, 276, 450
  black, 278
Marine bass, 316-57
Marine Laboratory (University of Miami), 33, 34, 35, 46, 71, 100, 156, 178
Marlin, 8, 25, 26, 29, 31, 35, 40-69, 70, 72, 73, 104, 138, 157, 160-62, 167, 169, 177, 287, 305
  Bermudian, 42, 69
  black, 39, 42, 47, 49, 50-57, 59, 162, 425
  blue, 26, 42-49, 63, 64, 69, 425
    Atlantic, 26, 42-47
    Pacific, 42, 43, 47-49, 59
  striped, 28, 40, 42, 54, 58-62, 169, 425
  white, 29, 42, 43, 62-69, 85, 202, 203, 425
Marlin swordfish, 61

Marmora, Sea of, 72
Marquesas, 77
Martha's Vineyard, Massachusetts, 44, 119, 128, 194, 205, 329
Maryland, 44, 62, 64, 85, 96, 119, 140, 191, 202, 249, 257, 310, 333, 343, 417
Mason Island, 331
Massachusetts, 32, 43, 44, 63, 64, 74, 76, 83, 85, 86, 96, 119, 123, 128, 133, 139, 148, 151, 156, 158, 159, 160, 170, 176, 184, 188, 191, 192, 193, 194, 196, 198, 205, 206, 207, 212, 220, 221, 227, 228, 245, 248, 250, 251, 256, 264, 279, 284, 285, 299, 307, 309, 310, 313, 320, 322, 326, 328, 329, 335, 340, 341, 343, 350, 353, 360, 361, 366, 382, 383, 385, 391, 392, 395, 396, 415, 417, 418
Massachusetts Bay, 331
Matanzas, Cuba, 64, 194
Matunuck, Rhode Island, 331
Matunuck Point, Rhode Island, 96
Mayor Island, 171
Mayport, Florida, 32, 244
Mazatlán, Mexico, 39, 58, 242, 287, 306, 357
Mazatlán yellowtail, 299, 306
Mediterranean bluefin tuna, 102
Mediterranean Sea, 32, 70, 72, 73, 77, 91, 100, 102, 124, 127, 139, 152, 165, 191, 194, 286, 302, 321, 415
Medway River, 383
MEGALOPIDAE, 408
Megalops, 408
Melanogrammus aeglefinus, 222
Menhaden, 79, 104, 137, 199, 200, 214, 230, 234, 244, 246, 328
Menticirrhus, 255
  americanus, 256
  littoralis, 257
  sexatilis, 256
  undulatus, 258
Merimbula, Australia, 132
Merrimac River, 320, 331
Merrit Island Causeway, 234
Messick, Virginia, 202
Mexican barracuda, 186-87
Mexican bonito, 142
Mexican Islands, 302
Mexican snapper, 402-4

Mexico, 38, 39, 47, 51, 58, 59, 60, 75, 84, 85, 102, 119, 143, 153, 161, 162, 185, 186, 226, 232, 233, 234, 238, 242, 243, 253, 287, 288, 290, 291, 294, 296, 302, 303, 304, 305, 311, 351, 354, 357, 373, 400, 407, 410, 412
  Gulf of, 32, 33, 34, 43, 45, 62, 76, 83, 119, 128, 139, 145, 156, 158, 159, 176, 185, 191, 201, 212, 213, 214, 232, 236, 238, 246, 248, 249, 250, 251, 252, 258, 279, 282, 296, 309, 313, 326, 333, 346, 363, 389, 390, 391, 392, 394, 397, 398, 400, 401, 406, 409, 415
Miami, Florida, 36, 45, 46, 68, 100, 167, 201, 296
Miami, University of, 42, 46, 314, 406, 410
Miami Beach, Florida, 36, 63, 180
Microgadus tomcod, 221
Micropogon undulatus, 248
Middle River, 338
Midway Islands, 167
Migration, 13-14
Milford, Connecticut, 331
Minas Basin, 328
Minnow, 199, 250, 345, 406
Minudie's sand flats, 385
Mira Bay, 329
Miramichi River, 383
Mississippi (state), 201, 214, 326
Mobile, Alabama, 214
Mollusk, 34, 115, 199, 208, 221, 230, 250, 256, 259, 286, 308, 419, 420
Mombassa, Kenya, 39, 40, 296
Monomy Island, 206
Monomy Point, 206
Montauk, Long Island, 44, 63, 75, 94, 171, 192, 216
Montauk Harbor, 203
Montauk Point, 96, 203, 331, 342
Monterey, California, 38, 371
Monterey Bay, 154, 163, 384, 421
Monterey halibut, 267
Monterey Spanish mackerel, 162, 163
Moonfish, 281
Moreton Bay, 132
Moriches, Long Island, 203
Morocco, 117, 345
Morone
  americana, 251, 317, 322, 342
  labrax, 345

Morro Bay, 126
Mount Desert Island, 329
Mount Desert Rock, Maine, 382
Mud dab, 269
Mud flounder, 266
Mud Hole, 203
Mullet, 36, 39, 86, 105, 136, 234, 300, 411
Mullet snapper, 403
Mullica River, 227
Mulloway, 259-260
Muskeget, Mass., 205
Muskelunge, 176
Mussel, 252, 263, 270, 419
Mutton snapper, 390, 391
Muttonfish, 180, 391-92, 401, 446
Mycteroperca
  bonaci, 317, 350
  microlepis, 351
  olfax, 352
  pardalis, 351
  venenosa, 350
  xenarcha, 352
Mystic, Connecticut, 331

Names, 10-12
Nantucket, Massachusetts, 64, 74, 119, 192, 198, 205, 206
Nantucket Shoals, 382
Nantucket Sound, 340
Nantucket Sound rip, 205
Napatree Point, Rhode Island, 331
Narooma, New South Wales, 120
Narragansett, Rhode Island, 92, 205
Narragansett Bay, 205
Narraguagus, Maine, 329
Narrow banded mackerel, 168
Nassau, 32
Nassau Anglers Club, 413
Nassau grouper, 353, 453
Navesink River, 336
Needlefish, 25, 36
NEMATISTIIDAE, 373
Nematistius pectoralis, 373
Neothunnus allisoni, 118
Nero, 372
New Brunswick, Canada, 324, 326, 329, 383
New England, 74, 85, 145, 148, 149, 158, 220, 221, 228, 263, 267, 269, 270, 326, 327, 332, 333, 341, 343, 360, 361, 383
New Hampshire, 329

Subject Index

New Hanover County, North Carolina, 202
New Jersey, 62, 85, 91, 92, 140, 148, 150, 203, 212, 216, 221, 227, 243, 244, 245, 248, 249, 250, 257, 301, 321, 324, 326, 327, 328, 332, 335, 336, 340, 341, 342, 418
New River Inlet, 202
New Smyrna Beach, Florida, 201
New South Wales, 51, 111, 112, 120, 132, 260, 288, 294, 303
New York (state), 119, 137, 139, 158, 159, 192, 198, 216, 220, 221, 227, 228, 229, 232, 251, 256, 262, 279, 296, 307, 309, 310, 311, 326, 327, 328, 331, 332, 342, 360, 366, 386
New York Bay, 382
New York City, 192
New York Harbor, 171, 203
New York State Conservation Department, 229
New York Zoological Society, 326
New Zealand, 45, 50, 51, 53, 58, 59, 60-62, 72, 110, 124, 134, 170-72, 191, 303, 305
New Zealand Swordfish and Mako Shark Club, 51
Newburgh, New York, 332
Newfoundland, 72, 73, 96, 193, 262, 380
Newport, California, 124
Niantic River, 324, 326, 331
Nicaragua, Lake, 411
Night snapper, 399
No Man's Land, Massachusetts, 83, 196, 197, 205
North America, 93, 119, 124, 127, 134, 153, 158, 220, 318
North Cape, Norway, 72
North Carolina, 44, 76, 85, 119, 128, 145, 147, 148, 156, 159, 165, 177, 184, 191, 193, 196, 198, 201-2, 205, 220, 228, 229, 237, 243, 244, 249, 250, 251, 257, 266, 275, 276, 279, 285, 286, 299, 307, 309, 310, 313, 320, 322, 324, 326, 327, 333, 340, 341, 342, 350, 351, 353, 355, 361, 363, 364, 365, 366, 367, 380, 382, 383, 420
North Equatorial Current, 113, 114
North Island (New Zealand), 51
North Island (South Carolina), 201
North Queensland, 349

North Sea, 91
Northern barracuda, 184, 432
Northern bluefin tuna, 131
Northern fluke, 264, 265-66, 267, 463
Northern king whiting, 256-57, 442
Northern porgy, 360-63, 448
Norwalk Islands, 331
Norway, 72, 91, 99, 145, 170, 262
Nova Scotia, 51, 63, 74, 83, 91, 92, 96, 97, 105, 106, 108, 109, 114, 136, 148, 150, 191, 196, 216, 218, 262, 282, 284, 294, 297, 316, 321, 324, 328, 329, 343, 382, 383, 385, 409, 413, 417, 419
Nymphs, 345

Ocean barracuda, 165
Ocean City, Maryland, 64, 85, 96
Ocean City Inlet, 66
Ocean whitefish, 358-59, 440
Oceanic bonito, 129, 133, 134-35, 136, 429
Oceanic skipjack, 133
Oceans, 16-22
Oceanside, California, 124
Octopods, 36, 64, 122
Octopus, 259
Ocyurus chrysurus, 303, 398
Office of Naval Research, 179
Ono, 165
Ontario, Lake, 380
Ophiodon elongatus, 315
OPHIODONTIDAE, 315
Orange, California, 186
Orange County, California, 336
Orange rockfish, 371
Orange-spotted rockfish, 371
Orangemouth corbina, 242
Oregon, 84, 127, 128, 325, 338
Orient, New York, 137
Orient Point, Long Island, 205
Oriental bonito, 131, 141-42
Orleans, Massachusetts, 322
Orthopristes chrysopterus, 279
Oslo, Norway, 99
Otehei Bay, New Zealand, 62, 171
Oysterfish, 417
Oysters, 246

Pacific amberjack, 299, 302, 306, 436
Pacific barracuda, 185-87, 432
Pacific bigeye tuna, 112-16
Pacific blue marlin, 42, 43, 47-49, 59

Pacific bluefin tuna, 92, 102, 114
  eastern, 93, 100, 111
Pacific bonito, 139, 141, 142
Pacific cultus, 315
Pacific halibut, 264
Pacific mackerel, 153-55, 430
Pacific mako shark, 170-72
Pacific Oceanic Fishery Investigations, 121
Pacific permit, 308-9
Pacific sailfish, 38-40
Pacific shortbill spearfish, 71-72
Pacific snapper, 400-401, 402, 403
Pacific yellowfin tuna, 118-23
Pacific yellowtail, 83, 303
Padre Island, 234
Painted mackerel, 160
Palawan, Philippines, 39
Palm Beach, Florida, 34, 66, 201
Palmer, 348
Palometa, 308, 311, 437
Pamet River, 329
Pamlico River, 382
Pamlico Sound, 326, 383
Panama, 42, 54, 58, 153, 158, 165, 187, 207, 241, 277, 287, 288, 290, 294, 302, 303, 308, 311, 346, 352, 400, 401, 406, 420
  Gulf of, 47
Panama Bay, 39, 53-54, 84
Panama Canal, 409
Panama Canal Zone, 51, 396, 409
Paralabrax, 356
  clathratus, 357
  nebulifer, 356
PARALICHTHYIDAE, 264
Paralichthys, 268
  brasiliensis, 268
  californicus, 267
  dentatus, 264, 266
  lethostigmus, 266
  oblongus, 267
Paranthunnus sibi, 112
Pargo, 392, 400-404
  amarillo, 403-4
  prieto, 402
  striped, 400-402, 446
Parrotfish, 177
Pauu'u, 287-88
Pemba Island, 287
Penobscot Bay, 329
Penobscot River, 329
Pensacola, Florida, 297, 390

Pensacola snapper, 389, 392
Perch, 279, 377
  black, 255, 343
  blue, 370
  bluenose, 343
  giant, 348
  gray, 343
  sea; *see* Seaperch
  silver, 251-52, 343, 444
  white, 251, 317, 318, 322, 340, 342-45, 434
  yellow, 345
Perchbass, white, 343
PERCIDAE, 343
Perlos Islands, 58
Permit
  Atlantic, 306-8, 437
  Pacific, 308-9
Persian Gulf, 91
Peru, 38, 50, 51, 54, 57, 58, 59, 60, 61, 75, 79, 84, 86, 113, 115, 120, 142, 162, 163, 187, 226, 238, 241, 283, 285, 356, 358, 373, 374, 375, 406
Peru Current, 54-57
Peruvian amberjack, 306
Peruvian bonito, 141, 142
Peto, 165
Petrometopon cruentatus, 355
Phanerodon furcatus, 379
Philippine Archipelago, 165
Philippines, 39, 58, 119, 144
Phytoplankton, 55
Pickerel, 176, 184
Pigfish, 279, 451
Pike, 176, 182, 184
Pilchard, 36, 127, 148, 243, 246, 300, 345
Pile seaperch, 378, 460
Pilotfish, 281
Pimelometopon pulcher, 421
Pinfish, 300, 365-66, 449
Pinopolis Dam (South Carolina), 333-34
Pinto broomtail grouper, 352
Plankton, 130, 150, 154, 384
Platichthys stellatus, 271
Pleurogrammus monopterygius, 274
PLEURONECTIDAE, 269, 271, 272
Plum Gut, 203
Plum Island, 205
Pneumatophorus
  australasicus, 153
  colias, 150

Subject Index

diego, 153
grex, 150
japonicus, 153
peruanus, 153
Pogonias cromis, 245
Point Abreojos, Baja California, 372
Point Arguello, California, 372
Point Conception, California, 58, 133, 185, 186, 252, 253, 258, 273, 279, 303, 315, 348, 356
Point Judith, Rhode Island, 83, 205, 331
Pollachius virens, 215
Pollock, 147, 191, 215-19, 222, 459
  harbor, 217
POMATOMIDAE, 190
Pomatomus saltatrix, 190
Pomfret, 115
Pompanito, 311
Pompano, 8, 281, 282, 297, 306-11, 437
  African, 289
  gaff-topsail, 311
  great, 307
  longfin, 311
  round, 307, 310-11, 437
Pompon, 278
Pond Point, Connecticut, 331
Porbeagle shark, 170
Porgy, 199, 342, 360-68
  grass, 364-65, 448
  jolthead, 365, 448
  littlemouth, 365
  northern, 360-63, 448
  saucereye, 364, 448
  sheepshead, 365, 449
  southern, 363
Porkfish, 279, 451
Porpoise, 82, 83
Port Antonio, 93
Port Aransas, Texas, 33, 71, 214
Port Aransas Rod and Reel Club, 33
Portland, Maine, 382
Portugal, 295
Potomac River, 202, 383
Pribilof Islands, 274
"Pride of Bermuda," 165
Priestfish, 370
Promicrops itaiara, 346
Provincetown, Massachusetts, 96
Pseudopleuronectes americanus, 268
Pteropods, 292
Puerto Rico, 44, 70, 117, 207, 299

Puffer, 177
Puppy drum, 243, 244

Quayaquil, Gulf of, 57
Queen Charlotte Sound, 371
Queenfish, 165, 296
Queensland, 260, 289, 294, 303, 349
Quillback rockfish, 371, 457
Quonochontaug, Rhode Island, 205, 331

Race, the, 205
Race Point, Massachusetts, 382
RACHICENTRIDAE, 212
Rachycentron
  canadus, 212
  pondicerianum, 212
Rainbow runner, 296-97, 440
Rainbow seaperch, 379, 460
Ray, 169
Rebecca Shoals, 157
Red drum, 242
Red grouper, 353
Red hind, 353, 454
Red rock cod, 370, 372
Red rockfish, 371
Red Sea, 31, 119, 132
Red snapper, 370, 389-90, 403, 446
Redfish, 242, 244, 421
Reedville, Virginia, 262
Rehoboth Beach, 203
Remora, 77, 213
Rhacochilus toxotes, 378
Rhincodon typus, 169
Rhode Island, 83, 92, 94, 190, 203, 205, 218, 229, 328, 331, 362, 417, 419
Rhomboplites aurorubens, 399
Riding Rocks, 100
Rigificola grandis, 111
Rio de la Plata, Argentina, 72
River kingfish, 259
Roanoke River, 319, 320
Robalo, 405
Roccus
  lineatus, 321
  saxatilis, 317, 321
Rock bass, 316-17, 350, 356-57
  spotted, 357, 455
Rock cod, 371
  yellowtail, 371
Rock grouper, 350
Rock hind, 352, 353, 453

Rock trout, 273
Rockaway Beach, New York, 204
Rockfish, 9, 127, 317, 322, 350, 369-72
  black, 372, 456
  blue, 370, 456
  brown, 371
  canary, 371, 456
  orange, 371
  orange-spotted, 371
  quillback, 371, 457
  red, 371
  sculpin, 372, 458
  speckled, 371
  vermillion, 370, 457
  yellowtail, 371-72, 457
Romano Bay, 214
Roncador stearnsi, 252
Ronco, 278, 451
Roosterfish, 373-76, 435
Rosefish, 263
Round pompano, 307, 310-11, 437
Rubberlip seaperch, 378, 461
Rudderfish, 188
  banded, 281
Runner, 283-285
  blue, 283-84, 285, 438
  rainbow, 296-97, 440
Rusty dab, 271

Sabalo, 408
Sachem's Head, 203
Sacramento Delta, 338
Sacramento River, 323, 338
Sailfish, 25, 26, 29-40, 41, 58, 66, 70, 72, 157, 167, 426
  Atlantic, 30-38, 64, 66
  Pacific, 38-40
Sailfish Conservation Club, 34
Sailfish Yacht and Beach Club, 34
Sailor's choice, 278, 279
St. Augustine, Florida, 246
St. Croix, Maine, 329
St. David's Island, 69
St. George River, 329
St. Helena, California, 123
St. John Harbor, New Brunswick, 329
St. John River (New Brunswick), 329, 383
St. Johns River (Florida), 334, 367, 380, 383, 406
St. John's River (Newfoundland), 380
St. Lawrence, Gulf of, 145, 148, 150, 216, 271, 343

St. Lawrence River, 316, 324, 328, 380, 383
St. Lucie Inlet, 201
St. Lucie River, 156
St. Mary's River, 201
St. Petersburg, Florida, 171
St. Simons Island, 201
Sakonnet Point, Rhode Island, 205
Salinas, Ecuador, 58
Salinity, of sea water, 16-17
Salmon, 40, 127, 218, 321, 329, 408
  black, 212
  king, 369
Salmon grouper, 371
Samar, Philippines, 39
Samsonfish, 294, 436
San Clemente, California, 124, 305
San Diego, California, 124, 128, 133, 136, 186, 267, 305, 372
San Diego County, California, 336
San Felipe, Mexico, 238
San Francisco, California, 128, 163, 240, 267, 338, 377
San Francisco Bay, 323, 336, 338, 339
San Joaquin Delta, 338
San Joaquin River, 323
San Juan, Puerto Rico, 44
San Juan River, 411
San Miguel Island, 372
San Pablo Bay, 338
San Pedro, California, 124, 128, 207, 285
Sand bass, 350, 356-57, 455
  California, 356
Sand fleas, 208, 310
Sand trout, 237
Sand weakfish, 236-37
Sandfish, 350, 355-56
Sandperch, 251, 355
Sandy Neck, Massachusetts, 329
Santa Barbara, California, 186, 238, 422
Santa Barbara Islands, 240
Santa Catalina Island, California, 59, 61, 74, 84, 305, 422
Santa Cruz Island, 39, 72, 75
Santa Monica, California, 161
Santee-Cooper Reservoir (South Carolina), 318, 333
Santee River, 333
Santo Tomas, Lower California, 370
Sapelo Island, 201

Subject Index

Sarda
  chiliensis, 141, 142
  chiliensis australis, 141
  lineolata, 141, 142
  orientalis, 141, 142, 144
  sarda, 136
  velox, 141, 142
Sardine, 39, 86, 104, 127, 136, 142
Sargasso Sea, 77
Sargo, 279, 451
Saucereye porgy, 364, 448
Scad, 281
  bigeye, 293
  mackerel, 294
Scandinavia, 136
School mackerel, 163-64
School tuna, 96
Schoolmaster, 392, 395, 396-97, 445
Sciaena
  antarctica, 259
  saturna, 255
SCIAENIDAE, 225, 226, 232, 236, 237, 238, 242, 245, 248, 250, 251, 252, 253, 255, 257, 258, 259, 260
Sciaenops ocellatus, 242
Scissors, 25
Scomber
  colias, 150
  scombrus, 145
Scomberomorus, 156
  cavalla, 155, 180
  commerson, 168
  concolor, 163
  guttatus, 164
  maculatus, 156, 158
  niphonius, 164
  queenslandicus, 163
  regalis, 160
  semifasciatus, 168
  sierra, 161
Scombrid, 90, 102, 137, 139, 141, 142, 155, 159, 165
SCOMBRIDAE, 90, 132, 134, 143, 155, 164, 165
Scombroid, 90
Scooter, 185
Scoots, 185
Scorpaena, 370
  guttata, 372
Scorpaenichthys marmoratus, 223
SCORPAENIDAE, 370
Scorpion, 372
Scorpionfish, 370, 372

Scorton Creek, Massachusetts, 329
Sculpin, 223, 263, 370
Sculpin rockfish, 372, 458
Scup, 230, 342, 361, 363
Sea bass, 190, 316, 317, 318-45, 434
  black, 340, 348
  California giant, 348
  California white, 238-39, 441
  giant, 316, 346-49
    black, 346, 348, 452
    California, 348
  shortfin, 240
  white, 226
    California, 238-39, 441
Sea Bright, New Jersey, 203
Sea catfish, 411
Sea cucumbers, 221
Sea herring, 381
Sea Island, 201
Sea trout, 227, 232, 238, 258, 273
Seaperch, 343, 377-79
  barred, 378, 460
  black, 378, 460
  pile, 378, 460
  rainbow, 379, 460
  rubberlip, 378, 461
  shiner, 379, 462
  striped, 378, 461
  walleye, 379, 461
  white, 379, 461
Searsport Harbor, Maine, 329
Seaside Park (Bridgeport, Conn.), 331
Sebastian Inlet, 201
Sebastodes, 370
  flavidus, 371
  goodei, 372
  maliger, 371
  melanops, 372
  miniatus, 370
  mystinus, 370
  paucispinis, 371
  pinniger, 371
Sebastolobus, 370
Selene vomer, 297
Senegal, 212
Sennet, 185
Sergeantfish, 212
Seriola, 294, 299
  colburni, 299, 302
  dorsalis, 299, 302, 303
  dumerili, 299, 301
  falcata, 299, 301
  grandis, 303

Seriola—Continued
 hippos, 294
 lalandi, 299, 301, 302
 mazatlana, 299, 303, 306
 peruana, 306
 rivoliana, 302
 simplex, 294
Serranid, 317, 340, 353, 355, 356
SERRANIDAE, 316, 317, 339, 342, 346, 347, 348, 349, 388, 415
Seychelles Islands, 39, 132
Shad, 380-87, 408, 435
 American, 380
 hickory, 381
 white, 380
Shagwong Reef, 331
Shark, 44, 73, 79, 105, 115, 169-72, 180, 182, 183, 213
 bonito, 170
 Greenland, 263
 hammerhead, 170
 mackerel, 170
 mako, 462
  Atlantic, 170-72
  Pacific, 170-72
 man-eater, 169, 170
 porbeagle, 170
 sharpnose, 170
 thresher, 170
 tiger, 170
 whale, 169
 white, 169
Shark Bay, 132
Shark sucker, 213
Sharpnose shark, 170
Sheepshead, 356, 366-67, 449
 California, 421-22, 458
Sheepshead porgy, 365, 449
Sherwood Island Park (Westport, Conn.), 331
Shiner, 206, 255
Shiner seaperch, 379, 462
Shinnecock, New York, 204
Shortbill spearfish, 426
 Atlantic, 70
 Pacific, 71-72
Shortfin barracuda, 187
Shortfin sea bass, 240
Shortnose spearfish, 71
Shrewsbury Rocks, 203
Shrimp, 104, 148, 154, 159, 161, 189, 199, 230, 234, 237, 239, 240, 244, 246, 250, 256, 265, 270, 271, 284,

298, 300, 305, 308, 310, 313, 317, 327, 345, 365, 384, 390, 393, 394, 397, 398, 399, 406, 411, 416, 420
Shubenacadie Lake, 328
Shubenacadie River, 328
Shumagin Islands, 274
Sicily, 83
Sierra mackerel, 161-63, 164
Silver bass, 343
Silver perch, 251-52, 343, 444
Silver squeteague, 237
Silver trevally, 288-89
Silver weakfish, 237
Silverhake, 263
Silverside, 199, 230, 234
Sinepuxent Beach, 64
Sinking, 21
Six Mile Reef, 203
Skate, 169
Skipjack, 90, 133, 143-44, 191
 black, 143, 152
 Hawaiian, 144
 oceanic, 133
Small dolphin, 85, 88
Small mackerel, 127
Smallmouth bass, 345
Smelt, 142, 305, 408
Snail, 270
Snake, 185
Snake mackerel, 115
Snapper, 190, 275, 303, 388-404
 Atlantic, 389-400, 401, 402
 bastard, 399
 black, 372
 chub-head, 399
 Colorado, 402
 Cuban, 394
 dog, 392, 393, 395-96, 401, 402, 445
 gray, 392
 green, 371
 Jordan's, 402-3
 lane, 397-98, 447
 mangrove, 392-94, 395, 396, 401, 402, 445
 Mexican, 402-4
 mullet, 403
 mutton, 390, 391
 night, 399
 Pacific, 400-401, 402, 403
 Pensacola, 389, 392
 red, 370, 389-90, 403, 446
 spotted rose, 403
 vermillion, 399-400, 447

Subject Index

yellow, 371
yellowtail, 87, 300, 398-99, 403, 447
Snapper bluefish, 191, 193, 195, 199, 203, 206
Snapping mackerel, 191
Snook, 236, 405-7, 433
Soldier's Rip, 105, 110, 196
Sole, 261
   lemon, 269
Solomon Islands, 39
South Africa, 130
South America, 39, 43, 45, 46, 51, 60, 63, 74, 75, 83, 91, 113, 119, 133, 134, 162
South Australia, 111, 187, 289, 303
South Carolina, 76, 176, 193, 201, 228, 264, 267, 299, 318, 333-34, 343, 360, 367, 390, 400, 415, 416
South China Sea, 77
South Equatorial Current, 54
South Island (South Carolina), 201
South Nyack, New York, 331
Southampton, 75
Southern bluefin tuna, 110, 131
Southern fluke, 266
Southern halibut, 267
Southern jewfish, 346
Southern king whiting, 257, 258
Southern kingfish, 257
Southern porgy, 363
Southwest Middle Grounds, 202
Spain, 99, 145
Spanish mackerel, 89, 155, 156, 157, 158-60, 161, 163, 164, 431
   Monterey, 162
SPARIDAE, 342, 360, 365, 366, 367
Spawning, 14-16
Spearfish, 25, 26, 31, 70-72
   longbill, 426
      Atlantic, 70-71
   shortbill, 426
      Atlantic, 70
      Pacific, 71-72
   shortnose, 71
Speckled rockfish, 371
Speckled trout, 232
Speckles, 232
Specs, 232
Sphyraena, 184
   argentea, 185
   barracuda, 175
   borealis, 184
   ensis, 186

guachancho, 184
novae-hollandiae, 187
obtusata, 187
picudilla, 184
sphyraena, 184
SPHYRAENIDAE, 175
Spiketail grouper, 352
Spiny boxfish, 177
Spot, 248, 249-51, 252, 328, 442
Spotfin croaker, 252-53, 443
Spotted bonito, 129, 134, 138-40, 141, 143
   Atlantic, 138-40, 143, 144, 429
Spotted broomtail grouper, 352
Spotted cabrilla, 354
Spotted jack, 287, 439
Spotted jewfish, 346-47, 452
Spotted mackerel, 163, 164
Spotted rock bass, 357, 455
Spotted rose snapper, 403
Spotted trout, 232
Spotted weakfish, 226, 232-36, 441
Spring Hill, Massachusetts, 329
Springer, 165
Squeteague, 227, 232
   silver, 237
Squid, 39, 51, 61, 64, 79, 80, 104, 115, 122, 130, 136, 137, 140, 142, 143, 155, 159, 161, 162, 167, 199, 221, 230, 239, 259, 265, 270, 292, 305, 313, 342, 345, 362
Squid hound, 321
Starry flounder, 271-72, 464
Staten Island, 198
Stenotomus
   aculeatus, 363
   crysops, 361
   versicolor, 360
Stony Brook, Long Island, 327
Strait of Belle Isle, 145
Straits of Juan de Fuca, 379
Streaked trout, 277
Striped barracuda, 187
Striped bass, 195, 205, 318-39, 340, 343, 344, 434
Striped bonito, 133
Striped corbina, 241
Striped grunt, 277
Striped mackerel, 153
Striped marlin, 28, 40, 42, 54, 58-62, 169, 425
Striped pargo, 400-402, 446
Striped seaperch, 378, 461

Subject Index

Striped tuna, 133
Striper, 322
Strongytura marinus, 25
Stuart, Florida, 32
Sucker, shark, 213
Suffield, Connecticut, 387
Suisun Bay, 338
Sumatra, 77
Summer blues, 191
Summer flounder, 264
Surf fish, 252, 253, 258
Surf whiting, 257
Swordfish, 25, 26, 54, 61, 72-81, 169, 171, 426
    broadbill, 54, 72-73, 74, 76-77, 79-80
    marlin, 61
Sydney, Australia, 110, 131

Taboga Island, 53
Taeniotoca lateralis, 378
Tahiti, 31, 39, 132
Talang, 295-96, 439
Tallapoosa River, 334
Tallassee, Alabama, 334
Tampa Bay, 194, 201, 214, 307
Tampico, Mexico, 410
Tanganyika, 131
Tanguigue, 168
Tarpon, 236, 280, 308, 312, 313, 365, 408-14, 433
Tarpon atlanticus, 408
Tasmania, 110, 111
Tautog, 417-420, 458
Tautoga onitis, 417
Tautogolabrus adspersus, 419
Tehuantepec, Gulf of, 135
Ten pounder, 312
Teraglin, 260
Tetrapturus
    angustirostris, 71
    belone, 70
    sp., 70
Texas, 45, 50, 71, 137, 159, 165, 201, 214, 232, 234, 237, 242, 244, 245, 248, 249, 250, 251, 257, 266, 287, 309, 346, 355, 363, 364, 366, 367, 392, 395, 410, 412, 413
Thames River, 324, 326, 331
Thimble-eye, 150
Threadfin, 281
Thresher shark, 170
Thunnine, 138

Thunnus
    alalunga, 123
    albacares, 118
    argentivitatus, 118
    atlanticus, 129
    maccoyii, 110, 131
    macropterus, 118
    obesus, 116
    sibi, 112
    thynnus, 90
Tides, 21-22
"Tiger of the sea," 180
Tiger shark, 170
Tinker, 150
Tinker mackerel, 148, 150
Tocopilla, Chile, 57, 59, 74, 80, 81
Tokyo, Japan, 126
Tomales Bay, California, 267
Tomcod, 215, 216, 221, 222, 255, 457
    microgadus, 221
Tonggol tuna, 130-32, 428
Tor Bay, 383
Totuava, 226, 239-40, 441
Trachinotus, 307
    carolinus, 307, 309, 310
    falcatus, 307, 310
    goodei, 306
    kennedyi, 308
    palometa, 311
    rhodopus, 311
Trachurops, 294
    crumenophthalmus, 293
    japonicus, 291
    lathami, 291
    symmetricus, 291
Trevally
    great, 289
    king, 289
    silver, 288-89
Triggerfish, 177
Tripletail, 415-16, 454
Trout, 408
    bastard, 237
    brook, 232
    brown, 232
    dolly varden, 272
    gray, 227
    rock, 273
    sand, 237
    sea, 227, 232, 238, 258, 273
    speckled, 232
    spotted, 232
    streaked, 277

SUBJECT INDEX

Tuckernuck, Massachusetts, 198
Tuna, 8, 89, 90-132, 136, 150, 152, 196
  Allison, 118
  Atlantic
    eastern, 97
    western, 97, 102
  bigeye, 54, 427
    Atlantic, 112, 115, 116-18, 130
    Pacific, 112-16
  blackfin, 116, 121, 129-30, 427
    Atlantic, 129-30
  bluefin, 28, 40, 51, 90-112, 121, 218, 427
    Atlantic, 92, 93, 100, 102, 111
    Australian, 110-12, 131
    California, 93, 111
    Mediterranean, 102
    northern, 131
    Pacific, 92, 93, 100, 102, 111, 114
    southern, 110, 131
  dogtooth, 132, 428
  European, 99
  great, 90
  little, 138
  longfin, 123, 127
  mackerel, 138
  school, 96
  striped, 133
  tonggol, 130-32, 428
  yaito, 144
  yellowfin, 29, 112, 113, 114, 117, 118-23, 135, 427
    Atlantic, 118-23
    Pacific, 118-23
Tuna Guides Association, 92, 103
Tunny, 90
  Indian longtail, 131
  long-tailed, 131
Turbot, 261
Turrum, 289
Tusket River, 419

Ulua, 287
  white, 288
Umbrina roncador, 253
Unimak Island, 272
United States, 44, 46, 51, 75, 76, 96, 97, 109, 128, 136, 176, 195, 200, 226, 236, 241, 255, 264, 318, 335, 340, 343, 360, 366, 380, 390, 417; *see also* names of states
Department of Interior, 385

Fish and Wildlife Service, 29, 33, 64, 71, 96, 114, 116, 119, 120, 121, 123, 124, 134, 140, 321, 386
National Museum, 78
Public Health Service, 178, 179
Upwelling, 21
Uruguay, 268, 415
Usacaranx georgianus, 288

Valparaiso, Chile, 54, 72
Vancouver, Canada, 255
Vancouver Island, 370, 372, 379
Vehuella, 78
Venezuela, 46, 68, 114, 128, 158, 406, 409, 410
Vermillion rockfish, 370, 457
Vermillion snapper, 399-400, 447
Victoria, 111, 289
Vineyard Sound, 205, 322
Virginia, 32, 85, 94, 147, 150, 191, 198, 202, 213, 243, 244, 246, 250, 262, 279, 333, 341, 343, 361, 387, 417

Wachapreague Inlet, 202
Wahoo, 36, 89, 164-68, 431
Walker Cay, 32, 45, 63, 94, 104, 105, 134, 140, 300, 392
Walleye seaperch, 379, 461
Walpole, Massachusetts, 196
Warsaw grouper, 346
Washington (state), 128, 336
Watch Hill, Rhode Island, 94, 331
Water fleas, 345
Water temperatures, 17-18
Weakfish, 195, 225, 226-42, 441
  sand, 236-37
  silver, 237
  spotted, 226, 232-36, 441
Wedgeport, Nova Scotia, 91, 92, 97, 99, 103, 105, 106, 109, 114, 196, 218, 219, 413, 419
Weekapaug, Rhode Island, 205, 331
Weldon, North Carolina, 320
Wellfleet Harbor, Massachusetts, 329
West Africa, 396, 406
West End (Bahamas), 177
West Indies, 86, 128, 156, 176, 185, 211, 276, 277, 278, 279, 284, 285, 290, 310, 311, 346, 350, 352, 353, 354, 355, 364, 365, 367, 391, 392, 396, 400, 406, 420

Subject Index

West Palm Beach Fishing Club, 34
West Point, 332
Western Atlantic tuna, 97, 102
Western Australia, 110, 112, 187, 289, 294, 349
Westport, Connecticut, 331
Wetumpka, Alabama, 334
Whale shark, 169
White chub, 188
White corbina, 241
White croaker, 255
White Frier Islands, 39
White grunt, 276, 450
White marlin, 29, 42, 43, 62-69, 85, 202, 203, 425
White perch, 251, 317, 318, 322, 340, 342-45, 434
White perchbass, 343
White sea bass, 226
  California, 238-39, 441
White seaperch, 379, 461
White shad, 380
White shark, 169
White ulua, 288
Whitefish, ocean, 358-59, 440
Whiting, 225, 255-60
  California, 258
  king, 256
    gulf, 257-58
    northern, 256-57, 442
    southern, 257, 258
    surf, 257
Wilderness Point, Fisher's Island, 331
Windsor Locks, 386
Windsor Locks Canal Company, 387
Windward Passage, 94
Winter flounder, 268-70, 463
Winter Harbor, Maine, 329
Winter Quarter Shoal Lightship, 66
Wood End, Massachusetts, 329
Woodmont, Connecticut, 331
Woods Hole, Massachusetts, 119, 128, 158, 197
Woods Hole Oceanographic Institution, 64, 94
Worms, 208, 221, 230, 250, 252, 253, 256, 265, 270, 271, 277, 279, 286, 345, 360, 362, 388, 398, 399, 419
Wrasses, 417-22

Xiphias gladius, 72
XIPHIIDAE, 72

Yaito tuna, 144
Yale–East African Expedition, 287
Yale Fishing Club, 298
Yale–New Zealand Expedition, 53
Yale Saltwater Fishing Team, 413
Yale–South American Expedition, 115, 375
Yale University, 39, 42, 47, 60, 109, 110, 218, 319, 412
Yarmouth County, Nova Scotia, 419
Yellow colorado grouper, 352
Yellow corbina, 241
Yellow fins, 227
Yellow grunt, 276, 277
Yellow jack, 285-86, 438
Yellow perch, 345
Yellow snapper, 371
Yellowfin croaker, 251, 253, 258, 259, 443
Yellowfin grouper, 350-51, 453
Yellowfin tuna, 29, 112, 113, 114, 117, 118-23, 135, 427
  Atlantic, 118-23
  Pacific, 118-23
Yellowtail, 251, 299, 302-6, 436
  Atlantic, 303
  California, 303
  mazatlán, 299, 306
  Pacific, 83, 303
Yellowtail flounder, 269, 271, 463
Yellowtail kingfish, 111, 303
Yellowtail rock cod, 371
Yellowtail rockfish, 371-72, 457
Yellowtail snapper, 87, 300, 398-99, 403, 447
York County, Virginia, 202
Yucatan Channel, 93

Zanzibar, 287
Zebra mackerel, 153
Zooplankton, 55, 135